THE TRANSFORMATION OF THE SOUTHEASTERN INDIANS, 1540–1760

The Transformation of the Southeastern Indians, 1540–1760

Essays by
MARVIN T. SMITH
PAUL KELTON
JOHN E. WORTH
HELEN C. ROUNTREE
STEVEN C. HAHN
PENELOPE B. DROOKER
R. P. STEPHEN DAVIS, JR.
CHRISTOPHER B. RODNING
MARVIN D. JETER
PATRICIA GALLOWAY
TIMOTHY K. PERTTULA

Edited by
ROBBIE ETHRIDGE
and
CHARLES HUDSON

UNIVERSITY PRESS OF MISSISSIPPI
Jackson

www.upress.state.ms.us

Copyright © 2002 by University Press of Mississippi
All rights reserved
Manufactured in the United States of America

Print-on-Demand Edition
∞
Library of Congress Cataloging-in-Publication Data available

British Library Cataloging-in-Publication Data available

Contents

Preface

This volume contains the proceedings of the 1998 Porter L. Fortune, Jr., History Symposium at the University of Mississippi. These symposia began in 1975 at the University of Mississippi as a conference on southern history. In 1983, its name was changed to honor Chancellor Emeritus Porter L. Fortune, who, along with his wife, Elizabeth Fortune, contributed much to the success of the symposium both during his tenure as chancellor and after his retirement. After Chancellor Fortune's death in 1989, Mrs. Fortune continued her support and enthusiasm for the symposium and has been an honored guest at almost all of the events. From its inception, the symposium has attracted an impressive roster of scholars. Past symposia have examined topics in southern history such as emancipation, the southern political tradition, childhood, the civil rights movement, religion, and the role of gender in shaping public power.

The 1998 Fortune symposium reaches further back in time—to the beginnings of Spanish, French, and English colonization—and places Native Americans at the center of the historical action. In the past twenty years, historians, anthropologists, and archaeologists have made considerable progress in interpreting the lifeways of the native peoples of the late prehistoric and early historic Southeast. From these works, we now understand that the first two hundred years of the historical era was a time when fundamental—even catastrophic—changes occurred in native societies of the South. The task of the 1998 symposium was to examine the various forces at play and to assess their role in the transformation of the native peoples of the Southeast between the era of Spanish exploration during the sixteenth century and the southern Indian uprising of 1715, known as the Yamasee War.

The seed for this particular topic was planted in 1996. After Dan Hickerson and I had completed our doctorates at the University of Georgia under the direction of Charles Hudson, Dan approached me about possibly co-organizing a symposium examining the social and political reorganization of the seventeenth- and eighteenth-century native Southeast—a topic that Hudson proposed as the next big question to be addressed in southeastern Indian studies. The following year was a busy one for both Dan and me—I took a position as McMullan Assistant Professor of Southern Studies and Anthropology at the University of Mississippi, and Dan's interest took him into a different field altogether. However, Hudson kept the idea of the symposium alive, and he encouraged me to seek funding and a venue. In the spring of 1997, I gave a lecture at the Center for the Study of Southern Culture's Brown Bag Series in which I roughly outlined some of the tasks at hand in understanding the early social history of the southeastern Indians. I closed with a comment about the need to organize a symposium focused on these and other questions. Afterwards, Ted Ownby, my southern studies and history colleague, suggested that Hudson and I submit a proposal to the University of Mississippi Department of History to organize the 1998 Porter L. Fortune, Jr., History Symposium. We did, and they accepted.

Charles Hudson then undertook to plan the content of the symposium, and I set about organizing and managing the program. The original participants in the symposium were Charles Hudson, who gave the keynote address, and leading scholars on various aspects that Hudson had identified as being crucial to the basic question at hand. These were Marvin Smith, John Worth, Steven Hahn, Helen Rountree, Chester DePratter, Patricia Galloway, and Timothy Perttula. Peter Wood and Vernon James Knight served as discussants. The following spring, Charles Hudson held a graduate seminar at the University of Georgia Department of Anthropology, to which he invited speakers who could address areas not covered in the symposium. These were Marvin Jeter, Dan Morse, Phyllis Morse, Penelope Drooker, Christopher Rodning, and Stephen Davis. That fall, I began collecting the majority of the papers presented at the 1998 symposium and in Hudson's 1999 seminar.

Many people were involved in organizing and taking on various tasks necessary for the Porter Fortune symposium and this publication. We first would like to single out for special thanks the symposium co-organizer Ted Smith, then a doctoral candidate in history and now executive director of the Southern Cultural Heritage Foundation. Much of the success of the symposium can be attributed to Ted's careful attention to detail, his quiet intelligence, his good temperament, and his refusal to take "no" for an answer. Dan Hickerson, likewise, deserves a special thanks for suggesting such a symposium in the first place, as does Ted Ownby for suggesting the Porter Fortune as a proper venue. The administration at the University of Mississippi has continued to support the symposium, and we would like to thank, in particular, Chancellor Robert Khayat, Provost

Emeritus for Academic Affairs Gerald Walton, Dean of University Librar-
ies John Meador, and Dean of Liberal Arts Glen Hopkins. For their guid-
ance and help, we would like to thank Robert Haws, chair of the Department of History, Charles Wilson, director of the Center for the Study of
Southern Culture, and Max Williams, chair of the Department of Sociology and Anthropology. The conference also owed much to the contributions and professionalism of the panel moderators—Jay Johnson, Janet
Ford, Robert Thorne, and Ted Ownby. Marvin Jeter graciously stepped in
to read Tim Perttula's paper when Tim was unable to attend. We would
also like to thank our copyeditor Carol Cox, as well as Craig Gill, Anne
Stascavage, and Shane Gong at the University Press of Mississippi.

Many others contributed in large and small ways to the success of the
symposium and to the completion of this volume, and we would like to
thank Ann Abadie, Alice Hull, Bert Way, Melissa McGuire, Ann O'Dell,
Betty Harness, Rona Skinner, Denton Marcotte, John Samonds, Katie
McKee, Jeff Jackson, Kirsten Dellinger, Karen Glynn, Bea Jackson, Dan
Sherman, M. K. Smith, Billy Stevens, Toni Stevens, Dave Kerns, Kelly
Drake, Shawna Dooley, Minoa Uffelman, Leigh McWhite, Virginia How-
ell, Kara Tooke, John Sullivan, Steve Budney, Jim Foley, Steve Chesebor-
ough, Susan McClamrock, Debra Young, Patricia Huggins, Ben Flem-
mons, Sabrina Brown, Herman Payton, Russell Cooper, Peter Lee,
Francine Green, Cliff Holley, and Terence Manogin.

We are grateful to the University of Mississippi Department of History
faculty for giving us the opportunity to participate in the Fortune symposia, and we gratefully acknowledge generous support from the Franklin
College of Arts and Sciences at the University of Georgia.

Robbie Ethridge

Introduction

Recent research on the expeditions of sixteenth-century Spanish explorers—Hernando de Soto (1539–43), Tristán de Luna (1559–61), and Juan Pardo (1566–68)—has made it possible to link up the historical experiences and observations recounted in the documents of these expeditions with the voluminous archaeological information that has been developed over the past half century by archaeologists. At least in a partial way, that linkage has now been accomplished.[1] We can now say with some confidence who lived where in the sixteenth-century Southeast, and we can also identify some rather large areas of land where no one lived. Previous to this research, the only way to map the Indians of the late prehistoric Southeast was as arbitrarily named archaeological cultures and phases. That is, the late prehistoric Indians of the Southeast could only be represented on a map by drawing circles or "jelly beans" around clusters of sites where archaeologists have found similar material remains.[2] This research on sixteenth-century exploration allows us for the first time to represent on maps what may properly be called polities, i.e., clusters of communities of people who were politically aligned with each other, and who might, in turn, have been aligned against other such clusters.[3]

I am putting it mildly when I say that there is still disagreement over the particulars of this reconstructed sixteenth-century social landscape of the Southeast, but we now have the beginnings of a map where none existed before.[4] When one compares this map with a map of the Indians of the early eighteenth-century South, the two (see Marvin Smith's maps #1 and #5 in this volume) are seen to be very different.[5] Most of the named sixteenth-century native polities are absent from the eighteenth-century map. And on the eighteenth-century map, new names—Creeks, Choctaws, Cherokees, Natchez—appear. A few sixteenth-century place names seemingly continue into the eighteenth century, but often they are situated at significantly different locations, sometimes hundreds of miles distant from where they were located in the sixteenth century. Many areas that were densely inhabited in the sixteenth century were uninhabited or only lightly populated in the eighteenth century. And some areas that were wilderness in the sixteenth century—for example, the Savannah

River basin—were populated in the eighteenth century. How are we to account for the differences between these two maps?

The question now before us is this: *What shaped the Indians of the eighteenth-century South?* That is to say, what historical forces, trends, and events were attendant to the formation of the Indians of the colonial South? Answering this question requires us to write the social history of the South between about 1539–43 and about 1715. What concepts are we to use in apprehending the changes depicted on these two maps, and how are we to conceive of the historical processes that shaped the destinies of the human actors?

CULTURE

I am afraid that the concept of culture will help us very little in the analytical task we are undertaking. The concept of culture is one of anthropology's most notable contributions to modern knowledge. For anthropologists "culture" refers to everything that one learns by virtue of living out one's life in a particular society. More than anything else, the capability of learning a human culture is what separates us from other primates. Perhaps anthropology's greatest contributions to a liberal education are the realizations that (1) as humans, our perception and grasp of the world are largely built upon the scaffolding of the culture we have learned, and (2) humans in various parts of the world differ, sometimes surprisingly, in the cultures they learn at their mother's knee.

Beyond this, however, the concept of culture has little analytical utility.[6] In spite of almost a century of research by social and cultural anthropologists, they have not devised ways of conceptualizing or measuring degrees of cultural difference. And despite a great deal of effort, they have not developed good ways of explaining or even describing cultural change.

Anthropologists do not even have a good answer to the first question anyone would ask: how different can cultures be? A related question is that since culture is the stuff that all human beings think and perceive with, how much of it is shared by *all* humans? One would think that cultural differences would be at their maximum in situations where Europeans first encountered the various preliterate societies of the world. The Hernando de Soto expedition, for example, was one such occasion in which cultural differences should have been at their greatest extent. For all that we presently know, the southeastern Indians had been cut off from human events in the Old World for more than twelve thousand years. And even if a few dugout canoes or rafts made it across the Atlantic or Pacific, it is difficult to see how such events could have resulted in significant cultural interchange.

When Spaniards first met Indians in the Southeast in 1539–43, at the time of the Soto expedition, was the cultural chasm between them unbridgeable? No, it was not. In a number of instances, the players changed sides. Indians went over to the Spanish side, and Spaniards went over to the Indian side. I am referring here to instances in which the changing of sides occurred with some apparent degree of volition. I say "apparent" because enormous power to punish and do harm lay in the hands of Soto and his captains, and the expedition carried with it such conflict, hardship, and risk that none of these decisions to change sides can be said to have been made entirely free of duress.

There were at least five instances in the course of the Soto expedition in which Spaniards and Indians changed sides. I will mention just two that seem to have been by choice. In the first one, an Indian changed sides. When Soto died, the chief of Guachoya, in southeastern Arkansas, delivered up two young boys to the Spaniards so they could be killed as retainers to accompany Soto's soul to the other world.[7] Retainer burial had been a part of southeastern elite funerary practices for hundreds of years. No one can be very definite about how the ones who were to be sacrificed were picked, but there is no reason to think that they were condemned to death for wrongdoing.

The Spaniards declined to sacrifice the two boys and scolded the Guachoyas for practicing this custom. Later, one of the boys declared to the Spaniards that he wished to accompany the Spaniards when they departed from Guachoya. He said that he did not wish to continue living among those who had consigned him to death, and he wished to live out his life among those who had spared him.

In the second instance, after Soto's death, a Spaniard changed sides as the survivors were trying to walk across Texas to reach safety in Mexico. This was Francisco de Guzmán, a bastard son of a gentleman of Seville, who was what we would today call a compulsive gambler. As the Spaniards were traveling through southwestern Arkansas, while they were in the chiefdom of Chaguate, Guzmán bet and lost his last possessions. By this time he had bet and lost his horse, most of his weapons, and some of his clothing, and finally he bet and lost a beautiful Indian concubine, enslaved during the course of the expedition, whom he loved.

While on the trail, a short time after the Spaniards took their leave from Chaguate, the Spaniards discovered that Guzmán had contrived to remain behind with his Indian lover. The Spaniards threatened the people of Chaguate with harm unless they handed over Guzmán, but the Indians insisted that Guzmán did not want to rejoin the expedition. The Spaniards could not wait any longer. They gave up on Guzmán and continued travel-ing toward the Southwest, but when they realized that they could not suc-ceed in reaching Mexico, they turned around and began marching back to the Mississippi River, retracing their route. When they returned to Cha-guate, they again attempted to retrieve Guzmán. They sent him a letter, accompanied with a pen and ink, saying that if he were being held pris-oner to inform them and they would force the Indians to release him. However, if he were not being held against his will, he should remember that he was a Christian man and should not be living among infidels. But the letter came back chillingly mute: Guzmán had signed his name—no more.[8] I should point out that his Indian lover was probably as much a stranger to Chaguate as Guzmán was.

We shall probably never know how successfully this Indian boy and this Spanish man changed sides, whether either of their lives was lived happily. But perhaps the most important thing to note here is that these instances seem to imply that the two sets of cultural players appear to have conceived of changing sides as an option. They saw it as a doable thing. And I think we have to conclude that even where cultural differ-ences might be expected to be at their greatest, there was in fact a deep substratum of cultural sameness shared by the two sets of players.

Now, if the concept of culture cannot help us sort out Spaniards from Indians as handily as we expected, can it help us sort out the native peo-ple of the sixteenth-century Southeast from each other? As my colleagues and I began fitting our new Soto route to archaeological evidence, plotting this on a map of the Southeast, I expected that the native polities would neatly coincide with archaeological cultures and language families. In some instances they seem to have done so. For example, sixteenth-century Caddoan social entities appear to coincide with Caddoan archaeo-logical cultures, and it may be that all of them spoke Caddoan languages. But analysis of the Soto experience elsewhere indicates that there were several dramatic exceptions. The paramount chiefdom of Coosa (Coza), located in the Tennessee Valley, included people of at least two different archaeological cultures and at least three Muskogean language divisions. The paramount chiefdom of Cofitachequi in South Carolina included peoples of at least three archaeological cultures and at least three different language families. My suspicion is that Indians all across the Southeast, from north Florida, Georgia, and the Carolinas and thence westward to east Texas and Arkansas, shared basic cultural understandings.

The concept of culture cannot be the analytical tool we use to analyze and explicate the history of the Indians of the Southeast in this early period. Moreover, I would venture to say that it has little analytical utility in *any* period of time. My saying so must sound odd to those who have read my 1976 book *The Southeastern Indians*.[9] Culture is the organizing concept in that book, which is still in print, and all I can say in my own favor is that it was the best I could do at the time in putting some initial coherence into the literature on the native peoples of the Southeast.

SOCIAL HISTORY

Along what lines, then, should a successor to *The Southeastern Indians* be written, whether by myself or someone else? I have to say that the general approach to the history of the early South that I advocated at the 1980 Porter Fortune symposium at the University of Mississippi I still advocate.[10] Namely, I still think that the approach of the social historians Marc Bloch, Fernand Braudel, and others is likely to be the most sustainable and productive approach to take.[11] It is a research paradigm that is capable of taking on world-sized systems, as in Braudel's great *Mediterranean and the Mediterranean World in the Age of Philip II*.[12] It is capable of grappling with exotic social orders with spotty documentation, as in Marc Bloch's *Feudal Society*.[13] It is capable of reconstructing communities in the remote past, as in Emmanuel Le Roy Ladurie's *Montaillou*.[14] And it is capable of examining the surface of life in remote eras, as in Natalie Zeamon Davis's *The Return of Martin Guerre* and in Carlo Ginzburg's *The Cheese and the Worms*.[15]

THE MISSISSIPPIAN WORLD

I would further advocate that our units of analysis for writing a social history of the early Southeast must be not cultures nor societies but polities:

that is, collections of human communities that were politically organized; moreover, these polities must be understood within the context of the world in which they existed. Let us use an analogy and think of a world-system as a particular kind of game (a serious game) that is played upon a delimited field—a definable area on the surface of the earth—and the players upon this field are polities. The play on such a field is of course constrained with respect to material and temporal limitations, and the actions of the human personnel making up the polities are governed by socially constructed rules and conventions. The question before us is how was the small, indigenous, native world in place in the Southeast at first contact destroyed and its remains absorbed into the vast and constantly expanding European world?

We can think of our task as scholars as being analogous to the hypothetical problem of describing and writing an account of the manner in which the game of cricket might be transformed over time into the game of baseball, or, perhaps as an analogy that would better reflect the true dimensions of this southeastern transformation, we might imagine the local game of cricket (played only in England and some of her former colonies) being transformed into the very different international game of soccer. A cricket player cannot be substituted for a soccer player, and I am persuaded that a member of the sixteenth-century chiefdom of Coosa could not be substituted for an eighteenth-century Creek or Choctaw.

In the past twenty years archaeologists have made enormous strides in reconstructing the world of late prehistoric southeastern Indians. This is the Mississippian way of life, and its era is the Mississippian period. Archaeologists are increasingly finding that quite a bit of variability existed within the area where the Mississippian way of life occurred, so much so that the usefulness of the term has been questioned. (I will continue to use it here, if only out of habit.) Of great importance in this recent Mississippian research has been the concept of the chiefdom, a type of society that is demographically small, numbering in the thousands or tens of thousands, but in whose structure and governance inherited social ranking was important. Archaeologists have gone furthest in reconstructing the economic base of these late prehistoric chiefdoms: hoe agriculture of corn, beans, and squash plus a few older southeastern cultigens in a varying mix with wild foods obtained by hunting, fishing, and gathering. This mix of domesticated and wild food varied throughout the course of a year, and it varied geographically, but recent research suggests that in some of its essentials, it was truly structural, enduring for centuries.[16]

Archaeologists have recently developed models of Mississippian societies that are much more dynamic and flexible than their initial models of twenty or thirty years ago. It is clear now that Mississippian chiefdoms were not peaceable kingdoms. Far from it. There was a lot of fighting going on in the late prehistoric Southeast, and this was an important part of what the Mississippian world was all about. Warfare was certainly the subject of many Mississippian artistic works, and I have to think that it must have been a subject of everyday concern.[17]

Of course, warfare was not the only thing that Mississippian peoples were concerned about. With conflict such as this, and with loss of life a constant worry, an adaptive advantage would have been realized by any Mississippian chiefdom that could contrive to create a wider peace, a peace over a larger area of land. Thus, I am sure that Mississippian peoples were motivated to experiment with ways of persuading people to get along with each other and to find ways to lay their vengefulness aside. I suspect that this was what prompted the formation of some of the paramount chiefdoms that Soto and his men encountered. Paramount chiefdoms were polities that were themselves composed of alliances of simple chiefdoms. Such alliances lessened the danger of violence on the part of close neighbors, while making it possible to put greater numbers of warriors on the field to oppose enemies who lived at a distance.

It can now be seen that the Mississippian social transformation was very much a theme with variations. That is, within a set of encompassing social and economic structures, the people of the late prehistoric Southeast came up with various localized expressions. Such a model—whose fine details are still to be worked out—allows us to think of Mississippian chiefdoms in present Georgia, Alabama, Tennessee, Mississippi, and Arkansas, but also in terms of more extreme variations in seventeenth-century Powhatan Virginia, in sixteenth- and seventeenth-century Timucuan north Florida, and in Caddoan east Texas. So far as I am aware, no scholar is now at work on the descriptive and analytical task of synthesizing this immense quantity of material. But much of the enabling research is now on the table. I am thinking, for example, of David Anderson's recent book on chiefdoms in Georgia and South Carolina,[18] Timothy Perttula's book on the Caddo,[19] and John Worth's recent book on the Timucuan chiefdoms.[20] And to this we can add newly published major works by

George Milner on Cahokia[21] and Vernon J. Knight, Jr., and Vincas Steponaitis on Moundville.[22]

The construction of this increasingly fleshed-out picture of the Mississippian world is a major scholarly achievement. This new picture represents the southeastern Indians at their cultural and social apogee, when
they were most distinctively themselves, because following European
contact they increasingly became players who were pushed and pulled
about in a world not of their own making.

How may this late prehistoric/early historic southeastern world be
briefly characterized? The playing field of the Mississippian world was
approximately the same as that of the territory included in the Old South.
It stretched from Florida, Georgia, the Carolinas, and possibly Virginia
westward across the South to Arkansas and east Texas and from present
St. Louis southward to the Gulf of Mexico. The players on this field were
simple chiefdoms which were sometimes aggregated into larger paramount chiefdoms. In some places and at some times, warfare reached a
high level, occasionally so high that a major river valley—such as the
Savannah River valley—might have to be abandoned. One assumes that
the principal concerns of these polities were affairs occurring within the
borders of their chiefdom; after that they were concerned with their allies
and after that with their enemies, who might not lie at a comfortable distance. Just what grasp these players had of other players who were located
in remote parts of the Mississippian world is a matter of some interest, but
I am not sure that anyone is presently able to make definitive statements
about it. For example, did the Caddoans have any knowledge of affairs in
the central Mississippi Valley chiefdoms? It is plausible, I think, to
believe that they did. But did they know about Coosa in the Tennessee
Valley, or Powhatan in Virginia, or the Timucuan chiefdoms in northern
Florida? In other words, what extent of "international" knowledge existed
in the minds of late prehistoric southeastern Indians? Recently I was
taken to task by a reviewer for arguing that the circle of knowledge was
rather small in the late prehistoric Southeast.[23] I still believe this to have
been the case. The evidence suggests that Mississippian chiefdoms were
composed of largely self-sufficient, local peoples who may have valued
exotic materials and things, but who probably did not know much about
faraway peoples and places.

As an aside, when I was writing my recent book on the Soto expedition,
Knights of Spain, Warriors of the Sun, I saw it as an opportunity to take my

readers on a walking tour of this late prehistoric world of southeastern chiefdoms. But it still remains for some archaeologist with expertise in social history (or a social historian with expertise in archaeology) to write a systematic and comprehensive reconstruction of this Mississippian world.[24]

THE MODERN WORLD-SYSTEM

The world that superseded this Mississippian world in the Southeast was immensely larger in territorial expanse, and its center lay across the Atlantic Ocean, in Europe. Indeed, in the course of time it knew no global limits. Immanuel Wallerstein has termed it the Modern World-System, though at times I will simply call it the Modern World.[25] It entailed a new way of doing business and of conducting international relations, and particularly of new economic arrangements for acquiring and administering colonies. For nations that could devise winning strategies in their contest with other nations for supremacy in this new world order, the rewards were to be enormous. Some nations possessed more successful strategies than others, and this can be seen as clearly in the American Southeast as anywhere in the world.

Nations in the Modern World-System developed the capability of crossing oceans, then sent their people to stand on foreign shores and to outrageously claim such places as their own. From the late sixteenth century until the eighteenth century the Southeast became one of the zones of conflict in the Modern World where Spain, the Netherlands, England, and France competed for supremacy, and the identities and characters of the native peoples were powerfully shaped when they were drawn into this contest. It is obvious to us now that seventeenth- and eighteenth-century Indian polities must be defined and understood as they existed within the context of this Modern World-System.[26] The native people of the Southeast were no longer Mississippian chiefdoms operating within an intimate world that they themselves defined and created. They were a new kind of people in a new kind of world. This may be obvious to us now, but I can tell you it was not at all obvious to me thirty-five years ago when I was doing my dissertation research. I remember how flummoxed I was in trying to come up with a satisfactory way of thinking about the Catawba Indians of South Carolina.[27]

What are we to call the Indian polities on this new Modern World playing field? Europeans in the seventeenth and eighteenth centuries often referred to the Indians of the old South as "nations."[28] Europeans themselves were avidly building and promoting the interests of their own nations at the time, and perhaps it is natural that they would extend this term to the Indians. But it is unclear to me whether they used this term in all seriousness, or whether they used it in some ironic, approximate, or as-if sense. Modern scholars have tended not to use "nation" because the Creeks, Cherokees, and Choctaws are hardly to be classed with eighteenth-century France, England, or Spain. Beginning in the nineteenth century, scholars have most commonly referred to them as "tribes," perhaps on the model of biblical usage or from classical European usage. But like many of the terms coined by nineteenth-century anthropologists, "tribe" turned out to have an unclear reference, and some anthropologists have more recently assigned "tribe" to a type of small-scale organization based on kinship and locality.[29] And I must say that in spite of the immense usefulness of the concept of the chiefdom, it does not convey an appreciation of the position of native polities in the larger world system.

So, the problem of developing a terminology to use in talking about seventeenth- and eighteenth-century southeastern Indians is a very real one. Using "nation" to refer to the native polities of this period is not as questionable as I once thought. These native southeastern polities surely were competing with European nations in the arena of a small piece of the Modern World, and it was a life-or-death struggle. To some of the players on both sides, these Indian "nations" may have been seen to have had a chance of surviving into the future. But we need a more refined vocabulary, because the seventeenth- and eighteenth-century native polities and collectivities obviously differed amongst themselves in their social and economic character, and we need terms that reflect these differences. For example, the Creeks and Cherokees should not be classed with the tiny groups of "settlement Indians" living hand-to-mouth in Carolina.[30] And are these "settlement Indians" to be classed with the *petites nations* Daniel Usner has described for the Mississippi Valley?[31] We need to begin working toward a commonly accepted analytical vocabulary.

Pulling some of these strands together, we have in the sixteenth century a late prehistoric southeastern world of Mississippian chiefdoms, and in the eighteenth century we have in its place the Southeast as a geopolitical zone in an expanding Modern World-System, peopled by colonists from European nations, their African slaves, and as yet ill-defined Indian polities and collectivities. The task before us is to reconstruct and explain what happened to the native peoples as this Modern World order replaced and superseded the old Mississippian order, but before I say more about this, I want to discuss a problem of evidence.

A PROBLEM OF EVIDENCE

Historical analyses of the Modern World-System are based on ample historical documentation. Documentation of the inner workings of the eighteenth-century Indian polities is always less then one would wish, but they were very definitely historical entities, with known actors, and in rare instances we can glimpse the thought processes of these native actors. And this documentary evidence is supplemented by archaeological information from historic sites.

Quite the reverse is true of the late prehistoric Mississippian world. For the bulk of what we know about this world, we must rely on archaeological evidence alone. Archaeological evidence derives from material stuff, and archaeologists are at their best in reconstructing the material and economic bases of life in the past. They cannot proceed with the same level of confidence in reconstructing kinship and community behavior, and even less so in analyzing social and political behavior above the community level. Their conclusions on such matters are inferential, and sometimes the inferences are pyramided one on top of the other. This material record can only be extended by using to the fullest degree the very earliest scant documentary record. I am speaking of the documents of the early Spanish and French explorers and missionaries, the documentary records of Spanish missions in Florida, and the English records of early colonial Virginia, Maryland, and North Carolina.

It seems to me inescapable that the scaffolding on which our picture of the Mississippian world is built is shakier, more inferential, and more subject to drastic revision than that of the Modern World-System. Hence, in tracing continuities and discontinuities between the Mississippian world and the eighteenth-century Southeast, we are confronted not so much with a case of comparing apples and oranges as of comparing corporeal apples with largely inferential apples. We need to frankly acknowledge this problem of uneven evidence on either side of the documentary divide and to devise ways of dealing with it.

THE TRANSFORMATION OF THE MISSISSIPPIAN WORLD

How do we begin accounting for why and how the Mississippian world was destroyed and its surviving peoples absorbed into the Modern World? The several causes are: (1) military losses at the hands of European explorers; (2) destabilization following initial European contact; (3) virulent Old World diseases; and (4) sustained political and economic incorporation into the Modern World-System as it evolved through time.[32]

Military Losses. Indian population losses at the hands of explorers like Hernando de Soto were small by modern standards, but they were in places very heavy for small-scale societies. This was the case in the battles at Napituca in northern Florida, Chicaza in Mississippi, Anilco in southeastern Arkansas, and most particularly Mabila in Alabama. But even when losses were great for particular native polities, it is unlikely that the aggregate of these losses was sufficient to tear apart the fabric of the Mississippian world.

Destabilization. By destabilization, I refer to the deleterious impact on native political relations from the actions of early European explorers, and this was particularly the case in instances where Europeans sided militarily with one group of Indians against another group. My impression of "normal" Mississippian warfare is that it was the Texas-draw type, in which hostility was constant, rather predictable, and low-level. Such appears to have been the case in northeastern Arkansas with the chiefdom of Casqui and their enemy, the paramount chiefdom of Pacaha. But it so happened that Soto sided with Casqui in a vicious attack on Pacaha at a much higher level of warfare than was normal, and chances are these two polities went at each other at an increased level of hostility after Soto departed and was out of the picture. Something similar may also have occurred between the people of Anilco and those of Guachoya.

Some have speculated that encountering the technologically superior Spaniards must have been demoralizing to the Indians, and may have weakened their respect for their leaders and even their regard for their gods. This is plausible, but I know of no direct evidence for it. As a causal factor in the transformation of the southeastern Indians, my inclination is to put destabilization in the same league as direct military losses, discussed above. That is, it was a contributing but not a major cause of social transformation.

Old World Diseases. We have long known that the impact of Old World

diseases on New World peoples was severe.[33] It caused such serious population loss that business as usual for the chiefdoms must have become
difficult and eventually impossible. There is no question that diseases
were one of the principal causes of structural social, cultural, and political
discontinuity in native polities between the sixteenth and nineteenth centuries. But serious questions remain—namely, which diseases struck the
Indians, and where, and when?

Epidemic diseases may explain some of the major perturbations in the
social history of the early Southeast. For example, it would seem that the
precipitous decline of population in the Mississippi Valley implies serious
epidemics, and the same is true for the dissolution of the paramount chiefdom of Coosa in the Tennessee Valley. This may also explain what seems
to be an anomaly in early Cherokee history: Cherokee-speaking peoples
do not appear to have been imposing in the sixteenth century, but they
were unusually prominent in the eighteenth century, and this seems contrary to historical trends elsewhere.

The crucial question is when and where did the first serious epidemics
occur? If copper from Basque fishermen could reach the Ohio Valley in
the sixteenth century, as Penelope Drooker argues (in this volume) was
the case, then we have to ask whether diseases might also have come into
the Southeast at this time from this direction. The problem lies in dis-
covering the evidence. Some of the epidemic diseases afflicting the Indians imparted little or no trauma to the bones, and in truly serious epidemics, many corpses probably lay unburied, to be consumed by scavengers.
Hence, it is difficult for archaeologists to adduce direct evidence of serious episodes of disease.

Paul Kelton argues in this volume that smallpox, the most dreaded Old
World disease, did not strike the interior of the Southeast until after 1696.
And he argues that other early diseases probably had little effect on the
native population of the region. Clearly, the smallpox epidemic that began
in Virginia in 1696 is the first major epidemic in the interior Southeast for
which there is ample historical documentation. The problem is that this
epidemic falls quite close to the time when the historical record on the
interior begins. And this raises the problem of uneven evidence mentioned earlier.

Kelton's paper flies in the face of the work of many archaeologists who
have concluded that severe population declines occurred in the Southeast
before 1696. This has been argued particularly regarding the Tennessee

Valley and the lower Mississippi Valley. It is notable, I think, that Kelton does not dispute the evidence that John Worth has adduced for an early population decline in Spanish Florida, because here the historical record is continuous from the second half of the sixteenth century onward.

Kelton's paper is a challenge for archaeologists. Can truly persuasive archaeological evidence be adduced for significant population decline in the Southeast before about 1700? If so, is this evidence persuasive enough to withstand the challenges of Kelton's thesis?

Political and Economic Incorporation into the Modern World-System. Epidemic diseases from the Old World were an ever-present cause of native population decline in the Southeast from the time of the introduction of the diseases until about the time of the American Revolution, when the population reached its nadir, stabilized, and recovered slightly.[34] In that diseases killed off the human repositories of knowledge and tradition, they were transformational. And when diseases reduced populations below the number that could support chiefdom level societies, they were transformational.

But an even more powerful cause of social transformation was the incorporation of native populations into the Modern World-System, the world sponsored by colonists from Europe. At different times from the sixteenth century through the eighteenth century, these colonists penetrated North America at several points along the Atlantic coast, and they developed three general colonial strategies by means of which they dominated the native peoples. These were: the Spanish mission system in Florida and eastern Texas, the fur trade in the Northeast, and the plantation system and Indian trade in the South. When these colonial strategies are seen in relation to the varying environmental and historical factors that existed between the St. Lawrence Valley and eastern Texas, much can be understood about how the native peoples of the eastern United States were transformed.

Spanish Missions in Florida. Spain was the first European power to penetrate the Mississippian world. For a long while, Spain failed at establishing viable colonies in the Southeast. The initiatives of Juan Ponce de León in 1513 and 1521, Lucas Vázquez de Ayllón in 1526, Pánfilo de Narváez in 1528, Hernando de Soto in 1539–43, and Tristán de Luna y Arellano in 1559–61 all ended in failure. None of these ventures was able to establish a colonial connection to a sufficiently complex native infrastructure and a sufficiently large and productive native population.

Pedro Menéndez de Avilés succeeded in colonizing Florida in 1565 because his aim was to establish a fundamentally defensive colony based upon a mission system. The purposes of this colony were to offer some protection and refuge to the Spanish fleet as it sailed through the Bahama channel and parallel to the Atlantic coast and also to prevent any other European nation from establishing a colony in the Southeast. As John Worth shows in his paper in this volume, the Spanish approach to colonization was to administer through the infrastructure of native social systems while gradually changing the people and incorporating them into the outer edges of the Spanish empire. In the Florida missions, the native chiefs possessed rights that were affirmed by the Spanish missionaries and officials.

The missions expanded out from St. Augustine from about 1587 to 1633, encompassing the Georgia and South Carolina coast to the north and the Timucuan and Apalachee provinces in and around present Tallahassee to the west. The missions were relatively stable after 1633 until the time when they began to be assaulted by the Carolina colonists and their Indian allies in the closing decades of the seventeenth century. Many native place names remained attached to the landscape for centuries in Spanish Florida.

One of the most notable characteristics of the Spanish mission system in Florida was its inability to shape Indian societies at a distance. Since the Spaniards' strategy was to transform Indians by changing them from within—by winning their hearts and minds—and to incorporate them into the colonial system, the Europeans had little direct impact on Indians who lived at any distance from the missions.

The Fur Trade in the Northeast. In light of the geographical constraints on the expansion of the Spanish mission system in Florida, it must seem odd that the next significant colonial penetration to affect the southeastern Indians took place in what is now the northeastern United States. The economic engine that set in motion this assault on the southeastern Indians was the fur trade, and the native agents who made it happen were the Iroquois. Perhaps no greater contrast than the Iroquois can be had to the kind of colonized Indian societies produced by the Spanish mission system.

Jacques Cartier discovered the mouth of the St. Lawrence River in 1535, and this became the avenue for French colonial penetration. The French found that the principal product of the north country was fur-bearing animals. Subsequently, they slowly developed a trade in furs with the Indians, and by about 1580 it had become significant enough to be the object of commercial speculation in Europe.[35] The French soon had competition from the Dutch, whose avenue was the Hudson River, and as time went on the French and the Dutch came into conflict with the English colonists in New England.

The people who were the nucleus of the Iroquois League and Confederacy were at first marginal to this trade. They lived in a series of clusters of towns—the Mohawks, Oneidas, Onandagas, Cayugas, and Senecas—that lay spread out from the Mohawk River (which emptied into the Hudson) westward over to the Genese River, to the south of Lake Ontario.

At first the Iroquois were impeded in their access to either the French or Dutch traders by other native peoples who lay in their way. But in time they were not only the preeminent people in this entire region; they became preemptive. They were so successful in the grim work they undertook that scholars are still trying to explain how and why they did it. As Daniel Richter has pointed out, the Iroquois did enjoy several advantages: (1) they were farmers, as opposed to many of their fur-trading neighbors who were hunter-gatherers, and therefore enjoyed the more abundant food supply that farming provided, plus perhaps some institutional advantages that came with farming; (2) they lived in a location that was somewhat out of the way, possibly sparing them some of the earliest epidemics; (3) they had water transport in all directions, making it easy for them to move goods that way; (4) they were located in proximity to several competing European colonial powers, and could at times play one of these off against the other to their own advantage.[36]

Embattled from without, the Iroquois dug in and remained in their territory, building heavily fortified towns to protect themselves from attacks by their enemies. After Henry Hudson sailed up the Hudson River in 1609, under the flag of the Dutch East India Company, the Dutch began competing with the French for the fur trade from their post at Fort Orange, at present Albany, New York. The Iroquois were initially hindered from trading with the Dutch by the Algonkian-speaking Mahicans, who blocked their way. But the Mohawks launched a concerted campaign against the Mahicans, defeating and driving them out, and in so doing they gained direct and convenient access to trade with the Dutch.

The Iroquois and other northern Indians exchanged furs for items of European manufacture on which they came to be dependent. European

cloth and metal tools were superior to what the Iroquois possessed, and
they had to do what was required to obtain these things. At first the Europeans were not eager to sell guns to the Indians. But eventually the Iroquois acquired guns in quantity. Perhaps the reason was that the competition for furs had grown keener. In 1640 the English in New England
captured the Mohawk trade by exchanging guns for their furs. The Dutch
quickly followed suit and themselves began trading guns to the Iroquois.[37]
This was the way of the modern world. In the future some English and
Dutch would be killed with these guns, but in the meantime there was
money to be made.

The earliest Jamestown colonists quickly learned that a deep fault line
lay between the mostly Algonkian-speaking Indians of Virginia and the
Iroquoian-speaking peoples to the northeast. They learned that the native
people living around Chesapeake Bay were worried about Iroquoian-
speaking Massawomeckes and Pocoughtraonacks who were attacking
them from the north. The Iroquois were pushing out other northern peoples—possibly Algonkian- and Siouan-speaking peoples. The Susquehannocks were obtaining metal tools in trade from the French, and they came
increasingly under severe pressure by the Iroquois.

As Penelope Drooker argues in this volume, people in the Ohio Valley
had probably been affected by some of these same forces before 1607.
Unfortunately, only the most indirect documentary evidence exists for
native societies in the Ohio Valley before 1750. But archaeological
research indicates that the same kind of prehistoric dynamic changes
occurred in this area as happened elsewhere in the Southeast. That is,
areas in the Ohio Valley with numerous villages at one time became
depopulated at a later time; evident coalescent populations formed in
some places; and old styles of material culture disappeared in some
places.

In the Ohio Valley, specific connections between historically identified
eighteenth-century polities and late prehistoric archaeological entities
continue to elude us. The several divisions of Algonkian-speaking Shawnee can definitely be placed in the Ohio Valley in the eighteenth century.
But as Drooker shows, there is no archaeological evidence persuasively
linking the Shawnee with the Fort Ancient archaeological complex.

One of the large questions about the protohistoric era is why there was
such a development of predatory polities in the Northeast whose members displaced peoples to their west and southwest, traveling surprisingly

long distances to do so. I am referring specifically to the Iroquois and the people they interacted with and affected. What were the peculiar environmental, cultural, economic, and historical conditions that account for this? How were these people organized? What were their motives? Why did this assault not proceed in the opposite direction? That is, why did southeastern peoples not raid northward, displacing people and wreaking havoc with old lifeways?

The Iroquois have to be explained in terms of their social formation having occurred in the historical crucible of their location between the French and their Algonkian allies on the one hand, and the Dutch on the other hand. The Iroquois traded not in a commodity—e.g., deerskins and Indian slaves—which they themselves worked to acquire and sell. Rather, they dealt in valuable furs, the best of which were trapped in the far north and which they could steal in piratical raids on other Indians. And they could replace their diminishing population at the same time by capturing people on these raids whom they could adopt into their societies. Can it be shown, therefore, that the Iroquois were as they were not because of their own Iroquois cultural genius but as a result of their adaptation to particular geopolitical and economic conditions?

These "wars of northern aggression" can be conceptualized as a series of shock waves radiating from the Northeast. From about the 1630s to 1650 the Iroquois attacks fell to their west, on the peoples of the St. Lawrence Valley, particularly on the Huron confederacy. By 1650 the Huron had been displaced. Then from 1650 to 1657 Iroquois attacks fell on the people to the south—on the Petun, the Erie, and the Susquehannock—displacing all but the latter. The survivors of these groups moved elsewhere. Some fled to the Ohio Valley. Others retreated to the Piedmont country to the west of the Virginia colony. After that, the Iroquois raided to the southwest over much longer distances into the Ohio Valley and west to the Great Lakes. Mainly Algonkian-speaking people in Ohio and Illinois moved west to the Mississippi River and also southward to areas previously occupied by Mississippian chiefdoms. Iroquois attacks continued on them in their new locations until the 1680s.

It also appears that the Iroquois caused other people who survived their onslaughts to organize themselves in similar ways. This seems to have been the case with the Westos, who appear to have been Erie who were displaced by the Iroquois. These people moved southward, through piedmont Virginia, North Carolina, and presumably South Carolina, to settle on the Savannah River before 1670. When the Carolina colonists first arrived, they found the Westos to be present and heavily armed with guns, living in the neighborhood of Indians who did not possess guns. The Westos lived in bark-covered longhouses, and the indigenous Indians were terrified of them, claiming that they were cannibals. They do appear to have had a trading connection with Virginia.

Is it fair to say that the Westos (and the Iroquois who shaped them) were to the late seventeenth-century Southeast what the Mongols with their superior cavalry were to medieval Europe? That is, they had a brief window of opportunity in which mobile people with a military advantage—in their case guns—could wreak great havoc on people who lacked guns and adequate defenses against such opponents.[38]

The Ohio Valley was not spared social dislocations. The occupation of Caborn-Welborn sites in the lower Ohio Valley appears to have ended around 1600. The eastern Fort Ancient occupations on the upper Ohio and Monangahela rivers appear to have ended in the 1630s. The Fort Ancient occupation of the central Ohio Valley appears to have ended at about 1650.

Historical evidence attests to the fact that Shawnees (the Algonkian word for southerners) were living in the Ohio Valley by the late 1660s and 1670s. Other named groups, including the Fox, were there as well. It is not known at present whether these peoples were coalescent people from elsewhere or whether they were made up wholly or in part of descendants of prehistoric Ohio Valley peoples. Certainly Gabriel Arthur, who penetrated the mountains of western Virginia in 1674, traveling to the confluence of the Kanawha and Ohio rivers, encountered people who were the victims of major historical dislocations, and it is noteworthy that the people he encountered did not possess guns by this date.

The Shawnees were certainly one of the distinctive peoples of the late seventeenth and early eighteenth centuries. They were organized into several distinct groups, though the interrelations among these several groups are poorly understood. They seem to have made decisions largely independently of each other, and they were noted for moving their places of residence over long distances. A group of them took up residence on the Savannah River by 1674, and they became allies of the Carolina traders. Another group was living in the Susquehannah country in southern Pennsylvania by 1692. Yet another group resided at a French fort in Illinois between 1683 and 1689. Their movements from the late 1600s to the early 1800s were extraordinarily complex.

The Shawnee were in great need of European trade goods. In 1674 Henry Woodward encountered two Shawnees who were engaged in a trade with Spaniards in St. Augustine. This encounter may have prompted the group of Shawnees who moved to the Savannah River a short time later, and who allied with the Carolinians in expunging the Westos. Some of these Shawnee may have moved in with the Tuckabachee on the lower Tallapoosa River after the Yamasee war of 1715.

The question is, what kind of historical formation were the Shawnee? Were they produced by the same forces that shaped the Iroquois and the Westos? Were the Shawnee in fact several coalescent groups of Algonkian-speaking peoples (or mainly Algonkian) who survived Iroquois aggression by becoming mobile and moving southward to seek any haven they could find by allying themselves with European colonists or other Indian political formations?

One of the greatest problems in accounting for the late prehistoric to early historic transformation of the native peoples of the Southeast is the massive changes in the Mississippi Valley. Like the Ohio Valley, the Mississippi Valley affords us no direct documentary evidence on the era between the 1540s and the 1680s, but historical evidence on either side of this "dark age" indicates that sweeping social change occurred during this interval. Hernando de Soto encountered some of the largest and most impressive chiefdoms here that he found in all his travels in the Southeast. But when Marquette and Joliet and La Salle again visited this area in the last two decades of the seventeenth century, the native population appeared to be tiny. And modern archaeological research confirms this. A particularly difficult interpretive problem is posed by the Quapaw, encountered at the mouth of the Arkansas River by the French, who described them as living in longhouses resembling those built by Iroquois and other northeastern Indians.

Over the years, archaeologists and historians have filled in this historical vacuum in the protohistoric Mississippi Valley with a complex series of hypotheses and counterhypotheses. Marvin Jeter's paper in this volume provides a summary of this extraordinarily intricate scholarly argumentation. Jeter proposes a novel scenario for the transformation of the central Mississippi Valley. He notes that on the basis of place names from the Soto expedition, the dominant languages of the lower Mississippi Valley were Natchezan and Tunican. Natchezan appears to have been spoken from just south of present Memphis southward down the valley on both sides of the Mississippi River, and this includes the lower Arkansas River. But around the northwestern rim of this area lay probable Tunican speakers, who also occupied the middle Arkansas River valley.

The scenario that Jeter proposes is that in the late sixteenth century or in the early to middle seventeenth century the population of the lower Mississippi Valley was affected by Old World diseases and underwent sharp decline. Perhaps feeling the impact of middle to late seventeenth-century native dislocations in the Northeast and Midwest, the Tunican and Natchezan survivors of these epidemics moved southward and coalesced into the societies encountered by the French: the Natchez, Koroa, Tunica, Taensa, and so on.

Jeter's scenario contains yet another novel solution. He proposes that the Quapaw, who spoke a Dhegihan Siouan language, were derived from eastern Fort Ancient peoples living on the upper Ohio River and its tributaries, who had been dislocated by Iroquois attacks. This accounts for the Quapaw longhouses, covered with bark, and his scenario is consistent with other evidence that many of the people in seventeenth-century back-country Virginia and the Carolina piedmont spoke Siouan languages.

This intrusion of the Quapaw into the Mississippi Valley probably occurred relatively late, at about the same time other northern peoples, namely the Westos and the Shawnee, were entering the Southeast. This pattern of long-distance movements of people from the north, it should be noted, is consistent with the broad patterns of population movements noted by Marvin Smith in his paper in this volume.

The Plantation System and Indian Trade in the South. The English approach to achieving colonial supremacy in the South was to establish plantations with mainly indentured and coerced laborers who produced commodities for the world market. At first these plantations were established near the coast on navigable waterways. As the Indians were progressively displaced and subdued, plantations pushed gradually inland. A second prong of the English strategy was to engage the Indians at a distance in trade for European-manufactured goods such as guns, cutting tools, woolen cloth, and other items in exchange for commodities such as dressed deerskins and Indian slaves.[39] A concomitant English strategy was to stimulate internecine conflict and attrition among the Indians to reduce and demoralize their population until the day when further agricultural penetration of the interior was possible, and the Indians could be pressured to cede their lands.

As Helen Rountree shows in her paper in this volume, this was the approach of the Virginians. The Jamestown colony faltered and almost foundered before it hit upon the cultivation of tobacco along the alluvial soils of the James River and its tributaries. Tobacco was an almost archetypal growth industry; once its devotees were addicted to its charms, demand for the product would only grow. But even with this, the Jamestown colony at first withered because of a very high death rate among the colonists.

It was with the beginning of the rule of Governor William Berkeley in 1640 that the Virginia colony got an infusion of new colonists, mostly royalists from southern England, and the colony began to expand vigorously. In 1646 the Powhatan paramount chiefdom was finally crushed and the Virginia colonists could begin paying more attention to Indians who lay to the west and southwest. Some Virginians penetrated to the south of Virginia in the 1640s, but their activities are poorly documented. The activities of Abraham Wood, particularly at Fort Henry on the Appomattox River after 1646 were important. After 1650 the Virginia government began encouraging adventurers to explore to the south and to pursue trade with the Indians. This culminated in a series of explorations in the 1670s that produced written reports.

What remains to be researched is to what degree and in what manner the Virginians affected Indians to their west and southwest between 1640 and 1670. Was this trade prosecuted by white traders going out with their wares? Or was it primarily conducted through Indian intermediaries, such as the Occaneechees, Tuscaroras, and others? What goods did the Virginians trade to the Indians, and what did they get in return? Was there a trade in Indian slaves, and if so, what was the volume? It is quite likely that a large chapter of this history will found in be the activities of Abraham Wood and his associates.

In general, until Bacon's rebellion in 1676, the Indian trade to the southwest was impeded by the Occaneechees, a group of people who occupied a crucial position on the Dan River where it intersected a trail that led to the southwest. This trail ran to the west of the territory of the Tuscaroras, an Iroquois-speaking people on the coastal plain who held out longer against the English colonists than the piedmont tribes did.

From the Mississippian chiefdoms along the Catawba-Wateree River, the heartland of old Cofitachequi, northward to backcountry Virginia, the piedmont was populated by tribal societies. Their houses were oval or circular, built of poles set in the earth, bent over, and covered with sheets of bark. They were typically laid out in a circular pattern around an open plaza and surrounded by a palisade. Typically these people did not possess public architecture (see Stephen Davis's essay in this volume). Many—but probably not all—of these people spoke Siouan or Catawban languages. For unknown reasons, people who lived in the coastal plain of Virginia and North Carolina—the Powhatans and the Tuscaroras—were able to put together polities that had greater ability to resist the English colonists than those of the piedmont tribes. It may be that the piedmont tribes were too exposed to the trail system from the north, the avenue of Iroquois raiders and their victims and later the thoroughfare of the Virginia traders. It is also possible that they had not developed the institutional means for building larger coalescent polities.

From 1650 onward—and particularly from 1676 onward—the piedmont tribes moved to take up positions on the trading path from Fort Henry to the towns on the Catawba-Wateree River, and from there to the Creeks and the Cherokees. In the next few decades, the piedmont tribes continually and rapidly dwindled in numbers. The main terminus for the Virginia traders was the cluster of people who coalesced on the Catawba River, who in time were collectively called "Catawbas."

After 1670, the center of the Indian trade to the southeast began to develop in Charles Town, the center of the Carolina colony. It began as a plantation trade among the planters who lived just inland, particularly those on Goose Creek. These traders had a far handier access to the larger interior populations of Indians than did the Virginia traders, whom they soon undercut. They established an interior trading post at Savannah Town on the Savannah River, somewhere in the vicinity of present Augusta. This became the entrepôt of the inland trade.[40]

Interestingly, the Indian trade prosecuted out of Charles Town would depend upon forging a trading path deep into the interior with reliable trading partners at its far end—in this case the Chickasaws.[41] Hence, it is likely that the Westoes and later the Catawbas at first served this same function for the Virginia traders. How successful the Virginia traders were in penetrating to the people on the upper Savannah River and those on the Chattahoochee River remains to be determined. It is clear enough, however, that the Virginia traders were firmly ensconced among the Catawbas at the time of John Lawson's excursion in 1700.

The Cherokees are seemingly exceptional in the Southeast for being more formidable in the eighteenth century than they were in the sixteenth century. The Cherokee-speaking peoples encountered by Hernando de Soto and Juan Pardo were hardly commented on in comparison to the Muskogean-speaking chiefdoms the Spaniards encountered on both sides of the Appalachian Mountains. But in the eighteenth century, the Cherokees were one of the powerful native entities in frontier politics. How did this come about?

As Christopher Rodning makes clear in his paper in this volume, there are still many questions to be answered about the origin and formation of the Cherokees. One environmental factor undoubtedly played a role: namely, they lived in and around the mountains. This would have given them some advantage with respect to mosquito-borne disease, such as malaria and yellow fever, and it was a habitat that was more defensible against invading enemies and slave raiders than were the piedmont and ridge and valley provinces on either side of the mountains.

Both historical and archaeological evidence suggests that at 1450 to 1600 the Cherokee-speaking peoples lived more to the northeast than was later the case. Some of them lived on the upper Nolichucky River and perhaps northward of that in the upper Tennessee Valley. Some of their towns were on the upper Pigeon River and quite possibly on the upper Catawba River in North Carolina. Then in 1600–1700 their territory contracted toward the southwest. The upper Tennessee Valley emptied out as did the upper Pigeon and probably the upper Catawba River. This contraction may have been partly caused by disease. But it may also have been partly caused by the action of predatory raiding parties from the northeast. It is possible as well that people displaced by the Iroquois may have had an impact on people who lay further down the Tennessee Valley.

In any case, the formation of the various divisions of the Cherokees may have been in place by about 1670–1700. That is to say: (1) the Lower towns were on the headwaters of the Savannah River, where they may have been a coalescence of descendants from earlier residents plus newcomers; (2) the Middle and Out towns were on the headwaters of the Little Tennessee River, and again they may have been a coalescence of old and new residents; (3) the Valley towns were on the headwaters of the Hiwassee River, and again they may have been a coalescence of old and new residents; and (4) the Overhill towns on the Little Tennessee River were mainly Cherokee-speaking peoples who reoccupied an area that had been occupied by Muskogean-speaking peoples in the sixteenth century and vacated by them in the seventeenth century.

The principal Cherokee trade connection in the early days appears to have been with Charles Town. Some Virginia trade surely reached them, perhaps mostly through Indian intermediaries. But once the Carolina trade was in motion, these traders had a shorter and much more direct route to the Cherokees than did the Virginia traders. An additional geopolitical advantage for the Cherokees was that they had good access to French trade items coming by boat up the Tennessee River.

Spanish Missions in Texas. In the sixteenth century Caddoan-speaking chiefdoms were located in parts of Arkansas, Oklahoma, Texas, and Louisiana, and their most complex development lay along the Great Bend of the Red River. Compared to the chiefdoms of the Southeast, the Caddo enjoyed something of a respite from early European contact. They were in the path of the Soto expedition of 1542. But subsequently they had little direct contact with Europeans until the La Salle expedition of 1684, from which they suffered little damage. They did not, however, escape the impact of Old World diseases. Cabeza de Vaca witnessed such diseases on the Gulf Coast of Texas after 1528, and he saw the effects of disease as he and his companions walked across the American Southwest to Mexico. As Timothy Perttula points out in this volume, the Caddo declined by as much as 75 to 95 percent between 1691 and 1816, and they may have suffered an initial loss of population between 1530 and 1691.

Their isolation from European colonists ended in the late seventeenth century with the simultaneous appearance of the French and of Charles Town deerskin and slave traders and their Indian trading partners. The Caddo fell under attack by Chickasaw slave raiders at an early date.

The Spaniards were always ready to act defensively when threatened by French and English colonists, and they did so as quickly as they could from Mexico. They established missions in east Texas in 1716–21.[42] But the Indians they missionized were little able to defend themselves because they lacked firepower. One trade advantage the Caddo enjoyed was that they had access to horses from the Southwest and also buffalo skins from the plains, which were desired both by the French and the English. They suffered at the hands of trading partners of the French, such as the Choctaws and Quapaw. Once they possessed both guns and horses, the Caddo began taking Apache slaves to trade to the French and the Spaniards.

There are some puzzles in the early history of the Caddo. One is that the languages spoken in this area are thought to have been exclusively Caddoan. On the surface, it seems that there was less multilingualism here than in the east. This needs to be examined closely, and if it is true, it needs to be explained. Another puzzle is that there is virtually no evidence of fortifications around late prehistoric Caddo towns. Does this mean that warfare was at a lower level here than in the east, or only that it was conducted differently? Certainly the Soto expedition encountered very capable fighters among the Caddo. But the conduct of war may have been different here.

The Caddo people coalesced into three groups: (1) the Hasinai, on the upper Neches River and its tributaries, as well as on the Trinity River, where they were affiliated with several Spanish missions and presidios; (2) the Kadohadacho on the Red River, above the Great Bend; and (3) the Caddo on the middle Red River, near the French post of Natchitoches. Both the Hasinai and the Natchitoches remained in place until the 1830s, but the Kadohadachos were forced to leave the Red River and settle in the Caddo Lake area in the 1780s.

NATIVE SOCIAL FORMATIONS IN THE COLONIAL SOUTHEAST

All of the major Indian polities in the seventeenth- and eighteenth-century eastern United States were formed out of coalescences and almagamations of the survivors of shattered prehistoric societies. The variability of these several societies was not so much produced by cultural causation as by the interplay of colonial politics and economics. Included were people like the Iroquois, who subsisted by preying on the wealth and population of their neighbors, and "traditional" societies like the Natchez, Apalachee, and Hasinai, who retained archaic features of social organization in French and Spanish colonial backwaters (it is notable that none of these "traditional" societies survived very far into the eighteenth century). There were "nations" of people like the Creeks, Chickasaws, Choctaws, and Cherokees, who enjoyed some protection by virtue of being located far in the interior, but whose internal structure is still poorly known. But by whatever means, these latter peoples were able to keep their numbers up at moderate levels, and hence they were forces to be reckoned with until after the American Revolution.

Others did not succeed in keeping up their numbers. These included the "settlement Indians" of the Carolinas, who ceased to have "ethnic" identities at an early date, and the "little nations" of Mississippi and Louisiana, who declined to such small numbers that they became socially vulnerable.

To what degree did this sixteenth-to-eighteenth-century social transformation in the Southeast represent a social, political, and economic discontinuity? In certain areas of life—in subsistence practices and kinship organization—surprising long-term continuities existed. But the Mississippian world surely disintegrated. The Mississippian world comprised a collection of simple and paramount chiefdoms who conducted their affairs with respect to each other in determinate ways and who probably agreed amongst themselves on the basic nature of the cosmos and of legitimate political power. When their world fell apart, the survivors found themselves on the fringes of a new world—the Modern World-System. When may we say that this transformation began to occur? Perhaps at 1650; perhaps earlier.

With the exception of Spanish Florida, can anyone adduce documentary evidence for social and political continuity between sixteenth- and eighteenth-century native societies in the Southeast? And I would venture to say that even in Spanish Florida the continuities were in name only. Outside of Spanish Florida, is there any evidence of eighteenth-century southeastern Indians asserting their rights to land on the basis of what we now know to have been sixteenth-century polities?

It is notable that even in the sixteenth and seventeenth centuries, a regional divide existed between North and South in eastern America. One major factor was the difference in agricultural potential. The South had the longest growing season and the best soils for plantation production of the commodities that fueled the burgeoning world economy. Colonies in the north were based on extractive economies, particularly a trade in wild animal furs, which were greatly desired in Europe. Later, trade, shipping, and manufacturing dominated the Northeast.

This geographical divide powerfully affected the history of the Indians in the seventeenth and eighteenth centuries. For example, in the seventeenth century, Indians in both North and South engaged in warfare for the purpose of taking captives. In the North, there was little market for

Indian slaves, so the Iroquois, who were the most powerful group, began adopting large numbers of the people they captured to compensate for their own loss of population through disease.[43] But in the South, to fuel the high demand for cheap labor on rice plantations, thousands of Indians were bartered away by other Indians as slaves.[44]

In the eighteenth century, when the English colonial officials appointed superintendents of Indian affairs, they appointed one for the North and a second for the South. The two regions were administratively distinct.

ON THE ANTIQUITY OF SOUTHERN HISTORY

An important implication of the papers in this volume is that the social history of the South extends much further into the past than most people realize. If we take what is most indubitably southern to be U. B. Phillips's house that Jack built, i.e., the nineteenth-century southern social order that was based on the production of cotton, tobacco, rice, sugar, and indigo by means of a slave-labor plantation economy, then a solid case can be made for the eighteenth-century colonial world's being a direct precursor of this.[45] That is, it was the British who devised the strategy that was victorious in the eighteenth-century struggle for colonial supremacy in the Southeast. As we have seen, it was a two-pronged strategy: (1) to establish slave-labor plantation economies, at first on the coast but later expanding inland, and (2) to manipulate the Indians through economic dependency and enslavement.

It is more difficult to make a case for the Mississippian world being, in turn, a historical predecessor of the eighteenth-century southeastern region within the Modern World, thereby linking it at one remove to the Old South. However, a case can be made on geographical grounds. Namely, one cannot fail to be struck with the degree to which a map of Mississippian archaeological complexes coincides with the area in which plantation agriculture came to reign.[46] The factors of soil, length of growing season, annual average rainfall, hydrology, and so on, conditioned both the plantation cultivation of cotton, tobacco, rice, sugar, and indigo and the Mississippian cultivation of corn, beans, and squash. In general, this is the area getting more than 210 freeze-free days per year and more than about 48 inches of rain per year.[47]

A more positive connection can be made with respect to food. Several of the basic Mississippian foods—gruels and stews made of dried corn processed with wood-ash lye (the hominy and grits of the Old South) as well as stewed beans, squash, and green corn—were the principal dishes of southern "soul food." Many contemporary southerners would agree with Mississippian people that roasted or boiled ears of green corn is the emblematic cuisine of early summer. It is probable that Mississippian people so thoroughly stewed their vegetables as to render them quite limp, as is the practice with traditional southern cooks. It is also appears that Mississippian people used animal fat in their cooking in much the same way that later southerners did. The only difference was that Mississippian cooks seasoned with bear fat instead of pork fat, although as the eighteenth century wore on the Indians also increasingly used pork. Mississippian people apparently realized, as do contemporary southerners, that barbecuing is a way of cooking meat that satisfies the soul as well as the palate, although if we are to trust the famous Theodore de Bry engraving, they were more eclectic in what they cooked than we are. (The word "barbecue," by the way, comes to us from *barbacoa*, a Carib word adopted by the Spanish explorers to designate this cooking technique.) Food is not trivial to civilization. Food is what fuels the people who build and run civilizations, and foodways can last for a very long time. In a nutshell, these are some of my reasons for saying that the social history of the South begins in the tenth century.

When the social history of the early South is conceived in this way, it can be seen that the Indians were not simply parts of the natural history of the region—mere background features. They were a part of the dramatis personae. Creeks, Choctaws, Chickasaws, Catawbas, Seminoles, and Cherokees were shaped by the same historical forces that produced white deerskin traders, frontier subsistence farmers, cattle herders, turpentiners, planters, and black slaves. The Indians were not alien from this world as cultural exotics. They were part and parcel of the colonial South. Indeed, how they came to be exiled from our southern history is to be explained, not merely assumed.

ACKNOWLEDGMENTS

I am grateful to Steven Hahn for reading and criticizing these pages.

Charles Hudson

THE TRANSFORMATION OF THE SOUTHEASTERN INDIANS, 1540–1760

Aboriginal Population Movements in the Postcontact Southeast

MARVIN T. SMITH

It is generally accepted that contact with Europeans set into motion a series of population movements that radically altered Native American societies and their interrelations. This paper seeks to determine the underlying causes of such movements, while cataloging many of the major shifts in a series of maps. These results are very preliminary, but will, I hope, serve to stimulate further research on the subject. In synthesizing these movements, I have relied on the scholarship of many colleagues.

It should be noted that the maps presented in this paper differ significantly from maps presented by John R. Swanton in 1946 in his *Indians of the Southeastern United States* (maps 1, 10, and 11). Research has made great strides in the half century since his book was published. First, archaeological knowledge and the recent reconstructions of the routes of various Spanish exploratory expeditions have significantly changed our knowledge of the locations of sixteenth-century groups. These locations must form the basis of any understanding of post-European contact population movements. I find Swanton's map 12, "Locations of Indian tribes in the Southeast" at different periods especially difficult to follow, since it includes multiple locations on a single map. I have attempted to break up movements into separate figures to better show movements at different intervals of time. Furthermore, I have created maps based on updated archaeological and historical research by many colleagues to produce what I believe are more accurate portrayals of population movements.

PUSH AND PULL FACTORS

There are many factors responsible for early native population movements. A number are discussed below, and I have no doubt that other factors will occur to other scholars. I do not believe that there is a mono-causal explanation for these movements; indeed, there is probably not even a single most important reason. We can distinguish between "push"

3

factors, which forced people to move away from their homes, and "pull" factors, which made other areas more attractive for settlement. Listed in no particular order are the factors I believe are important.

1. The push of disease. In earlier research, I relied heavily on the notion that introduced European epidemic disease was a big factor in population displacements of the sixteenth and seventeenth centuries.[1] While I am still convinced that this was an important factor, I now believe it must be seen as only one of several factors causing movement. I have no doubt that major epidemics occurred and forced people to migrate, but I am less convinced of the frequency of these epidemics. I now suspect that this explanation has been given undue weight.

2. The push of political factionalism. With the breakdown of native societies following the stresses of contact by alien European nations and the introduction of diseases, there must have been increased competition for traditional leadership positions. As heirs to political positions died before attaining office, competition must have accelerated. Given that factional competition was already a fact of life in Mississippian societies before contact,[2] it is likely that the stresses of contact led to more conflicts. It is also likely that decimated native societies had diminished means of managing disputes between kinship groups, as, for example, in cases of clan or lineage vengeance.[3] With desirable habitation areas opening up as a result of other factors, the opportunity for fissioning was greater than ever. A faction could decide to pick up and move to a recently deserted area. Thus, for example, a number of Shawnee moved to the Savannah River following the destruction of the Westos by the English in 1681. But note that only a few Shawnee moved, and not all of them called themselves Shawnee. The breakdown of aboriginal societies into various factions may also explain why some Natchez fled to the Chickasaws, while others went to the Cherokees and Creeks. Massive depopulation by disease and warfare against Europeans or Native Americans recently armed with European weapons meant that societies were suddenly less socially circumscribed, and thus had more options for fissioning and resettlement. As chiefly organization disintegrated, the "glue" that held society together lost its strength, sometimes resulting in social atomization.

Because there is evidence of population coalescence in the late sixteenth and early seventeenth centuries, I suspect that this fissioning response was a late protohistoric factor. By the late protohistoric, aboriginal groups were so reduced and relocated as to open up large vacant areas for resettlement by dissident factions.

3. The pull of European settlement and trade. I believe this factor has often been exaggerated. While Native Americans clearly wanted exotic materials from Europeans, they had conducted long-distance trade for millennia before European contact. They did not need to move closer to the Europeans to obtain material. Nevertheless, this factor may have been responsible for movements toward the Spanish missions on the coast. The desire for European materials is often cited as the reason many Lower Creeks left the Chattahoochee River in 1690 and moved to the Ocmulgee, Oconee, and even the Savannah rivers.[4] However, it should not be forgotten that there was also a simultaneous "push" for the Lower Creeks to get away from the Spaniards who had recently burned their towns on the Chattahoochee.[5]

4. The pull of favorable environmental zones. Certain areas had been favored for settlement for hundreds of years before European contact. Of particular interest was the fall line zone separating the coastal plain from the piedmont uplands. This region has many favorable characteristics, including fertile soil, excellent fishing, natural fords across rivers making for good access for trade and communication, a favorable mesh with the trail system, lithic resources from two very different biotic areas, and so on. As this area emptied out from depopulation and migration, other settlers were quick to fill it in. Thus, as the burial urn peoples of the Montgomery, Alabama, area abandoned such sites as Taskigi, probably around the middle of the seventeenth century, the Koasati-speaking people from the upper Tennessee River valley and the Alabamu from Mississippi quickly moved in. Such movements are documented by the Spaniard Marcos Delgado in 1686.[6] Delgado reminds us that fear of armed natives and the slave trade also prompted the movement from the Tennessee area. Thus there were both "pushes" away from an area and "pulls" to determine where the people went.

5. The Iroquois wars. I have wondered for years whether the heavily armed Iroquois warriors had any major effects in the Southeast. I suspect that they did play a role, but it was mostly an indirect one until nearly the eighteenth century. We know from historical sources that the Iroquois rapidly conquered their western neighbors—the Wenro by 1638, the Huron by 1649, the Neutral by 1652, and the Erie by 1656—displacing many people westward into the western Great Lakes region. By 1675,

combinations of Iroquois and Europeans eliminated the Susquehannocks who lay to the south. Although many of these people were assimilated into the Iroquois league to replace a rapidly diminishing population, many others were forced westward and perhaps southward. Other groups are known primarily through archaeology. For example, the Monongahela culture, of southwestern Pennsylvania and adjacent portions of West Virginia, Maryland, and Ohio, may be the archaeological manifestation of the Massawomeck, who are sketchily described in historic accounts. According to a recent study by William Johnson, "[A]rchaeological and ethnohistoric data indicate the dispersal of the Monongahela by ca. A.D. 1635, almost surely at the hands of the Seneca."[7] According to recent studies of the Fort Ancient culture by Penelope Drooker, as well as my own studies of European trade materials from Kentucky and West Virginia, most Fort Ancient sites in the Ohio Valley appear to have been abandoned by the middle of the seventeenth century. I suspect that some of these displaced people probably affected the Deep South, either by direct movement or by forcing other movements in a domino effect. Marvin Jeter suggests that the Quapaw may have moved to present Arkansas from the eastern Fort Ancient area, noting especially the use of longhouses by both groups.[8]

It is well documented that the Iroquois displaced many people into the western Great Lakes region. These newcomers, in turn, pushed other groups out onto the plains. I suspect that some of the Great Lakes people may have also turned to the south. Thus the Mitchigamea, an Illini group, were found by Marquette and Jolliet in northeastern Arkansas in 1673.[9] The Ilini were also documented enemies of the Chickasaw.[10] I suspect that their southern excursions were a recent event brought about by movements into the Great Lakes area by groups of people fleeing the Iroquois. The Quapaw also may have moved into Arkansas in the late seventeenth century from the Ohio Valley.[11]

James Merrill notes that our earliest documented attack by Iroquois on southern Indians (Occaneechees?) was in 1677.[12] Iroquois aggression probably accounts for the appearance of the Savannahs (Shawnee) on the Savannah River in 1674. The Iroquois were a big factor in the early-eighteenth-century Carolina frontier, according to Thomas Nairne. They had formerly attacked the Chickasaw and were still plaguing the Cherokee in 1708.[13] Their influence on the historically undocumented southeastern interior is harder to measure. Groups such as the Westos, who moved into the Deep South from an intermediate location in Virginia, were probably pushed from their original homeland by various Iroquois depredations. Far more research is needed in this area.

6. The pull of captured territory. It has been well documented that warfare was waged between Mississippian societies.[14] When a group's traditional enemies became weakened by disease, or when one group obtained firearms earlier than another group, such an imbalance of power allowed the victorious group to take over the loser's territory, and the loser could be forced to move long distances or even to amalgamate with the victors. Marcos Delgado documents many such movements of Tennessee Valley peoples south into the vicinity of present Montgomery, Alabama, in the late seventeenth century.[15] Another example is the dispersion of the Apalachee in 1704 and the subsequent reoccupation of northern Florida by the Seminole.

7. The pull of Indian elites seeking to bolster their power by forming connections to the Spaniards. John Worth makes an interesting observation that native elites often moved their followers to be closer to the Spaniards to bolster their own power.[16] The Spaniards gave presents to native leaders, often in the form of fancy clothing. These served as sumptuary goods to bolster the power of native chiefs. I suspect, however, that this factor was limited mainly to Spanish Florida. While Worth has clearly documented such movements of northern Timucuans to be closer to St. Augustine, I doubt that the pull extended very far into the interior Southeast.

8. The pull of missions. Worth notes that some interior natives were attracted to the coastal missions and apparently moved there voluntarily.[17] I suspect that much of the upper Oconee River in Georgia was depopulated by 1650, as seen in the lack of mid to late seventeenth-century European trade materials in sites above the fall line, and that many of these people moved downstream to the coastal missions. Others became known as the Yamasees. But these movements might also be related to Westo depredations. Further south, the history of the Florida missions seems to be a continuing story of population reduction and relocation.[18]

9. The pull of cultural similarities. James Merrill points out that as groups amalgamated, they usually coalesced with people speaking similar languages.[19] His example is based on the Catawba of the Carolina piedmont. While his observation is generally true, notable exceptions are known. Not all of the group that became known as the Catawba were Siouan speakers.[20] Consider also that some of the Natchez moved in with

the Overhill Cherokees, while others moved in with the Chickasaws and Upper Creeks, very different linguistic groups. However, following Merrill's model, the various Coosa groups had amalgamated into the Coosa-Abihka Upper Creeks by the eighteenth century.

10. The slave trade. The English-run trade in aboriginal slaves dates to the last half of the seventeenth century and the first quarter of the eighteenth. J. Leitch Wright notes that slavery was not important in early Jamestown because the colony was economically unstable and there was no real market for slaves. Caribbean islands were settled later and the market for slaves grew. Bermuda was established as an English colony in 1612, Barbados in 1627, and Jamaica in 1655. Indian slaves were first mentioned in Virginia statutes in 1660. Thus, when the Carolina colony was founded in 1670, the trade in Indian slaves may have been just expanding. The slave trade was often run by native middlemen preying on people who were sometimes their traditional enemies. This feature worked in combination with the warfare mentioned above. The Carolina slave trade began in coastal areas and gradually moved inland. The trade reached its height in the raids on Florida missions, and later during the Tuscarora and Yamasee wars. James Moore captured over four thousand "slaves" from his Florida raids in 1704, although it is probable that many of these people relocated voluntarily.[21] Areas that had been depopulated by the slave trade often became attractive locations for settlement by natives from elsewhere. Thus in the eighteenth century, Creeks and Yamasees moved to northern Florida to occupy the former territory of the Apalachees.

All of these factors, and probably others, caused linked population movements during the protohistoric period. Although it is difficult to prove with available data, I suspect that native movements accelerated during this period of the Indian slave trade, reaching a peak in the early eighteenth century. Soon thereafter, many of the population aggregates known from the last two-thirds of the eighteenth century until the removal of the nineteenth century were pretty much in place. That is not to say that more population movements did not occur after the first third of the eighteenth century, but they were more gradual and the movements were for shorter distances. Thus, for example, the Cherokee gradually moved into northern Georgia during the eighteenth century. By and large, the period of long-distance leaps was over until Indian removal, a long-distance movement of a different sort.

There are important lessons to be learned here. While I have previously taken the view of assuming that most Native American movements were for short distances and usually downstream, history teaches us that long distances were often involved. Some native groups fissioned and went in several directions.[22] For example, after the Natchez Revolt of 1729, some Natchez joined the Chickasaws while others joined the Overhill Cherokees or the Upper Creeks. The Shawnees traveled to many places in both the Southeast and the Northeast. Having proposed this list of push and pull factors, I have to add the qualification that it is entirely possible that the population movements suggested in this paper, as well as in some of my previous efforts, are in reality oversimplifications of the truth.

THE MAPS

I have compiled a series of maps showing major movements of people in the Southeast at various times. It is much more difficult to be certain of the timing of early movements than of later ones, which are historically documented. Starting with a baseline map of the Soto era population locations produced by George Milner in a study he coauthored with David Anderson and me, which in turn relies heavily on the reconstruction of the Hernando de Soto expedition by Charles Hudson and his associates, I have produced maps showing major movements at 1600–1650, 1650–1675, 1675–1700, and 1700–1735.[23] These maps do not attempt to document the locations of all populations at these times, but merely show major movements. The earlier movements are often inferred from archaeological data, while the majority of the later movements are known from documents. Reliance on historical sources makes data from the eastern portion of the Southeast much more complete than that for the western area. I certainly make no claim that the maps show all movements of native people, or even all the *major* movements. I have included some archaeological sites which can be dated to those intervals to show areas which were occupied. For the most part, these are sites with datable European trade materials. Not all sites are shown by any means.

It has not been my goal to create finely detailed maps, such as those produced by John Worth in his recent study of the Spanish missions of the Georgia coast, but to show major movements across the wide expanse of the Southeast in the hope of seeing an overall pattern to movements at a larger scale.[24] Finely detailed maps must be left to area specialists.

Poorly Known Areas

In trying to produce an overview of population movements in the Southeast from the mid-sixteenth to the early eighteenth century, one quickly finds that there are large areas that are poorly known with regard both to historical and to archaeological evidence. Such areas include the interior of Tennessee, coastal Carolina, western Virginia/ West Virginia, and the interior of Kentucky. For the most part, it is not known whether populations existed in these regions during the protohistoric era, and it is virtually impossible at this point to discuss movements into, out of, or through these regions.

Discussion

Let's take a brief look at the maps overall. The first map (fig. 1), from a study by Milner, Anderson, and Smith, illustrates our combined archaeological and historical evidence (primarily from the Soto expedition) of the locations of people in the mid-sixteenth century.[25] This map shows a region filled with dense nodes of population separated by uninhabited buffer zones. It should be noted that the size of the shaded area of an archaeological phase is not indexed to the size of the population.

The first of the migration maps (fig. 2) is my attempt to see population movements of the early seventeenth century. This map is based almost entirely on archaeological data, and is sketchy at best. Nevertheless, some areas occupied in the sixteenth century appear to have been abandoned by the middle of the seventeenth century, and this map presents my best guess for some of these movements. I have relied heavily on studies by Jeter, Braley, Dickens, Ward, and Davis, among others, for information synthesized in this map.[26]

By the period 1650–1675 (fig. 3), historic sources begin to document important moves. Worth documents movements of people from South Georgia into Florida.[27] Galloway has reconstructed the Choctaw formation, and I have used my knowledge of datable trade materials to suggest movement of Alabama River phase peoples at this time.[28] Historical sources indicate movements by the Westo and Mitchigamea.[29]

Fig. 1. Locations of indigenous groups in the mid-sixteenth-century Southeast.

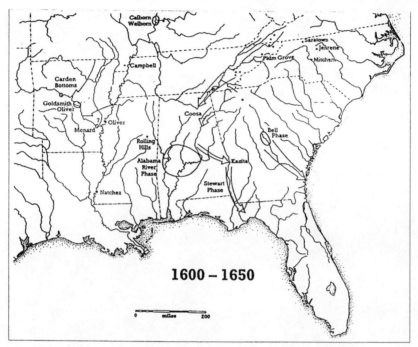

Fig. 2. Population movements of the early seventeenth century.

The period 1675–1700 (fig. 4) shows a flurry of movements. Spanish and English sources document movements in and out of the fall line of the Tallapoosa, Chattahoochee, Ocmulgee, Oconee, and Savannah rivers. The Catawba amalgamation solidifies at this time.[30] The Cherokee probably begin moving into the Tennessee Valley.[31] The Tunica appear in the lower Yazoo region.[32] Many of these movements may be due to changing political relations between Native Americans, Spaniards, the French, and the English.

The early eighteenth century (fig. 5) was the occasion of many long-distance movements, especially following the Yamasee and Tuscarora wars. There is much movement across the fall line again. The Natchez were destroyed and dispersed, while the Choctaw solidified their hold on central Mississippi. Some southern groups, such as the Shawnee and Tuscarora, moved to the Northeast to join the Iroquois. Remnants of Timucuan mission Indians converged on St. Augustine.[33]

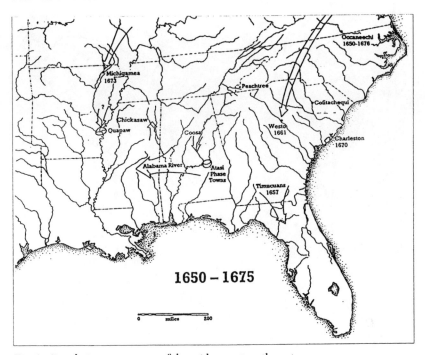

Fig. 3. Population movements of the mid-seventeenth century.

SOME CASE STUDIES

Focused studies of population movements could be organized in a number of ways. Three of these are particularly notable: (1) we can look at
movements by starting with a society principally identified on the basis of
archaeological information, though perhaps partly identified from historical information, and then attempt to trace its movement through time
using both archaeological and historical data; (2) we can look at a historical
tribal group and attempt to trace its movements using historical sources,
perhaps supplemented with archaeological data; or (3) we can look at a
particular region on the map, and trace the movements of people in and
out. Each of these approaches has its strengths and weaknesses. The first
method relies heavily on archaeological data, while the other two methods
are more suited to historical data. Some examples will serve as illustra-
tions of these approaches.

  1. An example of the following of an archaeological society through

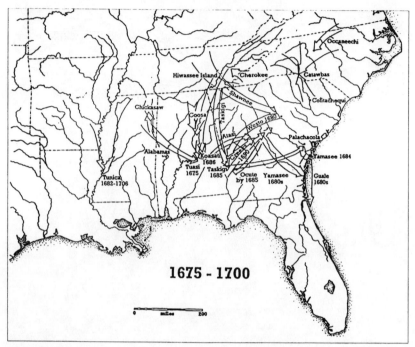

Fig. 4. Population movements of the late seventeenth century.

time is my own research on the Coosa chiefdom of the sixteenth century. We have excellent archaeological data on prehistoric peoples of eastern Tennessee, northwestern Georgia, and eastern Alabama.[34] Historical research on the expeditions of Hernando de Soto, Tristan de Luna, and Juan Pardo enables us to identify these archaeological remains as the paramount chiefdom of Coosa.[35] However, this brief illumination by historical information quickly fades into the dark age of the seventeenth century, requiring a return to archaeological data as the only information upon which to base population movements. These people do not reenter history until the last quarter of the seventeenth century.

My scenario is that movements in Coosa were short and generally downstream, because a sequence of archaeological sites seems to warrant this conclusion. By analyzing aboriginal ceramic styles, I have attempted to demonstrate that the same people were involved in this series of sites. I recognize that my interpretation could oversimplify a complex situation. Not only could other people have moved into the Coosa territory, but

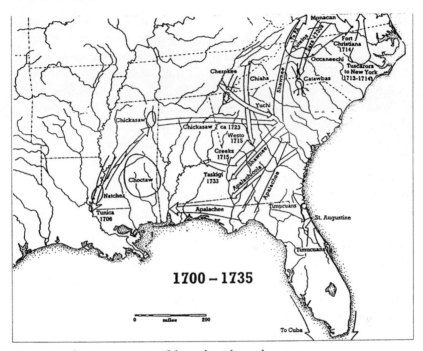

Fig. 5. Population movements of the early eighteenth century.

some or all Coosas could have moved elsewhere. I have reconstructed the movements of the Coosa people as follows.[36]

By the beginning of the seventeenth century, three site clusters in northwestern Georgia known archaeologically and identifiable in the Soto narratives as the simple chiefdoms of Coosa, Itaba, and Ulibahali had been abandoned. The survivors regrouped into one site cluster in the area of the present Weiss Reservoir in northeastern Alabama. This was essentially a simple downstream movement, but it did create a coalescence of three formerly individual chiefdom constituents of the Coosa paramount chiefdom. After roughly three decades in this area, these towns again migrated approximately twenty-five miles downstream to a location near present Gadsden, Alabama. With this move, further amalgamations took place, as indicated by the fact that fewer villages existed. Around 1670, the population again moved downstream approximately fifteen miles to establish one large settlement on Woods Island, where they appear to have been joined by some refugees from the Tennessee River drainage. By ca. 1715 they had moved another forty miles to the present Childersburg, Alabama, area to settle with other groups. These people became known to later history as the Coosa-Abihka people.

2. The second methodological approach is to trace a known group through time. Patricia Galloway's recent study of the Choctaws is a good example. Starting with a well-documented eighteenth-century group, Galloway attempts to reconstruct their genesis from a diverse group of archaeological cultures using cartographic, archaeological, and historical sources.[37] I have incorporated her interpretations into the maps in this study. It is necessary only to attempt to define the timing of the movements she has so well described. She sees a coalescence of several groups of people into what became the Choctaw country in the eighteenth century. According to Galloway, Alabama River people from western Alabama, groups from the Mobile area of southwest Alabama, Plaquemine peoples from south-central Mississippi, and Summerville-phase people from eastern Mississippi moved into east-central Mississippi. Archaeological dating based on European trade materials can be brought to bear on the question in only one of her regions at this time. The dating of the Alabama River phase can be approximated. The general lack of European material, as well as the types present at such sites as Taskigi to the east and Liddell (1WX1) further west on the Alabama River suggest that these sites were abandoned by the middle of the seventeenth century.[38] Thus, aggregation in the present state of Mississippi may have begun at approximately that time. Galloway adds that near the turn of the century, people from the Mobile delta area moved in because of conflict with armed groups to the east.[39]

But why did these people congregate in a region that had never supported Mississippian societies? Galloway suggests that rich hunting and unused farmlands lured people into the region.[40] During the eighteenth century, the Choctaw remained in this basic location, although some spread into the Yazoo basin. Later Choctaw movements, such as removal to Oklahoma, can be understood largely through historical documentation.

3. The third method is to look at a particular place, such as a river valley or portion of a river valley, and see which group or groups were attracted to this region. The Savannah River fall line region, the present location of Augusta, Georgia, was a popular location of aboriginal settlement. Large societies were found there in middle Mississippian times, although the region was abandoned in the late prehistoric period perhaps

because of political competition between major chiefdoms to the east and west or because of climatic change.[41] The attractions of the fall line have been described earlier in this paper. The Savannah River fall line location was quickly filled in as the chiefdoms collapsed in the seventeenth century. The Westo moved into the area ca. 1661.[42] Shawnee (Savannah) peoples were in the area by 1674, and helped extirpate the Westo by 1681. There were still three towns of Shawnee as late as 1708. Most if not all Shawnee left the region following the Yamasee War of 1715. The Hogaloge group of Yuchi appeared in the area (actually some twenty miles north of the fall line) in 1715, but left the following year.[43] They were followed by the Chickasaw around 1723. The fall line regions of the Ocmulgee, Chattahoochee, and Coosa/Tallapoosa had similar histories of successive (and in many cases cumulative) settlement.

Other regions had favorable settings, yet were abandoned fairly early. The middle Mississippi Valley is an interesting case study. The area from the Missouri bootheel south into Arkansas and across the Mississippi River into present northeastern Mississippi was home to dense Mississippian populations at the time of initial European contact with the Soto expedition.[44] In my opinion, the disappearance of these peoples is one of the greatest mysteries of southeastern archaeology. They lived in densely settled towns, and newly introduced disease may have been a contributing factor, but survivors must have moved somewhere for the region to have been largely depopulated by the time the French arrived late in the seventeenth century. Some people must have been in the area into the early seventeenth century, given the existence of documented European trade goods at sites such as Campbell in Missouri, Bradley in Arkansas, and Oliver in Mississippi.[45] Sites containing seventeenth-century European goods are fairly common on the Arkansas River in present Arkansas, suggesting an early concentration of people in that drainage. For example, early-seventeenth-century European items have been found at Carden Bottoms, Goldsmith-Oliver near Little Rock, Noble Lake, and perhaps Sarassa Lake.[46] I believe that it is possible that this large Arkansas-Mississippi-Missouri region collapsed, and the survivors consolidated in the Arkansas River drainage. Linguistic evidence from the Soto era suggests that some, if not all, of these people were Tunican speakers, and Marvin Jeter has provided a Maximum Tunican Scenario suggesting that all were Tunican-speaking peoples.[47]

The Little Rock, Arkansas, area is near the junction of the Ouachita

Mountains, the west gulf coastal plain, and the lower Mississippi Valley, and is only sixty-five kilometers from the Ozark Plateau.[48] Given the diverse resources of these regions along with the attraction of a major river valley, it is easy to see why this was (and continues to be) an important settlement location. I believe that this region served as a focal point for Tunica-speaking survivors in the middle seventeenth century.

The mouth of the Yazoo River and adjacent Yazoo bluffs regions had a number of attractions, the most obvious of which was the confluence of the Yazoo River with the Mississippi. This was a favorable location for trade, and was rich in alluvial soil for farming. It was also the approximate location of the junction of the southeastern evergreen forest region and the oak-pine forest region and was near the junction of the Mississippi Valley, loess hills, southern pine hills, and Jackson Prairie.[49] This area was the locus of Tunica amalgamation in the late seventeenth century. The Tunica eventually migrated to the south in a series of eighteenth-century moves documented by Jeffrey Brain.[50] Today, their descendants live near Marksville, Louisiana.

The Natchez bluffs region provided a home to dense Mississippian populations, and served as a magnet for many refugee groups who became associated with the Natchez.[51] The archaeology of the region suggests a relatively permanent population throughout the protohistoric period. At the very least, it can be said that finds of early-seventeenth-century European trade materials document the existence of some people in the area. Assuming that these people were at least culturally similar to each other, we might interpret the groups present when the French arrived as the descendants of various prehistoric Plaquemine peoples. That is, I suggest that the Natchez were a coalescent population, comparable to the Upper Creeks, Lower Creeks, Choctaws, Catawbas, and other contemporary societies, rather than a chiefly survival as has been commonly argued. Such an interpretation might help explain the diverse towns of the Natchez and the apparent political factionalization that can be documented historically. This interpretation might also help to demystify their vexingly unusual social system.

But why settle in the Natchez area? There is no close interdigitation of multiple physiographic provinces here as we see in many other areas popular in aboriginal settlement.[52] Of course, the Natchez loess bluffs do come right down to the Mississippi River at Natchez, making it a somewhat strategic location vis-à-vis commanding the river for trade or warfare. Perhaps the draw of the long-standing political power of the region, seen in the preceding Emerald and Anna chiefdoms, made it an important location. Or perhaps it was the lure of rich agricultural soils in an upland setting, in contrast with flood-prone alluvial valleys. For whatever reason, the Natchez area held an important concentration of native people in the early eighteenth century.

The final dispersal of the Natchez people took place as an aftermath of the 1729–30 Natchez Revolt. Many Natchez people moved in with the Chickasaw, the Cherokee, and the Upper Creeks, and some were even shipped to Caribbean islands by the French to serve as agricultural slaves.[53]

The junction of major rivers was also a favored location for settlement. Thus the junction of the Coosa and Tallapoosa, the Yazoo and the Mississippi, the Arkansas and the Mississippi, the Red and the Mississippi, and other major confluences held important protohistoric and historic era populations.

CONCLUSIONS

There were many factors causing population movements in the early historic Southeast. Many no doubt worked in conjunction with one another. Thus, disease may have led to new power imbalances which stimulated warfare, and this led to movements to take over an enemy's territory, and so forth. If one observation can be made from the scant information available at this time, it is that the very earliest population movements appear to have been over short distances. The best documented case is still the Coosa drainage, where successive movements were fifty miles or less. Late in the seventeenth century, primarily because of armed slave raids, there were many long-distance moves such as those described by Marcos Delgado in 1686. There were also late-seventeenth-century moves prompted by changing political relations between Native Americans and European powers. Thus, for example, elements of the Creek Confederacy moved away from the Chattahoochee and Tallapoosa valleys to flee the Spanish and join the English.

Aboriginal population movements clearly had complex causes, and far more research is needed regarding historical sources as well as archaeological sites before we can hope to unravel this crucial period of history. As Patricia Galloway has pointed out (in a personal communication), another avenue of study would be to combine tribal migration myths with archaeological and historical evidence. The migration myths should be reinvestigated with a more sophisticated understanding of both historical and archaeological sources. We may be sure that the resulting synthesis will dramatically change our understanding of the social history of the early Southeast.

The Great Southeastern Smallpox Epidemic, 1696–1700: The Region's First Major Epidemic?

PAUL KELTON

Smallpox infection is now eradicated from the world thanks to an effective global vaccination program, but people of an earlier time, especially American Indians, tragically experienced the virus's destructive power. Smallpox was absent from the Americas before European contact, making indigenous peoples particularly vulnerable when Europeans introduced it. Without previous exposure that would have produced acquired immunity, Indian societies were in effect "virgin" populations, in which small-pox quickly erupted into catastrophic epidemics, producing immensely high death tolls. These "virgin soil epidemics" often struck all members of an entire village or tribe at one time, leaving no one able to fulfill basic social services such as caring for the sick, defending against enemies, or gathering food, water, or firewood. Smallpox, of course, was not the only newly introduced disease to result in virgin soil epidemics, but its unique characteristics made it the most common agent of mass destruction that Indians throughout the Americas had to confront.[1]

While scholars agree that smallpox had a catastrophic impact on American Indians, uncertainty still exists concerning the timing in which partic-ular regions and tribes first experienced this deadly disease. European observers recorded the occurrence of outbreaks at various times among a multitude of Indian groups, but did smallpox epidemics erupt that went unrecorded? Certainly they did; the virus spread beyond the point of direct contact and hence beyond the view of literate observers, infecting Indians who may have never seen Europeans or Africans. But without available documents, can scholars reasonably determine when native peo-ples of specific areas initially suffered from the virus? Although the ques-tion of timing is difficult and will never be answered with a high degree of certainty, this essay will offer some conclusions in regard to the Indians of the American Southeast.[2]

Specifically, this paper suggests that the first major smallpox epidemic to spread through the entire Southeast occurred between 1696 and 1700. The virus had made its presence known in Spanish Florida and possibly Virginia much earlier and damaged the native population there, but it was unlikely that smallpox spread beyond the borders of these colonies until the acceleration of the Indian slave trade in the late seventeenth century. At the height of such trade, documentary evidence clearly shows that smallpox erupted with a fury, beginning in Virginia in 1696, sweeping south into the Carolinas, spreading into the interior, and traveling all the way to the Mississippi River, where it devastated aboriginal societies into 1700. This outbreak, which merits the title the Great Southeastern Small-pox Epidemic, was not the first region-wide epidemic merely because it was the first one documented. Rather, it was the first because conditions in the Southeast did not become ripe for the transmission and spread of smallpox until the 1690s.[3]

This paper, thus, questions prevailing assumptions that one or more region-wide smallpox epidemics occurred before 1696. Some scholars have suggested that southeastern Indians fell victim to hemispheric pan-demics, which occurred as early as the 1520s. Smallpox supposedly trav-eled from Mexico along aboriginal exchange routes, causing devastation from Chile to Canada. The spread of smallpox from Mexico in the 1520s has been questioned, but scholars can point to other possible ways in which the deadly virus made an early entrance and set off large-scale outbreaks. Smallpox either accompanied sixteenth-century Spanish explorers or arrived later in Virginia and Florida, spreading subsequently beyond these colonies by aboriginal trade. Whatever mechanisms were responsible for the introduction and spread of the disease, scholars pro-pose that population loss must have been severe, perhaps as high as 90 percent.[4]

Previous scholars may be correct that it was possible for smallpox to strike the Southeast at an early date, but it does not follow that a region-wide epidemic of the disease was probable. An examination of the epide-miological nature of smallpox, the characteristics of European contact with southeastern Indians, and the dynamics of intertribal exchange indi-cate that smallpox most likely failed to penetrate the region outside of either Virginia or Spanish Florida before the 1690s.

Smallpox was one of several diseases that accompanied Europeans and Africans to the Americas. The most deadly of these new illnesses belonged to a category known as acute infectious diseases, which in addition to smallpox included measles, yellow fever, typhus, whooping cough, influenza, and plague. All of these were dangerous diseases in Europe and Africa, and when introduced to virgin soil populations in the Americas they produced severe mortality rates. Among these highly lethal acute infectious diseases, however, smallpox could be transported for the greatest distances through the most dispersed populations. If an undocumented region-wide epidemic and catastrophic population loss did in fact occur in the Southeast during the early colonial period, then smallpox should be suspected as the most likely cause.[5]

The spread of smallpox exceeded that of all other diseases with comparable mortality rates for three main reasons. First, smallpox had longer periods of incubation and communicability than most acute infectious diseases. Once a person inhales the smallpox virus, the pathogen incubates for a twelve-to-fourteen-day period before symptoms appear. Smallpox symptoms—chills, severe fever, delirium, possible coma, and the characteristic pox sores—appear over a two-week period in which the disease is highly contagious. In contrast, influenza incubates one to two days, while its communicable period usually runs from three to five days. Smallpox, thus, remains alive within a human host for a significantly long time, twenty-six to twenty-eight days, giving a victim a relatively lengthy period in which to carry the disease from place to place and infect other nonimmune people.[6]

The unique ability of smallpox to survive outside of a human host is the second reason that it could spread farther than other highly lethal diseases. Measles, in contrast, has an equivalent period of incubation and communicability but cannot live on its own and needs to be passed directly from one person to another through exhalation and inhalation.[7] Smallpox, on the other hand, could be transmitted indirectly. After its two-week period of direct communicability expires, the virus can be transmitted for approximately two to four weeks longer to nonimmune persons who come in close contact with the scabs of victims, or even scabs that have fallen off a victim. In addition, the virus can live for several months on cloth in a dry and cool environment and consequently can infect any nonimmune person who handles such contaminated material.[8]

Finally, smallpox spread more easily than other highly lethal diseases because of a relative lack of environmental limitations. The transmission of some acute infectious diseases, for example, requires animal vectors. Yellow fever is spread by a species of mosquito, *Aedes aegypti*, whose hab-

itat is generally restricted to waterfront areas.⁹ Typhus is spread by particular species of lice and fleas, which thrive in unsanitary settings such as
urban slums or large army encampments.¹⁰ Similarly, plague depends on
the presence of specific species of fleas and rodents. Plague epidemics
therefore have been historically associated with densely settled and filthy
urban areas. For this reason, some scholars have argued that plague did
not make the trip to the Americas until the nineteenth century.¹¹ But in
the absence of such environmental limitations, smallpox could escape
waterfront areas or dense congregations of people, spread into the countryside, and infect a wide array of people living in a dispersed fashion.¹²

While several pathogens are comparably lethal to smallpox but not able
to travel as far, a number of illnesses are more transmittable but considerably less deadly. Typhoid fever, another acute infectious disease, is one of
these. Victims come in contact with the bacteria that cause typhoid by
consuming food or water contaminated by the feces or urine of an infected
individual. The bacteria incubate one to three weeks before symptoms
appear. A victim can transmit bacilli into the environment for various
amounts of time. Ten percent of those infected can transmit the disease
for up to three months, while 2 to 5 percent become permanent carriers.¹³
Symptoms can be quite excruciating, involving headache, sustained fever,
despondency, anorexia, slowness of heartbeat, enlargement of the spleen,
cough, rose-colored spots on the body, and bowel problems. The chance
of death, however, is considerably smaller than is the case with smallpox.
In modern times, epidemiologists have found a case fatality rate of 10 percent among untreated victims.¹⁴

Several illnesses classified as chronic infectious diseases are also more
transportable but less deadly than smallpox. Chronic diseases differ from
acute diseases in that there is a longer period during which the pathogen
induces symptoms and remains alive within a human host. Chronic diseases, such as malaria, tuberculosis, syphilis, fungal infections, and many
others, progress rather slowly. Once infected, an individual can carry the
affliction over years or even a lifetime. In some cases, an infected victim
may not show symptoms but can transmit the pathogen to another living
being. Such hosts can consequently carry the disease great distances and
potentially infect people over a wide geographic area.¹⁵

Chronic infectious diseases are rarely lethal to victims immediately
after infection. Death commonly occurs among only immune-deficient
people, including the elderly, the malnourished, and people suffering

from multiple infections. Generally, chronic diseases leave their victims debilitated, making their bodies less able to fight off more serious infections from acute illnesses. By themselves, however, chronic diseases have low mortality rates. For example, the case fatality rate of the most common form of malaria, a disease that in all probability came to the Southeast shortly after European contact, seldom exceeds 10 percent among untreated individuals.[16]

The epidemiological nature of smallpox indicates that, among the diseases capable of causing severe death tolls, it was the one most likely to accompany Europeans, to spread beyond the point of direct contact, and to produce undocumented virgin soil epidemics. But even when fully considering the ease with which smallpox spread, one cannot conclude that an undocumented region-wide virgin soil epidemic did occur or that such an event was even probable. Because it is an acute infectious disease, its spread to potential victims still required their direct contact with an infected person within a limited amount of time or contact with virus-laden cloth kept under cool and dry conditions. Whether southeastern Indians had a significant chance to become infected and whether they themselves facilitated the spread of the virus throughout the region before the 1690s are questions that deserve serious attention.

The dynamics of the various sixteenth-century Spanish expeditions to the Southeast indicate only a small possibility that smallpox arrived in the region by direct contact with Europeans. The exploratory parties were composed primarily of adult men, a population in which one would not expect to find active cases of an illness that normally occurred during childhood in Europe and Africa. The available records further suggest that none of the Spaniards were suffering from smallpox infection. To be sure, there were reports of sickness, but the illnesses did not appear to be smallpox. In most of the episodes of sickness, symptoms appeared several weeks or months after Europeans arrived. If any of these bouts of illness were smallpox, one would expect symptoms to erupt from twelve to fourteen days, at most, after departure.[17]

Indirect transmission also seems unlikely. A possibility exists that Indians, who had close physical contact with the Spaniards, may have contracted smallpox from viruses that clung to the cotton fabric of the visiting Europeans. For this to have happened, the Spaniards would have had to be in contact with smallpox victims before they left their points of departure, most often the Caribbean islands. Then, the viruses would have had to survive exposure to the heat and humidity that existed during transit and after arrival in the Southeast. Finally, contact between Spaniards and Indians would have had to be quite intimate in order for successful transmission to occur. That all of these conditions occurred simultaneously, however, is doubtful.

Of course, smallpox could have infected southeastern Indians by ways other than physical contact with Spanish explorers. Scholars suggest that the virus may have spread through the region along aboriginal trade routes that linked the southeastern interior with places that Europeans visited. Early epidemics, some argue, originated in places as far away as Mexico.[18] Later outbreaks began in the colonies of St. Augustine or Jamestown, or even with shipwrecked victims or other undocumented coastal visitors. Native American travelers then carried the pathogenic microbes through the region even to remote peoples, who may never have seen a European. The question, then, is did southeastern Indians engage in intertribal exchange to such an extent that it was probable that smallpox arrived from distant locations and then spread throughout the entire region?

Trade between Mexico and the Southeast can hardly be considered significant. It has been assumed that some goods found in southeastern archaeological sites came from Mexico or displayed direct Mesoamerican influence, but scholars lately doubt such long-distance origins. Even if some goods in the Southeast did come from so far away, they are rare components of archaeological sites, indicating that long-distance trade was also rare.[19] The idea of smallpox viruses surviving passage from Mexico to the Southeast, by way of sporadic aboriginal trade and through mountains, deserts, swamps, and other formidable geographic barriers, stretches the imagination.[20]

Aboriginal exchange among southeastern Indians themselves also indicates that the volume of trade was too small to make the spread of smallpox likely.[21] Natives had traditionally traded such raw materials as minerals, marine shells, feathers, and animal skins. They also exchanged finished goods, from common items such as hoes to ceremonial objects such as gorgets. Despite the occurrence of intertribal trade, the volume of such activity should not be inflated. Production and consumption of goods, as archaeologist Jon Muller notes, was "profoundly domestic." Southeastern Indians acquired the resources they needed near their towns or villages and produced their food, clothing, utensils, and other everyday items themselves.[22] This independent production and consumption and the subsequent low volume of trade stands in stark contrast to the continual flow of goods in the late seventeenth century, when southeastern Indians' dependency on English and French items began.[23]

To be sure, the Spanish introduced European trade goods to southeastern Indians before the English and French did, but Spaniards only slowly increased trade contacts with natives after the founding of St. Augustine in 1565. Not until 1639 did the Spanish, who held that conversion to Catholicism was more important than commerce, begin trading in earnest with their most significant partners, the Apalachees of northern Florida. The Apalachees were probably in direct contact with the Lower Creeks living in the interior up the Chattahoochee River. The Spanish themselves had established direct relations with the Lower Creeks by 1647.

Commercial contacts between the Spanish and Indians of the interior, though, were weak at best throughout the seventeenth century. Periodic hostility with Indians, official prohibition, and a lack of goods at their disposal meant that the Spanish initiated only a minor increase in commercial traffic in the Southeast. In addition, the archaeological record verifies such minimal trade. Virtually no everyday items of Spanish origin that Indians came to depend on, such as guns and metal utensils, appear in sites outside of Florida.[24]

Unlike the Spanish, the English out of Virginia did foster a significant expansion in the volume of trade within the Southeast. Such expansion occurred only after 1650, however. Before then, English goods if present were rare and were disseminated by Indian middlemen, but over the next twenty years, Englishmen leading packhorses loaded with goods penetrated the Carolina piedmont. The Tuscaroras and Westos were especially involved with the English, supplying them with deerskins and slaves in exchange for guns and other manufactured items.[25] While this growing trade set the stage for the Great Southeastern Smallpox Epidemic, it did not initiate an epidemic. Except for a localized outbreak in 1667 that struck the eastern shore, no smallpox epidemic appears to have occurred in Virginia from 1650 to 1696.[26]

In addition to the low volume of trade, buffer zones between rival native groups would have made it difficult for smallpox to spread from Florida, Virginia, or other places of direct contact throughout the entire region. European accounts describe a land full of people who seldom engaged in trade but instead jealously guarded their hunting, gathering,

and fishing territories from numerous enemies. Such enmity created multiple contested areas between enemy tribes that were unsafe for travel.[27]
For example, when the Soto expedition advanced through the Savannah
valley they found themselves in what they described as wilderness. For
one hundred thirty leagues, they found neither people nor villages, only
pine groves and large rivers.[28] The area stood vacant, seemingly because
of warfare between the Ocute and Cofitachequi chiefdoms. A century earlier the Savannah valley had been the home of many people, but before
Soto came, the Indians had withdrawn to safer locations.[29]

The Savannah valley was not the only buffer zone. Soto and his men
also found contested areas that separated groups living in both the Tennessee and the Mississippi valleys.[30] Aboriginal warfare continued to isolate Indian groups from each other throughout the seventeenth century.
One Frenchman, writing in the late seventeenth century but commenting
on long-standing conflict between coastal and interior groups, noted that
members of several chiefdoms feared traveling into the delta region,
claiming that native tribes there would "eat" any intruders.[31] Another
Frenchman reported that before the massive epidemics of the late seventeenth century, Indians of the valley had used a red post as a boundary
marker between rivals who competed for scarce resources. The Bayagoulas and the Oumas, he wrote, "were so jealous of the hunting in their territories that they would shoot at any of their neighbors whom they caught
hunting beyond the limits marked by the red post."[32] It is doubtful that
smallpox viruses passed through the maze of buffer zones that characterized the social landscape of the Southeast.

The epidemiological nature of smallpox, the dynamics of early exploration, the characteristics of aboriginal trade, and the existence of buffer
zones suggest the improbability of an undocumented catastrophic outbreak before the 1690s. Still, ethnohistorical and archaeological evidence
does appear to support the conclusion that a demographic collapse
occurred at an early date. Hernando de Soto and his expedition encountered several powerful and sophisticated societies or chiefdoms, but after
their departure these chiefdoms dissolved and in their place less complex
tribal confederacies emerged. In addition, native peoples apparently
abandoned several river valleys that remained vacant at the time of
English arrival in the late seventeenth century. While many scholars
assume that a region-wide smallpox epidemic and demographic disaster

must be the cause for these changes, other explanations not associated with a conjectured smallpox epidemic should be considered.[33]

The disintegration of southeastern chiefdoms was not a new phenomenon that came as a result of European invasion. Before contact, several chiefdoms underwent cycles of evolution and devolution. Devolving societies may have encountered military pressure from rival groups; they may have overutilized the soil and been forced to seek more fertile land; droughts, floods, and other natural disasters could have caused crop failure; and leaders of chiefdoms may have lost access to prestige goods that legitimized their power and thus lost their followers. Faced with such stress, these chiefdoms broke up into smaller tribes that dispersed to safer places or better farmlands. One can reasonably assume that these same indigenous causes of chiefdom devolution were common in the first two centuries of contact.[34]

Spanish exploration may have in fact accelerated the natural causes of chiefdom disintegration. The presence of strange white men carrying metal weapons and riding horses certainly threatened the leadership of chieftains. How could these leaders, whose legitimacy was based on the assumption of divine origin, explain the presence of these mysterious human beings? Followers of chieftains probably questioned the authority of their leaders, abandoned them after the Spaniards departed, and consequently lived in smaller, more decentralized tribal confederacies.[35]

The introduction of new diseases, which were more mobile than smallpox but not as deadly, may have also contributed to the devolution of chiefdoms. Malaria, for example, often occurs during the summer, consequently interfering with agriculture and causing a decline in crop yields. Chiefdoms depended heavily on maize agriculture and may have experienced declining production, the subsequent results being social disarray, population dispersion, and abandonment of some river valleys. Still, malaria would have caused much less damage than smallpox. Malaria would have been restricted to swampy environments, the habitat of the anopheles mosquito responsible for the spread of the disease, and mortality rates for the disease would be far from the catastrophic levels that some scholars propose.[36]

Finally, a closer examination of the archaeological and ethnohistorical evidence reveals that population collapse and chiefdom disintegration may not have been as complete as would be suspected if a region-wide smallpox epidemic had occurred. Excavations and surveys of the Black

Warrior valley, for example, reveal that Indians continually resided in the area until enemy tribes forced them to evacuate in the 1690s. The inhabitants of the valley had been associated with the Moundville chiefdom, which declined sometime before contact, and showed little evidence of rebuilding a powerful chiefdom after the sixteenth century. But their population remained stable or perhaps even grew to such an extent that they surpassed the carrying capacity of the land.[37] Similarly, archaeologists have observed no differences between a pre-Columbian site in Georgia and a post-Columbian site that suggest the occurrence of virgin soil epidemics. These sites, Etowah and King, lay near the center of the Coosa chiefdom, which both the Soto and Luna expeditions visited.[38] Apica, a town on the Coosa River that members of the Luna expedition visited, as well as two towns that Soto visited, Talisi on the Tallapoosa River and Mauvilla on the Alabama, also remained permanently inhabited, displaying no signs of population loss.[39]

The lower Mississippi valley, according to ethnohistorical sources, also displayed a degree of stability.[40] To be sure, in 1673 Marquette and Joliet failed to observe chiefdoms along the Mississippi between present-day Memphis and the Arkansas River, an area where Soto encountered several powerful groups.[41] If the two French explorers had advanced to the Yazoo Basin, however, they would have found populous societies. La Salle and his followers explored the Yazoo in 1682 and found numerous Indians.[42] At the junction of the Yazoo with the Mississippi, a companion to La Salle remarked that "as this river and land is very fertile in these places, it is densely populated with many different nations."[43] And, of course, even more to the south, the Natchez chiefdom still existed at the time of French exploration and settlement. If the Southeast had faced catastrophic epidemics and massive depopulation, the lower Mississippi valley would not have been as densely populated as it in fact was at the time when the French arrived.

With little possibility of an undocumented virgin soil epidemic of smallpox before 1696, the period between 1526 and 1696 is best described as the false dawn of epidemiological disaster. Nevertheless, disaster would strike the entire region in the 1690s, when changing conditions facilitated the spread of smallpox. The number of European and Africans who came to the Southeast dramatically increased in the late seventeenth century. In Virginia, the importation of African slaves, including men, women, and children, substantially rose after 1676 as laws made race-based slavery a permanent institution in the colony.[44] In 1670, the English founded South Carolina, and, in addition to European settlers, copious numbers of African slaves flooded into the new colony.[45] After 1682, French traders and missionaries increasingly penetrated the lower Mississippi valley, and in the late 1690s, the French established a permanent colony on the Gulf Coast. With thousands of non-Indians arriving in the Southeast in the late seventeenth century, the chances for the introduction of acute infectious diseases substantially increased.

Most significantly, the conditions that led to the spread of smallpox improved as the nature and volume of Indian trade changed. Following the lead of the Virginians, South Carolinian traders began in 1670 to accelerate commerce with southeastern Indians. Carolinians especially increased the volume of particular commodities that substantially increased the chances of spreading infectious diseases, and those commodities were Indian slaves. This trade, in which Indians supplied the English with captives in exchange for guns, cloth, and other items, dramatically expanded the volume of human traffic through the Southeast. This traffic not only involved numerous Indian slaves being sent overland to Carolina but also myriad tribes moving their villages hundreds of miles to escape slave raids.[46]

By 1698 and perhaps earlier, South Carolinians had established a slave trade network that linked their colony with tribes living as far away as the Mississippi River. In 1685, Henry Woodward, a South Carolinian, ventured west into Georgia and Alabama, seeking to purchase native captives and to form an alliance with the Creeks. Woodward sent traders even farther west to establish ties with the Chickasaws.[47] Thomas Welch, another Carolinian, was one who followed Woodward's lead. In 1698, Welch traveled to the Chickasaws, crossed the Mississippi, and descended the river to the mouth of the Arkansas. Welch mapped his journey, showing the way for other ambitious English slave traders to follow.[48]

When French colonists arrived on the Gulf Coast and in the Mississippi valley in the late 1690s, they discovered an English-inspired trade network firmly in place. In 1699 the governor of the new French colony, Pierre Le Moyne, Sieur d'Iberville, found several traders doing an "extensive" business in Alabama and Mississippi.[49] At Mobile Bay, one native informant told a French officer that British traders frequently visited villages up the Alabama River and its tributaries, the Coosa and Tallapoosa. Thirty-six "nations," or towns, resided in these river valleys, including

many recognizable members of the eighteenth-century Creek Confederacy.[50] English slave dealers also utilized the Tennessee as a trade route. In
1700, Iberville learned that British traders had descended the Tennessee,
entered the Mississippi, and reached the Arkansas.[51] One year earlier, a
French missionary reported that an Englishman, perhaps Thomas Welch,
had lived among the Quapaw Indians at the mouth of the Arkansas at least
since 1698. The trader took two Quapaw wives and supplied his adopted
people with two to three guns and "a lot of merchandise."[52]

The Quapaws' enemies, the Chickasaws, were an important link in the
slave trade network. One particular Englishman took a major role in
inspiring Chickasaw slave raids. "For several years this Englishman has
been among the Chicachas where he does a business in Indian slaves,"
Iberville complained, "putting himself at the head of Chicacha war parties
to make raids on their enemies and friends, and forcing them to take prisoners whom he buys and sends to the islands to be sold."[53] Most likely, the
Englishman sent his captives overland to South Carolina, but before the
French established themselves in the area, British ships rendezvoused
with traders along the gulf.[54] One of these ships made the mistake of
entering the Mississippi at the same time that Iberville's forces were
building their colony. French officials interrogated the English captain,
who informed them that his ship was not the first British vessel to penetrate the river. He claimed that, "[s]everal years before," English ships
from South Carolina had come to the area seeking to link up with traders
among the Chickasaws. These ships failed to meet their objectives and
departed from the river, but they represented an example of the extensive
efforts of British subjects to acquire slaves from distant places and send
them back to the new colony of South Carolina.[55]

The number of American Indians shipped to the West Indies or
enslaved on Carolinian plantations was considerably smaller than the
number of Africans imported to America. Nevertheless, the significance of
the slave trade to southeastern Indian history should not be underesti-
mated. The pernicious exchange of human captives, which resulted in
thousands of people moving, trading, and coalescing, set the stage for one
of the worst tragedies in southern history. Once introduced into the slave
trade network, the deadly smallpox virus spread from the Atlantic Coast to
the Mississippi River, sparing few nonimmune people in its path.

The first signs of the Great Southeastern Smallpox Epidemic appeared
in Virginia in 1696. While smallpox seemed inconsequential to the colo-

ny's first generations, population dynamics began to change in the late seventeenth century, making Virginia ripe for a major outbreak. Through most of its early history, Virginia was predominantly populated by British-born males, who probably had been exposed to smallpox as children in England. But with the expansion of slavery after Bacon's Rebellion, the increasing importation of Africans, and the development of Anglo-American families, the number of children and others never exposed to smallpox substantially increased. When introduced to the colony from an unknown source in 1696, the virus caused a major epidemic. It spread throughout the population, especially in Jamestown, forcing the colonial assembly to recess.[56]

The disease traveled rapidly from Virginia into North Carolina. The governor of South Carolina, John Archdale, reported that in 1696 "a great Mortality" struck tribes living in North Carolina near the Pamlico River.[57] When the English traveler John Lawson toured the area in 1701, the terrible destruction of the Great Southeastern Smallpox Epidemic was still visible. Lawson discovered that the epidemic had almost obliterated Sewees, Congarees, and other piedmont tribes in communication with the British. "Neither do I know," he wrote, "any savages that have traded with the English, but what have been great losers by this distemper." The traveler estimated that "the Small-Pox and Rum have made such a Destruction amongst them that, on good grounds, I do believe, there is not the sixth Savage living within two hundred Miles of all our settlements, as there were fifty years ago."[58]

By February 1697, smallpox had made its way to South Carolina. Some representatives to the South Carolina assembly could not meet in February and March because they, their families, or servants were sick.[59] The disease continued to rage throughout the year. In March 1698, colonial officials reported back to Britain that "[w]e have had ye Small Pox amongst us Nine or ten Months, which hath been very Infectious and mortall, we have lost by the Distemper 200 or 300 Persons."[60]

The worst casualties occurred among Native Americans. Carolinian officials reported that "the Small-pox hath killed so many of [the Indians], that we have little Reason to Believe they will be Capable of doing any Harm to us for severall Years to Come, that Distemper haveing Swept off great Numbers of them 4 or 500 Miles Inland as well upon ye Sea Cost as in our Neighbourhood."[61] One Carolinian commented further that "[s]mallpox . . . has been mortal to all sorts of the inhabitants & especially the Indians who tis said to have swept away a whole neighboring nation, all to 5 or 6 which ran away and left their dead unburied, lying upon the ground for the vultures to devouer."[62] The colonial governor, John Archdale, even looked on the event as a divine act to absolve the English of their brutal treatment of Indians. "But again, it as other times pleased Almighty God to send unusual Sicknesses amongst [the Indians], as the Smallpox, &c to lessen their Numbers," Archdale wrote, "so that the English in Comparison to the *Spaniard* have but little *Indian* Blood to answer for."[63] Obscured from the governor, of course, was the fact that the noxious trade in Indian slaves had facilitated the rapid spread of a deadly disease throughout southeastern Indian societies. Nevertheless, he saw what he thought was "the Hand of God . . . thinning the Indians, to make room for the English."[64]

With a trade network extending across the Southeast, it was not long before smallpox had spread far beyond South Carolina. In 1699, Iberville and his men arrived at Mobile Bay and witnessed the results of the epidemic. They discovered, according to one Frenchman, such "a prodigious number of human skeletons that they formed a mountain."[65] Iberville thought that the Indians had died in a massacre and hence named the place Massacre Island.[66] One Frenchman later learned that the Indians belonged to "a numerous nation who being pursued and having withdrawn to this region, had almost all died here of sickness."[67]

The identity of the sickness became more obvious as the Frenchmen visited other villages near present-day Biloxi, Mississippi. Iberville came upon the Mougoulacha and Bayogoula Indians and described these people as two nations "joined together and living in the same village." They probably did so to combine forces and defend themselves against slave raids. Smallpox, though, severely afflicted them both. "The smallpox, which they still had in the village," Iberville reported, "had killed one-fourth of the people." The scene was horrifying; the stench of rotting bodies made the French sick.[68] A year later, Iberville found even more deserted villages in the area. The French governor reported that the Biloxi Indians, whom he described as "formerly quite numerous," had contracted disease in 1698 and by 1700 had deserted their village.[69]

At the same time smallpox was taking the lives of numerous Indians on the Gulf Coast, native societies living in the Mississippi valley were also feeling the destructive power of the deadly virus. In January 1699, French missionaries descended the lower Mississippi and found smallpox among

Quapaws and other Arkansas tribes. One Catholic priest wrote: "We were sensibly afflicted to see this [Arkansas] nation once so numerous entirely destroyed by war and sickness. It is not a month since they got over the smallpox which carried off the greatest part of them. There was nothing to be seen in the village but graves."[70] The death scene continued as the missionaries traveled even farther south. After departing the Quapaws, they arrived at the Tonicas, where one priest reported that the Indians "were dying in great numbers."[71] The missionaries unfortunately caught smallpox themselves and helped spread the disease farther down the valley.[72]

Documentary evidence makes it clear that smallpox raged in an extensive area between 1696 and 1700 and that many indigenous people who inhabited the piedmont, the Atlantic and gulf coasts, and the Mississippi Valley perished. But it is not clear what impact the disease had on the major Indian confederacies of the interior—the Chickasaws, Creeks, Cherokees, and Choctaws.

The Chickasaws and Creeks most likely experienced the Great Southeastern Smallpox Epidemic. Their heavy involvement in slave raids and frequent communication with Carolinian traders made them vulnerable to exposure. Moreover, the massive number of people moving into the dominions of the Lower and Upper Creeks provided another opportunity for the disease to spread into the interior. Unfortunately, documentation dating to the 1690s concerning both the Creeks and Chickasaws remains sparse and prevents a definite conclusion that smallpox struck them during that time. Thomas Nairne, an English official who traveled through Creek and Chickasaw villages in 1708, reported that sometime before his journey the deadly virus had afflicted Indians of the region. Smallpox and other calamities, Nairne claimed, obliged Indians "to break up their Townships and unite them for want of inhabitants."[73] Unfortunately, one does not know whether Nairne specifically meant the Creeks and Chickasaws or was referring to Indians in general.

It is even more difficult to determine whether the Choctaws and Cherokees suffered from smallpox during the late 1690s. These two groups were primarily victims of early slave raids, and thus their villages were not in continuous communication with the English or their Indian allies. In addition, both groups lived in the most remote areas of the Southeast; it took visitors several days to reach them, decreasing the chances that anyone carrying smallpox would arrive among the villages before the virus

either ran its course or the carrier died. Since the Cherokees and Choctaws had the largest populations of all the southeastern tribes in the early
eighteenth century, they may indeed have escaped the ravages of
smallpox.[74]

Despite the possibility that the Great Southeastern Smallpox Epidemic
failed to strike the Cherokees and Choctaws, the outbreak resulted in
demographic catastrophe. It is unlikely that an epidemic of equal proportion preceded it. Neither Spanish explorers nor aboriginal exchange were
likely to spread smallpox through the region during the sixteenth and
most of the seventeenth centuries. Typhoid and chronic diseases such as
malaria may have spread through the Southeast and caused some alterations in southeastern Indian societies, but these diseases would not have
caused casualties anywhere near the number caused by smallpox. Indeed,
without smallpox ravaging Indians across the region, demographic losses
before the 1690s estimated as high as 90 percent appear to be grossly
exaggerated. A more reasonable conclusion concerning the timing of population collapse is that European contact resulted in the loss of more
southeastern Indian lives between 1696 and 1700 than in all of the previous years combined.

The reason for this relatively late timing of demographic collapse in the
Southeast is that conditions had not emerged to facilitate a region-wide
epidemic of smallpox until the late seventeenth century. At that time,
thousands of Europeans and Africans, including children, the most common carriers of smallpox, poured into the region. Most important, aboriginal trade became reoriented to meet the English demands for slaves, providing an avenue for the rapid spread of disease from the coasts into the
interior. When introduced in 1696 at a time of an unprecedentedly high
volume of human traffic, the smallpox virus produced population loss
unparalleled in any other period of southeastern Indian history.

Following the Great Southeastern Smallpox Epidemic, a series of outbreaks of smallpox and other diseases erupted in the region in 1718–1722,
1728–1733, 1738–1742, 1747–1750, 1759–1760, 1763–1765, and 1779–
1783. Many of these epidemics were part of global outbreaks associated
with the migration of European settlers, the importation of African slaves,
and troop movements during the various colonial wars. Epidemics then
spread into the interior, most often along with English and French trade
goods. Nevertheless, when smallpox again struck the Southeast, it did not
spread as thoroughly through the region and never produced the cata-

strophic mortality rates associated with the Great Southeastern Smallpox Epidemic.[75]

What subsequent epidemics did do, however, is make recovery from the Great Southeastern Smallpox Epidemic for the total Native American population impossible. If the unlikely event of a region-wide smallpox epidemic did occur in the sixteenth or early seventeenth centuries, native populations had time to recover because of the infrequent reintroduction of the disease.[76] If smallpox did in fact spread by way of early explorers or aboriginal trade routes linking the Southeast with Mexico or Florida, the lack of continual intercourse with Europeans and Africans meant that other diseases would not follow in rapid succession. Thus, some generations of southeastern Indians would never face disease, giving their populations time to grow by natural reproduction. The 1700s then should be considered the century of population collapse. Indeed, demographic studies have shown dramatic losses in the eighteenth century. As Peter Wood has estimated, native population in an area that includes present-day North Carolina, South Carolina, Georgia, Kentucky, Tennessee, Alabama, Mississippi, and Louisiana fell from 152,500 in 1685 to 46,700 in 1790.[77] If Wood's numbers and this paper are both correct, then 152,500 may be a close approximation of the population of Indians in these areas in 1492.

The Great Southeastern Smallpox Epidemic is thus even more significant because it was a turning point, ushering in nearly one hundred years of repeated epidemics and continual population decline. Some individual tribes suffered less than others and even experienced demographic recovery during the eighteenth century, but for the total population of Indians in the Southeast there was no reprieve. The same conditions that made the scope and magnitude of the outbreak of the 1690s so severe persisted through the 1700s, bringing more diseases and continuing the demographic disaster for subsequent generations.

ACKNOWLEDGMENTS

Many people have generously shared their time and insight. I especially appreciated the help of Gary Anderson, Paul Gilje, Charles Hays, Charles Hudson, James Knight, Donald Pisani, Terry Rugely, Cameron Wesson, and Peter Wood.

Spanish Missions and the Persistence of Chiefly Power

JOHN E. WORTH

JOHN E. WORTH

CONTRASTS

In the fall of 1728, fully a quarter century after the last Guale mission had been withdrawn to St. Augustine, an elderly Guale chief named Francisco Ospogue petitioned the king of Spain for an official military post from which he might draw a salary on which he and his descendants could live. Then approaching seventy years of age, the cacique Francisco based his petition on two primary facts: his more than forty years of active service in the Spanish militia (including a 1717 attack in which his wife and four children were captured and enslaved by English-allied Indians), and his noble birthright as the legitimate heir of the chiefly matrilineage of the Guale town of Ospogue, the remnants of which were at that time situated in the refugee mission called Nombre de Dios Chiquito.[1] As specifically noted in his petition, Francisco was "the legitimate son of Francisco Joseph and Augustina María, noble Indians," and was confirmed as cacique during the term of then-governor Laureano de Torres y Ayala, as is separately documented to have occurred on February 9, 1695, during the visitation of Guale by Captain Juan de Pueyo.[2] As was reported subsequently, Francisco "was of the age of thirty six when he made him cacique, his ancestors having also been [caciques], as was certified by all the caciques of this time." Given that Francisco's predecessor during the visitations of 1685 and 1695 is separately documented to have been named Antonio,[3] his succession to the office of cacique of Ospogue was probably matrilineal, following Guale custom.

What is perhaps most notable about this curious eighteenth-century petition is the fact that Chief Francisco Ospogue was probably the direct heir of a chiefly matrilineage that had been directly involved with the Spanish for more than a century and a half. The Guale town of Ospogue, also known simply as Ospo, was originally located on the southern side of Sapelo Island. In 1576 it was the site of the murder of Spanish royal officials during the widespread Guale-Orista rebellion that year, and follow-

39

ing its destruction by Governor Pedro Menéndez Márquez in 1579, the town's chief sued for peace in March of 1580.[4] It was formally missionized by Franciscan friars in 1595, but was a center of unrest during the 1597 Guale rebellion (Fray Francisco de Avila was captured here), and was burned again in October of that year, followed by yet another suit for peace in 1600.[5] The town and its lineage appeared briefly in visitation records over the next decade, and only reappeared during the late seventeenth century as a subordinate lineage within the relocated mission of San Phelipe, at that time situated on Amelia Island following more than a decade on Cumberland Island through 1684.[6] After their violent destruction in 1702, the remnants of these and other Guale towns regrouped far to the south near St. Augustine, where they were subjected to yet another disastrous raid in 1717.[7] By 1728, the refugee mission at Nombre de Dios Chiquito, still called Santa Catharina de Gualecita, held only seventy-one men, women, and children, including some thirteen immigrant Yamasee Indians and the remnants of most of the rest of Guale.[8]

Despite this 150 years of trauma, including at least four episodes of destruction by fire and at least four separate relocations, all during a period of at least 90 percent population decline among the Guale,[9] Francisco Ospogue's chiefly matrilineage survived to form a major component in his social and political standing among the remaining inhabitants of mission Nombre de Dios Chiquito. When he finally received a yearly pension, or alms, of two silver *reales* after 1734, one of the justifications used was that "the other caciques, by his example and in view of Royal mercifulness, will be more secure in their vassalage, and will be encouraged to distinguish themselves in Royal service, with the experience of seeing this cacique rewarded."[10] Even two centuries after first Spanish contact, the hereditary leaders of southeastern chiefdoms still exercised real political power, and they and their subordinate populations were viewed as noble vassals of the Spanish crown.

Contrast this with the contemporary statement of Spanish Friar Joseph Ramos Escudero, who had lived among the Florida mission Indians, and made the following statement regarding the leadership of the Lower Creeks in 1734. At the time, Fray Ramos was in London disguised as a Dutchman secretly observing the visit of Tomochichi, a Creek chief, and was able to have a conversation with Tomochichi's interpreter over a beer. Ramos explained in his subsequent communique that "[t]he present King is cacique of a large town called Apalachicol[a], which is the first after

Caveta, and the aforementioned interpreter gave me to understand that the stated present King is today the first in esteem on account of his great wisdom and counsel, and that of Caveta is very crazy [*alocado*] and desperate (and we know him to be thus in those parts), all of which should be believed to be so, because the Indians are not as subject to their Kings as the Europeans, at times good, at times bad, and although they do not recognize others as their caciques, but rather those who are such by birth, but in cases of wars and grave matters, they only give their attention to the cacique of greatest wisdom and age, and from the extremes that are seen here, it seems that this one is such, notwithstanding his being the second cacique of that province."[11]

This and many subsequent accounts suggest that while the early-eighteenth-century Creeks retained the notion of hereditary leadership titles and traditional ranking, in actual practice the power of their chiefs derived from a combination of achieved and ascribed status. Specifically, Creek political organization seems to have been somewhat less rigidly hereditary than that of their mission counterparts at the same time, and this fluidity manifested itself in the increased importance of individual achievement and perceived wisdom within the context of the new European colonial world.

Admittedly, the distinction is a subtle one, but there can be no doubt that the political structure of the eighteenth-century Creeks, including the ancestral chiefdoms of Apalachicola, Tallapoosa, and Abihka, was evolving in a direction different from that of the missionized Timucua, Guale, and Apalachee.[12] Not only had chiefly succession lost its strictly hereditary character—female chieftains had been common, and teenagers and even children from the chiefly matrilineage could govern with the assistance of their noble relatives—but even the office of chief had lost its elevated and privileged character. In stark contrast to mission chiefs, who chose rebellion in 1656 to avoid being seen carrying sacks of corn on their backs, who as late as 1678 and 1695 had to be persuaded by Spanish officials to even participate in planting their fields and grinding corn because of localized population decline, and who were still preferentially given expensive Spanish cloth as late as 1687,[13] Creek chiefs were described as early as 1708 as being little removed from their ordinary neighbors. As noted by experienced trader Thomas Nairne, "[T]hese honest men don't pretend that their subjects should contribute too much, to maintain a needless grandure. They are content to share with their people in assisting and setting them a good example the better and more patiently to endure the necessary toils of life."[14] In stark contrast to mission caciques, Creek chiefs were not exempt from manual labor, and according to William Bartram, by the late eighteenth century they differed little in both appearance and behavior from their common counterparts. In his words, the chief "associates, eats, drinks, and dances with them in common as another man; his dress is the same, and a stranger could not distinguish the king's habitation from that of any other citizen, by any sort of splendour or magnificence."[15] Compare this description to those of the ancestral chieftains of the late prehistoric Southeast, known from archaeological and ethnohistorical data to have lived on platform mounds, to have been carried on litters, and to have worn and possessed ornate clothing and ornaments of copper, shell, and stone with elaborate iconographic symbols and mythical creatures.[16] Clearly, substantial social transformations were in operation during the colonial era, and were most pronounced among nonmission groups.

Admittedly, there are methodological difficulties involved in forming a direct comparison between the ethnohistorical record for mission groups such as the Timucua, Mocama, Apalachee, and Guale and that for unassimilated frontier groups such as those involved in the emergent Creek Confederacy. Not only is there a substantial chronological difference between these two sets of documentary data, but they also derive from differing types of colonial interaction with completely different European cultures. Specifically, the vast bulk of ethnohistorical data relating to the mission Indians dates to the seventeenth century, and derives from Spanish documentation surrounding these assimilated components of the broader Florida colonial system, while in contrast the majority of the ethnohistorical data relating to unassimilated frontier groups dates to the eighteenth century, and derives in large part from English and French documentation surrounding long-distance interaction focusing on the slave and deerskin trade. These difficulties are not insurmountable, however, and a direct comparison between relevant sources of data, including not just historical but also archaeological data, makes it possible to assert that there were indeed some very fundamental and substantive differences between the colonial experiences of these two broad groups of southeastern Indians. In sum, Indian groups who were assimilated into the Spanish mission system seem to have exhibited a greater degree of cultural stability with regard to traditional sociopolitical systems than those who remained in the deep colonial frontier. Simply put, from an anthropological perspective, chiefdoms evidently changed less and lasted longer within the context of the mission system. But in the same connection, this cultural persistence in the face of steep demographic collapse ultimately left mission chiefs governing dysfunctional societies, while ongoing social transformations in the deep frontier resulted in cultural adaptations that were uniquely suited for the European colonial era. In the end, prolonged cultural stability among mission Indians was illusory and ultimately fatal. The survival of frontier groups such as the Creeks to the present day serves as a tragic contrast to the effective extinction of all mission groups attached to Spanish Florida. Nevertheless, an examination and comparison of the details of these processes provides many important clues as to the nature of social transformation in the context of colonization, and even regarding culture change in general.

The basic difference between missionized and frontier groups is one of trajectory. I would argue that by the first decades of the eighteenth century, mission groups such as the Timucua, the Guale, and the Apalachee comprised the surviving remnants of more or less traditional southeastern chiefdoms which were at that time experiencing the final death throes of long-term demographic collapse and flight in the face of recent armed aggression. In contrast, unmissionized frontier groups such as the Apalachicola, the Tallapoosa, and the Abihka comprised the remnants of similar chiefdoms that were at that very time experiencing the birth of a new social order that would ultimately lead to more egalitarian and fluid tribal confederacies without direct precedent among the chiefdoms of the late prehistoric Southeast. Mission chiefdoms were on their way out, and frontier chiefdoms were on the verge of transformation into new, and ultimately successful, social formations.

I do not believe that this difference in evolutionary trajectory can be attributed solely to the fact that mission groups were literally outcompeted by these very same frontier groups by the beginning of the eighteenth century. To be certain, many of the frontier groups noted above had by this time become musket-toting slave raiders with English support, and many of their primary victims were poorly armed mission towns with only limited Spanish protection. And indeed, by the end of 1706 all mission groups were physically reduced to a handful of refugee towns clustered around St. Augustine, while frontier groups ravaged the abandoned hinterlands in search of fresh sources of slaves. Moreover, by 1711 the entire Spanish mission population had been reduced to fewer than three hundred men, women, and children, while English records dating to 1715 reveal that the constituent groups of the later Creek Confederacy alone amounted to almost nine thousand individuals, or nearly thirty times the mission population.[17] What is notable here is not simply the fact that mission populations had dwindled from just over seventy-three hundred to fewer than three hundred in perhaps only a single generation, amounting to a 96 percent decline between 1681 and 1711 alone.[18] The extraordinary element of this equation for my purposes here is the fact that even in the face of unprecedented demographic collapse, Spanish documents reveal that the essential elements of chiefly political structure survived much longer in the context of the mission system than they did among isolated frontier chiefdoms that eventually became involved in English trade.[19] This contrast is even more impressive when one considers the fact that missionization preceded the expansion of the English slave and deerskin trade by as much as a century in some cases, and in all cases by at least fifty to a hundred years. Despite this lengthy saturation within the colonial system of Spanish Florida, fourth- and fifth-generation mission chiefs retained more hereditary power and privilege than did Creek chiefs whose parents had witnessed the arrival of Carolina traders in the 1680s.

While my primary focus in this paper is to elaborate on the specific characteristics of the mission experience that tended to promote sociopolitical stability and the persistence of chiefly power, I have also found it necessary to step back and take a broader view of the overall colonial experience for southeastern Indians both within and outside the mission system, focusing on the easternmost region dominated by Spanish and English colonial interests. This larger perspective makes it possible to identify specific differences among what I identify as the three primary categories of colonial interaction following first contact. The first category is *isolation*, referring to chiefdoms that remained in the deep colonial frontier after the period of first contact, and which were characterized by only sporadic and typically indirect long-distance interaction with European colonists, including limited exchange. The second category is *missionization*, referring to chiefdoms that were assimilated into the expanding mission system of Spanish Florida, and which were characterized by intensive and direct interaction with Spanish colonists. The third category is *commerce*, referring to chiefdoms that accepted resident English trad-

ers who supplied them with firearms and munitions for use in the slave
and deerskin trade.

After the initial period of first contact during the mid-sixteenth century,
all southeastern chiefdoms diverged into either missionization or isolation, which lasted for more than a century until the first two decades after
the establishment of Carolina in 1670, after which the period of intensive
trade began for many groups. Some groups, such as the Timucua and
Guale, experienced only missionization, while most other groups, such as
the constituent chiefdoms of the later Creek Confederacy, experienced
more than a century of isolation followed by well over a century of commerce. For this reason, I have found it necessary to compare and contrast
all three categories in order to assess the mechanisms for social transformation that might have been involved in each case.

I should add a word of caution here: the following discussion represents
an initial and thus very preliminary exploration of some of the issues
involved in social transformation during the European colonial era. Since
this paper is based on conclusions that I have only recently reached
regarding the nature and function of the broader colonial system of Spanish Florida and how aboriginal chiefdoms were assimilated into that system,[20] the following discussion should be viewed as a beginning rather
than an end. Furthermore, many of the comparisons and contrasts made
in this paper are intentionally broad and unidimensional, and in this sense
will ultimately require considerable refinement as the ideas and concepts
proposed here are subjected to more detailed scrutiny. Nevertheless, I
would hope that these preliminary interpretations might serve as a useful
framework for future research.

My point of departure for the discussion that follows is the observation
that chiefly social organization lasted longer and changed less within the
context of the Florida mission system than it did in the deep frontier.[21]
Specifically, assimilation into the mission system of Spanish Florida seems
to have actually fostered stability in that chiefly system, countering the
inherently destabilizing effects of early demographic collapse and later
English trade. My primary thesis in this regard is that the broader colonial
system of Spanish Florida reinforced internal chiefly power by providing
a tributary exchange system in which aboriginal land and labor were harnessed through hereditary chiefs to produce surplus foodstuffs such as corn
which were then exchanged for Spanish luxury goods and military support. In this way, by providing a new and substantial external market for

aboriginal corn, the Spanish colonial system not only reinforced the primary economic sources of chiefly power, namely land and labor, but also satisfied the additional preexisting need for ostentatious public display and for external military backing. In effect, Spanish Florida thus became a sort of modified paramount chiefdom through which the chiefly matrilineages of destabilized chiefdoms bolstered their own internal power by subordinating themselves to the Spanish crown.

CONTACT AND DIVERGENCE

For my purposes here, I will not attempt to frame my discussion of aboriginal social organization within the broader context of the rise and spread of agricultural chiefdoms during the late prehistoric period, nor will I attempt to provide an overview of the initial stages of European exploration in the Southeast.[22] It is sufficient to note that following initial contacts along coastal regions by expeditions under Juan Ponce de León, Lúcas Vázquez de Ayllón, and Pánfilo de Narváez between 1513 and 1528, and after the monumental expedition of Hernando de Soto between 1539 and 1543, during which prehistoric chiefdoms across much of the interior Southeast experienced first contact with the European world and its pathogens, the decade of the 1560s marked several important benchmark events for the already-collapsing chiefdoms of the Southeast. First, there were no fewer than three Spanish exploratory expeditions launched into the deep interior regions of northern Alabama, northern Georgia, eastern Tennessee, and western North Carolina. These expeditions, including a large detachment of soldiers under Tristán de Luna in 1560 and two successive expeditions by Juan Pardo between 1566 and 1568, marked the last direct European presence in most of these regions until more than a century later, after the beginning of direct English trade after 1685.[23] As a consequence, the Luna and Pardo expeditions prefaced more than a century of physical isolation from the European colonial world, during which time epidemic population collapse apparently functioned independently to spur transformations in both social geography and organization.

The second watershed event of the 1560s was the establishment of several European colonial settlements along the Atlantic seaboard, including French Charlesfort and Fort Caroline and Spanish St. Augustine and Santa Elena, all established between 1562 and 1566.[24] While only St. Augustine survived past the 1580s, these early colonial endeavors resulted in the establishment of a permanent European colonial hub on the eastern seaboard, and thus the beginning of incrementally more direct and intense interaction between European colonists and the chiefdoms of the Florida and Georgia coastal plain. All surviving societies within a two-hundred-mile radius west and north of St. Augustine were eventually assimilated into the expanding mission system of Spanish Florida between roughly 1587 and 1633, where they remained through the retreat of the missions between 1702 and 1706 and the final removal to Cuba and Mexico in 1763.

As will be seen below, until the 1560s the colonial experience of all these groups had been largely similar, marked by occasional though certainly notable visits by European explorers and would-be colonists and by the apparently rapid spread of European plagues in their aftermath.[25] After that point, however, these colonial experiences diverged radically. Chiefdoms neighboring St. Augustine in the coastal plain became increasingly integrated into the expanding Spanish colonial system through the mechanism of missionaries, including scattered Jesuit and early Franciscan efforts between 1568 and 1575 and substantial renewed Franciscan activity after 1587. During this same time, chiefdoms of the deep interior Southeast remained in virtually complete isolation from direct European contact for nearly a century before the Virginia firearms revolution after 1659, only accepting a resident English presence after 1685.[26] While it is of course possible that the early seventeenth-century Iroquois wars and other colonial conflicts in the Northeast may have had an indirect impact on the southeastern interior during this interval, my strong impression is that neither firearms nor direct English commerce penetrated this region until 1659, despite the possibility of one or more long-distance population relocations prompted by such activity.[27]

Despite this radical divergence in the colonial experiences of mission and frontier groups after the 1560s, however, one factor might be argued to have remained a more or less constant effect of the European colonial presence: disease. In this regard, the end result of colonial depopulation is relatively well documented: by the mid-eighteenth century, global southeastern Indian population levels had almost certainly dropped to well below 10 percent of their original levels in the early sixteenth century.[28] In some of the more well-documented cases, population losses were even steeper, clearly exceeding 95 percent in less than a century.[29] While a variety of probable and possible causes for this radical depopulation rate may be identified during this broader period, including factors relating to intergroup warfare and early English slaving, fugitivism and out-migration, and reduced fertility and birthrate caused by increased levels of stress and decreased community health, in my judgement the single most important factor in the overall demographic collapse of the southeastern Indians was epidemic disease.[30] Whether such plagues were episodic or continuous, and whether they were localized or multiregional, their ultimate effect was to act as an independent and ongoing drain on the human resources of each aboriginal chiefdom.

CHIEFDOMS AND DEMOGRAPHY

In order to judge the potential and actual effect of such demographic collapse on aboriginal sociopolitical structure, it is first necessary to explore the relationship between chiefdoms and their demographic base. Specifically, what was the connection between the political power of hereditary southeastern chiefs and the substantial subordinate populations they claimed as traditional subjects or vassals? Or, to rephrase the question, what was the real source of chiefly power in an agricultural chiefdom? Basing my case on a combination of archaeological data from the late prehistoric and early historic period, as well as ethnohistoric documentation relating primarily to mission groups, I would argue that chiefly power in the Southeast was constituted in the ability to appropriate and amass agricultural surpluses for the exclusive use of the chiefly matrilineage and other designated public officials, including warriors, artisans, and laborers involved in public works.[31] The key here is the word "surplus"; chiefs presumably were not in a position to regularly cut into the minimum subsistence base of their subordinate populations. Chiefly tribute, including both direct tribute of foodstuffs and indirect tribute of labor to produce foodstuffs, was constituted in the surplus production "above the line" of minimum survival. Such surpluses were largely made possible with the dawn of intensive agriculture based on highly productive crops such as corn, beans, and squash. In this sense, surplus agricultural production provided the tool with which chiefs and their families and heirs financed their power.[32]

Agricultural production also tied subordinate populations to the land, and thus traditional notions of chiefly ownership of land formed an essential component in the equation. Tribute was owed by subordinate lineages precisely because they lived and worked on lands owned by the chiefly lineage.[33] Furthermore, agricultural land was only valuable as a source of surplus and thus tribute if it were worked, and thus subordinate families and lineages held an obligation to farm their respective parcels of the chiefly domain. Spanish documentary evidence reveals, for example, that widows unable to work their husbands' fields could be dispossessed of their land, unless the chief made arrangements for public labor to be temporarily diverted for this purpose.[34] In sum, land without labor served no function, making both land and labor a fundamental source of real chiefly power.

During the European colonial period, depopulation in general, and epidemic population decline in particular, resulted in a substantial net loss of human labor, reducing the available labor pool from which these chiefly surpluses were generated. What can be said about the hypothetical effects of such demographic collapse in the absence of mitigating circumstances? In essence, a reduction in agricultural labor meant a reduction in agricultural surpluses, and a reduction in these surpluses left hereditary chiefs with little real basis for traditional chiefly power. In particular, as the amount of surplus foodstuffs declined, so too did the possibility of supporting artisans or laborers for public projects, or warriors for military action. Moreover, with the disappearance of substantial chiefly corn reserves came increased vulnerability to drought and famine, removing the protective buffer represented by these storehouses.

The primary result of rapid depopulation for southeastern chiefdoms was instability at a societal level. The system of public finance represented by chiefly tribute was undermined or even eliminated as populations dwindled to unprecedented lows. Even minimal losses could have profound effects. As the local and regional labor pool shrank, so too did the agricultural surpluses that once supported chiefly craftsmen and mound builders. This is not to say that the basic annual subsistence of subordinate families and lineages was necessarily affected; even in cases of agricultural crop failure, individual families within affected chiefdoms possessed a wide range of options for subsistence, and thus probably retained a strong degree of self-sufficiency with regard to food production. Nevertheless, the political superstructure overarching domestic life within southeastern chiefdoms almost certainly suffered the earliest and most severe impact of demographic collapse.

Indeed, archaeological evidence confirms that some of the most visible

markers of chiefly social organization vanished within only a few generations after first contact; sumptuary goods crafted from copper, shell, and
stone had fallen into disuse by the beginning of the seventeenth century,
and earthen platform mound construction ceased during the same
period.[35] Presumably warriors and defensive works were maintained as
long as possible, particularly given the broader regional context of localized political destabilization. But there seems little doubt that as populations declined, so too did the agricultural power base of chiefly matrilineages.

RESPONSES

With instability came increased vulnerability, both to natural and social
forces. In broad perspective, agricultural surpluses constituted both the
mechanisms and the means for surviving not only short-term fluctuations
in yearly crop production, but also both internal and external social ten-
sions. Chiefly food reserves could be harnessed for a variety of purposes,
not all sumptuary, and thus any diminishment of these reserves represented not only a decrease in chiefly power, but also a weakening of the
primary buffer against societal collapse and fragmentation. In essence, it
might be argued that the internal system of public finance by chiefly tribute represented the economic "glue" of southeastern chiefdoms, and that
any threat to this system also represented a threat to the chiefdom.

Using available archaeological and ethnohistorical evidence relative to
the period 1540–1685, I would hypothesize several specific responses that
appear to characterize southeastern chiefdoms experiencing demographic
collapse. These may be grouped in the following five broad categories,
which I will define below: contraction, relocation, aggregation, confederation, and assimilation. To greater or lesser extents, most chiefdoms ultimately experienced several of these responses at one time or another during the colonial era. It should be noted that these responses are not
necessarily mutually exclusive, nor are they intended to describe the
entire range of possible responses to demographic collapse. Nevertheless,
for purposes of clarification and contrast, it is useful to review these
responses individually.

Contraction may be defined as the abandonment of subordinate satel-
lite communities within a single local or regional chiefly domain and their
relocation to larger and more centrally situated communities. Documen-

tary evidence from the Florida missions indicates that this phenomenon, called *congregación*, was typically a response to declining population levels in small outlying villages and hamlets, and represented an attempt to "draw in" surviving populations from communities that were no longer viable entities.[36] The end result of such contraction was an overall reduction in the number of occupied community sites, and at least a temporary boost in the declining populations of primary communities to which these survivors relocated. This phenomenon appears to be confirmed by archaeological evidence in many areas, as indicated by a decrease in the number of archaeological sites within specific localities, in some cases corresponding to occupational continuity or even expansion in central sites.[37]

Relocation represented the physical movement of individual communities or chiefdoms from one previously occupied locality to another unoccupied area. Such relocations might be prompted by localized crop failure caused by drought or flooding, or by intergroup warfare or hostility, and were undoubtedly exacerbated by the destabilizing effects of demographic collapse. In particular, many recurrent episodes of natural or social trauma that would not normally have caused significant problems to chiefdoms during the prehistoric period were instead cause for regional abandonment and relocation during the colonial era, precisely because of the increased instability and vulnerability of chiefdoms experiencing epidemic depopulation. As early as 1584, for example, one of the survivors of the 1566–1568 Pardo expeditions noted the relocation of an unnamed chief and his vassals from the western side of the Appalachian summit across the mountains to the east as a result of increased intergroup warfare, which was said to have resulted in the abandonment of a lengthy section of an entire river valley.[38] The best archaeological evidence for relocations of this kind is in the sixteenth-century Coosa chiefdom of northwest Georgia, which has been traced through a series of short-distance migrations downriver to a single eighteenth-century location within the upper Creek region.[39]

Aggregation represents a response that is similar to relocation, but is here defined as a physical relocation from a previously occupied area to an area still occupied by a preexisting chiefdom. In this sense, immigrant communities or entire chiefdoms attached themselves to other chiefdoms, presumably negotiating a subordinate position within the existing social order as tributaries to the local chiefly matrilineage. Abundant documentation from the Spanish mission era describes this process in detail, revealing that immigrants were normally incorporated into the chiefly organization of the matrilineage on whose lands the immigrants settled, and that tributary obligations were normally expected of the newcomers. This was certainly the case among Yamasee immigrants to the Mocama chiefdom in the 1670s, and Chisca immigrants to the Timucuan chiefdoms in the 1640s, and undoubtedly occurred in other areas as well.[40] Archaeological evidence for the long-term persistence, and even expansion, of aboriginal occupation in specific areas during the early colonial has been interpreted as an indirect measure of population influx from other regions, probably prompted by localized demographic collapse, warfare, or societal instability.[41]

Confederation may be defined as a process similar to aggregation, in which two or more relocated chiefdoms or groups of communities band together in a new social formation that does not derive primarily from a preexisting local chiefly order. In this sense, leaders of confederated societies did not necessarily have any preexisting claim to matrilineal ownership of land or other resources, and thus presumably established structural relationships that may have been somewhat more egalitarian, or at the very least less strictly hierarchical, than would have been the case under circumstances of aggregation. An early example of this in the study area is the Yamasee confederacy, which crystallized along the lower South Carolina coast in the early 1660s, and which evidently represented an amalgam of relocated communities and chiefdoms forced together along the northern mission frontier as a result of early English slaving.[42]

A final, though pivotal, response to demographic collapse may be identified as *assimilation*, which I would define as the incorporation of preexisting chiefdoms as subordinate elements within the political and economic infrastructure of the expanding colonial system of Spanish Florida. This process of assimilation manifested itself as missionization in the Southeast, and thus forms the core discussion that follows in this chapter.[43] As a potential response to depopulation during the colonial era, assimilation differed from all other responses described above in that assimilated chiefdoms actually became functional components of a much broader sociopolitical system centered locally at St. Augustine, but which ultimately found its core in Europe. This distinction is extremely important, since all other responses to depopulation were strictly aboriginal in their character, while assimilation involved conscious and intentional subordination and linkage with a European-centered system.

In this sense, foreshadowing the final section of this paper, I would note that there were fundamental differences between the assimilation of chiefdoms into the Florida colonial system through missionization and the later involvement of frontier chiefdoms in the English slave and deerskin trade. As will be seen below, missionization directly subsumed participating chiefdoms within the political hierarchy of the Spanish colonial system, while the English trade system involved no such structural integration or explicit political subordination. Even though this commercial linkage undoubtedly led to a degree of mutual economic dependency, English colonists and traders for the most part interacted with independent and effectively autonomous aboriginal societies that had already experienced (or were undergoing at that time) the transformations resulting from some or all of the first four responses noted above, namely contraction, relocation, aggregation, and/or confederation. As a consequence, the trajectory of societal change in the absence of assimilation (i.e., missionization) was in most cases radically different.

MISSIONIZATION[44]

As a mechanism for societal assimilation within the context of the early European colonial era, missionization had far more important consequences for the aboriginal chiefdoms neighboring Spanish St. Augustine than the simple construction of churches and convents and the placement of resident Franciscan friars for purposes of religious conversion and indoctrination. Indeed, the most significant consequences reached far beyond even the relatively dramatic introduction of European material culture and foodstuffs and their incorporation into the domestic economy of mission households, an important and commonly addressed topic of interest to mission archaeologists.[45] What missionization actually signified for the chiefs and chiefdoms that chose this route was functional assimilation into the political and economic structure of the colonial system of greater Spanish Florida. In this sense, missionized chiefdoms ultimately became peripheral components of a nearly global political and economic system centered in Europe.

The process of missionization has been the subject of considerable research not only in the southeastern United States, but also across the European colonial world of the modern era. Particularly along the frontiers of the vast Spanish colonial empire of the sixteenth to eighteenth centuries, aboriginal societies were gradually assimilated into the broader colonial system by a process initiated and fostered by Christian missionaries, whose efforts to convert and catechize these groups served as an important step in the structural linkage between what was known at the time as the "Republic of Indians" and the "Republic of Spaniards." While its name tends to emphasize the religious and spiritual dimension, missionization was actually a much more intricate and complex process, with implications far beyond the simple conversion of the members of aboriginal societies to Catholicism. Indeed, the establishment of mission provinces along the frontier of established Spanish colonial zones was primarily a secular political process, in which localized aboriginal societies became integrated into the globally oriented Spanish colonial system. The construction of small mission compounds within principal aboriginal towns was actually only a small part of a much more complicated and far-reaching process that was supervised by political leaders of both republics.

The key to understanding the process by which southeastern chiefdoms were assimilated through missionization into Spanish Florida, as well as the ultimate impact on the societies involved, lies in the structure and function of the broader colonial system of Spanish Florida. Viewed within the context of the vast colonial empire ruled by Spain during the sixteenth to eighteenth centuries, Spanish Florida actually served as a strategic military outpost on the northern periphery of a complex web of productive colonies centered on the Caribbean basin and mainland Central and South America. Because Florida lacked the direct economic benefits afforded by richly populated New World provinces that routinely produced gold, silver, and other valuable commodities, its primary function was strategic—to guard the sea routes of the Bahama channel, through which all the treasures of the Americas passed on their way to Spain. As a consequence, direct royal support for the Florida garrison-town of St. Augustine was only scarcely sufficient for the majority of the garrison, and occasionally lacking altogether, for which reason St. Augustine ultimately developed a reputation as a wretched frontier town to which few colonists would relocate willingly. During the seventeenth century, external support became even less reliable, and delays in the shipment of wheat, corn, and other products from New Spain and Havana and in the delivery of cash from the *situado*—the royal dole from the coffers of Mexico—left the inhabitants of St. Augustine in the precarious position of having too many poor military families and not enough colonial farmers.

The survival of this garrison-town, therefore, was ultimately based on an extensive support system, including not only periodic infusions of cash, armaments, provisions and other supplies from Spanish colonies external to Florida, but also the vast pool of human and natural resources making up greater Spanish Florida. This reservoir was, of course, the mission system. Without readily available internal sources of wealth with which to supplement purchasing power based on royal support, St. Augustine's population was in many ways almost wholly dependent upon Indian labor, both directly and indirectly, to make up for substantial shortfalls in vital foodstuffs (principally corn) and other supplies. As a consequence, the colonial system of seventeenth-century Spanish Florida was fundamentally based on the structural assimilation of largely self-sufficient centers of Indian population distributed across an unevenly productive landscape. In this sense, Florida's mission provinces served a truly pivotal function for the residents of St. Augustine: the maintenance of a vast Indian labor pool comprising an interconnected web of population centers subordinated beneath the Spanish crown and church. In effect, then, Florida was not so much an independent Spanish outpost interacting with neighboring and autonomous Indian societies, as was the case with later English colonies to the north, but was instead a broader community of interdependent Spanish and Indian populations woven into a functioning, though inherently flawed, colonial system.

At its core, the internal economic structure of the colonial system in seventeenth-century Florida revolved around the production and distribution of staple food crops, particularly corn. While this is of course a gross simplification of a far more complex economic system, local corn production does seem to have played a determining role in the overall structure of Florida's economic system, particularly as regards the role of the missionized chiefdoms in that system. It was the production and distribution of Florida's yearly corn crop that constituted the primary economic relationship between St. Augustine and its mission provinces. Together, the missions provided both surplus corn and surplus labor for producing more corn, all of which was subsidized at least in part by funds derived from Florida's yearly royal subsidy, the *situado*. While local officials normally skimmed personal profits from all such transactions, the end result of this system was the yearly production of substantial supplementary food reserves for the garrison-town of St. Augustine. Given existing limitations both in available Spanish agricultural labor in St. Augustine (including royal slaves and prisoners at forced labor) and in subsidy funds which could have been used to purchase staple foods from other Spanish colonies, Spanish officials ultimately came to rely on the food and labor provided by the mission provinces as a relatively inexpensive local solution to food-supply problems in St. Augustine. In times of crisis, Florida's corn reserves were the primary buffer against privation.

An ongoing dilemma in this system was the fact that St. Augustine was situated in a comparatively unproductive region of broader Spanish Florida, and had few resident Indians remaining by the first decades of the seventeenth century, a consequence of epidemic depopulation resulting from early and sustained European contact since the 1560s. The most agriculturally productive areas in colonial Spanish Florida (both in terms of soil fertility and human population) were located far to the west and north of St. Augustine, in the missionized chiefdoms of Apalachee and Guale. While surplus corn and other foodstuffs were regularly transported by ship from coastal ports in these provinces, as many as three hundred laborers also marched annually across the less-productive mission provinces of Timucua and Mocama, once in winter and once in summer, to provide the labor force needed to produce St. Augustine's yearly corn crop through a draft labor system known as the *repartimiento*. This important crop amounted to perhaps a million pounds of corn each year during the mid-seventeenth century, providing something on the order of eight times the amount of surplus corn available for purchase annually from Apalachee and Guale.

The driving force behind the entire economic system of colonial Spanish Florida was aboriginal labor. Without resident aboriginal labor, the fertile soils of Apalachee and Guale could yield neither the agricultural surpluses regularly purchased by Spanish agents nor the subsistence-base of resident Indian and Spanish populations, including friars and garrisoned soldiers. Without aboriginal labor, the missions of Timucua and Mocama could not produce the staple foods that supported resident and transient populations along the Camino Real and the northern intracoastal waterway, nor could they provide ferry services across the rivers of northern Florida. Furthermore, without aboriginal labor from both these regions (and particularly Apalachee), the yearly corn crop in St. Augustine would effectively vanish, leaving the Spanish residents of St. Augustine without any important local source of staple foods as a backup in case of the failure of external supply lines. Finally, without aboriginal labor on a local level, Florida's aboriginal chiefs would have little real basis to their hereditary positions of leadership, undermining not only traditional aboriginal sociopolitical systems, but also the overlying Spanish administrative structure on which the entire colonial system was based. In these fundamental ways, aboriginal labor was easily the most important commodity in seventeenth-century Spanish Florida.

The primary personal motivation on the part of aboriginal chiefs for establishing relations with the Spaniards at St. Augustine seems to have been related to maintaining or enhancing internal political power within their own chiefdoms or communities. In formally rendering obedience to the Spanish governor as a local representative of the Spanish crown, chiefs not only established powerful military alliances, but also received exotic Spanish clothing and other goods for purposes of ostentatious display, a mechanism already well established within prehistoric chiefly societies. In converting to Christianity and accepting resident Franciscan friars within their local jurisdiction, chiefs gained not only the largesse of the Catholic church and the Spanish crown, but also a resident cultural broker and advocate to act on their behalf with respect to the Spanish military government. All things being equal, the establishment of a tributary labor arrangement with the governor of St. Augustine must have seemed a small price to pay in return for the anticipated benefits of assimilation through missionization.

Indeed, there seems good reason to assert that the assimilation of chiefdoms in Spanish Florida actually served to reinforce and bolster the internal power of mission chiefs. Within the Spanish colonial system, these chiefs managed both the selection of *repartimiento* laborers and the distribution of their wage goods, as well as the production and sale of surplus corn and other foodstuffs to Spanish officials. As noble leaders of the Republic of Indians, they maintained substantial internal autonomy over secular matters, and theoretically held a more or less autonomous position with respect to the Spanish governor and military officials. Resident Franciscan friars only held authority over religious affairs within mission communities, and were nominally subject to chiefly authority in regard to secular matters. In this sense, missionaries simply acted as subordinate religious practitioners within and beneath chiefly authority, just as indigenous religious practitioners had done before contact. Public labor and goods were indeed directed for the sole use of the friars and for church beautification, but all under the supervision of mission chiefs. In the final analysis, mission chiefs actually lost little internal power and authority within the Spanish colonial system.

The benefits, moreover, were substantial, especially given the tendency toward systemic instability during the plague years of early European colonization. As a part of Spanish Florida, mission chiefs not only had a ready market for surplus agricultural products grown on lands belonging to their matrilineage, but they were also provided an abundance of new tools and new crops which increased efficiency and presumably increased the local productivity of their lands. Surplus foodstuffs and surplus labor were readily converted into Spanish cloth, beads, tools, and other items, reinforcing preexisting norms regarding ostentatious display as a legitimizing factor for hereditary office. Chiefs were also regaled with a range of specialized gifts, including ornate cloth and articles of Spanish clothing, and were additionally provided luxury foods such as wheat, wine, and cheese during visits. An important benefit was that mission chiefs had direct and more or less immediate access to Spanish military protection and support, and through the standing Indian militia, they and their noble relatives and other warriors were given access to Spanish firearms and munitions, though perhaps on a less than consistent basis. It seems no surprise that most aboriginal chiefs struggled to gain entry into the mission system, and remained there for so long. Only in cases where their own internal authority was directly challenged did rebellion flare, as was the case with Guale in 1597 and Timucua in 1656. Rampant epidemic population loss and abuses in the labor system were largely tolerated as long as the chiefs maintained power.

Ultimately, assimilation into the mission system of Spanish Florida fostered stability in chiefly sociopolitical organization precisely because it strongly reinforced the preexisting source of chiefly power, land and labor, while providing the kinds of external support and internal legitimacy that served to maintain the structural integrity of aboriginal systems. In virtually the same way that prehistoric aboriginal paramount chiefdoms may have functioned to reinforce the internal leadership of their constituent societies, the mission system of Spanish Florida promoted long-term stability in southeastern chiefly social organization. Even in the face of near-total demographic collapse, accompanied by English-sponsored raiding that ultimately forced the retreat of all surviving mission communities to St. Augustine, chiefly matrilineages persisted, even in some cases of lineage extinction. Ultimately, the Spanish colonial strategy served to preserve these ancient social systems in a way unparalleled by other forms of European interaction.

Despite this conclusion, I would also comment here that this aboriginal social system, based fundamentally on the hereditary control of land and labor for the purposes of surplus accumulation, long outlived its functional role within Spanish Florida. In the context of broader systemic inertia within the colonial system, hereditary chiefs stubbornly clung to their traditional privileges of rank, in some cases ignoring the consequences of population loss until it was literally too late. By the end of the seventeenth century, there were too many chiefs and nobles, and not enough subordinate Indians to support their existence. I would argue that as a form of social organization, the traditional southeastern chiefdom was incapable of surviving such immense and widespread demographic collapse. Only through a process of adaptation and evolution, as is known to have occurred in the deep colonial frontier among nonmission groups, were these chiefdoms able to transform into new social formations more appropriate for the world in which they found themselves. While in the short term, the mission system of Spanish Florida provided hereditary chiefs with an effective solution to their internal instability, in the long term, this stability was only ephemeral. In clinging to their traditional power by birthright, the mission chiefs ultimately ensured the persistence of a dysfunctional sociopolitical system that would not survive the trauma of the colonial era. Their complete extinction by the end of the eighteenth century serves as a tragic contrast to the obvious success of the adaptations of frontier chiefdoms, the descendants of which survive to the present day.

SOME THOUGHTS ON SOCIAL TRANSFORMATION IN THE
DEEP FRONTIER

The stabilizing effect of missionization can be contrasted directly with the effects of both frontier isolation and, later, intensive English trade. As noted above, more than a century of near-total isolation in the deep colonial frontier evidently resulted in a wide range of transformations on both a local and regional scale. These included not only the apparent cessation of monumental public architecture and luxury craft specialization as an indirect measure of a concurrent decrease in agricultural surpluses under chiefly control, but also the short- and long-distance relocation of villages and entire chiefdoms, some of which clearly aggregated to existing chiefdoms. Moreover, during the brief interval of early English slave raiding after 1659, in which a single armed group called the Westo terrorized the entire region, population movements only accelerated in the face of increased societal instability, exaggerating these earlier transformations.[46] But unquestionably the most substantial and profound social transformations for these frontier chiefdoms accompanied the rapid expansion of English trade after 1685.[47] As the Southeast was reshaped into an armed borderland between competing European powers, the truly immense new market for deerskins and Indian slaves suddenly and radically altered the internal economic structure of unmissionized frontier chiefdoms, uprooting populations from their traditional ties to the land and diverting virtually all surplus labor toward commercial hunting and raiding. The agricultural infrastructure of chiefly social organization effectively collapsed as the surpluses which financed chiefly power vanished, and as the hereditary control of land and labor at the societal level dissolved in the face of English commerce. The nature of chiefly authority was constituted anew as frontier groups largely reverted to subsistence farming only as a supplement to their newfound role as primary producers in the European market economy.

Parenthetically, an important question that has yet to be answered in this context is whether or not unmissionized frontier chiefdoms would have eventually reformulated their indigenous chiefly social systems had they not been influenced by the spread of direct English commerce after 1685. Despite widespread demographic collapse and the consequent "reshuffling" of the social geography of the interior, would surviving societies have attempted to reconstitute their traditional chiefly order in new locations and with new subordinate populations? Would platform mound construction have continued after a brief interval of traumatic change? At present, this question is difficult to answer, but future archaeological research may ultimately be the best avenue for exploring such issues. Ethnohistorical evidence indicates that a number of partially or wholly reformulated chiefdoms of this sort may have been in existence as late as the 1650s or later, including not only the Apalachicola, Tallapoosa, and Abihka chiefdoms noted above, but also Altamaha (or "Tama") and Cofitachequi in eastern Georgia and central South Carolina, respectively.[48] If archaeologists can identify markers of continued or renewed chiefly organization in these areas during the period ca. 1600–1685 (as distinguished from both earlier and later occupations), it might be possible to develop an argument that depopulation alone might not have substantially shifted the developmental trajectory of these indigenous societies, but rather that later English commerce was actually the primary culprit in radical social transformation. In either case, the expansion of the English trade network after 1685 unquestionably had a profound and fundamental impact on surviving societies of the deep interior frontier.

As a fundamental part of a broader colonial strategy, the English trade system formed a marked contrast with the Spanish mission system in its primary focus on commerce as opposed to assimilation. Not only were the political and economic relationships fundamentally different in each system (i.e., lateral and relatively egalitarian as opposed to vertical and rigidly hierarchical), but the primary commodities of value in each system were similarly different: deerskins and Indian slaves in the English system and agricultural foodstuffs and wage labor in the Spanish system. The importance of these differences cannot be understated, especially with regard to the relative degree of impact on aboriginal social systems. Whereas the Spanish assimilative system tapped into preexisting chiefly tributary arrangements based on the accumulation of surplus foodstuffs through the management of subordinate labor in farming chiefly land, the English commercial system actually undermined indigenous socioeconomic structures by placing preeminent value on commodities that had little or no prior connection to the economic basis of hereditary chiefly power.

For example, the commercial hunting of slaves and deer generally did not occur on lands owned by chiefly matrilineages, presumably eliminating tributary obligations, and thus probably minimizing any role for chiefs as intermediaries in individual commercial transactions. While the acquisition of captives for sale as slaves commonly occurred as part of organized group raids, deer hunting was evidently far more individualistic, especially after the introduction of English firearms. In this sense, the production of commodities of value in English commerce presumably centered to a far greater extent on individual hunters and their nuclear families, resulting in a concurrent decentralization of broader lineage- or community-based labor management associated with intensive agricultural production. In addition, even though slave raiding may have been a corporate effort initiated by entire communities or societies, the commercial acquisition of captives was likely managed by warriors and war leaders whose social rank was achieved rather than ascribed. Indeed, the increasing value of commodities acquired through individual prowess in warfare and hunting (as opposed to hereditary power based on land, labor, and agricultural production) might possibly help in explaining the emergence of a certain "dualism" in political power that evidently became prevalent among southeastern Indian tribes in the eighteenth and early nineteenth centuries, where war chiefs (associated with the color red) occupied positions of parallel importance with peace chiefs (associated with white).[49] This pronounced dualism, markedly different from indigenous social organization within southeastern chiefdoms during the European contact and early colonial era, seems likely to have been a product of the new trajectory of social change among unassimilated frontier chiefdoms within the English marketplace economy, especially since it was not a component of sociopolitical organization among the missionized chiefdoms in Spanish Florida at the same time.

In addition to the decreased role of hereditary chiefs in managing the production of valuable commodities under the new economic regime of the English frontier, the redirection of labor simultaneously reduced the capacity of these same chiefs to amass warehouses of surplus foodstuffs to finance their hereditary power. As increasing amounts of surplus community labor were diverted away from intensive agricultural production and funneled into hunting and slave raiding, the amount of surplus foodstuffs available for chiefly appropriation and use diminished at the same time. This reduction would have been directly proportional to the decline in community labor available for farming fields that had previously been dedicated either to chiefly and noble lineages or to other public office holders or community functions. In the end, increasing amounts of surplus labor in each aboriginal community were directed toward pursuits that served individual rather than chiefly needs, supplying English marketplace demands more than traditional tributary obligations. Such a rapid and widespread reorganization and redirection of labor might ultimately have resulted in considerable decentralization of chiefly power, if for no other reason than the fact that chiefs were no longer able to depend on the accumulation of substantial surpluses of agricultural products (and particularly staple foods like corn) as a source of real economic power. In this same connection, the spread of English trade after 1685 also witnessed the participation of largely autonomous frontier chiefdoms in a true market economy in which individual labor was readily converted into commercial gain, and thus material wealth. As it developed in the eighteenth century, English commerce therefore diminished kinship as a primary basis for individual and family status, especially since material wealth was no longer achieved and defined through the allocation of labor toward agricultural production on chiefly lands. Rank societies like the southeastern chiefdoms of the late prehistoric and early colonial era were therefore rapidly transformed from rigid kin-based hierarchical systems based on the chiefly management of land and labor into more egalitarian and dynamic social entities where hunting and slave catching were a readily available means for converting human labor into individual wealth and power.

As a final comment, I would note that the argument that the expansion of European (and particularly English) trade resulted in significant social transformations among aboriginal groups is not a new one; archaeologists in particular have examined the impact of advanced European technology on southeastern Indians for decades, and have explored both the reasons why they became such voracious consumers of English goods and what the impact of this consumption was on aboriginal life in both public and domestic contexts.[50] Comparatively little work has been done on similar consumption of Spanish goods, in large part because Spanish gifts and trade were so completely dwarfed by English and later French commerce during the eighteenth century, but also because Spanish and English colonial systems were so radically different from one another. Nevertheless, I hasten to point out here that in broad perspective, the differing effects of Spanish and English colonial strategies had far less to do with what these European powers offered southeastern chiefdoms as consumers of European luxuries and innovative European technology and foods through trade, and much more to do with the radical shift in production on a local level and in the consequent allocation of human labor. It was, after all, this shift in production that disconnected hereditary chiefs from their original source of power in the surplus products of agricultural land and labor. Both mission and frontier groups ultimately became significant consumers of European goods, and an examination of the changing contexts and roles of these introduced European items within public and private life over the duration of the colonial era reveals much regarding the ongoing transformation of these aboriginal societies. Nevertheless, consumption was only half of the equation, and in many ways it was only an indirect reflection of more fundamental social transformations spurred by radical changes in local economic production and by comparatively profound alterations in the relationship between chiefly matrilineages and aboriginal land and labor.

Ultimately, the Creeks and other English trading partners were quickly transformed into commercial deer and slave hunters, which almost completely devalued surplus agricultural production from lands traditionally owned by chiefly matrilineages. I would argue that it was this fact more than perhaps any other that led to a reformulation of the nature of chiefly power among surviving frontier chiefdoms. By the same token, the increased value placed by Spaniards on land and labor managed by chiefly intermediaries resulted in the long-term persistence of indigenous social systems, even in the face of eventual extinction. While the early English colonial strategy may have been more overtly insidious in its emphasis on the slave trade and in its radical reformulation of the economic basis of chiefly power, the Spanish mission system ultimately ensured the persistence and eventual stagnation of a social system that could not survive the trauma of the colonial era.

Trouble Coming Southward: Emanations through and from Virginia, 1607–1675

HELEN C. ROUNTREE

It has been common for scholars of the mid-Atlantic coast, myself included, to view the century before 1670 as a time of limited native movements and scant overland exploration by Europeans. We knew that Iroquoian-speakers variously called Massawomecks and Pocoughtraonacks were coming in from the northwest and causing consternation among the Chesapeake Bay peoples. We heard, through John Smith, that the man Powhatan had single-handedly built up his paramount chiefdom to cover most of eastern Virginia. We had Smith's references to the Jamestown colony sending parties southward from Virginia in 1607–8 in search of survivors of the "Lost Colony." We also saw that an English expedition tried unsuccessfully to establish a trading relationship with the Tuscaroras (why them?) in 1650.[1] But that is all. The surviving records in Virginia do not speak loudly about either Englishmen or other native peoples engaged in long-distance travel through or from Virginia before 1670. Then in the early 1670s came several famous English expeditions to the southwestward: Batts and Fallam, Lederer (three trips), and Needham and Arthur.[2] Those endeavors, government sponsored and prying bravely into a vast, cruel wilderness,[3] seem to have been followed by an "explosion" of long-distance trading which caused a much-changed world for southeastern Indians and Europeans alike.

A view as limited as that one needs to be revised. For one thing, a more careful sifting of many early records shows that native people throughout the Eastern Woodlands were already making long-distance journeys—sometimes across hundreds of miles—for diplomatic, trade, and warring purposes when the first accounts by European visitors were committed to paper. The routes were well established and probably ancient.[4] For another thing, from the protohistoric period onward there are scattered references to both English and Indian activities in and through Virginia, adding up, on closer consideration, to a picture of considerably more movement, both voluntary and forced, on everyone's part than scholars have previously realized. The scene was set in the sixteenth and early seventeenth centuries; the curtain began to go up around 1650, not 1670.

At the time the English founded Jamestown and began recording their observations in detail, the native people of coastal Virginia were already involved in a pattern that would continue for another century.[5] There were hostilities, which Henry Spelman saw at firsthand,[6] with Iroquoian-speakers called Massawomecks or Pocoughtraonacks to the northwest[7]; these invaders apparently pushed other people, Algonquians and possibly Siouans, out of the Maryland piedmont by the end of the sixteenth century (fig. 1). There were guarded relations at a distance with the Susque-hannocks, who said they got metal tools from the French[8]; wary and often pugnacious dealings with Siouan-speaking Monacans and Mannahoacks to the west since at least 1570[9]; and usually friendly relations with various Algonquians, Iroquoians, and Siouans to the south and southwest. Powhatan's paramount chiefdom had originated near the James River's fall line (fig. 2). There the Virginia Algonquians, with their food-rich territory and their access to valuable shell beads and pearls, received copper and puc-coon (dyeing roots) from farther away, while staving off regular raids from the Monacans. That combination of luxury trade with one set of neighbors and war with another set made the upper James River estuary a logical starting place for the rise of a powerful and ambitious chief.[10]

The Powhatan Indians' trading to their south and southwest had estab-lished routes for moving people and goods before Jamestown was ever founded, according to evidence that is both archaeological and historical. The major protohistoric pottery types in the original Powhatan heartland are Gaston-Cashie wares, which are also the major types found in a swathe of land continuing down into the North Carolina piedmont. The first English expedition up the James found a part-European boy among the Arrohatecks, one of Chief Powhatan's original domains.[11] It is a pity that there was no qualified interpreter available yet to find out whether or not the boy was descended from a refugee from the Third (and Lost) Roa-noke Colony. Moving down the James, the Weyanocks, added fairly early to Chief Powhatan's domains, had by 1607 become his major conduit to the Tuscaroras,[12] who may have been middlemen on a trading route to South Carolina for puccoon.[13] And farther down the James, the Nansem-onds and Chesapeakes were known to be friendly with the Algonquian-speakers of the Pamlico Sound region, as evidenced both by the predomi-

Fig. 1. The mid-Atlantic region in 1607.

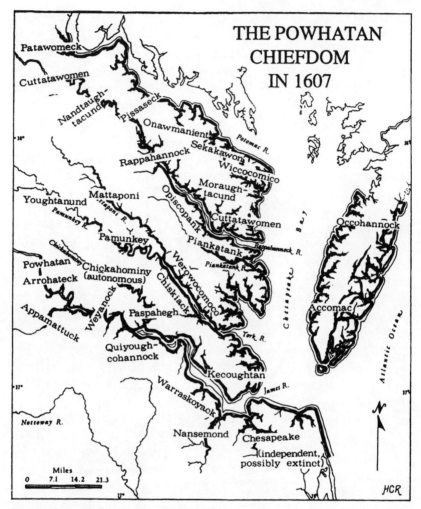

Fig. 2. The Powhatan chiefdom in 1607.

nance of Roanoke ceramic wares throughout those areas and by Ralph Lane's account from the First Roanoke Colony of an exploring party wintering among the Chesapeakes.[14] Once the English established their colony and began unraveling the fabric of Powhatan's paramount chiefdom, the "Southside" tribes like the Weyanocks resisted the English in order to remain middlemen—for both Indian and English customers in Virginia.

For several decades after 1607 the English took only a minor interest in

the Indian nations living south and southwest of Virginia. The wariness
they encountered from both the Southside Powhatans and the Monacans,
all of whom were militarily strong through the mid-1640s, was only one
reason. The "terrors" of the "wilderness," inhabited by warlike people
and also by predators such as bears, wolves, and the occasional cougar,
may have been another factor, though perhaps a peripheral one. Far more
salient in English thought, however, was the prospect of getting rich
quick, which directed their attentions not to the south but to the Virginia
coastal plain and the territories north of it. In the first half of the seventeenth century, there were two routes to immediate wealth: tobacco cultivation and the fur trade. The best tobacco lands anywhere in the mid-
Atlantic states were the naturally fertile floodplains along the rivers of
Virginia's inner coastal plain, where shipping was also easily available.
Those were also the best corn-growing lands the Powhatans had, so they
did not give them up readily. It took until 1646 for the English to subdue
the native people, after which they began to spread eagerly into the prime
farmlands in the York, Rappahannock, and Potomac river basins. The
pinch of diminishing prices and used-up land that pushed avid Englishmen into the Indian trade began a little later. As for the fur trade, a limited number of Virginia Englishmen pursued that avenue to riches near
the northern end of Chesapeake Bay, where a somewhat colder climate
produced a better grade of furs. Always in hot competition with the Maryland English, the Virginia traders lost interest after 1670.

The fur trade and especially the tobacco industry played an immense
role in Virginia English economic thinking in the first half of the seventeenth century, and consequently also in the records those people made.
Yet they knew that there were native people to the south and southwest
who were potentially friends and trading partners. The indications of it in
the surviving records are fragmentary, but they are indicative.

English people went southward into Indian country on numerous occasions before 1650. In the very early days of the Jamestown colony, they
went with Weyanock guides to try to find the Lost Colonists.[15] Later some
of them went unofficially as runaways: in 1643 the Virginia colony passed
a law requiring the death penalty if "any servant running away as afore-
said shall carrie either peice. powder and shott, And leave either all or any
of them with the Indians."[16] Some of those runaways may have headed
southward. Meanwhile, Powhatan Indian people continued to deal with
neighbors to their south, though the incidents the English heard about

were hostile ones. The Bland expedition of 1650 learned of raids between the Tuscaroras and the Powhatans under Opechancanough (coruler after 1618, sole ruler ca. 1629–1646), as well as between the town of Powhatan and the Chowanocs.[17]

The Third Anglo-Powhatan War (1644–1646) did much to set the stage for the major trading efforts that would occur later. For one thing, it broke the power of the Southside Powhatan tribes, leading the Weyanocks and part of the Nansemonds into a wandering life far south of the James (fig. 3).[18] Only the Appamattucks seem to have made peace and been able to stay in place, which left them available and willing as guides later on. For another thing, part of the English defenses involved setting up "frontier" forts, one of which was Fort Henry on the Appomattox River. Abraham Wood was made proprietor of that fort in 1646, with orders to maintain a military force there.[19] Receiving information and also trading with local Appamattucks would have been a natural part of Wood's activities, giving him a head start in his later rise to becoming one of the major Indian traders in the colony. Lastly, the English deliberately expanded their ter-

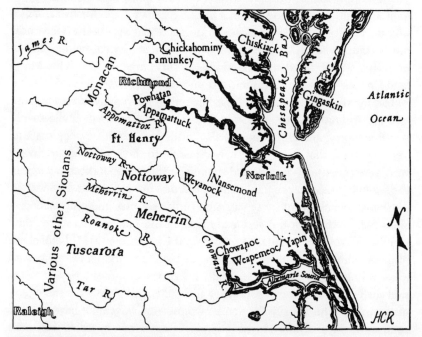

Fig. 3. Tribal territories after the 1644–1646 war.

ritorial ambitions to include the north side of Albemarle Sound during
that war, even though there is no evidence at all that the people native to
that region had allied themselves with Opechancanough. The people
appear in English records as Yapin or Yawpim (now spelled Yeopim), a
corruption of Weapemeoc. In Ralph Lane's time they held a swathe of
land running from the lower Chowan River through modern Edenton
(where several of their towns are shown on John White's map) eastward to
the Perqimans River.[20] An English military expedition from Lower Norfolk County went there in 1645.[21] The treaty made with Opechancanough's successor—who did not rule the Weapemeocs—in the next year
specified a boundary south of which all native people were to remain: a
line running eastward from the Monacan town above the James River falls
to the head of Blackwater River (near modern Franklin, Virginia) then
eastward along "the lymits of Yapin."[22] Whether or not the eastern extent
of that line corresponded with the modern Virginia–North Carolina line,
it is plain that the English had investigated and were now staking a claim
to some of the land south of the James River drainage.

The 1650 Bland expedition, which included Abraham Wood in its personnel, was officially organized not because of trade but because of other
English people who had gone south: the party was to visit the Tuscaroras
"and speake with an Englishman amongst them, and to enquire for an
English woman cast away long since, and was among those Nations."[23]
Trade, however, was in the back of everybody's mind. Some time before,
an unnamed Englishman had tried to hire Weyanock guides for trading
with the Tuscaroras, but the Weyanocks had checked with the English
militia colonel nearest them and had been discouraged from the project,
since "the Governour would give no licence to go thither."[24] The Bland
party's meetings with the Tuscaroras were brief and apparently unproductive, thanks to the machinations of the Nottoway guide, the Meherrins,
the Weyanocks—everyone except the Appamattuck guide, who had a
Meherrin "Sweet-heart."[25] News came that "at that time there were other
English amongst the Indians." The party further learned that the Meherrins had "intended divers times to have come in [to English settlements in
Virginia to trade], but were afraid, for the Wainokes had told them that the
English would kill them, or detaine them, and would not let them goe
without a great heape of Roanoake middle high." The Meherrins were
unfamiliar with English guns, for they asked to hear them shot off.[26]

The Englishman mentioned above, who wanted Weyanock guides to help him trade with the Tuscaroras, was never named, but he was operating, or trying to, before 1643. It was in March of that year that the governor of Virginia issued the first license to explorers going southward. Four men and any others they wanted to include were to have exclusive rights for fourteen years to make "the discovery of a new river [probably the Roanoke] or vnknowne land bearing west southerly from Appomattake river." The object was to find "profit" in general, and the Crown was to claim one-fifth of all "Royall Mines whatsoever."[27] The license was to date from the four men's first application for it, in June 1641. Further information on the outcome of the licensees' activities is lacking, the 1640s being a time of sparse documents in general in Virginia. But it is probably safe to say that this license, and also the military expedition to "Yapin" in 1645, represented only a fraction of all the journeys southward by English people that could have been made without ever having been recorded. As long as the middleman position of the Weyanocks, Nottoways, and Meherrins was not seriously threatened—and small-scale *private* trading would not have been threatening—then there would not even be Indian "unrest" to catch the attention of the English authorities and appear in the written records.

The two decades after 1650 did produce records of "unrest," all kinds of it. Those decades were a period of drastically shrinking Powhatan lands,[28] of increasing English exploration as tobacco lands were patented up, and of lamentably poorly recorded movements of "foreign" Indians into, out of, and through Virginia—usually heading southward.

Let us examine the Indian movements first (fig. 4). They involved northern Iroquoians, Maryland Algonquians, piedmont Siouans, and perhaps other people from farther west. The English and native Algonquian-speakers of Maryland had been pressured throughout the 1640s by Susquehannocks trying to move south; peace was not made until 1661.[29] Meanwhile, Maryland passed a law in 1651 that encouraged English people to settle around Indian towns, especially those of the Piscataways and Doegs.[30] The Piscataways understandably responded angrily to the invasion, and they also suffered rapid changeovers in their own leadership in 1659–63.[31] Complicating matters still further were incursions from the Five Nations Iroquois. The Senecas begin appearing by name in Maryland documents in 1661, as harassers of the Delaware Bay Indians, who in turn made a treaty with the Maryland English in that year.[32] From then on, there are records of skirmishes between the Senecas, Oneidas, and

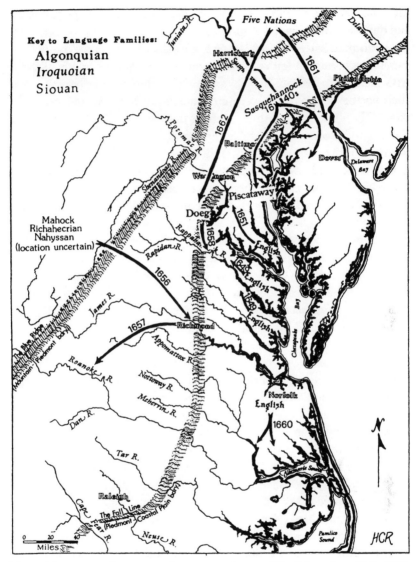

Key to Language Families:
Algonquian
Iroquoian
Siouan

Five Nations

Harrisburg

Philadelphia

Susquehannock
16 40s

1661

Potomac R.

Baltimore

Dover

Delaware Bay

Shenandoah R.

Mahock
Richahecrian
Nahyssan
(location uncertain)

Washington

Piscataway

Doeg

1651

1662

1658

Rapidan R.

Rappahannock R.

English

English

English

Chesapeake Bay

1656

James R.

Richmond

1657

Roanoke R.

Appomattox R.

Nottoway R.

Meherrin R.

Norfolk
English

1660

Dan R.

Tar R.

N

Raleigh

The Fall Line
(Piedmont / Coastal Plain Bdry.)

Albemarle Sound

Neuse R.

Cape Fear R.

Pamlico Sound

0   20   40
Miles

HCR

Fig. 4. Movements of native people, native raiders, and English settlers, 1640–1660.

Mohawks on one side and the Maryland English, the Susquehannocks, and the Piscataways on the other.[33]

Alarms like these were not lost on the English to the south. By 1662 the Virginia government felt sufficiently threatened that it forbade all trade with "northern Indians."[34] The preamble to the law shows how active such northerners already were on a north-south route, and how concerned the Virginia English were about the status of tributary Indians as useful middlemen: ". . . it appearing that the Susquehannock and other northern Indians, in considerable number[s], frequently come to the heads of our rivers, whereby plain paths will soone be made which may prove of dangerous consequence, and alsoe affront the English and destroy their stocks and gett the whole trade from our neighbouring and tributary Indians . . ."

Some of the local Algonquian-speakers that the Maryland colony had been dealing with headed southward to get away from the settlers, a strategy that worked only for a little while until settlers moved in on them from the James River English colony. The Doegs' movements were annoying the Virginia English of Westmoreland County by 1658.[35] In the early 1660s they and the Portobaccos of Maryland both settled near the Rappahannock River, where their names are preserved in place-names.[36] The Doegs soon moved back north, while the Portobaccos stayed until after 1700. But life was unrestful in the interim. Unidentified Indians, possibly from the Doegs, murdered some English people in that area in 1661.[37] Two years later the English pursued some Doegs for murdering Monacans and Occaneechis (piedmont Siouans located about 65 and 170 miles respectively from the Doegs' town), at the same time that they tried to draw the Patawomecks into a firmer Anglo-Indian alliance against the Doegs and "others."[38] That partnership failed, for in the summer of 1666 Virginia declared war on the Doegs, Portobaccos, Nanzimonds (possibly transplanted Southside Nansemonds),[39] and Patawomecks, after which the latter two groups disappear from the records.[40] Troubles between the Virginia English and the Piscataways and Susquehannocks then increased steadily up to Bacon's Rebellion in 1676.

Life among the other piedmont Siouan-speakers was not much more settled. In early 1656 a large body of them moved from parts unknown, for reasons unknown, and settled in what was still Monacan territory upriver from the falls of the James. The Virginia English found it alarming: "many western and inland Indians are drawne from the mountaynes [hills of the

piedmont, possibly the mountains beyond], and lately sett downe neer the
falls of James River, to the number of six or seaven hundred."[41] By July of
that year they or others had moved southeast to the lower Appomattox
River, possibly with the permission of the still-strong Appamattuck Indians.[42] The tribal identity of the newcomers is uncertain. The Charles City
County court called them "Massahocks," the Virginia Grand Assembly
labeled them "Richahecrians," and John Lederer later spoke of them as
"Mahocks and Nahyssans" or Nessans. Whoever they were, their experience of the Virginia English was a painful one. An English force was sent
out to try to send them away peacefully, but the commander slipped up
and there was bloodshed. The English tried to make peace with them
again in December 1656, but after that they seem to have gone south,
where John Lederer met them later.[43]

After 1650 English people from Virginia began pushing southward into
areas that were "new"—but only relatively new—to them. The surviving
records do not speak as yet of trading. Instead they speak of "entertaining," i.e., hiring, Indians. Beginning in 1655, the colony required prospec-
tive employers to acquire licenses, in an attempt to ensure that only
responsible, law-abiding Englishmen would be dealing with such possibly
"dangerous" workers.[44] Most of the Indians were probably men hired as
hunters, but the potential was always there for a knowledgeable hunter to
serve at times as a guide through a wilderness that was *not* trackless.
Among the many Englishmen along the James River who took out
licenses, Abraham Wood was a major employer.[45] The tribal identity of
the Indians he hired was never mentioned, though they were probably
Appamattucks.

English people also began moving southward out of the James River
valley as settlers. They began to patent land along the Appomattox River
in the 1630s, and after the 1644–46 war a wave of people moved steadily
upriver past the fall line (marked by modern Petersburg) and into the
adjacent piedmont.[46] By 1660 English farmers were beginning to take up
land along the Albemarle Sound as well. In that year the chief of the Yeo-
pims (Weapemeocs) sold a tract of land that ran down to the mouth of the
Pasquotank River; he had previously sold it, without getting payment, to
the leader of the 1645 Norfolk County expedition.[47] Other Englishmen
began patenting land from the Chowan River eastward in 1663.[48]

After 1650 the Virginia government began encouraging trusted individuals to explore even farther afield. In 1653 three Orders of Assembly were

passed with that in mind. The twelve-year-old license to explore south-westward was rescinded and a new fourteen-year license given for exploring and taking up land, the direction outward from Virginia not being specified. The recipients were William Clayborn and Henry Fleet, whose interests lay northward, and Abraham Wood. Once they had established claims, others could do likewise.[49] The second order promised large tracts of land to settlers from the Nansemond River area who moved to the lower Chowan River (the heartland of the Weapemeocs, who had not legally given up their claim) and on to the Roanoke River.[50] The Virginia land patents do not indicate very many people hazarding their luck that far afield as yet. The third order noted that divers people wanted to "discover the Mountains," so now any one making the attempt with enough people and ammunition (so that the colony would not be put the expense of bailing them out) had the assembly's permission to proceed.[51] In 1656 Col. Thomas Dew was authorized to organize an exploring expedition "to make a discoverie of the navigable rivers to the southward between Cape Hatteras and Cape Feare."[52] And in 1660 an even more expansive license was given to Francis Hamond and his associates to "enjoy such benefitts, profitts & trades for fourteen yeers as he or they have found or shall find out in places where no English ever have been or had perticular trade, And to take vp such lands by pattents (proving their rights) as they shall think good." Other English people were to have permission to take up land after them, but not to trade.[53] The logical direction for Hamond et alia to go would have been southwest. The items to be bought from Indian people were not specified, but deer hides were temporarily legal commodities just then. Virginia periodically tried (futilely) to encourage the crafts of tanning and weaving, rather than tobacco farming, by making the export of all hides and skins illegal: there were bans from 1632 to 1646, again from 1658 to 1659, and from 1662 to 1671.[54]

By 1670 the Nottoways and Meherrins were beginning to be surrounded by English settlements except to the south and southwest, while the Appamatucks were left on an island of tribal territory. Too many English neighbors usually impelled Indian men to hire themselves out to Englishmen, to give them some protection as they hunted farther afield. Abraham Wood would have been a major "patron" for such "clients." Protective friends were *needed*, too. The English put continual pressure on Indian parents to let their children be reared "properly" on English farms, where coincidentally their labor was in high demand.[55] Some of the parents may have been Nottoway, Meherrin, or even Tuscarora and Siouan ones living well away from English settlers. There were also unscrupulous Englishmen who sold arms to Indian people (at times it was legal), got them into debt, and then stripped them of their possessions. The Virginia Grand Assembly passed repeated orders and laws against such practices from the mid-1650s onward. The identities of the Indians being abused were never mentioned, but some of them may have been non-Powhatans to the south and southwest. Interestingly, liquor was not mentioned as being involved in these matters until 1670,[56] and there was no legislation in Virginia against selling it to Indians until 1705.[57]

Altogether, there are enough indications of English movements into the North Carolina coastal plain and lower piedmont that it is not surprising that trouble broke out between the Virginia English and the Tuscaroras by 1663. The grand assembly felt impelled in that year to forbid the "entertaining" of any Indians who did not bring an identifiable badge with them into the English settlements.[58] It is a pity that the surviving records say so little about who and what had caused the trouble and whether or not any of the Tuscaroras' Siouan neighbors were affected.

By the early 1670s, Virginia's interest in what is now the North Carolina piedmont and points southwest was becoming pressing. The Virginia English already knew, apparently from considerable firsthand experience, that there were riches to be acquired by trading in that direction, including Indian children as laborers (the trade in them reached its peak in the 1680s). They were also acutely aware that their tobacco farming was in trouble, at the same time that they were not willing to adopt slower-yield methods of accumulating wealth. The legalization of the deerskin trade in 1671 provided a new get-rich-quick commodity for would-be merchants to pursue. English settlements were being harassed by unfriendly Indians from the north. Although relations with native people to the south and southwest had already hit rough spots, the promise of allies in that direction was tempting. So it was time for the Virginia colony to send out official expeditions, to go farther afield and—note well—report back in more detail than had been done previously.

That was what was "new" about the three expeditions of John Lederer (1669–70) and the two sponsored by Abraham Wood (1671, 1673): they were recorded in detail and the accounts have survived. Lederer's trips may or may not have gone farther than his predecessors'; Batts and Fallam's did, and Gabriel Arthur went the farthest of all because he was a captive of Indian people who were genuinely long-distance travelers. But the reports made afterward opened the door—not to a new wave of traders and would-be settlers, but to an intensification of a decades-old movement that had started unofficially, in a piecemeal way. And the English coming southward were dealing with native people who themselves were being pressured by other natives: northern Iroquoians pushing Maryland and Virginia Algonquians, and also piedmont Siouans who were living unrestfully in Virginia and the Carolinas after the midpoint of the seventeenth century.

The best evidence that John Lederer came late upon an already active scene is his 1671 license for fourteen years of exclusive trade in hides and other commodities with the "Naasones Askeneethees Oenokes, Sharberies, Queyonks, Waterees, Nuntaniekes, Mahokes Sarus, Rickahokons Wissackies and Usheryes or any other Nations of the South West Indians." Lederer got that license from the colony of Maryland.[59] Francis Hamond and other, more shadowy, entrepreneurs had long since beaten him to it in Virginia.

The Mother of Necessity: Carolina, the Creek Indians, and the Making of a New Order in the American Southeast, 1670–1763

STEVEN C. HAHN

On May 27, 1715, a small boat carrying four Indian men arrived in St. Augustine, the epicenter of power in Spanish Florida. On board were Alonsso and Gabriel, two Yamasee chiefs, and Istopoyole and Brave Dog, two Creek Indians, who hinted that they had come to "renew" their obedience to the king of Spain. Eager to behave amicably with their Indian guests, Spanish officials feted them with food and drink later that evening.[1] This was, as it turned out, a remarkable occurrence, because the Creeks had not paid Spanish officials a friendly visit in more than twenty years. Quite the contrary. Since the erection of a Spanish fort on the Chattahoochee River in 1689, the Creek Indians had waged a war of revenge and attrition against Spanish Florida, and played a major role in destroying the Florida Indian missions in the years before 1706. Creek Indians were also known to have attacked the Florida garrison at Pensacola as late as 1714. Why, after a generation of killing, looting, and plundering, had these Indians come to talk peace? And why had they chosen to do so precisely at that time?

Such questions undoubtedly occurred to Francisco de Corocoles y Martinez, the governor of Florida, who interviewed the four Indian men the following day, on May 28. After first demanding that the four Indians identify themselves, Governor Corocoles asked the men to reveal the purpose of their visit. Then a Creek "war captain" named Brave Dog stepped forward to proclaim that he had come at the behest of the "great cacique of Coweta," then the most influential Creek chief, who had assumed authority to speak for "all of the caciques and micos of the towns of all the provinces" that bordered Britain's southernmost North American colony, Carolina. Brave Dog explained that they had recently risen up against the English and that he had come "to renew the obedience in the name of the

79

infidel and Christian casiques that they originally gave to this Government [Florida] in the name of the King of Spain." To demonstrate the impressive size of this ad hoc Indian alliance, Brave Dog then displayed eight knotted fathom-long strands of deerskin, each knot representing the Indian towns that made up the alliance, which totaled one hundred sixty-one towns.[2]

After handing the knotted strands to the governor, Brave Dog went on to discuss the underlying causes of the revolt. Brave Dog explained that their grievances with the Carolinians had begun about three years earlier, when English "lieutenants" (commissioned Indian traders) started seizing their women and children "relatives" in lieu of the trade debts that had recently accrued. "By the order of the English," Brave Dog added, they went to the "southern coast" of Florida, in the provinces of Jororo and Mayaca. The Indians had little choice but to look for Indian prisoners in these remote parts, Brave Dog continued, to pay for the "muskets, powder, shot, cutlasses, pistols, coats, hats . . . and brandy" which the English had sold to them on credit. The English warned the Indians that "if they failed to pay them in slaves, they had to cover [their debts] by making slaves of their kinsmen, and their children and wives."[3]

Initially, the allied Indians chose not to act upon those dire warnings, and Brave Dog related that the Indians "stayed quiet in their hearts" to see if the English "lieutenants" would carry out their threats. For several years, the southern Indians had tolerated the arbitrary seizure of their own "relatives," hoping that such acts were no more than a ploy to induce them to search for more slaves. More recently, however, an English "lieutenant" had killed the Usinjulo of Coweta, the "grand cacique's" eldest and most esteemed son, over an "accounting mistake," undoubtedly a debt dispute. This violent act, Brave Dog concluded, had led the Indians to believe that the English were serious about collecting their debts.

Having lost his most esteemed son to a debt dispute, the chief of Coweta then took it upon himself to fashion a compromise that might have enabled his people to restructure their debt payments. Brave Dog proceeded to relate that the chief of Coweta had proposed to Carolina officials a method by which the Indians might pay their debts "little by little." They would do this, he added, by paying the English not in slaves, which were hard to come by, but in "pork, corn . . . animal skins, oil, and beans," products to which the Creeks and most southern Indians had ready access. Furthermore, the chief of Coweta offered to supplement their payments with products which could easily be plundered from Spanish Florida, such as pigs, rice, cattle, chickens, and lard.

Through the grapevine, the chief of Coweta's plan appears to have reached the ears of South Carolina governor Charles Craven, who, according to Brave Dog, "put them at apparent ease, by saying that the bad lieutenants would leave and they would put good men in their place." But when the Indians learned that Governor Craven intended to fortify the Carolina frontier and that the traders had rejected the plan for debt payment, the chief of Coweta convened a large gathering of the chiefs at the Yamasee town of Pocotalico. There, the chief of Coweta and his Yamasee hosts debated whether or not to "liberate" themselves from the English, by force if necessary. As Brave Dog explained, on the morning of Good Friday, April 15, 1715, the Indians assembled at Pocotalico learned that Governor Craven had sent his Indian agents there to "inquire into the causes of the meeting"—to spy. Believing that the Carolina agents harbored bad intentions, Yamasee and Creek warriors stripped naked, painted themselves red and black—the grim gear of war of the southeastern Indians—and fired their flintlocks indiscriminately upon the Carolina agents, torturing those who had managed to survive the initial volley. With this bold stroke, Carolina's former Indian allies sparked a smoldering frontier conflict that, with the passage of time, became known as the Yamasee War.

*   *   *

Few single events in the early history of the Southeast have so captured the attention or the imagination of historians as the Yamasee War of 1715. And rightly so. As the eminent historian Verner Crane once argued, the Yamasee War caused a "revolution in frontier politics" that had a lasting effect on Carolina colonists and the southeastern Indians alike. For this reason, many historians rightly believe that the Yamasee War brought an end to what might be called South Carolina's "first system" of trade and exploration. In South Carolina, for instance, the war produced a variety of reforms in frontier defense and trade that would guide wary South Carolinians for generations to come. And the Yamasees, who bore the brunt of the fighting, fled to the Spanish presidios to eke out a marginal existence as dependent clients of La Florida.[4]

Because of the Yamasee War's indisputable influence on both the colonists and Indians, it should come as little surprise that the Carolina colonists and later historians inquired and continue to inquire into the causes of the war. Most contemporary accounts blamed the English traders for abusing the Indians in many unspeakable ways. Others were more willing to blame the influence of the Spanish and French. Verner Crane, for example, argued that the war was a "sui generis" revolt against the Carolina traders, who had committed unspeakable atrocities against the Indians in their effort to secure payment for debt. One scholar has suggested more recently that the war stemmed from the erosion of the Indians' economic base, principally deerskins. The most recent analyses of the Yamasee War suggest that the Indians' fear of being made slaves may also have been a contributing factor. Others still caution that the search for the Yamasee War's origins remains elusive, because each Indian nation that joined in the revolt had different motives, a fact which led ultimately to the revolt's collapse in 1717.[5]

Though there is an element of truth to most of the above interpretations, Brave Dog's discussion suggests that the roots of the revolt were much deeper than either the Carolina colonists or later generations of historians have recognized. As Brave Dog's interpretation suggests, the trade in Indian slaves had trapped the Creek and other Indians in a downward spiral of warfare, debt, and more warfare, fueled by the Creeks' own desire for English trade goods. Briefly put, Brave Dog's discussion leads one to believe that the establishment of Carolina as a center of trade caused a remarkable, if not radical, shift in the political economy of the Creek Indians, who had become fully "dependent" upon English trade goods before the year 1715. This assessment contradicts most current studies of Indian behavior in the Atlantic marketplace, which emphasize continuity in Indian life and portray dependency as a gradual, rather than an immediate, process.[6] By drawing upon Brave Dog's analysis, however, this essay will argue that Creek dependency occurred quickly—before the outbreak of the Yamasee War. It will argue further, though, that this dependency did not occur because of the inevitable spread—or imposition—of the so-called "modern world system." Rather, it will argue that Creek dependency was partially a function of the Creeks' own tendency to define European "luxuries" as essential "needs."

CAROLINA AND THE CREEKS: COMMERCIAL OVERTURES

Any study of the changes in economic behavior of the Creeks, or of any other southeastern Indian group, must begin with a discussion of the Carolina colony, founded upon the Ashley River in the year 1670. While documentary and archaeological evidence confirm beyond a shadow of a doubt that the Creeks' forbears had traded in Spanish Florida since the mid-seventeenth century, the real transformation in economic behavior did not occur until the English first established this important colony.

In a sense, the seeds of South Carolina were sown in 1660, when the English Parliament welcomed the exiled King Charles II, living as an expatriate in France, back to his home country. His father, King Charles I, had been deposed nearly eighteen years before and beheaded in 1649, becoming the most famous casualty of the civil wars between monarchist and republican forces that raged for the better part of the 1640s and 1650s. After the death of the "protector," Oliver Cromwell, in 1658, the country soon descended into political and economic chaos, prompting the Parliament to recall the exiled king from France in an attempt to restore order to the country.[7]

As a newly restored monarch, Charles owed a considerable political debt to his loyalist allies, many of whom worked diligently with Parliament to restore the Stuart monarchy. In an attempt to repay this political debt, on May 23, 1663, Charles issued a charter to a group of his supporters—Edward Earl of Clarendon, George Duke of Albemarle, William Lord Craven, Anthony Earl Ashley, Sir George Carteret, Sir William Berkeley, and Sir John Colleton—for lands in the American Southeast between the thirty-sixth and thirty-first parallels, known to posterity as "Carolina."[8]

Positioned as such, the new colony was likely to exert influence among the natives, including isolated nations such as the Apalachicolas, Talapoosas, and Abikas, whom the English would one day call "Creeks." But it was the timing of the colony's founding, not simply its proximate location, which made it a likely center of influence. As historians have come to recognize in recent years, England's Restoration period marked the beginning of a long spell of economic growth, culminating eventually in Britain's later commercial and colonial triumphs in the eighteenth and nineteenth centuries over lesser imperial powers, such as the Netherlands, Spain, and France.[9]

Although English colonies had existed continuously since the founding of Jamestown in 1607, it was not until the middle of the seventeenth century that English government officials and would-be colonizers alike first began to recognize the importance of the colonies as a source of imperial

and economic strength. This new theory of empire and commerce—
mercantilism—first became official government policy in 1651, when the
British Parliament under the "protector," Oliver Cromwell, passed the
first of a series of Navigation Acts. The Navigation Acts, inspired by a
recent upsurge in mercantilist theoretical writings, sought to confine colonial trade within the nascent British empire by placing duties on colonial
imports and exports and by requiring that the colonies do business solely
in the mother country or its dependencies. Proprietary colonies, such as
the ones founded in the wake of the Restoration in Carolina, Pennsylvania, and New Jersey, fit well into this new mercantile model. By granting
charters to a select group of proprietors, each of whom had a vested economic interest in the colony, the English crown hoped to create a climate
of industry and commerce which would produce tangible benefits to the
proprietors—and by extension to the mother country itself.

Like most proprietary colonies chartered during the Restoration
period, South Carolina was intended from the beginning to be a commercial enterprise, an important cog in England's burgeoning trans-Atlantic
mercantile empire. The proprietors stood to gain the most from the enterprise because the king's charter allowed them to funnel much of the
wealth generated in the colony to themselves and their heirs. To foster
economic development, the king's charter granted the proprietors certain
exemptions from the regulations of mercantilist legislation that would
have imposed an undue burden on the fledgling colony. To encourage
agricultural production, for instance, the king granted the proprietors a
seven-year exemption from mercantilist legislation, which would enable
them to develop Carolina's fledgling economy free from the burden of
import restrictions or duties. The Crown and the proprietors expected
that Carolina would eventually yield products such as silks, wines, raisins,
and olives, reflecting their prediction that the Southeast's climate was
similar to that of the Mediterranean.[10] Furthermore, the proprietors
received the exclusive rights to the profits derived from "[a]ll wracks,
mines, minerals, quarries, of ge'ms and precious stones, with whale fishing, and pearle fishing."[11]

Given the commercial nature of the Carolina enterprise, it was not clear
at first how the Indians figured into the proprietors' plans to develop the
colony. The king's charter, for instance, granted the proprietors the right
to raise a militia, expecting that any plantation established in the midst of
"savage and barbarous" people would require a measure of self-defense.

The charter did, however, grant the proprietors the right to "trade with the natives" free of restrictions, indicating that there was some expectation of drawing the Indians into a commercial relationship, but the colonial charter did not elaborate what that trade might entail.[12]

Nonetheless, the Indian trade appears to have figured prominently in the proprietors' scheme from the beginning. For this reason, they ordered the first colonists to set up a store for "Victualls, cloathes, Tools &c" from which trade with the Indians could be carried out. The colony's first storekeeper, Joseph West, received instructions "to deliver such quantitys of the Indian trade for presents to the Indian Kings, as our Governor and any three of our Deputies . . . shall direct you."[13] Initially, then, it appears that the proprietors intended to use the trade as a tool of diplomacy, directed at purchasing the "friendship and allyance" of Indian chiefs.[14]

But the proprietors also had a vested interest in creating a commercial relationship with the Indians so that the profits derived from the Indian trade could be channeled into their own pockets. To assure that the fruits of this trade would flow into such privileged channels, the proprietors established a legal monopoly of the Indian trade, forbidding private persons from making discoveries in the interior. To do otherwise, they argued, would allow private individuals to develop trade contacts with Indians in the deep interior and thereby subvert the proprietors' monopoly. To stifle the competition of private individuals, the proprietors urged the Carolina governor to "bind the peoples' minds to planting" and leave exploration and Indian trading to themselves.[15]

Although the proprietors' monopolization of western exploration may have actually delayed the Carolinians' "discovery" of Creek country, the initial obstacle seems to have been the Westos, who were by 1670 living at the falls of the Savannah River near present-day Augusta. Recall that well before the landing of the Carolinians, the Westos had established themselves as the Southeast's most feared Indian group, working as slave raiders for the Virginia planters. Initially, the Westos did not look upon the Carolinians as allies, and vice versa; instead, they lurked on the margins of the new colony stealing crops, killing livestock, and occasionally killing English colonists.[16] Relations between the Carolinians and Westos were so hostile, in fact, that on September 3, 1673, the Grand Council ordered Lieutenant Colonel Jonathan Godfrey and Maurice Matthews to raise a militia to "march against the [Westos] and kill and destroy them or otherwise subject them in peace."[17]

The Carolinians did not, as it turned out, choose to "kill and destroy" the Westos. Instead, they cultivated an alliance with them that allowed the Carolinians to push farther into the southern interior. Responsibility for opening up the interior rested on the shoulders of one of the colony's original proprietors, Anthony Ashley Cooper, whom King Charles had recently made the first earl of Shaftesbury. Shaftesbury, it appears, had developed an intense personal interest in interior exploration and economic development after reading accounts of earlier western explorations from Virginia by John Lederer, James Needham, and Gabriel Arthur. Furthermore, Henry Woodward's 1670 reconnaissance of the land of Cofitachequi, located several days' march to the northwest of Charles Town, revealed that there were significant profits to be derived from the Indian trade for skins and furs.[18]

Infatuated by reports of minerals, skins, and furs, Shaftesbury promptly sought to turn his St. Giles plantation on the upper Ashley River into a center of exploration and commerce. The Spanish at St. Augustine, for instance, offered one enticing avenue for trade. In May 1674, Shaftesbury instructed his principal agent in Carolina, Andrew Percival, to "endeavor to begin a trade with the Spaniards for Negroes, cloathes, or other commodities."[19] Through Percival, Shaftesbury also instructed Henry Woodward to write a letter to the Spanish governor, Pedro de Hita Salazar, "to let him know he is employed by English nobility the most affectionate with the Spaniards, who desire commerce with them."[20]

Shaftesbury's plans for establishing trade, however, did not end with the Spanish. Evidence indicates that he also desired to contact the Indians of the deep southern interior—Creek country—to form a peaceful alliance and open up a profitable trade. To accomplish these ends, on May 23, 1674, Shaftesbury ordered Henry Woodward to explore the interior and "to consider whether it be best to make peace with the Westos or Cussitaws, a more powerful nation, said to have pearl and silver, and by whose assistance the Westoes may be rooted out, but to include our neighbor Indians at amity with us."[21]

An analysis of Shaftesbury's orders to Woodward suggests that the English had their sights set on Creek country at a very early date. Shaftesbury's reference to the "Cussitaws," for instance, could have only referred to the town of Cussita, one of the northernmost towns on the Chattahoochee.[22] Evidently, Woodward had learned of this Indian province from some of the Indians he met during his many years of exploration, or perhaps from the Spaniards themselves during his confinement in St. Augustine. Not much was known about the "Cussitaws" at the time, but they were thought to be more powerful than the Westos, and it was believed that their lands contained freshwater pearls and a silver mine.[23]

Shaftesbury's decision to send Dr. Henry Woodward for this task was a wise one, for there was no one in Carolina who could match his knowledge of the Indians or the southern backcountry. Woodward, a London surgeon, first came to Carolina in 1666, during Robert Sandford's reconnaissance mission of the coast near Port Royal. When Sandford's party weighed anchor to return to England, Woodward voluntarily remained with the Indians at Port Royal and spent several months learning their languages and customs. Soon thereafter, Woodward fell into the hands of the Spanish, who arrested and imprisoned him at St. Augustine. Woodward escaped from prison in 1668 when an English buccaneer named William Searle attacked the city, releasing all English prisoners into Spanish custody. Upon his eventual return to Carolina in 1670, he became a valuable asset to the proprietors, who regularly employed his services for exploration and discovery.[24] According to all accounts, Woodward was an astute student of Indian culture and customs, and was said to know five different Indian languages.[25]

Given the Westos' apparent hostility toward the fledgling colony, Woodward's charge to forge an alliance with them might have proven to be a difficult task. But fortunately for Woodward and the Carolinians, the Westos themselves made the first overtures to establish a peaceful commercial relationship. On a cold and rainy Saturday, October 10, 1674, ten Westo Indians arrived at Shaftesbury's St. Giles plantation, where they met Henry Woodward, whom they proceeded to lead on a six-week march to the Westo town on the Savannah River.

While Woodward's voyage to the Westo town was important for the Carolinians and Westos because it catalyzed their short-lived trade alliance, Woodward's excursion also brought the Carolinians a step closer to the inhabitants of Creek country. Woodward, adhering to Shaftesbury's admonition to determine whether the Westos or the Cussitaws were more powerful, used his ten-day stay among the Westos to "view the adjacent part of the country" and to learn more about the interior South and the political configurations of its Indian inhabitants.

In the course of his stay among the Westos, Woodward learned of several other remote Indian nations, which undoubtedly captured his imagination as potential trade partners. Among Woodward's most important acquisitions was a young Indian boy, whom the Westos had kept as a "slave." According to Woodward, the Westos took the boy "from the falls of that river," which, in this context, apparently referred to the Chattahoochee. The evidence is sketchy at best, but if the young Indian boy came from the falls of the Chattahoochee River, then Woodward was now the master of an inhabitant of Coweta, Cussita, or another town located nearby.[26]

Soon after Woodward's Westo voyage in the fall of 1674, vague reports of Englishmen traveling through the interior Indian provinces began to reach the leery Spanish officials at St. Augustine, which hints at the possibility that Woodward had garnered enough information about the interior from the Westos and from his Indian servant to penetrate into the deep interior. On May 23, 1675, an Indian woman who had escaped from a Westo slave raiding party arrived in St. Augustine to report to Governor Hita Salazar that the Carolinians had entered into an alliance with the Westos and that they planned to attack the Christian Indian provinces of Timucua and Apalachee that summer. She also claimed that a mysterious English settlement existed somewhere in the interior, five days' travel from Apalachee.[27] Since Spanish officials generally believed the Westo settlements to be thirty days' march from Apalachee, the Indian woman was probably describing the intrusion of English traders into the heart of the Chattahoochee River valley.[28]

Although the Indian woman's account was vague and more than likely obtained by word of mouth, Florida officials also testified that there were Englishmen exploring the interior that spring.[29] Governor Hita Salazar reported, for instance, that a Franciscan stationed at the Chacato missions named Fray Rodrigo "has had news from Indians of other nations that five days travel from his town in a town called Chicasas, four Englishmen have arrived who have come from a new population that has formed at the mouth of a large river, if only to reconnoiter and desolate the land."[30]

Clearly, the reference to the "new population" of Englishmen inhabiting the mouth of a large river was a description of Charles Town. Fray Rodrigo's claim that the Englishmen were in a town called "Chicasas," however, is more difficult to reconcile with available evidence. The name bears a striking semblance to that of the Chickasaws of northern Mississippi, but they lived several hundred miles away and could not possibly have been reached in a mere five days. But the Spanish used the term "chicasa" in reference to an old abandoned town and its surrounding agricultural fields. It is possible, then, that a group of English traders had set up temporary residences in an abandoned town site somewhere in Apalachicola territory on the Chattahoochee River.

It is evident from later sources that, in the year or two following his Westo voyage, Woodward had unquestionably reached the town of Cussita and established a multilateral peace agreement between the Carolinians, the Westos, and the "Cussetoes." In January of 1677, the Lords Proprietors issued a statement acknowledging the efforts that Shaftesbury and Woodward had undertaken, recognizing that "the discovery of the country of the Westoes and the Cussatoes . . . hath been made at the charge of the Earl of Shaftesbury . . . and by the industry and hazard of Doctor Woodward."[31] The proprietors further asserted that the Westos and "Cussetoes" were both fierce, warlike nations who were now "at peace" with the Carolinians. Their loyalty, the proprietors assumed, would offer the fledgling colony a measure of protection from the Spaniards at St. Augustine.[32]

The "Cussetoes," too, had much to gain by entering into peace with the English. For instance, by becoming common allies of a European power, the Chattahoochee towns achieved an immediate truce with the Westos, thereby ending years of chronic fighting. What was most important, however, was that Woodward apparently achieved this truce by promising to open up trade. The Indians would have undoubtedly concurred with the Lords Proprietors, who argued that "it is absolutely necessary that the trade be carried on with those nations so that they may be supply'd with commodities according to agreement made with them by which rewards a firm and lasting peace shall be continued and by this way wee become necessary and useful to them."[33] To assure that the Indians would find Carolina "useful" and that a select group of men would receive a lion's share of the profits, the proprietors established a seven-year monopoly over the Westo and "Cussetoe" trade in April 1677.[34]

But did Woodward or other traders working in the proprietors' employ actually begin trading with the Creek peoples at such an early date? Although the proprietors were zealous in their determination to establish a commercial relationship with the "Cussatoes," English contact with the inhabitants of the Chattahoochee valley remained infrequent at best for several years to come. A Spanish report of English activity in the interior in the fall of 1678 remains one of the few pieces of evidence for English activity in the region before 1685.[35] For this reason, we may suspect that Woodward had little direct contact with the Creeks. Still, Woodward's own account book covering the years 1674–1678 makes mention of a trade with certain "Indians to ye Southward," a convenient label which may have included the Westos and their newfound allies to the west living in Creek country. Moreover, Spanish accounts attest to the fact that the Creeks had traded with certain unnamed Englishmen for two years before 1685, the year that Henry Woodward first established a permanent trade with the Creeks. The Creek trade with the English at Carolina thus began in fits and starts and not with Henry Woodward's later celebrated arrival on the Chattahoochee in 1685, a subject to which we shall soon return.

Despite these early trade overtures, it should not be assumed that the Creeks were destined to forge a commercial alliance with the English. Woodward did appear to have some sway via the Westos over northern Chattahoochee towns such as Coweta and Cussita. But the towns that lay to the south, such as Apalachicola, continued to seek a Spanish alliance. In the waning months of 1678, for instance, Governor Salazar reported that the Apalachicolas were currently trading regularly with the Apalachees and were still "desiring a priest."[36] Consider also the fact that it was the English from Virginia and, later, Carolina, who had sponsored Westo slave raids against the Apalachicolas between 1659 and 1674.

Moreover, after Henry Woodward and other like-minded Carolina slave dealers began a brief war with the Westos in the fall of 1680, a significant number of the Westos fled to Coweta the following spring. We will probably never know the horror stories the Westos told to their new hosts on the Chattahoochee, but it is apparent that the Westos' forced migration prompted the Apalachicolas to reconsider the potential of a Spanish alliance. For this reason, between 1681 and 1685, no fewer than five delegations of Apalachicola chiefs—including the chiefs of Apalachicola, Coweta, and Colomme—made the journey to St. Augustine to "confirm" their peaceful relationship, thereby flirting with the political and economic "neutrality" that characterized Creek politics in the eighteenth century.

THE SCRAMBLE FOR APALACHICOLA

The scramble to establish economic influence in Creek country began in Apalachicola, the Indian province consisting of approximately eleven towns which was then located near the falls of the Chattahoochee River. This scramble, which pitted the English against the Spanish, was actually a three-way affair involving the Carolina traders, the Florida military, and an upstart band of Scottish traders whose initiative to open the western Indian trade catalyzed the struggle for this coveted province. Although Henry Woodward may have agreed to establish trade with the "Cussetoes" as early as 1675, serious efforts to trade with the Apalachicola province stalled until January 1685, when a group of one hundred Scottish colonists headed by a nobleman, Lord Cardross, arrived at Port Royal to establish a new colony under the proprietors' royal charter.

This new colony, dubbed Stuart's Town in honor of the Scottish royal family, was intended to serve as a safe haven for Scottish Presbyterians fleeing religious persecution in their homeland. As such, the proprietary government of Carolina guaranteed the Scottish colonists the right to practice their own religion and allowed them to establish a separate judicial system. Both the Lords Proprietors and Lord Cardross hoped that this favorable arrangement would attract a large number of Scottish colonists, and thereby create a much-needed human buffer against the Spanish to the south.[37]

But the Scots, who held expansionist aspirations of their own, were not content merely to serve the Carolina regime as its frontier buffer. In fact, Stuart's Town's two most prominent residents, Lord Cardross and William Dunlop, had learned within three months of landing on Carolina's shores that the trade with the interior Indians, most notably the Cowetas and Cussetas, promised to be profitable. By late March they had already hatched a plan to establish "a method for correspondence and treade with Cuita and Cussita nations of Indians, who leive upon the passages betweixt us and New Mexico, and who have for severally yeirs left off any Comercie with the Spanirds."[38]

Although it is doubtful that the Indians had entirely ceased trading with the Spaniards, there can be little doubt that news of the Scots' plans soon reached the ears of Henry Woodward, who, after a long sabbatical in England, had recently returned to Charles Town armed with a proprietary commission to explore the "undiscovered" western frontier.[39] Woodward, who was to receive a one-fifth share of the profits derived from the western Indian trade, clearly viewed the Scots' pretensions as a threat to his economic interests.[40] To preempt the Stuart's Town trade, Woodward hastily departed from Charles Town in late April with his own cache of trade goods destined for the Chattahoochee River.[41] Though Lord Cardross would eventually arrest Woodward that May as he made an attempt to pass through the Stuart's Town colony, Woodward, with the help of at least fifty Yamasee guides and burdeners, appears to have reached his destination sometime that summer, most likely in July 1685.

News of the English interlopers quickly reached Spanish officials in St. Augustine, who considered the Apalachicolas as their own subjects. Rightly fearing that the intrusion of the traders was a sign that Apalachicola political loyalties were beginning to assume an English accent, the governor of Florida sent his lieutenant of Apalachee, Antonio Matheos, into Apalachicola in September 1685 and January 1686 to capture the pesky English traders and restore the Indians to their proper "obedience."

Events surrounding Matheos's *entradas* on the Chattahoochee illustrate that the vectors of human history do not always proceed gradually in predictable paths; rather, human history appears to be punctuated by critical epochs in which decisive decisions are made that alter history's course. For the Creeks, the fall and winter months of 1685–86 constituted such a critical historical crossroads, for, rather than comply with Matheos's demands to oust the traders, the inhabitants of the Chattahoochee fled their towns, hid the traders, and pleaded ignorance to their whereabouts.[42] By pleading ignorance, though, many Creeks suffered torture, the confiscation of their important corn surpluses, and, most important, the loss of four towns, which Matheos put to the torch. But by tolerating such oppressive acts, the Apalachicolas effectively set the Creek peoples on a path different from that of the Timucuas or the Apalachees to the south, choosing to become commercial clients of an economic power rather than a part of Florida's so-called "republic" of Indians. But, by zealously guarding their allies-in-commerce, the Creek peoples unwittingly enabled the English to gain a firmer foothold in the Southeast and become, in time, the South's most dominant European presence.

And just what were those trade goods, for which the Creeks sacrificed four of their towns and upon which, scholars argue, the Creeks eventually became dependent? A preliminary analysis of the rare documentary evidence of the English trade assemblage suggests that, initially, items of personal adornment were among the most coveted objects traded. When the Spanish lieutenant Antonio Matheos broke open a hastily erected English trading house on the Chattahoochee in the fall of 1685, he found an assortment of items used for personal adornment. Matheos uncovered, for instance, five pairs of "embroidered" socks, five red and three white pairs of socks, a yard and a half of scarlet cloth, a stitched cloth with an embroidered gold border, and other goods of "little value," most likely beads and other trinkets.[43]

If the cache of English trade goods uncovered by Matheos gives us any indication of the Creeks' wants, then it might be easy to conclude that personal adornment figured prominently. But there were more practical matters to be considered as well. In fact, in the spring and summer months of 1686, the alliance between the Apalachicolas and the Carolina traders appears to have grown stronger, mostly because the English began supplying these Indians with the trade item they wanted most—guns.

In May 1686, several months after Matheos carried out his scorched earth tactics against the Apalachicolas, a party of more than forty Yamasees and a lone Englishman arrived in the town of Apalachicola on a trade mission undertaken in the name of the governor of Carolina. While gun-bearing Yamasees guarded the town against anticipated Spanish resistance, the Englishman called a meeting, which was attended by the men, women, and children of the town, as well as by forty-five Yamasees and a variety of "new people" of unknown provenance. At this particular meeting, the Englishman gave the town's inhabitants twenty-six new muskets and a supply of hatchets, not as payment for deerskins, but as a gift from the governor.[44] This rather handsome gift may have been the first such shipment, but it was not to be the last, for later that summer spies reported to Lieutenant Matheos in Apalachee that Carolina's Yamasee allies had entered the province bearing gifts of guns and munitions for "all of the towns."[45]

Although the South Carolina governor was clearly seeking to win the Apalachicolas' loyalty with guns, it would be wrong to say that the Apalachicolas sought an English alliance solely for the sake of having an English alliance. Rather, the Apalachicolas had their own reasons for enlisting English military technology, namely, to fight a war against the Chiscas. The Chiscas, a nomadic group originally from the Virginia mountains that had preyed upon a variety of southeastern Indian societies since the 1620s, were currently at war with the Apalachicolas and had recently killed at least a dozen Apalachicola men, whose deaths required the Apalachicolas to seek vengeance.[46]

For reasons unknown, the Apalachicolas blamed these deaths on the English, who, despite the governor's gifts, apparently had not yet done enough to help them fight their enemy. The Apalachicolas were so displeased with the English, in fact, that they briefly refused to feed the traders who inhabited their towns. Upon hearing of the ill usage of the traders, Henry Woodward, who was then living at an undisclosed place in the woods nursing a snakebite, returned to the Apalachicola towns seeking to redress the Indians' grievances. He did not have any more firearms to give at the time, but distributed clothes and beads to all of the chiefs, telling them that if they returned with him to Charles Town, he would be able to obtain the governor's permission "to exterminate the Chiscas."[47] Woodward, it seems, needed Indian burdeners to carry the heavy loads of deerskins back to Charles Town and hoped to exchange their services for military assistance quid pro quo.

And while documentary evidence attests to the importance of clothing and guns in this early Carolina-Creek trade, archaeological evidence reveals that the Creeks traded for a wide array of goods in the years following 1685. Carol Mason, in her classic archaeological investigation of the remains of the English trade house at Ocmulgee, found an assortment of "utilitarian" goods such as guns, knives, scissors, needles, axes, and hoes. Decorative items such as bells and beads also continued to be popular, particularly for the adornment of their clothes, which, with a steady supply of English cloth, were undoubtedly beginning to take on a more English appearance.[48] Assuming the trappings of the English may have been a wise choice at the time, but, as we shall see, it also had its drawbacks.

THE "COLONIZATION" OF THE CREEK ECONOMY

Matheos's excessive actions, which were intended to bring the Apalachicolas to their former "obedience," had the opposite effect, steering the Apalachicolas into a more intimate alliance with the Carolina traders in the years that followed. In the summer of 1689, reports that English traders were still making "repeated incursions" into the Chattahoochee River prompted Governor Quiroga y Losada of Florida to order his subordinates to construct a fort near Coweta in order to prevent the traders from returning. By Christmas, the fort, dubbed "Apalachicola" after the Spaniards' name for that Indian province, was completed, and a garrison of

Spanish soldiers and Apalachee warriors arrived there in early April 1690.[49]

At first, relations between the Creeks and the Spaniards appeared to be on a good footing. In May of 1690, the commander of the Apalachicola fort conducted a general conference in the town of Coweta, during which the Indians made their usual promises to "obey" the Spaniards, while, conversely, the Spaniards tried to convince them that the new fort was for their own good. Soon after this amicable conference, however, the Creeks began abandoning their homes on the Chattahoochee en masse for friendlier territory in proximity to the English at Charles Town. By April of 1691, the Chattahoochee River was devoid of its entire population, and its inhabitants had reconstituted their towns at various new locations on the Ocmulgee, Oconee, Ogechee, and Savannah rivers.[50]

Although scholars have paid more attention to later historical events, such as the Creeks' participation in the Yamasee War of 1715, or the formation of their "neutral" foreign policy during the eighteenth century, the exodus to central Georgia in 1691 and their occupation of that territory until 1715 deserves examination as a formative period in Creek history. One reason for considering this particular epoch of Creek history important was that during this twenty-five-year time span the consumer revolution in Creek country occurred, an event which made them a "new people" in many respects. From the English trading house constructed near the remains of three ancient earthen mounds at Ocmulgee, the Creeks acquired their eighteenth-century tool kit, quite literally making a technological jump from the stone age to the eighteenth century in the space of a single generation. We should also note that the length of time spent at this location—twenty-five years—allowed an entire generation of Creek children to be raised to adulthood without knowing what life was like without a reliable supply of English trade goods.

It is important to realize, however, that the incorporation of the Creeks into the Atlantic economy occurred not in peacetime but in an epoch fraught with war. A Creek-led war of revenge against the Spanish and their Christian Indian allies ensued shortly after the migration to Ochese Creek in 1691. As it turned out, though, this war of vengeance dovetailed with a more widespread imperial conflict brewing across the Atlantic Ocean.

As was so often the case in a world that was becoming smaller by way of exploration, colonization, and imperial rivalry, events in Europe had marked effects on aboriginal populations in out-of-the-way places. Creek country was no exception. Such a precipitous event occurred in 1700, when Charles II, the last Hapsburg king of Spain, died without leaving an heir to the throne. Austrian Hapsburgs, who wished to see the Spanish crown remain in the family, sought to install the dead king's nephew as the new Spanish king. King Louis XIV of France, seeking to aggrandize the Bourbon family, asserted that his grandson Phillip, Charles's grand-nephew, had an equal, if not greater, claim to the throne, and had him installed in 1701. Fearing that Phillip might unite Spain and France under a single crown, in May 1702, England, Holland, and Austria together declared war on France and Spain. Their declaration of war thereby initiated the War of Spanish Succession, known in America as Queen Anne's War.[51]

In the American Southeast, the declaration of war in Europe allowed the festering territorial disputes between Carolina and Florida to erupt into a full-scale war, which, as we shall see, resulted in a number of stunning English victories. Spain, which claimed territory that extended as far north as Virginia, had never fully recognized the Carolina proprietors' claim to the same lands. A treaty signed between Spain and England in 1670 in Madrid specified that England had a right to keep all the territory that it "now possesses," but diplomats and colonial officials continued to haggle over the exact definition of the term. The Spanish, naturally, adhered to a strict interpretation of the treaty's provisions, and sought to keep English expansion to a minimum. For this reason, Spanish officials considered the intrusion of English traders into Apalachicola, as well as the spread of plantations southward toward Port Royal, to be encroachments on "their" territory. Carolina imperialists, who dreamed of making the American Southeast a part of the British empire, began considering a variety of schemes to occupy the Mississippi River valley and the Gulf of Mexico.[52]

Complicating matters further still was the fact that Spain's new allies, the French, initiated their own colonial projects in the Southeast as the seventeenth century drew to a close. In 1698, fearing English encroachment in the Mississippi valley, Louis XIV of France consented to the establishment of a new colony, dubbed "Louisiana" in his honor. The colony's first governor, Pierre Le Moyne, Sieur d'Iberville, conducted three voyages between 1698 and 1702 that led to the establishment of the first French forts in the gulf region. In the spring of 1699, Iberville and his men completed Ft. Maurepas, near present-day Biloxi, Mississippi, and by 1702 he had constructed forts on the Mississippi River and on Mobile Bay.[53] The Carolinians, who were well aware of the ravages the French had precipitated against English colonists in Massachusetts and Connecticut in the 1690s, rightfully began to fear French and Spanish encirclement.[54]

Not only did the migration to central Georgia enable the Creeks to acquire the fruits of the English trade, but it allowed them to score major victories against the Spanish regime and thereby become the virtual "masters" of northern Florida. In this way, the Creeks essentially used the English alliance as a means to a particular end. Because the English were useful, permitting traders to enter their towns and become a permanent part of the landscape seemed like a good compromise—perhaps even a liberating development—at a time when Spanish missionaries and soldiers threatened their freedom. As Queen Anne's war progressed, however, this symbiotic relationship underwent a near-complete reversal, and it was the English who began using Indians for their own imperialist purposes. In the course of this reversal, the Creeks and their allies witnessed a number of disturbing developments that sowed the seeds of discontent with the English regime, as evidenced in part by their decreasing willingness to fight for English causes.

Discontent began to simmer among the Creeks because the intrusion of the Carolina trade regime wrought tremendous changes in the Indian political economy. Before the European intrusion into the Southeast, the Creeks' ancestors' economy had remained isolated from the general economic currents that had begun to draw disparate parts of the world—from Europe to Asia to Africa—together in a nascent capitalist system in the late Middle Ages. Until the late seventeenth century, the Creeks' ancestors practiced small-scale agriculture based primarily on the production of corn, beans, and squash, supplemented by the hunting of game animals. As such, their economies remained local in nature, and surplus production was limited to the corn reserves and deerskins that commoners set aside as tribute for chiefs.[55]

Once English traders ensconced themselves among the Creek peoples living in central Georgia and on the Tallapoosa and Coosa rivers, the native inhabitants began regularly exchanging deerskins and Indian slaves for European manufactures. Contemporaries often described the Creeks as a people who "consumed a lot of goods," and it is evident that they became consumers in a very modern sense within a generation after regular trading commenced.[56]

Because the Creeks had regular access to the English traders, they were quickly becoming the South's wealthiest Indians, in terms of acquiring European goods. While the acquisition of European goods was something that the Indians desired greatly, their economy, as a consequence, began to acquire a distinctly "colonial" appearance. By definition, a colonial economy is a peripheral one, usually rural or agrarian, which provides raw materials for manufacturing centers in core capitalist regions. Because raw materials make up the bulk of the exports in these regions, profits usually remain small owing to the overemphasis on resource extraction, which consequently tends to stunt economic diversification and growth. Core capitalist regions, in contrast, possess the ability to take these raw materials, turn them into finished manufactured goods, and in turn sell them at high profits to domestic and foreign markets, including the peripheral regions from which the raw materials came. The very structure of this system virtually guarantees that the core regions will reap the greatest rewards from these raw materials, rendering the peripheries "dependent" on consumer goods produced elsewhere, as well as on price fluctuations on the world market.[57]

Being a "poor" agricultural society, the Creeks had little choice but to provide the English with their only salable commodities—agricultural produce, furs, and Indian slaves—in order to participate in the burgeoning trans-Atlantic economy. The principal problem was that the acquisition of guns, powder, and cloth, especially from traders willing to extend credit, eventually made the Creeks dependent upon European technology and severely indebted to English traders.[58]

It is significant, for example, that Thomas Nairne's ethnographic description of the Tallapoosas included a discussion on debt. According to Nairne, in addition to the chiefs' more traditional duties, Tallapoosa chiefs also played a role in "haranguing" people to pay their debts to the English so as not to suffer the "ill effects." Likewise, Governor James Moore's attempts to end the traders' practice of trading on "trust" (a seventeenth-century English term equivalent to the modern "credit") and the absolution of Indian debts in 1703 illustrate that debt had become a way of life in Creek country during this time period. By 1711, the Ochese Creek Indians were collectively one hundred thousand deerskins in debt, or approximately two hundred fifty deerskins (several years' work) per Indian man.[59]

Although the deerskin trade has received the most attention from scholars who study the southeastern Indians' economy, it was the trade in Indian slaves—founded in the context of an imperial war—that initially drew the Ocheses and others into a subordinate role vis-à-vis the English in the Atlantic marketplace. Because traders were willing to pay a high price for Indian slaves—usually a gun, some powder, and perhaps a shirt—the practice of trading on trust had dire consequences. When the supply of slaves was readily available, paying debts to the traders was possible. But when the Spanish missions—the principal source for Indian slaves—collapsed at the turn of the eighteenth century, the Creeks had to search farther afield for new sources of their human commodity. For this reason, Creek warriors began making slave raids against the Choctaws and other Indians groups living in the Mississippi-Tombigbee river basins to the west. Spanish and English sources alike attest to the fact that Creek warriors also made excursions into the Florida Keys in search of slaves. Evidence further suggests that the Creeks participated in the Tuscarora War in the fall of 1712 primarily to cover slave debts.[60]

By the end of the eighteenth century's first decade, the combination of debt and slave trading had created a variety of problems in Creek society, both among Indians and between Indians and English traders. Among Indians, one of the principal problems with amassing debts, particularly for a people who traditionally held communal notions of property, was the fact that indebted individuals sometimes sought to call upon the "traditional" notion of property to meet their personal obligations. For instance, on June 12, 1712, the newly created Indian Trade Commission of South Carolina heard the complaint of a Chehaw man named Tuskenaw, who argued that while he was off to war, the town of Cusseta stole two of his Indian slaves to cover their influential war captain's debt. After ordering the slaves to be returned to the said Tuskenaw, the commission mandated that "towns or relations" should not be responsible for individual debts, thereby forcing new rules of individual property ownership on a people who clearly retained collective practices. This is not to say, however, that the Creeks did not welcome individual notions of property. Clearly, Tuskenaw and others like him stood to gain from the enforcement of the new rules, and in this sense, "traditions" concerning property would remain a contested issue within Indian societies.

A further problem stemmed from the fact that many of the Creeks' so-called "slaves" constituted an important component of the local social fabric. For centuries, southeastern Indians had practiced a form of slavery in which prisoners of war remained among their captors' families, either as laborers of uncertain social status or, quite commonly, as ritually adopted members of the family. The English slave trade, which defined these persons as chattel property, strained this ancient practice when debts accrued. In Tuskenaw's case, the two Indian "slaves" for whom he sought redress—both Apalachee captives—were not chattel, but his relatives. One woman, named Toolodeha, was Tuskenaw's wife, and the other female "slave" was his mother-in-law.[61]

Although such disputes among Indians may have signified that there was something rotten about the English trade regime, it was the differences between Indians and English traders/creditors that ultimately led the Creeks and their neighbors to the conclusion that they might become slaves themselves if debts continued to mount. Since the beginning of the slave trade, Carolina officials had lamented the "abuses" that traders committed against Indians who were supposed to be their allies. By the turn of the eighteenth century, complaints of trader abuses had become so common that the Carolina assembly deemed it necessary to set up a special commission to regulate the trade in 1707.[62]

While trader abuses, such as beatings, whippings, and the molestation of women, clearly drew the ire of the Creeks, the real problems began in the waning years of Queen Anne's War. By that time, the Creeks had become so indebted that English traders began taking away the Apalachee "slaves" when they were unable to acquire slaves by other means. Recall, however, that, as in Tuskenaw's case, the Apalachees were not chattel, but relatives of many of the Creeks. By enslaving the Apalachees, then, English traders were, in effect, enslaving the Creeks' own people.[63]

Because English traders threatened, in turn, to enslave the Creeks themselves if they could not meet their debts, the specter of slavery loomed large in the minds of the people who had zealously enslaved others for more than a generation. By 1715, English-speaking Indian slaves who had escaped from Carolina plantations began to spread rumors that the English traders were considering a plan to enslave the Creeks and force them to cede their "ancient" lands. When the Indian agents John Wright and Thomas Nairne conducted a census of the Indians in the spring of 1715, the Creeks and many of their neighbors viewed this intrusive action as a first step toward their enslavement.[64]

Adding to the fear of slavery was the fact that during Queen Anne's

War, the English traders played a dual role as military commanders, leading expeditions against Spanish missions and forts and inciting the Indians to go to war against other Indians in order to obtain slaves to cover
their debts. In this way, the presence of English traders in the Indian
towns began to assume the appearance of a military occupation. According to Spanish soldiers from Pensacola, whom English-allied Indians captured and dragged to Charles Town for a reward, the entire Southeast,
from Ochese Creek to the Alabama River system, was a militarized zone.
Several soldiers, for instance, interviewed by Spanish officials upon their
return to St. Augustine in January 1710, claimed that each Indian town
had at least one resident English "lieutenant"[65] who gave gifts of powder
and shot and traded for furs. Some towns, such as Talisi on the Tallapoosa
River, had two English "lieutenants," and others appear to have been the
headquarters for more important English officials. Tuckebatchee, for
example, harbored a man named "Captain Chanchon" (perhaps the trader
John Cochrane) who commanded sixteen subordinates.[66] At Tiguale, the
southernmost Tallapoosa town, John Musgrove was said to command
three other English "lieutenants."[67] Although it is not certain whether or
not these traders were actually commissioned officers in the Carolina
militia, it is significant that they appeared as such to their Spanish prisoners. Such evidence indicates that the English traders were not merely
humble merchants plying their wares, but the militaristic taproots of an
increasingly aggressive British empire.

Even as they fought against the Spanish, French, and their Indian
allies, the Creeks began to recognize that the English regime had trapped
them in an oppressive spiral of warfare, debt, and more warfare. For this
reason, Carolina's Indian allies began to look upon the Spanish and
French not as a threat, but as allies and a potential source of trade. For
example, in 1707, while transporting a Spanish soldier named Juan
Gabrial de Vargas to Charles Town for a monetary reward, a party of "Tallapoosa" warriors asked the Spanish prisoner "if they were to go to the
Spanish with a white flag, if they would have peace with them, and if so,
would they sell them powder and bullets?"[68] Vargas, hoping to earn their
good favor, responded in the affirmative, prompting English traders privy
to the conversation to separate the Tallapoosa warriors from the Spaniard,
sending them to an undisclosed location in Charles Town.

Though English traders stationed in Charles Town had the power to
limit familiar conversations between their Indian allies and Spanish pris-

oners, they could do little to prevent them from making similar peace overtures to the French in Mobile. For instance, when Thomas Nairne sought to drag the Tallapoosas into a war against Mobile in 1708, his effort not only generated a lukewarm response, but appears to have had the opposite of its intended effect. Soon after Nairne's infamous journey, the Alabamas, who had fought and traded with the English for more than a decade, began to make tentative peace overtures toward the French at Mobile. Although the exact timing is not known, by July of 1709, the king of France had already received word of the peace overtures, and he urged Jean-Baptiste, Sieur de Bienville, the acting commander of Mobile, to seize this opportunity because "they were asking you for it."[69]

Evidently, Bienville continued to make peace overtures to the Alabamas and other Indians nominally allied to the English, for in the coming years, French officials consistently speculated that peace was at hand.[70] In March 1712, Bienville eventually secured a truce with the "Alabamas, Abikas, and to other nations of Carolina," thereby preventing a major English-led expedition against Mobile planned for the fall.[71] Curiously, in February 1715, the governor of Florida reported a sudden influx of "pagan and Christian Indians," who came to talk peace. Anticipating that St. Augustine might see a sudden influx of friendly Indians, Governor Corocles petitioned the Crown for an increase in the annual Indian fund, arguing that such expenditures would be necessary to cultivate newfound alliances. In light of this evidence, we may suspect that the Yamasee War came as little surprise to the Spanish and French, who would seek to accommodate the Creeks and other Indians in their attempt to forge a new world order.

THE LEGACY

In light of the above analysis, Brave Dog's explanation of the causes of the Yamasee War can be viewed as one man's attempt to untangle the meaning of dependency, as it was experienced by the southeastern Indians nearly three hundred years ago. Brave Dog's insights confirm that imperial warfare and the commodification of human beings, combined with the Indians' own desire for the things Europeans made, had compromised the Indians' political and economic autonomy. Thus, the collective revolt against the Carolina trade regime—the Yamasee War—was a necessary, if drastic, step toward achieving a measure of independence. If Brave Dog is to be believed, then, it appears that the Indians staged their revolt in order to evade their debt obligations and to put an end to the cyclical violence which constituted the dark and bloody heart and soul of the slave trade.

What is equally interesting about the Yamasee War is what it did not attempt to bring to an end: the consumption of European trade goods. After establishing regular contact with the Catholic powers, Creek leaders pleaded in vain with Spanish officials to erect a fort and a trading store in Apalachee. The Spanish made numerous attempts to establish such an enterprise, in 1718, 1738, and 1745, but could never turn their lowly *tienda* into much more than an understocked dram shop. Likewise, when Creek leaders began descending upon Mobile in the fall of 1715, they pleaded with the acting governor to send traders into their towns to barter with them for deerskins, corn, and other useful commodities—anything but slaves.

Neither of the Catholic powers, however, could initially meet the Creeks' demands for European trade goods, thereby prompting them to reestablish contact with the English in 1717. As one Englishman put it, the Creeks reestablished contact "not out of love, but want to be supplied."[72] Likewise, Spanish officials noted that Creek women had begun to lobby for a return to the English alliance, presumably in order to restore the trade in cloth that had enabled them to fashion an entirely new wardrobe for themselves in recent decades.

However much the Creeks may have wanted the restoration of the English trade, it is clear that they did not want a return to the status quo of 1715, for the Creeks had no intention of becoming pawns of the British empire. Rather, their goal was to use the now-competitive political environment established after the Yamasee War to their advantage, by drawing the English into a strictly commercial relationship, while using their putative alliances with Spain and France to thwart Carolina's imperial and territorial ambitions. For the first decade or so after reestablishment of contact with the English, however, the trade between the two former allies proceeded only sporadically. The Creeks occasionally disrupted this restored trade by murdering traders and plundering their stores, by refusing to end their relationship with the French and Spanish, and, most important, by continuing their war against Carolina's newest Indian allies, the Cherokees.

To counteract this sustained belligerence, the Carolina government dispatched a series of agents to Creek country to force the Indians to behave in a more peaceable manner. One such agent was a young captain in the South Carolina militia named Tobias Fitch, who in the summer and fall months of 1725 made the first of his two trips to Creek country. His mission was to scold the Creeks for attacking and plundering English traders. The arguments he employed to exact concessions from the Creeks suggest that England's ability to meet Creek consumer demand was his strongest selling point.

On July 20, 1725, Fitch delivered a speech to a delegation of sixty headmen at Oakfuskee, an Upper Creek town on the Tallapoosa River. At Oakfuskee, Fitch pleaded with the headmen to control their young people, who, most agreed, were guilty of committing these "rogueish proceedings." Before concluding his speech, Fitch delivered this final salvo to induce the Upper Creeks to behave kindly to the English: "I must tell your Young Men that if it had not been for us, you would not have known how to [go to] War, nor yet have anything to war with. You have had nothing but bows and arrows to kill deer; You had no hoes or axes then [but] what you made of stone. You wore nothing but skins; But now you have learned the use of firearms as well to kill deer and other provisions as [well as] to [wage] war against your enemies, and yet you set no greater value on us who have been such good friends unto you than on your greatest enemies. This all [of] you that are old knows to be true. And I would have you make your young men sensible of it."[73]

By drawing a contrast between the past, using the imagery of bows and arrows and skins, and the present, by reminding them of the effectiveness of firearms, Fitch made an argument that played to the Creeks' recognition of their own recent history. It is particularly telling that he directed his salvo at the old men, not only because they held the authority in Creek society, but because they could remember the time before they began trading regularly for English goods—most especially guns. By doing so, Fitch was able to remind the Creeks that their recent rise to power could not have occurred with the "primitive" weapons of their forefathers. Fitch's arguments thus prompted Creek leaders to accede to his demands rather than act upon their deep-seated distrust of the English.

Because the efforts of Fitch and others put the Anglo-Creek trade on a firm footing, historians have tacitly or overtly portrayed the thirty-to-forty-year period following the Yamasee War as a kind of golden age for British/Creek relations, a "middle ground" of cooperation in which nei-

ther party had the means (though did not necessarily lack the will) to sub-
jugate the other. There is some justification for this portrayal, because
trade continued virtually uninterrupted, and there were no major wars
between the Creeks and English until the outbreak of the American Revolution.[74]

One reason that the Creeks were able to establish a kind of detente
with the English was their ability to carve a favorable "neutral" niche for
themselves among the English, French, and Spanish. This famous Creek
"neutrality" policy has received some attention from scholars in the past,
who have characterized it as a "national" foreign policy implemented by
the Creek chief Brims in the 1720s.[75] Although in recent years this view of
Creek foreign policy has fallen somewhat out of favor, and we now know
that there was no such thing as a "national" policy among the Creeks, the
characterization still has merit.[76]

It is probable that this famous Creek neutrality policy began in late
March 1718 during a large gathering of Creek chiefs at Coweta. The resolution decided upon during that meeting, however, was not necessarily to
be "neutral" in any kind of ideological sense, but in their words "to live in
peace with the people of Charlestown, St. Augustine, San Marcos, Pensacola, and Mobile." The often unstated (in front of the English, at least)
second facet of this neutrality policy was to get from each European outpost the largest amount of gifts and trade goods possible. In other words,
the Creeks wanted to acquire European trade goods by any means necessary.[77]

As we might expect, however, England's favorable economic situation
and its ability to deliver greater quantities of trade goods gave Creek
"neutrality" a distinctively English accent, the underlying goal of which
was to keep open the trade routes to Charles Town, Augusta, and Savannah. This "English first" policy reveals that the world's so-called peripheral peoples, like the Creeks and other southeastern Indians, found mercantile empires quite attractive, even seductive. This was so because, in
their ideal form, mercantile empires required few political or territorial
concessions from the local inhabitants other than the necessary fort or two
on the coast, which served merely as bases for trading operations.[78]

The Creeks' goal during the fifty-year period following the Yamasee
War was to allow the English to maintain a series of such outposts on the
peripheries of what they regarded as "their" territory (including much of
Georgia and north Florida), and yet to keep English settlement confined

to the tidal regions on the coast. To limit English encroachment, the Creeks effectively propped up the anemic Spanish and French colonial enterprises, hoping that their continued presence would prohibit the English from making any extraordinary western land claims.[79]

But by the 1740s and certainly by the 1750s this mercantile empire, which the Creeks eagerly courted, had begun to evolve into a new kind of empire, an empire of land.[80] By the mid-eighteenth century, English settlers were pouring into the southern backcountry to places like the Ogeechee River in Georgia, which once served the Creeks as important hunting ground. These initial migrations initiated the wave of English settlement that would sweep across the continent. In this way, the Creeks' "English first" policy backfired on them, for eventually they had to begin making political and territorial concessions to keep the peace, as well as to maintain a steady flow of trade goods. In 1763 the Creeks' foreign policy system collapsed after the signing of the Treaty of Paris. Not only did the Treaty of Paris end the Seven Years' War, but it forced Spain and France to relinquish their territorial claims in the Southeast to Britain, which then began its systematic attempt to bring all of eastern North America under its dominion.

THE MOTHER OF NECESSITY

Although it is often difficult to see into the future with clarity, the Creeks understood that the English posed a particular threat to their well-being. As both the actions taken during the Yamasee War and Brave Dog's analysis of the causes of that conflict suggest, the Creeks and other Indians were well aware of this danger rather early in the eighteenth century. What remains to be answered, however, is why the Creeks chose to continue to trade with the English, despite their recognition that this trade seriously compromised their political autonomy.

It has been argued here and elsewhere that the Creeks (and Indians throughout eastern North America) made political compromises with the English because they were "dependent" upon the English for trade goods, which, over the course of the eighteenth century, became necessities of life. As originally construed, dependency theory seeks to explain how the world's "peripheral" regions—like the aboriginal Southeast— become "dependent" when representatives of European core capitalist countries penetrate the peripheries, draw local inhabitants into an unequal economic relationship, extract economic surpluses, and thwart the local inhabitants' attempts to regain control of surplus production. In short, by linking themselves to the emerging world capitalist system— centered in Europe—southeastern Indians and other such "peripheral" peoples became inextricably tied to the fluctuations of the emerging world market and the currents of world geopolitics, a complex situation of which the Indians were only dimly aware and over which they certainly had no control.[81]

Studies of the Anglo-Indian trade system, which all rely to some degree on this concept, have successfully shown the ways by which the southeastern Indian economy evolved from a local, self-sufficient precapitalist system based upon hunting, gathering, and horticulture into a nascent capitalist system in which southern Indians produced deerskins and a few other commodities for the trans-Atlantic marketplace. The critical link between the southeastern Indians and their European counterparts, of course, was European trade goods, upon which most historians assume southeastern Indians became irreversibly and inevitably "dependent" after several generations of sustained contact and the subsequent loss of aboriginal handicraft skills.[82]

Because of its emphasis on the structure of the world economic system, dependency theory provides a usable context through which to explain how the southeastern Indians became "dependent." Being Marxist in inspiration, though, dependency theory possesses a materialist bias that places greater emphasis on the changing modes of commodity production than on the behavior of consumers. Consequently, studies of economic dependency generally assume that consumerism was and is the consequence of this changing pattern of surplus production. Moreover, such studies typically portray peripheral peoples as victims of foreign aggression and highlight the various methods by which people caught in the jaws of history, so to speak, resist the intrusion of impersonal, individualistic market forces into their communal societies. It should also be noted that many historical studies of the Indians portray their incorporation into this world system as an inevitable occurrence, consistent with Marx's own scientific view of history.

Theories of economic dependency, which emphasize the gradual incorporation of peripheral peoples into the modern world system, thus fail to explain Brave Dog's dilemma. How was it possible that the Creek Indians, who had lived for millennia without the things Europeans made, could find themselves dependent upon the English for the very necessities of life within a generation? How did trade render the English so "indispensable and necessary"? The answer, as we shall see, can be found in the changing ways in which the Creeks and other southern Indians defined the word "necessary."

To understand why the Creeks considered the English to be "necessary," one must see the trade goods themselves as the very stimulus for the consumer revolution that occurred during Brave Dog's time. Guns are the most obvious case in point. Although most historians recognize that the early smooth-bore muskets were inferior weapons when compared to the firearm technologies developed in subsequent centuries, most concur that even these primitive firearms were far superior to the bows and arrows carried by the Indians. As such, the smooth-bore musket gave certain Indians a decided advantage over other Indians who lacked the new military technology. This technological advantage, when placed in the context of the Indian slave trade and the imperial warfare waged during the age of Queen Anne, allowed the Creeks to ascend to prominence to a degree which was unthinkable in an earlier epoch—hence their obvious attraction to guns and other tools of the military trade, such as powder, shot, and metal hatchets.

As with guns, cloth appears to have been attractive to the Indians because of its particular advantages over dressed deerskin, which the Indians had commonly used to clothe themselves before the arrival of the Europeans. As anyone who has spent time outdoors knows, deerskin, when wet, tends to shrink, dries slowly, and does not permit the skin to "breathe." Deerskin, therefore, is ill equipped to keep a person warm in cold, wet weather. Wool cloth, in contrast, repels moisture, allows the skin to "breathe," and provides ample resistance to wind and cold. Because of these particular qualities, wool cloth enables the human body, even when exposed to cold, wet weather, to conserve heat, thus making it ideally suited for life in the damp, chilly winters characteristic of southeastern North America.

Because of these obvious advantages, it might be easy to assume that the Creeks and other southeastern Indians had little choice but to embrace English-furnished guns, cloth, and other superior merchandise. Perhaps. But what made the Indians realize that deerskin garments were insufficient? What made them recognize, after centuries, if not millennia, of wearing such garments, that they were now "cold"? Moreover, how do we explain why certain items of European manufacture, such as brass kettles, failed to supplant the Indians' native technology, in this case earthen pottery, the manufacture and use of which flourished throughout the eighteenth century? And finally, how do we explain the Indians' tendency to define European "luxuries," such as mirrors, beads, and brandy, as the very "necessities" of life? Why did this occur so quickly? And why did English trade goods exert such an enduring influence over the Creeks and other southeastern Indians?

One answer to these questions worth proposing is that Indian "dependency" upon European trade goods was intrinsic to the goods themselves, which is to say that European trade goods created "needs" that previously did not exist. Southeastern Indians, then, did not necessarily become dependent upon trade goods because of their greater utility or because of the loss of native crafts, but because their aesthetic changed to fit "modern" standards. Devoid of any romanticist sentimentality for the "sublime" past, southeastern Indians were loath to return to the "primitive" technologies of their forefathers.

To probe the nature of the Creeks' so-called "dependency," it might be useful to look forward briefly to the year 1738, when the Spanish governors of both Florida and Cuba campaigned to establish a trading post at San Marcos in order to compete with the English traders and draw the Creeks to the Spanish interest. To initiate this new campaign, in February of 1738, the governor of Cuba sent Alonso Marquez del Toro to San Marcos with a ship laden with a generous supply of trade goods and food. His mission was to bestow gifts upon the Lower Creeks and to acquire information about English trade practices.[83]

On March 12, 1738, while at San Marcos, Toro received an unexpected visitor named Tickhonabe from one of the Upper Creek towns. Tickhonabe, known to the Spanish as Balero, was once a familiar friend to the Spanish, and had met the viceroy of New Spain during a visit to Mexico City in 1717. In those days, Tickhonabe was known as the "war captain" of the Tallasees, and his Spanish name, Balero, supports his assertion that he had received Christian baptism during his stay in Mexico City, the viceroy himself serving as Tickhonabe's godfather. Tickhonabe, then, had a long history of interaction with the Spanish before his arrival at San Marcos in 1738.

But it is also important to point out that Tickhonabe was likely born after the English had established a permanent presence in Creek country and would not have had a firsthand recollection of a world without English trade goods. Thus, it is highly unlikely that Tickhonabe could have lived comfortably without the English, to whom his allegiance would eventually return after the Yamasee War. In the 1720s, for example, Tickhonabe became a zealous pro-English partisan and led Upper Creek efforts to root out the last of the Yamasees, who continued to wage a low-scale guerrilla war against Carolina. Though Tickhonabe's motives for changing allegiances are difficult to uncover, it appears that his political affections gravitated toward the English because only the English traders could satisfy his desire for European manufactures. The Spanish, as Tickhonabe explained, "have always made promises, and always they deluded them." "When they go down to the English," Tickhonabe noted in contrast, "they bring them every thing they need and they take their furs."[84]

The reason Tickhonabe made this particular journey to San Marcos was to plead with Toro and the Spanish to supply trade goods for his own people, the "Tallapoosas," whom the governors of Cuba and Florida had ignored or forgotten to include in the disbursement of presents. Toro, although unable to give Tickhonabe the presents he wanted, seized this opportunity to interview him about English trading practices, demanding to know the kinds of goods traded and their relative prices. In the process of this conversation, Tickhonabe dictated to Toro a massive list of trade goods and corresponding prices that reveal much about the changing Creek aesthetic and their radical redefinition of "necessity."[85]

Balero's "Wish List"

Rum
Cloth: Blue, and Red.
Heavy Cloth: Blue, White, colored, Green
Blouse Shirts
Blouse Shirts: White, Printed
Chintz Cloth: of several colors
Wool Yarn: various colors
Wool: uncombed
Shoes:
[ditto]: with metal base
Brimmed Hats
Brimmed Hats: with a false braid

[ditto] : in a larger size
Silk Ribbons: assorted, by halves
Cotton Belts: coarse, striped
Wool Belts: striped, smooth, in bright colors
Linen Belts: with loose stitching
Narrow Belts: half length [presumably for children]
Large Wool Spindles
Small Wool Spindles
Small mirrors: with a wood frame
Scarves: linen
[ditto]: of cotton
Combs : of glass
[ditto]: of wood
[ditto]: of bone
Scissors: medium sized
Scissors: small
Clasp Pins
Sewing Needles
Thimbles: large, for the ears
Buttons: metal, yellow, mixed
Buttons: with bells
Earrings: silver plated
Earrings: with glass beadwork, false stones
Rings: silver
[ditto]: metal
Beads: medium sized, all colors
Belts: tanned leather, with metal loop and buckle, gold workings
Tobacco Pipes: plain and painted
Cowbells: yellow and thick
Powder
Muskets: long variety
Carbines or Pistols
Gunflints Ramrods or wormers
Sabres: ³/₄ length
Machetes: ³/₄ length, with a sleeve
[ditto]: ½ length, with a holster of corresponding size
Pans: light

[There is a break here. Tickhonabe argues that this is but a fraction of
    what one finds.]

Small tin cups
Gloves: (purvidas) and plain (zapatos de manos)
Roasting skewers
Drills
Planking Nails
Ordinary Nails
Gunsmith files: medium
[ditto] : small
Cheap saws
[ditto]: of ¾ length
Knives
Pocket knives
Folding Razors
Straight Awls
Chain Links
Fish Hooks: small
Harpoons: small
Cauldrons: of brass
Vermillion
Soap
Molasses
Salt
Carafes
Jars: for drinking asi (asiete)
Glass Vessels: for drinking liquor

[At this point the scribe quits, stating that this was not in his job
    description.]

An examination of Tickhonabe's "wish list" reveals first that the Creeks
appreciated the utility of European technology. For this reason, items that
would presumably reduce the amount of energy expended to complete
day-to-day tasks, such as knives, axes, fish hooks, and saws, figured prominently on the list. What is perhaps more telling is the degree to which
decorative items, or things we might classify as "luxuries," appear on the
list, such as bells, buttons, ribbons, and beads. Significantly, Tickhonabe

did not merely list cloth as a preferred trade item, but mentioned several kinds of varying styles and quantities, indicating that the Creeks, or Tickhonabe at least, had a true sense of fashion.

However revealing Tickhonabe's list might be to us, the conditions under which it was composed are even more so. Consider, for example, the fact that Tickhonabe's rather detailed list was a response to Toro's very general question about the "ordinary" types of English trade goods found among his people. Furthermore, Tickhonabe caused Toro's scribe, a member of the San Marcos garrison, to develop a somewhat severe hand cramp, which caused Tickhonabe to pause briefly while dictating. As the list continued to grow, the scribe eventually quit, stating that he was not paid to do that sort of work. Tickhonabe's list, while extensive, is nonetheless incomplete.

Tickhonabe's ability to compile such a lengthy and detailed list of trade goods after being asked a simple question must have caused Toro to suspect that the crafty Creek headman was up to something. Several days later, Toro presented Tickhonabe's list to an Irishman named James Hamilton, who had traded with the Creek Indians for some years before coming to live with the Spanish at San Marcos. Upon perusing Tickhonabe's list, Hamilton replied that it was too long and that it contained many things "that the English do not trade."[86] Hamilton then provided Toro with a new list, which was much shorter, and, according to Hamilton, was a much more accurate description of the trade goods commonly found in Creek country. Evidently, Tickhonabe had exaggerated the diversity of English trade goods currently circulating among his people in an attempt to acquire more of the things that his people, the Upper Creeks, deemed "necessary" but found difficult to acquire. Tickhonabe's behavior before Toro thus indicates that the Creeks did not merely have needs: they had wants that even the well-supplied British traders could not satisfy.

*   *   *

Tickhonabe's brazen attempt to procure more trade goods from the Spaniards than the English themselves were capable of furnishing explains in part why Brave Dog's proclamation of "obedience" to the Spanish in 1715 would ultimately ring hollow in the ears of most Creeks. Like Brave Dog, Tickhonabe had once looked to the Spanish in an attempt to evade the ill effects of the Carolina trade system. We do not know what ultimately happened to Brave Dog. But Tickhonabe, his contemporary, behaved in a manner which suggests that English trade goods held an enduring power over and appeal for the Creeks, even though many Creeks may have secretly loathed the very men who supplied them with their "necessities." In this light, it becomes apparent that trade goods were the important tool of hegemony that permitted the English to wrest important political concessions from the Creeks and exploit their "dependency" upon the English. Although it has often been said that necessity is the mother of invention, the Creek experience in the late seventeenth and early eighteenth centuries suggests that quite the opposite may also be true: invention is the mother of necessity. And the "inventions" of the time period—English trade goods—could be said to be the mother of the British empire in America.[87]

The Ohio Valley, 1550–1750: Patterns of Sociopolitical Coalescence and Dispersal

PENELOPE B. DROOKER

Before the middle of the eighteenth century, the Ohio River valley was known to Europeans almost entirely through statements by Indian informants. Through the mid-1670s, these accounts depict a populous, prosperous region. After that, the record is extremely fragmentary, but the area appears to have been significantly depopulated until the 1720s, when Shawnees, Delawares, Senecas, and others began to move there from Pennsylvania and western New York.

From the archaeological record, we know that such movements were not without precedent. During the fourteenth and fifteenth centuries, there were major population shifts in the region.[1] Large areas previously dotted with villages apparently became uninhabited. In some locations, regional populations coalesced into larger settlements located within relatively smaller areas; in others, settlements and the typical styles of material culture associated with them disappeared entirely.

These changes typically have been attributed to single, monolithic causes. Without much consideration of alternatives, scholars have usually invoked climatic change to explain the earlier population movements. Late-seventeenth-century depopulation almost invariably is blamed on Iroquois warfare. When a variety of evidence is considered, however, a more complex picture emerges.

MODELS OF POPULATION MOVEMENT

A recently developed archaeological migration model discusses the theoretical bases for major population movements.[2] Conditions favorable to migration include three factors: "negative . . . stresses in the home region," or *push factors*, "positive . . . attractions in the destination region," or *pull factors*, and acceptable transportation costs.[3] Information

115

about new regions usually comes from relatives or friends there, and/or from short-term visits; migration is unlikely to take place without such previous knowledge. Motivation often is economic. One good predictor of movement is "great differences in economic opportunities between two regions."[4] Factors such as lower population densities or higher energy uptake per person in the destination region would "pull" migrants, while factors such as drought or military invasion in the home region would "push" them.

In a recent paper, Marvin Smith discussed ten factors responsible for early historical population movements in the New World, particularly in southeastern North America: the push of disease, the push of political factionalism, the pull of European settlements and trade, the pull of favorable environmental zones, the pull of captured territories, the pull of Indian elites seeking to bolster their own power by forming connections to the Spaniards, the pull of missions, the pull of cultural similarities, the slave trade, and Iroquois warfare.[5]

Iroquois League[6] warfare actually involved both a push and a pull. Fear of Iroquois attacks did result in major population shifts in the Great Lakes area, with many groups moving hundreds of miles westward in an attempt to escape attack.[7] Those who were captured in Iroquois raids often were taken to Iroquoia, either to be tortured and killed or to be adopted into the tribe to replace family members who had died as a result of disease or warfare.[8] From the mid-1630s onward, as guns became more widespread and warfare became more lethal, and as epidemics became more frequent, more and more Iroquois attacks appear to have been motivated by the necessity to replenish their dwindling population by an influx of captives from other groups.[9]

The brunt of Iroquois League warfare fell on different regions during different time periods.[10] From the 1630s through the 1650s, attacks fell mainly on other Iroquoian peoples in the St. Lawrence Valley and directly west of Iroquois League territory, especially the trade rivals of the Huron Confederacy in what is now southern Ontario.[11] By 1649, most Huron villages were abandoned. Between 1650 and 1657, the Petuns, Neutrals, and Eries were dispersed, leaving far western New York and southeastern Ontario virtually abandoned. Attacks widened after that, to all surrounding areas. During or soon before this period, Algonquian peoples of northwestern Ohio, northern Indiana, and Michigan moved westward, beyond Lake Michigan,[12] where their settlements were described by Frenchmen such as Nicolas Perrot from the late 1600s onward; some Illinois people moved southward, and west of the Mississippi River. Iroquois attacks—not always successful—continued in the midwest through the 1680s, not only against native groups there, but also against French enclaves, such as at the Grand Village of the Kaskaskia on the Illinois River in 1680 and the nearby Fort St. Louis, established in 1682. Until 1675, when English settlers destroyed their main village, the Susquehannocks of southeastern Pennsylvania were another major target. French attacks on Iroquois League territory escalated in the 1680s and 1690s, culminating in a 1701 peace treaty. For fifty years after that, Iroquois warfare was directed southward, at Catawbas, Choctaws, and other groups.

In movements into and out of the Ohio Valley during the sixteenth, seventeenth, and eighteenth centuries, several of these push-pull factors appear to have been operational. *Iroquois warfare* probably became a significant "push" factor in the late seventeenth century, precipitating significant out-migration. However, movement from the region appears to have begun well before that time. The waning of Iroquois influence during the first half of the eighteenth century was associated with an equally significant in-migration to the region.

The push of "political factionalism," or at least *political differences*, and the pull of "cultural similarities," or *political alliances*, appear to have acted in concert to influence the direction and result of migration. Archaeological evidence shows that different populations within the Ohio Valley had different prehistoric long-distance exchange relationships; when they left the valley, they may well have moved toward the territories of their allies. Social segmentation also played a part. For example, the historically known Shawnees, whose homeland probably was somewhere within the Ohio River drainage, were composed of five or six divisions that are known to have repeatedly separated and come together from the late seventeenth century onward.

The pull of *European trade* and of *European protection* from Iroquois attacks probably played a part. In addition, the pull of *favorable environmental zones* was a factor: the rise of bison as an important subsistence item during and just before this period may have drawn people westward to the prairies where these animals were more abundant.

I will discuss each of these factors in turn, but first let me give you a bit more background on the Ohio Valley and its residents. I will start by summarizing the archaeological evidence, then the sparse historical information.

OHIO VALLEY ARCHAEOLOGY TO 1650

The Ohio is a major tributary of the Mississippi River. Its upper reaches incorporate the Allegheny and Monongahela rivers in Pennsylvania and New York. The Tennessee and Cumberland rivers join its lower reaches at the Kentucky-Illinois state line, just upstream from where the Ohio enters the Mississippi River. I will be referring to several tributaries, including the Cumberland (which goes through Nashville), the Wabash (which partially delineates the Illinois-Indiana state line), the Scioto (which flows southward through central Ohio), and the Kanawha-New River system (which flows northwesterly through a gap in the Allegheny Mountains to join the Ohio north of Huntington, West Virginia).

Both the river system and an extensive system of trails provided access to other regions,[13] and Ohio Valley residents interacted prehistorically with many groups in surrounding territories, including southeastern peoples from the Cumberland, Tennessee, and Mississippi River valleys.

During the sixteenth and seventeenth centuries, European exploration and settlement increasingly circled the Ohio Valley, but did not penetrate the valley itself.[14] Almost all of our information about this region until around 1750 comes from archaeology.

In the mid-sixteenth century, people were living along the main trunk of the Ohio River primarily in three locations: at the mouth of the Wabash at the Illinois-Indiana state line; in the area between southeastern Indiana and western West Virginia; and along the upper reaches of the Monongahela (which flows north to join with the Allegheny River at present-day Pittsburgh, forming the Ohio). The archaeological traditions in these three regions during this time are called Caborn-Welborn, Fort Ancient, and Monongahela, respectively. Between Fort Ancient and Monongahela settlements were a few villages attributed to the Wellsburg tradition. Each of these traditions is distinguished archaeologically by its architecture and settlement patterns, its burial customs, and the styles of its artifacts, particularly pottery. My main focus here is on the Fort Ancient people.

Just before the European contact period, large portions of the Ohio River drainage had become devoid of permanent settlements.[15] Up to that time, much more of the central and lower Ohio Valley had been occupied. During the fifteenth century, the *Cumberland River valley* lost all or most of its population.[16] Along the Ohio upstream from the mouth of the Cumberland, smaller, relatively widespread villages coalesced into larger ones, most of which were located on or near the main river.

Before 1400, a series of small Mississippian chiefdoms had been located in the lower Ohio Valley.[17] By the sixteenth century, only one group of settlements remained, surrounded by a large buffer zone or hunting territory, which archaeologists call *Caborn-Welborn*. From analysis of burial practices and ceramic styles, David Pollack has proposed that the western villages of this tradition were occupied by peoples whose ancestors had lived in Mississippian chiefdoms downriver, and that eastern villages were populated by people derived from the Mississippian Angel chiefdom immediately upriver.[18] Because there is no evidence of Mississippian-style ranked social organization, Pollack suggests that the polity might have functioned as a confederacy rather than a chiefdom.[19]

From the evidence of exotic ceramics at Caborn-Welborn communities, we know that their residents interacted with Oneota groups in the upper Mississippi Valley (southern Wisconsin, northeastern Iowa, and southeastern Minnesota) and with Late Mississippian groups in the lower Mississippi Valley.[20] Although no Fort Ancient ceramics have been found at Caborn-Welborn sites, both Oneota-style disk pipes and Fort Ancient-style vasiform pipes were present.[21]

Pipes, of course, were very important in greeting ceremonies among upper Mississippi Valley people, and pipe bowls often were presented or exchanged during such ceremonies.[22] Thus, the presence of nonlocal pipes at a settlement often is an indicator of external relationships. In eastern North America, external diplomatic relations were a male sphere of activity, so interaction patterns signified by pipes often differed considerably from those signified by pottery, which was made and used primarily by women.[23]

Only four Caborn-Welborn sites have produced European-related artifacts,[24] indicating that they were occupied beyond the mid-sixteenth century. All such artifacts of which I am aware are late-sixteenth- to early-seventeenth-century types.[25] The region may or may not have been populated much past that time.

Within *Fort Ancient* territory, there also was a coalescence of population during the fifteenth century. Whereas earlier settlements were located almost up to the headwaters of many Ohio River tributaries, after 1450 almost all settlements were located on the Ohio River or along the lower reaches of its tributaries.[26]

These late prehistoric and protohistoric sites are recognized by the presence of "horizon marker" artifacts. The Late Fort Ancient time period, about 1450 to 1650, which is designated the Madisonville Horizon, is defined by the presence of typical shell-tempered Madisonville-style pottery, among other artifacts,[27] although east-west attribute differences do occur.[28] Because women made the pottery, the relative stylistic homogeneity indicates that during this time there was frequent interaction—visiting and intermarriage—all along this stretch of the Ohio. The protohistoric period,[29] starting around 1550, is defined archaeologically by the presence of European metal and glass artifacts.[30]

Many of the Late Fort Ancient villages, like the last surviving Caborn-Welborn villages, were quite large in size. Some protohistoric Fort Ancient villages, such as the Madisonville site at present-day Cincinnati, which has been the focus of my own research,[31] may have appeared very similar to an artist's reconstruction of the Caborn-Welborn Slack Farm site,[32] with houses clustered around several small plaza areas, but others, such as the Buffalo site in West Virginia,[33] were more circular in plan. Buffalo and other Fort Ancient sites of this time period included very large houses in which probably lived extended kin groups.[34] The populations of such villages were significantly greater than most earlier communities.

In spite of much similarity in material culture, there were notable differences between eastern and western Fort Ancient peoples in personal adornment, burial patterns, settlement layouts, subsistence, and exchange networks.[35]

Western Fort Ancient people maintained their strongest interregional ties with groups living in northern Ohio and with Oneota peoples in northern Illinois and western Iowa.[36] The presence of many Oneota-style disk pipes with important male burials at the Madisonville site indicates formal, and strong, diplomatic relationships between the regions.[37] Western Fort Ancient people also interacted with Mississippian peoples in the central Mississippi River valley.[38]

Eastern Fort Ancient people interacted most intensively with Wellsburg people farther upriver along the Ohio,[39] with Whittlesey people in northeastern Ohio[40] and with Mississippian peoples in and around eastern

Tennessee;[41] they also may have received European glass beads and metal through Susquehannock groups in West Virginia and Pennsylvania.[42]

Burial patterns and grave goods at the Madisonville site indicate the likelihood that a two-tiered social organization, achieved rather than ascribed, was in place during the protohistoric period.[43] The large-sized, similarly shaped copper pendants buried with adults at four different western Fort Ancient sites[44] are interpreted as symbol badges probably signalling highest-level leadership and intervillage ties, and perhaps a regional peer polity or confederacy organization.[45] This appears to have been a late-sixteenth- to early-seventeenth-century phenomenon, because at least some of these badges were made from European kettle metal.

Upstream to the northeast of Fort Ancient territory in the sixteenth century were a few *Wellsburg* settlements.[46] By the second half of the century, these people seem to have moved southward, and started to form combined villages with eastern Fort Ancient people.[47] Note that this was well before the historically documented period of intense Iroquois warfare, which began in the 1640s.

There is no positive archaeological evidence for continued occupation of the Caborn-Welborn area or the Wellsburg area beyond the early 1600s. The small numbers of European artifacts from Caborn-Welborn and Wellsburg sites all would have been available before that time, so it seems likely that these settlements were depopulated by then. In the upper reaches of the Ohio, *Monongahela* settlements do not appear to have been occupied beyond the mid-1630s.[48]

The Fort Ancient area was occupied beyond that time, but exactly how long is uncertain. Much greater numbers and a greater variety of European-related artifacts, representing a longer time range, have come from Fort Ancient sites than from Caborn-Welborn or Wellsburg sites. This may reflect an extended occupation in Fort Ancient territory or simply a better and more continuous access to trade goods. However, the supply of European goods to the central Ohio Valley appears to have been cut off by the mid-seventeenth century.

At the western Fort Ancient Madisonville site, exchange relationships represented by European items are amazingly far-ranging and start remarkably early.[49] A child was buried with a brass Clarksdale bell, a type of artifact that has been associated with the 1539–43 Soto expedition in the Southeast but also is present at sites in the region occupied into the early seventeenth century.[50] Pieces from a distinctive style of copper kettle with iron fittings that was supplied by Basque fishermen in the St. Lawrence estuary during the late 1600s probably were obtained through Iroquoian middlemen in or near southern Ontario.[51] Glass beads are particularly sensitive horizon marker artifacts. The only type present at Madisonville dates to around 1600.[52] Artifacts made from thin metal tubes may have been manufactured at the site. The metal, the concept, and the technology probably came from the Iroquoian northeast, where spiral-shaped tubes originated.[53] Madisonville people seem to have been making coil shapes and serpent shapes, which were exchanged with people to the south and northwest.[54] Metal blanks, as well as many whole and broken finished pieces, have been found at the site. So, too, have a phenomenal number of pipe styles, confirming northeastern, southeastern, and midwestern contacts.[55] All European-related artifacts at the Madisonville site would have been available by the early 1600s; there is no evidence that the site was occupied much past that time.[56]

Eastern Fort Ancient settlements have produced some somewhat-later European artifacts, including a much greater variety of glass beads, a few of which were not available until after 1630, and large brass arm bands, otherwise known mainly from southeastern sites occupied after 1630.[57] These artifacts, plus the relatively large numbers of shell beads and engraved shell gorgets at eastern Fort Ancient sites[58] are evidence for significant interaction between eastern Fort Ancient and interior southeastern peoples.[59]

Neither eastern nor western Fort Ancient territory has produced midseventeenth-century gun parts, Jesuit rings, late-style brass bells, or any other typical trade items from the last half of the century.[60] Nor have any distinctive indigenous artifacts, such as pipe bowls, in late-seventeenth-century styles been excavated. While this does not prove that Fort Ancient territory was abandoned after the mid-1600s, population may well have dwindled dramatically. At the very least, judging from the dearth of European and other exotic artifacts, contacts with other regions appear to have been drastically curtailed.

It seems that archaeology takes us to the mid-seventeenth century in the central Ohio Valley, then leaves us dangling. Brief mentions of this region begin to appear in the historical record just after that time. Is it possible to connect the two records? Can we learn from the written records which historically known groups might have occupied the region and for how long, and where they might have gone? How does the archaeological chronology, obtained from radiocarbon dating and horizon marker artifacts such as European goods, fit in with the timing of historical events?

OHIO VALLEY HISTORY, 1660–1680

In the late 1660s and early 1670s, at least some portions of the Ohio River valley were still well populated. In 1668, La Salle in Montreal was told by a group of Seneca Iroquois that the river rose three days' journey from their homeland in western New York, "and that after a month's travel one came upon the *Honniasontkeronons* and the *Chiouanons* [southerners or Shawnees; usually interpreted as the latter], and that after having passed the latter, and a great cataract or waterfall that there is in this river [the falls of the Ohio, near Louisville], one found the *Outagame* [Fox] and the country of the *Iskousogos*."[61] In 1671, La Salle was told by Senecas about the Touguenhas, who lived on the Ohio; according to Hunter, this name was "the general Iroquois designation for the Algonquians to their west."[62] When Marquette and Joliet passed the mouth of the Ohio on their way down the Mississippi in 1673, they were told that the Chaoüanons who lived in the Ohio Valley had "as many as 23 villages in one district, and 15 in another, quite near one another."[63]

In 1670, some English explorers advanced to the headwaters of the New River, near the Virginia–West Virginia line, where they met some Mohetan Indians who informed them of "a great company of Indians that lived upon the great Water" to the northwest, presumably the Ohio River.[64] In 1674, an illiterate trader, Gabriell Arthur, was captured by Tomahittan Indians, with whom he visited the Monetons and probably traveled to the area near the confluence of the Kanawha and Ohio rivers, north of present-day Huntington, West Virginia.[65] Arthur, whose adventures later were recorded by his employer, spoke of a populous "nation" dispersed along a large, westward-flowing river, twenty days' journey from end to end. He gave a hatchet and knife to their "king" but saw no other iron tools during his stay, nor did the people he met know how to use guns.

Franquelin's map of 1684, based on secondhand information, placed "destroyed" villages of the Kentaientonga, the Oniassontke, the Casa, and the Mosapelea north of the Ohio from east to west, and the Chaskep and Meguatchaiki on a tributary south of the Ohio.[66] From the latter location ran a trail labeled as "a road by which the *Casquinampo* and the *Chaouenons* go to trade with the Spanish."[67]

Only a few of these names can be identified with historically known peoples,[68] and most of those were known from other evidence to have lived only on the periphery, not in the central Ohio Valley proper. The Chaouenons probably were Shawnees, who spoke a Central Algonquian language, although this term also was used more generally for "southerners." The Meguatchaiki mapped in the 1680s as living on a southern tributary of the Ohio are thought to have been the Mekoche division of the Shawnees, while the Chaskepe were "associated with the Shawnee."[69] Some historians have identified that river as the Cumberland, and have suggested the Cumberland River valley as the Shawnee homeland,[70] but this is questionable since there is no archaeological evidence that the valley was significantly populated during the protohistoric period.[71] The Outagame were the Fox, another Central Algonquian group, whose prehistoric homeland probably was north of the Ohio Valley proper; by the late 1660s, they had migrated to Wisconsin.[72] The Kentaientonga perhaps were related to the Eries,[73] who in the early seventeenth century lived close to the Lake Erie shore south of Niagara Falls. The Mosopelea, whom James Griffin places along the Mississippi River south of the Ohio during the 1670s, were of unknown linguistic affiliation.[74]

SHAWNEE ARCHAEOLOGY AND HISTORY, 1670–1750

Of all these named groups, only the Shawnees can be clearly identified as residents of the Ohio Valley proper, and traced in the historical record. Many historians and ethnohistorians have assumed or concluded that Fort Ancient people were the ancestors of the Shawnee.[75] To date, this has not been demonstrated from the archaeological record.

Although the locations, or approximate locations, of quite a few late-seventeenth- and early-eighteenth-century Shawnee settlements are known, at a variety of locations far from the Ohio Valley,[76] no large-scale excavation of such a site has yet taken place to test whether there is significant continuity with any protohistoric Ohio Valley archaeological tradition. Small-scale excavations, or data from ethnically mixed sites, have provided tantalizing clues, but not enough information to prove a hypothesis. For example, Fort Ancient-like pottery has been found at a 1655–1670 Seneca Iroquois site where Shawnee captives might have lived,[77] at a 1670s Susquehannock site in southeastern Pennsylvania near where Shawnees are known to have resided starting two decades later,[78] and at a French fort in Illinois, near where a group of several hundred Shawnees lived between 1683 and 1689.[79] The pottery at the Seneca village included both non–shell-tempered vessels that probably were locally made and two shell-tempered vessels that had contained red ochre.[80] In Alabama, no nonlocal artifact types were excavated at Tuckabatchee Town, said to have been strongly associated with one or more refugee groups of Shawnees.[81] Although Madisonville-style Fort Ancient pottery and typical Fort Ancient lithic artifacts have been excavated at a site within the bounds of Lower Shawneetown, a mid-eighteenth-century English-Shawnee trading town at the confluence of the Ohio and Scioto rivers, more excavation is necessary to confirm that the Fort Ancient materials are contemporaneous with the eighteenth-century settlement, rather than associated with an earlier occupation.[82]

Three burials in stone-lined graves were excavated adjacent to a known early-eighteenth-century "Shawanese town" in Pennsylvania.[83] Extant grave goods all were European trade items—there were no artifacts to provide ties to any sixteenth- or seventeenth-century Ohio Valley archaeological tradition. Stone-lined graves are the hallmark of pre-1500 Cumberland River valley people and also occur at some pre-1400 Fort Ancient sites. Only a few are known from later sites. They have been reported from small-scale excavations at one protohistoric Fort Ancient site, Larkin, in central Kentucky,[84] described further below, and in extremely small percentages from two more extensively excavated protohistoric eastern Fort Ancient sites, Hardin and Buffalo.[85] This possible connection bears further investigation.

In 1732, a Shawnee explanation to the governor of Pennsylvania of why their group had moved away from the Susquehanna Valley was that the Five Nations had told them to go, saying, "[Y]ou Shawanese, look back toward Ohio, the place from whence you came; and return thitherward."[86] Again, a westward connection, but no proof that they were descendants of the Fort Ancient people.

At present, what we can say from the archaeological and historical evidence is that at least some Shawnee groups definitely came from the larger Ohio River valley, but not necessarily from Fort Ancient territory.

Thus, of all the groups named in Euroamerican documents as Ohio Valley residents during the seventeenth century, only the Shawnees can be clearly identified and traced in the historical record. In terms of coalescence and dispersal, their historically recorded movements are extraordinarily complex. They are also instructive, in terms of the options and choices available to Native American groups of the interior during the early colonial period, so I will briefly summarize some of them.

Historically, the Shawnees consisted of five divisions, the Chalaakaatha, the Thawikila, the Mekoche, the Kishpoko, the Pekowi, and, perhaps in earlier times, a sixth, named Shawnee. These divisions embodied different functions within the tribe—for example, the Kishpoko were concerned with warfare and the Pekowi with ritual—and they maintained separate villages.[87] They also seem to have traveled separately. Members of different divisions turned up at different locations during the early colonial period; for instance, it was mainly Thawikila people who migrated to the Charles Towne, South Carolina, vicinity (see below). Only during a relatively short period of history, between about 1740 and 1775, did most of them reside together and act as a tribal entity. After that, they dispersed again, and now are settled in three separate locations in Oklahoma.[88]

Reconstructions of their movements from the late seventeenth through the early nineteenth centuries have been attempted by many researchers,[89] but they are extraordinarily complex.[90] Barry Kent has summarized the difficulties in tracing these people: "Their apparent proclivity for moving frequently and fragmenting into new bands makes them difficult to follow historically, and a real challenge to trace archaeologically." He remarks on "a great confusion of movements by the Shawnee, in and out of their towns, to new places, to towns with multi-ethnic compositions, etc."[91]

Individuals and groups of Shawnee people were first encountered by Europeans far from their putative homelands and from each other. They surfaced inland from Charles Towne soon after 1674, in Illinois in 1682, and in the newly established Commonwealth of Pennsylvania by 1692. Shawneetowns, Piquas, and Chillicothes—and the Savannah River—named after the tribe and its divisions, dot the map across this entire region.

In the south, near Augusta, Georgia, Henry Woodward in 1674 encountered two Shawnees traveling from St. Augustine.[92] His descriptions of trading possibilities at the newly established Charles Towne probably were instrumental in the arrival of a larger group of Thawikila Shawnees to the area somewhat later, who were well established on the upper reaches of the Savannah River by 1680[93] and became important middle-men in trade with the English. Many of them later migrated to Pennsylvania, but some moved west in 1715 after the Yamasee War, to the Coosa-Tallapoosa River region, perhaps joining Kishpoko Shawnees among the Creeks on the Tallapoosa; the latter may have lived among the Susque-hannocks until their 1675 defeat, then migrated south.[94] The Shawnee affiliation with the Creek Tukabatchee Town was so strong that a late-eighteenth-century Creek spokesman "professed that Tuckabatchee and Shawnee fires were one."[95]

A group of several hundred Shawnees resided for a time at the newly established French Fort St. Louis, on the Illinois River. In early 1681, reported René-Robert Cavelier, Sieur de La Salle, "[A] Shawanoe chief commanding a hundered and fifty warriors, living on the banks of a large river which flows into the Ohio, . . . sent [to La Salle] to ask for the protec-tion of the king"; La Salle's counterproposal was that the group should join him.[96] They arrived by the following year, first living among the Miami (another Algonquian group), then moving close to the fort, some remaining until 1689.[97]

For several decades starting in the early 1690s, Shawnees resided in eastern Pennsylvania. One of the first groups to be recorded, in 1692, came from Fort St. Louis at the invitation of some eastern Algonquians ("Wolf Indians," either Mahicans or Delawares).[98] Other groups arrived from the Savannah River region and the Ohio drainage.[99] To remain in Pennsylvania, Shawnee groups made peace with the League of the Iro-quois, assuming a subordinate status within the Covenant Chain and a special relationship with Delaware groups.[100]

By the mid-1720s, many Delaware and Shawnee groups were moving toward the upper Ohio, seeking better hunting and more land,[101] as did Seneca Iroquois from western New York, Wyandots (refugee Hurons), and others. By the 1740s, the two largest settlements in the Ohio Valley were Logstown (near present-day Economy, Pennsylvania), populated with Shawnees, Seneca Iroquois, Mahicans, and Algonkins, and Lower Shawneetown, at the mouth of the Scioto, with sixty cabins of Shawnees as well as members of other groups. During the late 1740s, Shawnees also occupied a village near the mouth of the Wabash,[102] and there were numerous small Seneca, Delaware, and Shawnee settlements along the main river, plus Miami villages on tributaries in western Ohio and Indiana, observed by Pierre-Joseph Céloron de Blainville during a 1749 mapping expedition.[103] Céloron's report and one from a similar French expedition in 1739 marked the first extensive eyewitness accounts of the valley.[104]

PUSH AND PULL FACTORS IN OHIO VALLEY POPULATION
MOVEMENTS

Now I will return briefly to "push" and "pull" factors influential in the seventeenth-century depopulation and the eighteenth-century repopulation of the central Ohio Valley. The archaeological evidence and the historical evidence, although useful in combination, are not always in complete agreement.

Iroquois Warfare. Was Iroquois warfare a major factor in depopulating the Ohio Valley? It seems to have played a part, but perhaps was not as major a factor as many researchers have assumed or implied. The Iroquois did claim the Ohio Valley in the eighteenth century through right of conquest, but recent historians have vigorously disputed the validity of this claim.[105]

During the 1660s and 1670s, the French recorded a handful of references to Iroquois raids into the Ohio Valley and/or the country of the Chaouanons, but no massacres or large numbers of captives—nothing to compare, for instance, with the six hundred dead and seven hundred captives that are said to have resulted from a 1681 raid against the Illini.[106]

French references to the Ohio Valley region during this period include the following. In the late 1660s, Nicolas Perrot stated that since the "Iroquois could no longer make war on their neighbors . . . they therefore sought to carry it into the country of the Andastes [Susquehannocks] and the Chaouanons, whom they routed in several encounters. From these tribes they considerably augmented their own forces . . ."; in contrast, in 1672 he reported that an Iroquois war party had failed to accomplish anything against the Chaouanons.[107] The famous 1673 quotation from Marquette's journal about the occupants of the Ohio Valley states that the Chaouanons who lived there "are not at all warlike, and are the nations whom the Iroquois go so far to seek, and war against."[108] The successor to Father Marquette's mission in Illinois, Father Alloues, described the Chaouanons whom he found living among the Miamis as "tribes who live much Farther away Toward the South, whom the Iroquois War has compelled to abandon their own country."[109] Franquelin's suspect map of 1684 labels all the villages along the Ohio drainage as "destroyed," but Griffin notes that an earlier draft of the map does not so label the villages.[110]

In the archaeological record, there is no "smoking gun" to indicate an escalation of warfare in the 1660s. There is no evidence for massacres at well-excavated protohistoric Fort Ancient settlements, although occasional male burials with healed or unhealed wounds from projectile points or war clubs indicate that low-level conflict was endemic both prehistorically and protohistorically.[111] Scalping was identified on one of nine burials excavated at the protohistoric Larkin site near Lexington, Kentucky, on one of two males who probably sustained traumatic injuries from associated projectile points.[112] Ceramic grave goods at the site were consistent in style (but not disposition) with Fort Ancient pottery, but the stone-lined graves are unusual for this late period. A comparison with stone-lined graves from a probable historical Shawnee cemetery in Pennsylvania (see above) would be of great interest.

Because few protohistoric Fort Ancient sites have been completely excavated, it is unclear whether palisades were consistently present. The three sites where they definitely were present are near the southeastern and northeastern edges of Fort Ancient territory.[113]

Another possible indicator of warfare would be the presence of refugee groups. At the western Fort Ancient Madisonville site, mortuary pottery from, or in the style of, northern Ohio indicates the presence of nonlocal people, but it is not concentrated at a single location within the site, so inmarriage and/or visiting are more likely than group migration.[114] To the east, Wellsburg settlements in the upper Ohio Valley did apparently move southward during the mid-1500s, with a Wellsburg site located close to Fort Ancient territory by the second half of the century.[115] Two of the most northerly eastern Fort Ancient settlements, both of which were palisaded, contained approximately equal proportions of Wellsburg- and Madisonville-style pottery.[116] At the late-sixteenth-century Bosman site, the different pottery types were segregated within the site, but at the early-seventeenth-century Neale's Landing site they were not, and a mixed-attribute style also was present, probably indicating integration. The timing, however, does not coincide with historically recorded fierce Iroquois warfare, which took place mainly after 1640.

European protection. A factor not specifically listed by Smith would be the "pull" of protection from attack. The historical records foreground this motive in several instances, such as the Shawnees from the Ohio River drainage who were induced to join La Salle at Fort St. Louis in 1682. Europeans, of course, often encouraged Native American groups to settle nearby in order to provide protection for the Europeans. Near Charles Towne, for instance, Shawnee settlements on the Savannah provided a buffer zone to protect the European settlement, and Shawnee warriors in 1680 helped rout the Westos, who had been attacking European settlements.

Alliances. In previous work, based more on archaeology than history, I have suggested that migrations from the Ohio River valley during the seventeenth century in many cases would have been toward peoples with whom there already were established exchange partnerships and alliances.[117]

The archaeological record led me to expect that western Fort Ancient people would have been most likely to have traveled northwest, toward Oneota groups with whom they seem to have had a relationship cemented by the ritual ceremonialism of pipe exchange. Fort Ancient-like pottery at mid-seventeenth-century Illinois sites and typical Illinois pottery types at the Madisonville site[118] are strong evidence of reciprocal visitation. Because of mid-seventeenth-century Iroquois depredations on the populations there, I ruled out northern Ohio, with which there seems to have been a strong prehistoric relationship, as a protohistoric migration destination for Fort Ancient people.

I expected that eastern Fort Ancient people would most likely have traveled south, toward Mississippian groups from which they had received engraved shell gorgets and other shell ornaments, and perhaps east, toward Susquehannock groups, who may have supplied glass beads and brass during the early seventeenth century. For eastern Fort Ancient people, there did seem to be evidence for a seventeenth-century relationship with proto-Creek and Creek villages on the Tennessee, Coosa, and Tallapoosa rivers, objectified by the distribution of large brass armbands.[119]

Upon further investigation of historical records, some of these suggestions have held up, but some have not been confirmed. For the one historically documented Ohio Valley group that I could investigate, the Shawnees, there were indeed connections to the historical Creek, at Tukabatchee Town, but the chronology and archaeology still are shadowy.[120] There are hints in the historical and archaeological literature that some Shawnees were living with Susquehannocks before the defeat of the latter in 1675,[121] but a more concerted effort is needed to bring this information together.

From the Euroamerican historical record, other late-seventeenth-century Shawnee locations—on the Savannah River, at Fort St. Louis in Illinois, and in eastern Pennsylvania—seem to have been more at the invitation or instigation of Europeans or the result of recently developed relationships with indigenous groups, rather than being associated with long-standing alliances visible in the archaeological record. This might perhaps be evidence against equating the Shawnee and Fort Ancient peoples. More research is needed here, too.

European trade. Until the early seventeenth century, there was a flow of metal into western Fort Ancient territory from Basque and French traders on the St. Lawrence, via Iroquoian middlemen living near Niagara Falls.[122] The establishment of a Dutch trading center on the Hudson River around 1614 apparently disrupted this link,[123] so these Ohio Valley people might have sought other sources.

From the historical record, European trade seems to have been a "pull" to the Shawnees who lived on the Savannah River between the mid-1670s and the Yamasee War. In 1680, they aided the English in ousting the Westos, assuming middleman status between Charles Towne and groups farther west and also becoming involved in the slave trade.[124] One Shawnee group that was induced to come to Pennsylvania was engaged in the fur trade,[125] but another seems mainly to have been concerned with finding land on which to settle.[126]

Disease. Archaeologists have speculated that epidemic disease might have been a factor in the depopulation of the Ohio Valley.[127] To date, however, no archaeological evidence, such as mass burials, has been uncovered to support this hypothesis.[128]

Subsistence. At the western Fort Ancient Madisonville site, early-seventeenth-century out-migration might have been related to a change of subsistence. Prehistorically, Fort Ancient people were maize horticulturalists, who also hunted local animals such as deer. At Madisonville, bison products became important during the protohistoric period, as evidenced by the late appearance of bison-bone hide scrapers in the archaeological assemblage. Their locations in refuse pits were statistically correlated with the presence of copper and brass, so this appears to have been a late-sixteenth- to early-seventeenth-century phenomenon.[129] Bison were more numerous to the west, in the prairie peninsula region of Illinois and beyond. The presence of Oneota-style disk pipes with important male burials at Madisonville indicates strong positive relationships with Upper Midwest groups, so it is possible that at least some Madisonville residents ultimately were drawn to that region.[130] If they were, they cannot be identified with the Shawnee group that arrived in Illinois in 1682, since its leader made his initial approach directly to the French leader, La Salle, rather than to or through an indigenous leader.

Since the Oneota archaeological tradition is strongly associated with Siouan speakers such as the Ioway,[131] who historically lived beyond the Mississippi River, it is possible that some western Fort Ancient people may have joined bison-hunting groups living west of the Mississippi. Further archaeological and historical research is warranted.

Shawnees who moved to Pennsylvania from Fort St. Louis in the late 1600s at the inducement of some Delawares seem to have been motivated by the desire for land on which to settle.[132] It is not clear why the eastern location was deemed preferable to the rich prairie lands of Illinois, but later accounts (ca. 1749) do report political friction between some Shawnees and some Illini.[133]

Certainly, the eighteenth-century migration from Pennsylvania to the Ohio Valley had to do with subsistence. Colonists in Pennsylvania were encroaching on land occupied by Delawares and Shawnees,[134] and Ohio Territory offered a much better opportunity for both horticulture and hunting.

Migration preparations. Many researchers have viewed the movements of peripatetic groups like the Shawnees as inexplicable "wanderings." Barry Kent, for instance, describes Shawnee migrations as "a great confusion of movements."[135] But there is evidence in the historical record that one of the tenets of David Anthony's migration model—scouting expeditions before mass movement—was indeed at work.[136] In the case of the Shawnees, even when long-distance travels were not necessarily associated with prior alliances, they did not occur haphazardly. For example, the inquiry that La Salle received from a Shawnee chief about protection from the French that brought an invitation to settle in Illinois took almost two years to come to fruition.[137] And Shawnees who accompanied Delawares east from Fort St. Louis turned out to be only a small portion of their group. They entered into negotiations with the English, then

requested that "some Christians" return with them to their settlement. A
year and a half later, a much larger group of Shawnees appeared.[138]

CONCLUSION

Tracing protohistoric and early historical population movements, fragmentation, and coalescence requires all the evidence we can muster.
Archaeological and historical records, used in concert, will provide a
much sounder basis for conclusions than either used alone. Regarding the
region that I have been studying, there clearly is much work yet to be
done.

The Cultural Landscape of the North Carolina Piedmont at Contact

R. P. STEPHEN DAVIS, JR.

In late December 1700, John Lawson and a party of six Englishmen and four Indians set out from Charles Town to conduct a reconnaissance survey of Carolina for the colony's Lords Proprietors. By the time he arrived at the English settlement on Pamlico Sound almost two months later, Lawson had traversed some six hundred miles through the Carolina backcountry, describing the natural and cultural geography he encountered along the way. During the first leg of his journey, along the Santee and Wateree rivers, he visited villages of the Santee, Congaree, and Wateree Indians. Next, he entered the territory of the eighteenth-century Catawba, where he encountered the Waxhaw, Esaw, Sugaree, and Kadapau. From Kadapau, Lawson's party left the Catawba-Wateree valley and headed northeast along the Great Trading Path, which ran from the James River in Virginia to the Savannah River at Augusta. Crossing the North Carolina piedmont and its swift-flowing rivers, he visited the palisaded villages of the Saponi along the Yadkin River, the Keyauwee along Caraway Creek, and the Occaneechi along the Eno River. Other tribes who lived in nearby villages, but who were not visited by Lawson's party, included the Tutelo, Sissipahaw, Shakori, Eno, and Adshusheer. Heeding the warning given him by a Virginia trader near Achonechy Town that an Iroquois raiding party had been sighted in the area, Lawson left the Trading Path and headed east toward the English settlements on the Pamlico River, a route that took him through the heart of Tuscarora territory.

LINGUISTIC AND ARCHAEOLOGICAL IDENTIFICATION

With the exception of the Tuscarora, who were an Iroquoian-speaking people, all of the tribes encountered by Lawson have since been identified as "eastern Siouan." This linguistic identification was made late in the nineteenth century by Albert Gatschet[1] for the Catawba and by Horatio Hale[2] for the Tutelo. James Mooney, using scanty linguistic evidence for some groups and ethnohistorical information for most others, further argued that over two dozen neighboring tribes mentioned by early travelers and explorers also were Siouan.[3] Given that no direct linguistic evidence exists for many of these groups, their classification as Siouan speakers cannot be substantiated. According to Mooney, the area of Siouan-speaking peoples during the seventeenth century extended from the upper Rappahannock River in north-central Virginia to the Congaree and Santee rivers of central South Carolina, and from the Blue Ridge to the fall line. In southeastern North Carolina and South Carolina, Siouan peoples also inhabited the lower reaches of the Cape Fear, Pee Dee, and Santee rivers as far as the Atlantic coast. To the east, the Siouans were bounded by the Algonkian-speaking tribes of the Powhatan Confederacy and the Nottoway, Meherrin, and Tuscarora, who spoke Iroquoian languages; to the west and south they were bounded by the Cherokee and Muskogean peoples.

Two separate divisions of Siouan peoples were proposed by John Swanton[4] and Frank Speck[5] based on significant linguistic differences between Tutelo and Catawba and the historical association of other groups with these two peoples. They included within a northern, or Tutelo, division the various tribes of the Manahoac and Monacan confederacies, located in central Virginia when Jamestown was established in 1607, and the Saponi, Tutelo, and Occaneechi who resided along the Roanoke River and its tributaries during the second half of the 1600s. This latter region is represented by the Dan River phase and related complexes during the late prehistoric period.[6] Archaeologically, these complexes reflect a continuation of a Late Woodland cultural tradition and show little Mississippian influence. Villages were located along streams with substantial bottomlands and were composed of simple circular or oval houses constructed of saplings and bark. These houses were arranged in a circle, facing an open plaza, and were surrounded by a palisade. With the exception of the Fredricks site, which had a large communal sweat lodge, none of the late prehistoric or historic villages excavated in piedmont North Carolina and Virginia has produced any evidence of public architecture (fig. 1).[7]

The other groups identified as Siouan, located in North Carolina and South Carolina during the early eighteenth century, were placed by Swanton and Speck in a southern, or Catawba, division. However, unlike the northern division, the usefulness of a southern division is problematic, given the cultural, geographic, and probable linguistic diversity repre-

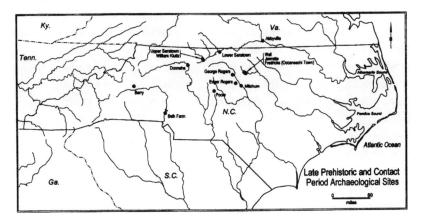

Fig. 1. Archaeological sites of the late prehistoric and contact periods.

sented by the groups contained within it.[8] Booker, Hudson, and Rankin refer to the languages of these people as Catawban and argue that they should not be called "Siouan."[9] The northern and central North Carolina piedmont was home to the Sara, Eno, Shakori, Sissipahaw, Adshusheer, and Keyauwee, while the Sugaree, Waxhaw, and groups collectively known as Catawba in the eighteenth century were located along the lower reaches of the Catawba River near present-day Rock Hill, South Carolina. Below the Catawba were the Wateree, Congaree, and Santee, and the coastal region between the North Carolina sounds and the Ashley River was home to the Woccon, Waccamaw, Cape Fear, Pedee, Winyah, and Sewee.

While the area inhabited by southern-division tribes also is much more diverse archaeologically for the late prehistoric period, many sites throughout the southern part of the region possess archaeological traits— such as evidence for public buildings and earthworks, distinctive mortuary and architectural patterns, and Lamar-style pottery—that are commonly associated with South Appalachian Mississippian.[10] The region occupied by the Congaree, Wateree, Waxhaw, Sugaree, and Catawba in the early eighteenth century approximates the territory controlled by the chiefdom of Cofitachequi during the mid-sixteenth century[11]; however, the archaeological data from this area are not sufficient to assess any possible relationship between the two. Chester DePratter has argued that the Cofitachequi abandoned the Wateree valley just before 1700.[12] To the north, the late prehistoric archaeological complexes along the middle and upper Catawba valley, as well as within the upper reaches of the Yadkin valley, also show strong Lamar influence. David Moore believes that the peoples of this region—whom he calls Catawba Valley Mississippians—gradually moved down the Catawba valley during the late sixteenth and seventeenth centuries and became the Catawba of the early eighteenth century.[13] Conversely, archaeological complexes associated with the Sara, Keyauwee, Sissipahaw, and Shakori—including Dan River, Hillsboro, Saratown, Caraway, and Jenrette phases—exhibit only slight South Appalachian Mississippian influence, mostly with respect to Lamar-like pottery surface treatments. This suggests that these groups are not closely related culturally to the Catawba-Wateree valley groups. Even more problematic is the likelihood that the late prehistoric Dan River phase of the upper Roanoke drainage is ancestral to both the southern-division Sara and the northern-division Tutelo and Saponi.

SIOUAN ETHNOHISTORY AND CULTURAL GEOGRAPHY

One problem that has plagued Siouan studies is the relative paucity of ethnohistoric information. As Mooney observed more than a century ago, the native peoples of piedmont Carolina and Virginia "were of but small importance politically; no sustained mission work was ever attempted among them, and there were but few literary men to take an interest in them. War, pestilence, whisky and systematic slave hunts had nearly exterminated the aboriginal occupants of the Carolinas before anybody had thought them of sufficient importance to ask who they were, how they lived, or what were their beliefs and opinions."[14] The written records that do exist present a picture of rapid culture change as native peoples sought to cope in a variety of ways with the forces of disease, trade, and conflict that were largely beyond their control.

Although John Lawson has left us with our most detailed account of the Siouan tribes of the North and South Carolina piedmont, the cultural landscape he witnessed bore little resemblance to the one that existed a century or even half a century before. Lawson recognized this, remarking that "[t]he Small-Pox and Rum have made such a Destruction amongst them, that, on good grounds, I do believe, there is not the sixth Savage living within two hundred Miles of all our Settlements, as there were fifty years ago."[15] This process of depopulation is reflected by the frequent abandonment and relocation of villages and the merging of tribes to create new societies; unfortunately, the details of this process are vague, due to the spotty nature of the ethnohistoric literature.

The ethnohistory of the piedmont begins with the explorations of Hernando de Soto in 1540 and Juan Pardo in 1566 and 1567. These Spanish explorers penetrated the Catawba-Wateree valley at the southwestern edge of Siouan territory. Here they contacted native peoples who later became known collectively as Catawba. David Moore has recently argued that the sixteenth-century ancestors of the eighteenth-century Catawba are represented in the middle and upper Catawba valley by the Low and Burke phases,[16] and Rob Beck has identified the Berry site, a Burke phase mound center located on a tributary of the upper Catawba River near Morganton, as the village of Xuala visited by Soto and Joara visited by Pardo.[17] Beck has argued further that the Joara (Xuala) to Chiaha routes of both explorers likely crossed the mountains along the Toe River valley and not the French Broad valley as Charles Hudson and others first hypothesized.[18]

After the Soto and Pardo expeditions, there were few recorded contacts between Europeans and piedmont Indians until the mid-1600s, when English traders and explorers began to penetrate the inner coastal plain and piedmont south and west of the James River. Before this time, direct trade between the English and Indians in Virginia was limited largely to the Chesapeake Bay. Following the Second Pamunkey War of 1644–1645, which reduced the members of the Powhatan Confederacy to tributary status, the Virginia colony established forts at the falls of the James, Pamunkey, and Appomattox rivers to protect the colony's western frontier. Fort Henry, located on the Appomattox River at present-day Petersburg, quickly became a commercial center for trade with the Siouan tribes to the southwest. The earliest reported expedition out of Fort Henry was led by Edward Bland in 1650 and sought to establish a trade with the Tuscarora to the south.[19] Bland's narrative was used by Lewis Binford to identify territories and settlements of the Nottoway, Meherrin, and Tuscarora along the fall line, and it also provides the first reference to the Occaneechi residing on the Roanoke River.[20]

Knowledge of the native cultural landscape of southern Virginia and northern North Carolina greatly increased during the early 1670s with the written accounts of three separate explorations. The first of these was by a German physician named John Lederer, who sought a route across the Appalachian Mountains.[21] In 1669 and 1670, Lederer made three westward journeys from tidewater Virginia. His first and third expeditions explored the York and Rappahannock valleys to the Blue Ridge; on his second expedition he traveled southwest from the falls of the James River through the Virginia and Carolina piedmont. According to Cumming, Lederer's second journey in 1670 took him to the Monacan and Mahock along the James River, the Saponi and Nahyssan on the Staunton River, the Occaneechi on the Roanoke River just below the confluence of the Dan and Staunton rivers at present-day Clarksville, the Eno and Shakori within the upper Neuse drainage, the Watary and Sara within the Yadkin or Deep River drainages, and the Wisacky and Ushery on the Catawba River.[22] Some researchers have dismissed Lederer's narrative, in large part because he described the Ushery, or Catawba, as living along the banks of a great lake of brackish water.[23] While this portion of his account probably is not based on firsthand information, most of the other villages that he visited appear to be accurately placed geographically; unfortunately, with the exception of the Jenrette site, which may be the Shakori village of Shakor, none of the other villages has been identified archaeologically, and no archaeological evidence exists for placing the Sara south of the Dan River before the eighteenth century.

The following year, Thomas Batts and Robert Fallam undertook a westward expedition from Fort Henry for Abraham Wood, the fort's commander and a trader.[24] The purpose of this enterprise was to establish a fur trade to rival the French, as well as to find a passable route westward beyond the mountains and to search for precious metals.[25] Batts and Fallam visited the Saponi village on the Staunton River that John Lederer had visited the previous year and also visited a Totero, or Tutelo, village further upriver, probably in the vicinity of Roanoke. From there, they proceeded further west and reached New River, a headwater of the Ohio. The Batts and Fallam and Lederer accounts provide our only documentary evidence for placing the Tutelo and Saponi along the Staunton River at first contact. If these groups were located there prehistorically, then they are almost surely represented archaeologically by the Dan River phase. Shortly after these two expeditions, the Tutelo and Saponi moved downstream and joined the Occaneechi near the confluence of the Staunton and Dan rivers.[26]

In 1673, Abraham Wood sponsored another expedition led by James Needham to establish trade with the Tomahittans, or Tomahitas, who lived beyond the mountains of western North Carolina, probably in eastern

Tennessee. The Tomahittans occupied a heavily fortified town and apparently were a Cherokee group; however, Waselkov has suggested that they were a relocated Hichiti-speaking group living in the upper Coosa drainage.[27] Information about this expedition is contained in a 1674 letter from Wood to John Richards of London and is the only significant ethnohistoric document about English explorations into the interior that was not available to James Mooney.[28] The expedition party, consisting of Needham, Gabriel Arthur, and eight Indians, departed from Fort Henry and traveled along the Trading Path to the Occaneechi settlement on Occaneechi Island. From there, they journeyed southwest for nine days to Sitteree and then another fifteen days to the Tomahittans' town. Sitteree has not been identified, but it may have been a Siouan village in the upper Yadkin valley. In his letter, Wood remarked that Sitteree was the last Indian settlement encountered until Needham's party was within two days of the Tomahittans. This is consistent with archaeological data which indicate that the western piedmont and northwest mountains of North Carolina were largely unoccupied during the seventeenth and early eighteenth centuries.[29]

After a short stay, Needham returned to Fort Henry and left Arthur with the Tomahittans to learn their language. Wood wrote that, on the journey back to retrieve Arthur, Needham and his Occaneechi guide Hasecoll traveled from Occhonechee (Occaneechi) to Aeno (Eno) and then to Sarrah (Sara). This sequence of villages, with the omission of Shakor and Watary, corresponds to the sequence of piedmont Siouan villages visited by Lederer three years earlier. From Sarrah, Needham traveled a short distance to a Yattken (Yadkin) town on the Yadkin River, where he was killed by his Indian guide during a violent argument. Gabriel Arthur eventually made his way back to Fort Henry after traveling extensively throughout the Southeast with his Tomahittan hosts; however, his story is not of concern here.

Archaeological evidence indicates that, during the 1670s, the Sara were living along the Dan River in the area known historically as Upper Saratown, and the topographic setting of the Upper Saratown site fits well with Lederer's description.[30] Furthermore, this area is only about twenty miles northeast of the Great Bend of the Yadkin River where the Donnaha site is located. Although excavations at Donnaha did not identify a seventeenth-century component, the site does have a substantial late prehistoric occupation.[31] The identity of the Yadkin village is unknown; however, Swanton suggests on geographical grounds that they may have been related to the Sara or Keyauwee.[32]

While there are no further ethnohistoric accounts of native peoples in piedmont North Carolina until John Lawson in 1701, historic documents do exist concerning the demise of the Occaneechi during Bacon's Rebellion in 1676.[33] At the time of the rebellion, the region below the confluence of the Dan and Staunton rivers, where the Trading Path crossed the Roanoke River, was occupied by the Occaneechi, Susquehannock, Tutelo, Saponi, and perhaps others. An anonymous writer of the period remarked that Occaneechi Island was "the Mart for all the Indians for att [sic] least 500 miles."[34] The congregation of tribes at this location was probably due as much to the protection it afforded against Iroquois raiding as to the attraction of the fur trade.

The year 1676 was clearly pivotal in the history of relations between Virginians and piedmont Indians. During the two decades before Bacon's Rebellion, the Occaneechi established themselves as middlemen and controlled much of the trade from Occaneechi Island. Archaeological evidence, as well as historical accounts, further suggest that the Occaneechi probably were successful in restricting direct access to the trade by more remote groups.[35] Following the rebellion, the Occaneechi abandoned their island home, and southern Virginia and the Carolina piedmont were opened up to Virginia traders. As John Lawson witnessed a few years later, the exchange of furs and deerskins for European goods now took place in Indian villages along the Trading Path and not at a more distant trading center at the edge of the Virginia colony. And, because the focus of the Virginia trade was on the more populous Catawba and Cherokee, participation in the trade probably caused many smaller tribes in the intervening region to reposition their settlements along the Trading Path.

One could easily argue that Lawson's view of the piedmont's cultural landscape in 1701 is biased, since he did not deviate from the Trading Path between the lower Catawba valley and Occaneechi Town. He did not visit any villages off the trail until he left the Occaneechi and headed eastward toward the village of Adshusheer, and some other groups such as the Sara and Sissipahaw clearly did not reside along the path at this time. Still, present archaeological evidence for the central and northern North Carolina piedmont suggests that most Siouan villages were aligned with the Trading Path (either directly on the path or close to it), and no areas of significant occupation have been identified away from this trail other than the upper Dan drainage where the Sara lived during the seventeenth and early eighteenth centuries.[36]

FACTORS OF CULTURE CHANGE

The character of the cultural landscape that Lawson witnessed was short lived due primarily to four factors: (1) depopulation; (2) the impact of Iroquois raiding; (3) changes in the fur trade; and (4) the Tuscarora, Yamasee, and Cheraw wars. Archaeological evidence suggests that significant depopulation of the Carolina piedmont did not occur until the latter half of the seventeenth century, and that the period of greatest population loss coincided with the opening of the piedmont for English traders after Bacon's Rebellion.[37] Early contact-period sites such as Lower Saratown, Mitchum, and Jenrette contain comparatively few burials, whereas sites that date to the period from about 1680 until the early 1700s, such as Upper Saratown, William Kluttz, and Occaneechi Town, reflect very high mortality rates. As an example, twenty-five burials in three cemeteries are associated with Occaneechi Town, a settlement that was probably occupied for less than a decade by no more than fifty to seventy-five people.[38] Additionally, excavations over a ten-year period at Upper Saratown uncovered about 25 percent of that site and exposed over one hundred burials. Lawson's observation in 1709 that the native population of Carolina had declined by five-sixths during the preceding fifty years probably was not too much of an exaggeration.[39] As individual villages diminished in size, their inhabitants combined with neighbors to form new communities. The Eno, Shakori, and Adshusheer had joined together by the time of Lawson's journey, and the Saponi and Tutelo at this time also were closely aligned and by 1714 had merged with the Occaneechi, Meipontski, and Steukenhocks at Fort Christanna.[40] The Sara and Keyauwee also merged sometime during the early 1700s and by 1743 were a constituent of the Catawba Nation.[41]

Iroquois raids clearly affected native peoples in the piedmont during this period, and they probably also contributed to the frequent relocation of Siouan villages.[42] Lawson was constantly reminded by Indians and English traders he met of the threat of "Sinnager" raiding parties, and William Byrd II, writing in 1733 about the Saras' abandonment of the Dan River valley, remarked that "the frequent inroads of the Senecas annoyed them incessantly and obliged them to remove from this fine situation about thirty years ago. They then retired more southerly as far as the Pee Dee River and incorporated with the Keyauwees, where a remnant of them is still surviving."[43] Even after the Saponi, Tutelo, and Occaneechi sought protection from the Virginia colonial government at Fort Christ-anna, depredations at the hands of the Iroquois persisted.[44] While the Albany Conference with the Five Nations in 1722 was largely successful in halting these raids, Mooney notes that Iroquois attacks on the Sara as late as 1726 caused them to incorporate with the Catawba.[45]

Changes in the fur trade also affected the cultural landscape of pied-mont North Carolina during the late 1600s. Before 1676, the trade was dominated by Virginians operating out of Fort Henry and working through the Occaneechi as middlemen. Following the establishment of an English settlement at Charles Town in 1670, South Carolinians were quick to engage the native population in trade. By 1700, South Carolina was Virginia's chief trade rival and, because Charles Town was in a much better position geographically to conduct commerce with the Catawba as well as the Cherokee and Creek, the Virginia merchants suffered greatly. Other factors, such as depopulation from disease and the economic rise of tobacco, also affected the gradual demise of the Virginia trade. The native population occupying the piedmont between Virginia and the Catawba had been so greatly reduced by disease that trade with these groups alone was no longer profitable. As the profits from trade declined, prominent Virginia merchants, such as William Byrd I, increasingly turned to grow-ing tobacco. With the decline of the Virginia trade, the Trading Path no longer offered the advantages it once had for settlement location, and it was gradually abandoned in favor of places nearer to the English settle-ments of South Carolina and Virginia.

Finally, the Southern Indian Wars of the early eighteenth century irre-versibly altered the native cultural landscapes of both Carolina colonies.[46] The first of these was the Tuscarora War, which began in 1711 with the capture and execution of John Lawson and attacks on settlers along the lower Pamlico, Neuse, and Trent rivers. Between 1711 and 1713, expedi-tions led by John Barnwell and James Moore of South Carolina defeated the lower Tuscarora along the Neuse River, the Tar River, and Contentnea Creek. Both expeditions were composed of large bodies of warriors from the Yamasee, Cherokee, Catawba, Sara, and several other piedmont tribes. After their defeat, most of the lower Tuscarora left the southern

coastal plain of North Carolina and fled north to live with the Five Nations
Iroquois.

The subsequent Yamasee and Cheraw wars of 1715–1718 had a greater
and more direct impact on the Siouan peoples of the Carolina piedmont.
Dissatisfied with unfair trading practices and the way they were treated
by their English allies during the Tuscarora War, and having seen firsthand how weak the English plantations and towns really were, most of the
Siouan tribes (including the Catawba, Sara, Sugaree, Waccamaw, and
Cape Fear) who had fought under Barnwell and Moore now joined the
Yamasee and Creek in their attack on the South Carolina low country.
These efforts were unsuccessful and resulted in heavy losses for many of
the Siouan groups. However, the wars also had a positive effect on native
peoples. Channels of communication were strengthened and cooperation
increased among these groups, and the Catawba emerged as the most
prominent of the Siouan tribes. Merrell has argued that the effects of making war and making peace were the same: they promoted cooperation
among the piedmont Siouans and permitted the subsequent consolidation
of most of the remaining native population along the lower Catawba
River.[47]

MAPPING THE CULTURAL LANDSCAPE

From the preceding discussion, it should be clear that geographical information for the North Carolina piedmont during the seventeenth century
is at best vague and sketchy. Still, the combining of such data with archaeological information makes it possible to map in preliminary fashion the
cultural landscape of this period. What follows is a series of eight maps
which convey our present understanding of how the piedmont was populated at different dates between about 1540 and 1720. The dates selected
are those about which we have sufficient ethnohistoric information to
form reasonable conceptions of the cultural landscape.

Many of the spatial gaps between the phases or territories shown on
these maps likely represent unpopulated areas or buffers between culturally distinct peoples; however, in some instances they may be simply a
product of inadequate ethnohistoric or archaeological survey data. Likewise, territory size varies depending on the quality of available information: that is, territories defined by "good" data tend to be smaller than
those defined by "poor" data. In general, archaeological survey coverage

for the North Carolina piedmont is incomplete, and the late prehistoric ceramic chronology for this region as a whole is not tightly defined. None of the maps is based on comprehensive, systematic study of all available information; instead, each can best be viewed as a first approximation.

Maps of the Cultural Landscape in 1540, 1567, and 1600[48]

Figures 2 and 3 show the locations of mid-to-late sixteenth-century cultural phases, as defined by archaeology, and the routes taken through the central South Carolina and western North Carolina piedmont by Hernando de Soto in 1540 and Juan Pardo in 1567.[49] Few sites have been excavated which date to this period, the most notable one being the Berry site on Warrior Fork in the upper Catawba drainage. Both Moore and Beck have suggested, based on the occurrence of sixteenth-century Spanish artifacts (including olive jar fragments, a Caparra Blue Majolica sherd, and a grayware sherd recovered from undisturbed mound fill and the surface), that this single-mound center may have been Soto's Xuala and Pardo's Joara.[50]

Although the Hillsboro phase Wall site on the Eno River probably had

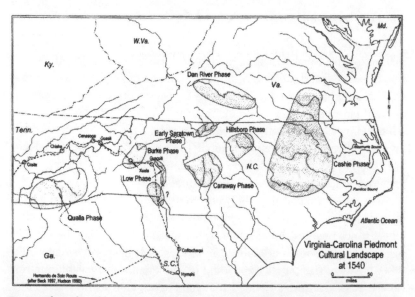

Fig. 2. The cultural landscape of the Virginia–North Carolina piedmont at 1540.

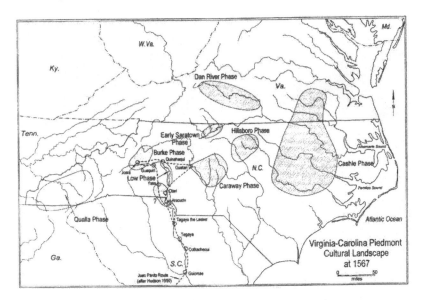

Fig. 3. The cultural landscape of the Virginia–North Carolina piedmont at 1567.

been abandoned by the mid-1500s, it appears to be typical of protohistoric settlements of the northern Carolina piedmont. It was a small, circular, palisaded village that covered about 1.25 acres and likely had no more than 150 residents. Other related Hillsboro phase sites, such as the George Rogers and Edgar Rogers sites in the nearby Haw River drainage, are located along smaller streams and represent clusters of scattered households.[51]

Figure 4 shows the piedmont cultural landscape at about 1600, based on archaeology and ethnohistory at earliest contact with the English. At this time, the northern-division Siouans, including the Manahoac, Monacan, Tutelo, and Saponi, were located in central Virginia, and the southern-division Siouans, with the possible exception of the Occaneechi, occupied piedmont North Carolina. The placement of the Occaneechi within the Hillsboro phase is at best tenuous, being based solely on general ceramic similarities between Hillsboro pottery and known Occaneechi pottery made nearly a century later. Archaeological evidence suggests that the resident populations of the Roanoke and Catawba-Wateree drainages were substantially larger than the population of the intervening Yadkin-Pee Dee, Cape Fear, and Neuse basins. And the upper Catawba val-

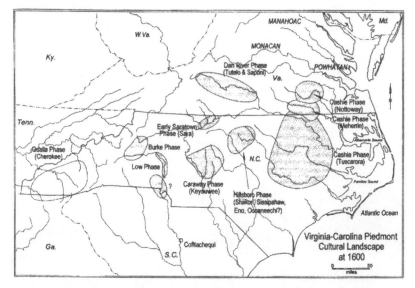

Fig. 4. The cultural landscape of the Virginia–North Carolina piedmont at 1600.

ley may have been largely vacant by 1600. The Siouan tribes of the southern North Carolina coastal plain and South Carolina have not been mapped because of insufficient information.

Map of the Cultural Landscape in 1650[52]

Figure 5 shows the piedmont cultural landscape at about 1650. The only ethnohistoric source for this period is Edward Bland, who traveled south from Fort Henry along the fall line and either encountered or mentioned the Nottoway, Meherrin, Tuscarora, and Occaneechi.[53] The placement of Siouan groups to the west is based on the occurrence of archaeological sites with small quantities of presumed early English trade goods (e.g., copper ornaments and certain glass bead types)[54] and the correspondence of these sites with places associated by John Lederer twenty years later with specific tribes.[55] The identification of the Iredell phase and a yet undefined phase along the middle and lower Catawba River is based on Moore's analysis of pottery samples from those areas.[56] The placement of the Occaneechi, Eno, Shakori, Sissipahaw, and Keyauwee along the corridor traversed by the Trading Path likely reflects the growing importance

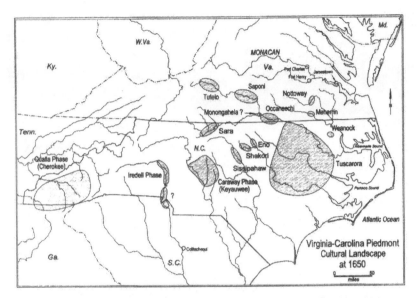

Fig. 5. The cultural landscape of the Virginia–North Carolina piedmont at 1650.

of this trail during the mid-seventeenth century. Perhaps the most interesting and intriguing aspect of this map is the placement of the Monongahela at the junction of the Staunton and Dan rivers, just upstream from Occaneechi Island. Evidence for this placement comes from the Abbyville site, excavated by members of the Archeological Society of Virginia in the late 1960s. Although the excavators believed that the site was a Susquehannock village dating to the period of Bacon's Rebellion, the pottery and trade artifacts from the site have been identified as Monongahela and as dating between about 1635 and 1650, following their dispersal from the upper Ohio valley at the hands of the Seneca.[57]

Maps of the Cultural Landscape in 1670 and 1676[58]

Figure 6 depicts the piedmont cultural landscape as seen by Lederer, Batts and Fallam, and Needham and Arthur.[59] With the exception of the Sara, most of the Siouan groups in North Carolina at this time lived in villages near the Trading Path, and all were engaged in the fur trade. Excavated archaeological sites that date to this period include Upper Saratown (Sara) on the Dan River, the Jenrette site (Shakori) on the Eno

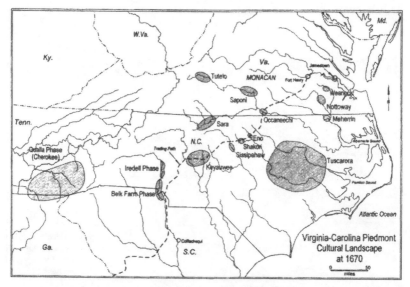

Fig. 6. The cultural landscape of the Virginia–North Carolina piedmont at 1670.

River, the Mitchum site (Sissipahaw) on the Haw River, the Poole site (Keyauwee) on Caraway Creek, and the Belk Farm site on the Catawba River. Excavations were sufficiently large at Upper Saratown, Jenrette, and Mitchum to reveal a circular arrangement of houses surrounded by a palisade.[60] While the Sara appear to have lived in multiple villages, there is no evidence to suggest that other Siouan communities of the central North Carolina piedmont were composed of more than a single settlement, and these communities probably were made up of no more than 150–200 individuals.

Figure 7 shows the period of Bacon's Rebellion in 1676 and reflects the consolidation of the native population in southern Virginia near the Occaneechi trading center. The Susquehannock moved into the area in 1675, after being driven out of the upper Chesapeake by Maryland and Virginia militias, and their subsequent attacks along the Virginia frontier precipitated the rebellion.[61] It is not known if the Tutelo and Saponi joined the Occaneechi before or after their massacre at the hands of Bacon's militia; however, Mooney, citing William Byrd II, places them on the two islands above and below Occaneechi Island "some time between 1671 and 1701."[62] This time bracket reflects the facts that these two

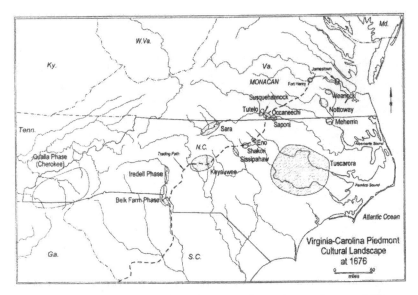

Fig. 7. The cultural landscape of the Virginia–North Carolina piedmont at 1676.

groups were encountered by Batts and Fallam along the middle and upper Staunton River in 1671 and were living along the Yadkin River when visited by John Lawson three decades later.

Map of the Cultural Landscape in 1700[63]

Figure 8 shows the cultural landscape of piedmont North Carolina and South Carolina that John Lawson saw. A comparison with the two preceding maps (see figs. 6 and 7) shows the substantial changes that occurred during the last quarter of the seventeenth century. These changes relate to effects on the fur trade that resulted from Bacon's Rebellion, the impact of depopulation as the exposure of piedmont Siouans to European-introduced diseases increased, and the consolidation of peoples along the lower reaches of the Catawba River.

While Bacon's Rebellion brought about the abandonment of the Roanoke valley by the Occaneechi, Tutelo, Saponi, and others, these tribes continued to engage in trade with Virginia. With the Occaneechis' elimination as middlemen in that trade, Virginians could now trade with individual tribes along the Trading Path and without restriction. By the 1690s,

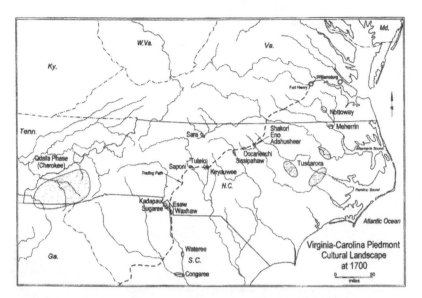

Fig. 8. The cultural landscape of the Virginia–North Carolina piedmont at 1700.

the Trading Path's crossing point over the Roanoke River had been relocated thirty miles downstream to Moniseep Ford, where it bypassed the Occaneechis' former territory altogether.

The kinds and quantities of trade goods found on sites of this period clearly reflect the extent to which the piedmont Indians relied on the trade.[64] Whereas before the 1670s the Trading Path was largely a trail that connected the population centers of the central North Carolina piedmont, after that time it became a commercial link to Virginia that attracted the native population. It is little wonder that Lawson encountered the Saponi, Tutelo, and Occaneechi while traveling along this path.

Archaeological evidence from sites such as Upper Saratown, William Kluttz, and Fredricks (i.e., Occaneechi Town) shows the impact that disease had on the late-seventeenth-century piedmont. All three sites contained large numbers of burials relative to estimated village size and settlement duration, and all represent smaller populations than late prehistoric and protohistoric sites located nearby.[65] Also, Lawson's journal indicates that a process of population coalescence and consolidation had begun along the lower Catawba River—with the Waxhaw, Sugaree, Esaw, and Kadapau living in nearby villages—and in the upper Neuse drainage where the Shakori, Eno, and Adshusheer now lived in a single village.[66] The coalescence of these latter three tribes at Adshusheer most likely was brought about by depopulation and the constant threat of Iroquois raiding.

Map of the Cultural Landscape in 1720[67]

The process of coalescence and consolidation evident at the beginning of the eighteenth century accelerated during the two succeeding decades, and by 1720 the North Carolina piedmont was largely vacant (fig. 9).[68] By 1713, remnants of Siouan tribes that Mooney identified as belonging to his northern, or Tutelo, division had moved north and resettled at Fort Christanna on the Meherrin River in southeastern Virginia.[69] There, the Tutelo, Saponi, and Occaneechi joined the Meiponski and Steukenocks, two tribes who formerly were part of the Manahoac or Monacan confederacies, and became known collectively as the Saponi, or Fort Christanna, Indians.[70]

Other Siouan tribes who once lived in central North Carolina, including many who fought against the English in the Yamasee and Cheraw

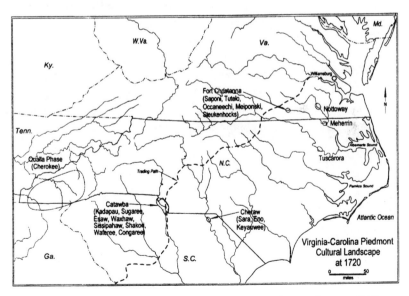

Fig. 9. The cultural landscape of the Virginia–North Carolina piedmont at 1720.

wars, moved south to the Catawba and Pee Dee valleys. The Sissipahaw and Shakori joined the Kadapau, Esaw, Sugaree, and other tribes who were now known to the English as Catawba, while the Sara, Eno, and Keyauwee moved to the Pee Dee River in South Carolina. By the 1740s, they too had joined the Catawba.[71]

CONCLUSION

One problem that has long plagued anthropologists studying the native peoples of the Carolina piedmont at contact is the apparent contradictions in cultural geography offered in the written accounts of early Europeans who traveled through the region.[72] For example, the accounts of Lederer, Batts and Fallam, and Needham and Arthur in the 1670s contain inconsistencies that have led some researchers to discount their validity, and by 1700 many of the tribes mentioned by Lawson or placed on contemporary maps were far removed from their earlier territories. As archaeological and ethnohistoric research into the contact period has progressed, it has become increasingly clear that many of these piedmont villages were occupied only briefly and, as European-introduced diseases took their toll on the native population, new societies were formed from the remnants of old ones. The economic transformations brought about by the fur trade, the persistent threat of Iroquois raiding, and finally the disruption of native life caused by the Southern Indian Wars of the early 1700s also contributed to a more fluid and ever-changing cultural landscape than existed previously. When viewed in this context, these geographical contradictions of the seventeenth and early eighteenth centuries are not contradictions at all; rather, they are clear evidence for the processes of culture change that affected all of the piedmont tribes.

Reconstructing the Coalescence of Cherokee Communities in Southern Appalachia

CHRISTOPHER B. RODNING

Several distinct groups of Cherokee towns formed within different areas of southern Appalachia during the late seventeenth and early eighteenth centuries (fig. 1). Several of the Lower Towns along the headwaters of the Savannah River were located at or near mounds that may have been community centers from the eleventh through sixteenth centuries[1]—during the 1700s, many people abandoned these towns because of conflicts with Creek and European groups.[2] The relationship between people in the Overhill Towns along the lower Little Tennessee River and earlier chiefdoms in the region before the sixteenth century is unclear[3]—during the 1700s, these settlements received many refugees from the Middle and Lower towns.[4] The Middle Towns were settlements in the upper Little Tennessee River valley in southwestern North Carolina. Some Middle Towns were less than fifty miles away from Lower Cherokee settlements located in what is now northwestern South Carolina. The Out Towns were built close to ancient mounds along the Tuckasegee and Oconaluftee rivers east of the Little Tennessee.[5] The Valley Towns were close to Peachtree and other mounds in the upper Hiwassee watershed in the westernmost corner of North Carolina.[6] People in these five different groups of towns shared a common cultural and linguistic background and were probably related through matrilineal kinship.[7] There was little political centralization between or even within towns.[8] Leaders of towns were spokespersons for their communities, but their status did not grant them power over people in other towns. Different towns likely formed alliances with each other in different situations, but there were not paramount chiefs that ruled whole groups of towns. How did these relatively small-scale polities form out of the vestiges of earlier chiefdoms that flourished in the greater southern Appalachian region in earlier centuries?[9] What processes drove the coalescence of native communities in this region into the particular configuration in which English traders found them during

155

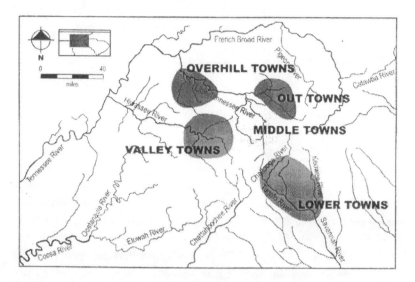

Fig. 1. Lower, Middle, Out, Valley, and Overhill Cherokee towns. Courtesy of the
Journal of Cherokee Studies, Museum of the Cherokee Indian, Cherokee, North
Carolina.

the early and mid-eighteenth century?[10] This paper outlines an archaeological approach to the Cherokee coalescence in southern Appalachia during the centuries bridging what archaeologists call the late prehistoric and
early historic periods.

The Cherokee spoke an Iroquoian language distinct from that of their
Muskogean and Catawban neighbors.[11] Language was probably one of
many ways in which native people in southern Appalachia made distinctions between different groups within the regional landscape. Specific
characteristics of material culture such as pots and architecture may have
communicated social distinctions between Cherokee and other groups as
well. However, archaeologically visible distinctions in ceramics and architectural styles are not necessarily correlated with salient ethnic distinctions within past communities in any straightforward way.[12] Moreover, it
is likely that eighteenth-century towns and much earlier sixteenth-
century chiefdoms included speakers of many different languages and
members of several distinct ethnic groups.[13] The implication of these points
is that not all residents of historic Cherokee towns formed one coherent ethnic group. Nor did speakers of common languages in southern Appalachia

necessarily make the same kinds of pottery or build the same kinds of houses.

Several Cherokee towns during the eighteenth century bore names derived from Muskogean rather than Iroquoian languages.[14] The place names Chota, Citico, Conasauga, Chilhowee, Tanasee, Tallassee, Tuskegee, and Tomotley all have Muskogean rather than Iroquoian etymologies, even though these are the names of Cherokee towns dating to the eighteenth century. Town names such as Nequassee, Seneca, and Kituwah likely have Iroquoian rather than Muskogean etymologies, and perhaps some place names blended Cherokee with Catawban and Muskogean elements. This linguistic blend in place names most likely reflects movements of people across the landscape over the course of many generations. It may even reflect negotiation and conflict between groups about access or ancestral claims to ancient mounds and towns.

Certainly there were significant historical reasons why Cherokee communities formed where they did in the late seventeenth and early eighteenth centuries. I am confident that many members of Cherokee towns could trace their descent from much earlier communities in southern Appalachia. I nevertheless would agree with others who have suggested that it was only at the end of the seventeenth century that there formed in southern Appalachia a social entity specifically identifiable as Cherokee. The following section of my paper argues that the greater Cherokee community was a diverse and perhaps even multiethnic congeries of towns in the early eighteenth century. This point has significant implications for the archaeological study of community formation and social dynamics in southern Appalachia during the sixteenth and seventeenth centuries. Certainly, the coalescence of native communities in southern Appalachia during these years was guided in some ways by the long-term histories of power within Mississippian chiefdoms.[15] However, the greater Cherokee community formed as such partly as a result of the short-term responses of native groups to the European presence in their midst and the opportunities for trade that came with them.[16] The concluding section of my paper outlines my current thoughts about politics within Cherokee towns at the dawn of their involvement in the deerskin trade.

CHEROKEE COMMUNITIES DURING THE EIGHTEENTH CENTURY

Cherokee communities of the eighteenth century are widely thought to have had an egalitarian political culture and social structure, less rigidly hierarchical than the earlier paramount chiefdoms present in some areas. Fogelson has attributed this phenomenon to an embedded Cherokee cultural tradition that prevented anybody from acquiring an excess of power and instead favored consensus building and tolerance of dissent.[17] Gearing has characterized the presence of peace chiefs and war chiefs in Cherokee communities as evidence that these groups vested different people with different kinds of power.[18] Town leaders generally did not outrank leaders of other Cherokee towns,[19] and their power was different in scale from that wielded by elites who lived at paramount centers in northern Georgia and eastern Tennessee in earlier centuries.[20] Leaders of Cherokee towns were spokespersons for people living within their towns and surrounding countryside,[21] not chiefs with power to exact tribute or prevent households from moving from one town to another.[22] This situation of relative socioeconomic and sociopolitical parity may have changed dramatically in the later eighteenth century, with opportunities for Cherokee men and women to enhance their wealth and status through trade with Europeans.[23] Before these opportunities, there seem not to have been individuals within Cherokee communities with significantly more wealth or power than their fellow Cherokees.[24]

Cherokee towns were composed of several different households, each of which may have been formed by local members of one matrilineal clan.[25] This seems to have been the case in native towns in the southern Appalachians during the eighteenth century.[26] This relationship between the social entities called towns and clans may have been part of a broader southeastern tradition.[27] Members of town councils may have served as representatives from their respective clans.[28] My extrapolation from these clues is that towns and clans were distinct if overlapping social domains in which women and men derived different kinds of power.[29] Traditional gender roles guided men towards leadership within towns and women to leadership within clans and households. Certainly, there must have been hierarchies within these social entities, and probably statuses within them related to age and lifetime achievement. However, it is unlikely that town leaders always outranked leaders of clans in any vertical political hierarchy, or that the converse was true.

Cherokee towns sometimes acted in concert with each other during the eighteenth century, but they were not bound together within any paramount chiefdom.[30] Town leaders were spokespersons for constituents whom they could persuade but not coerce. Dissenters within towns were not necessarily bound to the decisions of town leaders. Towns often pursued their own interests with or without the collaboration of neighboring towns.

This negotiable relationship between towns seems comparable to Galloway's model of the genesis of the historic Choctaw tribal community from residents of different areas in Mississippi and western Alabama.[31] She has shown that the Choctaw tribe of the eighteenth century was composed of several distinct groups whose own ancestors lived in different areas outside the historic Choctaw homeland.[32] She has shown that the coalescence of the Choctaw confederacy as such owed much to the geopolitics of the late Mississippian and protohistoric periods.[33] Towns were fundamental social and political entities, and many Choctaw towns may have been home to people from several different ethnic groups. Some towns may have been relatively homogeneous in their ethnic and linguistic composition, but the social composition of distinct ethnic groups and groups speaking common languages probably varied from one generation to another and from one Choctaw town to another. Memberships within certain clans were major determinants of social identities, as were affiliations with one town or another. Choctaw towns were not ethnic groups in and of themselves, although different towns banded together in response to the geopolitics of the seventeenth and eighteenth centuries to advance their own interests.

Formations of alliances between towns and groups of towns are one major component of Knight's model of the origins of the Creek confederacy in Georgia and eastern Alabama.[34] The variety of pottery made by people in different areas where Creek towns were concentrated during the eighteenth century has led him to conclude that residents of these towns had diverse cultural backgrounds. The presence of speakers of different languages in both the Upper Creek and Lower Creek towns of the eighteenth century further attests the diverse social composition of Creek communities in the eighteenth century. Many residents of Creek towns did speak Muskogean languages such as Koasati and Hitchiti.[35] Other residents of Creek towns seem to have spoken closely related Muskogean languages such as Alabama and Apalachee.[36]

The formation of the Choctaw and Creek confederacies and the greater Cherokee community as such took place within the context of significant movements of native groups from one region to another during the sixteenth and seventeenth centuries. These movements often were responses to episodes of conflict with colonial or native neighbors, epidemic diseases, or more likely combinations of these and other developments.[37] Series of maps can trace multiregional patterns in movements of and social interactions between these groups, and meanwhile archaeologists are developing an ever-better understanding of the spatial layout and social composition of towns themselves.[38] What is not well known but very conducive to further archaeological study in many areas of southern Appalachia is the layout of the cultural landscape around and between towns. The study of settlement patterns at the corresponding spatial scale should shed some light on the regional significance of towns as hubs of social activity in southern Appalachia where power relations would have been negotiated and communicated during rituals and other events. This approach will contribute much to knowledge about the social and political dynamics within Cherokee towns whose members likely included those living close to town council houses as well as people living in farmsteads between town centers themselves.

CHEROKEE ANCESTORS BEFORE THE EIGHTEENTH CENTURY

Archaeology has offered several different perspectives on the formation of Cherokee communities as such in different parts of their historic homeland. One reason for this is the diversity of material culture found in these areas. Another reason is that archaeologists have tended to study these and other problems through archaeological materials from one state or another. There are significant environmental differences in these distinct areas of the historic Cherokee homeland.[39] The Lower Towns in Georgia were located in the upper Savannah Valley south of the Blue Ridge escarpment. The Overhill Towns in Tennessee were located within the Ridge and Valley province. The other groups of Cherokee towns were carved out of the more rugged landscapes of the Appalachian Summit province south of where the Soto and Pardo expeditions crossed the Appalachian Mountains in the sixteenth century.[40] The continuing archaeological study of early Cherokee social history needs to draw from the archaeology of each of these areas, and perspectives from these different areas are reviewed here. The emergence of Cherokee communities as such was guided by social and political interactions that took place at several different spatial scales, from the interregional level to the level of social dynamics within towns.

Gerald Schroedl has developed an archaeological model of the origins of eighteenth-century Cherokee groups in eastern Tennessee from more hierarchical chiefdoms in the region predating the sixteenth century.[41] His model posits that Mississippian chiefdoms in these regions collapsed during the sixteenth century, and that communities were eventually reformed without the ranked social hierarchy characteristic of those earlier chiefdoms. This model envisions a historical relationship between historic Cherokees and much earlier chiefdoms in the region, albeit neither an unbroken nor unchallenged ancestral relationship. One unresolved archaeological problem related to the study of the Cherokee emergence in Tennessee is the unclear relationship between several different late prehistoric and protohistoric archaeological phases in the region.[42] Another problem relates to the major demographic changes that may have taken place in the lower Little Tennessee Valley and in the lower Hiwassee River valley during the seventeenth century.[43] Were parts of the lower Little Tennessee Valley and other areas in eastern Tennessee abandoned during the seventeenth century? Or did towns disperse? What ethnic groups formed in these areas and when? How is it that Cherokee groups and not others built towns along the lower Little Tennessee River during the eighteenth century? Some towns were probably built at and around ancient mounds because of their prominence as visible landmarks. Mound building practices had changed significantly by this point even though some council houses were built on old mound summits. Perhaps building Cherokee towns and council houses beside ancient mounds like Toqua and Citico effectively laid claims to places that had symbolic significance to native people in the region because of the presence of these ancient landmarks in eastern Tennessee. The same may have been true of Cherokee towns built at the Estatoe and Tugalo mounds in northeastern Georgia.

David Hally has argued that similarities in archaeological ceramics indicate that eighteenth-century Cherokee groups in northeastern Georgia practiced the same ceramic tradition as local residents of the sixteenth century.[44] His paper outlines the major characteristics of sixteenth-century Tugalo-phase ceramics from the Tugalo, Estatoe, and Chauga mounds—including complicated stamp motifs on globular jars and incised designs near the rims of carinated bowls. These ceramic characteristics are very comparable to those in eighteenth-century Estatoe-phase pottery from sites along the Tugalo, Keowee, and Chauga rivers—

although check stamping is much more prevalent in Estatoe-phase than in Tugalo-phase assemblages. I would add that Tugalo and Estatoe ceramics are very similar to what archaeologists call Qualla pottery in southwestern North Carolina.[45] I gather from Gerald Schroedl and Brett Riggs that there are similarities as well between Qualla ceramics and the pottery from the Cherokee town of Chattooga in northwestern South Carolina.[46] Despite continuities in ceramics dating to the sixteenth and eighteenth centuries, there is a gap in the archaeological record of northeastern Georgia corresponding to the seventeenth century. This problem is unresolved, although there are archaeological clues that major centers and settlement concentrations did shift across the landscape in some areas of northern Georgia at different points in the past. In some areas, centers of power shifted from one mound center to another. In some cases, abandoned mounds were later reoccupied. Mark Williams has demonstrated this phenomenon in the middle Oconee Valley in Georgia from the eleventh through fifteenth centuries, when different mound centers rose and declined in regional prominence.[47] David Anderson has argued that similar changes are visible in the Savannah River watershed, although there was somewhat greater continuity of settlement at the headwaters of the Savannah than further downstream.[48] I am confident that some Cherokee groups of the eighteenth century could trace their ancestry to residents of the upper Savannah River valley in the sixteenth and earlier centuries. I think it is less clear whether regional leaders lived continuously at Savannah River Mississippian mound centers in this region or if Cherokee towns were built at these localities in deliberate efforts to claim some historical or ancestral relationship with seats of earlier chiefs that had been temporarily abandoned.

Hally has demonstrated the close similarities between archaeological ceramics from the Savannah River headwaters during the sixteenth and eighteenth centuries, leading to his reasonable conclusion that there were significant ancestral relationships between the residents of these areas during these different eras.[49] Hally has written: "Tugalo and Estatoe phase ceramics differ in many important respects from those of Lamar phases located south and west of the Tugalo River in Georgia. I do not have access to pottery collections from sixteenth-century sites on the headwaters of the Hiwassee, Little Tennessee, and Keowee rivers in North Carolina and South Carolina, and therefore can not evaluate the extent of ceramic similarity existing between them and the Tugalo and

Estatoe phase assemblages. It is clear to me, however, that we do not have to look outside the Tugalo River drainage for the ceramic antecedents of the eighteenth-century Lower Cherokee."[50]

Anderson and colleagues have shown that much of the Savannah River watershed was abandoned during the fifteenth century, at which point people may have moved southwest to the Oconee Valley and upstream towards what became the Lower Cherokee towns.[51] Anderson has commented that "[o]rganizational change in the Mississippian populations occupying the headwaters of the Savannah River basin at the beginning of the Tugalo phase is indicated by the new mound construction at Chauga, at Estatoe, and possibly at Tugalo. All of these events took place around or shortly after 1450, when the lower portion of the basin was abandoned. An influx of people from the collapsing chiefdoms to the south may have occurred, resulting in social reorganization. This is suggested in part by symbolic termination and rebuilding episodes in the mound at Estatoe and by the reoccupation of other previously abandoned centers such as Chauga and Tugalo. While the occupations that emerged in the late fifteenth century appear to have continued into the historic period and hence represent the formation of the Lower Cherokee towns, this is a subject of some debate. Appreciable stylistic and technological continuity is evident between the ceramic assemblages of the Tugalo and Estatoe phases,[52] although assemblages from the interval between these phases, from circa 1600 to 1700, remain to be documented."[53]

Interestingly, there are gaps in the archaeological records of both northeastern Georgia and southeastern Tennessee representing the seventeenth century. Meanwhile, there has been rather little comprehensive treatment of material culture dating to that century in southwestern North Carolina and northwestern South Carolina in the widely published archaeological literature.

Dickens has argued that ancient traditions of living in highland environments of western Carolina characterize the core of Cherokee lifeways and social dynamics in the eighteenth century.[54] Societies in western North Carolina from A.D. 1000 to 1450—related to the archaeological complex known as the Pisgah phase—are thought of as chiefdoms with villages and farmsteads spread around mound centers in a hierarchical settlement pattern. Native groups in western North Carolina from A.D. 1450 to 1838—represented by archaeological materials and sites attributable to the Qualla phase—are generally thought of as the direct descendants of these prehistoric forebears. One problem with this model is that archaeologists really have not yet excavated whole towns in western North Carolina that clearly date to the sixteenth century, although mounds like Peachtree must have been significant regional centers of some kind before and during this period.[55] Another problem is that there may not have been any linear development from what archaeologists recognize as the Pisgah phase to the Qualla phase in every river valley, with the identification of these phases resting primarily upon certain diagnostic characteristics of ceramics.[56] Pisgah pottery is common in the French Broad valley, where there are not many sites with distinctively Qualla ceramics. Pisgah material is found far less often in the Hiwassee and Little Tennessee valleys, where Qualla pottery is commonly present at archaeological sites. Generally, this spatial distinction has been interpreted to represent the movement of communities represented by Pisgah sites southwest to areas where Qualla sites are most common.[57] However, the incising and complicated stamp motifs on Qualla jars and carinated bowls are as much or more similar to Tugalo and Estatoe ceramics as they are to Pisgah pottery.[58] Groups of people represented by the Pisgah phase in western North Carolina certainly would have become part of Cherokee communities in the eighteenth century. My point here is simply that there may be archaeological complexes in the upper Hiwassee and Little Tennessee watersheds that are contemporary with but not the same as the Pisgah phase as it is represented further northeast. Ward and Davis suggest that "[a]n as-yet-unrecognized early Qualla (or Lamar) phase culture was thriving in the western mountains (including the Snowbird, Nantahala, Unaka, Cowee, and Cheoah ranges) at about the same time Pisgah influence was being felt in the central Appalachian Summit. Once detailed studies of Qualla ceramics from the western mountains are completed and more excavated samples are analyzed, archaeologists will probably find that this early Qualla phase is characterized by pottery related to that of the Wilbanks phase of northern Georgia, the Dallas phase of eastern Tennessee, and other ceramic series described as Early Lamar."[59]

The earliest well-known Qualla site described as such in the archaeological literature is Coweeta Creek, located in the upper Little Tennessee River valley close to the locations of several historically known Middle Cherokee towns.[60] Native ceramics at Coweeta Creek seem comparable to Estatoe or Tugalo phase pottery, potentially placing them between the end of the sixteenth and beginning of the eighteenth centuries.[61] Archaeologists have found glass beads in the Coweeta Creek council house, and these artifacts would seem to date this town to the seventeenth century.[62] Coweeta Creek is thus not an Early Qualla site, given the time frame that is usually associated with this phase. Coweeta Creek is certainly significant for its clues about town layout and native lifeways in western North Carolina during the early historic period, but it does not span the end of the Pisgah phase and beginning of the Qualla phase as these phases are currently understood.

The development from Pisgah to Qualla material culture and the lifeways of the groups represented by these archaeological phases may characterize some areas of western North Carolina, including the French Broad and Pigeon watersheds.[63] This developmental model is not necessarily applicable elsewhere, including the areas where Cherokee towns were concentrated during the eighteenth century in southwestern North Carolina, such as the Middle and Valley town areas. If that is the case, the model of continuous development from the Pisgah to Qualla phases may be only one piece of the puzzle of Cherokee origins in western North Carolina, albeit an important piece.

Williams and Anderson have shown that there were significant movements of people *within* and *between* regions in the Savannah and Oconee watersheds during the fifteenth and sixteenth centuries.[64] Were any of these movements triggering movements of people north into western North Carolina? Were there movements of groups in many different directions within western North Carolina? Ward and Davis have noted recently that the "Qualla phase of western North Carolina is best understood when placed within a broader regional context. Most archaeologists working the Southeast consider Qualla to be a manifestation of the widespread Lamar culture that is found across the northern half of Georgia and Alabama, most of South Carolina, and eastern Tennessee—as well as the western one-third of North Carolina."[65]

SPATIAL SCALES AND CHEROKEE ARCHAEOLOGY

The foregoing review outlines some significant building blocks for the continuing archaeological study of early Cherokee social history. We know where the major groups of Cherokee towns were concentrated in southern Appalachia during the eighteenth century[66]—interestingly, there may not have been major hubs in northeastern Georgia during the seventeenth century.[67] We know something about the social composition of earlier chiefdoms in these different areas[68]—however, the development of historic Cherokee communities out of the vestiges of these earlier hierarchical chiefdoms probably reflected both cultural continuity and changes in the geopolitics of native and colonial groups.[69] Archaeologists have learned much about the layout of Mississippian and protohistoric towns.[70] Archaeologists also know something about the distribution of wealth within towns before and after European contact.[71] What are yet unresolved with enough precision to speak specifically about how Cherokee polities formed are problems of archaeological chronology and knowledge of what cultural landscapes looked like between towns.

The first point has been noted by Jack Wynn, who has written that "[l]ate Lamar will doubtless need to be broken down into short-term phases in different areas. . . . From the Appalachian Summit area of western North Carolina a 'Qualla phase' may also be appropriate here. However, lack of a tighter definition of what Qualla is and when it is makes it less useful in this context. It is likely that there is a relationship between the Qualla culture of the Appalachian Summit and the cultures of the 'north slope' drainages in the Georgia Blue Ridge which will prove important to our understanding of either or both of them."[72] Archaeologists in Georgia and Tennessee have developed more precise chronological frameworks than current ceramic chronologies in western North Carolina. Further fieldwork and collections studies will help with this problem and further elucidate the relationship between the Pisgah and Qualla phases in western North Carolina.

The second problem has been noted by Gerald Schroedl, who has argued that periodic declines in the productivity of farmlands would have forced towns "to considerably reduce and disperse their populations or to relocate their towns at 50- to 150-year intervals. Village abandonments as a response to land-use patterns would tend to have archaeological visibility, like the kinds of episodic patterns of palisade rebuilding, major changes in mound construction, and multiple structural placements such as those seen at Toqua and elsewhere. Series of proximally located and sequentially occupied villages, such as the three Mouse Creek sites and the Dallas-Hixon-Davis sites, also are potential outcomes of these land-use dynamics, as are the paired sites tentatively interpreted as primary and secondary mound centers of chiefly polities."[73] This point is applicable to the archaeological study of town layout and patterns of rebuilding at the Coweeta Creek site and to regional settlement patterns during the sixteenth and seventeenth centuries in southwestern North Carolina. The following are some of my current thoughts about significant points for archaeological consideration through the study of extant archaeological collections from the upper Little Tennessee River valley and surrounding areas and through further fieldwork in this part of North Carolina.

The town at Coweeta Creek is located north of the confluence of that stream and the upper Little Tennessee River (fig. 2).[74] Dwellings were built in the village, and when the village was built its residents constructed a council house and created a town plaza in the area northwest of the village itself. The council house was built and rebuilt here at least six times, though not on top of a pyramidal mound built specifically as a platform for elite architecture in earlier centuries. The compact town plan clearly contrasts with the dispersed settlement pattern characteristic of the Cherokee landscape during the late eighteenth and early nineteenth centuries.[75]

Archaeologists have conducted surveys in many areas of western North Carolina including the upper Little Tennessee Valley (fig. 3).[76] Aside from schematic maps of settlement patterns in western North Carolina,[77] the archaeological materials gathered during these surveys have received little archaeological study in and of themselves. Nevertheless the study of these sites would complement maps of towns like that at Coweeta Creek,[78] perhaps clarifying the relationships between different towns and the ways in which people living in areas between town centers affiliated themselves with one polity or another. Understanding relationships between people living within towns themselves and in rural areas around them are significant for understanding the role of towns within the regional political dynamics of southern Appalachia during the seventeenth century.[79]

What was the relationship between towns in the upper Little Tennessee Valley? Was Coweeta Creek the center of a major town even when there were towns centered at the more visibly prominent Nequassee and Cowee mounds? Did Coweeta Creek become a major town after people from the Lower Towns along the Keowee and Tugalo rivers began moving north towards the Middle Towns in the late seventeenth century? How did the interregional movements mapped by Marvin Smith affect social dynamics and politics within the upper Little Tennessee Valley?[80] How

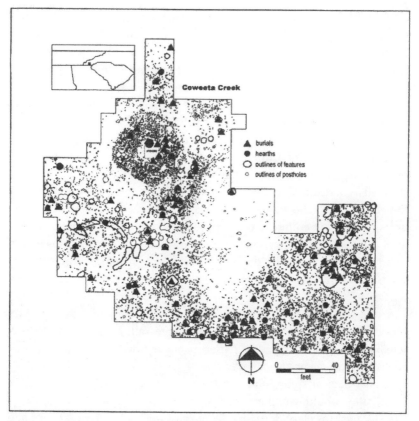

Fig. 2. Archaeological map of the town plan at Coweeta Creek. Courtesy of the *Journal of Cherokee Studies*, Museum of the Cherokee Indian, Cherokee, North Carolina.

did trade opportunities like those outlined by Joel Martin affect the social structure and spatial layout of communities along the upper Little Tennessee River?[81] The consideration of these questions through settlement pattern studies will contribute to better understandings of what kinds of polities are represented by clusters of towns in southwestern North Carolina and how these polities interacted with each other.

Without doubt, the council house and public plaza area at Coweeta Creek served as the symbolic center of town. But it is less clear how far the township spread outward from this space. People living in farmsteads and hamlets between this and other towns in the region probably chose to affiliate themselves with one town or another.[82] Only by studying artifacts

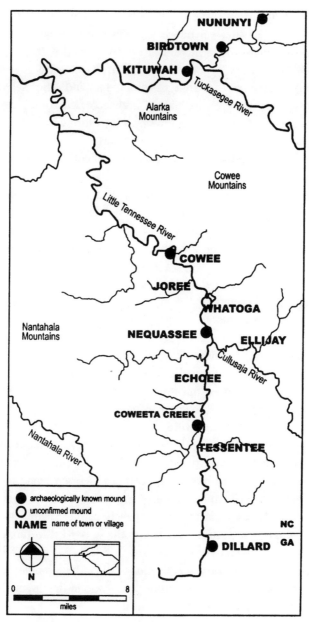

Fig. 3. Towns and sites in the upper Little Tennessee River valley. Courtesy of the *Journal of Cherokee Studies*, Museum of the Cherokee Indian, Cherokee, North Carolina.

collected during surface surveys and perhaps through conducting excavations at the smaller sites surrounding towns can archaeologists begin to identify how people living in rural areas interacted with people living close to town centers.[83] These kinds of archaeological investigations should help determine the range of settlements and other activity areas within any given region. This kind of archaeological knowledge should help place major towns and their public architecture within the context of the regional landscapes of which they were part.

As currently understood, native ceramics and colonial trade beads suggest that the town at Coweeta Creek dates to the seventeenth century and perhaps the very early eighteenth century. It does not date much earlier than the early seventeenth century, if at all. This means that it probably was built well after the mounds at Cowee and Nequassee had become prominent town centers or something akin to great towns. Perhaps the creation of this relatively new town reflects the movement of people to the region from points further south, including refugees from towns along the Keowee and Tugalo rivers.

How did native residents recognize boundaries between towns along the upper Little Tennessee River? Perhaps the towns centered at the Cowee and Nequassee mounds were more significant political centers than Coweeta Creek because of longer histories of settlement and mound building at these localities, but it is difficult to assess settlement hierarchies with currently available evidence and understanding of chronology in the region. Perhaps there were major centers along the Cullusaja and Ellijay rivers contemporary with the Coweeta Creek town, but survey collections from these areas are still unanalyzed. Some excavations have been done at the Dillard mound in northern Georgia,[84] and this mound seems to date primarily to the century before the tenure of the town center at Coweeta Creek. Considerable excavations have been conducted at the Macon County Industrial Park site in the upper Little Tennessee Valley,[85] and this settlement is roughly seven miles northwest of Coweeta Creek. These sites and survey collections hold valuable clues about how people were spread across the cultural landscape in the upper Little Tennessee Valley at different points in the past.

Archaeologists know much about the regional and even continental geopolitics in which native groups in southern Appalachia became enmeshed as early as the late sixteenth century. Meanwhile, archaeologists have learned much about social dynamics within individual towns.[86] However, archaeologists know less about what the cultural landscape between towns looked like.[87] Spatial patterns in archaeological evidence from areas around and between towns in southern Appalachia are significant sources of evidence about the composition of individual polities and interactions between them.

SOCIAL DYNAMICS IN CHEROKEE COMMUNITIES

Compared to earlier Mississippian chiefdoms, historic Cherokee polities seem to have been relatively egalitarian. Hereditary rank distinctions were not communicated through elaborate mortuary ritual as they were in some Mississippian chiefdoms, especially before the fourteenth century.[88] Whereas earlier pyramidal mounds created platforms for architecture accessible only to elite echelons of Mississippian societies, communal council houses of the eighteenth century were much less exclusive architectural spaces.[89] I would argue that egalitarianism prevailed within Cherokee towns of the eighteenth century as a result of continuous negotiations between leaders with power in different social domains. I would suggest further that native community formation in southern Appalachia took place at different social and spatial scales.

Residents of Cherokee towns could claim descent from earlier residents of mountain ranges and valleys in the greater southern Appalachians. Although their traditional language is indeed related to that of northern Iroquois groups of the seventeenth century, their material culture and traditional lifeways nevertheless resemble those of earlier groups in the Southeast in many respects. Ceramics by historic Cherokee potters are part of a long tradition known to archaeologists as Lamar, and architectural forms present at Cherokee towns have antecedents at earlier settlements in the southern Appalachians. People in Cherokee towns probably traced their own ancestry from many different areas in southern Appalachia. Nevertheless the specific label of several groups of towns as Cherokee originated at the point when the deerskin trade and the global economic forces driving it reached remote areas of southern Appalachia.

People living in Cherokee towns were culturally related to but independent of other towns and groups of towns clustered along major rivers in the southern Appalachians. Town leaders were spokespersons for residents of their towns, but that authority did not spread to other Cherokee towns.[90] Towns were social entities composed of several and even dozens of households in some cases, and these households may have represented local members of the seven traditional Cherokee clans.[91] Clan kinship thus bound people of different towns together. Doubtless other ties linked members of one town to residents of many others. Indeed, Cherokee towns often did act in concert with each other, perhaps in part because of clan relationships that crossed town borders. However, Cherokee towns were not bound together within any political structure greater than towns themselves, as may have been the case in earlier paramount chiefdoms in some areas.

Within local communities, the power of prominent Cherokee men would have been balanced by the power of prominent women. As in many other societies of the native Southeast, Cherokee people traced kinship through matrilineal clans. As in other areas of the Southeast, Cherokee households were likely matrilocal groups. Certainly, some Cherokee men would have gained prestige as warriors and traders, and prominent male elders undoubtedly commanded respect and deference. However, leaders within Cherokee clans and households were most likely women, and this status within matrilineal and matrilocal communities would have given them significant voice to advance their own interests. Leaders of towns— mostly adult men—would have had significant authority within their local communities.[92] Leaders of clans—probably most often adult women— would have been prominent leaders within social domains in which they tended to outrank men.[93]

Not only would clan leaders have been powerful in their own ways, but significant economic resources in Cherokee communities would have been the province of specific households. Households traditionally kept gardens and fields of their own.[94] Houses themselves were architecturally linked to certain household groups.[95] Access to resources and social relationships through kin networks would have ensured the power of women within their matrilineal communities. People were members of households and clans by virtue of specific kin relationships with women. Membership in one Cherokee clan or another gave a person a place within his or her community and access to many kinds of resources and significant social relationships.[96]

At least some households kept storehouses of their own, and households made significant contributions to feasts and other ritual events in their towns.[97] There is neither archaeological nor ethnohistoric evidence of major socioeconomic differences between households in the seventeenth century, and stored resources likely did not correlate with vertical distinctions in the rank of some households relative to others. There is no evidence of pronounced wealth and power distinctions within towns, although some towns may have been especially well positioned to capitalize upon major trade routes. Contributions to feasts may not have been tribute given to chiefs but perhaps represented widespread beliefs in rituals that would ensure good harvests and resources to last through even the lean seasons of the year.[98] Of course the presence of surpluses within towns may have given aspiring leaders tempting opportunities to enhance their own standing within their communities by seeking control of stored resources.[99] Nevertheless there were not rigidly pronounced differences in socioeconomic status of different households within Cherokee communities during the seventeenth and early eighteenth centuries, as there were later.[100]

This situation may have changed dramatically at the dawn of the eighteenth century, when there developed opportunities to trade deerskins with European colonists from Virginia, Carolina, and even Canada in exchange for European material culture such as beads and blankets.[101] These opportunities may have offered significant enticements for some towns to pursue trade relationships with French, English, and Spanish colonists to enhance their wealth and standing within the regional cultural landscape. Men may have even sought to enhance their power within their hometowns through their trading activities and access to material wealth from Europeans. By the late eighteenth century, Cherokee women were trading with their new colonial neighbors on their own, sometimes in ways that contradicted the wishes and policies of men in their towns.[102] But at the outset of the deerskin trade in the late seventeenth century, Cherokee men may have been major players in the kind of hunting that fit within traditional male roles, and in the actual exchange of deerskins for European goods because the European traders themselves were men.[103]

These points are meant to underscore the different sources of power available to women and men in Cherokee communities of the eighteenth century. The egalitarianism characteristic of historic Cherokee towns probably derived from decades or even centuries of negotiations and interactions between people with power in these distinct social domains. My suggestion is that within protohistoric native communities of southern Appalachia, this spread of power across different social domains effectively prevented any aspiring paramount chiefs from forming regional polities ruled by them and their close relatives. These dynamics have likely left some mark in the archaeological record of native towns in southern Appalachia and in the countryside between them. There are no major multimound centers at the top of multilayered settlement hierarchies like those centered at Moundville and Etowah during earlier eras. Nor is there clear evidence of elite households at Cherokee towns in southern Appalachia during the seventeenth and early eighteenth centuries.

Different models in the archaeological literature of the formation of Cherokee towns in southern Appalachia each contribute something significant to our knowledge of this interesting development spanning the late prehistoric and early historic periods. Schroedl is right that Cherokee towns formed out of the vestiges of earlier south Appalachian Mississippian chiefdoms, and that both the long-term history of these chiefdoms and the short-term geopolitical developments of the seventeenth century contributed to their formation as such.[104] Hally is right that there are significant parallels in historic Cherokee pottery and earlier ceramics in the Lamar tradition, and that these similarities in material culture relate in some way to cultural descent and ancestry.[105] Dickens is right that lifeways tailored to rugged mountain environments in western North Carolina form one major component of historic Cherokee culture.[106] Dickens is correct as well in arguing that movements of people between and within river valleys of western North Carolina and surrounding areas are one major dimension of the genesis of Cherokee communities as such.[107] Many people living in the Appalachian Summit province of western North Carolina indeed may have moved south during the sixteenth and seventeenth centuries to the Savannah headwaters and surrounding areas, which seem to have been wholly or partially abandoned during the seventeenth century or earlier. Many residents of the upper Savannah River watershed and southwestern North Carolina moved to what became known as the Overhill settlements during the eighteenth century, where they became members of towns spaced closely together near much more ancient mounds.

These movements are reflected in interregional spatial patterns in the archaeology of southern Appalachia. Archaeologists have mapped the movements of people from one region to another during the late prehistoric and protohistoric periods, although chronological frameworks in many valleys of western North Carolina are still rather broad, making it difficult to pinpoint the timing of these movements with precision.[108] Social dynamics within towns represent another social scale at which people came together to form the regional group known historically as the Cherokee. The social structure and spatial layouts of late prehistoric and protohistoric towns in western North Carolina deserve further study in their own right, and archaeologists still have much to learn about how towns were rebuilt, periodically abandoned, and in some cases resettled.[109] These topics deserve further archaeological consideration, as does the regional landscape of different river valleys between town centers. Mapping the landscape between towns is significant because people living in these outlying areas likely affiliated themselves with one or more towns, and it may well have been that there were alternating periods of nucleation and dispersal of people within different areas.

Ethnohistoric evidence of Cherokee culture and community in the eighteenth century gives archaeologists a model of social and political dynamics within and between towns, and archaeologists have learned much about the nature of towns as social entities related to specific points within the landscape. Archaeology in southern Appalachia offers opportunities to place these social entities called towns within the regional cultural landscapes of which they were a part, and further study of this scale of patterning in the archaeological record is an especially promising path for archaeologists to pursue.

ACKNOWLEDGMENTS

This paper was originally given as a contribution to Charles Hudson's anthropology graduate seminar at the University of Georgia about social coalescences in the native Southeast. I am grateful to professors and graduate students for my stimulating visit to Athens, and to my fellow grad students at Chapel Hill for our interesting conversations about archaeology and ethnohistory. Thanks to Professor Hudson, David Hally, Gerald Schroedl, Mark Williams, David Moore, and Brett Riggs for their advice and brainstorming. Thanks to Steve Davis, Trawick Ward, Vin Steponaitis, Margie Scarry, Brian Billman, Rob Beck, Bram Tucker, Greg Wilson, Tony Boudreaux, Amber VanDerwarker, Kathy McDonnell, and Steve Williams for their thoughtful and helpful comments. I appreciate the invitation from Robbie Ethridge to contribute to this book. I am grateful to Hope Spencer for her palpable support and encouragement. My paper owes much to these people. Any problems with this chapter are of course my own responsibility.

From Prehistory through Protohistory to Ethnohistory in and near the Northern Lower Mississippi Valley

MARVIN D. JETER

This chapter will begin with a discussion of general problems in correlating archaeological and ethnohistorical data. I will then scrutinize the terminal prehistoric to early historic situations in and near the northern portion of the Lower Mississippi Valley (LMV), with emphasis on the intervening protohistoric processes of sociocultural change, continuity, and discontinuity, as indicated by my readings of the relevant literature. I will close with critical summaries of several competing "scenarios" for relating the archaeological record to the ethnohistorical data, concluding with two compatible scenarios which I think have several important points in their favor.

DISCORDANT DIMENSIONS IN ARCHAEOLOGY AND ETHNOHISTORY

Protohistoric or ethnohistoric archaeology involves theoretically and methodologically difficult, but crucially important, attempts to link the completely undocumented (as far as written "eyewitness" or even hearsay accounts are concerned) prehistoric past with the situations described in early historic documents. We attempt to correlate the data provided by several distinct and independent (if not incommensurable) disciplines, in search of concordance,[1] if not complete consilience.[2]

Some time ago, I remarked that in the LMV, correlations between/among material culture, ethnicity, and language were likely to be significantly less than one-to-one, and cited Franz Boas's well-known dictum about the independence of race, language, and culture.[3] After I made further reviews of and reflections on the protohistoric archaeological literature and situations,[4] especially during a 1998 sabbatical, it dawned upon me that much of the difficulty derives from the different quantitative and qualitative characteristics of the data that are the stocks-in-trade of archaeology and ethnohistory. This can be clearly illustrated with regard

177

to the basic "dimensions of archaeology,"[5] namely space, time, and culture,[6] as shown in table 1.

	Archaeology	*Ethnohistory*
Space	Resolution can be very fine	Resolution often poor, uncertain
Time	Resolution often poor, $+/-$ factor	Resolution can be fine
Culture	Material/etic, via archaeologists	Behavioral/mental/emic, via observers/participants

Table 1. Dimensional contrasts between archaeology and ethnohistory.

Space. Archaeology's primary dimension, it seems obvious to me, is the spatial one: in the field, we can pinpoint horizontal and vertical locations down to the decimeter or centimeter, or even (really getting into "spurious accuracy") to the millimeter. Beyond mere measurement, we "read the dirt" to interpret strata, features, and associations in space.

Ethnohistory, though, often has problems with the spatial dimension. This is especially, and maddeningly, true for the documents of the Soto *entrada*: although some individual site identifications have been claimed, spatial resolution is often on the order of several kilometers at best—sometimes several tens of kilometers. Brain has argued for some time that a "swath" of variable width (up to several tens of km) is the best that the evidence permits.[7] More recently, he has stated that differences of opinion about the location of Soto's 1541 Quizquiz-Aquixo Mississippi River crossing, on the order of 50 miles (c. 80 km), are "insignificant" but that differences of placement for Anilco, Guachoya, and Aminoya in 1542–43 are "significant," as they are on the order of 150 miles (c. 240 km).[8]

With regard to spatial resolution, then, the difference of scale between archaeology (c. 1 cm) and this particular kind of ethnohistory (c. 10 km = 1,000,000 cm) is sometimes as much as six orders of magnitude, or one vs. one million. To a lesser degree, this also applies to the later chronicles of the French explorers; e.g., in Arkansas we are still not sure that we have precisely relocated even one of the four (or five?) classic Quapaw settlements of the 1670s to early 1700s.

Time. In contrast, time is almost always something of a struggle for archaeologists. It is approached only indirectly, through interpretations of the spatial data (especially associations); our accuracy and precision are always fuzzy, with plus/minus factors. Archaeologists dealing with proto-historic sites in the Southeast would generally be quite pleased with accuracy down to the nearest decade, and often have uncertainties within spans of several decades.

Instead, time is the strong suit of most of our ethnohistoric documents. The Soto chronicles are generally accurate down to the level of a few days, and sometimes agree on specific days, or even fairly specific times (morning, midday, afternoon, evening) within specific days.[9] Here, the difference in scale of resolution between archaeology (c. 10 years or 3,650 days) and ethnohistory (c. a fourth of a day) is often something like four orders of magnitude, or more than ten thousand to one.

Culture. With regard to the always-problematical cultural dimension, archaeology and ethnohistory often "discourse" past each other. "Culture" to many if not most archaeologists is expressed mainly in terms of material remains (artifacts, features, etc.) and their forms, styles, and (once again) spatial relationships (especially associations). It is basically "etic" in the anthropological sense of being imposed by Western scholarly or scientific worldviews and somewhat biased toward the "infrastructural" level of technology and economic production.[10]

The "structural" level of domestic and sociopolitical organization may also be approached, via intensive work at a number of sites, particularly via studies of settlement patterning at various scales, burial associations, etc. Although we all project our own "emic" views into our interpretations in various ways, we do not have much access through archaeology to the "superstructural" level, involving "emic" views of the long-deceased pre-literate people being studied, except through our own interpretations of their surviving artistic works. Archaeology has long involved the additional complexities of idealist-essentialist "typological thinking" with regard to artifacts, especially ceramics.

Ethnohistorically, aboriginal "culture" (both material/behavioral description and oral expression) comes to us in the documents filtered through and distorted by the European explorers' own "emic" views, motives, and hidden agendas, to be filtered and distorted further by our own. But at least this literature has a chance of communicating something of the Native Americans' "emics" as well, especially in the "superstructural" realms of ideology, religion, and ceremonialism, plus the "structural" level of sociopolitical organization.[11] What it generally does not communicate is adequate, let alone detailed, information about the archaeologists' most basic data sources, namely ceramic and lithic artifacts, nor indeed about major features such as mounds, although there is some tantalizing information about house types.

It has long been the hope of Harvard–Lower Mississippi Survey archaeologists that their basic unit of archaeological synthesis, the phase, could be closely correlated with, or equated to, the ethnohistorians' tribal/ ethnic groups.[12] But some of their attempted correlations have been strongly contested,[13] and there are doubts about the degree of correlation that can be expected[14] and the validity of the phase concept itself.[15]

In the "cultural" realm, then, the problems are not merely those of quantitative differences in scales of resolution. We are also struggling to find ways to deal with qualitative discordances between archaeological and ethnohistorical data.

Oral traditions. A special kind of ethnohistorical data is that derived from the oral traditions of Native Americans. Archaeologists have tended to avoid these traditions, or to dismiss them out of hand as hopelessly ethnocentric, inextricably entangled with the stuff of mythology, etc. In terms of the "dimensions" just discussed, they tend to be even more vague than Euro-ethnohistory with regard to space, even more imprecise than archaeology with regard to time, and predominantly "emic" culturally. Yet, they may contain kernels of information that can be correlated with "etic" data, and some attempts to do so will be made in the "scenarios" summarized below.

ARCHAEOLOGY AND ETHNOHISTORY IN AND NEAR THE
"NORTHERN LMV"

These are indeed contentious issues—in fact, we archaeologists cannot even seem to agree on the proper name for the major area under consideration here. Before plunging into scenarios, I will set the stage in terms of place, time, and actors.

Space: The "Northern LMV" and Beyond

Following the long-established usages of geologists[16] and several influential archaeologists,[17] I regard the LMV as the alluvial lands extending southward from around the mouth of the Ohio to the Gulf of Mexico. For the purposes of this paper, the "northern LMV" is regarded as approximately that portion between the mouths of the Ohio and Arkansas rivers.[18]

As indicated by this chapter's title, I will range somewhat beyond those boundaries (fig. 1). In the LMV proper, I will look southward as far as the Vicksburg and even Natchez localities, mainly with regard to Natchezan connections. I will also refer to regions well to the north and northeast, in search of Quapaw origins. West of the usually defined boundaries of the LMV, I will venture far up the Arkansas Valley, and also into the Ozarks north of that valley. This will enable me to deal more comprehensively with the Tunican-Quapaw question, and to incorporate relevant archaeological data from a number of Arkansas Valley sites and localities that have seen significant investigations in the past decade or two.

Near the mouth of the Arkansas, the Menard site and locality, brought to modern archaeological prominence by Ford, have seen important new work very recently.[19] A short distance upstream in the Pine Bluff vicinity, House has also reported on recent work at other "Menard complex" sites.[20] I have been involved for some time with the related Goldsmith Oliver 2 site on the eastern outskirts of Little Rock, most recently during my sabbatical and by comparative research related to the famous Oliver site in northwest Mississippi.[21] Hoffman synthesized data from 1930s excavations at the closely related Kinkead-Mainard site, just up the river from Little Rock, and since then has periodically reviewed aspects of the greater Arkansas Valley situation.[22] The very similar Carden Bottoms complex, farther upvalley, has long been infamous because of pot hunting,[23] but recent documentary and oral-history work has clarified the situation somewhat,[24] and new fieldwork has started on a limited scale.[25] Finally, in the Oklahoma-Arkansas borderlands, Schambach has argued that the famous Spiro site and related sites should be reinterpreted in a number of ways that are relevant here.[26]

I will also call upon my own primary research base in southeast Arkansas, where I have a long-standing interest in the late prehistoric to protohistoric situations.[27] This has been a good vantage point for observing related research by my colleagues, not only in the lower Arkansas Valley to the north and the Caddoan country (the Trans-Mississippi South, or TMS) to the west, but also in the Yazoo basin of Mississippi to the east[28] and the Tensas, Boeuf, and Ouachita basins to the south in northeast Louisiana.[29]

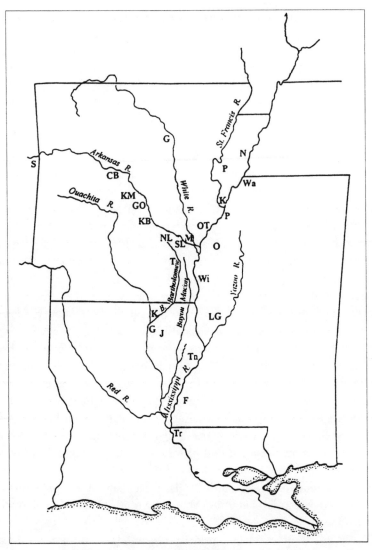

Fig. 1. Archaeological sites and phases in and near the lower Mississippi Valley.
Arkansas: CB = Carden Bottoms; G = Greenbrier; GO = Goldsmith Oliver; K =
Kent; KB = Kuykendall Brake; KM = Kinkead-Mainard; M = Menard; N =
Nodena; NL = Noble Lake; OT = Old Town; P = Parkin; SL = Sarassa Lake; T =
Tillar. **Oklahoma:** S = Spiro. **Mississippi:** F = Fatherland ("Grand Village of the
Natchez"); LG = Lake George; O = Oliver; P = Parchman; Wa = Walls; Wi =
Winterville. **Louisiana:** G = Glendora; J = Jordan; K = Keno; Tn = Taensa; Tr =
Trudeau (the "Tunica Treasure" site).

Time Span: The Protohistoric Period, Plus or Minus

I concur with generally established LMV usage in setting the prehistoric-protohistoric boundary at about A.D. 1500, and the protohistoric-historic one at around 1700.[30] Dye has further suggested a three-way division of the Protohistoric period, with the Early portion ending in the early 1540s with the Soto *entrada*; the long Middle portion (also called the "Protohistoric Dark Ages") continuing until the appearance of the first French explorers in 1673; and a short Late portion, marked by increasingly frequent contacts as the French colonial enterprise intensified (and the Native American cultures were increasingly modified by the culture-contact processes).[31] The most critical problem here is bridging the Middle Protohistoric gap, which has increasingly appeared to entail significant cultural changes, and even discontinuities, as archeological data have accumulated and the ethnohistorical accounts have been reexamined.

Although some successes have been claimed for linking specific archaeological sites to specific settlements of ethnohistorically documented Native American groups (specifically, the Quapaw and Tunica) in the northern LMV regions surveyed here,[32] I have my doubts about all of these cases.[33] So far, the nearest apparently successful attempts to apply the "direct historical method" in the entire LMV have been well to the south, at the Fatherland site, "the Grand Village of the Natchez."[34] West of the LMV, there have been more general identifications of groups of sites as Caddoan. Those TMS regions seem to have been relatively stable in protohistoric times, perhaps due to their relatively remote situation, far from Mississippi River traffic, and their dispersed-hamlet settlement pattern, relatively nonconducive to the spread of epidemics.

The northern LMV situation seems to me similar to that described by Marvin Smith for eastern portions of the "interior Southeast" where essentially undocumented Middle Protohistoric period disease decimations and population movements have made use of the "direct historical method" extremely difficult.[35] Such disruptions may well have been at their very worst in and near northeast Arkansas and the lower Arkansas Valley, where the Spaniards of the 1540s found the densest Native American populations they had encountered. Ironically, these seemingly strong "paramount chiefdom" societies may have been the most vulnerable to European diseases (either brought in by Soto's people or later via trade), because of their concentrations of people with no resistance to Old World pathogens and the lack of knowledge of the actual causes of these diseases.

For the first time, the archaeological record is augmented by sketchy ethnohistorical descriptions, left to us by the Spanish chroniclers. But, as is all too well known, attempts to identify known sites (or archaeological phases) with specific settlements (or "provinces") named in the chronicles are arguable at best in this area.[36]

The "Dark Ages" certainly must be represented at a number of archaeological sites, although we have been generally uncertain as to just which components at these sites actually date to these times. The Goldsmith Oliver 2 site[37] has been something of a revelation and turning point in this regard, mainly because of a revision in dating based on European trade goods.[38] Now it and other "Menard complex" sites are regarded as having had significant occupations in the "Dark Ages" span.[39] Previously, they would have been assigned to the Late Protohistoric to Early Historic periods, as much as a century later.

Some 130 years after Soto, the Native American situations are described more and more regularly, and in increasing detail, by documents derived from the earlier (1673; 1682 to early 1700s) French explorations. However, we also begin to encounter a sort of "uncertainty principle" in that, as a general tendency, the more detailed the description, the more likely that the Native American group in question had been changed by various direct impacts and side effects of European contact. And now, with the earlier dating for trade goods and site components, these have become the periods for which we have the most glaring gap in the archaeological record.

Archaeo-Cultures

Given these spatial and temporal boundaries, this chapter must be bounded in the cultural sense as well. Its coverage begins in the 1400s with two relevant terminal prehistoric (late Mississippi period) to early protohistoric cultural traditions known only via archaeology. These are (1) the Mississippian tradition in and near the northern LMV, up the Arkansas Valley, and expanding southward into southeast Arkansas and beyond; and (2) the Plaquemine tradition just to the south, in southeast Arkansas and adjacent western Mississippi, and shrinking southward.[40]

Mississippian. As is well known, this cultural tradition is characterized by predominantly shell-tempered pottery and other distinctive artifact types and by subsistence involving significant maize agriculture.[41] More to the point in this volume on "social history" is that Mississippian social organization, inferred mainly from site-plan and settlement pattern studies at various scales of analysis (but also to some extent from the Soto chronicles), was obviously fairly complex, probably ranging from "big man" tribes to more or less ordinary chiefdoms, but with several societies in and near northeast Arkansas apparently attaining a sort of "paramount chiefdom" status.

Mississippian archaeological/artifactual "culture" (whatever this may represent in terms of tribal/ethnic societies and linguistic groups) seems to have spread southward down the LMV rather gradually, on the order of a few tens of km/miles per century, and had reached northeast Louisiana and adjacent Mississippi by late prehistoric to early protohistoric times.[42] My own impression is that this was mainly a process of diffusion of technology (including shell-tempering of pottery),[43] subsistence practices, stylistic motifs, and religious beliefs/practices, quite probably crossing tribal/ethnic and linguistic boundaries, rather than a southward expansion of "Mississippians."[44]

Mississippian houses were "typically" relatively small and rectangular to squarish, with wattle-and-daub walls and thatched roofs. However, evidence is accumulating that at least some of these structures, perhaps those occupied in the warmer seasons, were not daubed.[45] The earlier Mississippian sites are characterized by farmsteads and more or less formally laid-out villages, plus ceremonialism centered on "temple mound" sites. Later, in late prehistoric to protohistoric times, there were nucleated (sometimes fortified) towns. In northeast Arkansas at least, generations of reoccupation at some sites produced large and deep accumulations of structural rubble and other debris, comparable at least in principle to Near Eastern Neolithic *tells*.[46]

Unfortunately, virtually all of these sites have been riddled by pot hunters for many decades. The work of nineteenth-century archaeologists and Clarence B. Moore at the beginning of the twentieth century, plus the "professional" excavations of the 1930s, all concentrated on recovering burial pottery, and did not produce much in the way of data on intrasite settlement patterning.[47] A praiseworthy effort at recording house locations at the Upper Nodena site, by Dr. James K. Hampson, led to a "tentative" site map, but the houses were not described in any detail and their contemporaneity was merely assumed.[48] Late prehistoric to protohistoric Mississippian sites in the northern LMV have seen nothing like the modern intensive area excavations that were done under the auspices of the FAI-270 project in the American Bottoms.[49] Such work here would have to be done on a truly massive scale, given the complex nature of the deep deposits. The major ongoing effort in this regard is being carried out by the Arkansas Archeological Survey's Parkin Research Station, primarily through summer field schools directed by Jeffrey Mitchem.[50]

There is some evidence that by middle protohistoric times, similar sites were accumulating along the lower Arkansas Valley.[51] But in the Mississippian frontier zone to the south, in southeast Arkansas, a simpler "rural Mississippian" settlement pattern apparently prevailed in terminal prehistoric and protohistoric times, with scattered farmsteads locally integrated by ceremonial/mortuary centers until virtual abandonment in the (earlier?) 1600s.[52] A similar dispersed-settlement situation also appears to have been the case in northeast Louisiana until middle to terminal protohistoric or early historic times, when relatively brief population nucleations occurred, perhaps the result of migrations and/or fusions of diverse remnant peoples after disease impacts.[53] The contemporary situation in the Yazoo basin, across the Mississippi from southeast Arkansas, is open to question; it will be discussed near the end of this chapter.

Plaquemine. The Plaquemine archaeological "culture" is a rather nebulous concept; its definitions and interpretations have varied over the years and from one authority to another.[54] In these regards, it rivals those other peripheral, not-quite-Mississippian but more or less contemporary archaeo-entities, Fort Ancient in the Ohio Valley and Oneota in the upper to central (in my sense) Mississippi Valley.

Artifactually, Plaquemine culture is recognized mainly by a more or less agreed-upon suite of grog-tempered pottery types, showing some continuity with those of the preceding Coles Creek culture, from which Plaquemine appears to have developed by around 1200.[55] In the earlier literature, it was seen as an interpolation between the previously defined Coles Creek and Natchez complexes, in the regions around Natchez to Vicksburg and adjacent Louisiana. Later, Jeffrey Brain contended that it was mainly a product of Mississippian (Cahokian) influences on the more northern Coles Creek cultures, as suggested by his work at the Winterville Mounds site near Greenville.[56] The Plaquemine emergence was accompanied by a major outburst of construction of flat-topped, Mississippian-like, "temple" mounds, between about 1200 and 1350 or 1400.[57]

Although it had long been speculated that Coles Creek culture had been significantly dependent on maize agriculture,[58] that has not been borne out by flotation and archaeobotanical analyses. Instead, it appears that although maize was present in late (or "transitional") Coles Creek times, c. 1000–1200, it was not an important part of the subsistence base until between 1200 and 1400, in Plaquemine contexts.[59]

In any event, the northernmost extent of Plaquemine culture in the lower Yazoo basin appears to have been just beyond Winterville, around the 1300s.[60] West of the Mississippi, it may have extended even farther north, well up into southeast Arkansas along Bayou Bartholomew and the Ouachita-Saline drainage, stopping just short of the lower Arkansas Valley. Again, there was an outburst of mound building, though on a smaller scale than along the Mississippi. During or after the 1300s, artifactually defined archaeological Plaquemine "culture" (but not necessarily groups of people) retreated as Mississippian culture spread southward.[61]

Plaquemine houses (or "temples," as a good proportion of the excavated structures have been atop mounds) generally but not uniformly changed from early circular forms with Coles Creek prototypes to rectangular forms suggestive of Mississippian influences.[62] Throughout the Plaquemine realm, the basic settlement pattern appears to have featured dispersed habitation sites, probably farmsteads, rather than towns or even large villages. Even the mound centers "do not seem to have become true towns" like some of their Mississippian counterparts.[63] In the lower Yazoo basin, there was apparently a tendency toward nucleation of small habitation sites around major ceremonial centers like Winterville and Lake George.[64] Brain suggested that this, and a new Mississippian-like pattern of one mound dominating the others at these sites, indicated that an "elite" with "theocratic trappings" was now in charge of a chiefdom-like redistributive system.[65]

By the 1400s, the former northern Plaquemine territory became part of the Mississippian sphere of influence, and the major mound centers declined.[66] To the south in the Natchez region, there was a "basic reorientation of settlement patterns" as major sites moved inland, away from the perhaps-dangerous Mississippi River.[67] This trend continued into protohistoric times.[68]

In late protohistoric times, major local depopulations, and immigrations of refugee groups, apparently occurred in the Mississippianized lower Yazoo basin.[69] In the Natchez bluffs, Plaquemine culture also suffered a "marked decline" in population, as occupation became "concentrated . . . around the historic home of the Natchez Indians" with some evidence of immigration.[70]

ETHNOHISTORICAL CULTURES: NORTHERN LMV TRIBAL-ETHNIC GROUPS

If we are trying to match archaeological findings to ethnohistorically documented groups, we should start by identifying which of those groups will be considered. The only specifically named ethnic/tribal/linguistic groups who have been seriously proposed in recent decades as being represented by these late prehistoric and protohistoric sites and phases in the northern LMV are the Quapaw and Tunicans. I will nominate a third group below.

Quapaw. Although some have argued (see "scenario" discussions, below) that the Quapaw were at least in the northernmost LMV by late prehistoric to early protohistoric times, and were contacted at least once (at "Pacaha") by the *entrada* in 1541, this is not generally accepted today. They were not definitely documented by Europeans until 1673 and the 1680s, when French explorers found them living in a few settlements within a rather restricted locality, mainly along the Mississippi River near the mouth of the Arkansas. One (ironically, the one called "Akansea") was actually in the present state of Mississippi, apparently very near the Mississippi River. Another, Osotouy (first reported by Tonti in 1686), was a short distance up the Arkansas.

During some of these first contacts, the Quapaw were described as living in bark-covered longhouses, and quite possibly using larger versions of these structures as "council houses."[71] This glaring discordance from the archaeological record (as so far known) of late prehistoric and protohistoric structures in these regions, and other problems with the "Quapaw phase" concept, resulted in the designation of a "Quapaw paradox."[72] My own opinion (elaborated below) is that they had not been in this locality, nor indeed in the northern LMV, for very long when the French appeared in 1673, but this is by no means proven.

There does not appear to be much in the way of definitive information about aboriginal Quapaw sociopolitical organization. Some of the earliest accounts mention structures used by "chiefs," but there is no detailed account of their powers and activities. There are some indications that they were recognized only or mainly on the individual-village level, that they were closely associated with warriors (and feasted with them on dog flesh on special occasions), and that there was at least a ceremonial seating arrangement of chief-elders-warriors-common people.[73] There were probably clans organized into moieties, with the village-chief position inherited in the male line; villages were apparently generally autonomous, although pan-village consensus could be sought in important matters.[74]

Along with at least one former believer in the "Quapaw phase,"[75] I have contended for some time that we do not really know what the Quapaw archaeological/artifactual record looks like, and think that much of what had been called "Quapaw" may actually be attributable to Tunicans and/ or others.[76] We have some renewed hopes, though, that a Quapaw assemblage from somewhere in the 1700–1750 period may soon be identified.[77] Meanwhile, most Arkansas archaeologists have turned to the ethnically/ linguistically neutral term "Menard complex" as a label for these protohistoric to early historic Arkansas Valley assemblages.[78]

Tunicans. A somewhat stronger case for time depth in the lower Mississippi and/or Arkansas valleys can be made with regard to the Tunicans. For the time of the Soto *entrada*, Jeffrey Brain has long argued that the village called Quizquiz, encountered in 1541 near the Mississippi River in present northwest Mississippi, was a Tunica settlement.[79] There are a few linguistic clues that the powerful chiefdom of Pacaha, in northeast Arkansas, may have been Tunican.[80] Some have argued that the province of "Coligua" (near North Little Rock, they believed; but in the Hudson reconstruction it is near Batesville, northeast of central Arkansas) was probably the protohistoric Koroa (Coroa).[81] The latter are believed by some, on very slender evidence, to have been Tunican speakers.[82] Kidder concurred on the "Coligua = Koroa" possibility, and also has suggested that the Kinkead-Mainard and Carden Bottoms archaeological remains might relate to the Koroa.[83] It is generally agreed that the Soto-documented settlement of "Tanico," in the province of "Cayas," somewhere in western Arkansas, was Tunican. Swanton and Dickinson placed it at Hot Springs, but Hudson puts it in the Carden Bottoms locality.[84]

During the French contact period much later, Marquette and Jolliet in 1673 reported (at second hand) that up the Arkansas Valley from the Akansea-Quapaw settlements were those of groups including the "Tanikoua" and "Akoroa," who are believed to have been Tunica and Koroa. At

least in the account of the La Salle expedition of 1682 (which did not mention the Arkansas Valley situation), the Tunica group (refugees?) reported
by hearsay in the Vicksburg vicinity were characterized as enemies of the
Akansea-Quapaw and the (probably Natchezan) Taensa.[85] The same expedition reported a group of Koroa living near the Natchez.[86] Subsequent
accounts in the 1680s and 1690s mention names closely resembling those
of the Tunica or Koroa in or near southeast Arkansas, but they are not
documented in the Arkansas Valley after 1673, and seem to have completely left Arkansas by about 1700, moving southward down the lower
valley.[87]

Tunicans, apparently displaced, were observed in the Vicksburg vicinity in 1700 and said to have had round houses, with cane lathing or wattle
and mud-plaster daub, covered (roofed?) with "straw."[88] At least, this is
a generic southeastern and LMV house type, in contrast to the Quapaw
longhouses. Round houses may have been a winter form used by people
who had rectangular houses in warmer weather. Another French source
of 1700 described the Tunica in the same locality as having seven "hamlets" with "50 or 60 small cabins."[89] Accounts of their later southward
movements have been summarized by Brain.[90] A sketch painted by
Dumont de Montigny between 1728 and 1742 shows a Tunica village with
rectangular houses, but this may be an artistic convention or might represent Houma houses taken over by Tunicans.[91]

If one assumes that Spanish-contacted settlements and provinces of the
1540s, such as Quizquiz, Pacaha, Coligua, and Tanico, were indeed Tunican, then a picture of populous, and in some cases powerful, Tunican
chiefdoms can be inferred, along with connections to early-middle protohistoric and late prehistoric archaeological sites and phases. There is
pathetically little information, though, about late protohistoric Tunicans
and their lifeways in the northern LMV. While conceding that the early
French accounts indicate more simply structured "remnant" groups of
Tunicans, Brain suggested that some elements of a sociopolitical hierarchy
survived.[92] Although he spoke of a "Tunica continuum," he conceded that
"change did not occur at a constant rate."[93] That may be an extreme
understatement; in any event there is a huge gap in the dates of his data
sources, from the putative Soto contact of 1541 to 1699.[94] The entire Middle and Late Protohistoric periods are missing.

Neighboring, Visiting/Trading, or Intruding Groups

A few archaeologically and/or ethnohistorically documented or hinted-at neighboring or "foreign"groups appear to have visited or intruded into the northern LMV or the Arkansas Valley during the protohistoric period. I will summarize them briefly here, but they will be essentially left out of the big-picture scenarios below. I will also mention some hypothetical "northern Natchezans" here, and will elaborate on this concept in a new scenario. I will not deal at all with groups such as the Chickasaw and Choctaw, mainly in the uplands east of the LMV, who have been studied extensively by others.[95]

Caddoans. These Indians of south-central to (especially) southwest Arkansas and adjacent portions of bordering states have been believed by some to have inhabited parts of the Arkansas Valley in the present Arkansas-Oklahoma borderlands, and lands northward into the Ozarks, in late prehistoric to protohistoric times. However, I agree with Schambach's recent arguments that they were basically restricted to the West Gulf Coastal Plains and Ouachita Mountains, centering on the Red and Ouachita valleys, and generally stopped short of the Arkansas Valley proper, not to mention the Arkansas Ozarks.[96]

There is, though, some evidence of a late prehistoric to protohistoric Caddoan expansion northeastward toward the Arkansas Valley in south-central Arkansas.[97] Also, there appear to have been Caddoan contacts with late protohistoric to historic Mississippians in the Arkansas Valley;[98] and perhaps even a Caddoan "ceremonial" site at the southern margin of the Arkansas Valley, below Little Rock.[99] The Caddoan situation is discussed in this volume, from a northeast Texas perspective, by Perttula.

Mitchigamea. These Illinoian-speaking people were described in the Marquette-Jolliet documents as having a village on the Mississippi River in eastern Arkansas above the Akansea-Quapaw.[100] However, they were mapped ambiguously, resulting in a "Mitchigamea problem."[101] Of their two "village" symbols on the Marquette map, one was indeed on the Mississippi, just above the "Akansea" (Quapaw) symbol on the east side, but the other was inland, apparently "about 50 miles west of the Mississippi" and a similar (lesser?) distance north of the Arkansas.[102]

Phillips et al., following the historian Jean Delanglez, leaned toward the interpretation that the Mississippi-bank settlement had actually been a

Quapaw village, the one later called "Kappa" (= "Quapaw"), and that the actual Mitchigamea village had been the inland one.[103] Morse and Morse, though, accepted the edge-of-the-Mississippi interpretation.[104]

But later, Dan Morse excavating at an inland site in northeast Arkansas, found European trade goods, and suggested that it had been the 1673 "Michigamea [sic] village" instead.[105] I doubt this; I have suggested that "this could well have been a village of the Michigamea, but it is not necessarily the one alluded to . . . in 1673."[106] Even if a component at Morse's site does date to the 1670s, although the trade goods may date somewhat later ("they seem to indicate a date of 1700, plus or minus thirty years" according to Morse), it is not only some 75 miles west of the Mississippi, but also nearly 150 miles north of the Arkansas.[107] That simply does not jibe at all with the inland "Mitchigamea" location indicated by the Marquette map.

However, Morse's suggestion that this may have been a temporary "summer village" of Mitchigamea traders is of great interest for comparative purposes (see the next section).[108] So is the location of this site with European trade goods, regardless of which Native American group was involved there. It is near a major trail leading from the Cahokia–St. Louis vicinity to the middle Arkansas Valley.[109]

Wichita. This rather distantly based group, or one or more of their several subdivisions, may also have been at least seasonal trading (and/or raiding?) visitors into what is now Arkansas. The proto-Wichita homeland appears to have been the "province" known as "Quivira" to sixteenth- and seventeenth-century Spanish explorers from New Mexico. It was probably located along the Arkansas River and its tributaries in what is now central Kansas, where the subsistence base involved maize agriculture and bison hunting.[110]

It has generally been believed that the "Tula" who were contacted by the Soto *entrada* in October 1541, almost certainly somewhere in western Arkansas, were the first Caddoan-speakers encountered, marking a sharp linguistic boundary.[111] Dickinson "speculate[d] that the Tula were Wichita rather than Caddo proper," noting that the Wichita were Southern Plains Caddoans.[112] Following Swanton, Dickinson believed that the Spanish-Tula contact took place around Caddo Gap, far south of the Arkansas Valley. Hudson's revision placed Tula well to the north, but still in the Ouachita Mountains.[113] However, Early suggested that a better fit would be in the Arkansas Valley near the present town of Ozark, upstream from Car-

den Bottoms (she did not speculate about Tula's cultural/tribal affiliation).[114] Hudson agreed that this location was quite plausible, and reiterated that this contact might have represented a cultural/linguistic "divide"
between some Mississippian ("possibly Tunican") variant and "a Caddoan
culture" represented archaeologically by the Fort Coffee phase.[115] More
recently, he has suggested that the Tula might have been either Caddoans
from the Ouachitas or "people who were ancestral to the Wichitas."[116]

It is likewise believed that names such as "Paniassa," which appears on
the Marquette 1673 map, apparently south of the Arkansas River and well
within present-day Arkansas, refer to a branch of the Wichita, as do names
such as "Mento(u)".[117] If Mildred Wedel is correct, some subgroup(s) of
the Wichita also had trading contacts with Puebloan Indians in New Mexico, and there is some archaeological evidence of this during late prehistoric and protohistoric times.[118]

There are also a few hints of Plains connections in the Middle Protohistoric period Native American artifact assemblage from the Goldsmith Oliver 2 site at Little Rock.[119] There is at least some possibility that European
trade goods found at that site, probably dating around the early 1600s,[120]
may have been derived from Spanish Colonial sources in New Mexico,
although the Spanish missions near St. Augustine, Florida, are probably
more likely sources.[121] Similar items have been found at related contemporary sites farther down the Arkansas Valley,[122] and more than one hundred turquoise beads, quite possibly from southwestern sources, were
found at the Oliver site in northwest Mississippi, just inland and northeast
of the mouth of the Arkansas.[123] One possibility is that some of this material could have been brought as far as "Quivira" by the 1601 expedition of
Juan de Oñate, and given to the proto-Wichita in central Kansas, then
traded down the Arkansas Valley.[124]

Dan Morse suggested that his putative Mitchigamea "village of Illinois
speakers" was "five days' travel" from the Akansea-Quapaw settlements
near the mouth of the Arkansas.[125] But, as I have pointed out, "this con-
flates two statements cited (confusingly) by Delanglez: that there was an
Illinois village *four* days away and a separate source's remark that *five*
days away there was 'a nation that trades with those of California.' "[126] I
suggest instead that the latter "nation" may have been a Wichita subgroup, visiting the Arkansas Valley as seasonal traders. I suspect that the
"California" allusion was an understandable mistake, a result of the
French explorers' confusion about Indians' vague hearsay allusions to

Spaniards and other Indians "way Out West," which was actually present-day New Mexico.[127]

Osage. This group is usually included in popular accounts of "Indians of Arkansas."[128] In fact, their hunting parties did range down into the Arkansas Ozarks, and they raided as far south as the Arkansas Valley in historic times, but they were based in western Missouri, well above the present state line. No archaeological sites in Arkansas have ever been conclusively linked to the Osage. I mention them here only for the sake of some semblance of completeness, and will discuss them later in a scenario of Quapaw origins.

Natchezans. As noted above, there appears to have been a substantial continuity from protohistoric Plaquemine culture to that of the Natchez in their historic homeland, far south of the "northern LMV" regions. However, the Taensa, apparently Natchezan-speakers, were found living in seven to nine villages on Lake St. Joseph, near the Mississippi River in what is now northeast Louisiana, by La Salle's expedition in 1682 and by later French observers. They were said to have had a "chief," wattle-and-daub structures including a temple with "perpetual fire" maintenance, and Natchez-like customs, including human sacrifice. They also already had some trade goods. They were forced to move southward in 1706, moved as far as Mobile, and gradually disintegrated as a tribal/ethnic unit during the later 1700s.[129]

The complex social organization of the Natchez themselves, with the "Great Sun" at the top and ranked classes below, has been a source of fascination and debate for many decades.[130] But it should be remembered that the archaeological record indicates a "marked decline" in population in the Natchez bluffs during the Plaquemine-Natchez transition, with evidence of some late immigration. In a new scenario, I will summarize evidence suggesting that groups of "northern Natchezans," including the Taensa, may have lived well up in the northern LMV in late prehistoric to early protohistoric times, and migrated southward from there during the middle to late protohistoric decades.

Languages

Since we are unavoidably verging into linguistics, some basic facts and conjectures about languages are also well worth reviewing. The Quapaw spoke a Siouan language, specifically the Quapaw variant of the Dhegiha division of Siouan; the other languages in this division are Omaha-Ponca and Osage-Kansa.[131] The most significant implications of linguistics in this regard are that migrations definitely must have occurred, to result in the widespread historic separation of the Dhegihans, and that earlier migrations must have been responsible for the other Siouan dispersals. But the times of these migrations and the locations of the former homelands are still matters for educated conjecture and debate.

The Tunica language was once believed to have been rather distantly related to the Muskogean languages of the Southeast, and to Natchez, all within a hypothesized "Gulf" macrogroup; but Tunican is now generally regarded as a "linguistic isolate."[132] The Koroa may have spoken a Tunican language, although the evidence is very skimpy. Other groups, shown (based on hearsay) along the Arkansas Valley between the "Tonikoua" and "Akoroa" on the 1673 Marquette-Jolliet expedition maps, may have been Tunican speakers.[133]

Natchez had been suggested as fairly close to Muskogean, but is now also regarded as an "isolate."[134] The extinct language of the Taensa was virtually omitted from the discussions in recent major reviews, but Swanton devoted considerable effort to demonstrating its close affinity to Natchez.[135]

Especially in the last of the "scenarios" which follow, I provisionally accept Swanton's linguistic interpretations of place names along the *entrada* route, but apply them to locations suggested by Hudson's revision of the route. Assuming for the moment that Swanton was wrong, even far off, about the route, it does not necessarily follow that he was also wrong about the languages themselves. Indeed, it seems to me that relocating his placements of them tends to clear up several long-standing problems.

Genetics?

In confining the discussion so far to archaeology, ethnohistory, and linguistics, I have not mentioned one kind of data which does not yet exist for this specific situation, but which appears to have the potential to make the others obsolete, or ancillary, as means of determining relationships. This would be genetic data, in the form of DNA analyses of samples from bones or other tissues. Comparing DNA from large numbers of samples from human remains found at these archaeological sites to samples (e.g., derived from hair) from large numbers of present-day Native American descendants of various groups might well essentially solve the problem of relative strengths of biological relationships.[136] I have been suggesting this for some time, and am pleased to see it recommended elsewhere in a similar situation.[137]

For the time being, though, this approach seems unlikely because of the reluctance of Native Americans to permit such sampling of archaeological skeletal remains or to submit samples themselves. If they do not want scientific information about their own biological relationships to past peoples, who are we to harangue them about obtaining it?[138] Instead, for the moment at least, we must fall back on attempting to improve the logical or hypothetical connections among the data sources that are available. There is no lack of alternative possibilities.

COMPETING SCENARIOS OF PROTOHISTORIC ARCHAEO-ETHNICITY

In 1990, I outlined three hypothetical "scenarios" for the protohistoric situation: a "maximum Quapaw" scenario; a sort of in-between Tunican-Quapaw amalgam; and a "maximum Tunican" scenario, which was then my own preference.[139] I essentially ignored the more cautious approach which avoided attempting to ascribe ethnicity to archaeological situations.[140] The "maximum" versions were purposely devised as logical opposites, to emphasize the differences between them, in an effort to stimulate discussion and research; the "in-between" version had then recently been proposed by Brain.[141]

A fair amount of discussion has indeed followed in Arkansas, though most of it has been informal and very little has been published. At least some discussions have tended to identify me exclusively with the "maximum Tunican" scenario that I favored in the 1990 report,[142] despite my emphasis on using such scenarios as "provocative" or "heuristic" devices, and my remark, adapted from Cyrus Thomas, that although I then believed it to be the best scenario, "I am not wedded to it."[143]

Here, after once again dismissing the "agnostic" approach, I will briefly update the three 1990 scenarios, interpolating a "moderate Quapaw" version in their midst. Next, I will summarize a colleague's recently proposed "Tunicans far west" scenario, followed by a "Tunicans and northern Natchezans" scenario, presented here for the first time. I will conclude with a "very late Quapaw/Dhegiha migration" scenario, which deserves a section of its own, involving more detail (and a later suggested dating) than my 1990 outline, which was part of the "maximum Tunican" scenario.

An "Agnostic" Approach

I will not call this version a "scenario" because it suggests that no assignments of archaeological remains to ethnohistoric tribal groups are possible in this particular case, at this time and state of our knowledge. Perhaps the principal practitioner of this approach in this vicinity has been my colleague John House, who has cautiously and consistently (and probably wisely) declined to speculate. He has insisted on separation between concepts like "ethnohistoric Quapaw" on one hand, and "Quapaw phase" or "Menard complex" or just plain "Mississippian" for the archaeological remains on the other.[144]

Taken to extremes, though, such approaches seem to deny our chances of ever getting satisfactory answers to such questions. This can perhaps be seen in the negative attitude toward archaeology (or at least that of the Soto *entrada* route) of the ultraskeptical nonarchaeologist David Henige.[145] Meanwhile, every now and then, a lost fort or La Salle ship gets found and rather conclusively identified. New approaches may also be able to bypass the old "archaeology vs. ethnohistory vs. linguistics" stalemates, or those caused by lack of sufficient data in these traditional approaches. As noted above, DNA analyses have the potential to characterize the strengths of biological relationships among sampled archaeological skeletal populations and of their relationships to possible descendant populations.

The "Maximum Quapaw" Scenario

The basic premises here are that every protohistoric phase or site that has ever been called or suggested as "Quapaw" or Quapaw-related by legitimate archaeologists does indeed represent the ethnohistoric Quapaw, and furthermore, that there was significant time depth to the Quapaw occupation of these regions, going well back into the last centuries of prehistory (before 1500).

This concept would include not only Phillips's Quapaw phase, but also its extension by Hoffman to the Kinkead-Mainard site above Little Rock (although Hoffman no longer argues for that),[146] plus the Carden Bottoms complex which is clearly closely related to the Quapaw phase–Menard complex, as noted by Hoffman.[147] The Goldsmith Oliver 2 site, and related sites in the "downstream from Little Rock" locality, would fit right in. Also included as "Quapaw" here would be at least the last occupation at Oliver, as hinted at by Phillips and Brain, and any related sites and phases in northwest Mississippi.[148]

Going back into late prehistoric times, this scenario includes not merely the Nodena phase (see below) of northeasternmost Arkansas, but also the rest of the major late "chiefdom" and "paramount chiefdom" phases of northeast Arkansas and adjacent Tennessee and northwest Mississippi. These would be Parkin, Kent, Greenbrier, Old Town, etc., in Arkansas, plus Walls, Hushpuckena, and Parchman in Mississippi.

In one sense, this is the "officially recognized" scenario for Arkansas, where NAGPRA agreements have designated the modern Quapaw as the tribe to be consulted for late prehistoric as well as protohistoric remains from the entire northeast quarter of the state and much of the Arkansas Valley as well, relegating the Tunicans to portions of southeast Arkansas. I think this may be grossly incorrect, but there it is, fait (or fiat?) accompli. It does appear that the system is working reasonably well, and I hold no particular brief in favor of Tunicans over Quapaws; in fact, as will be seen, I am perfectly willing to reconsider the "maximum Tunican" scenario.

My opposition to the "maximum Quapaw" scenario is based primarily on the "Quapaw paradox" that has been noted in publications for well over a decade now, but has never been resolved.[149] In my opinion, the discrepancies between the former "Quapaw phase" (now "Menard complex") and ethnohistoric descriptions of the Quapaw are stronger than ever, a result of the recent earlier dating for the Menard complex plus the increasing likelihood that the Quapaw arrived very late indeed to the Lower Mississippi Valley.

A "Moderate Quapaw" or "Nodena-Quapaw" Scenario

This might be better characterized as a "minimalist Quapaw" scenario, as about all it does is to get a Quapaw foot in the northern LMV's door, as it were, in late prehistoric to early protohistoric times. But at least it does not shut them out completely in those times, and it allows for recognition of the somewhat later "Quapaw phase" as at least partially, if not totally, ethnic Quapaw. It was not spelled out in my Goldsmith Oliver 2 contract report, wherein it was absorbed into the deliberately provocative "maximum Quapaw" scenario.

Here, I attempt to paraphrase Dan and Phyllis Morse.[150] They suggest that the Quapaw may have arrived in northeast Arkansas by around 1400–1450, and that certain artifacts (e.g., catlinite disk pipes and Matthews Incised pottery) attest the arrival of Siouans from farther north in or near the Mississippi Valley (but not from well up the Ohio Valley).

The Morses have generally claimed only (or mainly) the Nodena phase, or portions thereof, as Quapaw-in-Arkansas at the time of the Soto *entrada* in 1541. This derives initially from a rendering of Soto's "Pacaha" province as "Capaha" (which resembles "Kappa" and "Quapaw") by Garcilaso de la Vega, the least reliable of the Soto chroniclers,[151] and follows from the Morses' belief that Pacaha is represented by the Nodena phase.

However, the leading linguistic scholar of the Quapaw language, Robert Rankin, has firmly rejected the Capaha-Quapaw equation and concluded that there is no evidence whatever of Siouan words recorded by the Spaniards at Pacaha or anywhere else; and, furthermore, that the three words that were (approximately) recorded looked like *Tunican* words, with meanings that appeared to reflect *Tunican* social organization and practices.[152] Dan Morse has protested that the sample size is totally inadequate, and that all complex societies had interpreters.[153] I can only counter that the Spaniards were at Pacaha for something like forty days, and not only did not record any Siouan words, but also did not mention any linguistic change from whatever they had encountered at Quizquiz and related provinces, which may have been Tunican or some other non-Siouan language.[154] This should be viewed in a broader context: the Spaniards instantly noted a change to an unknown language when they later encountered the Tula (possibly Caddoan-speakers, perhaps a Wichita subgroup), probably in western Arkansas; I would emphasize that Soto's own highly valued interpreter of southeastern Indian languages, Juan Ortiz, was still alive during the Tula episode.

As far as I know, the Morses have never published an argument, or even a statement, that contemporary phases adjacent to—and quite similar to—the Nodena phase (e.g., Parkin, Kent) were Quapaw at the time of the *entrada*. Indeed, I do not know that they have ever suggested *any* ethnic identification for any of these phases in their classic locations. Phyllis Morse did suggest that a difference in ceramic tempering between Parkin (overwhelmingly coarser shell) and Nodena (more use of finer shell,

"Bell" paste) was "probably a tribal difference, not a temporal one" but did not suggest what tribe might be involved.[155]

The Morses for some time regarded the "Quapaw phase" as fully Mississippian, but felt that it was being overly expanded, and welcomed its replacement by the "Menard complex" term.[156] They have suggested, in various ways, that the Quapaw of the 1670s to early 1700s, in the Arkansas-Mississippi juncture locality, were a relocated amalgamation of survivors of decimated Soto provinces such as Casqui, Pacaha, and Aquixo,[157] that is, of phases such as Nodena, Parkin, and "societies farther to the south,"[158] consistently favoring Pacaha-Nodena (or its decimated successor in the Missouri-Arkansas-Tennessee borderlands before c. 1650) as the major constituent in this mixture of province or phase remnants.[159] This sort of situation has also been suggested by Brain, with different phase mixes.[160] But the linguist Rankin found that the implications, such as evidence of pidginization and creolization, loan words, etc., were *not* met in the Quapaw language, which instead appeared to be a rather pure example of Dhegiha Siouan.[161] Hoffman has summarized other evidence against what he called the "Quapaw were shreds and patches" scenario.[162] I, of course, take all this as evidence for a very recent arrival of the Quapaw in the Arkansas-Mississippi juncture locality.

A "Combined Quapaw-Tunica(n)" Scenario

A close reading of Brain's report on Tunica(n) archaeology, wherein he subdivided the "Quapaw phase" into early ("Quapaw I") and late ("Quapaw II") portions, infers that despite its name, he regarded the "Quapaw I" subphase as basically representing Tunicans![163] Only with the "Quapaw II" subphase did he mention the ethnic/tribal Quapaw, and even then, he regarded the ceramics as basically Tunican, showing "continuity" with his "Yazoo 7" ceramic set, which he elsewhere related directly to his "Hushpuckena II" subphase, equated in turn with his ur-Tunicans, the people of Quizquiz of the Soto *entrada* narratives.[164]

Based on a hypothesis by Belmont, Brain suggested that the "Quapaw II" people included Quapaw males, bearers and users of the "Oliver lithic complex," and Tunican females continuing to make Tunican ceramics.[165] I doubt this, as it says nothing of the Quapaw females, and postulates a probably nonexistent lithic "complex" as having an ethnic/tribal correlation that would be highly questionable even if the "complex" were a reality.[166]

This could also be seen as an attempt by Brain to bridge, on the regional level, the slight temporal gap at the Oliver site, between the Hushpuckena and Oliver phase components, which had clearly similar ceramics at the type level, though there were obvious differences at the variety and modal levels. Brain expanded another of Phillips's northwest Mississippi phases, Parchman, southward and inserted it into the Hushpuckena-Oliver temporal hiatus.[167] His regional map for the Parchman phase did not show a Parchman component at Oliver, although the surrounding landscape was included in the Parchman territory.[168] I will leave it to my Mississippi colleagues to deal with this.

The "Maximum Tunican" Scenario

This reconstruction includes as "Tunican" every site and phase and Soto "province" or settlement that any serious archaeologist or ethnohistorian or linguist has referred to as Tunica or Koroa (or simply "Tunican"). It also embraces any others located between the aforementioned sites or phases, and implies a very late, limited-scale arrival for the Quapaw in the LMV.

Thus, following the route of the *entrada*, it accepts Brain's equation of Quizquiz with "the" Tunica (or at least, as some kind of Tunican settlement).[169] Wherever Quizquiz may have actually been, this clearly would put Tunicans in northwest Mississippi. Across the Mississippi from Quizquiz, in present-day Arkansas, was Aquixo, which according to Brain was closely related to Quizquiz, and is therefore claimed as Tunican.[170] Northward, the Spaniards went to Casqui and beyond, as far as Pacaha, which is equated with the Nodena phase in the Morse-Hudson reconstruction, which is the most popular at present, and is used exclusively in this scenario, for the sake of brevity. Although Dan Morse has suggested that the people of Pacaha-Nodena were the protohistoric Quapaw, the Quapaw linguistic expert Rankin rejected that interpretation and suggested that Pacaha was more likely Tunican.[171] The "maximum Tunican" scenario, of course, follows Rankin here. It infers that the Quapaw had not yet arrived in even the northeasternmost corner of Arkansas by the 1540s, and attempts to embrace, as Tunican, everything from Quizquiz to Pacaha—and beyond.

Soon after leaving Pacaha (and Casqui again), and passing through the populous province of Quiguate, the Spaniards headed westward, encountering the province of Coligua, which Hudson places near modern Batesville. Continuing west up the Arkansas Valley, they arrived at the settlement of Tanico, in the province of Cayas, somewhere in western Arkansas, among several others. This scenario also claims all of these Soto provinces and settlements as Tunican.

Still farther west, the Spaniards encountered the people of Tula (which is not claimed as Tunican in this version, but is in a very different new scenario; see below). Returning eastward, they went down the Arkansas Valley to the region of the Arkansas-Mississippi juncture, encountering (among others) a populous province called Anilco, perhaps in the Menard locality. In the Hudson version, Soto's subsequent death was in southeast Arkansas, at the settlement of Guachoya. The "maximum Tunican" scenario claims all of these Arkansas Valley polities below Tanico-Cayas, and those nearby in interior southeast Arkansas. The protohistoric archaeological remains of this latter region are generally believed to have strong affinities to Brain's concept of Tunican remains.[172]

Well over a century later, the maps derived from the 1673 Marquette-Jolliet expedition suggest strongly that at least two of the eight groups shown (apparently) in the lower Arkansas Valley at that time were Tunicans.[173] Their hearsay information shows "Tanikoua" and "Akoroua" and other groups upvalley from the Akansea-Quapaw. Rankin suggests that at least one of the other groups shown between those two on these maps, Papikaha (= relocated Pacaha?) was also Tunican;[174] of course, this scenario also claims it, and perhaps some of the others shown in the Arkansas Valley, although at least one or two may have been subgroups of the Wichita.[175]

In summary, the "maximum Tunican"scenario claims that there was a huge area of the LMV (sensu lato), centered on eastern Arkansas but extending eastward into northwest Mississippi and (briefly in late prehistoric times, around Spiro) westward even into Oklahoma, that had been occupied by various Tunicans with significant time depth back into late prehistory, when Soto and his army appeared on the scene in the 1540s. These Tunicans would have included not only the populous and nucleated Mississippian "paramount chiefdoms" in and near northeast Arkansas and the Arkansas Valley, but also "rural Mississippians" with dispersed settlement patterns in southeast Arkansas. At some time(s) after the entrada, but not necessarily because of it, these populations, especially the dense, nucleated ones in northeast Arkansas, were decimated by European diseases. Northeast Arkansas was essentially abandoned during the early to middle 1600s, with survivors regrouping among kindred Tunicans along the Arkansas Valley and leaving the remains that have come to be known as the "Menard complex" (formerly "Quapaw phase"). At a relatively late date, perhaps around or even after 1660, the actual Quapaw—themselves refugees from better-armed enemies—came down the northern LMV and pushed aside the Tunican remnant, settling in a few villages near the Arkansas-Mississippi juncture, as summarized in the final scenario.

A "Tunicans Far West" or "Neither Quapaw nor Tunican" Scenario

Recently, my southwest Arkansas colleague Frank Schambach has proposed a radical and intriguing reinterpretation of Tunican late prehistory and protohistory,[176] following up on his reinterpretations of the Spiro site and related situations in the Arkansas Valley, western Arkansas, eastern Oklahoma, and northeast Texas.[177]

Schambach has, in effect, excommunicated the Arkansas Valley and regions to the north of it from the Caddoan cultural realm, and I generally agree with him. More specifically, he has argued that the great Spiro site, on the Arkansas River in Oklahoma just west of the Arkansas state line, was not basically Caddoan as has been believed for decades, but was basically Mississippian, rather neatly accounting for the Mississippian style of the numerous "Southern Cult" and other artistic items found there. Again, I agree wholeheartedly. Furthermore, he argues that the Mississippians at Spiro were late prehistoric Tunicans. Once again, I think this is quite likely, representing the ceremonial and trading center of their westernmost expansion (see the "maximum Tunican" scenario above). He argues that certain unusual smaller sites to the west, including the Sanders site on Bois d'arc Creek near the Red River in northeast Texas, were entrepôts, or trading stations, for Spiro-based Tunicans, involved in complex trade relations for highly desirable bois d'arc (so-called "Osage orange") bows from Caddoans (who monopolized it and got prestige goods in return), and for bison products from Southern Plains groups (who got bows in return). Yet again, I think this is quite likely, and a real tour de force of reinterpretation.

In his new extension of Tunican reinterpretations into the protohistoric period, Schambach suggests that Soto's 1541 "Tanico" was perhaps another Tunican trading entrepôt, this time among the non-Tunican province of Cayas, somewhere in western Arkansas near the Arkansas River.[178] So far, even this is still plausible to me (that is, Tanico, like Spiro before it, as a western outpost of Tunican groups based to the east); but after this we begin to part company.

Schambach also suggests that the "Tula" people, next encountered by Soto west of Tanico, were in fact the major Tunicans.[179] The Tula have generally been regarded as some sort of Southern Plains people, possibly a branch of the Wichita, who spoke a Caddoan-related language, so this is a major departure. His main argument is that the Tula, according to Garcilaso, practiced an unusual kind of head deformation, which Schambach identifies with the "annular" style of deformation found on skeletons from the Sanders site, and with possible practices of historically observed Tunicans.

I think this may be stretching (if not deforming) the evidence a bit too far; any attempts to rely on Garcilaso are fraught with difficulties in the first place,[180] and it is also a stretch from Sanders in the 1300s to Tula in 1541 to LMV Tunicans around 1700. Also, by claiming Tula as Tunican, Schambach is forced to deny that Tunicans were present to the east of Tula, since (as noted above) Soto's chroniclers recorded an abrupt linguistic shift, to an incomprehensible language, at Tula. But, if Schambach still accepts "Tanico" as Tunican, why did the Spaniards not remark on the linguistic change there?

Schambach and I have for some time agreed that the Quapaw were probably not present in or near northeastern Arkansas and the Arkansas-Mississippi river junction until around 1600 or later (around 1660, I now suggest), and so were not the people of the various late "chiefdom" phases (Nodena, etc.) or Soto's provinces (e.g., Pacaha) in the same regions.[181] However, with his new "Tunicans far west" reinterpretation, he also denies that those peoples were Tunicans.[182]

Schambach's critique has at least had the valuable effect of forcing me to reexamine the "LMV Tunicans" evidence more critically. In the early 1980s, influenced by Brain's writings about Tunican archaeology and ethnohistory east of the Mississippi, plus Dickinson's ethnohistoric study which mentioned Tunicans in Arkansas, I tried to correlate the ethnohistoric and archaeological data on "Tunicans west of the Mississippi" in a 1983 meeting paper, later expanded and published.[183] There and subsequently, I more or less took Brain's case as proven, though I had noted in passing that "Quizquiz" did not sound like "Tunica" and carped about Brain's not dealing with the Winterville site and Soto's "Tanico" in relation to his concept of "Tunica(n)."[184]

But now, recalling that Swanton regarded "Quizquiz" (like several other Soto "province" or town names in the lower valley; see below) as a *Natchezan* word, it appears to me that the only "evidence" for Quizquiz as Tunica(n) in the 1540s is Brain's scantily supported, archaeologically based assertion that "our penetration into the prehistoric past of the Yazoo Basin has been successfully consummated: the protohistoric morass has been bridged [I would say, skipped over[185]], and Tunica origins founded in sixteenth-century Quizquiz."[186] Maybe so, but more support is needed.

Schambach has also pointed out that the oft-cited Chickasaw-Choctaw "tradition" of "Tunica old fields" in or near what is now Tunica County in northwest Mississippi was actually recorded very late, around 1830 to the 1840s.[187] It could easily refer to Tunicans who had moved into that region during or after the middle-late protohistoric disruptions or even in early historic times, rather than Tunicans who had been there from late prehistoric to early protohistoric times.

If Schambach is right about Tunicans not being in the LMV prehistorically, and if we are both right about the Quapaw being late arrivals, who, then (I asked him), were the ethnic/tribal groups represented by all those major late prehistoric to protohistoric Mississippian sites and phases in the northern LMV? His response was that they may have been other peoples, possibly Muskogean-speakers, who were essentially wiped out by European diseases and/or left the lower Mississippi Valley during the "Protohistoric Dark Ages" after the *entrada*.[188] I will make an alternative (to Muskogeans) suggestion below, but before that I will note that the "Tunicans far west" scenario has some problems of its own.

In support of his contentions, Schambach also makes a number of arguments based on archaeological ceramic typology and formal modes.[189] He suggests that the true late prehistoric to protohistoric Tunican pottery was that of the Fort Coffee phase, the successor to the Spiro phase in those regions of the Arkansas Valley, and that it was distinguished by various attributes, including flat bases on shell-tempered vessels. He has long denied that Brain's "Winterville Incised, *var. Tunica*" was really a Tunican type, suggesting instead that it derives from the Caddoan (or pan-cultural?) type Foster Trailed-Incised.[190] I have not accepted that argument in the past, and still do not. He also suggests that the later protohistoric to historic Tunicans had essentially ceased making their own pottery, and instead emphasized the use of Caddoan and Natchezan ceramics.

Space does not permit a detailed counterargument here, but I would contend that Schambach has not sufficiently considered the ceramics of the Arkansas Valley from Carden Bottoms on down and of related materials from adjoining regions (including my own southeast Arkansas regions) to the east of his area of expertise. In my opinion, these ceramics collectively represent a continuous sequence of late prehistoric, protohistoric, and historic developments leading more directly to Brain's later historic "Tunican" assemblage found down valley in Louisiana. For instance, the apparently indigenous utilitarian/mortuary ceramics of the Tillar and Hog Lake complexes in southeast Arkansas commonly include shell-tempered vessels with flat bases, and have many resemblances to the vessels from Brain's "Tunican" sites to the south.[191]

A New "Tunicans-and-Northern-Natchezans" Scenario

Here, I will outline yet another more or less plausible interpretation. Noting that the "maximum Tunican" scenario has been regarded as "not proved, nor even generally accepted,"[192] and inspired by portions of Schambach's critique, I have gone "back to the drawing board" and tried to find a credible alternative to the provocative extremes of that scenario.

My starting point, hinted at above but ignored or dismissed by Brain,[193] is the likelihood that "Quizquiz" may well have been not only a Natchezan word,[194] but also the name of a Natchezan-speaking settlement. Quizquiz in 1541 was almost certainly in northwest Mississippi, well to the north of the later-documented Natchezan territory, and it seems rather unlikely that Soto, en route westward from a long stay in northeast Mississippi among probable proto-Chickasaws, would have had Natchezan guides.

Additional suspicions are raised when we scan the place names and occasional other Native American words recorded by the Soto chroniclers in Arkansas. According to Swanton, although there are five probable or possible Tunican words, namely Pacaha, Coligua, Calpista, Palis(e)ma, and Tanico, significantly more of the Arkansas settlements and provinces have Natchezan names.[195] And, the "northern Natchezans in Arkansas" possibilities increase significantly if we use the northerly placements suggested by the Hudson route.

Settlement names listed as possibly Natchezan by Swanton, and placed in various Arkansas locations by him and Hudson, are Quiguate, Quixila, Tutilcoya, Quipana, Anoixi, Quitamaya, and Utiangue/Autiamque. Other probably Natchezan settlement names, including Tietiquaquo, Ayays, Tutelpinco, Anilco, and Guachoya, were placed well down into eastern Louisiana by Swanton (and Dickinson, and Brain), but Hudson puts them in southeast Arkansas, just below the mouth of the Arkansas. After Soto's death, the expedition was led westward by Moscoso, into Texas and back. Swanton placed that route across northern Louisiana, and assigned the province names of Aminoya, Taguanate, Catalte, Chaguate, and Aguacay in those regions to Natchezan also; but Hudson places them in southern Arkansas. If Swanton was right about the linguistic affiliations, and if Hudson is right about the route, then we have seventeen (!) Natchezan place names in eastern, central, and southern Arkansas—and some explaining to do. So, the "Tunicans and northern Natchezans" scenario is born.

Sketching out the geographic pattern of these names, using Hudson's placements (fig. 2), I note that this relegates all five of the probable/possible Tunican names to the north of the probable/possible Natchezan distribution. As already noted, Pacaha is in northeast Arkansas, on the Mississippi River, by all accounts. Swanton placed Coligua around North Little Rock, but put Tanico at Hot Springs. However, there are serious problems with placing any Native American group other than Caddoans in that Ouachita Mountains–Ouachita Valley locality.[196] The Hudson reconstruction solves these problems by placing Coligua at the southeastern margin of the Ozarks, near Batesville, and Tanico on the north side of the Arkansas River, in non-Caddoan Mississippian archaeological territory just south of the Ozarks.[197] In late prehistoric to early historic times, these locations would have been along or near major trails and routes linking the American Bottoms and Cahokia, near modern St. Louis, with the Arkansas Valley—and with Schambach's postulated Mississippian (Tunican?) traders at Spiro.[198]

One particularly interesting implication here is the possibility of linkage with a Tunican oral tradition, referring to origins from a mountain or to a mountainous homeland.[199] Brain, following the Swanton reconstruction, interpreted this as possibly referring to the Ouachita Mountains of central Arkansas, but doubted its literal truth and suggested as an alternative that it simply referred to the Mississippian mound-building tradi-

Fig. 2. The "Tunicans and northern Natchezans" scenario for the early-middle
1500s. This reconstruction is based on Hudson's version of the 1540s Soto route and
Swanton's attributions of linguistic affiliations to place names in the Soto narratives,
with some allowance for names likely to have been obtained from Native American
guides for places beyond their own linguistic regions. Probable or possible **Tunican**
names (●) are along the Ozark margin. Probable or possible "**northern Natchezan**"
names (▼) are along the Mississippi and Arkansas river valleys. The names Aquixo
and Casqui may refer to northern Natchezan, Tunican, or Muskogean settlements.
Apparent "northern Natchezan" names possibly given by guides for settlements that
were *probably* **Caddoan** (□) are in the Ouachita mountain/valley region. Names
farther west and southwest are *definitely* **Caddoan** (■). A group with an
unintelligible language, possibly a **Wichita** subdivision or other Plains Caddoans,
was given the name Tula. Down the Mississippi Valley, **Natchezan** chiefdoms (▲)
were in place, including Quigualtam in the lower Yazoo basin and those who later
became known as "Theloel," or the Natchez. In this scenario, the **Quapaw** have not
yet arrived.

tion.[200] Recently, evidence has gradually accumulated about late prehistoric Mississippian occupations in at least the eastern and central Ozarks.[201] It may also be relevant that flat-based shell-tempered pottery (see above) has been documented in the Ozarks.[202] Perhaps this was the legendary mountainous portion of the Tunicans' homeland.

Returning to figure 2, we see that the probable/possible "northern Natchezan" place names of the 1540s now include Quizquiz in northwest Mississippi and twelve others (Quiguate, Quixila, Tutilcoya, Autiamque, Tietiquaquo, Ayays, Tutelpinco, Anilco, Guachoya, Catalte, Aminoya, and Taguanate) in adjacent eastern to central Arkansas. (The names Aquixo and Casqui are of uncertain attribution, and could be northern Natchezan, Tunican, or even Muskogean. In any event, like Pacaha they are not Siouan, and it is assumed here that the proto-Quapaw had not yet arrived on our scene.) Notably, the putative "northern Natchezan" names include and surround the Menard locality, and extend well up the Arkansas Valley. Down the Mississippi Valley, Natchezan chiefdoms were in place, including Quigualtam in the lower Yazoo basin and those who were later documented as calling themselves "Theloel" and became known historically as "the" Natchez.

Following mainly archaeological considerations, I have assumed that five other "Natchezan" place names (Quipana, Anoixi, Quitamaya, Chaguate, and Aguacay), in what is generally considered to be Caddoan territory in the Ouachita mountain/valley country of Arkansas, may have been names given by Natchezan-speaking guides for places that were actually Caddoan. (Names farther west and southwest are definitely Caddoan.) The "Tula" group with the unintelligible language may have been Plains Caddoans, such as a Wichita subdivision, or some other non-Tunican, non-Natchezan tribe of traders and/or raiders.

The possibility of Natchezan-speakers in Arkansas has been staring us in the face for some time now,[203] but I, at least, had been sidetracked and dissuaded from thinking about it by at least three mental blocks. Like Swanton, I had assumed that Natchezan-speakers had "always" been in the southerly latitudes where they were first definitely described by the French.[204] Also, I had been bedazzled by Brain's assertions about Quizquiz being Tunican, and about linkages of the Native American ceramics accompanying the "Tunica treasure" to those found in northwest Mississippi, plus the obvious similarities to those in my own southeast Arkansas territory. A final factor was some degree of satisfaction with my own pet "maximum Tunican" scenario, which at least had the virtue of resolving the "Quapaw paradox" as noted above. This new "Tunicans and northern Natchezans" scenario treats the Quapaw question in the same manner (see below).

This new scenario also meshes well with several other phenomena and problems noted in studies of LMV archaeology and ethnohistory in recent decades. For one thing, there is the question of the Koroa: whether or not they were Soto's Coligua, they (or some subgroups of them) are fairly certainly known to have lived during the late 1600s and early 1700s on the lower Arkansas and in southeast Arkansas and northeast Louisiana and believed to have possibly spoken a Tunican language. Attempting to surmise what their archaeological record might have looked like, I suggested some sort of Tunican-Natchezan mixture.[205] Whether or not they spoke a Tunican language, at least some of them must have been closely associated with the Natchez by 1682, when La Salle found a Koroa group living with the Natchez.[206]

Ceramic typology and other analyses also have indicated a sort of gradation from the largely grog- or fine-shell-and-grog-tempered wares and types of the Plaquemine-Natchez heartland, northward well into Arkansas and adjacent latitudes of Mississippi, where coarser shell-tempered wares, expanding gradually southward, became dominant after about 1400. I have suggested that this may have been more a process of southward-spreading technological change than of a southward expansion of people.[207] This is particularly noteworthy in the cases of Leland Incised and closely related types such as Fatherland Incised.[208] Hally noted that Leland designs occurred on much coarser shell-tempered pottery in southeast Arkansas.[209] The Lower Mississippi Survey later designated a new type, Cracker Road Incised, as "a fully shell-tempered counterpart to Fatherland Incised" in the Vicksburg vicinity;[210] as will be seen, it also occurs farther north.

Then, there is the question of the Taensa. First documented by the French in northeast Louisiana during the period between 1682 and 1706, they almost certainly spoke a Natchezan language and were fairly certainly located along Lake St. Joseph.[211] Yet, they have not been securely identified archaeologically. Phillips designated a "Taensa phase" to accommodate them, but was disappointed to note that the surface collections "failed to reflect an integrated Natchezan culture as expected" but instead showed a "mixture of Natchezan and Mississippian elements" characterized by "some Natchezan sherds together with shell-tempered pottery more suggestive of relationships to the north" and a "few stone artifacts" that "also appeared to be related to historic complexes in the north, e.g., Quapaw and Oliver."[212] The new scenario suggests that perhaps the Taensa of 1682–1706 were themselves "northern Natchezans" with basically coarse-shell-tempered ceramic assemblages, recently departed from the lower Arkansas and/or adjacent Mississippi valleys.[213]

It should also be noted that Phillips was puzzled by finding in Natchezan culture "a strong Mississippian strain that it didn't get from Plaquemine." He mentioned "Mississippian influences from the north" and a "slightly wild hypothesis" of "Moundville-Fort Walton influences" from the east and southeast, but did not consider the possibility, suggested here, of actual southward migrations of refugee "northern Natchezan" groups bearing Mississippian archaeological assemblages.[214]

For what it may be worth, this scenario is also supported by Natchezan oral traditions of contraction from a much larger territory. In one version, "Our nation . . . was formerly very numerous and very powerful. It extended for more than twelve days' journey from east to west and more than fifteen from north to south . . ."[215] A figure of about 30 km, or 20 miles, for a day's journey would suggest an east-west extent on the order of 360 km, or 240 miles, and a north-south extent of about 450 km, or 300 miles. In another version, more geographically specific, "The reported territory *claimed* by the Natchez ran from Bayou Manchac [in southern Louisiana] . . . to the Ohio . . .";[216] that is a north-south airline distance of more than 700 km (c. 450 miles), including all but the southern tip of the entire LMV.

Finally, looking back to the time of the *entrada* once more, we see that this scenario calls for renewed attention to the question of Quigualtam, the apparently powerful chiefdom down the Mississippi a short distance below Guachoya. Swanton suggested that "Quigualtam" was a Natchezan word, and Brain has long contended that it represented the Natchez themselves, in their historic location.[217] However, the Hudson reconstruction moved Guachoya far north, to southeast Arkansas just below the Arkansas-Mississippi juncture, and Quigualtam to the Winterville-Greenville vicinity in the lower Yazoo basin. Brain has recently reopened the debate, reasserting that the Winterville site and surrounding related sites "appear to have been abandoned long before the first conquistador arrived on the scene."[218] With the Mississippian-Plaquemine frontier having moved well to the south of the Greenville locality, to the Vicksburg vicinity, by the 1400s, there was no reason, in the traditional normative paradigm, to expect Plaquemine-affiliated Natchezans in the Winterville vicinity.[219] But the "northern Natchezan" scenario, as already noted, has no problem with the notion of a basically (or partially) Mississippian artifact assemblage for Natchezan-speakers.

The last known Winterville occupation, that of the Lake George phase, was representative of "the high-water mark of the Mississippian culture in the Yazoo Basin."[220] Occupation was "extensive and intensive."[221] There was "an overall growth in population and some continuing mound construction but instead of occupying a few large centers the population dispersed somewhat. This rather dispersed settlement system is not typical of the usual Mississippian mode."[222] However, it is quite familiar for the more or less contemporary "rural Mississippian" phases across the Mississippi in southeast Arkansas.[223]

Brain believes that the Lake George phase had ended by around 1500 or shortly thereafter, and the only radiocarbon dates for this phase are indeed in the pre-1500 range, at both Winterville and Lake George.[224] However, "the terminal occupation is not dated at either site,"[225] and there appear to be some reasonable grounds to suggest that the phase (if not the occupation of Winterville itself) continued on until the time of the *entrada* and beyond in the Greenville locality. Nearby in southeast Arkansas, Mississippian occupations are regarded as having continued until the 1600s.[226]

The Lake George phase assemblage itself includes items such as ground/polished and chipped stone pebble "celts" (or chisels, or adzes), triangular Madison points, "pipe" drills, and "trade" occurrences of the pottery types Bell Plain, Nodena Red and White and Avenue Polychrome.[227] Elsewhere, such artifact classes and types are associated with terminal prehistoric to (at least) middle protohistoric phases such as Nodena and Parkin, which are believed to have been very much extant at the time of the *entrada*.[228]

Phillips defined the Lake George phase as rather limited in extent, around the Lake George site, and regarded it as related to the more extensive Deer Creek phase, above and (especially) below the Winterville site.[229] Williams and Brain "sank" the Deer Creek phase and included its sites in an expanded Lake George phase.[230] As I noted in a review, Brain's *Tunica Archaeology* volume skips over the "Dark Ages" and also leaps (backward in time and northward in space) from the Vicksburg locality to northwest Mississippi, not addressing the question of Tunica relationships, if any, to the Winterville site and locality, though he suggested two varieties of the pottery type Winterville Incised were among the key diagnostics of Tunica(n) culture.[231]

In a contract survey and testing project (not cited by Brain) along upper Steele Bayou, immediately south of Greenville and just west of the Deer Creek meander belt, Weinstein et al. found a "striking" number of "Deer Creek phase" sites, but assigned only a very rough date range of 1400–1700.[232] Their illustrated ceramics include several sherds that would be at home in the early to middle protohistoric complexes of nearby southeast Arkansas.[233] In another contract project, in Bolivar County just above Greenville and opposite the mouth of the Arkansas, Weinstein and Hahn surface-collected at the Neblett Landing, Clark Mound, and Clark Village sites.[234] They found only generic Mississippian sherds at Neblett, but possibly very late (i.e., protohistoric) Mississippian materials, including Cracker Road Incised and Winterville Incised pottery and Madison points, at the Clark sites. They compared some Clark Mound finds to items representing "most of the Hushpuckena phase, and possibly part of the subsequent Parchman phase" and even mentioned in passing the possibility of "a very late occupation . . . equivalent in time to the Oliver phase."[235] In Brain's scheme, those phases are, respectively, just before, just after, and long after the *entrada*.[236] More intensive field work, involving excavations and comparative research, is needed at outlying sites in the Winterville locality.

The "Very Late Quapaw/Dhegiha Migration" Scenario

The "maximum Tunican" scenario, and the two that followed it, all solve the key riddles of the "Quapaw paradox" by making the Quapaw very late arrivals on our scene. Perhaps the most important, or at least the most obvious, of these riddles has been the glaring discrepancy between the archaeological record of relatively small late Mississippian houses, often of wattle-and-daub wall construction with thatched roofs (perhaps daubed near smoke holes), vs. the ethnohistorically documented Quapaw bark-covered longhouses, which have not been identified yet by excavations at "Quapaw phase" (Menard complex) sites.[237] Another has been the large region(s) involved in the "maximum" Quapaw phase archaeological sce-

nario vs. the very restricted locality of the early descriptions of the ethnohistoric Quapaw. In the scenario espoused here (fig. 3), the longhouses
and limited spatial extent are among several indicators of the very late
arrival of the Quapaw from far to the northeast (or north) where such
structures were commonly used.

In a possibly analogous and more or less simultaneous situation well to
the east, Native Americans from the north known as the "Westo" were

Fig. 3. The "late Quapaw/Dhegiha migration scenario" of long-distance population
movements in the 1650s–1660s. Under pressure from the League Iroquois, the non-
League Iroquoian Erie (E) leave their homeland in the mid-1650s and move
southward through Virginia and the Carolinas, becoming known as the Westo (W)
and settling on the Savannah River in Georgia around 1660. Under expanding
Iroquois pressure in the 1660s, the eastern Fort Ancient (EFA) proto-Dhegiha
Siouans move down the Ohio Valley to the Mississippi River, where they separate
and migrate to the historic locations of the Omaha-Ponca (Om), Osage-Kansa (Os),
and Quapaw (Q). (The Chiwere Siouans, or Oneota archaeological culture, had
separated from the Dhegiha Siouans in prehistoric times.) Some remnant Tunicans
(T) remain in the Arkansas valley, but others and northern Natchezans (NN; see
fig. 2) have moved south, closer to the historic Natchez (N). The Plains Caddoan
Wichita (Wi) and Algonquian (Illini) Mitchigamea (M) send seasonal trading parties
down the Arkansas and Mississippi valleys and back. This accounts for the situations
found by Jolliet-Marquette in 1673 and La Salle in 1682.

documented as causing disturbances as they traveled south through Virginia and the Carolinas, finally settling in the vicinity of Augusta, Georgia, in their own bark-covered longhouses around 1660.[238] The "Westo" are generally believed to have been originally a western New York non-League Iroquoian group, quite possibly the Erie, who were displaced and forced to flee in the mid-1650s, soon after the League of the Iroquois started acquiring technologically superior flintlocks in the 1640s.[239]

Similarly, the proto-Quapaw may have been displaced from an original homeland very far from the Arkansas-Mississippi river juncture. One possibility, but a rather remote one in my estimation, is that they came downstream from far up the Mississippi Valley's drainage basin. The "Classic" Oneota sites of Wisconsin have produced numerous large longhouses, dating around 1400 to 1650;[240] at least the chronology is about right. But the Oneota archaeological complex has often been suggested, in some cases fairly convincingly, as ancestral to at least some of the Chiwere Siouan tribes, and has generally been discounted as ancestral to Dhegiha Siouans.[241] A recent review of Siouan languages and the Oneota question by Rankin reaffirmed the Chiwere-Oneota connection, and again suggested that Dhegiha Siouans "likely . . . were not in close contact with Oneota culture during its developmental phases."[242] However, his colleague John Koontz holds out for the possibility of Oneota-Dhegiha connections, and a source region for the Dhegihans in the upper Mississippi Valley (UMV), around present-day Minnesota.[243]

A much more promising source region, in my estimation, is the Ohio Valley, but I believe that recent speculations in that direction may have not looked far enough upvalley. The Caborn-Welborn protohistoric archaeological complex of southwestern Indiana,[244] sometimes invoked as a possible Quapaw antecedent or relative,[245] appears to lack longhouses,[246] and is probably not far enough north-northeast to have had them. The Caborn-Welborn artifact assemblage appears to reflect both northern LMV Mississippian and Oneota influences.[247] Also, the Caborn-Welborn complex may not have survived beyond the early 1600s, i.e., not late enough for the "very late Quapaw migration" scenario that I favor.[248]

The next major late prehistoric to protohistoric manifestation up the Ohio Valley is non-Mississippian: the Fort Ancient complex. Although data are spotty, it appears that none of the "western Fort Ancient" sites, such as the recently reanalyzed Madisonville site in southwest Ohio near Cincinnati, have yet produced definitive evidence of longhouses.[249] (However, posthole sizes and depths at Madisonville suggest that large or long houses may have been present, but not recognized by early excavators.)[250] The closest (to Arkansas) archaeologically documented occurrences that I am aware of in the Ohio drainage are in the "eastern Fort Ancient" complex, in northeastern Kentucky and western West Virginia, where numerous large longhouses have been found at sites such as Hardin Village and Buffalo.[251] These sites were apparently abandoned, again very conveniently for this scenario, by around 1650.[252]

In his classic study of the Fort Ancient "aspect" (trait cluster), James B. Griffin discounted the possibility of a Siouan connection and doubted that "any specific historic tribe or tribes" could be identified with it, but did believe that "only one linguistic stock . . . namely, the Algonquian" could not be eliminated.[253] But even if some Fort Ancient groups were Algonquian, not all of them need have been; perhaps something deeper is reflected in Griffin's geographical "foci" and/or others' more recent tendency to split Fort Ancient into "eastern" and "western" portions.[254]

In a brief but provocative modern synthesis, the late Patricia Essenpreis criticized previous "normative" studies and concluded that the Fort Ancient concept "subsumes a number of different tribal or ethnic units."[255] According to a much more thorough recent review by Drooker, the general preference still seems to be the Central Algonquian group that Griffin favored, the Shawnee.[256] However, there are other possibilities, involving several ethnic groups, including Siouans. Various Algonquian groups (including the Illinois-Peoria-Miami) called the Ohio "the River of the Kansa" (a Dhegiha Siouan group very closely related to the Osage), and the Shawnee called the pecan the "Kansa nut."[257]

This scenario also agrees with the Quapaws' own oral traditions, as they have been generally interpreted, with regard to geography. They relate a story of a homeland in the Ohio Valley, and also one of having defeated Tunicans somewhere around the mouth of the St. Francis River and perhaps elsewhere, on their way down the Mississippi to the Arkansas-mouth locality.[258] Somewhat ironically, given their well-known sympathies to the Quapaw, the Morses have been reluctant to credit this tradition, discounting it as a "myth" recounted very late (in the 1820s) to a biased, racist territorial governor;[259] they concede at most only a "near the mouth of the Ohio" origin.[260]

Still further support for this scenario comes from comparative historical linguistics and geography. The Osage, known historically to have been based in west-southwest Missouri, were Dhegiha Siouan speakers, like the Quapaw.[261] Even farther from the Quapaw in historic times, well up the Missouri Valley in the Nebraska-Iowa-Minnesota borderlands, were the Omaha-Ponca.[262] Springer and Witkowski asserted that "within Dhegiha, Omaha-Ponca is more similar to both Osage and Quapaw than these two are to each other" which contrasts strongly with the historic geographical configuration.[263] But Rankin and Koontz regard the Springer-Witkowski study as very inadequately documented, and quite possibly flawed in its methods and conclusions; instead, they see the three subgroups as more or less equidistant from each other linguistically.[264] Even so, the more or less linear historical configuration still contrasts strongly. How did this strange alignment of linguistic relatives come into existence?

I suggest that in late prehistoric to middle protohistoric times, the Dhegihans, in whatever configuration, were the (or among the) "eastern Fort Ancient" groups (perhaps the easternmost). When the Iroquois attacks or threats became intolerable, they left. Drooker regards the "legendary all-out external warfare conducted by the Iroquois League from the 1640s onward" as only one (possibly small) factor among many that played a part in pushing the Fort Ancient people from their Ohio Valley homeland,[265] but from my remote perspective it appears a likely candidate as the major factor. The League of the Iroquois began getting significant numbers of improved flintlocks in the 1640s.[266] Eastern Fort Ancient groups were a relatively short distance down the Ohio drainage from the Seneca, the westernmost members of the League of the Iroquois, and would have been literally "under the gun" in short order. The League had defeated the Erie (Westo?) and forced them out of western New York by around 1656; then, the Iroquois may have intensified attacks on the eastern Fort Ancient people.[267] The latter may have been forced to migrate by around 1660; several sources state that during the 1660s and especially after 1670, the Iroquois were attacking the more distant Shawnee, who may have been the next major group (western Fort Ancient people?) downstream.[268]

When the Dhegihans reached the mouth of the Ohio, the Osage went up the Mississippi-Missouri system, then "turned left" and settled in what were to become known as the Osage and Little Osage river valleys. Very shortly thereafter (according to traditions summarized by Baird 1980:6), the proto-Omaha and proto-Quapaw parted at the Ohio-Mississippi juncture. The former group proceeded up the Mississippi and Missouri rivers and became known as the "upstream people," or *Omaha*; the latter turned south, down the Mississippi, and became known as the "downstream people," or *Quapaw*—just as in their oral traditions.

Assuming for the moment that the "Quapaw paradox" has indeed been solved, how do these scenarios of very late migrations into new territories match the archaeological records (or rather, lack of same) in the other Dhegiha groups' historic "homelands"? Very well indeed.

The Omaha, on the northeastern Great Plains margin, "have no satisfactory prehistoric archaeological manifestation" and "are archaeologically detectable only in the late eighteenth century . . . documentary descriptions [beginning in the 1670s, which sounds familiar] precede any authenticated Omaha archaeological site."[269] Longhouses (which require ample supplies of timber and suitable bark, scarce resources on the Plains) are not attested, and the Omaha "claimed that they began building earthlodges only after their move to the Missouri River."[270] During the 1670–1700 period, they were "on the move, and possibly on the run, being forced westward by better-armed Algonquin tribes."[271] And finally, "the whole question of Omaha origins remains as obscure now as before. Where did they come from? How rapidly did they migrate from their former homeland to the Missouri Valley? Can these migration sites be located and identified?"[272]

As for the Osage, despite decades of investigation, archaeologists have been unable to establish indigenous "roots" for them in the late prehistoric to early-middle protohistoric remains found in their historic "homeland," the Plains-Woodland borderlands of western to southwestern Missouri. Instead, after a recent thorough review of the subject, Vehik credited an "origin in the Ohio Valley, as suggested by the oral histories," and concluded that the record "is indicative of a comparatively late Dhegihan arrival on the Plains, probably during the seventeenth century."[273] Similarly, O'Brien and Wood concluded, "[W]e see no reason to think that the proto-Osage ever spent much time in southwestern Missouri."[274]

In sum, this scenario (or perhaps its Oneota-UMV variant) fits the linguistic, oral-tradition, and negative archaeological evidence very well. Glaringly absent, though, is the positive archaeological evidence, especially in the ethnohistorical Quapaw locality. Where are the Fort Ancient diagnostics, especially the shell-tempered, cord-marked pottery,[275] which is so abundant at eastern Fort Ancient sites?[276] For the moment, it can

only be postulated, rather lamely, that we have not yet found a well-pre-
served Quapaw component. No one has even claimed to have located any
of the primary Quapaw villages on the Mississippi River. Claims have
been made for the village of Osotouy on the lower Arkansas River, at
"Menard locality" sites such as Wallace and Menard itself, but doubts
have been cast on these.[277] Indeed, a new candidate site has been found,
but so far has only been surface-collected.[278] We await its thorough testing
with great interest.

CONCLUDING REMARKS

The foregoing discussions have been, to a large extent, exercises in pat-
tern-recognition in the patchy and weedy fields of ethnohistorical, linguistic, and archaeological data. We are probably not going to get much in the
way of rediscoveries of "new" ethnohistorical documents, lost for centuries, nor of new data on the relevant Native American languages, although
there may be no end to argumentation about, and reinterpretation of, the
little we already have. However, despite the recent and ongoing tide of
destruction, there are still numerous "new" late prehistoric to early historic archaeological sites, or site remnants, out there waiting to be discovered by (or shown to) archaeologists, and there are still major unexcavated
portions of the known site remnants. There is still some hope that the
"Tunicans and northern Natchezans" and "Quapaw migration" scenarios
(and others) outlined above can be tested archaeologically.

Yet, what kind(s) of archaeology will suffice to deal with these matters?
I am of two minds on this subject. There is still a major place for traditional culture history, perhaps not so much as a particularistic end in itself
(although many of the stories it has to tell are indeed fascinating), but as a
necessary basis for large-scale comparisons of cultural processes—some of
them of rather short duration, closer to the "event" end of the continuum
than the evolutionary end. In particular, the scenario of a very late, very
long-distance migration by the proto-Quapaw (and their Dhegihan relatives) demands supporting evidence in the form of recognizably "intrusive
diagnostic" artifacts and features, from both the technological and typological viewpoints. While I continue to doubt any high correlations
between material culture and tribal/ethnic/linguistic groups, I also continue to doubt that there are no such correlations.[279] Until and unless
someone comes up with bark-covered longhouse remains or (preferably,

and) eastern Fort Ancient-like shell-tempered, cord-marked pottery near the Arkansas-Mississippi juncture, this fine-on-paper scenario must be regarded as conjectural.

Beyond the short-term "event" level, I suspect that the most productive works of the future will not be based on traditional, normative, monothetic, essentialist "typological thinking,"[280] let alone "nihilistic" postprocessual relativism.[281] Instead, I expect that they will come through developments of the no-longer-"new" processual school, in conjunction with aspects and attitudes of neo-Darwinian evolutionary ecology, evolutionary archaeology, and evolutionary psychology, all of which share a basis in dealing with variation via "population thinking."[282] This is not to say that the culture-historical typologists have not had their insights, but they have been more like those of connoisseurs than those of scientists; a "philosophical stance . . . oriented more toward humanism and historicism than scientism."[283] A lot more in the way of scientific (if not "scientistic")[284] archaeology is needed, in my estimation.

A few barbarians have been grumbling at the LMV elite's typological gates for some years now, and indeed, there are now some signs that the walls are beginning to crumble.[285] Just as Phillips, Ford, and Griffin remarked at the end of their classic survey, "We stand before the threat of the atom in the form of C14 dating. This may be our last opportunity for old-fashioned uncontrolled guessing,"[286] Phillips commented near the end of his classic synthesis, "New statistical devices are now available about which I know nothing; the factor of expense is no longer a problem, now that computers are being installed in college dormitories like Coke machines."[287] Starting from a qualitative standpoint, Schambach has pointed out some major inadequacies of the Phillips type-variety system, and devised a new ("collegiate") descriptive classification system which is much more inclusive and versatile.[288] In effect, it analyzes nominal-level attributes, some of which are amenable to at least ordinal-level quantification. It has been applied in several southern and western Arkansas situations, but not yet in the LMV proper, nor yet combined with cutting-edge statistical analyses.[289]

On the other hand, recent applications of multivariate statistics in the LMV regions of southeast Missouri and in northeast Arkansas and western Tennessee have claimed that the traditional phases are "inconsistent sets of assemblages"[290] and that "existing ceramic typology . . . is simply inadequate . . ."[291] Nevertheless, both of these studies were based on the old LMV literature's type counts—not even on the type-variety system, let alone actual reanalyses of the materials on the attribute level, and at least one of them appears methodologically flawed.[292] I hope the new millennium soon produces some LMV reanalyses on that finer level, combined with appropriate statistical manipulations.

More along comparative, and even processual, lines, I find it of some interest that this chapter's preferred scenario, for a good portion of the western interior Southeast, more or less parallels Smith's suggestions of short-distance moves just after the *entrada*, intermediate-distance southerly moves by around 1600, and longer-distance southerly moves in the middle to late 1600s, in the eastern interior Southeast.[293] It also harmonizes well with Galloway's scenario for Choctaw tribal formation by various peoples moving into a new "homeland" between 1500 and 1700.[294] And speaking of harmony, it is good to find, after a decade or so of some acrimony in the wake of NAGPRA, that archaeologists and ethnohistorians are finding substantial concordance with at least some elements of Native American oral traditions.[295]

I do not intend to let the ethnohistorical and linguistic records off scot-free, let alone insinuate that protohistoric archaeology's main problem is to correlate its findings with their truths. A glance at the linguistic literature relevant here reveals widely differing points of view.[296] The ethnohistorical documents cannot be taken at anything like face value, and do not have an inherently privileged position over archaeology.[297] This is going to be a difficult intellectual struggle.

Yet, archaeology may have the "final" word. Lacking new ethnohistoric and linguistic data, support or disproof of this chapter's preferred scenarios—late prehistoric to protohistoric "northern Natchezan" and Tunican occupations in the northern LMV, interrupted by the Soto *entrada* and subsequent disease decimations, soon followed by their own generally southward movements and emigrations and ultimately by very late Quapaw immigration—will have to come out of the ground, and out of our analyses.

ACKNOWLEDGMENTS

First, I am grateful to Robbie Ethridge and Charles Hudson for organizing the October 1998 Porter L. Fortune, Jr., History Symposium (which led to this book) at the University of Mississippi, and for their hospitality there (I "sang for my supper" by reading Tim Perttula's faxed-in paper when he couldn't make it to the meeting). Later, Charles prevailed on me to fill in a rather large geographical gap in the symposium's coverage by presenting my thoughts on the "northern LMV" situation to his class and colleagues at the University of Georgia during a memorable March 1999 visit to Athens and by expanding that presentation into this chapter. I also appreciate Robbie's patience in dealing with my virtually endless revisions, despite her own difficult circumstances.

I have especially benefitted from conversations, communications, and civilized disagreements with my Arkansas Archeological Survey colleagues Dan and Phyllis Morse (retired but still active), and Frank Schambach. George Sabo kindly provided a number of references and reprints on the subject of social organization. Survey director Tom Green came up with the creative financing for my sabbatical leave within the University of Arkansas System during the first half of 1998, which permitted me to expand my perceptions of the protohistoric scene in all directions, especially eastward.

I gained added perspectives from the symposium papers and other works by, and/or conversations with, Penny Drooker, Patricia Galloway, Helen Rountree, Chester DePratter, and especially Marvin Smith, who really opened my eyes to the big picture more than a decade ago. With regard to linguistic matters, I have also benefitted for more than a decade from Robert Rankin's publications and communications; more recently, Bob gave me an "e-introduction" to his colleague John Koontz, who also graciously shared his perspectives on linguistic prehistory and protohistory. None of the above are to blame for my errors of commission, omission, or distortion of their views. I am, as always, grateful to my wife, Charlotte Copeland, for her companionship and encouragement through these adventures.

This chapter is dedicated to my mentor and friend C. Roger Nance, as a sort of "one-paper *festschrift*" on the occasion of his retirement after thirty years of teaching and research at the University of Alabama in Birmingham. Yes (and incredibly), it was about three decades ago (in 1971) that Roger got me started in archaeology back at UAB in the classroom and lab, and in the field along the Alabama River east of Selma. It was he who showed me the value (and fun) of archaeology—and of critical thinking about the archaeological literature, theory, and methods, including nontypological approaches such as attribute analysis.[298] Since those days, my family and I have greatly enjoyed our visits with Roger, Vally, and family, at meetings and especially back in Birmingham. Best wishes, Roger, for a very long, enjoyable, healthy, and productive retirement.

Colonial Period Transformations in the Mississippi Valley: Dis-integration, Alliance, Confederation, Playoff

PATRICIA GALLOWAY

THE USUAL EXCUSES ON SOURCES

It took me a long time to get started on this paper, because it was not entirely clear what would be left for me to say once my colleagues had finished dealing with their topics: disease, population movements, and the influences of the Spanish in Florida and the English from colonies along the eastern seaboard would already have been dealt with. But as I looked over the list of papers, I saw that French colonial contacts had not been covered, nor did it seem apparent that anyone else would be concerned with the Indian view of events. As a result, I took up my assignment of dealing with the early part of the most recent[1] social history of the eastern side of the lower Mississippi Valley[2] with the intention of trying to accomplish four things: (1) recount the state of research on the ethnogenesis, political environment, and agency of four major tribes (Choctaw, Chickasaw, Natchez, and Tunica), with relevant comments on several "small tribes" who figured in the political economy of the region but are now virtually extinct as groups and on whom very little research beyond Swantonian surveys has been done (Chakchiuma, Yazoo, Ofo, Tioux, Grigra, Koroa, Houma, Capinan, Acolapissa, Biloxi, Pascagoula, etc.); (2) pay special attention to the impact of the French as they entered the region as explorers and colonials; (3) focus also on Native origin histories and other traditions that cast light on the period of interest; and (4) pay attention to how what people *knew* (or thought they knew) about one another affected the ways they acted or were able to act. In practice, the materials uncovered through attention to the three latter concerns will facilitate the accomplishment of the first.

Although Paul Kelton is of Cherokee ancestry, in this symposium we are hearing mostly Euroamerican voices describing other people's history, at a time when the very topic, the connection between the precon-

tact past and the "historic tribes," is a foregrounded political issue
because of the fate of archaeological collections under NAGPRA. Charles
Hudson is to be congratulated for his persistent efforts to help establish
these historical connections when many others are avoiding the issue, but
we need to be aware that like the European "diligent writers of early
America,"[3] we are putting forward our modern academic "imaginary" as
an approximation of truth at a time when Native people are increasingly
contesting that view and the right of academics to assert its authoritative
claims.

Professor Hudson long ago suggested that the relevant paradigm for
this protohistoric–early contact ethnohistory is that of the *Annales* school
of French historians. The *Annales* historians have, however, been quite
explicit in their historiographical discussions of the use of documentary
sources,[4] and I have argued elsewhere that their standards would all but
evict the early exploration narratives from consideration, while retaining
the quantitative evidence constructed in the routine records of regular
colonies. That much is clear, and it means that cliometrics just can't do
much of a job on exploration narratives. The *Annales* historians have been
less helpful with respect to the application of the *Annales* paradigm to
traditional oral sources and archaeological evidence, both of which are
available for the writing of European history, of course, but neither of
which is much used by *Annales* historians,[5] certainly not on the massive
scale that archaeological evidence is used to reconstruct the indigenous
history of the Americas. I would like to make some suggestions here about
how precisely we may apply the *Annales* categories of *histoire événementielle, conjoncture,* and *longue durée* to these two kinds of evidence so crucial to our enterprise. It will be seen that, since archaeological categories
are built on the same modernist, rationalist, "scientific" worldview as
Annales historiography, archaeological evidence better fits *Annales* categories than does Native traditional historical knowledge—or indeed the
late medieval flights of exploration rhetoric.

Southeastern archaeology has been carried out for the past hundred
years mostly under the paradigm of "culture history": in all its avatars,
regional archaeological research has sought to find chronological and spatial patterns in the distribution of the objects and structures found by surface collection and excavation, and has subsequently reified those patterns
as "cultures," which most archaeologists feel (and many are now more
than ever protesting) do not and cannot be mapped precisely onto any

actual polity or group.[6] But that is not to say that the chronological and
spatial developments do not provide a background for very clear understanding of the shape of the *longue durée*: long-term and large-scale cultural developments like the results on landscape and culture of significant
climatic trends; how people used and modified that landscape and perhaps even affected at least restricted microclimates; the rate of increase
and decrease of their populations; what kind of settlement regimes they
favored; and what foods they ate and how it affected their health. Unquestionably archaeology presents appalling epistemological problems: terrible contingencies of sampling, drastically differential survival of evidence
unrelated to behaviors of interest, destruction of evidentiary context in
the recovery of evidence, and the significant variation over time of recovery procedures themselves. But it also seems that, as archaeologists
deeply believe, if you superimpose just the right spatial and temporal
grids on your evidence, they will in fact reveal historically meaningful patterns. At least they will if the patterns are really big.

Because many of these sequences present discontinuities, it is also possible to suggest that different kinds of *conjoncture* may appear in archaeological evidence. On a regional scale we can easily show the emergence
and swift dominance of certain technologies: technologies of weaponry
(bows and arrows), shelter and transportation construction (woodworking
tools), agriculture (cultivating tools, grain-storage artifacts and structures),
and (perhaps, if our interpretation is correct) power and the sacred (various forms of communal architecture). It is also possible to demonstrate
that some groups were deprived of these technologies for a time—or
chose to opt out—and even to suggest whether they were adversely
affected—or not—as a result. In other words, archaeological evidence can
be used to look at significant *shifts* in material and political economies and
at *changes* in gender and age roles, and it is this kind of archaeological
evidence that has been most fruitfully used to address the early period of
European contact.

Finally, the excavation of individual sites frequently reveals elements of
histoire événementielle, the specific incidents that can be articulated in
terms of individual people (who must usually remain anonymous but not
less individual for that), particularly when those sites include "closed
finds," evidence of one-time events that have been intentionally or accidentally sealed immediately and have lain undisturbed since: burials of
the dead, whole sites buried as they stood by deep flood-borne silts, and

buildings reduced to their most perdurable substances by fire. Professor Hudson and his colleagues have been looking assiduously for this kind of evidence to track the Soto expedition, and have been rewarded with the discovery of good evidence at Tallahassee and Parkin.

But I will be a spoilsport and mention the existential limitations on archaeological evidence, which mean that some of these stories cannot be told at all using it. Because organic materials have been particularly subject to disintegration in the climate of the Southeast, organic remains—including also organic portions of human bodies—are very rare except for those accidentally preserved by burning or in anaerobic conditions: hence we can practically never know directly that a dead body was killed by a European disease. And we must rely upon European trade numbers to show how many deer and other animals were killed to satisfy European markets, because unless the meat was consumed at home, even the bones of the prey cannot be counted. Population is a crucial issue, but although the scale of population loss can be debated using proxy data like number of sites, archaeological evidence is also unlikely even to reveal the number of dead, since in the grip of widespread epidemic disease burials may not have been carried out.

And how in the world are we to construe clusterings of like material practices as cultural continuities, when anthropologists have a hard time limning ethnogenesis among their contemporaries who can be observed alive? Archaeologists have been patiently building up sequences of pottery types for more than a hundred years, calling wells of similitude "peoples"; following objects to strange places on the landscape and calling it "trade" (or even "peer polity interaction"); and constructing thresholds of difference that become the temporal borders marking "social change." What is hard for archaeologists to see is continuity: it makes them think time has not passed—hence it is possible for a big and obvious site to become something of a temporal sink, making it only too easy for long-term accretion to look like short-term power.[7] Further, the base assumption is always that changes in pattern mean changes in worldview; yet where is the guarantee of that? In a very real sense, archaeologists are artists of *différance*, and this is what their evidence does best.

This is all the more reason why Native oral tradition is important. Though much maligned by historians and anthropologists alike until recently, the work of Jan Vansina and David Henige in Africa, of Richard Price in South America, and of archaeologists and ethnographers in the southwestern United States has shown that purely oral tradition—never once written down until modern times—can preserve quite accurate facts about the past pertaining to specific kinds of events, facts that are often hundreds of years old and that can even sometimes supply us with meaning for objects more than a thousand years old.[8] Oral tradition is difficult to deal with, however, because it can collapse in one "document" evidence pertaining to the *longue durée* and the *conjoncture*, both expressed in an example taken from *histoire événementielle*. There are limitations as far as specific events are concerned—researchers have carefully developed methods for finding them in such traditions as genealogical lists and migration histories—but then they may not be of greatest value in understanding the changes that prehistoric polities underwent. We are limited also both by what ethnographers have chosen to collect and by what Native people have seen fit to reveal to people who seemed to them intrusive, ceremonially impure, and likely to appropriate and misuse intellectual property. Still, we should not simply assume that there are no Native sources for information about the past. Native tradition is still capable of revealing where people came from, what their aspirations were, and how they lived.[9]

STATE OF RESEARCH FOR THE "OLD SOUTHWEST"

The state of research on the period of interest for early contact tribal histories in the "Old Southwest" region is uneven. I am of course most familiar with my own work on the Choctaws, which several archaeologists are in the process of testing[10] and which I have extended somewhat into the eighteenth century. On a larger temporal scale, Jeffrey Brain has done a fairly complete job on the evidence for Tunica history,[11] though ongoing discussions about Marvin Jeter's "Maximum Tunica Hypothesis" and the Tunica-Biloxi's own concern with their history promise additional information in the future.[12] Research on the Chickasaws for this period is sparse and in the near future not likely to be much amplified except incrementally, but again, modern Chickasaw Nation interest in their own history and the development of a Chickasaw museum is already encouraging additional archaeological and historical research.[13] The Natchez, on the other hand, have relatively few modern descendants, but because of their status as a presumed working model for a chiefdom they have received a great deal of relatively recent archaeological research from two generations of researchers originally based in the Lower Mississippi Survey[14] and at least a comment from every other archaeologist obliged to address the issues of chiefdom organization;[15] yet perhaps it is the apparent completeness of the eighteenth-century account of the Natchez from Du Pratz (or the lack of a good modern translation of that work[16]) that has discouraged an extended effort to reconstruct the protohistoric story of the Natchez. As for the generous number of what the French referred to as the "small tribes" of the lower Mississippi and Gulf Coast, their small size, early demise, lack of significant European documentation, or obscure location—or several of those factors—have conspired to discourage research on most individual groups.[17]

REGIONAL POLITICAL ECONOMY BEFORE CONTACT

I suppose the first question that should be asked about the late precontact political economy in the region of the Old Southwest is whether it is properly called a "Mississippian world" at all. I think most archaeologists would agree that the zenith of Mississippian development of mound building and agriculture had probably passed, since we know that Cahokia was already centuries past it, while more local powers like Moundville had also shown evidence of scaling back noticeably; archaeologists have spoken for years of a "Mississippian Decline" that resulted in smaller sites and less flashy remains, though of late they have reconsidered the use of the term "decline."[18]

I am persuaded by the climatological evidence that the global cooling known as the Little Ice Age may well have had negative cultural effects on the great Mississippian chiefdoms that can be compared to the positive effects of the "hypsithermal" maximum that apparently propelled the Late Archaic florescence.[19] To the north, where short growing seasons could make maize crops impossible, Cahokia saw its decline already in the fourteenth century. In the South, where large populations probably depended upon the ability to harvest more than one planting of maize, multiple crop failures in multiple years could and probably did mean a failure of central organization where it existed. I suspect that it is not coincidental that southeastern legends about the origin of corn include an explanation (in terms of human failure) of why so few successional crops are possible.[20]

Mississippian chiefdoms could have declined because food shortages placed undue strains on the fallbacks of trading networks and stored foods. Or they could have failed because the leading edge of a change in climatic regime destroyed the credibility of priest-chiefs who could no longer plan reliable harvests. The result would be the same. Constituent (kinship, geographical) groups within Mississippian polities would fission off and vote with their feet as they followed now-necessary game to less crowded regions where again they could develop a workable planting schedule or change their dietary mix.[21]

The point is that by the time Columbus bumbled into the Americas, former "Mississippians" were well into an adjustment to a climatic regime somewhat less favorable for agriculture than that which had nurtured the Mississippian florescence, and it seems very likely that relationships across the Old Southwest region remained somewhat unsettled. But that is not to say that some underlying continuities were not in effect. The Mississippi and Tombigbee valleys were rich providers of croplands and hunting grounds, with the Mississippi preeminent. The lands in between were still not very densely populated by maize farmers, and the Pearl valley may even have been partly vacated. All the people of the region were still quite aware of one another's existence, yet communication and trade would have been brisker with allies than with enemies.

It is reasonable to assume that if climate was a factor, peoples from the North would start moving southward.[22] Jeffrey Brain has argued that between 1500 and 1600 the Tunicans were pushed south and east across the Mississippi by movements of people from the north (I am happy to leave the Quapaw question to Marvin Smith) to occupy the northern half of the Yazoo Basin, where he reifies Parchman phase pottery distributions as "Tunica" because features seen here can arguably be shown to be connected developmentally with later pottery defined unequivocally as Tunica. He sees this whole process as continuous in a sense with the original expansion of "Mississippian-ness" from Cahokia southward, which he believes had already gradually "Mississippianized" underlying Coles Creek traditions in the southern part of the basin from 1200 to 1400.[23]

Further south along the Mississippi below the Yazoo confluence, Plaquemine culture had remained distinctive enough for its makers to be assumed to have held firm in resisting the full Mississippian influence, implying that they had little need of or interest in what the northerners had to offer (never mind that they could well have taken to wearing buffalo robes by the millions or have chanted borrowed formulae over their same old crops). There is no doubt that the Plaquemine peoples would in fact be the Natchez of history, for the continuity of their pottery tradition is obvious. The major question here is when and why they felt they had to move away from sites overlooking the Mississippi to build other mounds on eastern tributaries and the Natchez Trace.[24]

Less activity apparently took place across the Central Hills physiographic divide into east Mississippi. Even in flush times, these uplands did not support large populations, and even the western side of the Tombigbee and its tributaries apparently did not offer significant subsistence resources, since the region entirely lacks significant multiple-mound sites. Archaeologists have talked in terms of "country cousins" of Moundville serving as middlemen between that polity and those of the Yazoo Basin and Natchez regions.[25] Although there are a few odd lots of pottery through the region that make this suggestion believable, it is also important to note that these ideas are given support by the picture of regional alliances revealed by later documented Native reactions to each other and to European contact. To the north, present research argues for a location of the Chickasaws around the Columbus region, though it has not been possible to connect them neatly with specific mound sites.[26] To the south, I have offered the argument that ancestors of the western Choctaws lived in the vicinity of Nanih Waiya, just as one of the Choctaw origin histories suggests, but archaeology shows that this small group was certainly not crowded by near neighbors in late prehistory.[27]

Arguments about the definitive dating of the decline and fall of Moundville will continue, but I think it is clear that Moundville was also well along past decline to reorganization by the time of European arrival,[28] and this may have made significant differences to both proto-Chickasaws and proto-Choctaws. The Chickasaws would perhaps have lost a significant trading partner, although there were still eastward trans-Tombigbee connections with peoples who represent Moundville remnants at the end of the seventeenth century and through the eighteenth.[29] The Choctaws may have already established marriage alliances with what would have become by this time the Summerville phase "small tribes" of the lower Black Warrior and adjacent Tombigbee, too. The fact that both Chickasaws and Choctaws shared connections into this area is supported by their continuing mutual claim to it in the late eighteenth and nineteenth centuries.[30]

Both of these peoples, who still share an origin story that explains their cleavage from an original whole, were undoubtedly linked in frequent communication, as both used the Tombigbee to reach regional resources like salt. And neither was significantly favored over the other by the Black Belt soils or the Flatwoods hunting territory they shared. The fact that their extraregional contacts varied (proto-Choctaws with the Natchez region and the Mobile delta via Pearl and Sucarnoochee rivers and overland trail; proto-Chickasaws with the Yazoo and the Natchez region via land and Yazoo tributaries) may have been an advantage, enabling the two groups to ally with one another selectively in order to take advantage of specific resources not directly available.

And what about the other named groups that showed up later in the documents of colonization? The Yazoos, it is generally believed, were in fact those Mississippianized Plaquemine people of the lower Yazoo Basin. It is not completely clear who the Ibitoupa, Chakchiuma, and Ofogoula might have been this early,[31] and the always less highly centralized tribes of the Mississippi below the Homochitto and the Gulf Coast west of Mobile seem to have been organized mainly around small single-mound sites on minor tributaries, probably depending less on agriculture than on fishing and hunting in the wet woodlands of those regions. Their fate, however, has been partly a product of their failure to establish active alliances with Europeans and thus make a big splash in European documentation, no matter how good their environmental situation or even their success in escaping from political domination or European disease. Smaller simply means harder to see in archaeological and historical terms.

1492–1519: RUMORS OF STRANGERS

With the coming of European strangers, the question of regional communication is cast into relief. Archaeologists have made the case that trade had spanned the entire Southeast for thousands of years, not by huge numbers of people wandering around, but by single adventurers or small parties who might span several polities along a river or by diplomatic moves between neighboring groups. Flashy "type fossils" of significant rarity and recognizability (like obsidian, turquoise, *Busycon* shell, and copper) play the part of Kula-like gifts or objects of exchange to trace these links, whose routes seem to have been remarkably persistent.[32] If there were communication routes, and it is clear that there were, there were also barriers of enmity.[33]

Linguistic barriers may have been less serious in specific regions. It is clear that from the Central Hills of Mississippi east through most of Alabama and Georgia practically everyone could understand each other if they had to, although specific diplomatic relationships may have forbidden them to admit it in certain situations. Yet the archaeologists see no borderline mixing of pottery types that they would expect where friendly relations are maintained (potluck suppers, perhaps?), so they reckon there was a rift of some kind: it was not a linguistic problem that stopped Moundville people from communicating with the people east of them along the Coosa, Tallapoosa, and Flint, but probably enmity.

On the Mississippi, on the other hand, language may have been more of a problem, as at least two and eventually three unrelated linguistic groups—Tunican, Natchezan, eventually Siouan—lived next to each other. Emmanuel Drechsel has made an argument for a Mississippian-period time depth for the so-called "Mobilian" trade language,[34] and that may indeed be the case, but it seems to me likely that Mobilian was a Western Muskogean koiné that was not used on the Mississippi until spread there somewhat later, during the protohistoric, when the power of Mississippi River polities was in decline.

Given these conditions, what is the likelihood that Native people in the Mississippi Valley region had heard of the Spanish advent before they ever saw a Spaniard? Certain painful experiences of early explorers suggest that at least some Native people had been warned of their coming. But it is doubtful that any Native people upon more than passing acquaintance considered them gods, as Europeans so fondly imagined. We know that traditions and stories can travel very far, probably because they explain common life events in some very perspicuous way, but the speed of such travel is something else again. Certain thematic elements making up the phenomenon of the Southeastern Ceremonial Complex did travel across the region, but not unchanged and not very fast—probably not quickly enough for people who had a run-in with Ponce de Leon in 1513 to have warned people along the Mississippi coast about what to expect by the time of the Pineda voyage of 1519 or the Narváez expedition of 1528. And though it is possible that word of the Spanish arrival traveled along with shells traded into the Mississippi Valley from Florida, it is likely that the cautious reactions of Native people reflected their already-established behaviors toward strangers in general. It looks as though *direct* contact, fairly nearby, was required for the peoples of the Old Southwest to begin to learn that their world had changed.

Perhaps we should discount Pineda. As it seems more and more unlikely that Pineda actually explored Mobile Bay, coastal people may have only had a glimpse of his ship offshore. But we cannot do the same with Narváez. There was a violent encounter between Native leaders—probably of the Pensacola culture—and Narváez and his men, likely between the Mobile and Pascagoula rivers. According to the Spaniards they met with several men distinguished by special dress; further, they left behind two hostages, a Greek and a black man, and then escaped with difficulty from what may have been a trap.[35] This encounter suggests that either Pineda's proceedings had been more violent than he reported, or undocumented slaving expeditions had taken place in the intervening nine years.

In the hostages the people of the Gulf Coast had possession of significant knowledge that they did not have before. It is nearly impossible to evaluate what they may have learned; we can only speculate on some possible effects. Much would depend upon how long the men lived, whether they were kept together, how they comported themselves, and what their captors wished to learn from them. The two may have been kept alive. If so they were probably taken into elite custody. Although they had apparently died or been killed by the time Soto appeared (note that Luna in turn received news of individuals lost from the Soto expedition, who had lived eleven or twelve years), clearly there was ample time to debrief them, to learn something of what they knew.

The examples of fellow Narváez survivors Cabeza de Vaca in the Southwest and Juan Ortiz in Florida may be instructive. Cabeza de Vaca and his companions survived by fitting into the decentralized hunting-gathering cultures they found, while Núñez himself prospered as a trader between the coast and the hinterland, doubtless brokering local information as well as trade goods and certainly not revealing the truth of their situation.[36] Juan Ortiz, taken captive by a sedentary chief, had hastened to learn the language of his captors, and using it he claimed to have imparted a positive account of his people. Yet the reaction to his account depended less on his claims than on the experiences and political concerns of the elites he encountered: Ucita abused Ortiz because his family had received cruel treatment from the Spanish, while Mococo treated him liberally and listened to what he had to say, possibly intending to draw political advantage against his more powerful neighbor from Ortiz's people.[37] The antagonism that the Narváez expedition met with on the Gulf Coast argues for a quick and nasty fate for the Greek and the black man, but against this the subsequent fates of Soto survivors suggest that like contemporary European royalty, some elites, at least, were in the habit of learning from freaks and prodigies. They may have learned just how persistent Spanish intentions would be and as a result prepared to meet them with force.

It is not beyond the bounds of possibility that the considerable fortifications of Mabila had actually been built to counter in some way just such a threat from strangers rather than from neighbors, but we won't have the answer to that until Mabila is found. The confusion of the Soto expedition reports does not cast a blinding light upon the scene, either, but his undeniably violent and dangerous passage must have made the prologue of Pineda and Narváez real, must have established for anyone who still doubted it a threat from these genuinely strange people as a pattern to be reckoned with: they were not likely to go away. Nor did they behave like sane people. They could not, in other words, be dealt with using well-understood diplomatic conventions.

I have already argued that what Soto saw between the Tombigbee and the Mississippi Valley were at best "countrified" simple chiefdoms along the Tombigbee and more hierarchically organized[38] groups immediately west of the Mississippi and in its valley. I am still convinced that in the Moçulixa, Zabusta, Pafalaya group the Spaniards saw at best a modest alliance of probably Summerville phase villages, one or several future components of the Choctaws, living on the lower Black Warrior or adjacent Tombigbee rivers. The core group of Choctaws, who would anchor the eighteenth-century homeland land base, was missed by the expedition.

Precursors of the Chickasaws were not missed, though I am not certain how much of them the Spaniards actually saw. What they described is much like the scattered and sprawling villages that would later be characteristic. Present scholarship holds that their location was in the vicinity of Columbus, where most of the few substructural mounds were probably not in use. The "Sacchumas," "Alimamu," and "Talapatica" are far more shadowy: there is no solid documentary evidence of any concrete relationship between them and the Chicasa, and the archaeology doesn't help, since possible identifiable Chakchiuma sites are too late for Soto. I am still convinced that at this point what we are seeing is a loose regional confederation of modest single-level polities, though clearly that situation could not remain unaltered after Soto's departure.

The expedition's long stay in Chicasa had to have significant impact on firewood as well as food resources and is likely to have passed pathogens via several vectors, not the least of which may have been porcine.[39] Recent archaeological efforts have shown pretty conclusively that in the hundred years that followed, the future Chickasaws moved north from this location and settled across present Lee and Pontotoc counties in some eight villages.[40] Doubtless they were affected to some degree by European disease, but I am now inclined to see that effect as serious rather than catastrophic. The violence of the battles they fought against the Spaniards suggests that they were fit enough in the short term and that at least some segment of the group could rally military activity. The Alimamu resistance need have been no more than a working coordination with allies.

The political structures west of the Mississippi Central Hills and Flatwoods were something else again. Clearly Quizquiz as Soto saw it was a functioning multilevel chiefdom, as were the rest of the polities the expedition encountered in the Mississippi Valley. They all had chiefly capitals for which the Spaniards sometimes mention mounds, but it is obvious, even if the Spaniards exaggerated their interpolity conflicts, that they did not communicate or form alliances as easily or as willingly with one another as had the less centralized groups of the Tombigbee or even the chiefdoms of the Coosa-Tallapoosa-Alabama river valleys, who at least spoke mutually intelligible languages. Archaeologists are not in agreement over which of the major multiple-mound centers of the northern Yazoo Basin Quizquiz was, or even where in the valley Quigualtam was. I will assume for the purposes of this paper that Quizquiz did in fact map onto the Parchman phase proto-Tunicas, while "Quigualtam" represented a rumor of the Emerald phase Plaqueminians of the Bluffs region south of the Yazoo who would become the later Natchez. Even if these identifications are wrong, the sequences of subsequent devolution would remain substantially the same.

The "polities" seen in the region of interest by the Soto expedition were clearly of two very distinct kinds. On the Tombigbee they were of modest size: the people lived in sometimes considerable villages, and if one of their villages contained a mound it was yet not a vacant ceremonial center: the leader, while honored, was not significantly separated from villagers—a *primus inter pares*, not a king.[41] They also depended as much on hunting as they did on farming. In the Mississippi Valley, on the other hand, the significant grandeur of chiefs reflected in the large ceremonial centers they occupied rested on the bounty of the maize fields of many villages and the tribute of lesser mound towns. There was still security and prosperity in both regions, but social functions had to be less costly in the less rich of the two valleys. The cost of hierarchy on the Mississippi, on the other hand, was justified by the efficiency it lent to supporting many on relatively little land and organizing those many as a whole for various purposes: the Spaniards witnessed more "civility" because more discipline was required to live in such societies.[42]

Granted that the immediate impact of contact with Soto in the interior was powerfully related to the violence of his passage, the most serious question for us is also what the long-term political impact was. These Europeans were clearly not simply powerful neighboring chiefs, and there was probably no precedent for powerful chiefs from afar to come soldiering in announcing de facto conquest. Chiefs or priests didn't have to travel to distant places to obtain rare knowledge of these strangers and their powers; this time all they had to do was restrict access to the strangers—and I think it is fairly obvious that they did that to some degree where they could. This effect is far more obvious in the more hierarchically organized societies where management of obscure knowledge is theoretically supposed to have been part and parcel of chiefly power.[43] Reportage from the Spanish explorers explicitly states that they sought out polity leaders in order to gain control, but polity leaders may have sought Spanish leaders out as well, if only to prevent possible rivals from doing the same; clearly in the Mississippi Valley, polity leaders competed with each other for custody of the cognitive goods the Spanish strangers brought.

What knowledge was gathered that might have affected the existing political economy of the region? Even the less powerful groups of the Tombigbee region evidently took a pretty dubious view of Soto's claimed divinity, since they were not afraid of attacking him. The attacks and threats offered by Native groups might even have had a strategic purpose, because they served to incite the Spaniards to reveal such powers as they had. The Spaniards' armaments allowed deadly action at a distance, but it was not so accurate or silent as that of the Native people. The din of musketry might have been seen as a sign of power and would certainly have been an instrument of terror: what if the din raised by the Chicasa in attacking Soto was designed to appropriate some of that power? We know very little of the noise of Native battle before conflicts with European observers had already had the chance to alter it!

The horses and other animals are another issue. Native people in the Southeast, like those in the Southwest and Plains, were quick to adopt the horse in spite of the inconvenience of using horses in dense woodland. Horses were both killed and left behind alive in the region of interest, just as pigs were, and although doubtless some horses were eaten by Native people, upon closer acquaintance they may have used their existing classification of quadruped mammals to exclude horses from the edible cloven-footed (i.e., deer, bison) just as they included pigs (and eventually cattle). Tunicas particularly, but also Chickasaws and Choctaws, were so prominent in the horse trade later[44] that it is very tempting to guess that a few horses were kept alive, perhaps even as talismans or trophies—just as European monarchs prized exotic animals. Animals kept, however, amounted to disease vectors nurtured.

1542–1682: FLEETING CONTACTS

I won't spend a lot of time on disease since it will have been dealt with in greater detail by others. I would simply stress the importance of nonhuman animal disease vectors and say that while I think epidemic disease did seriously strike the Old Southwest during this period, it was certainly not the only disruptive factor. There is very little other than disease plus famine or war carnage on the scale of the nearly contemporary European Thirty Years' War to explain the scale of population loss in the more heavily populated areas of the Mississippi Valley. It would have required European weapons, which we know were not available in large numbers, to have inflicted that scale of carnage, even if we can imagine how and why it might have broken out in the context of existing regimes of diplomacy, alliance, and warfare—and in the absence of Europeans. Hence disease still must bear the responsibility for much population loss during this period and the one to follow. I have suggested that the emphasis on secondary burial and particularly the presence in Choctaw origin history of the notion of carrying the bones of ancestors may be linked to the disruptions of this period: that perhaps in a sense the Choctaw constituents accomplished a sort of ethnic "translation of empire" by bringing along the remains that still rested in ossuaries when they came to join the Nanih Waiya people in the homeland.[45] But it still seems to me that *secondary* burial practices would not survive mass mortality; the fact that they did persist may point toward lesser disease impact.

Direct physical evidence for disease is inevitably sparse in both regions, so diminution in sites has to proxy for it. That certainly happened; by now the statistical drop-off in known protohistoric-period sites is obviously not only an artifact of the recency of the "protohistoric" construct.[46] It also seems to have happened in both regions. But while the people of the Mississippi Valley worked out their own fates beyond European observation, on the Tombigbee the people got a second exposure both to European greed and European disease. Almost twenty years after Soto's expedition sliced its swath, Luna and his company spent enough time in the Mobile River valley to provide some observations about how things were going in the interior.[47] We should not assume that Luna & Co. were the only observers during this time, but they are the only Europeans who left us with substantive observations and who in turn added significantly to the change they were observing. If the Bottle Creek chiefdom still functioned and was reflected in Luna's Nanipacana, as I think likely, the activities of Luna's people and the diseases they left behind almost certainly led to its diminution, at least, and I suspect partly to its further dispersal. But the Spanish observations definitely showed that in twenty years the larger polities east of our region had seen serious decline in population and accordingly in hierarchical organization, while *the smaller ones nearer by seemed about the same*.

Population movements have also been treated in other essays, so I will simply reiterate here that their effects in the region in question touched all of the groups I am following in varying degrees. If Brain is right the Tunica people made a significant move from the northern Delta to the lower Yazoo, where they settled in coresidence with Yazoos and Koroas and Grigras; if I am right new Choctaws moved west from the Tombigbee and Mobile delta; if Neitzel and Brown are right several Yazoo Basin peoples moved south to join the Natchez; and if Johnson is right the Chickasaws moved northward into Lee County. In this last case little suggestion has been made that the Chickasaws took in additional groups before the eighteenth century, and I still doubt that they did so wholesale, but we know that they would soon do so, and the three southern towns of Ackia, Apeony, and Chukafala should be examined carefully as possible precolonial accretions, perhaps from Summerville peoples or perhaps from the northern Yazoo Basin.

The results of all these disruptions and effects of new knowledge were clearly felt in the social landscape and political economy of the region, but remarkably, the relative ranking of groups remained constant. By 1682 proto-Tunicas and proto-Natchez still used mounds and had important chiefs, though the mounds were not as many and the chiefs doubtless ruled less territory. By this time also proto-Chickasaws and proto-Choctaws still lived in dispersed settlements and displayed far fewer hierarchical tendencies than their Mississippi River neighbors. The strength of preexisting historical developments and cultural patterns, combined with the relatively steady state of the underlying subsistence base, seems to have kept individual groups on the same paths they had already defined for themselves.

Can Native traditions tell us something more about why these continuities were so strong? It is easy to point to environmental determinism and list constraints, but people *construct* the constraints that they obey. Muskogean origin traditions in the Southeast are of two kinds, earth-emergence and "walkabout," and both have significant things to say about the cognitive landscape of the region, yet in recent years few have taken them seriously enough to apply them in detail to the real physical and human landscape. As better understanding of the historicization of landscape by indigenous Australians has emerged, the possibility of similar practice would seem a fruitful area of investigation in North America as well.[48] If we could see ways in which the southeastern landscape was made sacred, we might better understand patterns of use, settlement, and polity formation that can now only be theorized in terms of pottery distributions.

1682–1715: COLONIZATION AND NEW EXPOSURE

The British and French came fully on the scene at the end of the seventeenth century. We point to 1682 because we know La Salle came down the Mississippi in that year, but there are bound to have been undocumented small forays into the interior by Florida Spaniards, Canadian Frenchmen, and Carolina Englishmen before that date, just as there were certainly documented forays out of it and into the edges of the European settlements by adventurous, curious, or rank-seeking Native people from our region. But now we begin to get some degree of permanent interaction: Frenchmen left behind with Chickasaws in 1682 by La Salle and with Quapaws by Tonti in 1686; Carolina trade with the Chickasaws from 1688, with traders establishing residence shortly afterward. The most significant of these contacts, which created the greatest disruption in the trans-Tombigbee interior, was that of the English traders seeking slaves.[49] Their alliances with the Upper Creeks, Chickasaws, and for a time the Quapaws turned Native groups (usually, I think, subtribal groups) into firearm-equipped slave catchers and enemies to their neighbors. Those neighbors were thus disposed to turn to any powerful Other who had assistance with defense to offer, and in the Mississippi Valley they were lucky that the relatively land-indifferent French were the potential allies who turned up. Rather than slavers, the French initially sent missionaries who sought souls rather than land, and their settlement on the Gulf Coast and at Mobile, which created a source for guns and trade goods, was just in time to contrast powerfully with the genocidal 1704 English raids on the Apalachee to the east that drove many of them, too, westward into the French orbit along with the Chatot.

The effects of the European establishment on the Chickasaws were perhaps most profound: they were the hinge of this new element in the region, and in return for English trade and support they immediately became very unpopular with all their neighbors. It should be said that most of the evidence indicates that Native peoples themselves practiced slavery of a kind, but it was not chattel slavery (just as much of the domestic slavery in Africa was not) and it did not become hereditary. Hence the kind of literally wholesale slave catching the English initiated was extreme in the numbers it sought and especially in removing its victims entirely from the continent.

It cannot have taken victimized Indian groups long to understand that this was different from anything seen before. I suspect that this move, with its drastic redefinition of "enemy" and "captive," may well have caused as much disruption in as short a time as any other European-borne change they had seen up to that point. I also think it is likely that from the first the Chickasaws were not all united in this or any other effort in relation to their English patrons, just as their victims were not unanimously happy to welcome the French. With the truly *Annales*-style, fine-grained evidence offered by the paper blizzard of a full-scale colonial bureaucracy, we begin to see the nuance and complexity of the Native response that was missing from the earlier swashbuckling tales of adventure; I would suggest that earlier avatars of the historic polities were similarly factional, but did not always reveal themselves so in the brief and one-sided glimpses explorers offered.

The Chickasaws were by this time a small polity of eight villages and perhaps five thousand people localized in northeast Mississippi, with others in two or three semipermanent camps in east and west Tennessee, over which they ranged to hunt and raid. The villages seem to have been autonomous to a degree and treated virtually equally, but the separation between the northern villages and the three to the south seems to have been more than geographical. As a result of their English alliance the Chickasaws began early to acquire not only guns, but all the accouterments that went with them, along with items that mimicked traditional prestige goods like cloth, clothing, and jewelry. Archaeological evidence has suggested that in moving to the Lee County region the Chickasaws had already adopted a subsistence base more focused on hunting and gathering than on agriculture, and guns would have made such arrangements more effective.

Besieged by former allies from the north and east, the Choctaws and their Mobile delta allies were driven together for security: even if they had not previously begun confederation for other reasons, it was now necessary for them to formulate some way of making common cause, some way that would prevent any member from throwing in with the enemy. Even so, the early French evidence shows that some Choctaws were somehow trading with the English—some members of the confederacy were spared the raids, and accumulated deerskins to obtain the precious guns. All that necessity initially went away when the French arrived. The French, eager themselves to obtain an ally of such proportions—some twenty thousand people in forty autonomous villages—with good reason to hate or fear the English, were generous with their guns and ammunition, and the Choctaws could have relinquished entirely the dangerous trade with the English.

But they didn't, at least not for long. Most Native peoples had realized, once they grasped that enmities among these tribes of strangers also existed, that danger from their technological power could be tempered if they were played off against one another, and that the less they knew of the others' activities, the better it would be for their "allies." So some Choctaws would trade with the English when they could, just as some Chickasaws, for most of the colonial period, would trade with the French. And both would tell Europeans what they wanted them to know. As groups who found themselves geographically situated between powerful Europeans, they would orchestrate their allegiances for survival, *just as they had when their powerful neighbors were chiefdoms*.

The Native groups on the Mississippi did not have quite the same luxury. In the early days of European penetration of the interior at the end of the seventeenth century, they could choose allies to some degree: the Quapaw tried to keep the French to themselves when they advised La Salle to keep away from the Tunicas—and shortly afterwards they were dealing with the English as well. The Tunicas therefore had to take initiative in looking for a European alliance, and they actively courted the French, going so far as to solicit and accept a missionary and tolerate his contempt for their temple worship. Much reduced in numbers from their former glory, yet still using their mound, they had joined in coequal settlement with several other Yazoo Basin peoples, most of them non-Tunican. This was apparently not a happy situation, however, and did not protect them adequately against Chickasaw slaving, so in 1706 they moved to join the Houmas on the Mississippi south of Natchez. Why the Houmas? What prior relations did they have with them? This alliance proved not to be comfortable for either group, and resulted in a deadly struggle that saw the Houmas driven from their home and the Tunicas left in possession. Had they done this before? Was this how they had been dispossessed in the northern Yazoo when Quapaws pushed across the river? As much as we know about the Tunicas, we don't know the answers to these questions, any more than we know the exact processes that transformed them from chiefdom to autonomous villages. For now, we have to think that it was the impact of European contact, but details are still hazy.

The Natchez story is similar in some respects. Although the genocidal retaliation by the French after the Natchez revolt of 1729 falls after this period of interest, they were in effect simply driven out of their very rich and desirable homeland by European action. They too were still firmly entrenched in their cultural traditions, though of course they had changed and moved like everyone else. They too had made coresidential arrangements with the Koroas and the mysterious Tioux and Grigra, and they had also taken in some Chitimachas; the mechanism of this alliance may have been the kinship arrangements anthropologists have so puzzled at—the so-called "Natchez Paradox."[50]

Yet the Natchez were different from all the others in ways that profoundly affected their interaction with Europeans and their success in the new environment. In the Suns they apparently retained a solid core of chiefdom structure, one with life and death control over non-Sun villagers, and a degree of hierarchy survived in the relative autonomy of at least some of the nine "villages." From the first, Sun comportment toward Europeans echoed the pride of Quigualtam's dismissal of Spanish power. From the first the Suns resented European presumption; from the first the relationship with the French was a rocky one. The Natchez also attempted to make a connection with the English, probably through the Chickasaws, to give them leverage against the French, but in the end they were geographically too isolated to make it work.

1715: FRENCH BREAKTHROUGH

The English had made several relatively successful attempts to win over the Native groups of the region of interest who had fallen under the influence of the French. The efforts of Thomas Nairne in 1708 and Price Hughes in 1713–14 had persuaded French allies to accept English trade, but the English traders' abuses when they had gained a favorable near-monopoly finally angered all the tribes of the Southeast. The Yamasee War in 1715, in which even the Chickasaws declared against the English, cut all the tribes of the trans-Tombigbee West off from English alliance and a potential balance for the French. With the English traders staying at home, the French were the only trading partners available, and they took advantage of that fact by placing two forts on the Mississippi (at Natchez in 1716 and the Yazoo confluence in 1718) and at the strategic confluence of the Coosa and Tallapoosa far to the east among the Alabamas (in 1717). These actions were quite consciously taken to rob the English of as many of their allies to the east of the Mississippi as possible, and their success, combined with the outcome of the War of the Spanish Succession, made John Law's venture at full-scale colonization seem promising.[51] As the cut-off point for this conference, then, the Yamasee War does have significant repercussions in the region of interest here.

The placement of the Natchez fort was ostensibly also punishment for the Natchez murder of five Frenchmen in 1716, which some alleged was actually the fault of the French governor Cadillac's failure to smoke the calumet with them shortly before, taken by the Natchez as a declaration of war. The French under Bienville, having killed three of the alleged murderers and received from the Natchez the head of a fourth, used their more docile allies the Tunicas—now located opposite the Red River mouth, where the French had already erected a small fortification—to support them in this punitive action. Natchez assistance in building the fort, as well as killing the chief of White Earth village, was the price of the subsequent peace. According to Bienville, "The chiefs of all the villages assembled at the house of the Great Chief agreed to execute all these articles" of the peace.[52]

This one incident is signal, because it shows one former chiefdom, the Natchez, still resisting outside dominance but forced to cooperate by threat of superior arms, while another, the Tunica, had adapted its insistence on autonomy to accommodate the discipline of a European alliance. One simple difference is obvious: the Natchez still occupied their virtually immemorial homeland, drawing strength from the evidence of their long residence written in the mounds and cleared lands that the French found so attractive. When eventually forced out they would fragment and disappear as a polity. The Tunicas, already less centralized before the coming of the French, had learned what it was to be landless, and had built the knowledge of strangers into a brokerage role. The price of survival in their case was to give up the apparent stability of structured authority for the flexibility of localized power.

The Choctaws were much less negatively touched by the temporary absence of the English, because the Chickasaws inevitably had to adapt by mending fences with Choctaw allies. But both groups were already positioned in many ways to become power brokers between the English and French and thereby to help maintain the Southeast as Indian country for much longer than it would remain so anywhere else east of the Mississippi (except the Florida swamps). They were geographically so placed, because for hundreds of years they had lived in and adapted to lands that for the time being Europeans did not covet. The English had chosen the Atlantic shore, and were reluctant to plunge in large numbers a distance into the "backcountry" that would be enough to bring them out on the other side of their own island. The French had reached their ice-free port by pioneering the Mississippi, but they were always more comfortable in the cooler prairies of the Midwest that would become the American equivalent of the Beauce. Because Choctaws and Chickasaws were placed between the European rivals, they had already attracted and over time would again attract additional villages and tribal fragments to join them: in spite of disease and war, they would grow and prosper. Their geographical position placed them at a choke point for knowledge, too: they could screen the French from the English or vice versa, but they could also hide what each was doing from the other. Finally, because they were each a congeries of autonomous villages, essentially acephalic, neither English nor French would ever be able to establish effective control over either of them or obtain more than segmentary cooperation at any given time.

CONCLUSION

If there is any general conclusion to be drawn from these observations it is that the pristine model of the hierarchical chiefdom was probably not implemented anywhere, or at least not for long, because it didn't respond that well to change: the cost could so easily exceed the benefit when the environment, climatological or geopolitical, changed. The male-headed "government" of hierarchical chiefdoms that Europeans recognized and attempted to control or crush was all too easy to cut off from its sources of power, as Soto had shown in Cuzco. Smaller village and lineage units— much more dependent upon the distributed authority of women and kinship not recognized by Europeans—were capable of providing most kinds of support including subsistence, as long as environmental resources were adequate. Hence the more decentralized the authority, the less easy it was to bring it under discipline and forcibly alter its construction of ethnic identity. Particularly as long as such groups were in a position to manage regional intelligence, they could do so for their own benefit. This is, if you will, the triumph of Redfield's "little tradition." And in the long term this is how most "subaltern" groups have managed to preserve their identities and resist cultural absorption.

Today the Natchez have been essentially absorbed by the Creeks and Chickasaws, but are once again politically emergent. The Tunicas have joined with Biloxis and other small tribes in Louisiana to establish a resilient tribal government. The Chickasaws, nearly all removed to Oklahoma, enjoy a strong and active tribal leadership devoted to the maintenance of tribal rights. The Choctaws in Oklahoma recently elected a new tribal government; Choctaws still in Mississippi are led by a chief whose successful economic policy of tribal self-sufficiency has made him the darling of fiscally conservative Washington leaders. All of these groups, more or less refreshed and empowered by NAGPRA, are working out a cultural renaissance for themselves: a new ethnogenesis. But chiefdoms are gone for good, and southeastern Indians are willing to leave it to Anglos to cling to civic fetishes.

Social Changes among the Caddo Indians in the Sixteenth and Seventeenth Centuries

TIMOTHY K. PERTTULA

Along with other native populations of the southeastern United States,[1] the Caddo Indian peoples who lived in what is now northeast Texas, northwest Louisiana, eastern Oklahoma, and southwestern Arkansas have withstood disease and demographic loss, colonization, and acculturation, the centuries-long and continuing interaction with Europeans.[2] They survived and apparently thrived at critical times amidst the onslaught of European and American empire-building on lands the Caddo had considered their own from time immemorial.[3] In this paper I focus on the period from about 1530 to 1715, that time between prehistory and history "for which few written records are available, and for which most evidence is derived from archaeology,"[4] to understand how Caddoan societies began to change and evolve following the initiation of contact and interaction with Europeans in the early sixteenth century.

The study of initial contacts between Europeans and Caddo peoples has focused on the effects of that contact on the nature of changes in Caddo societies. In my use of "initial contact," I am following Trigger and Swagerty in referring to the period that "extends from the earliest evidence of European goods or diseases in a region to the start of detailed and continuous written records."[5] In the Caddoan area, this traditionally begins about the time of the earliest possible contacts between the Caddo and Europeans and ends with the mid-1680s expeditions of La Salle. The period of initial contact can be extended into the first several decades of the eighteenth century, before the 1716–1721 Spanish establishment of several permanent missions and the first presidios among the Hasinai Caddo.[6] After this time, a relatively voluminous archival and historical record of the Caddo peoples is available,[7] although the archaeological record remains meager.[8]

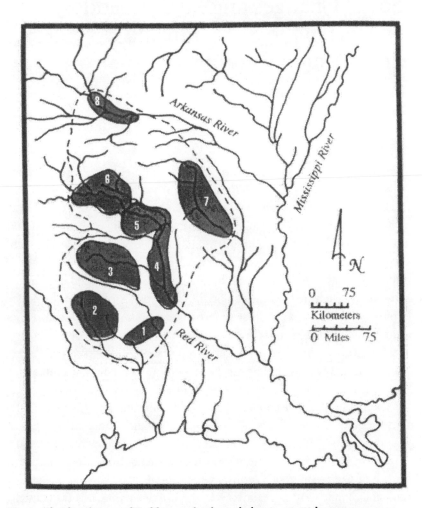

Fig. 1. The distribution of Caddoan archeological phases at initial contact, ca. A.D. 1520: (1) Angelina phase, (2) Frankston phase, (3) Titus phase, (4) Belcher phase, (5) Texarkana phase, (6) McCurtain phase, (7) Mid-Ouachita and Social Hill phases, and (8) Fort Coffee phase.

THE CADDO PEOPLE IN THE PRECONTACT AND CONTACT ERAS

During prehistoric and historic times, the Caddo peoples were a powerful group of related theocratic chiefdoms with a political and religious elite that had great political skill and trading savvy.[9] The Caddo people shared with their Mississippian neighbors maize agriculture and a hierarchical political organization, along with "a set of religious cult institutions and iconographic complexes."[10] Nevertheless, when boundaries of Mississippian societies are drawn, most of the Caddoan area—other than the Arkansas and Red River basin Caddoan groups[11]—has frequently been excluded from the Mississippian world.

The archaeological record of the Caddo peoples from ca. A.D. 800 indicates that they lived in parts of Arkansas, Oklahoma, Texas, and Louisiana. The Great Bend of the Red River valley—with its fertile soils, broad valley, sacred hills, and rich aquatic resources—was the cultural heartland of the Caddo peoples. Caddoan populations reached from the Arkansas and Red River valleys into the western Ozarks as well as south into deep east Texas and east into central Arkansas, in what has been called the Trans-Mississippi South.[12]

Despite archaeological investigations beginning in the latter years of the nineteenth century, and many major research efforts since that time, current knowledge about the early social history of the Caddo Indian peoples is still not well known. In the period between 1530 and 1715, archaeological evidence of Caddoan populations includes the Social Hill and Deceiper phases along the Ouachita River in southwestern Arkansas;[13] the McCurtain, Texarkana, and Belcher phase communities along a two-hundred-mile stretch of the Red River and tributaries in northeastern Texas and southeastern Oklahoma;[14] Titus phase groups in the Cypress Creek and upper Sabine River basins of northeast Texas;[15] and the Allen phase communities and hamlets in deep east Texas (fig. 1).[16] These Caddo polities are recognizable in the archaeological record by distinctive differences in ceramic vessel and pipe forms and styles, diverse arrowpoint forms and other tools, and the use and decoration of shell tools and ornaments, including Gulf Coast marine shell.[17]

From at least the late seventeenth century, the Caddo peoples comprised at least twenty-five distinct but closely affiliated groups, all speaking their own dialects.[18] Shortly thereafter, because of population loss, tribal movements, and village abandonments, these Caddo-affiliated

groups became coalesced into the Hasinai, Kadohadacho, and Natchitoches confederacies in the Neches and Angelina river valleys, the Great
Bend of the Red River, and in the vicinity of the French post of Natchitoches in northwestern Louisiana, respectively. The Hasinai Caddo
groups continued to live through the 1830s in their traditional east Texas
homelands, while the Natchitoches did the same in western Louisiana,
but the Kadohadacho were forced to move off the Red River in the late
1780s to the Caddo Lake area, along the boundary between the territory
of Louisiana and the province of Texas.

The Caddo peoples trace descent matrilineally. They also recognized
and ranked clans, with marriage typically occurring between members of
different clans. Religious and political authority in historic Caddoan communities rested in a hierarchy of key inherited positions shared between
the various affiliated communities and groups. The *xinesi* (pronounced
"chenesi," meaning Mr. Moon)[19] inherited the position of spiritual leadership; the *caddi* was the principal headman of a community, a position that
passed from father to son; and the *canahas* were village elders or subordinate headmen. The Caddo people looked to the *xinesi* for mediation and
communication with their supreme god, the *Caddi Ayo*, for religious leadership and decision-making influence, and in leading certain special rites,
including the first-fruits, harvest, and naming ceremonies. In essence, the
xinesi imbued everyday life for the Caddo peoples with the supernatural.
The *caddi* was primarily responsible for making the important political
decisions for the community, sponsoring other major ceremonies of a diplomatic nature, leading councils for war/raiding expeditions, and conducting the calumet (or peace pipe) ceremony with important visitors to the
communities.[20]

The precontact Caddoan cultural tradition is characterized by widely
dispersed but sedentary settlements, a horticultural to agricultural economy, and a complex sociopolitical structure marked by a heterarchical
network of centers controlled by the political and religious elite. The
Caddo polities engaged in extensive interregional trade in items such as
bison hides, salt, and bois d'arc (i.e., Osage orange) bows, along with copper, turquoise, marine shell, pottery vessels (and their contents), and
exotic lithic raw materials.[21] These items were often accumulated as grave
goods to be placed in the burials of the Caddo social and political elite.
After about A.D. 1400/1500, however, long-distance trade efforts were

diminished, and elaborate mortuary ceremonialism ceased to flourish outside of the Red and Little river areas of the Great Bend region.

In precontact times, beginning about A.D. 800/900, the premier civic and ceremonial centers were marked by mounds for the burial of the elite in elaborate mortuary rituals and as platforms for structures and public architecture used by the elite.[22] The development of these well-planned mound centers went hand-in-hand with the development of elite status positions within powerful Caddoan communities. These larger communities were primarily located along the major streams—the Red, Arkansas, Little, Ouachita, and Sabine rivers—crossing the Caddoan area. In historic times, after Caddoan mound-building activities were discontinued,[23] elite-controlled rituals and ceremonies were conducted among the Caddo in specialized and centrally located public structures and plazas[24] and probably also at the community cemeteries common, for example, throughout the Cypress Creek basin in northeast Texas.[25]

Into the world of the Caddo peoples entered the Spanish *entrada* of Hernando de Soto, now led by Luis de Moscoso, who passed through Caddo lands in present-day Arkansas, Texas, and Louisiana in 1542–1543.[26] The Gentleman of Elvas noted that when the Spaniards reached the Caddo province of Naguatex on the Red River in August of 1542 "[t]he cacique [of Naguatex], on beholding the damage that his land was receiving [from the Spanish forces], sent six of his principal men and three Indians with them as guides who knew the language of the region ahead where the governor [Luis de Moscoso] was about to go. He immediately left Naguatex and after marching three days reached a town of four or five houses, belonging to the cacique of that miserable province, called Nisohone. It was a poorly populated region and had little maize. Two days later, the guides who were guiding the governor, if they had to go toward the west, guided then toward the east, and sometimes they went through dense forests, wandering off the road. The governor ordered them hanged from a tree, and an Indian woman, who had been captured at Nisohone, guided them, and he went back to look for the road."[27]

Not far behind apparently were the epidemic diseases introduced by the Europeans,[28] although the Caddoan archeological record is still mostly silent concerning when the population declines caused by disease occurred and how substantial they were (see below).

When the Europeans next arrived among the Caddo in 1686, the Caddo peoples lived primarily in small groups on the Red River and in east Texas. Populations had diminished. While the establishment of the Spanish missions between 1690 and 1721 failed completely to convert the Caddoan peoples, and did not lead to the resettlement of Caddoan communities around the missions, a few Caddo apparently chose mission life rather than remain in east Texas. Eyeish (Ais) and Tejas (Hasinai) individuals were enrolled at missions San Jose and Valero in San Antonio in the mid-to-late 1700s.[29]

Through their missions, ranches, trading posts, and fur traders, the far edges of the French and Spanish empires laid claim to the land and loyalties of the Caddo Indians.[30] The Caddo were well situated to participate in the French fur trade, and to trade guns, horses, and other essential items to other Indian groups and Europeans, and in the process they developed new trade and economic networks. The resulting economic symbiosis between the Caddo groups and Europeans was the key to the political success and strength of the Caddo tribes through much of the colonial era.[31] Sabo's ethnohistorical studies of late-seventeenth- and early-eighteenth-century Caddoan societies show how significant structural relationships within Caddoan society—such as village organization and the hierarchical ranking of peoples—were explicitly extended to Europeans.[32] The Caddo used symbols of sacred and secular rituals and greeting ceremonies (including the weeping during greeting ceremonies of the Caddo leaders noted by the Soto chroniclers; see Hudson) to draw out these relationships, as well as what La Vere terms "fictive kinship," and "to extend to their relations with Europeans those basic principles and themes that ordered and gave shape to their own distinctive societies."[33]

The Caddos' participation in the fur trade had important consequences for them, as well as for their European partners. As with the fur trade elsewhere in North America,[34] the participation of the Caddo led to their acquiring and accumulating large quantities of desirable European-manufactured goods, which they in turn exchanged with other Indian groups for furs and horses, all the while exploiting existing trade networks to their advantage. The success of the fur trade for the Caddo also allowed them to expand their hunting activities into new territories, and/or reoccupy once-abandoned river valleys (such as the upper Sabine River basin after about 1740)[35] for the same purposes. Their contribution to the European frontier economy, and their military presence, was recognized by the French and Spanish governments through their program of annual gifts and presents, reflecting the existence of political and economic commitments between the Caddo peoples and the Europeans.[36] These all had considerable economic, military, and social values to the Caddoan peoples in their dealings with other Indian groups.

SIXTEENTH- AND SEVENTEENTH-CENTURY CADDO SOCIAL HISTORY

Fundamental changes in Caddo society in the sixteenth and seventeenth centuries appear to be the product of depopulation from European-introduced diseases, increased tribal conflicts to the east and west with groups moving across the Southern Plains and the lower Mississippi Valley, access to European goods such as the horse and gun, and their participation in the European market economy. In what had been powerful precontact era chiefdoms, disease, population movements, and trade opportunities created a "new cultural geography" among the Caddo,[37] one where once-distinct Caddo polities coalesced to form small-scale confederacies of kin-based affiliated groups of Caddo communities.[38]

Disease and Health

There is no question that epidemics greatly reduced Caddo populations—possibly by as much as 75 to 95 percent between 1691 and 1816.[39] How much Caddo populations may have declined between ca. 1530 and 1691 is still unresolved, however, although population losses are thought to have been significant. According to archaeological evidence and historically recorded population estimates of the Hasinai, Kadohadacho, and Natchitoches confederacies, population declines were more substantial among the Caddo groups living along the major rivers (such as the Kadohadacho) than they were among "rural" Caddo groups[40] and more substantial than among neighboring mobile hunter-gatherers.[41] It was mainly the small dispersed Caddo groups like the Hasinai Caddo that survived to be described ethnographically by Europeans and Anglo-Americans,[42] and it is about them that we know the most in historic times.

With one exception, however, there is no direct bioarchaeological evidence for the presence of epidemic diseases in any Caddoan historic bioarchaeological assemblages.[43] However, acute epidemic diseases rarely leave specific direct evidence on archaeologically recovered skeletal samples,[44] limiting in this respect the interpretive significance of bioarchaeological remains to directly address the issue of disease. Nevertheless, the population and disease effects on native Caddo groups have been closely scrutinized through both archaeological and bioarchaeological evidence,[45] with the work concentrating especially on reconstructing Caddoan population histories—determining when epidemic diseases were introduced among Caddoan groups, when postcontact population declines occurred, and what the long-term cultural impacts of disease and population declines on Caddoan societies and communities were. Trends and discontinuities in the abandonment of regions and major sites, abrupt changes in settlement patterning, and the discontinuation of mound building appear to relate to, or denote, more fundamental cultural changes in demographic or health conditions of Caddoan polities. This point is reiterated by Kealhofer and Baker, who state that "changes in mortality and health patterns, and the imprint of epidemic-based demographic decline, must be correlated with the detailed settlement data and chronology."[46]

Burnett's bioarchaeological study of the Ouachita River basin in southwestern Arkansas is one of the most comprehensive bioarchaeological studies of post–A.D. 1500 Caddoan skeletal remains.[47] Her work seems to suggest that between A.D. 1500 and 1600, Caddoan adults lived shorter lives than before, and that infection rates among subadults and adults were higher than at any other time in the Caddoan occupation of the basin. Might this evidence reflect population declines resulting from European diseases? However, Burnett detected that after A.D. 1600 infection rates declined and adult age at death increased, which she attributes to improved adaptive efficiency among these Caddoan populations; after 1700, the Caddo groups completely abandoned the Ouachita River basin.

The recent bioarchaeological work on protohistoric assemblages from the Red River in northeast Texas provides a view of Caddo health conditions during the sixteenth and seventeenth centuries.[48] These Caddo populations were generally healthy, but "biologically adapted over many generations to this regimen [of a maize diet]."[49] From patterns of arthritis and bone inflammations, we know their agricultural lifeway was a hard one, and patterns of infant mortality were comparable to that seen in other southeastern United States Mississippian societies. They suffered from endemic treponematosis, an infectious disease, and bioarchaeological studies have shown that some 11 percent of the individuals had experienced severe iron deficiency anemia before the age of four.[50]

Population declines and settlement changes appear to have been more substantial along the major rivers, as seen by the complete abandonment of the Ouachita and Little rivers by 1700 and the Arkansas River earlier in the 1600s but no major abandonment of much of east Texas by the Hasinai Caddo in historic times. The area between the Sabine and the Sulphur rivers, occupied by Titus phase groups,[51] appears to have been essentially abandoned, however, by about 1680, if not earlier. The Caddoan groups who lived in this once densely populated region were not directly visited or contacted by either the Spanish or the French. The introduction of European epidemic diseases is thought to be primarily responsible for the virtual abandonment of the region by these Pineywoods Caddo peoples.

Times of Conflict

Caddoan communities, towns, and mound centers were never fortified, and there is no hint of a defensive posture in the widely dispersed prehistoric and historic Caddoan communities.[52] Similarly, there is virtually no evidence in the archaeological record for warfare or violent conflict between the Caddos and other peoples; that is, evidence of fortifications is rare, as is evidence of individuals dying from wounds inflicted from an arrowhead, scalping, or forms of mutilation after death, certainly when compared to contemporaneous Indian groups in the Southern Plains and the Southeast.[53] This is also quite a contrast with the sedentary agriculturists living in the Mississippi Valley and interior Southeast, where heavily populated towns were palisaded, and Indian polities asserted political and economic authority through warfare.[54] Thus, it is difficult to credit Hickerson's assertion that the threat of Apache aggression played a major role in the formation of the Hasinai Caddo confederacy in the late seventeenth century.[55] This is not to say that there were not conflicts between the Caddo peoples and their neighbors that played a role in defining the character of Caddo society in the sixteenth and seventeenth centuries.

Interestingly, some of the enemies of the Hasinai and Kadohadacho in the late 1600s included other Caddoan-speaking groups such as the Nabiri (or Nabiti), the Nondacau (or Nondacao), and Nauydix (or Naouydiche; table 1).[56] These were groups who later were more closely allied with the Hasinai confederacy. From this, we may conclude that population coalescence and confederation was not a simple bonding process among surviving Caddo groups, but one of fragmentation and changing intergroup alliances. Other possible Caddoan-speaking tribal groups mentioned by Henri Joutel as enemies of the Kadohadacho include the Nadaho, Nadeicha, Nacoho, Nacassa, Nahacassi, Nadatcho, and the Nardichia (table 1.).[57] All these tribal names begin with the Caddoan *na*, a locative prefix in the Caddoan language.[58]

Regarding their other enemies, it is suspected that relations between them and Caddoan peoples alternated over the years between alliances and hostility, depending upon the needs of the moment, particularly the willingness to trade. All this was to change with the appearance and adoption of the horse and gun among the Caddo and their Southern Plains neighbors. With the horse and gun, the Caddos were able to increase their bison hunting in the prairies and plains well west and southwest of their territory, which probably exacerbated existing animosities, but did

Enemies

Cannaha	Caiasban	Nacoho
Nasitti	Tahiannihou	Nardichia
Houaneiha	Natsshostanno	Nacassa
Catouinayos	Cannahiss	Tchanhie
Souanetto	Hianagouy	Datcho
Quiouaha	Hiantatsi	Aquis
Taneaho	Nadaho	Nahacassi
Canoatinno	Nadeicha	
Cantey	Chaye	
Caitsodamme		

Allies

Senis	Nondaco*	Douesdonqua
Nassoni	Cahaynnohoua	Dotchetonne
Natsohos	Tanico	Tanquinno
Cadodaquis*	Cappa	Cassia
Natchittos	Catcho	Neihahat
Nadaco*	Daquio	Annaho
Nacodissy	Daquinatinno	Enoqua
Haychis	Nadamin	Choumay
Sacahaye Nouuista		

* The Cadaquis and Nadatcho were listed by Joutel as enemies, but these appear to be the same name as Cadodaquis and Nadaco or Nondaco, respectively.

Table 1. Enemies and allies of the Kadohadacho, 1687[59]

not prevent them from moving into and using new areas (i.e., new hunting territories and in settlements astride Indian and European trade routes). It also assured the Caddoan peoples of continued trade with the Europeans and an active role in arranging political and economic measures between other Native Americans and the Europeans that directly affected their well-being.

By the 1680s, those hunting-gathering groups to the west and southwest of the Hasinai Caddo tribes had horses in numbers, but lacked guns, which the Caddo peoples began to obtain (if sometimes only periodically) in trade with the French fur traders. The Hasinai Caddo peoples also had horses obtained through trading with their allied groups on the prairies and plains of central and southern Texas and through raiding on their enemies. The Caddoan groups were well placed along the "Horse Frontier" and the "Gun Frontier," and "as of about 1716, the Hasinai and the Cadohadachos marked, respectively, the saturated frontier of horses moving eastward, and of muskets moving westward in trade."[60]

This accessibility of such desirable goods as guns and horses contributed strongly to the maintenance and expansion of Caddoan social and political power relationships among their Native American neighbors, allies, and enemies. The Caddo increased their bison and deer hunting in the prairies and plains well west and southwest of their territory[61] to obtain deer and bison hides for trade with the French. By the 1680s, the Caddoan societies south of the Red River were well supplied with horses obtained in trade, such that "there were four or five about each house."[62] The acquisition and use of the horse by the Caddo facilitated the rapid movement and transportation of goods (both aboriginal and European), were highly sought trade items of great value, and brought increased mobility and range to hunting forays. Thus, the seemingly rapid adoption of the horse conferred a considerable selective advantage to Caddoan groups over their non-Caddoan neighbors when considered together with an increased accessibility to French guns, Spanish mission horse herds, and the expanding Southern Plains bison herds.[63]

Fighting between the Caddo and their enemies was mainly that of "hit-and-run raids upon an enemy in which an attempt was often made to capture a foe,"[64] rather than battles with large numbers of casualties on either side. This enmity did not prevent the Caddo peoples from hunting and trading regularly in both areas before and after they had the horse, as noted above, and indeed the Hasinai Caddo peoples were quite familiar with these regions, giving Fray Mazanet in 1691 their names for each of the streams from the Nabedache village on San Pedro Creek (just west of the Neches River) as far west as the San Antonio area.[65] After the Caddo peoples had horses, they began to regularly use central and south Texas as hunting territory, obtaining deer and bison hides for trade with the French.[66]

For the Kadohadacho tribes, on the other hand, according to Joutel in 1687, "most of the hostile tribes are to the east . . . and have no horses; it is only those towards the west which have any."[67] The hostile tribes to the east had plentiful supplies of guns obtained from both French and British sources, and their aggressive raids focused on obtaining Caddoan slaves, horses, and furs.

This disparity in supplies of the coveted horses and guns led to a profitable trade for the Caddo peoples, either in direct exchange or through their acting as middlemen, but over the long run, the trade bounty did not serve to better protect them against the Osage and Chickasaw, also well supplied with guns, who, from the late 1600s to the early 1700s, ceaselessly raided the Caddo for slaves.[68] Shortly thereafter, the Caddo became involved in the thriving traffic in Apache slaves, one outcome of the Southern Plains warfare between the Comanche and Apache that began about 1700,[69] trading European goods for Apache children to the French and Spanish markets at Natchitoches and Los Adaes.[70] By the 1760s, the Osage were expanding their hunting and trapping territory to obtain more furs, however, and their depredations against the Caddo changed to a "war of conquest."[71]

Settlements, Communities, and Landscapes

When first visited by the Soto *entrada* in 1542, the Caddo in southwestern Arkansas and eastern Texas were described as living primarily in scattered settlements with abundant food reserves of corn in several of the provinces (Naguatex on the Red River and Guasco near the Neches River).[72] Archaeological investigations confirm that Caddoan communities were widely dispersed throughout all of the major and minor river valleys of the region from at least A.D. 800 until the early 1700s. Their settlements had great permanence: the people had for a thousand years or more lived and sustained themselves in the forested and well-watered landscape of the Trans-Mississippi South.

Looking more closely at the historic territory of the Caddo about 1520/ 1530, we see that the Hasinai Caddo groups lived in permanent communities throughout the upper Neches and Angelina river basins. They are represented by the Frankston (ca. 1400–1600) and Allen (ca. 1600–1750) phases,[73] and are likely related to the Guasco province described by the Soto chroniclers.[74] Although occasional Hasinai Caddo groups or bands lived west of the Neches and Trinity rivers in historic times, they usually did not go beyond that boundary "unless going to war."[75] The Hasinai groups continued to live in the upper Neches and Angelina river basins until they were driven out of northeast Texas by the Republic of Texas after 1836.

Groups such as the Naguatex and Nisoona were Red River Caddo communities living in the Great Bend of the Red River, and they are ancestral to the Kadohadacho and other affiliated groups of the Kadohadacho confederacy. To their east were the "Chagus" or Chaguate, a mid–Ouachita River Caddo "province" involved in the salt trade. The Chaguate may be ancestral to the Cahinnio Caddo, since they were living on the Ouachita River when Joutel first encountered them in 1687. Other Caddo groups encountered by Soto's men include the Lacane, the Ayx, and the Xualatino in the Pineywoods of northeast Texas. The province of Lacane may be related to the Titus phase Caddo groups living south and west of the Red River[76] and north of the Hasinai Caddo affiliated groups.

European maps of the late 1500s to the mid-1600s located Caddoan groups such as the Naguatex, Nisoone (Nasoni), Pato, Lacane, Ays, Xualatino (or Soacatino) and Guasco on a western tributary of a drainage labeled Rio de Leon or Rio de Spiritu (Espiritu) Santo, the Mississippi River, but it is clear from similarities between 1572 and 1656 maps that geographic knowledge of the territory of the interior-living Caddo and other Texas tribes had not improved over that period.[77] It was not until Europeans (principally La Salle[78]) ventured again into the Caddoan area in the 1680s that the territory of the various Caddoan tribes and of their non-Caddoan allies and enemies became better understood.

Delisle's map of 1702 places a series of related Caddoan groups along a considerable stretch of a western tributary of the Mississippi River, obviously the Red River. Beginning on the lower Red River with the Nachitoches (Natchitoches) and proceeding upriver, other Caddoan groups included the Nakasa (one of the enemies of the Kadohadacho in 1687, according to Joutel),[79] Yatache (Yatasi), Natsoos (Nanatsoho), Cadodaquiro

(Kadohadacho), the (upper) Nachitoches, and the Nassonis (Nasoni). The Cahinoiia (Cahinnio) Caddo were living east-northeast of the Natchitoches, while the Ouachita Caddo were living downstream from them on the Ouachita River in southwestern Arkansas. The Cahinnio Caddo lived in one large town, according to Joutel in 1687, but by 1700 they were living with the Kadohadacho on the Red River. Most of the Ouachita Caddo had gone to live with the lower Natchitoches sometime between 1690 and 1700.[80] Upstream from the Nasoni on the Red River were the Canouaouana and Chaquanhe tribes, apparently enemies of the Kadohadacho, again according to Joutel.

The westernmost Caddoan groups were shown by Delisle as living on and near the Rio aux Cenis (probably the Neches River), Cenis (or Senys) being the French name for the Hasinai Caddo. Other than containing the mistake of having the Rio aux Cenis run into the Red River, Delisle's map indicates that the French had a good understanding of the locations of the various Hasinai Caddo groups, from the Inahe (Hainai) to the east (on the Angelina river), the Nadaco and Nassonis (Nasoni) to the north and west, and a series of Cenis or Hasinai communities along the western boundaries of their territory. No Caddoan communities are depicted north of the Rio aux Cenis or between the Hasinai and the Red River, nor are there any Caddo communities west of the Trinity River (Rio Baho), with the closest non-Caddoan communities living between the Trinity and Brazos (La Maligne R.) rivers. On the Brazos River lived the Canohatino tribe, one of the enemies of the Hasinai Caddo (see table 1), who felt the brunt of a French-Caddoan attack in 1687 in which more than forty Canohatino were massacred by the joint armed forces.

From Delisle's time to the mid-eighteenth century, the Caddo landscape did not change much, and the Caddo populations remained in deep east Texas and on several stretches of the Red River (fig. 2). While European civil and religious settlements were now more permanently established in their midst, there were at most small-scale shifts in populations, first towards the European settlements and then again away from them as the Caddos' involvement in the fur trade expanded.[81] The population contraction or amalgamation that occurred between ca. 1540 and 1700, and left much of the Caddoan area abandoned by 1700, meant that by the middle of the eighteenth century local Caddo chiefdoms remained only where direct and permanent European settlements existed throughout much of the eighteenth century—the French town of Natchitoches, the French

Nassonite Post, and the Spanish missions and presidios from Los Adaes to the Neches River. It was in these settings that new economic and political relationships developed between Europeans and the Caddo peoples.[82]

When Alonso de Leon came among the Hasinai Caddo in 1690, he described their community along the Neches River as follows: "The principal settlement encompasses fourteen to fifteen leagues, but we were unable to see all of it because of a river [the Neches] that passes through the middle. In the part that we did see there were more than four thousand people."[83] He went on to note that there were many other Caddo settlements in the area. According to French testimony, there were nine or more Caddoan communities,[84] as well as "the large settlements of the Cadohadacho [to the north and northeast], whose people plant and store [enough produce] for the year."[85] Indeed, the Soto-Moscoso *entrada* noted the agricultural capabilities of the Kadohadacho in 1542, when they pillaged the maize stores on their way west; when they returned some

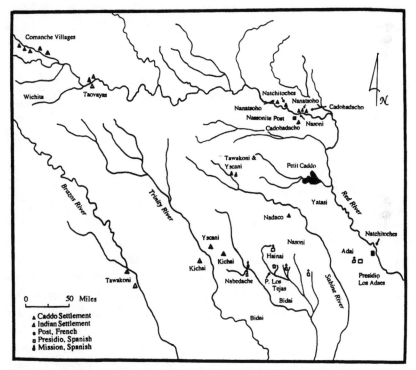

Fig. 2. Late eighteenth-century locations of the Caddo or Kadohadacho and Hasinai tribes on the Red River and in east Texas, the Wichita tribes (Taovayas, Tawakoni, Yscani, and Kichai), the Bidai, and a band of Red River Comanche (after Carter 1995: 182).

months later to the same villages, the maize stores had been replenished.[86]

As in prehistoric times, the Caddoan people during the protohistoric era lived principally in year-round sedentary, dispersed communities, or *rancherías*, containing single homesteads and/or farmsteads with one or two structures and small family cemeteries. At the McLelland site on the Red River, the 1650–1710 Nakasa Caddo community consisted of two circular structures (11–12 m in diameter), a possible ramada, several burials, a sheet midden deposit covering ca. 450 m², and an assortment of extramural pits and features that likely represent cooking and working areas.[87] Hamlets and/or larger villages with a number of houses, middens, burials and cemeteries, and open plaza areas are also known archaeologically, particularly along the Red River and elsewhere across the Caddoan area that evidently had higher population densities, including the "heavily settled valley" of San Pedro Creek in deep east Texas noted by de Leon in 1689.[88] Occasionally these hamlets or villages had small earthen mounds that capped important public structures.[89] Along Big Cypress Bayou in the Pineywoods of northeast Texas, protohistoric Titus phase communities also had large community cemeteries, sometimes containing 150–300 burials, in addition to the family cemeteries at the farmsteads and hamlets.[90] The distribution of the large community cemeteries appears to reflect the overall density of Titus phase populations and the distribution of Titus phase settlements across the region.

Caddoan settlements and communities in prehistoric and protohistoric times were regularly associated with the important (though usually vacant) centers that had earthen mounds and/or public architecture.[91] As Schambach notes, the main mounds dating after ca. A.D. 1300 "contain the remains of important buildings rather than important people," as was not the case among ca. A.D. 900–1300 Caddoan groups whose mounds contained the shaft burials of elite members of Caddoan society.[92]

Archaeological investigations along the major streams and tributaries document the construction and use of earthen mounds among the Caddo in the sixteenth and seventeenth centuries. These mound centers have been categorized as "vacant in the sense that there was no domestic occupation off the mounds, with the population living in small farmsteads scattered around the countryside,"[93] but some other mound centers occupied about this time along the middle reaches of the Red River (among the

McCurtain phase) had dense settlements strung out along the natural levees and alluvial landforms.

One of these dispersed Caddoan communities was mapped in 1691–1692 by Don Domingo Teran de los Ríos during his expedition to the Kadohadacho.[94] Teran's map shows that the Caddo village was divided into individual compounds, or *ranchitos,* containing one to three grass- or cane-covered structures, above-ground granaries, and outdoor ramadas or arbors, as well as compound cultivated plots.[95] A *templo,* or temple mound, was in use at the far western end of the village, seemingly "half buried in the top of the mound" from earth placed there to bury the temple after it had been ritually burned and extinguished.[96]

William Stinson Soule's 1874 photographs of a Caddoan village in western Oklahoma (Long Hat's camp) depict the same relationship of structures, ramadas or arbors, and open plaza-like areas within the compound as Teran's map did some 180 years earlier.[97] Alonso de Leon was told in 1689 by a Frenchman that each Caddo "has his own house and large garden, enough to plant corn for his use."[98] The similarity in Caddoan settlement between these historical sources is the basis for the Teran-Soule settlement model proposed by Schambach, where "the settlement pattern . . . at the time of European contact was the dispersed farmstead, vacant ceremonial center."[99]

The four-to-nine-km-long Upper Nasoni community mapped by Teran appears to have been located at the Hatchel-Mitchell-Moores archaeological complex in Bowie County, Texas.[100] The archaeological remains at this important Caddoan center had at least five mounds, including one platform mound used for several hundred years that contained sixteen circular structures, as well as extensive habitation and cemetery areas.[101] Creel suggests that the complex was continuously occupied from ca. A.D. 1200 to the early nineteenth century.[102] The nearby Upper Kadohadacho village (including sites 3MI3/30 and 3MI4) described in the seventeenth and eighteenth centuries was apparently as extensive as the Upper Nasoni *ranchería,* with village areas, cemeteries, and seven earthen mounds.[103]

Mortuary Behavior and Mounds

At the time of European contact, there were considerable differences in the complexity of Caddo mortuary practices that relate to the treatment at death of the social elite. Caddoan groups living along the Red River, the

Little River, and the Ouachita River interred their social elite (usually a paramount male) in shaft/pit tombs in the burial mounds, accompanied by exotic prestige goods as well as large numbers of other kinds of grave goods.[104] Burial mounds do not appear to have been constructed or used by Caddo groups after about A.D. 1650.

The rest of the population of these Caddo groups were buried in family cemeteries near the houses they lived in, possibly with the same rituals and ceremonies as the elite but without many of the exotic grave goods.[105] Among the Titus phase Caddo groups (see below), the social elite and nonelite began to be buried in large community cemeteries. While some elite individuals were treated at death in a manner comparable to elites in Caddoan populations on the major rivers, generally the individuals were buried in the same manner of body preparation, treatment, and position in either the family or community cemeteries.[106]

The diversity in mortuary practices and rituals that existed among protohistoric Caddo groups is well illustrated by an examination of the kinds of grave goods included with the deceased, particularly the kinds of ceramic vessels. Fray Casañas had commented in 1691 that the Caddo buried "their dead with all their arms and utensils which each possess,"[107] and it is evident that the grave goods represent, in a symbolic and material sense, the items used by that individual in life, as well as goods needed to accompany the deceased on their journey to the other world. The archaeological evidence from across the Caddoan area indicates that sixteenth- and seventeenth-century ceramic mortuary assemblages differ from region to region in the composition of jars, bottles, bowls, and carinated bowls.[108] In fact, no two contemporaneous Caddo mortuary vessel assemblages from different groups are similar, and Perttula and Nelson interpret this to "mean that there was a very considerable diversity among Caddoan groups in their cultural practices, beliefs, and world-views about what males and female adults and children needed in life and death and that there were cultural boundaries between Caddoan groups not regularly crossed by networks of personal and group contacts."[109] Inverse relationships in the representation in mortuary contexts of food-serving vessels, cooking and storage jars, and bottles (probably used for holding liquids, cornmeal, and offerings) between eastern and western Caddoan groups express a basic dichotomy in belief and cultural practices, one that highlights the existence of well-defined social boundaries in protohistoric times. Interestingly, Derrick and Wilson note an analogous east-west dichotomy in the styles of cranial modeling used by Caddoan groups, as well as a similarity in cranial modeling styles between most of the Caddoan groups living in northeast Texas.[110]

Looking in more detail at the mortuary practices of Caddoan groups living in the Pineywoods of northeast Texas (where relatively abundant information is available on more than 110 cemeteries[111]), we see that mortuary behavior among the ca. A.D. 1430–1680 Titus phase Caddoan groups suggested that most adults had the same social status. Burial accompaniments followed lines of age and sex, as well as group philosophical and religious precepts and beliefs about the kinds, amounts, and placement of grave offerings that were important to include for the deceased's journey to the next life.[112] Nevertheless, 46 percent of the known community cemeteries and 12 percent of the family or hamlet cemeteries had individuals of apparent high rank or elite social position.[113]

In some of the larger community cemeteries dating to the sixteenth and seventeenth centuries, the social elite appear to have been placed in central burial locations, signifying their central and powerful place in the community, and rows of the nonelite radiated out from the center. The long-term group memory of grave locations suggests that differences in social position of individuals and social groups were as important to maintain after death as they had been expressed among the living.

The mortuary treatment of the Caddo social elite during Titus phase times was quite diversified. The burials of the Titus phase elite included: (a) burial in a shaft tomb; (b) burial in a mound; (c) burials with large chipped bifaces; (d) individual extended supine burials with large quantities of grave goods, especially quivers of arrow points; and (e) double extended supine burials with quantities of grave goods, particularly ceramic vessels.[114] Most of the apparent Titus phase elite were adult males, though at least one was apparently an adult female (Burial 19 at the Tuck Carpenter site).[115]

We know from chronological and seriation studies that the majority of the presumed Titus phase social elite burials (in community cemeteries and the smaller family-farmstead-hamlet cemeteries) date after ca. A.D. 1550–1600. They occur across the Big Cypress basin, but cluster in the Titus phase "heartland," a sixty-by-twenty-km area along the middle reaches of Big Cypress Bayou.[116] From all indications, the large community cemeteries lasted only two or three generations, these generations representing a time of coalescence and population aggregation. They were used intensively only in portions of the Pineywoods, and certainly ended by ca. A.D. 1680. After the community cemeteries were no longer used, most of the region was abandoned by the Caddo.[117]

Community cemeteries occurred first in this "heartland," and the density of cemeteries and burial numbers suggests relatively high Caddo populations, larger than in other parts of the region. The community cemeteries also lingered longer in use there than in any other part of the Titus phase area, while small family-farmstead-hamlet cemeteries continued to be used as long as Caddoan peoples lived in the Pineywoods and the rest of the Caddoan area.[118]

SUMMARY AND CONCLUSIONS

Caddo social history between ca. 1530 and 1715 was vibrant and dynamic, as it was in prehistoric times, and as it is down to the present day. The Caddo peoples always played important political, economic, and social roles with other Native American groups of the Southeast and Southern Plains, and were mediators and alliance-builders between European explorers/colonists and Native American groups. In the face of ever-increasing contact and conflict, the Caddo lost territory and populations were greatly diminished, but their societies and sociopolitical relationships were transformed and enhanced through the formation of the Hasinai, Kadohadacho, and Natchitoches confederacies from remnant groups and the strong leadership of the *caddices* from the premier local chiefdoms.

The Caddos were powerful agricultural chiefdoms when visited by the Spanish *entrada* led by Soto and Moscoso in the 1540s. They were recognized as the "Great Kingdom of the Tejas," a populous nation, by the Spanish and French in the seventeenth and eighteenth centuries. And they incorporated these European traders and settlers into long-standing aboriginal trading networks and de facto kinship networks across the Caddoan area and beyond.

The Spanish were unsuccessful in establishing missions among the Caddo, or in converting the Caddo to Catholicism. This has been attributed to the "strength of the culture of the Caddo people—their spiritual belief and long-standing customs and traditions, both for the conduct of their everyday life and the conduct of taking care of spiritual needs."[119] The Caddo did not need the religion brought by the Spanish, having their own strong spiritual beliefs, as well as strong political and civil leaders who were also spiritual leaders in Caddo communities.[120]

When it suited the Caddo, they cooperated and interacted with the European intruders, mainly through trade. The Caddo traded deer hides, salt, horses, and other items to Europeans for a variety of European goods that improved the lives of the people.

The hereditary chain of Caddo leadership—with strong, able, and peace- and alliance-building *caddis*—seems to have continued unbroken among the Hasinai and Kadohadacho throughout most of the contact era,[121] and this was the source of their strength. The Caddo political leaders shaped the important political decisions of the day to favor and strengthen the Caddo peoples, and arranged and brought to fruition alliances between the Caddo, other powerful Native American groups, and competing European nations.

Given the permanent Anglo-American settlement of the region in waves of immigration after about 1815, it was the Caddos' misfortune to have been living on choice and fertile farmlands desired by the Anglo-Americans.[122] In a few short years, they were dispossessed of their traditional homelands, their lands and goods swindled from them by U.S. Federal Indian agents in the Caddo Treaty of 1835, and eventually they were forced in 1859 to relocate from Texas to Indian Territory.

However, the Caddo peoples have survived, and had a powerful influence over other Native Americans in Texas during much of that time. For their survival, they called on all their religious faith, their political strength, influence, and leadership, and their continued traditions and beliefs.

ACKNOWLEDGMENTS

I would like to thank Dr. Charles Hudson and Dr. Robbie Ethridge for the opportunity to participate in the 1998 Porter L. Fortune, Jr., History Symposium held at the University of Mississippi.

Notes

Notes to INTRODUCTION

1. Charles Hudson, *The Juan Pardo Expeditions: Exploration of the Carolinas and Tennessee, 1566–1568*; Charles Hudson, Marvin T. Smith, Chester B. DePratter, and Emilia Kelley, "The Tristán de Luna Expedition, 1559–1561"; Jerald Milanich and Charles Hudson, *Hernando de Soto and the Indians of Florida*; Charles Hudson and Carmen Chaves Tesser, *The Forgotten Centuries: Indians and Europeans in the American South*; Charles Hudson, *Knights of Spain, Warriors of the Sun: Hernando de Soto and the South's Ancient Chiefdoms*.

2. James B. Griffin, "Eastern North American Archaeology: A Summary," p. 185; Judith A. Bense, *Archaeology of the Southeastern United States: Paleoindian to World War I*, pp. 244–245.

3. Charles Hudson, Marvin Smith, David Hally, Richard Polhemus, and Chester DePratter, "Coosa: A Chiefdom in the Sixteenth-Century Southeastern United States," pp. 44–50; David J. Hally, Marvin T. Smith, and James B. Langford, Jr., "The Archaeological Reality of de Soto's Coosa," pp. 121–138.

4. Hudson, *Knights of Spain*, pp. 472–481.

5. See also Lester J. Cappon, *Atlas of Early American History*, p. 19.

6. For a critique of the concept of culture on different grounds, see Patricia Nelson Limerick, "The Startling Ability of Culture to Bring Critical Inquiry to a Halt."

7. Hudson, *Knights of Spain*, pp. 350–351. This indicates, by the way, that the Indians perceived and treated Soto as a principal chief.

8. Hudson, *Knights of Spain*, pp. 357–358, 377.

9. Charles Hudson, *The Southeastern Indians*.

10. Published with some revisions as "An Unknown South: Spanish Explorers and Southeastern Chiefdoms."

11. Fernand Braudel, "History and the Social Sciences: The *Longue Dureé*."

12. Fernand Braudel, *The Mediterranean and the Mediterranean World in the Age of Philip II*.

13. Marc Bloch, *Feudal Society*.

14. Emmanuel Le Roy Ladurie, *Montaillou: The Promised Land of Error*.

15. Natalie Zeamon Davis, *The Return of Martin Guerre*; Carlo Ginzburg, *The Cheese and the Worms: The Cosmos of a Sixteenth-Century Miller*.

16. Jon Muller, *Mississippian Political Economy*.

17. James Brown, "A Reconsideration of the Southern Cult"; David Dye, "Warfare in the Sixteenth-Century Southeast: The de Soto Expedition in the Interior," pp. 211–222.

18. David Anderson, *The Savannah River Chiefdoms: Political Change in the Late Prehistoric Southeast*.

19. Timothy K. Perttula, *"The Caddo Nation": Archaeological and Ethnohistoric Perspectives*.

20. John E. Worth, *The Timucuan Chiefdoms of Spanish Florida*.

21. George R. Milner, *The Cahokia Chiefdom: The Archaeology of a Mississippian Society*.

22. Vernon J. Knight, Jr., and Vincas P. Steponaitis, *Archaeology of the Moundville Chiefdom*.

23. Ronald Wright, "On the Rampage in Florida: Hernando de Soto's Cruel Life and Death."

24. Peter N. Peregrine, *Mississippian Evolution: A World-System Perspective*.

25. Immanuel Wallerstein, *The Modern World-System: Capitalist Agriculture and the Origin of the European World-Economy in the Sixteenth Century*.

26. Robbie Ethridge and Charles Hudson, "The Early Historic Transformation of the Southeastern Indians," pp. 34–50.

27. Charles Hudson, *The Catawba Nation*.

28. See James Adair, *Adair's History of the American Indians*. Adair describes the "Katahba, Cherokee, Muskohge, Choctah, and Chickkasah Nations," pp. 221–373. For more recent uses of the term, see Hudson, *The Catawba Nation*, and Duane King, *The Cherokee Indian Nation: A Troubled History*.

29. Elman R. Service, *Primitive Social Organization: An Evolutionary Perspective*, pp. 99–132; for a critique, see Morton H. Fried, *The Evolution of Political Society: An Essay on Political Anthropology*, pp. 154–184.

30. Edmund Atkin, *The Appalachian Indian Frontier: The Edmund Atkin Report and Plan of 1755*, p. 45.

31. Daniel H. Usner, Jr., *Indians, Settlers, and Slaves in a Frontier Exchange Economy: The Lower Mississippi Valley Before 1782*, pp. 45, 60–63.

32. Hudson, *Knights of Spain*, pp. 417–426.

33. Marvin T. Smith, *Archaeology of Aboriginal Culture Change in the Interior Southeast: Depopulation During the Early Historic Period*; Ann F. Ramenovsky, *Vectors of Death: The Archaeology of European Contact*.

34. Peter H. Wood, "The Changing Population of the Colonial South: An Overview by Race and Region, 1685–1790," pp. 90–91.

35. Bruce G. Trigger, "Early Iroquoian Contacts with Europeans," p. 346.

36. Daniel K. Richter, *The Ordeal of the Longhouse: The Peoples of the Iroquois League in the Era of European Colonization*, pp. 2–3.

37. Trigger, "Iroquoian Contacts," pp. 352–353.

38. Eric E. Bowne, "The Rise and Fall of the Westo Indians: An Evaluation of the Documentary Evidence."

39. See Steven Hahn, "The Mother of Necessity: Carolina, the Creek Indians, and the Making of a New Order in the American Southeast, 1670–1763," this volume.

40. Verner W. Crane, *The Southern Frontier, 1670–1732*, pp. 22–46.

41. Crane, *Southern Frontier*, pp. 133–136.

42. Elizabeth A. H. John, *Storms Brewed in Other Men's Worlds: The Confrontation of Indians, Spanish, and French in the Southwest, 1540–1795*, pp. 196–225.

43. Richter, *Ordeal*, pp. 65–74.

44. Kathryn E. Holland Braund, *Deerskins and Duffels: The Creek Indian Trade with AngloAmerica, 1685–1815*, pp. 31–34.

45. Ulrich B. Phillips, *Life and Labor in the Old South*, pp. 3–13.

46. Sam Bowers Hilliard, *Atlas of Antebellum Southern Agriculture*, map 102, p. 71.

47. Hilliard, *Atlas*, maps 9 and 10, p. 17.

Notes to ABORIGINAL POPULATION MOVEMENTS IN THE POSTCONTACT SOUTHEAST
by Marvin T. Smith

1. Marvin T. Smith, *Archaeology of Aboriginal Culture Change in the Interior Southeast: Depopulation During the Early Historic Period*; Marvin T. Smith, "Aboriginal Population Movements in the Early Historic Period Interior Southeast."

2. David G. Anderson, *The Savannah River Chiefdoms: Political Change in the Late Prehistoric Southeast*.

3. Charles Hudson, personal communication.

4. Swanton, *Indians of the Southeast*.

5. John Worth, "The Lower Creeks: Origins and Early History."

6. Mark F. Boyd, "Expedition of Marcos Delgado, 1686."

7. William C. Johnson, "The Protohistoric Monongahela and the Case for an Iroquois Connection."

8. Penelope Drooker, *The View from Madisonville: Protohistoric Western Fort Ancient Interaction Patterns*, p. 99, table 4-9; Marvin Jeter, "From Prehistory through Protohistory to Ethnohistory in and near the Northern Lower Mississippi Valley," this volume.

9. Dan F. Morse, "The Seventeenth-Century Michigamea Village Location in Arkansas."

10. George T. Hunt, *Wars of the Iroquois*.

11. See discussion in Michael Hoffman, "The Protohistoric Period in the Lower and Central Arkansas River Valley in Arkansas," pp. 24–37. For a contrary argument that the Quapaw were indigenous to the Arkansas valley, see Dan F. Morse, "On the Possible Origin of the Quapaws in Northeast Arkansas," pp. 40–54.

12. James Merrell, *The Indians' New World: Catawbas and Their Neighbors from European Contact through the Era of Removal*.

13. Thomas Nairne, *Nairne's Muskogean Journals: Journal of Expedition to the Mississippi River, 1708*, pp. 37, 76.

14. David Dye, "Warfare in the Sixteenth-Century Southeast: The de Soto Expedition in the Interior," pp. 211–224.

15. Boyd, "Expedition."

16. John Worth, *The Timucuan Chiefdoms of Spanish Florida*, vol. 1, p. 37.

17. Worth, *Timucuan Chiefdoms*, vol 1., p. 37.

18. Worth, *Timucuan Chiefdoms*, vol 1., p. 37; John Worth, *The Struggle for the Georgia Coast: An Eighteenth-Century Spanish Retrospective on Guale and Mocama*.

19. Merrell, *Indians' New World*, p. 25.

20. Charles M. Hudson, *The Catawba Nation*.

21. J. Leitch Wright, *The Only Land They Knew*, pp. 133, 138, 114.

22. Smith, *Archaeology of Culture Change*; Smith, "Aboriginal Population Movements."

23. George Milner, David Anderson, and Marvin T. Smith, "The Distribution of Eastern Woodlands Peoples at the Prehistoric and Historic Interface."

24. Worth, *Struggle for the Georgia Coast*.

25. Milner, Anderson, and Smith, "Distribution of Woodlands Peoples."

26. Marvin Jeter, "Ethnohistorical and Archaeological Backgrounds," pp. 32–96; Jeter, personal communication; Chad Braley, "Yuchi Town (1Ru63) Revisited"; Roy Dickens, Trawick Ward, and R. P. Stephen Davis, *The Siouan Project: Seasons I and II*; H. Trawick Ward and R. P. Stephen Davis, *Indian Communities on the North Carolina Piedmont* A.D. 1000–1700.

27. Worth, *Timucuan Chiefdoms*.

28. Patricia K. Galloway, *Choctaw Genesis: 1500–1700*.

29. Verner W. Crane, *The Southern Frontier, 1670–1732*; Dan F. Morse, "Seventeenth-Century Michigamea."

30. Merrell, *Indians' New World*.

31. Smith, *Archaeology of Culture Change*.

32. Jeffrey P. Brain, *Tunica Archaeology*.

33. Worth, *Timucuan Chiefdoms*.

34. David Hally, Marvin Smith, and James B. Langford, "The Archaeological Reality of De Soto's Coosa," pp. 121–138.

35. Charles Hudson, Marvin Smith, David Hally, Richard Polhemus, and Chester DePratter, "Coosa: A Chiefdom in the Sixteenth Century Southeastern United States."

36. Smith, *Archaeology of Culture Change*; Smith, "Aboriginal Population Movements"; Marvin T. Smith, "In the Wake of De Soto: Alabama's Seventeenth-Century Indians on the Coosa River"; Marvin T. Smith, *Coosa: The Rise and Fall of a Southeastern Mississippian Chiefdom*.

37. Galloway, *Choctaw Genesis*.
38. For Taskigi, see Smith, *Archaeology of Culture Change*. For Liddell, see Caleb Curren, *The Protohistoric Period in Central Alabama*, p. 53.
39. Galloway, *Choctaw Genesis*, p. 353.
40. Galloway, *Choctaw Genesis*, pp. 352–353.
41. Anderson, *Savannah River Chiefdoms*.
42. Worth, *Struggle for the Georgia Coast*.
43. Swanton, *Indians*.
44. Charles M. Hudson, *Knights of Spain, Warriors of the Sun: Hernando de Soto and the South's Ancient Chiefdoms*; Dan Morse and Phyllis Morse, "The Spanish Exploration of Arkansas," pp. 197–210.
45. James Price and Cynthia Price, "Protohistoric/Early Historic Manifestations in Southeastern Missouri," pp. 59–69; David Dye, "Reconstruction of the De Soto Expedition Route in Arkansas: The Mississippi Alluvial Plain," pp. 36–57; Clarence B. Moore, "Some Aboriginal Sites on the Mississippi River"; Dan Morse and Phyllis Morse, *Archaeology of the Central Mississippi Valley*; Dan Morse, "The Nodena Phase," pp. 69–97. The Oliver collection is being analyzed by Marvin Smith.
46. Leslie Stewart-Abernathy, "The Carden Bottom Project, Yell County, Arkansas: From Dalton to Trade Beads, So Far"; Jeter, "Ethnohistorical and Archaeological Backgrounds"; John House, "Continuing Field Studies at the Sarassa Lake Site"; John House, "Noble Lake: A Protohistoric Archaeological Site on the Lower Arkansas River."
47. Robert Rankin, "Language Affiliations of Some de Soto Place Names in Arkansas," pp. 210–221; Marvin Jeter, "Tunicans West of the Mississippi: A Summary of Early Historic and Archaeological Evidence," pp. 38–63; Jeter, "Ethnohistorical and Archaeological Backgrounds."
48. Marvin Jeter, Kathleen Cande, and John Mintz, *Goldsmith Oliver 2 (3Pu306): A Protohistoric Archaeological Site Near Little Rock, Arkansas*, p. 9.
49. E. Lucy Braun, *Deciduous Forests of Eastern North America*; Nevin Fenneman, *Physiography of Eastern United States*, p. 68.
50. Brain, *Tunica Archaeology*.
51. Jeffrey Brain, "Late Prehistoric Settlement Patterning in the Yazoo Basin and Natchez Bluffs Regions of the Lower Mississippi Valley," pp. 331–368.
52. Fenneman, *Physiography*; Lewis Larson, "Settlement Distribution during the Mississippi Period."
53. Wright, *Only Land They Knew*.

Notes to THE GREAT SOUTHEASTERN SMALLPOX EPIDEMIC, 1696–1700: THE REGION'S FIRST MAJOR EPIDEMIC?
by Paul Kelton

1. The most influential scholar to address the impact of European and African diseases on Native Americans is Alfred Crosby. See Alfred Crosby, *The Columbian Exchange: Biological and Cultural Consequences of 1492*; Alfred Crosby, "Virgin Soil Epidemics as a Factor in the Aboriginal Depopulation in America." See also Russell Thornton, *American Indian Holocaust and Survival*.
2. Establishing the timing of virgin soil epidemics is important in deriving estimated precontact native populations. This article's main focus is timing, but the conclusion suggests how its findings affect current demographic assessments of southeastern Indian population. For a survey of southeastern Indian population, see Peter Wood, "The Changing Population of the Colonial South." For a useful summary of the various demographic studies of North American Indians, see John D. Daniels, "The Indian Population of North America in 1492." Scholars focusing on areas other than the Southeast have addressed the issue of timing. See Dean Snow and Kim M. Lanphear, "European Contact

and Indian Depopulation in the Northeast: The Timing of the First Epidemics" and Daniel Reff, *Disease, Depopulation, and Culture Change in Northwestern New Spain, 1518–1764.*

3. Epidemics among the mission Indians of Spanish Florida, which included modern-day Florida and coastal Georgia, have been well documented, and this paper takes no issue with the conclusion that a demographic tragedy occurred among the Timucuan, Guale, and Apalachee Indians well before the 1690s. For the most reliable accounts of the demographic upheaval that the Indians of Florida faced, see John Worth, *The Timucuan Chiefdoms of Spanish Florida,* and John Hann, *Apalachee: The Land between the Rivers,* pp. 160–180. The demographic impact of Old World diseases on the natives of Virginia remains unclear. This paper assumes that epidemics did erupt in colonial Virginia and proposes reasons why such epidemics most likely did not spread farther south and west. For a general history of disease in colonial Virginia, see Wyndham B. Blanton, *Medicine in Virginia in the Seventeenth Century.*

4. Henry Dobyns has been the leading proponent of the idea that major epidemics and large-scale demographic disaster occurred among all of the indigenous peoples of the American South during the sixteenth century. See Henry Dobyns, *Their Number Become Thinned.* Alfred Crosby has utilized Dobyns's ideas in his latest work, *Ecological Imperialism.* Ann Ramenofsky argues, counter to the evidence presented in this paper, that archaeological and epidemiological factors support Dobyns's views. See Ann Ramenofsky, *Vectors of Death.* Marvin Smith agrees with Dobyns and Ramenofsky that demographic losses and epidemic diseases struck the southeastern interior in the sixteenth century and early seventeenth century, and he adds that such catastrophe was responsible for major population movements that he has skillfully detailed. This paper does not refute the movements that Smith has clearly demonstrated, but it does suggest that the underlying reason for them must have been something other than massive depopulation and epidemic diseases before the 1690s. See Smith, *Archaeology of Aboriginal Culture Change in the Interior Southeast.* Insightful critiques of Dobyns include George Milner, "Epidemic Disease in the Postcontact Southeast," and David Henige, "Primary Source by Primary Source? On the Role of Epidemics in New World Depopulation."

5. It is not the intention here to pursue a detailed discussion of the entire disease inventory that Europeans brought with them to America. Rather, I wish to generally discuss why smallpox had the most detrimental impact. Other scholars agree that smallpox was the most consequential of all diseases. For a more thorough discussion of diseases, see Ramenofsky, *Vectors of Death,* 137–162; Ann Ramenofsky and Patricia Galloway, "Disease and the Soto Entrada."

6. To compare the characteristics of smallpox and influenza, see Abram S. Benenson, *The Control of Communicable Diseases in Man: An Official Report of the American Public Health Association,* pp. 224–229, 394–399.

7. Benenson, *Control of Communicable Diseases,* pp. 269–275.

8. Benenson, *Control of Communicable Diseases,* pp. 395–399; Joel N. Shurkin, *The Invisible Fire: The Story of Mankind's Victory over the Ancient Scourge of Smallpox,* pp. 26–27; Snow and Lanphear, "European Contact and Indian Depopulation," p. 26. Whooping cough can also be transmitted in a similar manner. Individuals who come into contact with material contaminated by the fresh discharges of a victim can possibly become infected. Despite the possibility of indirect transmission, whooping cough was still less mobile than smallpox. The bacteria that cause the disease incubate for a shorter period, usually seven days, almost uniformly within ten days, and never longer than twenty-one days. In addition, whooping cough was not as deadly as smallpox, with death disproportionately striking children. See Benenson, *Control of Communicable Diseases,* pp. 364–367.

9. The nature of this specific mosquito restricted the spread of yellow fever. The mosquito lives year-round only in areas where the temperature does not fall below seventy-one degrees Fahrenheit, thus becoming endemic in tropical regions of the Americas.

In addition, this mosquito typically lives only in close association with human communities, especially seafront populations. The disease could be epidemic in more temperate climates of the continental United States, but only seasonally, erupting in port cities whenever ships arrived carrying both the disease and the mosquitoes. The epidemic would subside after the warm season ended. See Benenson, *Control of Communicable Diseases*, pp. 486–490, and Erwin Ackerknecht, *History and Geography of the Most Important Diseases*, pp. 51–55.

10. On the role of typhus in world history, see Hans Zinsser, *Rats, Lice, and History*.

11. William McNeill, *Plagues and Peoples*, pp. 123–127, 165–166; William Cronon, *Changes in the Land*. Henry Dobyns, however, argues that plague struck the Americas in the sixteenth century; see Dobyns, *Their Number Become Thinned*, pp. 18–19.

12. Benenson, *Control of Communicable Diseases*, pp. 12–15, 250–257. Most diseases that animal vectors transmit to humans, such as malaria, are chronic infectious diseases, discussed elsewhere in this paper. There are, of course, other acute infectious diseases that require animal vectors, including anthrax and rabies, which are not necessarily limited to densely settled areas. Anthrax historically has been associated with communities that depend heavily on raising domestic livestock. Rabies is a rare disease, which only infects humans after a bite by a rabid animal. Neither rabies nor anthrax can be directly transmitted from one human to another. Thus, one would expect that neither could have had an impact as detrimental as that of smallpox.

13. Most commonly these permanent carriers are middle-aged women, such as "Typhoid Mary," who unknowingly exposed many Americans to the disease in the twentieth century.

14. Benenson, *Control of Communicable Diseases*, pp. 469–470. It is probable that Spanish explorers carried typhoid with them and contaminated the drinking supply of at least some southeastern Indians. However, the impact of the disease would be comparable to that of malaria, as discussed in both the text and the notes below. One encounter between Europeans and Native Americans does appear to have introduced typhoid fever. In 1585 during their failed attempt to colonize Roanoke, the English exposed Indians to a fatal disease. Thomas Harriot reported that numerous Indians died in villages that the English visited but that none of the British fell ill. Typhoid is indicated because none of the English had an active infection, which would be expected if the epidemic was a result of most other acute infectious diseases. The English, many of whom could have had typhoid months earlier, may have defecated near local drinking water and left before Indians had a chance to display symptoms. One cannot rule out malaria, however. See Thomas Harriot, "A Briefe and True Report of the New Found Land of Virginia (1588)," p. 152.

15. The introduction of chronic diseases to the Americas was less significant than the introduction of acute diseases not only because chronic diseases were less deadly but also because several chronic diseases were already present. Tuberculosis, blastomycosis, and treponematosis had a long history in the Americas. Malaria, however, was absent. See Charles Merbs, "A New World of Infectious Diseases."

16. Benenson, *Control of Communicable Diseases*, pp. 261–264. On the spread of malaria in North America, see Mark F. Boyd, "An Historical Sketch of the Prevalence of Malaria in North America," p. 224; Ackerknecht, *History and Geography of the Most Important Diseases*, pp. 90–91; Darret B. Rutman and Anita H. Rutman, "Of Agues and Fevers: Malaria in the Early Chesapeake."

17. The expeditions referred to include those of Lucas Vázquez de Ayllón (1526), Pánfilo de Narváez (1528), Hernando de Soto (1539–1543), Tristan de Luna (1559–1561), and Juan Pardo (1566–1568). None of the primary documents for these expeditions indicate that the Spaniards had active cases of smallpox. After a voyage of less than a month from their Caribbean base, the Ayllón expedition arrived in South Carolina. After arrival some of the members became sick, and gradually others did. The death toll was quite high; within three months, 450 of the 600 men perished. Still, if smallpox was the culprit,

illness most likely would have erupted while the Spaniards were in transit. In addition, the high percentage of male casualties indicates a disease other than smallpox or measles, diseases that many of the Spaniards certainly had contracted during childhood. Exposure, famine, and lack of drinking water may have caused many of the deaths, but it was highly likely that malaria, dysentery, and typhoid were accompanying Ayllón's men. Combined with famine and exposure, these diseases could have produced heavy mortality among the Spaniards. Members of the Pánfilo de Narváez expedition also became sick but only several months after arrival. The Hernando de Soto expedition seemed to be the healthiest of all the Spanish expeditions, which may explain why it was the most successful. None of the chronicles of the expedition include reference to illness during the first year of Soto's journey. After a year, some of Soto's men became sick with fever, indicating that they possibly picked up malaria introduced earlier by the Ayllón expedition. Tristan de Luna's expedition suffered immensely, but instead of disease it was famine that plagued them. Sickness was not reported immediately after their arrival, but the Spaniards quickly ran out of food and found that the Indians were unwilling or unable to help them. Dobyns's argument that Luna's men carried influenza with them is not credible. One would expect the disease to erupt while Luna's men were in transit and to spread quickly through Spanish ranks. It was nearly ten months after arrival that Luna's men suffered from "*la enfermedad*," which most likely was related to starvation rather than infectious disease. No one accompanying the Juan Pardo expeditions reportedly became sick. See Gonzalo Fernández de Oviedo, "*Historia General y Natural de las Indias*," pp. 260–261, 263; Alvar Núñez Cabeza de Vaca, "*La Relación dio Alvar Núñez Cabeza de Vaca*," pp. 24–25; Lawrence Clayton, Vernon J. Knight, Jr., and Edward C. Moore, *The De Soto Chronicles: The Expedition of Hernando de Soto to the United States, 1539–1543*, vol. I, p. 281; Tristán de Luna, *The Luna Papers*, vol. I, pp. 132–197; Charles Hudson, *The Juan Pardo Expeditions*.

18. Epidemics did wreak havoc in Mexico and the Caribbean in the sixteenth century. Settlers, slaves, and children who flooded into this area certainly represented vastly larger numbers than nonnatives who visited the Southeast. Pathogenic microbes thus followed the main thrust of Spanish colonization. For the disease history of early Latin America, see Noble David Cook and W. George Lovell, "Secret Judgements of God."

19. Jon Muller, *Mississippian Political Economy*, p. 363.

20. Henige, "Primary Source by Primary Source," p. 299.

21. Saul Jarcho is also critical of the idea of aboriginal trade networks as vehicles for the spread of disease. See Saul Jarcho, "Some Observations on Disease in Prehistoric North America," p. 14.

22. Muller, *Mississippian Political Economy*, pp. 225–287, 363–384.

23. For an example of an archaeological site that shows little evidence of circulation of goods beyond the confines of a particular chiefdom, see Alfred K. Guthe and E. Marian Bistline, *Excavations of Tonnotley, 1973–74, and the Tuskegee Area*, p.119.

24. Gregory Waselkov has characterized Spanish trade with Indians in the seventeenth century as "substantial" but trade to the interior as "small-scale." He surveyed the archaeological and ethnohistorical evidence and found the presence of possible Spanish items, notably brass objects and Old World cultigens such as peaches and black-eyed peas. While such items indicate a degree of trade and possible avenues for the spread of pathogens, the small volume of items found and the noncommercial nature of the Spanish colonial project lessen the likelihood of disease transmission into the interior. See Gregory Waselkov, "Seventeenth-Century Trade in the Colonial Southeast."

25. James Merrell, *The Indians' New World*, pp. 27–43.

26. Blanton, *Medicine in Virginia*, pp. 60–61; Thomas B. Robertson, "An Indian King's Will," p. 193.

27. The classic study of Native American contested areas is Harold Hickerson, *The Southwestern Chippewa; an Ethnohistorical Study*.

28. Clayton, Knight, and Moore, *The De Soto Chronicles*, vol. I, pp. 168, 229.

29. David Anderson, "Stability and Change in Chiefdom-Level Societies," p. 208.

30. The palisaded villages that Soto encountered among towns belonging to the Coosa chiefdom, for example, most likely indicated warfare with rivals such as Cherokee-speaking groups or others living in the general area of the Tennessee valley. Clayton, Knight, and Moore *De Soto Chronicles*, vol. I, pp. 232, 283.

31. "Voyage made from Canada inland going southward during the year 1682 by order of Monsieur Colbert Minister of State," in Galloway et al., *La Salle, the Mississippi and the Gulf: Three Primary Documents*, pp. 50–51.

32. André Pénicaut, *Fleur de Lys and Calumet: Being the Pénicaut Narrative of French Adventure in Louisiana*, pp. 25–26. After 1700 when epidemics had in fact struck, human depopulation fostered the multiplication of wild game herds, and the former rivals abandoned their animosity. "They hunt everywhere," the Frenchman claimed, "the ones with the others, and are good friends."

33. Jon Muller argues that many scholars have exaggerated the size and complexity of Indian polities in the sixteenth century and even earlier societies such as Cahokia and that the same scholars have unnecessarily underappreciated the size and complexity of eighteenth-century polities such as the Choctaws and Creeks. See Muller, *Mississippian Political Economy*, pp. 55–116. If Muller is correct, then the lack of declension strengthens my argument. However, if Muller is incorrect, scholars still need not see the radical declension of native polities as evidence of a disastrous virgin soil epidemic and population collapse.

34. On the evolution and devolution of chiefdoms, see Anderson, "Stability and Change in Chiefdom-level Societies," p. 199; Christopher Peebles, "The Rise and Fall of Moundville in Western Alabama"; Randolph J. Widmer, "Structure of Southeastern Chiefdoms," pp. 145–146; and Patricia Galloway, *Choctaw Genesis: 1500–1700*, pp. 348–349, 354.

35. Mark Williams, "Growth and Decline of the Oconee Province," pp. 191–193.

36. If a European-introduced disease was responsible for the "plague" that, according to the Soto chronicles, struck the chiefdom of Cofitachequi, malaria was a likely culprit. One of Hernando de Soto's chroniclers recorded that "about the town [of Cofitachequi] within the compass of a league and a half league were large uninhabited towns, choked with vegetation, which looked as though no people had inhabited them for some time." Indians informed the Spaniards that "two years ago there had been a plague in that land and they had moved to other towns." Another chronicler verified the account, calling the disaster both a "pestilence" and a "plague." The disease, if it was a disease, seems most likely to have been malaria. Since the spread of malaria depends on the presence of anopheles mosquitoes, whose habitat is generally restricted to areas of stagnant water, infection does not occur uniformly throughout a given territory. The "plague of Cofitachequi" indeed appears to have spread unevenly; the main town of Cofitachequi and other villages remained occupied and served as receptacles for people whose communities suffered. An acute infectious disease such as smallpox would have caused more widespread and uniform damage and most likely would have destroyed the Cofitachequi chiefdom, which was still functioning by the time Soto arrived. For Spanish observations at Cofitachequi, see Clayton, Knight and Moore, *De Soto Chronicles*, vol. I, p. 83, and vol. II, p. 286. A few scholars have suggested that the "plague" was not a disease of European origin but crop failure or other calamity; see Widmer, "Southeastern Chiefdoms," pp. 137–138; Chester DePratter, "The Chiefdom of Cofitachequi," pp. 215–216.

37. Christopher S. Peebles, "Paradise Lost, Strayed, and Stolen," pp. 32–34.

38. Robert L. Blakely and B. Detweiler Blakely, "The Impact of European Diseases in the Sixteenth Century Southeast: A Case Study."

39. Keith J. Little and Caleb Curren, "Conquest Archaeology of Alabama," pp. 174, 177.

40. Archaeologists know that the region experienced population loss before the eighteenth century, but none has successfully demonstrated that such loss predates the 1690s. Two scholars who address this issue are Ian W. Brown, "An Archaeological Study of Cul-

ture Contact and Change in the Natchez Bluffs Region" and Jeffrey P. Brain, "Late Pre-historic Settlement Patterning in the Yazoo Basin and Natchez Bluffs Regions of the Lower Mississippi Valley."

41. Charles Hudson and his associates have put tremendous effort into revising John Swanton's earlier reconstruction of the route that Hernando de Soto took through the Southeast. Although the specific route remains debated, I rely on Hudson's conclusion that Soto went as far north on the Mississippi as Memphis. If Soto did not go as far north as Hudson proposes, one cannot be sure that the area between Memphis and the Arkansas was abandoned sometime after contact. For an excellent synopsis of his research and a useful map, see Charles Hudson, "The Hernando de Soto Expedition, 1539–1543."

42. Henri de Tonti, "Tonty's Account of the Route from the Illinois, by the River Mississippi to the Gulf of Mexico," vol. I, p. 82.

43. "Voyage Made from Canada" in Galloway et al., *La Salle*, p. 49.

44. On the development of slavery in Virginia, see Edmund S. Morgan, *American Slavery, American Freedom*.

45. On the development of slavery in South Carolina, see Peter H. Wood, *Black Majority: Negroes in Colonial South Carolina from 1670 through the Stono Rebellion*.

46. Some of the population movements that Smith found were in fact associated with the growth of the slave trade in the late seventeenth century. See Smith, *Archaeology of Aboriginal Culture Change*, pp. 129–142.

47. Thomas Nairne, *Nairne's Muskogean Journals: Journal of Expedition to the Mississippi River, 1708*, p. 50; Verner Crane, *The Southern Frontier, 1670–1732*, p. 30.

48. Crane, *Southern Frontier*, pp. 46–47.

49. Pierre Le Moyne, Sieur d'Iberville, *Iberville's Gulf Journals*, pp. 119, 132.

50. Charles Levasseur, "A Voyage to the Mobile and Tomeh in 1700, With Notes on the Interior of Alabama."

51. Iberville, *Iberville's Gulf Journals*, p. 144.

52. Father James Gravier, "Journal of . . . Gravier," pp. 126–127.

53. Iberville, *Iberville's Gulf Journals*, p. 110.

54. Daniel Coxe, "Coxe's Account of the Activities of the English in the Mississippi Valley in the Seventeenth Century," pp. 246–248.

55. Iberville, *Iberville's Gulf Journals*, p. 107–109; De Sauvole de la Villantray, *The Journal of Sauvole [1699–1701]*, p. 35.

56. Edmond Andros to Duke of Shrewsbury, June 27, 1696, Class Five Files, Colonial Office, 5:1307, p.83, British Public Record Office, London, microfilm transcript in the Library of Congress, Washington.

57. John Archdale, "A New Description of that Fertile and Pleasant Province of South Carolina," vol. II, p. 89.

58. John Lawson, *A New Voyage to Carolina*, pp. 17–18, 34, 237–238.

59. Alexander S. Salley, *Journal of the Commons House of Assembly of South Carolina, 1697*, pp. 9–12.

60. Joseph Blake and Council to Lords Proprietors of Carolina, March 12, 1698, in Alexander S. Salley, *Commissions and Instructions from the Lords Proprietors of Carolina to Public Officials of South Carolina, 1685–1715*, p. 103.

61. Joseph Blake and Council to Lords Proprietors, April 23, 1698, in Salley, *Commissions and Instructions*, p. 105.

62. Quoted in Edward McCrady, *History of South Carolina*, p. 308.

63. Archdale, "A new description," p. 12. Archdale emphasized "Spaniard" and "Indian."

64. Archdale, "A new description," p. 12.

65. Pénicaut, *Fleur de Lys and Calumet*, p. 11.

66. Iberville, *Iberville's Gulf Journals*, p. 38.

67. Pénicaut, *Fleur de Lys*, p. 11.

68. Iberville, *Iberville's Gulf Journals*, p. 59.

69. Iberville, *Iberville's Gulf Journals*, p. 139.
70. J. F. Buisson St. Cosme, "Letter to Bishop of Quebec, 1699," p. 73.
71. Thaumer de la Source, "Letter of Mr. Thaumer de la Source, 1699," pp. 81–82; Montigny, "Letter of Mr. De Montigny, January 2, 1699," p. 78.
72. Thaumer de la Source, "Letter," pp. 81–82.
73. Nairne, *Nairne's Muskogean Journals*, p. 63.
74. John Philip Reid misleadingly concluded that the first documented smallpox epidemic struck the Cherokees in 1697, and other scholars have followed Reid in coming to the same conclusion. Reid's source is Verner Crane, who quoted the same primary document as I did above. (See note 61 and Crane, *Southern Frontier*, p. 142). The document in question, however, does not specifically mention the Cherokees, saying only that the virus spread hundreds of miles inland from Charles Town. Thus, one cannot conclude with certainty that the Great Southeastern Smallpox Epidemic affected the Cherokees. See John Philip Reid, *A Better Kind of Hatchet*, p. 30; Russell Thornton, *The Cherokees: A Population History*, p. 22; Wood, "Changing Population," p. 63; M. Thomas Hatley, *The Dividing Paths: Cherokees and South Carolinians through the Revolutionary Era*, p. 6.
75. For some tribes subsequent epidemics may have been more severe. Smallpox struck the Cherokees especially hard in 1738–39. This outbreak may have been their first encounter with the virus. But for the entire southeastern Indian population, no subsequent outbreaks equaled the Great Southeastern Smallpox Epidemic. Subsequent epidemics and their impact are examined in more detail elsewhere. See Paul Kelton, "Not All Disappeared: Disease and Southeastern Indian Survival, 1500–1800," pp. 215–283; Peter H. Wood, "The Impact of Smallpox on the Native Population of the 18th-Century South."
76. Russell Thornton, Tim Miller, and Jonathan Warren, "American Indian Population Recovery Following Smallpox Epidemics."
77. Wood, "Changing Population," pp. 38–39. Wood tabulated estimates for ten different subregions of the Southeast. The figures 152,500 for 1685 and 46,700 for 1790 are total populations for the seven subregions that are within the scope of this paper. Wood divides these subregions into the following: North Carolina (east of the mountains), South Carolina (east of the mountains), Creeks (Georgia and Alabama), Cherokees, Choctaws/Chickasaws, Natchez/Louisiana, and Shawnee Interior (Kentucky and Tennessee). Wood also provided estimates for Virginia, Florida, and east Texas, subregions that are not considered in this paper.

Notes to SPANISH MISSIONS AND THE PERSISTENCE OF CHIEFLY POWER
by John E. Worth

1. Francisco Ospogue, Petition to the King, October 18, 1728. Archivo General de Indias, Santo Domingo 2584 [hereafter cited as AGI/SD].
2. See published translation by John H. Hann, "Visitations and Revolts in Florida, 1656–1695," p. 234.
3. See translations by John E. Worth, *The Struggle for the Georgia Coast: An Eighteenth-Century Spanish Retrospective on Guale and Mocama*, pp. 115, 125, and Hann, "Visitations and Revolts," p. 229.
4. Gonzalo Méndez de Canço, Auto, October, 1597, AGI/SD 224; Pedro Menéndez Márquez, Letter, April 2, 1579, AGI/SD 168; Thomás Bernaldo de Quirós, Petition and service record, 1584 (date in Council), AGI/SD 125.
5. Gonzalo Méndez de Canço, Auto, October, 1597, AGI/SD 224; Gonzalo Méndez de Canço, Auto, July 1, 1598, AGI Patronato 19, Ramo 28; Gonzalo Méndez de Canço and Juan Ximénez, Certification, May 18, 1600, AGI/SD 231.
6. Worth, *Struggle*, pp. 115, 125; Hann, "Visitations and Revolts," p. 229.
7. Charles W. Arnade, *The Seige of St. Augustine in 1702*; Francisco Ospogue, Peti-

tion to the King, October 18, 1728; AGI/SD 2584; John E. Worth, *The Timucuan Chiefdoms of Spanish Florida. Vol. 2, Resistance and Destruction*, pp. 147–150.

8. Worth, *Timucuan Chiefdoms*, vol. 2, p. 152.

9. Compare probable Guale populations of more than 1,000 people in 1595 to just 296 people in the census of 1681 and finally to only 61 people in 1711, amounting to a reduction of well over 90 percent during this period alone; see John E. Worth, *The Timucuan Chiefdoms of Spanish Florida. Vol. 1, Assimilation*, p. 128; Worth, *Timucuan Chiefdoms*, vol. 2, 148.

10. Francisco Ospogue, Petition to the King, October 18, 1728; AGI/SD 2584.

11. Fray Joseph Ramos Escudero, Letter, October 15, 1734; AGI/SD 2591.

12. See, for example, Vernon J. Knight, "The Formation of the Creeks," pp. 373–392.

13. Worth, *Timucuan Chiefdoms*, vol. 1, p. 142; vol. 2, pp. 49–50, 59; Hann, "Visitations and Revolts," pp. 141, 208.

14. Thomas Nairne, *Nairne's Muskhogean Journals: The 1708 Expedition to the Mississippi River*, p. 34.

15. William Bartram, *Travels of William Bartram*, p. 389.

16. For an excellent summary of this prehistoric southeastern world, see Charles Hudson, *Knights of Spain, Warriors of the Sun: Hernando de Soto and the South's Ancient Chiefdoms*, pp.11–30.

17. Francisco de Córcoles y Martínez, Letter to the King with attached census, April 9, 1711, AGI/SD 843; Thomas Nairne, John Wright, Price Hughes, and John Barnwell, "An exact account of ye number and strength of all the Indian nations that were subject to the Government of South Carolina and solely traded with them in ye beginning of ye year 1715," British Public Records Office, Records Relating to South Carolina, vol. 7, 238–239 [hereafter cited as BPRO/SC]. I have excluded allied Yamasees from the Creek population figure since they later fled to the missions.

18. Worth, *Timucuan Chiefdoms*, vol. 2, pp. 136–137, 147–148.

19. Worth, *Timucuan Chiefdoms*, vol. 1, pp. 77–102; Worth, *Struggle*, p. 47; and see John H. Hann, "Political Leadership among the Natives of Spanish Florida," pp. 188–208.

20. Worth, *Timucuan Chiefdoms*, vols. 1–2.

21. A similar pattern of cultural persistence may have characterized early French Louisiana and Spanish east Texas, as discussed by Hudson, *Knights of Spain*, pp. 417–440.

22. Sound overviews of these subjects may be found in the following selected volumes: David G. Anderson, *The Savannah River Chiefdoms: Political Change in the Late Prehistoric Southeast*; Charles Hudson and Carmen Chaves Tesser, *The Forgotten Centuries: Indians and Europeans in the American South, 1521–1704*; Jerald T. Milanich, *Florida Indians and the Invasion from Europe*; Jerald T. Milanich, *Laboring in the Fields of the Lord: Spanish Missions and Southeastern Indians*.

23. For the most current overviews of these early expeditions, see Hudson, *Knights of Spain*; Charles Hudson, Marvin T. Smith, Chester B. DePratter, and Emilia Kelley, "The Tristán de Luna Expedition, 1559–1561"; Charles Hudson, *The Juan Pardo Expeditions: Exploration of the Carolinas and Tennessee, 1566–1568*.

24. Overviews of this earliest French and Spanish colonial era may be found in the following works: Eugene Lyon, *The Enterprise of Florida*; Sarah Lawson and W. John Faupel, *A Foothold in Florida: The Eye-Witness Account of Four Voyages made by the French to that Region*; Milanich, *Invasion from Europe*, pp. 143–166; Milanich, *Laboring*, pp. 78–103; John H. Hann, *A History of the Timucua Indians and Missions*, pp. 35–72.

25. See, for example, Marvin T. Smith, *Archaeology of Aboriginal Culture Change in the Interior Southeast: Depopulation during the Early Historic Period*.

26. See notes 43 and 44 below.

27. The enigmatic Chisca Indians, for example, apparently made a sudden and dramatic move from their Appalachian homeland along the Virginia–North Carolina border, relocating far southward to arrive on the Florida peninsula shortly before 1624, precisely

during the time when rumors of English or Dutch horsemen along the northern Florida frontier prompted no fewer than five Spanish reconnaissance expeditions into the deep interior. Whether or not their relocation was caused by the ongoing spread of European firearms and commerce in the Northeast, the immigrant Chisca apparently possessed no firearms before 1676, instead maintaining a sort of parasitic existence within the Spanish mission frontier until their formal expulsion in 1651 and their subsequent relocation to the northwest Florida panhandle. See John E. Worth, "Late Spanish Military Expeditions in the Interior Southeast, 1597–1628"; Worth, *Timucuan Chiefdoms*, vol. 2, pp. 18–21, 34–35, 208.

28. Peter H. Wood, "The Changing Population of the Colonial South: An Overview by Race and Region, 1685–1790," presents data suggesting a nearly 75 percent population decline among all southeastern Indians between 1685 and 1760 alone. Extreme depopulation figures are posited by Henry F. Dobyns, *Their Number Become Thinned: Native American Population Dynamics in Eastern North America*, while Paul Kelton, in this volume, takes a much more conservative view of depopulation in the broader Southeast.

29. Worth, *Timucuan Chiefdoms*, vol. 2, pp. 10, 148.

30. Worth, *Timucuan Chiefdoms*, vol. 2, pp. 1–26; and see John E. Worth, "The Ethnohistorical Context of Bioarchaeology in Spanish Florida."

31. Worth, *Timucuan Chiefdoms*, vol. 1, pp. 162–168.

32. Worth, *Timucuan Chiefdoms*, vol. 1, p. 11; Anderson, *Savannah River Chiefdoms*, pp. 121–126.

33. Worth, *Timucuan Chiefdoms*, vol. 1, pp. 162–168, 224. Apart from the fact that chiefs had the right to confiscate the lands of widows who did not remarry and work their fields, additional documentary support for indigenous concepts of chiefly land ownership in the Southeast can be found in various petitions by chiefs for obligatory tribute from immigrants living on lands presently or formerly owned by them or their ancestors, or for the protection of their right to their traditional lands and the natural resources on them against incursions or abuses by Spaniards or other Indians (some of which were resisted or even denied by Spanish authorities, suggesting that the custom was not of Spanish origin). See, for example, Worth, *Struggle*, p. 35; Worth, *Timucuan Chiefdoms*, vol. 1, pp. 198–209; Worth, *Timucuan Chiefdoms*, vol. 2, pp. 34–35, 98–99, 192–197.

34. Worth, *Timucuan Chiefdoms*, vol. 1, pp. 164–165.

35. Smith, *Aboriginal Culture Change*.

36. Worth, *Timucuan Chiefdoms*, vol. 2, pp. 27–29; Worth, *Struggle*, pp. 10, 47.

37. See, for example, Knight, "Formation," pp. 382–383; Smith, *Aboriginal Culture Change*, pp. 68–75.

38. John E. Worth, "Recollections of the Juan Pardo Expeditions: The Domingo de León Account."

39. Smith, *Aboriginal Culture Change*, pp. 75–77.

40. Worth, *Struggle*, pp. 20–22, 35; *Timucuan Chiefdoms*, vol. 2, pp. 34–35.

41. E.g., Knight, "Formation," pp. 384–390; Marvin T. Smith, "Aboriginal Population Movements in the Early Historic Period Interior Southeast."

42. E.g., John E. Worth, "Yamassee Origins and the Development of the Carolina-Florida Frontier"; Worth, *Struggle*, pp. 19–22; William Green, "The Search for Altamaha: The Archaeology and Ethnohistory of an Early 18th-Century Yamasee Indian Town."

43. Worth, *Timucuan Chiefdoms*, vol. 1, pp. 35–43.

44. The following discussion derives substantially from my more in-depth treatment of the entire Spanish colonial system in Worth, *Timucuan Chiefdoms*, vols. 1–2, although it has been adapted to address the more focused theme of this chapter.

45. See, for example, the range of papers in Bonnie G. McEwan, *The Spanish Missions of La Florida*, and mission-related papers in David Hurst Thomas, *Columbian Consequences: Archaeological and Historical Perspectives on the Spanish Borderlands East*; and see Brent R. Weisman, *Excavations on the Franciscan Frontier: Archaeology at the Fig Springs Mission*.

46. For details of the arrival and early impact of the Westo, also known as Rechahecrians to the Virginians and Chichimecos to the Floridians, see Worth, *Struggle*, pp. 15–20. While other such groups involved in the early slave trade might possibly have taken part in raids farther to the west, documentary evidence from Florida and Carolina sources underscores the clear dominance of the Westo in the region under consideration here, at least until their destruction by the Carolinians after 1680.

47. See, for example, Verner W. Crane, *The Southern Frontier, 1670–1732*; Kathryn E. Holland Braund, *Deerskins and Duffels: Creek Indian Trade with Anglo-America, 1685–1815*; and Steven C. Hahn, this volume.

48. E.g., Knight, "Formation"; Worth, "Late Spanish Military Expeditions"; Mark Williams, "Growth and Decline of the Oconee Province"; Chester B. DePratter, "The Chiefdom of Cofitachequi."

49. See, for example, the overview by John R. Swanton, "The Social Significance of the Creek Confederacy."

50. See an early work by Carol I. Mason, "Eighteenth-Century Culture Change among the Lower Creeks," and more recent work by Vernon James Knight, "Tukabatchee: Archaeological Investigations at an Historic Creek Town, Elmore County, Alabama, 1984"; for the most up-to-date work on items traded by the English, see Gregory A. Waselkov, "The Eighteenth-Century Anglo-Indian Trade in Southeastern North America."

Notes to TROUBLE COMING SOUTHWARD: EMANATIONS THROUGH AND FROM VIRGINIA, 1607–1675
by Helen C. Rountree

1. Edward Bland et al., "The Discovery of New Brittaine, Began August 27, Anno Dom. 1650."

2. Robert Fallam, "A Journal from Virginia beyond the Appalachian mountains, in Sept. 1671, Sent to the Royal Society by Mr. Clayton, and read Aug. 1, 1688, before the said Society"; John Lederer, *The Discoveries of John Lederer*; Abraham Wood, "Letter to John Richards, August 23, 1674."

3. Alan Briceland, *Westward from Virginia: The Exploration of the Virginia-Carolina Frontier, 1650–1710*, p. 13.

4. Helen Hornbeck Tanner, "The Land and Water Communication Systems of the Southeastern Indians"; Helen C. Rountree, "The Powhatans and Other Woodland Indians as Travelers."

5. Helen C. Rountree, *The Powhatan Indians of Virginia: Their Traditional Culture*, p. 120.

6. Henry Spelman, "Relation of Virginea," p. cxiv.

7. James Pendergast, *The Massawomeck: Raiders and Traders into the Chesapeake Bay in the Seventeenth Century*.

8. John Smith, "A Map of Virginia" p. 232.

9. Clifford M. Lewis and Albert J. Loomie, *The Spanish Jesuit Mission in Virginia, 1570–1572*, p. 161.

10. Helen C. Rountree and E. Randolph Turner III, "On the Fringe of the Southeast: The Powhatan Paramount Chiefdom in Virginia"; Helen C. Rountree and E. Randolph Turner III, "The Evolution of the Powhatan Paramount Chiefdom in Virginia."

11. George Percy, "Observations Gathered out of a Discourse of the Plantation of the Southern Colonie in Virginia by the English 1606," p. 140.

12. William Strachey, *The Historie of Travell into Virginia Britania*, pp. 56–57.

13. Rountree, "The Powhatans," pp. 47–48.

14. David Beers Quinn, *The Roanoke Voyages, 1584–1590*, pp. 257–258.

284   Notes to Pages 69–75

15. John Smith, "A True Relation," p. 91; John Smith, "The Generall Historie of Virginia, New England, and the Summer Isles, 1624," pp. 193, 215.
16. William Waller Hening, *The Statutes at Large, Being a Collection of all the Laws of Virginia from the First Session of the Legislature*, vol. 1, p. 255.
17. Bland et al., "Discovery," pp. 13–14, 16.
18. Helen C. Rountree, *Pocahontas's People: The Powhatan Indians of Virginia Through Four Centuries*, pp. 105, 108–109.
19. Hening, *The Statutes*, vol. 1, p. 326. At this writing, as far as I can determine, there is no scholarly treatment of any real length of Wood's life and activities. The task of writing his history would be complicated, certainly, by the fact that Charles City County, where he spent so much time, had most of its colonial records burned in the Civil War.
20. David Phelps, personal communication, 1998.
21. Minutes 1637–46, 294, Norfolk County Virginia Records, City of Chesapeake, Virginia [hereafter cited as NCVR/GBC].
22. Hening, *The Statutes*, vol. 1, p. 325.
23. Bland et al., "Discovery," p. 10.
24. Bland et al., "Discovery," p. 10.
25. Bland et al., "Discovery," p. 18.
26. Bland et al., "Discovery," p. 12.
27. Hening, *The Statutes*, vol. 1, p. 262 (brackets mine).
28. Rountree, *Pocahontas's People*, pp. 89–127.
29. Browne et al., *Archives of Maryland*, vol. 1, passim, treaty; vol. 3, p. 420–422.
30. Browne et al., *Archives of Maryland*, vol. 1, pp. 329–332. The Doegs, shown as Tauxenents on John Smith's map of 1608, were based on Occoquan Bay in what is now northern Virginia. However, in the 1650s most of their dealings were with Maryland, whose colonial seat of government was located considerably closer to them than Jamestown.
31. Browne et al., *Archives of Maryland*, vol. 1, p. 348; vol. 3, pp. 360 [1659], 402–403 [1661], 453–454 [1662], 481–483 [1663].
32. Browne et al., *Archives of Maryland*, vol. 3, pp. 431–433.
33. Browne et al., *Archives of Maryland*, vols. 1, 3; vol. 5, passim.
34. Hening, *The Statutes*, vol. 2, p. 153.
35. DW 1653–59, p. 110, Westmoreland County, Virginia Records, Virginia [hereafter cited as WCVR].
36. H. R. McIlwaine, *Minutes of the Council and General Court of Virginia, 1622–1632, 1670–1676*, pp. 488–489.
37. Deeds 2, pp. 201–202, Old Tappahannock County, Virginia Records, Essex County Courthouse, Tappahannock, Virginia [hereafter cited as TCVR/ECC].
38. Hening, *The Statutes*, vol. 2, p. 194.
39. Martha McCartney, personal communication, 1984.
40. McIlwaine, *Minutes*, pp. 488–489.
41. Hening, *The Statutes*, vol. 1, p. 402 (brackets mine).
42. Orders 1655–65, p. 61, Charles City County, Virginia Records 1655–1665, Library of Virginia Archives [hereafter cited as CCCVR/LVA].
43. Hening, *The Statutes*, vol. 1, pp. 402, 422–423; Lederer, *Discoveries*, p. 16; Thomas Mathew, "The Beginning, Progress and Conclusion of Bacon's Rebellion in Virginia in the Years 1675 & 1676," p. 14; Lionel Gatford, "Publick good Without Private Interest," quoted in Edward D. Neill, *Virginia Carolorum*, pp. 246–247.
44. Hening, *The Statutes*, vol. 1, p. 410.
45. Orders 1655–65, p. 72, CCCVR/LVA.
46. Nell Marion Nugent, *Cavaliers and Pioneers: Abstracts of Virginia Land Patents and Grants, 1623–1800*, vol. 1 (1934); vol. 2 (1977), passim.
47. Deeds & Wills Book D, 1656–66, p. 293, NCVR.
48. Nugent, *Cavaliers and Pioneers*, vol. 1, pp. 425–428.

49. Hening, *The Statutes*, vol. 1, pp. 376–377.

50. Hening, *The Statutes*, vol. 1, pp. 380–381.

51. Hening, *The Statutes*, vol. 1, p. 381.

52. Hening, *The Statutes*, vol. 1, p. 422.

53. Hening, *The Statutes*, vol. 1, p. 548.

54. Hening, *The Statutes*, vol. 1, pp. 174, 198–199, 307, 314, 488, 515; vol. 2, pp. 124, 179, 183, 216, 287.

55. Hening, *The Statutes*, vol. 1, pp. 326, 410, 481–482.

56. Lederer, *Discoveries*, p. 42.

57. Hening, *The Statutes*, vol. 3, p. 468.

58. Hening, *The Statutes*, vol. 2, p. 193.

59. Browne et al., *Archives of Maryland*, vol. 5, pp. 84–85.

Notes to THE MOTHER OF NECESSITY: CAROLINA, THE CREEK INDIANS, AND THE MAKING OF A NEW ORDER IN THE AMERICAN SOUTHEAST, 1670–1763
by Steven C. Hahn

1. For a summary of this event, see Francisco Corocles y Martinez to the King, July 5, 1715, Archivo General de Indias, Santo Domingo 843 (hereafter cited as AGI/SD), Stetson Collection, Reel 35.

2. Francisco Corocles y Martinez to the King, July 5, 1715, AGI/SD 843, Stetson Collection, Reel 35.

3. Francisco Corocles y Martinez to the King, July 5, 1715, AGI/SD 843, Stetson Collection, Reel 35.

4. On the fate of the Yamasees, see Verner Crane, *The Southern Frontier, 1670–1732*, p. 255; John Hann, "St. Augustine's Fallout from the Yamasee War."

5. Steven James Oatis, "A Colonial Complex: South Carolina's Changing Frontiers in the Era of the Yamasee War, 1680–1730."

6. See especially Richard White, *The Roots of Dependency: Subsistence, Environment, and Social Change among the Choctaws, Pawnees, and Navajos*, and Richard White, *The Middle Ground: Indians, Empires, and Republics in the Great Lakes Region, 1650–1815*.

7. For a summary of the events leading to the Restoration, see Alan G. R. Smith, *The Emergence of a Nation State: The Commonwealth of England, 1529–1660*, pp. 364–368.

8. On the proprietors, see Crane, *Southern Frontier*, p. 4; for a copy of Charles II's Carolina Charter, see William Laurence Saunders, *The Colonial Records of North Carolina. Vol. 1, 1662–1712*, pp. 20–33.

9. For an examination of Britain's rise to power after the Stuart Restoration, see Linda Colley, *Britons: Forging the Nation, 1707–1837*.

10. Carolina Charter, Saunders, *Colonial Records*, p. 27.

11. Fundamental Constitutions of Carolina, by John Locke, July 21, 1669, South Carolina Historical Society, *Collections of the South Carolina Historical Society*, p. 116.

12. Carolina Charter, Saunders, *Colonial Records*, p. 26.

13. Instructions for Joseph West, South Carolina Historical Society, *Collections*, pp. 127–128.

14. Instructions for the Governor and Council, July 27, 1669, South Carolina Historical Society, *Collections*, p. 123.

15. See Lord Ashley to William Sayle, May 13, 1671; Lord Ashley to Henry Woodward, April 10, 1671, South Carolina Historical Society, *Collections*, pp. 316, 327–328; see also Crane, *Southern Frontier*, pp. 13–17.

16. Joseph Dalton to Anthony Lord Ashley, January 20, 1672, William Noel Sains-

bury, *Calendar of State Papers, Colonial Series: America and West Indies, 1574–1660*, vol. 5, pp. 319–320.

17. Grand Council of Carolina, Journals, September 3, 1673, South Carolina Historical Society. *Collections*, pp. 427–428.

18. Crane, *Southern Frontier*, p. 15.

19. Shaftesbury to Andrew Percival, May 23, 1674, Sainsbury, *Calendar*, vol. 5, p. 585.

20. Shaftesbury to Andrew Percival, May 23, 1674, Sainsbury, *Calendar*, vol. 5, p. 585

21. Shaftesbury to Andrew Percival, May 23, 1674, Sainsbury, *Calendar*, vol. 5, p. 585.

22. Shaftesbury to Henry Woodward, May 23, 1674, Sainsbury, *Calendar*, vol. 5, p. 58.

23. Shaftesbury to Henry Woodward, May 23, 1674, Sainsbury, *Calendar*, vol. 5, p. 58.

24. Crane, *Southern Frontier*, pp. 12–21; Eirlys Mair Barker, "Much Blood and Treasure: South Carolina's Indian Traders, 1670–1755."

25. Juan Marques Cabrera to the Viceroy of New Spain, May 19, 1686, AGI/SD 839, Worth Collection, Reel 6, no. 2, f. 555.

26. Juan Marques Cabrera to the Viceroy of New Spain, May 19, 1686, AGI/SD 839, Worth Collection, Reel 6, no. 2, f. 134.

27. Hita Salazar to the King, June 8, 1675, AGI/SD 839, Stetson Collection, Reel 14.

28. Hita Salazar to the King, November 10, 1678, AGI/SD 839, Stetson Collection, Reel 15.

29. Spanish officials began reiterating the statements of Fray Rodrigo and the Indian woman, which indicates their belief in the veracity of their reports. See Auto, May 23, 1675, AGI/SD 839, Stetson Collection, Reel 15; Governor Hita Salazar to the King, June 8, 1675, AGI/SD 839, Stetson Collection, Reel 15.

30. Hita Salazar to the King, June 8, 1675, AGI/SD 839, Stetson Collection, Reel 15.

31. Declaration of the Lords Proprietors, April 10, 1677, British Public Record Office, Colonial Office, Class Five Files, London, England, microfilm transcript in the Library of Congress, Washington DC (hereafter cited as BPRO/CO) 5/286, f. 120; see also Crane, *Southern Frontier*, p. 15.

32. Declaration of the Lords Proprietors, April 10, 1677, BPRO/CO 5/286, f. 120; see also Crane, *Southern Frontier*, p. 15.

33. Articles of Agreement of the Lords Proprietors Concerning Trade, April 10, 1677, BPRO/CO 5/286, f. 124.

34. Declaration of the Lords Proprietors, April 10, 1677, BPRO/CO 5/286, f. 120.

35. Hita Salazar to the King, November 10, 1678, AGI/SD 839, Stetson Collection, Reel 15.

36. Hita Salazar to the King, November 10, 1678, letter in response to a November 5, 1677, Royal Cedula, AGI/SD 839, Stetson Collection, Reel 15.

37. George Pratt Insh, *Scottish Colonial Schemes, 1620–1686*, pp. 186–211; Crane, *Southern Frontier*, pp. 27–28.

38. Lord Cardross and William Dunlop, "Cardross and William Dunlop to Peter Colleton, March 27, 1685," p. 104.

39. BPRO/CO 5/287, f. 198–202; Crane, *Southern Frontier*, p. 30.

40. Woodward to John Godfrey, March 21, 1685, Sir John William Fortescue, *Calendar of State Papers, Colonial Series: America and West Indies, 1574–1660*, vol. 12, p. 19.

41. It is difficult to pin down the exact date of the departure of Woodward and company. It must have occurred sometime between March 21, 1685, when Woodward was known still to be in Charles Town, and May 6, 1685, when Woodward can be found at Stuart's Town interviewing Yamasees. It is probable that Woodward set out in late April. See BPRO/CO 5/287, f. 140.

42. Several years later, the Creeks admitted to their subterfuge. See Don Faviano de

Angelo to the Governor, May 24, 1690, AGI/SD 58-1-26, and Mary L. Ross Papers, f. 90, n. 36, Georgia Department of Archives and History, Atlanta (hereafter cited as GDAH).

43. Antonio Matheos to Governor Juan Marques Cabrera, January 12, 1686, AGI/SD 839, Mary L. Ross Papers, f. 88, no. 27, 220–221.

44. Antonio Matheos to Juan Marques Cabrera, May 29, 1686, AGI/SD 839, Worth Collection, Reel 6, no. 1, f. 628.

45. Matheos to Governor Marques, May 29, 1686; Antonio Matheos to Juan Marques Cabrera, August 21, 1686, Archivo General de Indias, Audiencia of Mexico (hereafter cited as AGI-MEX) 616, Worth Collection, Reel 6, no. 48, p. 1.

46. Matheos to Governor Marques, August 21, 1686, AGI-MEX 616, Worth Collection, Reel 6, no. 48, p. 1.

47. Matheos to Governor Marques, August 21, 1686, AGI-MEX 616, Worth Collection, Reel 6, no. 48, p. 1.

48. Carol Mason, "The Archaeology of Ocmulgee Old Fields, Macon, Georgia," pp. 140–180; Gregory Waselkov, "The Macon Trading House and Early European-Indian Contact in the Colonial Southeast."

49. Governor Quiroga y Losada to the King, September 29, 1689, AGI/SD 234, Stetson Collection, Reel 20; Quiroga y Losada to Enrique Primo de Rivera, October 6, 1689, AGI/SD 234, Worth Collection, Reel 6; Enrique Primo de Rivera to Quiroga y Losada, AGI/SD 234, Worth Collection, Reel 6.

50. Auto, September 18, 1690, AGI/SD, Stetson Collection, Reel 22; Quiroga y Losada to the King, April 10, 1691, AGI/SD, Stetson Collection, Reel 22; Fray Jacinto de Barreda, Petition, April 30, 1691, AGI/SD, leg. 227-B.

51. Howard Peckham, *The Colonial Wars, 1689–1762*, p. 59.

52. Crane, *Southern Frontier*, p. 9; Herbert Eugene Bolton and Mary Ross, *The Debatable Land, A Sketch of the Anglo-Spanish Contest for the Georgia Country*, chapter 3; J. Leitch Wright, *Anglo-Spanish Rivalry in North America*, p. 61.

53. Marcel Giraud, *A History of French Louisiana. Vol. 1, The Reign of Louis XIV, 1698–1715*; Jay Higginbotham, *Old Mobile: Fort Louis de la Louisiane, 1702–1711*, pp. 15–86.

54. Crane, *Southern Frontier*, pp. 47–70.

55. Jon Muller, *Mississippian Political Economy*, chapter 6; John E. Worth, *The Timucuan Chiefdoms of Spanish Florida*, vol. 1, pp. 9–11.

56. Thomas Nairne, *Nairne's Muskhogean Journals: The 1708 Expedition to the Mississippi River*, p. 34

57. On Indian "dependency" in the modern world capitalist system, see White, *Roots of Dependency*, pp. xiv–xix; Theotonio Dos Santos, "The Structure of Dependence," pp. 231–236; Wilma Dunaway, "Incorporation as an Interactive Process: Cherokee Resistance to Expansion of the Capitalist World System"; James Merrell, *The Indians' New World: Catawbas and Their Neighbors from European Contact through the Era of Removal*, pp. 49–91.

58. On the Creeks' early trade activities, see Kathryn Braund, *Deerskins and Duffels: The Creek Indian Trade with Anglo-America, 1685–1815*, pp. 28–39.

59. June 13, 1711, Journal of the Commons House of Assembly, South Carolina (hereafter cited as JCHA-SC).

60. May 4, 1714, William L. McDowell, Jr., *Journals of the Commissioners of the Indian Trade, September 20, 1710–August 29, 1718*, p. 53.

61. June 12, 1712, McDowell, *Journals*, p. 26.

62. Crane, *Southern Frontier*, p. 120.

63. Corocoles y Martinez to the King, July 5, 1715; Corocoles y Martinez to the King, December 23, 1715, AGI/SD 843, Stetson Collection, Reel 35.

64. Corocoles y Martinez to the King, July 5, 1715; Corocoles y Martinez to the King, December 23, 1715, AGI/SD 843, Stetson Collection, Reel 35.

65. It is curious that the Spanish soldiers interviewed used the term "theniente" or

"capitan" to describe the traders, rather than "mercador," the word used in subsequent years when English traders were discussed.

66. Declarations of Juan Gabriel de Vargas, Joseph Fernandez, and Joseph de Rojas, January 9–10, 1710, enclosure with Governor Corocoles y Martinez to the King, January 22, 1710, AGI/SD 841, Stetson Collection, Reel 34.

67. Spanish soldiers referred to Musgrove as "Chanlacta Maestechanles," which resembles the name Barcia used to describe Musgrove in his 1722 Ensayo Chronologico. Declaration of Joseph de Rojas, January 9, 1710, AGI/SD 841, Stetson Collection, Reel 34.

68. Testimony of Juan Gabriel de Vargas, January 9, 1710, AGI/SD 841, Stetson Collection, Reel 34.

69. Ponchartrain to Bienville, July 9, 1709, Dunbar Roland and A. G. Saunders, *Mississippi Provincial Archives: French Dominion, Vol. 3, 1704–1743*, p. 127.

70. On the proposed Alabama peace, see Ponchartrain to Bienville, July 11, 1709; Ponchartrain to Bienville, May 10, 1710; King Louis XIV to Governor Lamothe Cadillac, May 13, 1710; Roland and Saunders, *Mississippi Provincial Archives: French Dominion, Vol. 3*, pp. 127–129, 139, 144.

71. Braund, *Deerskins and Duffels*, p. 34.

72. Creeks often complained of their "disappointment" over the Spanish failures to meet their demand for trade goods. For one example, see Diary of Juan Marquez del Toro, entries for March 12–15, 1738, AGI/SD 2593, Worth Collection, Reel 3. On Fort Toulouse, see Daniel H. Thomas, *Fort Toulouse: The French Outpost at the Alabamas on the Coosa*.

73. Journal of Tobias Fitch, BPRO/CO 5/12 (microfilm copy in the possession of the author).

74. J. Russel Snapp claims that in the period before 1763, a "middle ground" existed between the Creeks and English. See J. Russel Snapp, *John Stuart and the Struggle for Empire on the Southern Frontier*, especially chapter 1. Although most other historians do not use this "middle ground" metaphor, the time period between the Yamasee War and 1763 has been portrayed in a rather favorable light; see David H. Corkran, *The Creek Frontier, 1540–1783*.

75. Corkran, *Creek Frontier*, p. 61.

76. Braund, *Deerskins and Duffels*, p. 22; Richard Sonderegger, "The Southern Frontier to the End of King George's War," p. 224.

77. Jose Primo de Ribera to Juan Ayala Escobar, April 28, 1718, AGI/SD, Stetson Collection, Reel 37.

78. On mercantile empires, see Eric Hinderaker, *Elusive Empires: Constructing Colonialism in the Ohio Valley, 1673–1800*.

79. E. Atkin to William H. Lyttleton, November 30, 1759, The Lyttleton Papers: The Papers of William Henry Lyttleton, Governor of South Carolina, Original Manuscripts and Letterbooks, William L. Clements Library, Ann Arbor, Michigan (hereafter cited as Lyttleton Papers).

80. For a discussion of this process in the Ohio valley, see Hinderaker, *Elusive Empires*.

81. Among historians who study trade, only Richard White has adhered to this strict definition of dependency, as defined by Marxist-inspired scholarship on third world countries. See White, *Roots of Dependency*; White, *The Middle Ground*, pp. 483–484. On colonialism and capitalism, see Karl Marx, "The Modern Theory of Colonization." For more general discussions of dependency, see Immanuel Wallerstein, *The Modern World System: Capitalist Agriculture and the Origins of the European World Economy in the 16th Century*; Fernando Henrique Cardoso, "Dependency and Development in Latin America"; Dos Santos, "Structure of Dependence"; Ronald Chilcote, *Theories of Development and Underdevelopment*; Florencia Mallon, *The Defense of Community in Peru's Central Highlands*.

82. See White, *Roots of Dependency*, pp. 16–146; Braund, *Deerskins and Duffels*; Merrell, *Indians' New World*, pp. 49–92; Crane, *Southern Frontier*.

83. Juan Francisco Guemes y Horcasitas to the King, January 18, 1738, AGI/SD 2582, Worth Collection, Reel 3.

84. Diary of Juan Marquez del Toro, entries for March 12–15, 1738, AGI/SD 2593, Worth Collection, Reel 3.

85. Diary of Juan Marquez del Toro, entries for March 12–15, 1738, AGI/SD 2593, Worth Collection, Reel 3.

86. Diary of Juan Marquez del Toro, entry for April 2, 1738, AGI/SD 2593, Worth Collection, Reel 3.

87. For an interesting discussion of this turn of phrase, see Jared M. Diamond, *Guns, Germs, and Steel: The Fates of Human Societies*.

Notes to THE OHIO VALLEY, 1550–1750: PATTERNS OF SOCIOPOLITICAL COALESCENCE AND DISPERSAL
by Penelope B. Drooker

1. R. Berle Clay, "The Mississippian Succession on the Lower Ohio"; Penelope B. Drooker, *The View from Madisonville: Protohistoric Western Fort Ancient Interaction Patterns*, pp. 6–76; David Pollack, Cheryl Ann Munson, and A. Gwynn Henderson, *Slack Farm and the Caborn-Welborn People*; Kevin E. Smith, "The Middle Cumberland Region: Mississippian Archaeology in North Central Tennessee," pp. 413–425.

2. David W. Anthony, "Migration in Archeology: The Baby and the Bathwater"; Richard F. Sutton, "New Approaches for Identifying Prehistoric Iroquoian Migrations."

3. Anthony, "Migration," p. 899.

4. Anthony, "Migration," p. 900.

5. Marvin T. Smith, "Aboriginal Population Movements in the Postcontact Southeast."

6. Members of the "League of the Iroquois," "Iroquois Confederacy," or "Five Nations" included (from west to east): the Seneca, whose villages were south of present-day Rochester, New York; the Cayuga, who occupied land between Cayuga and Owasco lakes in the Finger Lakes region of New York; the Onondaga, whose villages were located south of the eastern end of Lake Ontario between Cazenovia Lake and Onondaga Creek; the Oneida, who lived directly southeast of Oneida Lake, which is southeast of Lake Ontario; and the Mohawk, of the Mohawk River drainage west of Albany, New York. As of 1722 or 1723, the Tuscarora, who had moved to New York from North Carolina after the 1711–1713 Tuscarora Wars, became a sixth member. The Five Nations are referred to as "Iroquois." Other speakers of Iroquoian languages, such as Hurons, Neutrals, and Susquehannocks, are referred to as "Iroquoian" in this chapter. Basic information about these groups, their languages, their territories, and their histories can be found in Bruce G. Trigger, *Northeast*.

7. For example, Richard White, *The Middle Ground: Indians, Empires, and Republics in the Great Lakes Region, 1650–1815*, pp. 1–49.

8. Daniel K. Richter, "War and Culture: The Iroquois Experience"; Daniel K. Richter, *The Ordeal of the Longhouse: The Peoples of the Iroquois League in the Era of European Colonization*, pp. 36–38.

9. Francis Jennings, *The Ambiguous Iroquois Empire: The Covenant Chain Confederation of Indian Tribes with English Colonies from Its Beginnings to the Lancaster Treaty of 1744*, p. 95; Richter, "War and Culture"; Richter, *Ordeal*, pp. 57–74; Dean R. Snow and Kim M. Lamphear, "European Contact and Indian Depopulation in the Northeast: The Timing of the First Epidemics"; Dean R. Snow and William A. Starna, "Sixteenth-Century Depopulation: A View from the Mohawk Valley."

10. Richard Aquila, "Down the Warrior's Path: The Causes of the Southern Wars of

the Iroquois"; Jennings, *Ambiguous Iroquois*, pp. 84–112, 143–213; Barry C. Kent, *Susquehanna's Indians*, pp. 33–58; James H. Merrell, " 'Their Very Bones Shall Fight:' The Catawba-Iroquois Wars"; Raoul Naroll, "The Causes of the Fourth Iroquois War"; Richter, "War and Culture"; Richter, *Ordeal*, pp. 60–65; Daniel K. Richter and James H. Merrell, *Beyond the Covenant Chain: The Iroquois and Their Neighbors in Indian North America 1600–1800*, pp. 2–3; Wayne C. Temple, *Indian Villages of the Illinois Country*; Bruce G. Trigger, "The Mohawk-Mahican War (1624–1628): The Establishment of a Pattern"; Bruce G. Trigger, "Early Iroquoian Contacts with Europeans," pp. 352–356; Anthony F. C. Wallace, "Origins of Iroquois Neutrality: The Grand Settlement of 1701."

11. During the early contact period, the Huron and their close associates the Petun lived just south of the tip of Georgian Bay, Lake Huron. The Neutral occupied area around the western end of Lake Ontario, with Wenro probably directly east, near Niagara Falls. Erie territory probably was close to the Lake Erie shore from perhaps as far west as the New York-Pennsylvania border to perhaps as far east as Buffalo. For more information, see Trigger, *Northeast*, and Chris J. Ellis and Neal Ferris, *The Archaeology of Southern Ontario to* A.D. 1650.

12. Drooker, *View from Madisonville*, fig. 3–7.

13. Drooker, *View from Madisonville*, pp. 48–49; Helen C. Rountree, "The Powhatans and other Woodland Indians as Travelers"; Helen H. Tanner, "The Land and Water Communication Systems of the Southeastern Indians."

14. Drooker, *View from Madisonville*, figs. 3-4, 3-5, 3-6.

15. David G. Anderson, "Examining Prehistoric Settlement Distribution in Eastern North America," figs. 3, 4, 5.

16. Smith, *Middle Cumberland*, pp. 413–425.

17. Clay, "Mississippian Succession."

18. David Pollack, "Intraregional and Intersocietal Relationships of the Late Mississippian Caborn-Welborn Phase of the Lower Ohio River Valley," fig. 1-3; David Pollack and Cheryl Ann Munson, "Caborn-Welborn Ceramics: Inter-Site Comparisons and Extra-Regional Interaction"; David Pollack and Cheryl Ann Munson, "The Angel to Caborn-Welborn Transition: Late Mississippian Developments in Southwestern Indiana, Northwestern Kentucky, and Southwestern Illinois"; Pollack et al., *Slack Farm*; see also Munson et al., *Archaeology at the Hovey Lake Village Site*.

19. Pollack, "Intraregional," pp. 446–448.

20. Pollack et al., *Slack Farm*, pp. 25, 26.

21. Warren K. Moorehead, *A Narrative of Explorations in New Mexico, Arizona, Indiana, etc.*, fig. 22; Munson et al., *Archaeology*, p. 23; Pollack et al., *Slack Farm*, pp. 24, 25.

22. For example, see Donald J. Blakeslee, "The Origin and Spread of the Calumet Ceremony"; Ian W. Brown, "The Calumet Ceremony in the Southeast and its Archaeological Manifestations"; Robert L. Hall, "The Evolution of the Calumet Pipe"; Robert L. Hall, "Calumet Ceremonialism, Mourning Ritual, and Mechanisms of Inter-tribal Trade."

23. Penelope B. Drooker, "Fort Ancient and the Southeast: Late Prehistoric and Protohistoric Interaction"; Drooker, *View from Madisonville*, pp. 56–58; Penelope B. Drooker, "Exotic Ceramics at Madisonville: Implications for Interaction"; Penelope B. Drooker, "Pots and Pipes as 'Smoking Guns'—Tracking the Early Historical Iroquois–Fort Ancient Relationship."

24. Pollack, "Intraregional," fig. 5-3.

25. Moorehead, *Narrative of Explorations*, fig. 23; Pollack et al., *Slack Farm*, p. 24; Cheryl Munson, personal communication; personal examination of metal artifacts from the Murphy site.

26. Drooker, *View from Madisonville*, figs. 4-4, 4-5.

27. For example, see Drooker, *View from Madisonville*, fig. 4-9.

28. For example, Lora A. Lamarre, "The Buffalo Site Ceramics: An Analysis of an Archaeological Assemblage from a Fort Ancient Village Site in West Virginia," pp. 152–153.

29. Within any given region, the protohistoric period is a shadowy time of indirect or short-term contact with Europeans. Bruce Trigger has defined it as the interval "between the first appearance of European goods and the earliest substantial historical records" (Bruce G. Trigger, *Natives and Newcomers: Canada's "Heroic Age" Reconsidered*, p. 116). In the Ohio Valley, this interval stretches from the mid-sixteenth century to the mid-eighteenth century, the period that is the focus of this paper.

30. Penelope B. Drooker, "Madisonville Metal and Glass Artifacts: Implications for Western Fort Ancient Chronology and Interaction Networks"; Drooker, *View from Madisonville*; Penelope B. Drooker, *Zoom-in to Madisonville*.

31. Drooker, *View from Madisonville*, pp. 106–219.

32. Pollack et al., *Slack Farm*, pp. 10–11.

33. Lee H. Hanson, Jr., *The Buffalo Site, A Late Seventeenth Century Indian Village Site (46 Pu 31) in Putnam County, West Virginia*.

34. Penelope B. Drooker and C. Wesley Cowan, "The Dawn of History and the Transformation of the Fort Ancient Cultures of the Central Ohio Valley"; Lee H. Hanson, Jr., *The Hardin Village Site*; Hanson, *Buffalo Site*.

35. Drooker, *View from Madisonville*, pp. 72–76, 95–103, 327–339.

36. Drooker, *View from Madisonville*, pp. 283–337.

37. Drooker, *View from Madisonville*, pp. 303–309, 331–332, table 7-18, figs. 6-20, 7-5a, 7-6, 7-30.

38. Drooker, *View from Madisonville*, p. 332, figs. 6-19b, 8-18, 8-37d, 8-38, 8–39.

39. Stanley W. Baker, "Neale's Landing Site Ceramics: A Perspective on the Protohistoric Period from Blennerhasset Island"; Jeff Carskadden and James Morton, *Where the Frolics and War Dances Are Held: The Indian Wars and the Early European Exploration and Settlement of Muskingum County and the Central Muskingum Valley*, fig. 9; Drooker, "Exotic Ceramics."

40. Cf. Lamarrre, "The Buffalo Site," p. 155.

41. Drooker, *View from Madisonville*, pp. 294, 301–302; Darla S. Hoffman, "From the Southeast to Fort Ancient: A Survey of Shell Gorgets in West Virginia" (1998); Darla S. Hoffman, "From the Southeast to Fort Ancient: A Survey of Shell Gorgets in West Virginia" (1999); Lamarre, "The Buffalo Site," p. 153.

42. Drooker, "Fort Ancient"; Drooker, *View from Madisonville*, pp. 72–74, 294–303, 328–329; Jeffrey R. Graybill, "The Eastern Periphery of Fort Ancient (A.D. 1050–1650): A Diachronic Approach to Settlement Variability"; Jeffrey R. Graybill, "Fort Ancient–East: Origins, Change, and External Correlations"; Jeffrey R. Graybill, "Fort Ancient–Madisonville Horizon: Protohistoric Archeology in the Middle Ohio Valley."

43. Drooker, *View from Madisonville*, pp. 279–282.

44. Drooker, *View from Madisonville*, figs. 6-21f, 7-31, 8-10.

45. Drooker, "Madisonville Metal," pp. 165, 166–169; Drooker, *View from Madisonville*, pp. 274–275, 292–293.

46. Drooker, "Madisonville Metal," p. 42; Drooker, *View from Madisonville*, fig. 3-3.

47. Baker, "Neale's Landing"; Jeff Carskadden, "The Bosman Site, Muskingum County, Ohio"; Jeff Carskadden and James Morton, "Fort Ancient in the Central Muskingum Valley of Eastern Ohio: A View from the Philo II Site"; Jeff Carskadden, Larry Edmister, and James Morton, "Scenes from the Bosman Site Excavation, Muskingum County, Ohio"; Carskadden and Morton, *Frolics and War Dances*, pp. 33–39; Drooker, *View from Madisonville*, pp. 56, 73–74; Janice K. Whitman, "An Analysis of the Ceramics from the Riker Site, Tuscarawas County, Ohio."

48. Anonymous, "Monongahela Village Site Donated"; William C. Johnson, "The Protohistoric Monongahela and the Case for an Iroquois Connection"; James F. Pendergast et al., "Discussion of Archaeological Evidence of the Massawomek."

49. Drooker, "Madisonville Metal"; Drooker, *View from Madisonville*, pp. 153–173, 283–296.

50. Cf. Jeffrey P. Brain, "Artifacts of the Adelantado"; Jeffrey M. Mitchem and Bonnie G. McEwan, "New Data on Early Bells from Florida."

51. Cf. William R. Fitzgerald, "Late Sixteenth-Century Basque Banded Copper Kettles."

52. Drooker, *Zoom-in,* Unpublished Report 4.

53. James W. Bradley and S. Terry Childs, "Basque Earrings and Panther's Tails: The Form of Cross-Cultural Contact in 16th Century Iroquoia."

54. Drooker, *View from Madisonville,* figs. 8-5 through 8-8.

55. Penelope B. Drooker, "External Relations: Exotic Materials and Artifacts at Madisonville"; Drooker, *View from Madisonville,* pp. 302–315, figs. 7-5, 7-6, 7-30, 8-25, 8-26, 8-27; Drooker, *Zoom-in.*

56. Drooker, *View from Madisonville,* pp. 135–219.

57. Drooker, *View from Madisonville,* pp. 293–296, table 4-9, fig. 4-18; Gregory A. Waselkov, "Seventeenth-Century Trade in the Colonial Southeast."

58. Janet G. Brashler and Ronald W. Moxley, "Late Prehistoric Engraved Shell Gorgets of West Virginia"; Drooker, *View from Madisonville,* pp. 294, 297–305, tables 4-9, 4-13, figs. 8-15, 8-16, 8-24; Hoffman, "From the Southeast" (1998); Hoffman, "From the Southeast" (1999).

59. Cf. Marvin T. Smith, *Archaeology of Aboriginal Culture Change in the Interior Southeast: Depopulation During the Early Historical Period;* Marvin T. Smith and Julie B. Smith, "Engraved Shell Masks in North America"; Waselkov, "Seventeenth-Century Trade."

60. Drooker, *View from Madisonville,* pp. 58–62, tables 4-9, 6-7.

61. Abbé Galinée quoted in Charles A. Hanna, *The Wilderness Trail; or, the Ventures and Adventures of the Pennsylvania Traders on the Allegheny Path, With Some New Annals of the Old West, and the Records of Some Strong Men and Some Bad Ones,* pp. 121–122.

62. William A. Hunter, "History of the Ohio Valley."

63. James B. Griffin, *The Fort Ancient Aspect: Its Cultural and Chronological Position in Mississippi Valley Archaeology,* p. 31.

64. Griffin, *Fort Ancient Aspect,* p. 31.

65. Clarence W. Alvord and Lee Bidgood, *The First Explorations of the Trans-Allegheny Region by the Virginians, 1650–1674,* pp. 210–226; Sigfus Olafson, "Gabriel Arthur and the Fort Ancient People."

66. Griffin, *Fort Ancient Aspect,* maps 7, 8; Hunter, "History," p. 589.

67. Hunter, "History," p. 589.

68. Cf. Ives Goddard, "Central Algonquian Languages," p. 587.

69. Hunter, "History," p. 589.

70. Cyrus Thomas, "The Story of a Mound: or, the Shawnees in pre-Columbian Times"; cf. Charles Callender, "Shawnee," p. 630.

71. Smith, *Middle Cumberland Region,* pp. 413–425; cf. Clay, "Mississippian Succession."

72. Charles Callender, *Social Organization of the Central Algonkian Indians,* fig. 1; Charles Callender, "Fox," p. 643, fig. 1.

73. Hunter, "History," p. 589.

74. James Griffin, *Fort Ancient Aspect,* pp. 12–27.

75. For example, see John Witthoft and William A. Hunter, "The Seventeenth-Century Origins of the Shawnee"; cf. Callender, "Shawnee," p. 630; Drooker, *View from Madisonville,* pp. 103–105; Griffin, *Fort Ancient Aspect,* pp. 11–35.

76. Cf. Callender, "Shawnee," fig. 1.

77. Drooker, *View from Madisonville,* p. 319, fig. 4-19; Drooker, "Pots and Pipes."

78. Drooker, *View from Madisonville,* pp. 104, 317, fig. 8-36; Kent, *Susquehanna's Indians,* p. 378.

79. James A. Brown and John Willis, "Re-Examination of Danner Pottery from the Starved Rock Area"; James A. Brown, *The Zimmerman Site: A Report on Excavations at the Grand Village of Kaskaskia, La Salle County, Illinois;* Drooker, *View from Madisonville,* p. 319, fig. 6-61; Drooker, "Exotic Ceramics."

80. Personal examination of vessels at the New York State Museum and the Rochester Museum and Science Center.

81. Vernon James Knight, Jr., *Tukabatchee: Archaeological Investigations at an Historic Creek Town, Elmore County, Alabama, 1984*, p. 27.

82. A. Gwynn Henderson, Cynthia E. Jobe, and Christopher A. Turnbow, *Indian Occupation and Use in Northern and Eastern Kentucky During the Contact Period (1540–1795): An Initial Investigation*, pp. 131–137; A. Gwynn Henderson, David Pollack, and Christopher A. Turnbow, "Chronology and Cultural Patterns," pp. 270–278; David Pollack and A. Gwynn Henderson, "A Mid-Eighteenth Century Historic Indian Occupation in Greenup County, Kentucky"; C. Wesley Cowan, personal communication.

83. Kent, *Susquehanna's Indians*, pp. 90–91; Gary D. Schaffer, "An Examination of the Bead Hill Site in the Wyoming Valley"; Christopher Wren, "Description of Indian Graves on Bead Hill, Plymouth, Pennsylvania."

84. David Pollack, Mary Lucas Powell, and Audrey Adkins, "Preliminary Study of Mortuary Patterns at the Larkin Site, Bourbon County, Kentucky."

85. Hanson, *Hardin Village*, pp. 29, 65–67; Hanson, *Buffalo Site*, p. 23, figs. 21, 22.

86. Hanna, *Wilderness Trail*, pp. 189–190.

87. Callender, "Shawnee"; Penelope B. Drooker, "The Shawnee Female Deity in Political Perspective," pp. 19–21, 28–32; Alford in William A. Galloway, *Old Chillicothe: Shawnee and Pioneer History: Conflicts and Romances in the Northwest Territory*.

88. Callender, "Shawnee," fig. 1; Drooker, "The Shawnee Female," pp. 28–32, fig. 3.

89. For example, Callender, "Shawnee"; Jerry E. Clark, *Shawnee*; Hanna, *Wilderness Trail*, pp. 119–160; Jennings, *Ambiguous Iroquois*, pp. 196–202; Kent, *Susquehanna's Indians*, pp. 78–91; Temple, *Indian Villages*; Witthoft and Hunter, "Seventeenth-Century Origins."

90. Cf. Callendar, "Shawnee," fig. 1.

91. Kent, *Susquehanna's Indians*, pp. 78, 91.

92. John R. Swanton, *Indians of the Southeastern United States*, p. 184.

93. Callender, "Shawnee," p. 630.

94. Knight, *Tukabatchee*, pp. 22–28.

95. J. Leitch Wright, Jr., *Creeks and Seminoles: The Destruction and Regeneration of the Muscogulge People*, p. 112.

96. René-Robert Cavelier, Sieur de la Salle, *Relation of the Discoveries and Voyages of Cavelier de La Salle from 1679 to 1681*, p. 259.

97. Henri de Tonti, *Relation of Henri de Tonti Concerning the Exploration of La Salle from 1678 to 1683*, pp. 111, 113; Callender, "Shawnee," p. 630; Hanna, *Wilderness Trail*, pp. 124–125.

98. Hanna, *Wilderness Trail*, pp. 126–127.

99. Hanna, *Wilderness Trail*, pp. 135–136, 140–143, 158; Jennings *Ambiguous Iroquois*, pp. 201–202, 206; Kent, *Susquehanna's Indians*, pp. 78–91.

100. Jennings, *Ambiguous Iroquois*, pp. 196–208; Callender, "Shawnee," p. 622.

101. Callender, "Shawnee," p. 631.

102. Temple, *Indian Villages*, pp. 145–146.

103. Reuben G. Thwaites, *The Jesuit Relations and Allied Documents; Travel and Explorations of the Jesuit Missionaries in New France, 1610–1791*, pp. 165–193, 296–301.

104. Drooker, *View from Madisonville*, p. 64.

105. For example, see Aquila, "Down the Warrior's Path," pp. 6, 12–13, 106; Jennings, *Ambiguous Iroquois*; Michael N. McConnell, "Peoples 'In Between': The Iroquois and the Ohio Indians, 1720–1768," p. 93.

106. Thwaites, *Jesuit Relations*, vol. LXII, pp. 71, 185.

107. Nicolas Perrot, *The Indian Tribes of the Upper Mississippi Valley and Region of the Great Lakes, as Described by Nicolas Perrot, French Commandant in the Northwest; Bacqueville de la Potherie, French Royal Commissioner to Canada; Morrell Marston, American Army Officer; and Thomas Forsyth, United States Agent at Fort Armstrong*, pp. 226, 227.

108. Thwaites, *Jesuit Relations*, vol. LIX, p. 145.
109. Thwaites, *Jesuit Relations*, vol. LXII, p. 209.
110. Griffin, *Fort Ancient Aspect*, map 7.
111. Drooker, *View from Madisonville*, pp. 93, 101–103, 204–207, 209–210, 213, 282; Hanson, *Buffalo Site*, fig. 27.
112. Pollack et al., "Preliminary Study."
113. Drooker, *View from Madisonville*, pp. 204–207; tables 4-2, 4-5, 4-11.
114. Drooker, *View from Madisonville*, pp. 206–209.
115. Raymond C. Vietzen, *Riker Site*; Janice K. Whitman, "An Analysis of the Ceramics from the Riker Site, Tuscarawas County, Ohio."
116. Baker, "Neale's Landing"; Carskadden, "The Bosman Site"; Carskadden, "Fort Ancient"; Carskadden et al., "Scenes," p. 60; Drooker, *View from Madisonville*, pp. 74–75.
117. Drooker, "Fort Ancient and the Southeast"; Drooker, *View from Madisonville*, pp. 4, 337.
118. Drooker, "Exotic Ceramics"; Drooker, "Pots and Pipes."
119. Drooker, "Madisonville Metal," fig. 8-14.
120. Knight, *Tukabatchee*, pp. 17–27.
121. For example, see Perrot, *Indian Tribes*, p. 226; Kent, *Susquehanna's Indians*, pp. 377–379; Knight, *Tukabatchee*, pp. 24–27.
122. Drooker, "Madisonville Metal."
123. Martha L. Sempowski, "Early Historic Exchange Between the Seneca and the Susquehannock."
124. Clark, *Shawnee*, p. 18.
125. Hanna, *Wilderness Trail*, pp. 138–143.
126. Hanna, *Wilderness Trail*, p. 138.
127. For example, see C. Wesley Cowan, "The Dawn of History and the Demise of the Fort Ancient Cultures of the Central Ohio Valley," p. 16.
128. Cf. Drooker, *View from Madisonville*, pp. 209–210.
129. Drooker, *View from Madisonville*, pp. 109–110, 153, 200–202.
130. Drooker, *View from Madisonville*, pp. 335–337.
131. Mildred M. Wedel, "Oneota Sites on the Upper Iowa River"; Mildred M. Wedel, "The Ioway, Oto, and Omaha Indians in 1700"; Mildred M. Wedel, "Peering at the Ioway Indians Through the Mist of Time: 1650–circa 1700."
132. Hanna, *Wilderness Trail*, p. 138.
133. Temple, *Indian Villages*, pp. 175–176.
134. For example, see Jennings, *Ambiguous Iroquois*, pp. 325–346.
135. Kent, *Susquehanna's Indians*, p. 91.
136. Anthony, "Migration."
137. Anderson, *Relation of Henri de Tonti*, pp. 111, 113; Anderson, *Relation of the Discoveries*, p. 259; Callender, "Shawnee," p. 630; Hanna, *Wilderness Trail*, pp. 124–125.
138. Hanna, *Wilderness Trail*, pp. 138–143, quotation from p. 139; Jennings, *Ambiguous Iroquois*, pp. 200–202, 206.

Notes to THE CULTURAL LANDSCAPE OF THE NORTH CAROLINA PIEDMONT AT CONTACT
by R. P. Stephen Davis, Jr.

1. Albert Gatschet, "Grammatic Sketch of the Catawba Language."
2. Horatio Hale, "The Tutelo Tribe and Language."
3. James Mooney, *The Siouan Tribes of the East*.
4. John Swanton, "Early History of the Eastern Siouan Tribes."
5. Frank Speck, "Siouan Tribes of the Carolinas."
6. R. P. Stephen Davis, Jr., and H. Trawick Ward, "The Evolution of Siouan Com-

munities in Piedmont North Carolina"; Howard A. MacCord, Sr., "Prehistoric Territoriality in Virginia."

7. Davis and Ward, "Evolution of Siouan Communities."

8. See Charles M. Hudson, *The Juan Pardo Expeditions: Spanish Explorers and the Indians of the Carolinas and Tennessee, 1566–1568,* pp. ix–x.

9. Karen M. Booker, Charles M. Hudson, and Robert L. Rankin, "Place Name Identification and Multilingualism in the Sixteenth-Century Southeast," p. 410.

10. David J. Hally, "An Overview of Lamar Culture."

11. Chester B. DePratter, "Cofitachequi: Ethnohistorical and Archaeological Evidence."

12. DePratter, "Cofitachequi."

13. David G. Moore, *Late Prehistoric and Early Historic Period Aboriginal Settlement in the Catawba Valley, North Carolina.*

14. Mooney, *Siouan Tribes,* p. 6.

15. John Lawson, *A New Voyage to Carolina by John Lawson,* p. 232.

16. David Moore, *Late Prehistoric.*

17. Robin A. Beck, Jr., "From Joara to Chiaha: Spanish Exploration of the Appalachian Summit Area, 1540–1568."

18. Beck, "From Joara to Chiaha; see also Charles M. Hudson, Marvin T. Smith, and Chester B. DePratter, "The Hernando De Soto Expedition: From Apalachee to Chiaha."

19. Edward Bland, *The Discovery of New Brittaine.*

20. Lewis Binford, *Cultural Diversity Among Aboriginal Cultures of Coastal Virginia and North Carolina.*

21. John Lederer, *The Discoveries of John Lederer.*

22. Lederer, *Discoveries.*

23. See Clarence W. Alvord and Lee Bidgood, *The First Explorations of the Trans-Allegheny Region by the Virginians, 1650–1674,* p. 68.

24. Alvord and Bidgood, *First Explorations,* pp. 183–205.

25. Alvord and Bidgood, *First Explorations,* pp. 59–61.

26. Mooney, *Siouan Tribes,* p. 38; William Byrd, *The Prose Works of William Byrd of Westover,* p. 384.

27. Gregory A. Waselkov, "Seventeenth-Century Trade in the Colonial Southeast," p. 118.

28. See Alvord and Bidgood, *First Explorations,* pp. 209–226; James Needham and Gabriel Arthur, "The Travels of James Needham and Gabriel Arthur Through Virginia, North Carolina, and Beyond, 1673–1674."

29. Moore, *Late Prehistoric.*

30. Jack H. Wilson, Jr., *A Study of Late Prehistoric, Protohistoric, and Historic Indians of the Carolina and Virginia Piedmont: Structure, Process, and Ecology.*

31. J. Ned Woodall, *The Donnaha Site: 1973, 1975 Excavations.*

32. John R. Swanton, *The Indians of the Southeastern United States,* p. 208.

33. Warren M. Billings, *The Old Dominion in the Seventeenth Century.*

34. Anonymous, "Virginias Deploured Condition; Or an Impartiall Narrative of the Murders Comitted by the Indians There, and of the Sufferings of His Majesties Loyall Subjects under the Rebellious Outrages of Mr. Nathaniell Bacon, June to the Tenth Day of August Anno Domini 1676," p. 167.

35. R. P. Stephen, Davis, Jr., and H. Trawick Ward, "The Occaneechi and Their Role as Middlemen in the Seventeenth-Century Virginia–North Carolina Trade Network."

36. Daniel L. Simpkins, *Aboriginal Intersite Settlement System Change in the Northeastern North Carolina Piedmont During the Contact Period.*

37. H. Trawick Ward and R. P. Stephen Davis, Jr., "The Impact of Old World Diseases on the Native Inhabitants of the North Carolina Piedmont."

38. Elizabeth I. Monahan, R. P. Stephen Davis, Jr., and H. Trawick Ward, "Piedmont Siouans and Mortuary Archaeology on the Eno River, North Carolina."

39. Lawson, *New Voyage*, p. 232.

40. Lawson, *New Voyage*; Mooney, *Siouan Tribes*.

41. James Adair, *Adair's History of the American Indians*.

42. For a discussion of the causes of Iroquois warfare during the seventeenth century, see Bruce G. Trigger, "Early Iroquoian Contacts with Europeans," pp. 352–354.

43. Byrd, *Prose Works*, p. 398.

44. See John Fontaine, *The Journal of John Fontaine, An Irish Huguenot Son in Spain and Virginia 1710–1719*, p. 9.

45. Mooney, *Siouan Tribes*, p. 6.

46. E. Lawrence Lee, *Indian Wars in North Carolina 1663–1763*.

47. James H. Merrell, *The Indians' New World: Catawbas and Their Neighbors from European Contact through the Era of Removal*, pp. 102–103.

48. Sources of information for the maps of the cultural landscape in 1540, 1567, and 1600 are John Smith, *Travels and Works of Captain John Smith*; Beck, "From Joara to Chiaha"; Binford, *Cultural Diversity*; Bland, *The Discovery of New Brittaine*; Douglas W. Boyce, "Iroquois Tribes of the Virginia–North Carolina Coastal Plain"; Davis and Ward, "Evolution of Siouan Communities"; Roy S. Dickens, Jr., "The Origins and Development of Cherokee Culture"; Hudson, *Juan Pardo Expeditions*; Mooney, *Siouan Tribes*; Moore, *Late Prehistoric*.

49. After Beck, "From Joara to Chiaha"; Hudson, *Juan Pardo Expeditions*.

50. Moore, *Late Prehistoric*; Beck, "From Joara to Chiaha."

51. Davis and Ward, "Evolution of Siouan Communities."

52. Sources of information for the map of the cultural landscape in 1650 are Beck, "From Joara to Chiaha"; Binford, *Cultural Diversity*; Bland, *The Discovery of New Brittaine*; Boyce, "Iroquois Tribes"; Davis and Ward, "Evolution of Siouan Communities"; Dickens, "Origins and Development"; Lederer, *Discoveries*; Mooney, *Siouan Tribes*; Moore, *Late Prehistoric*.

53. Bland, *The Discovery of New Brittaine*.

54. H. Trawick Ward and R. P. Stephen Davis, Jr., *Indian Communities on the North Carolina Piedmont*, A.D. 1000 to 1700.

55. Lederer, *Discoveries*.

56. Moore, *Late Prehistoric*.

57. William C. Johnson, "The Protohistoric Monongahela and the Case for an Iroquois Connection"; William C. Johnson, personal communication, 1998.

58. Sources of information for the maps of the cultural landscape in 1670 and 1676 are Alvord and Bidgood, *First Explorations*; Binford, *Cultural Diversity*; Boyce, "Iroquois Tribes"; Davis and Ward, "Evolution of Siouan Communities"; Dickens, "Origins and Development"; Lederer, *Discoveries*; Mooney, *Siouan Tribes*; Moore, *Late Prehistoric*.

59. Alvord and Bidgood, *First Explorations*; Lederer, *Discoveries*.

60. Ward and Davis, *Indian Communities*.

61. Francis Jennings, "Susquehannock."

62. Mooney, *Siouan Tribes*, p. 38.

63. Sources of information for the map of the cultural landscape in 1700 are Boyce, "Iroquois Tribes"; Davis and Ward, "Evolution of Siouan Communities"; Dickens, "Origins and Development"; Lawson, *New Voyage*; Mooney, *Siouan Tribes*.

64. R. P. Stephen Davis, Jr., Patrick C. Livingood, H. Trawick Ward, and Vincas P. Steponaitis, *Excavating Occaneechi Town: Archaeology of an Eighteenth-Century Indian Village in North Carolina*; Roy S. Dickens, Jr., H. Trawick Ward, and R. P. Stephen Davis, Jr., *The Siouan Project: Seasons I and II*; Ward and Davis, *Indian Communities*.

65. Ward and Davis, "Impact of Old World Diseases."

66. Lawson, *New Voyage*, pp. 39–50, 61.

67. Sources of information for the map of the cultural landscape in 1720 are Boyce, "Iroquois Tribes"; Dickens, "Origins and Development"; Mooney, *Siouan Tribes*; Adair, *Adair's History*; Byrd, *Prose Works*.

68. Byrd, *Prose Works*, pp. 307–309.
69. Mooney, *Siouan Tribes*.
70. Mooney, *Siouan Tribes*, pp. 21, 37.
71. Adair, *Adair's History*.
72. See Mooney, *Siouan Tribes*; Douglas L. Rights, *The American Indian in North Carolina*; Speck, "Siouan Tribes"; Swanton, "Early History."

Notes to RECONSTRUCTING THE COALESCENCE OF CHEROKEE
COMMUNITIES IN SOUTHERN APPALACHIA
by Christopher B. Rodning

1. David G. Anderson, *The Savannah River Chiefdoms: Political Change in the Late Prehistoric Southeast*, pp. 302–307.
2. David H. Corkran, *The Creek Frontier, 1540–1783*, pp. 145–159; M. Thomas Hatley, *The Dividing Paths: Cherokees and South Carolinians Through the Revolutionary Era*, pp. 156–159.
3. Lynne P. Sullivan, "Mississippian Community and Household Organization in Eastern Tennessee," pp. 100–103.
4. William W. Baden, *Tomotley: An Eighteenth Century Cherokee Village*, pp.10–17; David H. Corkran, *The Cherokee Frontier, 1740–1762*, pp. 25–37.
5. Lance K. Greene, "The Archaeology and History of the Cherokee Out Towns."
6. Roy S. Dickens, Jr., "The Route of Rutherford's Expedition Against the North Carolina Cherokees."
7. G. Gary C. Goodwin, *Cherokees in Transition: A Study of Changing Culture and Environment Prior to 1775*, p. 113; Charles M. Hudson, *The Southeastern Indians*, pp. 191–194.
8. Duane Champagne, "Symbolic Structure and Political Change in Cherokee Society," p. 56; Hudson, *Southeastern Indians*, pp. 237–238.
9. See Anderson, *Savannah River Chiefdoms*; John F. Blitz, "Mississippian Chiefdoms and the Fission-Fusion Process"; David Hally, "The Settlement Pattern of Mississippian Chiefdoms in Northern Georgia"; Adam King, "De Soto's Itaba and the Nature of Sixteenth Century Paramount Chiefdoms"; John F. Scarry, "The Late Prehistoric Southeast"; Mark Williams, "Growth and Decline of the Oconee Province."
10. See Goodwin, *Cherokees in Transition*, pp. 38–48; Hatley, *Dividing Paths*, pp. 3–16; Schroedl, "Mississippian Towns in the Eastern Tennessee Valley"; p. 64; Sullivan, "Mississippian Community," p. 120.
11. Karen M. Booker, Charles M. Hudson, and Robert L. Rankin, "Place Name Identification and Multilingualism in the Sixteenth-Century Southeast," pp. 410–411; Charles M. Hudson, *The Juan Pardo Expeditions: Explorations of the Carolinas and Tennessee, 1566–1568*, pp. 95–96.
12. Mark S. Aldenderfer and Charles Stanish, "Domestic Architecture, Household Archaeology, and the Past in the South-Central Andes," pp. 7–8; Geoffrey Emberling, "Ethnicity in Complex Societies," pp. 310–320; David J. Hally, "The Cherokee Archaeology of Georgia," pp. 118–119; David J. Hally, "Lamar Archaeology," pp. 172–173; Sian Jones, *The Archaeology of Ethnicity: Constructing Identities in the Past and Present*, pp. 125–127; Catherine Morgan, "Ethnicity and Early Greek States: Historical and Material Perspectives," pp. 131–135; Stephen J. Shennan, "Archaeological Approaches to Cultural Identity," pp. 20–21; Charles Stanish, "Household Archaeology: Testing Models of Zonal Complementarity in the South Central Andes," pp. 7–8; Gregory A. Waselkov and John W. Cottier, "European Perceptions of Eastern Muskogean Ethnicity," pp. 28–29.
13. Hudson, *Juan Pardo*, p. 109; Scarry, "Late Prehistoric," p. 25.
14. Booker et al., "Place Name," pp. 432–433; Hudson, *Juan Pardo*, pp. 98–105.
15. See Anderson, *Savannah River Chiefdoms*, pp. 324–332; Blitz, "Mississippian

Chiefdoms"; Timothy K. Earle, *How Chiefs Come to Power: The Political Economy in Prehistory.*

16. See Penelope B. Drooker, *The View from Madisonville: Protohistoric Western Fort Ancient Interaction Patterns*, pp. 39–62; Michael A. Harmon, *Eighteenth Century Lower Cherokee Adaptation and Use of Material Cultures*; Hatley, *Dividing Paths.*

17. Raymond D. Fogelson, "Cherokee Notions of Power"; Ralph J. Randolph, *British Travelers Among the Southern Indians, 1660–1763*, p. 151.

18. Frederick O. Gearing, *Priests and Warriors: Social Structures for Cherokee Politics in the Eighteenth Century*; Randolph, *British Travelers*, p. 152.

19. Champagne, "Symbolic Structure," pp.88–90; Duane Champagne, "Institutional and Cultural Order in Early Cherokee Society: A Sociological Interpretation," pp. 14–20.

20. Hally, "Lamar Archaeology"; David J. Hally, "The Chiefdom of Coosa"; King, "De Soto's Itaba"; Williams, "Growth and Decline."

21. Champagne, "Institutional and Cultural Order," pp. 28–29.

22. Theda Perdue, *Cherokee Women: Gender and Culture Change, 1700–1835*, pp. 40–46.

23. M. Thomas Hatley, "Cherokee Women Farmers Hold Their Ground," p.37; Sarah H. Hill, *Weaving New Worlds: Southeastern Cherokee Women and Their Basketry*, p. 98.

24. Roy S. Dickens, Jr., "The Origins and Development of Cherokee Culture," p. 28; Hatley, *Dividing Paths*, p. 10.

25. Perdue, *Cherokee Women*, p. 42.

26. Hill, *Weaving New Worlds*, p. 27.

27. Vernon J. Knight, Jr., "Social Organization and the Evolution of Hierarchy in Southeastern Chiefdoms," p. 5.

28. V. Richard Persico, Jr., "Early Nineteenth-Century Cherokee Political Organization," p. 93.

29. Perdue, *Cherokee Women*, p. 17.

30. Champagne, "Symbolic Structure"; Champagne, "Institutional and Cultural Order"; Frederick O. Gearing, "The Structural Poses of the Eighteenth-Century Cherokee Villages"; Gearing, *Priests and Warriors*; Persico, "Early Nineteenth-Century," p. 93.

31. Patricia Galloway, "Confederacy as a Solution to Chiefdom Dissolution: Historical Evidence in the Choctaw Case"; Galloway, *Choctaw Genesis*; see also Duane Champagne, *Social Order and Political Change: Constitutional Governments Among the Cherokee, the Chickasaw, the Choctaw, and the Creek*, p. 26; John F. Blitz, *An Archaeological Study of the Mississippi Choctaw Indians*; John F. Blitz, "Choctaw Archaeology in Mississippi"; Timothy Paul Mooney, "Migration of the Chickasawhay into the Choctaw Homeland"; Timothy Paul Mooney, "Choctaw Culture Compromise and Change Between the Eighteenth and Early Nineteenth Centuries: An Analysis of the Collections from Seven Sites from the Choctaw Homeland in East-Central Mississippi"; Timothy Paul Mooney, *Many Choctaw Standing: An Archaeological Study of Culture Change in the Early Historic Period.*

32. Galloway, *Choctaw Genesis*, pp. 352–260.

33. Galloway, "Confederacy," pp. 393–394.

34. Knight, *Tukabatchee*; Vernon J. Knight, Jr., "The Formation of the Creeks"; see also Champagne, *Social Order*, p. 27; Braund, *Deerskins and Duffels*; Frederica R. Dimmick, "A Survey of Upper Creek Sites in Central Alabama"; Terry L. Lolley, "Ethnohistory and Archaeology: A Map Method for Locating Historic Upper Creek Indian Towns and Villages"; Gregory A. Waselkov, "Historic Creek Indian Responses to European Trade and the Rise of Political Factions"; Gregory A. Waselkov, "The Macon Trading House and Early European-Indian Contact in the Colonial Southeast."

35. Booker et al., "Place Name," p. 411; Knight, "Formation of the Creeks," p. 379.

36. Booker et al., "Place Name," p. 411; Braund, *Deerskins and Duffels*, p. 7.

37. Betty A. Smith, "Distribution of Eighteenth-Century Cherokee Settlements," pp.47–52; Marvin T. Smith, *The Archaeology of Aboriginal Culture Change: Depopulation During the Early Historic Period*, pp. 140–142.

38. David J. Hally and Hypatia Kelly, "The Nature of Mississippian Towns in Northern Georgia: The King Site Example," pp. 55–63; Schroedl, "Mississippian Towns," p.91; Lynne P. Sullivan, "Household, Community, and Society: An Analysis of Mouse Creek Settlements," p. 120; H. Trawick Ward and R. P. Stephen Davis, Jr., *Time Before History: The Archaeology of North Carolina*, pp. 158–190.

39. Charles M. Hudson, *Knights of Spain, Warriors of the Sun: Hernando de Soto and the South's Ancient Chiefdoms*, pp. 190–199.

40. Robin A. Beck, "From Joara to Chiaha: Spanish Exploration of the Appalachian Summit Area, 1540–1568," pp. 163–167.

41. Gerald F. Schroedl, "Toward an Explanation of Cherokee Origins in East Tennessee," p. 132; see also Baden, *Tomotley*; Jefferson Chapman, *Tellico Archaeology: Twelve Thousand Years of Native American History*; Kurt C. Russ and Jefferson Chapman, *Archaeological Investigations at the Eighteenth Century Overhill Cherokee Town of Mialoquo*; Alfred K. Guthe, "The Eighteenth Century Overhill Cherokee"; Richard R. Polhemus, *The Toqua Site: A Late Mississippian Dallas Phase Town*; Gerald F. Schroedl, "Louis-Phillipe's Journal and Archaeological Investigations at the Overhill Town of Toqua."

42. Schroedl, "Toward an Explanation," pp. 123–129.

43. Schroedl, "Toward an Explanation," pp. 129–132.

44. David Hally, "Cherokee Archaeology," p. 112; see also Anderson, *Savannah River Chiefdoms*, pp. 205–217; Jack T. Wynn, *The Mississippi Period Archaeology of the Georgia Blue Ridge*, pp. 54–58.

45. Brian J.Egloff, "An Analysis of Ceramics from Historic Cherokee Towns," pp. 72–73; Marvin T. Smith, *Historic Period Indian Archaeology of Northern Georgia*, pp. 66–68; see also Hally, "Cherokee Archaeology"; David J. Hally, "The Identification of Vessel Function: A Case Study from Northwest Georgia."

46. A. Eric Howard, *An Intrasite Spatial Analysis of Surface Collections at Chattooga: A Lower Cherokee Village*; Gerald F. Schroedl, *A Summary of Archaeological Activities Conducted at the Chattooga Site, Oconee County, South Carolina*; see also Gerald F. Schroedl, *Overhill Cherokee Archaeology at Chota-Tanasee*, pp. 307–315; Gerald F. Schroedl and Brett H. Riggs, "Investigations of Cherokee Village Patterning and Public Architecture at the Chattooga Site."

47. Williams, "Growth and Decline," pp. 187–193; see also King, "De Soto's Itaba."

48. Anderson, *Savannah River Chiefdoms*, pp. 326–329; see also David J. Hally, "The Territorial Size of Mississippian Chiefdoms."

49. Hally, "Cherokee Archaeology," pp. 98–112.

50. Hally, "Cherokee Archaeology," p. 112.

51. David G. Anderson, David J. Hally, and James L. Rudolph, "The Mississippian Occupation of the Savannah River Valley," pp. 47–48.

52. Hally, "Cherokee Archaeology," p. 111.

53. Anderson, *Savannah River Chiefdoms*, p. 304.

54. Roy S. Dickens, Jr., "An Evolutionary-Ecological Interpretation of Cherokee Cultural Development," p. 90; see also Roy S. Dickens, Jr., *Cherokee Prehistory: The Pisgah Phase in the Appalachian Summit*, pp. 210–214; Bennie C. Keel, *Cherokee Archaeology: A Study of the Appalachian Summit*, pp. 214–218.

55. Roy S. Dickens, Jr., "Mississippian Settlement Patterns in the Appalachian Summit Area: The Pisgah and Qualla Phases," pp. 125–126; Frank M. Setzler and Jesse D. Jennings, *Peachtree Mound and Village Site, Cherokee County, North Carolina*, pp. 50–57.

56. Greene, "Archaeology and History," pp. 29–37; Ward and Davis, *Time Before History*, pp. 179–183.

57. See Dickens, "Mississippian Settlement," pp. 132–135.

58. See Dickens, "Origins," pp. 20–28.

59. Ward and Davis, *Time Before History*, p. 180.

60. Dickens, "Mississippian Settlement," p. 124; Ward and Davis, *Time Before History*, pp. 183–190.

61. Egloff, "Analysis of Ceramics," p. 38; see also Dickens, "Origins," p. 24.

62. Keith T. Egloff, "Methods and Problems of Mound Excavation in the South Appalachian Area," p. 62; see also Dickens, "Mississippian Settlement," p. 131.

63. Burton L. Purrington, "Ancient Mountaineers: An Overview of the Prehistoric
Archaeology of North Carolina's Western Mountain Region," pp. 142–151; Ward and
Davis, *Time Before History*, pp. 180–181.

64. Williams, "Growth and Decline," pp. 188–193, and Anderson, *Savannah River
Chiefdoms*, pp. 326–329.

65. Ward and Davis, *Time Before History*, p. 178.

66. Crane, *Southern Frontier*, pp. 130–131; Goodwin, *Cherokees in Transition*, pp.
117–123; William Bartram, *William Bartram on the Southeastern Indians*, pp. 74–78.

67. Smith, *Historic Period*, pp. 24, 30.

68. Hally, "Lamar Archaeology"; Hally, "Chiefdom of Coosa"; Hudson, *Southeastern
Indians*, pp. 237–239; Hudson, *Juan Pardo*, pp. 94–101; Hudson, *Knights of Spain*, pp.
190–199; Ward and Davis, *Time Before History*, pp. 158–178.

69. Smith, *Historic Period*, pp. 112, 128.

70. Dickens, "Mississippian Settlement"; Richard R. Polhemus, "Dallas Phase Architecture and Sociopolitical Structure"; Schroedl, "Mississippian Towns"; Sullivan, "Mississippian Community."

71. Harmon, *Eighteenth Century*; Brett H. Riggs, "Interhousehold Variability Among
Early Nineteenth Century Cherokee Artifact Assemblages"; Gerald F. Schroedl, "Over-
hill Cherokee Household and Village Patterns in the Eighteenth Century"; Sullivan,
"Household."

72. Wynn, *Mississippi Period*, p. 58.

73. Schroedl, "Mississippian Towns," p. 89.

74. David G. Moore, "An Overview of Historic Aboriginal Public Architecture in
Western North Carolina"; Christopher B. Rodning, "Archaeological Perspectives on Gender and Women in Traditional Cherokee Society," p. 9.

75. Richard Pillsbury, "The Europeanization of the Cherokee Settlement Landscape
Prior to Removal: A Georgia Case Study," p. 59; Douglas C. Wilms, "Cherokee Settlement Patterns in Nineteenth-Century Georgia," pp. 46–53; Douglas C. Wilms, "Cherokee Land Use in Georgia Before Removal."

76. Dickens, "Route of Rutherford's Expedition"; Rodning, "Archaeological Perspectives," p. 8.

77. Dickens, "Mississippian Settlement," pp. 133–134.

78. Rodning, "Archaeological Perspectives," pp. 12–13.

79. Goodwin, *Cherokees in Transition*, p. 113; Hudson, *Southeastern Indians*, p. 238.

80. Marvin T. Smith, "Aboriginal Depopulation in the Postcontact Southeast"; see
also Anderson, *Savannah River Chiefdoms*; Williams, "Growth and Decline."

81. Joel W. Martin, "Southeastern Indians and the English Trade in Skins and
Slaves"; see also Crane, *Southern Frontier*; Gregory A. Waselkov, "Seventeenth-Century
Trade in the Colonial Southeast."

82. See Gregory A. Waselkov, "Changing Strategies of Indian Field Location in the
Early Historic Southeast."

83. See James W. Hatch, "Lamar Period Upland Farmsteads of the Oconee River
Valley, Georgia."

84. Wynn, *Mississippi Period*, pp. 54–55; David Hally, personal communication,
1997.

85. Susan M. Collins, *A Prehistoric Community at the Macon County Industrial Park
Site*, pp. 17–39; David Moore, personal communication, 1999.

86. See Schroedl, "Mississippian Towns"; Sullivan, "Mississippian Community."

87. But see C. Michael Baker, "Archaeological Investigation of a Late Prehistoric Settlement in the Little Tennessee Drainage, Macon County, North Carolina"; Brett H.
Riggs, M. Scott Shumate, and Patti Evans-Shumate, *Archaeological Site Survey and Test-*

ing at Site 31Jk291, Jackson County, North Carolina; Brett H. Riggs, M. Scott Shumate, and Patti Evans-Shumate, *Archaeological Data Recovery at Site 31Jk291, Jackson County, North Carolina*; Brett H. Riggs, M. Scott Shumate, Patti Evans-Shumate, and Brad Bowden, *An Archaeological Survey of the Ferguson Farm, Swain County, North Carolina*; M. Scott Shumate and Larry R. Kimball, *Archaeological Data Recovery at 31Sw273 on the Davis Cemetery Tract, Nantahala National Forest, Swain County, North Carolina*; Waselkov, "Changing Strategies"; Bartram, *William Bartram.*

88. Anderson, *Savannah River Chiefdoms*, pp. 311–313; Chester B. DePratter, "The Chiefdom of Cofitachequi"; King, "De Soto's Itaba," p. 114; Scarry, "Late Prehistoric," p. 30; Schroedl, "Mississippian Towns," p. 91; Marvin T. Smith and Julie Barnes Smith, "Engraved Shell Masks in North America," pp. 14–16.

89. Anderson, *Savannah River Chiefdoms*, pp. 308–309; Chester B. DePratter, *Late Prehistoric and Early Historic Chiefdoms in the Southeastern United States*; Vernon J. Knight, Jr., "Moundville as a Diagrammatic Ceremonial Center," pp. 47–53; Marvin T. Smith and Mark Williams, "Mississippian Mound Refuse Disposal Patterns and Implications for Archaeological Research," pp. 32–33.

90. Gearing, *Priests and Warriors*, p. 38; Persico, "Early Nineteenth-Century," p. 95.

91. Hill, *Weaving New Worlds*, p. 32; Perdue, *Cherokee Women*, p. 42.

92. Gearing, *Priests and Warriors.*

93. Richard A. Sattler, "Women's Status Among the Muskogee and Cherokee."

94. See Waselkov, "Changing Strategies," p. 183.

95. See Hill, *Weaving New Worlds*, p. 28.

96. Perdue, *Cherokee Women*, p. 46.

97. Perdue, *Cherokee Women*, pp. 27, 43; Schroedl, *Overhill Cherokee*, p. 228.

98. See Hill, *Weaving New Worlds*, p. 73; Ruth Y. Wetmore, "The Green Corn Ceremony of the Eastern Cherokees," p. 47.

99. See H. Trawick Ward, "Social Implications of Storage and Disposal Patterns," pp. 97–101; Cameron B. Wesson, "Chiefly Power and Food Storage in Southeastern North America," pp. 157–158.

100. See Riggs, "Interhousehold Variability," p. 328.

101. James Axtell, *The Indians' New South: Cultural Change in the Colonial Southeast*; Champagne, *Social Order*, pp. 50–86; Crane, *Southern Frontier*; Hatley, *Dividing Paths*, pp. 32–41; Martin, "Southeastern Indians"; Waselkov, "Seventeenth-Century Trade."

102. See Hatley, "Cherokee Women Farmers," p. 47; Hill, *Weaving New Worlds*, p. 98; Perdue, *Cherokee Women*, pp. 74–76.

103. See Hatley, "Cherokee Women Farmers," p. 52; Hill, *Weaving New Worlds*, p. 17; Perdue, *Cherokee Women*, pp. 70–81.

104. Schroedl, "Toward an Explanation"; see also Anderson, *Savannah River Chiefdoms*, p. 328; Leland G. Ferguson, "South Appalachian Mississippian," p. 11.

105. Hally, "Cherokee Archaeology"; see also David J. Hally and James B. Langford, *Mississippi Period Archaeology of the Georgia Valley and Ridge Province*, pp. 67–79; David J. Hally and James L. Rudolph, *Mississippi Period Archaeology of the Georgia Piedmont*, pp. 63–80.

106. Dickens, "Evolutionary-Ecological Interpretation," p. 90; see also Joffre Lanning Coe, "Cherokee Archaeology," p. 61.

107. Dickens, "Mississippian Settlement," p. 136; see also Hudson, *Knights of Spain*, p. 194.

108. See James B. Griffin, "Foreword," pp. xx–xxi.

109. See Schroedl, "Mississippian Towns," pp. 88–89.

Notes to FROM PREHISTORY THROUGH PROTOHISTORY TO ETHNOHISTORY IN AND NEAR THE NORTHERN LOWER MISSISSIPPI VALLEY
by Marvin D. Jeter

1. Christopher Carr, *For Concordance in Archaeological Analysis: Bridging Data Structure, Quantitative Technique, and Theory.*

2. Edward O. Wilson, *Consilience: The Unity of Knowledge*.
3. Marvin D. Jeter, "Tunicans West of the Mississippi: A Summary of Early Historic and Archaeological Evidence," pp. 39, 42.
4. Marvin D. Jeter, "Review of *Tunica Archaeology*, by Jeffrey P. Brain"; Marvin D. Jeter et al., *Archeology and Bioarcheology of the Lower Mississippi Valley and Trans-Mississippi South in Arkansas and Louisiana*; Marvin D. Jeter, Kathleen H. Cande, and John J. Mintz, *Goldsmith Oliver 2 (3PU306): A Protohistoric Archeological Site near Little Rock, Arkansas*.
5. Cf. Albert C. Spaulding, "Review of 'Method and Theory in American Archaeology' by Philip Phillips and Gordon R. Willey"; Gordon R. Willey and Philip Phillips, *Method and Theory in American Archaeology*; Jeter et al., *Archeology and Bioarcheology*, p. 57ff.
6. Instead of the Willey-Phillips term "culture," some (especially followers of the "evolutionary archaeology" movement) would prefer "form" or "content" (see Michael J. O'Brien and Robert C. Dunnell, *Changing Perspectives on the Archaeology of the Central Mississippi Valley*, pp. 20–21, and Michael J. O'Brien and W. Raymond Wood, *The Prehistory of Missouri*, pp. 6–32, 358–365), or simply "material" (see Ann F. Ramenofsky and Anastasia Steffen, *Unit Issues in Archaeology: Measuring Time, Space and Material*).
7. Jeffrey P. Brain, "Update of De Soto Studies Since the United States De Soto Expedition Commission Report," pp. xlvi–xlvii.
8. Jeffrey P. Brain, "A Note on the River of Anilco," pp. 116–117.
9. John R. Swanton, *Final Report of the United States De Soto Expedition Commission*, pp. 325–331.
10. Cf. Marvin Harris, *The Rise of Anthropological Theory: A History of Theories of Culture* and *Cultural Materialism: The Struggle for a Science of Culture*.
11. Harris, *The Rise of Anthropological Theory* and *Cultural Materialism*.
12. Cf. Willey and Phillips, *Method and Theory*; Philip Phillips, *Archaeological Survey in the Lower Yazoo Basin, Mississippi, 1949–1955*; Jeffrey P. Brain, "The Archaeological Phase: Ethnographic Fact or Fancy?"; Brain, *Tunica Archaeology*; Stephen Williams and Jeffrey P. Brain, *Excavations at the Lake George Site, Yazoo County, Mississippi, 1958–1960*.
13. Phyllis A. Morse, *Parkin: The 1978–1979 Archeological Investigation of a Cross County, Arkansas, Site*; Dan F. Morse and Phyllis A. Morse, *Archaeology of the Central Mississippi Valley*; Charles Hudson, "De Soto in Arkansas: A Brief Synopsis"; Charles Hudson, "Reconstructing the de Soto Expedition Route West of the Mississippi River: Summary and Comments."
14. Jeter, "Tunicans West"; Jeter, "Review of *Tunica Archaeology*"; cf. John H. House and Henry S. McKelway, "Mississippian and Quapaw on the Lower Arkansas."
15. Spaulding, "Review of 'Method and Theory,'" p. 86; Marvin D. Jeter, "The Archeology of Southeast Arkansas: An Overview for the 1980s," p. 110ff.
16. Harold N. Fisk, *Geological Investigation of the Alluvial Valley of the Lower Mississippi River*; Roger T. Saucier, *Quaternary Geology of the Lower Mississippi Valley*; Roger T. Saucier, *Geomorphology and Geologic History of the Lower Mississippi Valley*.
17. Philip Phillips, James A. Ford, and James B. Griffin, *Archaeological Survey in the Lower Mississippi Alluvial Valley, 1940–1947*, p. 5ff; Phillips, *Archaeological Survey*.
18. I reject the usage "Central Mississippi valley" (CMV), recently promulgated by my colleagues Dan and Phyllis Morse (see Morse and Morse, *Archaeology*; Dan F. Morse and Phyllis A. Morse, "Changes in Interpretation in the Archaeology of the Central Mississippi Valley since 1983"; Dan F. Morse and Phyllis A. Morse, "Northeast Arkansas") as referring to the alluvial lands between the mouths of the Ohio and the Arkansas, and note with some dismay that it seems to be catching on, with variable "archaeocentric" meanings, in some quarters (e.g., Charles H. McNutt, *Prehistory of the Central Mississippi Valley*; O'Brien and Dunnell, *Changing Perspectives*). The territory under consideration here also has a large amount of overlap with the "Mid-South" as defined in terms of present-

day behavior and ideology by participants in the annual Mid-South Archaeological Conference (cf. Marvin D. Jeter, "Edward Palmer and Other Victorian Pioneers in Mid-South Archeology" and other papers in Martha Ann Rolingson, *The History of Archeology in the Mid-South*), centered more or less on Memphis, but that concept generally includes uplands east of the Mississippi Valley that I do not survey here.

19. James A. Ford, *Menard Site: The Quapaw Village of Osotouy on the Arkansas River*; John H. House, " 'The Most Historic Place in Arkansas': The 1997 Society-Survey Training Program at the Menard-Hodges Archeological Site, Arkansas County, Arkansas"; John House, Mary Evelyn Starr, and Leslie C. Stewart-Abernathy, "Rediscovering Menard"; David R. Jeane, "Osotouy: The Quapaw Village Relocated Again?"

20. John H. House, "Continuing Field Studies at the Sarassa Lake Site"; John H. House, "Noble Lake: A Protohistoric Archeological Site on the Lower Arkansas River."

21. Jeter et al., *Goldsmith Oliver 2*; Charles Peabody, *Exploration of Mounds, Coahoma County, Mississippi*; John M. Connaway, *The Oliver Site in Northwest Mississippi*; Marvin D. Jeter, "Oliver, as Seen from Goldsmith Oliver—and Beyond"; Marvin D. Jeter, *The Goldsmith Oliver 2 Site (3PU306): Protohistoric Archeology, Ethnohistory, and Interactions in the Arkansas-Mississippi Valleys and Beyond*.

22. Michael P. Hoffman, "The Kinkead-Mainard Site, 3PU2: A Late Prehistoric Quapaw Phase Site near Little Rock, Arkansas"; "The Protohistoric Period in the Lower and Central Arkansas River Valley in Arkansas"; "The Terminal Mississippian Period in the Arkansas River Valley and Quapaw Ethnogenesis"; "Quapaw Structures, 1673–1834, and Their Comparative Significance"; "Protohistoric Tunican Indians in Arkansas"; "Ethnic Identities and Cultural Change in the Protohistoric Period of Eastern Arkansas"; "Protohistoric Tunican Indians in Arkansas."

23. Mark R. Harrington, "A Pot-Hunters' Paradise."

24. Phyllis Clancy, "The Carden's Bottom Puzzle Elucidated."

25. Leslie C. Stewart-Abernathy, "The Carden Bottom Project, Yell County, Arkansas: From Dalton to Trade Beads, So Far."

26. Frank F. Schambach, "Some New Interpretations of Spiroan Culture History"; Frank F. Schambach, "Spiro and the Tunica: A New Interpretation of the Role of the Tunica in the Culture History of the Southeast and the Southern Plains, A.D. 1100–1750."

27. Jeter, "Archeology of Southeast Arkansas"; Jeter, "Tunicans West"; Marvin D. Jeter, David B. Kelley, and George P. Kelley, "The Kelley-Grimes Site: A Mississippi Period Burial Mound, Southeast Arkansas, Excavated in 1936"; Jeter et al., *Archeology and Bioarcheology*; Marvin D. Jeter and Ann M. Early, "Prehistory of the Saline River Drainage Basin, Central to Southeast Arkansas"; cf. also H. Edwin Jackson, *The Ables Creek Site: A Protohistoric Cemetery in Southeast Arkansas*; Martha Ann Rolingson, "Archeology along Bayou Bartholomew, Southeast Arkansas"; Frank F. Schambach, "A Description and Analysis of the Ceramics."

28. Williams and Brain, *Excavations at the Lake George Site*; Connaway, *The Oliver Site*.

29. David J. Hally, "The Plaquemine and Mississippian Occupations of the Upper Tensas Basin, Louisiana"; Tristram R. Kidder, "Excavations at the Jordan Site (16MO1), Morehouse Parish, Louisiana"; Tristram R. Kidder, "The Glendora Phase: Protohistoric–Early Historic Culture Dynamics on the Lower Ouachita River."

30. David H. Dye and Ronald C. Brister, *The Protohistoric Period in the Mid-South: 1500–1700*.

31. David H. Dye, "Introduction."

32. Ford, *Menard Site*; Brain, *Tunica Archaeology*; Dan F. Morse, "The Seventeenth Century Michigamea Village Location in Arkansas."

33. Jeter, "Review of *Tunica Archaeology*;" Marvin D. Jeter, "Review of *French Colonial Archaeology*, edited by John A. Walthall, and *Calumet and Fleur-de-Lys*, edited by John A. Walthall and Thomas E. Emerson"; Jeter et al., *Goldsmith Oliver 2*.

34. Robert S. Neitzel, *Archaeology of the Fatherland Site: The Grand Village of the*

Natchez; Robert S. Neitzel, *The Grand Village of the Natchez Indians Revisited: Excavations at the Fatherland Site, Adams County, Mississippi, 1972.*

35. Marvin T. Smith, *Archaeology of Aboriginal Culture Change in the Interior Southeast: Depopulation During the Early Historic Period,* pp. 7ff, 146–147; also cf. Melburn D. Thurman, "Conversations with Lewis R. Binford on Historical Archaeology," pp. 32–33.

36. Brain, "The Archaeological Phase"; Brain, "Update of De Soto"; Brain, "A Note"; Samuel D. Dickinson, "Historic Tribes of the Ouachita Drainage System in Arkansas"; Samuel D. Dickinson, "The River of Cayas: The Ouachita or the Arkansas River?"; Hudson, "De Soto in Arkansas"; Hudson, "Reconstructing"; Gloria A. Young and Michael P. Hoffman, *The Expedition of Hernando de Soto West of the Mississippi, 1541–1543*; David Henige, "Millennarian Archaeology, Double Discourse, and the Unending Quest for de Soto."

37. Jeter et al., *Goldsmith Oliver 2.*

38. Smith, *Archaeology of Aboriginal Culture Change*; Marvin T. Smith, "Glass Beads from the Goldsmith Oliver 2 Site."

39. Cf. House, "Noble Lake."

40. Phillips, *Archaeological Survey,* pp. 923–946; Morse and Morse, *Archaeology,* p. 271ff; Jeter et al., *Archeology and Bioarcheology,* p. 171ff, figs. 19–22.

41. Morse and Morse, *Archaeology*; Jeter et al., *Archeology and Bioarcheology,* p. 171ff.

42. Jeter et al., *Archeology and Bioarcheology,* figs. 15–22.

43. Cf. Morse and Morse, *Archaeology,* p. 208ff.

44. Jeter, "Tunicans West"; Jeter et al., *Archeology and Bioarcheology*; cf. Hally, "The Plaquemine"; Rolingson, "Archeology along Bayou Bartholomew," p. 134.

45. Jeffrey M. Mitchem, "Results of 1998 Research at Parkin."

46. The "St. Francis-type" sites of Phillips et al., *Archaeological Survey,* p. 329ff; cf. also Morse and Morse, *Archaeology,* p. 280ff.

47. Jeter, *Edward Palmer's*; Jeter, "Edward Palmer"; Dan F. Morse and Phyllis A. Morse, *The Lower Mississippi Valley Expeditions of Clarence Bloomfield Moore*; Dan F. Morse, *Nodena: An Account of 90 years of Archeological Investigation in Southeast Mississippi County, Arkansas.*

48. Morse, *Nodena,* p. 97ff, fig. 44.

49. Charles J. Bareis and James W. Porter, *American Bottom Archaeology: A Summary of the FAI-270 Project Contribution to the Culture History of the Mississippi River Valley*; plus numerous individual site reports.

50. Jeffrey M. Mitchem, "Village Life at Parkin in the 1500s"; Jeffrey M. Mitchem, "Investigations of the Possible Remains of de Soto's Cross at Parkin"; Jeffrey M. Mitchem,"The 1996 Field Season at Parkin Archeological State Park"; Mitchem, "Results of 1998."

51. House, "Noble Lake," pp. 55, 93.

52. Jeter, "Tunicans West"; Jeter et al., "The Kelley-Grimes Site"; Jeter et al., *Archeology and Bioarcheology*; Jackson, *The Ables Creek Site.*

53. Kidder, "The Glendora Phase," pp. 255–257.

54. See Jeter et al., *Archeology and Bioarcheology,* pp. 172, 205ff for a review.

55. Phillips, *Archaeological Survey*; Hally, "The Plaquemine"; Williams and Brain, *Excavations at the Lake George Site.*

56. Jeffrey Brain, "Late Prehistoric Settlement Patterning in the Yazoo Basin and Natchez Bluffs Regions of the Lower Mississippi Valley"; Jeffrey Brain, *Winterville: Late Prehistoric Culture Contact in the Lower Mississippi Valley*; Williams and Brain, *Excavations at the Lake George Site,* p. 409.

57. Brain, "Late Prehistoric Settlement," p.344ff; Brain, *Winterville,* pp. 122–123; Williams and Brain, *Excavations at the Lake George Site,* p. 413; Ian W. Brown, *Natchez Indian Archaeology: Culture Change and Stability in the Lower Mississippi Valley,* p. 253.

58. E.g., Williams and Brain, *Excavations at the Lake George Site,* p. 408.

59. Gayle J. Fritz and Tristram R. Kidder, "Recent Investigations into Prehistoric Agriculture in the Lower Mississippi Valley."

60. Brain, *Winterville*, fig. 82.

61. Jeter et al., *Archeology and Bioarcheology*, figs. 17–21; cf. Schambach, "A Description"; Rolingson, "Archeology along Bayou Bartholomew"; Jeter and Early, "Prehistory of the Saline River."

62. Brown, *Natchez Indian Archaeology*.

63. Brain, "Late Prehistoric Settlement," p. 347.

64. Brain, "Late Prehistoric Settlement," p. 344ff; Williams and Brain, *Excavations at the Lake George Site*, p. 413.

65. Brain, "Late Prehistoric Settlement," pp. 345, 347–350.

66. Brain, "Late Prehistoric Settlement"; Brain, *Winterville*; Jeter et al., *Archeology and Bioarcheology*; Rolingson, "Archeology along Bayou Bartholomew."

67. Brain, "Late Prehistoric Settlement," p. 352.

68. Brain, "Late Prehistoric Settlement," pp. 354–355.

69. Brain, "Late Prehistoric Settlement," pp. 358–360.

70. Brain, "Late Prehistoric Settlement," p. 360; cf. Williams and Brain, *Excavations at the Lake George Site*, pp. 414–415; Brown, *Natchez Indian Archaeology*, p. 254; Ian W. Brown, "Plaquemine Architectural Patterns in the Natchez Bluffs and Surrounding Regions of the Lower Mississippi Valley."

71. Hoffman, "Quapaw Structures."

72. Hoffman, "The Protohistoric Period."

73. Hoffman, "Quapaw Structures," pp. 60–61.

74. George Sabo III, *Paths of our Children: Historic Indians of Arkansas*, pp. 31–33.

75. Hoffman, "The Kinkead-Mainard Site."

76. Jeter, "Review of *Tunica Archaeology*"; Jeter, *The Goldsmith Oliver 2 Site*; Jeter et al., *Goldsmith Oliver 2*; Hoffman, "Protohistoric Tunican" (1992); "Protohistoric Tunican" (1995).

77. Jeane, "Osotouy"; House et al., "Rediscovering Menard," pp. 170–173.

78. Jeter, "Review of *Tunica Archaeology*"; John H. House, "Time, People, and Material Culture at the Kuykendall Brake Site, Pulaski County, Arkansas."

79. Jeffrey P. Brain, Alan Toth, and Antonio Rodriguez-Buckingham, "Ethnohistoric Archaeology and the De Soto Entrada into the Lower Mississippi Valley"; Jeffrey P. Brain, *On the Tunica Trail*; Jeffrey P. Brain, *Tunica Treasure*; Brain, *Tunica Archaeology*, p. 288ff.

80. Robert L. Rankin, "Language Affiliations of Some de Soto Place Names in Arkansas."

81. E.g., Swanton, *Final Report*, pp. 52, 54; Dickinson, "Historic Tribes."

82. E.g., John R. Swanton, *Indian Tribes of the Lower Mississippi Valley and Adjacent Coast of the Gulf of Mexico*, pp. 33, 327ff.

83. Tristram R. Kidder, "The Koroa Indians of the Lower Mississippi Valley," pp. 15ff, 22.

84. Swanton, *Indian Tribes*, p. 306; Swanton, *Final Report*, pp. 52, 54; Dickinson, "Historic Tribes"; Hudson, "De Soto in Arkansas"; Hudson, "Reconstructing."

85. Swanton, *Indian Tribes*, p. 307.

86. Jeffrey P. Brain, "La Salle at the Natchez: An Archaeological and Historical Perspective."

87. Brain, *On the Tunica Trail*; Brain, *Tunica Treasure*; Brain, *Tunica Archaeology*; Dickinson, "Historic Tribes"; Jeter, "Tunicans"; Tristram R. Kidder, "The Koroa Indians of the Lower Mississippi Valley."

88. Hoffman, "Quapaw Structures," p. 65; cf. Sabo, *Paths of our Children*, pp. 63–64.

89. Swanton, *Indian Tribes*, p. 309.

90. Brain, *Tunica Archaeology*, pp. 30ff, 297ff.

91. Brain, *Tunica Archaeology*, p. 298 and cover illustration.

92. Brain, *Tunica Archaeology*, pp. 319–321.

93. Brain, "Tunica Archaeology," p. 315ff.

94. Brain, "Tunica Archaeology," table 79.

95. James R. Atkinson, "Historic Chickasaw Cultural Material: A More Comprehensive Definition"; Patricia K. Galloway, *Choctaw Genesis: 1500–1700*; Patricia K. Galloway, "Colonial Period Transformations in the Mississippi Valley: Dis-integration, Alliance, Confederation, Playoff," this volume; Jay K. Johnson, "Stone Tools, Politics, and the Eighteenth Century Chickasaw in Northeast Mississippi."

96. Schambach, "Some New Interpretations" and "Spiro and the Tunica."

97. Jeter and Early, "Prehistory of the Saline River."

98. Morse and Morse, *Archaeology*, pp. 284, 300; Jeter et al., *Archeology and Bioarcheology*.

99. House, "Time."

100. Phillips et al., *Archaeological Survey*, p. 396.

101. The map (Phillips et al., *Archaeological Survey*, fig. 71) has been more clearly reproduced in a redrawn version (see House, "Noble Lake," fig. 49); Phillips et al., *Archaeological Survey*, pp. 397–398.

102. Phillips et al., *Archaeological Survey*, p. 397.

103. Phillips et al., *Archaeological Survey*, pp. 397–398.

104. Morse and Morse, *Archaeology*, p. 316.

105. Morse, "Seventeenth Century Michigamea."

106. Jeter, "Review of *French Colonial Archaeology*," p. 355.

107. Morse, "Seventeenth Century Michigamea," p. 63.

108. Morse, "Seventeenth Century Michigamea"; Morse and Morse, "Changes in Interpretation," p. 25; Morse and Morse, "Northeast Arkansas," pp. 133–134.

109. Joni L. Manson, "Trans-Mississippi Trade and Travel: The Buffalo Plains and Beyond," p. 392, fig. 1.

110. Waldo R. Wedel, *An Introduction to Kansas Archeology*; Mildred M. Wedel, "The Indian They Called *Turco*."

111. Swanton, *Final Report*; Hudson, "Reconstructing," p. 147.

112. Dickinson, "Historic Tribes," pp. 2, 4.

113. Hudson, "De Soto in Arkansas," p. 7.

114. Ann M. Early, "Finding the Middle Passage: The Spanish Journey from the Swamplands to Caddo Country," pp. 74–75.

115. Hudson, "Reconstructing," pp. 246–247.

116. Charles Hudson, *Knights of Spain, Warriors of the Sun: Hernando de Soto and the South's Ancient Chiefdoms*, p. 327.

117. Dickinson, "Historic Tribes," p. 6; Wedel, "The Indian"; Susan C. Vehik, "Wichita Culture History."

118. Wedel, *An Introduction*; M. Wedel, "The Indian"; Manson, "Trans-Mississippi," pp. 387–390, fig. 1.

119. Jeter et al., *Goldsmith Oliver 2* ; Jeter, *The Goldsmith Oliver 2 Site*.

120. Smith, "Glass Beads."

121. Jeter "Oliver"; Jeter, *The Goldsmith Oliver 2 Site*.

122. Clarence B. Moore, "Certain Mounds of Arkansas and of Mississippi"; House, "Noble Lake," pp. 73–74, 83, 86.

123. Peabody, *Exploration of Mounds*; Connaway, *The Oliver Site*.

124. Jeter, "Oliver"; Jeter, *Goldsmith Oliver 2 Site*; Marc Simmons, *The Last Conquistador: Juan de Onate and the Settling of the Far Southwest*.

125. Morse, "Seventeenth Century Michigamea."

126. Jeter, "Review of *French Colonial Archaeology*, p. 355.

127. Cf. also Louis De Vorsey, Jr., "The Impact of the La Salle Expedition of 1682 on European Cartography," p. 67. The French at that time were obsessed with routes to California and the Pacific, and would have been eager to believe in such contacts. Schambach (personal communication, 1999) suggests that shell beads from (Baja?) California

may actually have reached the Arkansas valley in late prehistoric to protohistoric times, via centers such as Pecos in New Mexico and a route involving the Red River valley to northeast Texas, thence over a trail to the Arkansas valley.

128. For example, see Sabo, *Paths of our Children*, pp. 42–48.

129. Swanton, *Indian Tribes*, pp. 257–272.

130. Swanton, *Indian Tribes*, p. 100ff; Charles Hudson, *The Southeastern Indians*, p. 205ff; Greg Urban, "The Social Organization of the Southeast," p. 179ff.

131. Hoffman, "Protohistoric Period," p. 30, fig. 3.2; Robert L. Rankin, "Quapaw: Genetic and Areal Affiliations."

132. Ives Goddard, "Introduction"; Ives Goddard, "The Classification of the Native Languages of North America."

133. Swanton, (*Indian Tribes*, p. 33, plate 1) also believed that Yazoo, Tioux, and Grigra, spoken along the eastern Mississippi Valley at the time of French contacts, were probably related to Tunica.

134. Swanton, *Indian Tribes*, p. 9; Goddard, "Introduction"; Goddard, "Classification."

135. Goddard, "Introduction"; Goddard, "Classification"; Swanton, *Indian Tribes*, 9–26.

136. Of course, as usual there are numerous potential cultural complexities that might have been superimposed over straightforward "etic" biological relationships, e.g., intermarriage, "fictive kin" arrangements, adoptions, etc. Even so, adequate numbers of DNA samples from skeletal and recent to modern sources might well be expected to make some archaeological-ethnohistorical linkages much more probable than others.

137. Penelope B. Drooker, *The View from Madisonville: Protohistoric Western Fort Ancient Interaction Patterns*, p. 105.

138. Nevertheless, it has for some time seemed strange (and indeed, inconsistent) to me that the "legal" processes involved in NAGPRA repatriation of archaeological skeletal remains to "related" groups have not insisted on such DNA analyses, which are now routinely used in court cases.

139. Jeter et al., *Goldsmith Oliver 2*, p. 520ff.

140. Cf. John H. House and Henry S. McKelway, "Mississippian and Quapaw on the Lower Arkansas."

141. Brain, *Tunica Archaeology*, p. 272ff.

142. E.g., Hoffman, "Protohistoric Tunican," pp. 74–75.

143. Jeter et al., *Goldsmith Oliver 2*, pp. 520–521, 537; Cyrus Thomas, "Burial Mounds of the Northern Sections of the United States," p. 80.

144. House and McKelway, "Mississippian and Quapaw"; House, "Noble Lake," pp. 87–93.

145. Henige, "Millennarian Archaeology."

146. Phillips's *Archaeological Survey*, pp. 943–944, Quapaw phase, but also its extension by Hoffman, "The Kinkead-Mainard Site."

147. Hoffman, "Protohistoric Period."

148. Phillips, *Archaeological Survey*, pp. 941–942, and Brain, *Tunica Archaeology*, p. 277ff.

149. House and McKelway, "Mississippian and Quapaw"; Hoffman, "Protohistoric Period."

150. Morse and Morse, *Archaeology*, pp. 277–278, 284, 300–301, 305ff, fig. 12.1; Morse and Morse, "Changes in Interpretation," pp. 24–27; Morse and Morse, "Northeast Arkansas"; Dan Morse and Phyllis Morse, personal communications, 1998–99; cf. also Dan F. Morse, "The Nodena Phase"; Dan F. Morse, "On the Possible Origin of the Quapaws in Northeast Arkansas," pp. 53–54.

151. Cf. Patricia K. Galloway, "The Incestuous Soto Narratives"; David Henige, " 'So Unbelievable It Has To Be True': Inca Garcilaso in Two Worlds."

152. Rankin, "Language Affiliations," pp. 213–216. Recall also that Swanton (*Final Report*, pp. 54, 61) suggested that "Pacaha" itself was a Tunican word.

153. Dan Morse, personal communications, 1993–99.

154. Also, the Soto chronicles indicate an ease of communication between the chiefs of Casqui and Pacaha. However, Dan Morse (personal communication, 1999) argues quite rightly that these complex societies must have had interpreters, and Soto's own interpreter Ortiz was also present.

155. P. Morse, *Parkin*, pp. 66–67.

156. E.g., Morse and Morse, *Archaeology*, pp. 300–301, fig. 12-1.

157. Morse and Morse, *Archaeology*, p. 320.

158. Morse and Morse, "Changes in Interpretation," p. 25.

159. Cf. also D. Morse, "On the Possible Origin," p. 54.

160. Brain, *Tunica Archaeology*, pp. 272, 280.

161. Rankin, "Quapaw."

162. Hoffman, "Terminal Mississippian," p. 221.

163. Jeter, "Review of *Tunica Archaeology*," p. 149; Brain, *Tunica Archaeology*.

164. Brain, "Tunica Archaeology," pp. 269, 277ff.

165. John S. Belmont, "The Peabody Excavations, Coahoma County, Mississippi, 1901–1902"; Brain, "Tunica Archaeology," pp. 281–283.

166. Jeter, "Review of *Tunica Archaeology*," p. 149; cf. Johnson, "Stone Tools."

167. Brain, *Tunica Archaeology*, pp. 272–277, figs. 195 and 196; Phillips, *Archaeological Survey*, pp. 939–940.

168. Brain, *Tunica Archaeology*, fig. 196.

169. Brain, *On the Tunica Trail*; Brain, *Tunica Archaeology*.

170. Brain, "Late Prehistoric Settlement," p. 311.

171. Morse, "The Nodena Phase"; Morse, "On the Possible Origin," pp. 53–54; Rankin, "Language Affiliations."

172. Jeter, "Tunicans West," p. 45ff; Brain, *Tunica Archaeology*, pp. 272–273; Jackson, *The Ables Creek Site*, pp. 113–114.

173. House, "Noble Lake," fig. 49.

174. Rankin, "Language Affiliations," pp. 216–217.

175. Dickinson, "Historic Tribes," p. 6.

176. Schambach, "Spiro and the Tunica."

177. Schambach, "Some New Interpretations"; Frank F. Schambach, "A Probable Spiroan *Entrepôt* in the Red River Valley in Northeast Texas."

178. Schambach, "Spiro and the Tunica," p. 195.

179. Schambach, "Spiro and the Tunica."

180. Galloway, "Incestuous Soto"; Henige, "So Unbelievable."

181. Frank F. Schambach, personal communications, 1990s.

182. Schambach, "Spiro and the Tunica."

183. Brain, *On the Tunica Trail*; Brain, *Tunica Treasure*; Dickinson, "Historic Tribes"; Jeter, "Tunicans West."

184. E.g., Jeter et al., *Archeology and Bioarcheology*; Jeter et al., *Goldsmith Oliver 2*; Jeter, "Review of *Tunica Archaeology*," p. 148.

185. Jeter, "Review of *Tunica Archaeology*," p. 148; cf. Swanton, *Final Report*, p. 61.

186. Brain, *Tunica Archaeology*, p. 277.

187. Frank F. Schambach, personal communication, 1998; Brain et al., "Ethnohistoric Archaeology"; Swanton, *Indian Tribes*, pp. 306–307; Brain, *Tunica Archaeology*, p. 25.

188. Frank F. Schambach, personal communication, 1998.

189. Schambach, "Spiro and the Tunica," pp. 190–193.

190. Frank F. Schambach and John E. Miller, "A Description and Analysis of the Ceramics," pp.113–114, fig. 11–10.

191. Cf. Brain, *Tunica Treasure*; Brain, *Tunica Archaeology*; Jeter, "Tunicans West"; Jackson, *Ables Creek Site*.

192. Hoffman, "Protohistoric Tunican," p. 74.

193. Brain, *On the Tunica Trail*; Brain, *Tunica Treasure*; Brain, *Tunica Archaeology*; Brain et al., "Ethnohistoric Archaeology."

194. Swanton, *Final Report*, p. 61.

195. Swanton, *Final Report*, pp. 54, 61.

196. Ann M. Early, *Standridge: Caddoan Settlement in a Mountain Environment*; Early, "Finding the Middle Passage"; Ann M. Early, *Caddoan Saltmakers in the Ouachita Valley: The Hardman Site*.

197. Hudson, "De Soto in Arkansas"; Hudson, "Reconstructing."

198. Manson, "Trans-Mississippi," p. 392, fig. 1.

199. Mary R. Haas, *Tunica Texts*, pp. 19, 141.

200. Brain, *Tunica Archaeology*, pp. 22, 288.

201. George Sabo III et al., *Human Adaptation in the Ozark-Ouachita Mountains*; Sabo et al., *Archeological Investigations at 3MR80–Area D in the Rush Development Area, Buffalo National River, Arkansas*.

202. John H. House, "Flat-bottomed Shell-tempered Pottery in the Ozarks: A Preliminary Discussion."

203. Cf. the listing of some of Swanton's place-name attributions by Dickinson, "Historic Tribes," p. 1.

204. Swanton, *Indian Tribes*; Swanton, *Final Report*.

205. Jeter, "Tunicans West," pp. 45, 49; Kidder later independently suggested something similar—see Kidder, "Koroa Indians," p. 22ff.

206. Brain, "La Salle at the Natchez," p. 50ff.

207. Jeter, "Tunicans West," p. 49; cf. Hally, "The Plaquemine," pp. 496–497, 529–532, 615–620. The similar and more or less simultaneous change in tempering of Caddoan pottery from grog to shell in late prehistoric to protohistoric times appears to be taken for granted as merely a technological change, rather than an indication of migration, by Caddoan archaeologists (cf. Schambach and Miller, "Description"; Early, "Finding the Middle Passage").

208. Phillips, *Archaeological Survey*, p. 104ff.

209. Hally, "The Plaquemine."

210. Brain, *Tunica Archaeology*, p. 350.

211. Swanton, *Indian Tribes*, pp. 9–24, 257ff.

212. Phillips, *Archaeological Survey*, p. 945.

213. A similar situation was actually suggested to me informally by Hester Davis (personal communication, 1981) during the preparation of the Arkansas state plan (see Hester A. Davis, *A State Plan for the Conservation of Archeological Resources in Arkansas*). At that time, she sent me a sketch map of tribal territories in Arkansas, on which she had sketched in "Taensa?" in southeast Arkansas, with no further comment. That sounded far-fetched to me then, as I was already attuned to the siren song of Tunican affiliations, but there may well have been something worth considering there.

214. Phillips, *Archaeological Survey*, pp. 954, 971.

215. Swanton, *Indian Tribes*, p. 171.

216. Jon Muller, *Mississippian Political Economy*, p. 64.

217. Swanton, *Final Report*, pp. 54, 61; Brain, "Late Prehistoric Settlement"; Brain, "A Note."

218. Brain, "A Note," pp. 117–118.

219. Brain, *Winterville*, fig. 83.

220. Williams and Brain, *Excavations*, p. 379.

221. Williams and Brain, *Excavations*, fig. 11.20.

222. Williams and Brain, *Excavations*, p. 380.

223. Jeter, "Tunicans West"; Jeter et al., "The Kelley-Grimes Site"; Jeter et al., *Archeology and Bioarcheology*.

224. Brain, *Winterville*, p. 106ff; Williams and Brain, *Excavations*, pp. 345–346.

225. Williams and Brain, *Excavations*, p. 346.

226. Jeter, "Tunicans West"; Jeter et al., *Archeology and Bioarcheology*; Jackson, *The Ables Creek Site*.

227. Brain, *Winterville*, pp.105–106; Williams and Brain, *Excavations*, pp. 341–342, 381.
228. Morse and Morse, *Archaeology*, p. 271ff.
229. Phillips, *Archaeological Survey*, pp. 560–565, fig. 249.
230. Williams and Brain, *Excavations*, pp. 378–381.
231. Jeter, "Review of *Tunica Archaeology*," p. 148; Brain, *Tunica Archaeology*.
232. Brain, "A Note"; Richard A. Weinstein et al., *Cultural Resources Survey of the Upper Steele Bayou Basin, West-Central Mississippi*, pp. 3–42.
233. Weinstein et al., *Cultural Resources*, figs. 3-10 and 3-11; Jeter, "Tunicans West"; cf. Jackson, *The Ables Creek Site*.
234. Richard A. Weinstein and Thurston H. G. Hahn III, *Cultural Resources Survey of the Lake Beulah Landside Berm, Item L-583, Bolivar County, Mississippi*, pp. 148–165.
235. Weinstein and Hahn, *Cultural Resources Survey*, p. 156.
236. Brain, *Tunica Archaeology*, pp. 266–280.
237. Dan Morse (personal communication, 1999) suggests that the "longhouses" may have merely been long rectangular houses, misinterpreted by translators, and that suitable bark, comparable to birchbark used to cover northeastern longhouses, may have been lacking in Arkansas. But the unusual bark-covered Quapaw structures are attested by more than one observer, and the bark of the common bald cypress trees may have been used; in fact, it is specifically mentioned or strongly implied by some early French observers (see Hoffman, "Quapaw Structures," pp. 57, 59, and Hoffman, "The Protohistoric Period," p. 30, 32).
238. Helen C. Rountree, "Trouble Coming Southward: Emanations Through and From Virginia, 1607–1675"; Smith, *Archaeology of Aboriginal Culture Change*, p. 133; Chester DePratter, "The Role of Carolina in the Transformation of Native American Societies."
239. Smith, *Archaeology of Aboriginal Culture Change*, pp. 22, 41, 132–134; Marvin T. Smith, "Aboriginal Population Movements in the Early Historic Period Interior Southeast," p. 30, fig. 3.
240. R. Eric Hollinger, "Residence Patterns and Oneota Cultural Dynamics," pp. 141, 144.
241. James B. Griffin, *The Fort Ancient Aspect: Its Cultural and Chronological Position in Mississippi Valley Archaeology*, pp. 309–312.
242. Robert L. Rankin, "Oneota and Historical Linguistics."
243. John Koontz, personal communication, 1999.
244. Thomas J. Green and Cheryl A. Munson, "Mississippian Settlement Patterns in Southwestern Indiana."
245. E.g., Hoffman, "Protohistoric Period," p. 33; Morse and Morse, "Northeast Arkansas," p. 134; Brain, *Tunica Archaeology*, p. 279.
246. Cheryl Munson, personal communication, 1998.
247. Green and Munson, "Mississippian Settlement Patterns," pp. 300–303.
248. Penelope Drooker, "The Ohio Valley, 1550–1750: Patterns of Sociopolitical Coalescence and Dispersal," this volume; Cheryl Munson (personal communication, 2000), while conceding the lack of post-1600 trade goods, suggests that Caborn-Welborn may have survived well into the 1600s, possibly even the late 1600s. In any event, the Caborn-Welborn people do not seem to have used longhouses, and I consider them very unlikely candidates for proto-Quapaw status.
249. Drooker, *View from Madisonville*.
250. Drooker, *View from Madisonville*, p. 133; personal communication, 1999.
251. Lee H. Hanson, *The Hardin Village Site*; Lee H. Hanson, *The Buffalo Site: A Late 17th Century Indian Village Site (46PU31) in Putnam County, West Virginia*; William F. S. Holmes, "Hardin Village: A Northern Kentucky Late Fort Ancient Site's Mortuary Patterns and Social Organization."
252. Holmes, "Hardin Village," p. 96. This scenario is by no means the first to suggest

that the Quapaw were relatively late emigrants from well up the Ohio valley. Their historian W. David Baird (*The Quapaw Indians: A History of the Downstream People*, pp. 3–8) opined that they had migrated from the regions around southern Ohio some time after 1600, forced out (just as suggested here) by Iroquoian warfare, which he saw as impinging significantly on the Ohio valley in the 1650s. His work seems to have made little impression on archaeologists, possibly partly because of his rather deprecatory remarks about their beliefs, but perhaps mainly because of his somewhat naive and mixed-up interpretations of the archaeological literature. He attempted to derive the Quapaw from the Adena-Hopewell tradition, which ended around A.D. 500 at the latest, without even mentioning subsequent cultures; the most glaring omission was Fort Ancient. In a later popular book, he drastically shortened his Quapaw-origins section, left out the Hopewellian thesis, referred only vaguely to "the Ohio Valley" (although he still mentioned the "aggressive Iroquois" in passing), and moved the migration significantly back in time, to "probably during the late 16th century" (Baird, *The Quapaws*, p. 14). Much earlier, at a 1932 conference, John R. Swanton, in "The Relation of the Southeast to General Culture Problems of American Pre-history," had noted that "[e]arly and consistent Quapaw and Osage legends point to the Ohio above its junction with the Wabash as their early home. . . ." (p. 66) and even claimed "that the homeland of five tribes—Quapaw, Osage, Ofo, Biloxi and Tutelo—proves to be in the region of the Fort Ancient culture and that the movements of several others were distinctly away from that region" (p. 67–68).

253. Griffin, *Fort Ancient Aspect*, p. 308ff.

254. Griffin, *Fort Ancient Aspect*, p. 36ff, map 1; Patricia S. Essenpreis, "Fort Ancient Settlement: Differential Response at a Mississippian–Late Woodland Interface"; Drooker, *View from Madisonville*; Drooker, "Ohio Valley, 1550–1750," this volume.

255. Essenpreis, "Fort Ancient Settlement," pp. 145–151, 164.

256. Drooker, *View from Madisonville*, pp. 103–105.

257. Robert L. Rankin, personal communication, 1999.

258. Baird, *Quapaw Indians*, pp. 3ff, 6; Hoffman, "Terminal Mississippian," p. 208; Hoffman, "Protohistoric Tunican," p. 73.

259. Morse, "On the Possible Origin," pp. 53–54.

260. Morse and Morse, *Archaeology*, p. 320; linguists Robert L. Rankin and John E. Koontz (personal communications, 1999) also advise some caution in dealing with reports of these "traditions" (e.g., in the secondary sources that Baird used), until someone produces a critical review of all the primary sources.

261. Modern "tribal" and linguistic maps often show the Osage and Quapaw territories as running continuously over a vast "Siouan" area from western Missouri through the Ozarks to the Lower Arkansas–Mississippi vicinity. However, there is no evidence for settled populations of either group in the huge gap between their distant base localities in late protohistoric to early historic times. The Kansa, whose language was very close to that of the Osage (they are often "lumped" as "Osage-Kansa" by linguists), lived somewhat north of the Osage, along the Missouri River, in historic times.

262. The Omaha and Ponca languages are "virtually identical" (John E. Koontz, personal communication, 1999).

263. James W. Springer and Stanley R. Witkowski, "Siouan Historical Linguistics and Oneota Archaeology," p. 75.

264. Robert L. Rankin and John E. Koontz, personal communications, 1999.

265. Drooker, *View from Madisonville*, p. 337; Drooker, personal communication, 1999; Drooker, "Ohio Valley, 1550–1750," this volume.

266. Smith, *Archaeology of Aboriginal Culture Change*, p. 135: Drooker, *View from Madisonville*, p. 56.

267. Baird, *Quapaw Indians*, p. 5.

268. Griffin, *Fort Ancient Aspect*, pp. 29–30; Drooker, "Ohio Valley, 1550–1750," this volume. Yet another possibility is that the Fort Ancient peoples, both eastern and western, were indeed the Shawnee and/or other Algonquians, as Griffin (*Fort Ancient Aspect*)

believed, and that the proto-Quapaw were still farther up the Ohio valley, where the archeology is apparently rather poorly known (cf. Drooker, *View from Madisonville*; Drooker, "Ohio Valley, 1550-1750," this volume).

269. John M. O'Shea and John Ludwicksonk, *Archaeology and Ethnohistory of the Omaha Indians: The Big Village Site*, pp. 16-17.

270. O'Shea and Ludwickson, *Archaeology and Ethnohistory*, p. 72.

271. O'Shea and Ludwickson, *Archaeology and Ethnohistory*, p. 290.

272. O'Shea and Ludwickson, *Archaeology and Ethnohistory*, p. 294.

273. Susan C. Vehik, "Dhegiha Origins and Plains Archaeology," p. 246.

274. O'Brien and Wood, *Prehistory of Missouri*, p. 348. Both Vehik ("Dhegiha Origins," p. 246) and O'Brien and Wood (*Prehistory of Missouri*, p. 348) gave some credence to possible Oneota origins for the Osage, and did not mention any possible Fort Ancient connection, which is certainly rather distant from their perspective and is postulated for the first time (as far as I know) in the present chapter. Vehik did remark that "Oneota might be too far north to account for Dhegihan similarities to southeastern societies . . . the Caborn-Welborn phase of the Ohio River Valley might be Quapaw . . ."

275. In fact, apparently very late shell-tempered cord-marked pottery *has* been found in Arkansas, but not in or near the Arkansas-Mississippi juncture locality. At the putative "seventeenth-century Michigamea village" west of the Missouri "bootheel," Dan Morse ("Seventeenth Century Michigamea," p. 66) found "very small" potsherds which were "shell-tempered, typical of Mississippi Plain. Most [apparently more than three hundred; Morse, "Seventeenth Century Michigamea," table 3.1] are plain or badly eroded; five are cord-marked, both coarse and fine. Morse added, "[W]hether this pottery is Illini [i.e., Mitchigamea] or Quapaw is not known. John A. Walthall's ["Aboriginal Pottery and the Eighteenth-Century Illini," pp. 167-170] thesis would indicate that Quapaw ceramics are to be expected [a result of de-emphasis of ceramics by the Illini and their trading relations with the Quapaw] . . . [This site] could constitute a major test of this hypothesis" (brackets added). Here, I find it very interesting that *none* of the traditional decorated ceramic "diagnostics" of the former "Quapaw phase" or "Menard complex" (which I think is basically Tunican and/or "northern Natchezan" rather than Quapaw) were found; and that the same is apparently the case so far at the newly found early-1700s site near Menard, although no cord-marked sherds have yet been found there either (Jeane, "Osotouy"; House et al., "Rediscovering Menard," p. 170).

276. Hanson, *The Hardin Village Site*, p. 76ff.

277. Phillips et al., *Archaeological Survey*, pp. 414-415; Ford, *Menard Site*; Jeter et al., *Goldsmith Oliver 2*.

278. Jeane, "Osotouy"; House et al., "Rediscovering Menard," pp. 170-173.

279. Cf. Jeter, "Archeology of Southeast Arkansas," pp. 113-115; Jeter, "Tunicans West," p. 39.

280. Cf. Phillips, *Archaeological Survey*; Williams and Brain, *Excavations*.

281. Cf. Thurman, "Conversations with Lewis R. Binford," pp. 52-53.

282. Lewis R. Binford, *An Archaeological Perspective*; James L. Boone and Eric Alden Smith, "Is It Evolution Yet? A Critique of Evolutionary Archaeology"; Timothy K. Earle, "Comment on 'Is It Evolution Yet?' by James L. Boone and Eric Alden Smith"; R. Lee Lyman and Michael J. O'Brien, "The Goals of Evolutionary Archaeology: History and Explanation"; Steven Mithen, "Comment on 'Is It Evolution Yet?' by James L. Boone and Eric Alden Smith"; Ernst Mayr, *The Growth of Biological Thought: Diversity, Evolution, and Inheritance*. Despite its name, the "type-variety" system (Phillips, *Archaeological Survey*) does not really deal with variation in a statistical way. It is just a continuation of "typological thinking" on a finer scale.

283. Brain, *Tunica Archaeology*, p. 4.

284. Brain, *Tunica Archaeology*, pp. 2-4.

285. E.g., Jon L. Gibson, "Review of 'Archaeology and Ceramics at the Marksville Site,' by Alan Toth"; Jeter, "Archeology of Southeast Arkansas," pp. 110-119; Jeter et al., *Archeology and Bioarcheology*, p. 57ff.

286. Phillips et al., *Archaeological Survey*, p. 455.
287. Phillips, *Archaeological Survey*, p. 973.
288. Schambach, "Description and Analysis."
289. Schambach, "Description and Analysis"; Schambach and Miller, "Description and Analysis"; Early, *Standridge*, p. 89ff; Early, "Finding the Middle Passage," pp. 102–109; Schambach and Waddell, "Pottery from the Bangs Slough Site."
290. Gregory L. Fox, "An Examination of Mississippian Period Phases in Southeastern Missouri," p. 58.
291. Robert C. Mainfort, Jr., "Late Period Phases in the Central Mississippi Valley: A Multivariate Approach," p. 167.
292. Charles H. McNutt, "Review of *Changing Perspectives on the Archaeology of the Central Mississippi Valley*, edited by Michael J. O'Brien and Robert C. Dunnell," pp. 79–82.
293. Smith, *Archaeology of Aboriginal Culture Change*, pp. 54ff, 129ff, figs. 4.2 and 7.1; Smith, "Aboriginal Population Movements."
294. Galloway, *Choctaw Genesis*, p. 338ff, fig. 9.1.
295. Hoffman, "Terminal Mississippian," p. 208; Vehik, "Dhegiha Origins," p. 246; Galloway, *Choctaw Genesis*, pp. 324–337.
296. Cf. Springer and Witkowski, "Siouan Historical Linguistics"; Rankin, "Quapaw"; Rankin, "Oneota."
297. Patricia K. Galloway, "The Direct Historical Approach and Early Historical Documents: The Ethnohistorian's View"; Galloway, *Choctaw Genesis*; Galloway, "Incestuous Soto"; Lewis R. Binford, "In Pursuit of the Future," pp. 474–476; Thurman, "Conversations with Lewis R. Binford," pp. 34, 49–50.
298. C. Roger Nance, "Artifact Attribute Covariation as the Product of Inter-level Site Mixing."

Notes to COLONIAL PERIOD TRANSFORMATIONS IN THE MISSISSIPPI VALLEY: DIS-INTEGRATION, ALLIANCE, CONFEDERATION, PLAYOFF
by Patricia Galloway

1. I wish that the title of this symposium had not offered aid and comfort to historians who still feel that "not paper-documented" is equivalent to "without history." *In fact we are working here on the LATE social history of southeastern Native people.*
2. I trust that others will deal with the western side, and confess that the Quapaw question is beyond me.
3. Wayne Franklin, *Discoverers, Explorers, Settlers: The Diligent Writers of Early America*, preceded Stephen Greenblatt's *Marvelous Possessions: The Wonder of the New World* in pointing out the degree to which European accounts of their "discoveries" were accounts of themselves.
4. In my paper "*Conjoncture* and *Longue Durée*: History, Anthropology, and the Hernando de Soto Expedition," pp. 283–294, I have already addressed some of the problems with attempting to extract *Annales*-style tabular data from early exploration narratives; the later regular and ongoing bureaucratic reports made to and sent home by colonial governments are much more suited to *Annales* treatment.
5. Even the brilliant microhistorical work of Emmanuel LeRoy Ladurie has been based primarily on written records.
6. Which in my humble opinion would seem to make law-like generalizations based upon them, which claim to describe the behavior of polities and the effects of ethnicity, dubious at best and daydreaming at worst.
7. This possibility has been argued about with reference to Poverty Point for the last twenty years.
8. Jan Vansina, *Oral Tradition as History*; David Henige, *Oral Historiography*. At the

1998 AASLH meeting Kurt Dongoske recounted how information that tallied with and clearly explicated a significant archaeological find of sacred objects dating to some 1200 years B.P. was gathered entirely independently from a modern Zuñi traditional specialist. See also Rober Anyon, T. J. Ferguson, Loretta Jackson, and Lillie Lane, "Native American Oral Traditions and Archaeology."

9. Much Native traditional history still remains to be gathered, but it is likely that in the future it will be gathered by Native people themselves in support of their own preservation programs, as is now taking place in the Mississippi Choctaws' language program.

10. Tragically, Timothy Mooney's promising Ph.D. work at the University of North Carolina on the origins of the southwestern Choctaws was left unfinished when he was killed accidentally, but it is now being pursued by Patrick Livingood at the University of Michigan.

11. Jeffrey P. Brain, *Tunica Treasure*; Jeffrey P. Brain, *Tunica Archaeology*.

12. Marvin Jeter, "Tunicans West of the Mississippi: A Summary of Early Historic and Archaeological Evidence." The Tunicas merged with the Biloxis in Louisiana in the nineteenth century, and today, as the Tunica-Biloxi, have taken over and fully developed a tribal museum in Marksville, Louisiana.

13. Excavations in Lee County planned as a joint venture between the Chickasaws, the University of Mississippi, and Mississippi State University for the near future will follow up on recent work by Jay Johnson (an attempt to locate the 1541 Soto winter camp) and work by Johnson's students and John O'Hear at Lee County sites on the eighteenth-century Chickasaw. The Chickasaw Nation in Oklahoma has organized a Chickasaw Historical Society which publishes a semiannual journal, and the Nation is actively engaged in the development of an expanded historical museum and archive.

14. The earliest professional archaeology of the eighteenth-century Natchez was carried out by Mississippi Department of Archives and History archaeologist Moreau Chambers, whose work was followed up on and completed by Robert Stuart Neitzel, *Archeology of the Fatherland Site: The Grand Village of the Natchez*; Robert S. Neitzel, *The Grand Village of the Natchez Revisited*. Lower Mississippi Survey archaeologist Jeffrey Brain included Natchez precursors in his influential essay on lower valley chiefdoms (Jeffrey P. Brain, "Late Prehistoric Settlement Patterning in the Yazoo Basin and Natchez Bluffs Regions of the Lower Mississippi Valley"), but primary field archaeology on late prehistory and the protohistoric period in the region has been carried out by Vin Steponaitis at Emerald and Ian Brown at several eighteenth-century sites and last summer at Anna; much of this has been waiting to appear as the fabled Brain, Brown, and Steponaitis opus *Archaeology of the Natchez Bluffs Region* for more then fifteen years.

15. A list of these citations would be longer than this paper, so for the moment I respectfully decline.

16. I have been trying for years to complete a translation of Antoine Simon Le Page du Pratz's *Histoire de la Louisiane*, and have completed two-thirds of one, but other assignments have always been given precedence.

17. Except when surviving descendants attempt to make a case for their authenticity, as in the case of the Houmas, who were recently denied federal recognition once again after many Houma-sponsored studies (among them Greg Bowman and Janel Curry-Roper, *The Houma People of Louisiana: A Story of Indian Survival*) and a responding 1994 BIA research effort amounting to nearly three hundred pages (Bureau of Indian Affairs, *Proposed Finding: United Houma Nation, Inc.*).

18. See Christopher Peebles, "Paradise Lost, Strayed and Stolen: Prehistoric Social Devolution in the Southeast."

19. Recent tree-ring studies have suggested definite local cooling in the Mississippi Valley beginning in the fourteenth century.

20. A convenient source for several Native versions of the origin of corn can be found in George E. Lankford, *Native American Legends*, pp. 147–156.

21. Some years ago David Anderson, in "Stability and Change in Chiefdom-Level

Societies: An Examination of Mississippian Political Evolution on the South Atlantic Slope," suggested (after Jonathan Friedman, "Tribes, States, and Transformations") that chiefdoms cycled through booms and busts as they repeatedly exhausted lands and resources and relocated. More recently John Blitz ("Mississippian Chiefdoms and the Fission-Fusion Process") has propounded a more complex model of "fission-fusion" that borrows from what is known of chiefdom splitting and confederation during the protohistoric period, suggesting that this model probably better fits the increasingly evident nonuniformity of social organization across the Mississippian-period Southeast.

22. Just as the North Germanic peoples did in another era of global cooling, setting in motion the fall of Rome and the birth of the Middle Ages.

23. See Jeffrey P. Brain, "Late Prehistoric Settlement Patterning in the Yazoo Basin and Natchez Bluffs Regions of the Lower Mississippi Valley"; Brain, *Tunica Treasure*; Brain, *Tunica Archaeology*; Jeffrey P. Brain, *Winterville: Late Prehistoric Culture Contact in the Lower Mississippi Valley*; and Stephen Williams and Jeffrey Brain, *Excavations at the Lake George Site, Yazoo County, Mississippi, 1958–1960*.

24. Jeffrey Brain in "Late Prehistoric Settlement" pointed to this phenomenon, and noted that the layout of the mounds on the top of Emerald quotes that of the then-abandoned Anna site, possibly implying that a descendant group occupied it.

25. See Jay K. Johnson and John T. Sparks, "Protohistoric Settlement Patterns in Northeastern Mississippi," and Craig T. Sheldon and Ned J. Jenkins, "Protohistoric Development in Central Alabama."

26. Jay K. Johnson, "From Chiefdom to Tribe in Northeast Mississippi: The Soto Expedition as a Window on a Culture in Transition"; James R. Atkinson, "The De Soto Expedition through North Mississippi."

27. See Patricia K. Galloway, *Choctaw Genesis: 1500–1700*, chapter 2.

28. See J. Vernon Knight, Jr., and Vincas P. Steponaitis, *Archaeology of the Moundville Chiefdom*.

29. Viz. Cahaba or Kaapa.

30. Choctaws and Chickasaws still argued over the place in the nineteenth century and even held a ballgame to decide the outcome—which decided only who should hand over to the Americans.

31. The Ofo, like the Biloxi, have long been viewed as inexplicable Siouan interlopers, but to my knowledge no archaeological evidence has yet so identified them. The Ibitoupa seem to have been absorbed by the Choctaws later—they had villages called "Ibitoupougoula"—while the Chakchiuma apparently joined the Choctaws and Chickasaws.

32. It cannot be mere coincidence that there are significant parallels between the route by which Florida shell passed as far west as Spiro and the Carolina traders' Upper Path to, through, and beyond the Creek and Chickasaw nations.

33. See James Brown, "On Style Divisions of the Southeastern Ceremonial Complex: A Revisionist Perspective"; Peebles, "Paradise Lost."

34. Emanuel J. Drechsel, "Mobilian Jargon in the 'Prehistory' of Southeastern North America."

35. See Carl Sauer, *Sixteenth Century North America: The Land and People as Seen by the Europeans*, pp. 43–44; Robert Weddle, *Spanish Sea: The Gulf of Mexico in North American Discovery, 1500–1685*, p. 193.

36. The story of their survival is told in Alvar Núñez Cabeza de Vaca, *The Account: Alvar Núñez Cabeza de Vaca's Relación*.

37. See Charles Hudson, *Knights of Spain, Warriors of the Sun: Hernando de Soto and the South's Ancient Chiefdoms*, pp. 78–85.

38. I am resisting here and throughout the term "complex," since it is a misnomer. Hierarchical organization has as its aim a *reduction* in complexity; and nothing is more complex than the nonuniform factional relationships of a face-to-face society, particularly when decisions and communal actions must be taken. This *real* complexity (the phrase "herding cats" comes to mind), while it made effective corporate resistance to European

conquest difficult or impossible, also made the imposition of European-style "capillary discipline" impossible and the management of supposedly "conquered" groups a nightmare.

39. See Ann Ramenofsky and Patricia Galloway, "Disease and the Soto Entrada." Interestingly, Bryan Foods of West Point, Mississippi, is one of the largest pork processors in the region, and Mississippi, the twenty-eighth-largest pork producer, today concentrates that production in the counties of Chickasaw, Clay, Monroe, Lowndes, Noxubee, and Simpson—all but the last in the region where the Chickasaws lived when encountered by Soto.

40. For the move, see Johnson, "From Chiefdom to Tribe."

41. John Blitz, Ancient Chiefdoms of the Tombigbee.

42. Norbert Elias, The Civilizing Process.

43. Mary Helms, Ancient Panama: Chiefs in Search of Power, introduced this notion of monopolized knowledge from afar as an aspect of leadership.

44. Eighteenth-century Indian groups of the Mississippi River, especially the Tunicas, used and especially traded horses obtained from western tribes by theft or trade with the Spaniards of Mexico, but clearly the Choctaws and Chickasaws had plenty of horses for their own use as early as the first third of the eighteenth century, when Régis du Roullet saw Choctaw horses corralled on a Pearl River island (see Régis du Roullet, "Itinerary from Mobile to the Choctaws, April to August 1732, Paris," Archives Hydrographiques V. LXVII, 2, No. 14–1, Portefeuille 135, Document 21) and Jean-Christoph de Lusser was forced to go along with a breakneck ride "in the Indian fashion" through the damp forest of south Mississippi (see Jean-Christoph de Lusser in Dunbar Roland and A. G. Saunders, Mississippi Provincial Archives, French Dominion. Vol I. 1729–1740, p. 99). The famous "Chickasaw ponies," still remembered today by Oklahoma Chickasaws, were certainly added to by trade from the English traders' horse caravans, from which the Choctaws stole animals, but may have begun with Spanish horses.

45. See Galloway, Choctaw Genesis.

46. Patricia K. Galloway, "Prehistoric Population of Mississippi: A First Approximation."

47. See Tristán de Luna, The Luna Papers.

48. Considering how obsessively many scholars have debated every stream and hill found in European exploration narratives, it is unfortunate that they are willing to ignore the often quite explicit environmental description found in traditional Indian narratives.

49. J. Leitch Wright's fine book The Only Land They Knew: The Tragic Story of the American Indians in the Old South outlines the fullest account of the slaving carried out by the "Goose Creek Men" and its geopolitical significance.

50. So named by Jeffrey Brain, "The Natchez 'Paradox.' "

51. Marcel Giraud, Histoire de la Louisiane Française: L'époque de John Law.

52. "Bienville to Cadillac, June 23, 1716," Dunbar Roland and A. G. Saunders, Mississippi Provincial Archives, French Dominion. Vol. III. 1704–1743, p. 214.

Notes to SOCIAL CHANGES AMONG THE CADDO INDIANS IN THE SIXTEENTH AND SEVENTEENTH CENTURIES
by Timothy K. Perttula

1. E.g., James Axtell, The Indians' New South: Cultural Change in the Colonial Southeast, pp. 43–44, 69; Patricia K. Galloway, Choctaw Genesis 1500–1700; Charles Hudson and Carmen C. Tesser, The Forgotten Centuries: Indians and Europeans in the American South 1521–1704.

2. See G. Avery, "Eighteenth Century Spanish, French, and Caddoan Interactions as seen from Los Adaes"; Cecile Elkins Carter, Caddo Indians: Where We Come From; Dayna Bowker Lee, "A Social History of Caddoan Peoples: Cultural Adaptation and Per-

sistence in a Native American Community"; Timothy K. Perttula, "French and Spanish Colonial Trade Policies and the Fur Trade among the Caddoan Indians of the Trans-Mississippi South"; Timothy K. Perttula, "Two Worlds Meet: The Caddoan People and Missions"; Willard H. Rollings, "Living in a Graveyard: Native Americans in Colonial Arkansas"; F. Todd Smith, *The Caddo Indians: Tribes at the Convergence of Empires, 1542–1854.*

3. See David La Vere, *The Caddo Chiefdoms: Caddo Economics and Politics, 700–1835.*

4. Lesley Adkins and Roy A. Adkins, *A Thesaurus of British Archaeology,* p. 242.

5. Bruce G. Trigger and William R. Swagerty, "Entertaining Strangers: North America in the Sixteenth Century," p. 326.

6. D. Hadley, Thomas H. Naylor, and M. K. Schuetz-Miller, *The Presidio and Militia on the Northern Frontier of New Spain: A Documentary History. Vol. 2, Part 2: The Central Corridor and the Texas Corridor, 1700–1765,* pp. 359–364.

7. John R. Swanton, *Source Material on the History and Ethnology of the Caddo Indians.*

8. Cf. J. S. Girard, "Historic Caddoan Occupation in the Natchitoches Area: Recent Attempts to Locate Residential Sites," p. 19; David B. Kelley, *Two Caddoan Farmsteads in the Red River Valley: The Archeology of the McLelland and Joe Clark Sites;* Timothy K. Perttula, *"The Caddo Nation": Archaeological and Ethnohistoric Perspectives;* Ann M. Early, " 'With their friends they keep unchangeable peace': The Caddo of the Trans-Mississippi South."

9. See James A. Brown, *The Spiro Ceremonial Center: The Archaeology of Arkansas Valley Caddoan Culture in Eastern Oklahoma;* Ann M. Early, *Caddoan Saltmakers in the Ouachita Valley: The Hardman Site;* Early, "With their friends"; La Vere, *Caddo Chiefdoms;* J. D. Rogers, "Markers of Social Integration: The Development of Centralized Authority in the Spiro Region"; George Sabo III, "Encounters and Images: European Contact and Caddo Indians."

10. John F. Scarry, "The Nature of Mississippian Societies," p. 13.

11. Cf. John F. Scarry, "Looking for and at Mississippian Political Change," fig. 1.1; John F. Scarry, "How Great Were the Southeastern Polities?," fig. 5.5.

12. Frank F. Schambach, *Pre-Caddoan Cultures in the Trans-Mississippi South: A Beginning Sequence,* pp. xii, 7–10.

13. Early, *Caddoan Saltmakers.*

14. James E. Bruseth, "The Development of Caddoan Polities along the Middle Red River Valley of Eastern Texas and Oklahoma"; Kelley, *Two Caddoan Farmsteads;* Frank F. Schambach, "The Archeology of the Great Bend Region in Arkansas."

15. Timothy K. Perttula, "Late Caddoan Societies in the Northeast Texas Pineywoods."

16. See Dee Ann Story, *The Deshazo Site, Nacogdoches County, Texas. Vol. 1, The Site, Its Setting, Investigation, Cultural Features, Artifacts of Non-Native Manufacture, and Subsistence Remains;* Dee Ann Story, *The Deshazo Site, Nacogdoches County, Texas. Vol. 2, Artifacts of Native Manufacture.*

17. See Timothy K. Perttula, *Caddo Archeological and Historical Workshop Sourcebook for the Caddo Tribe of Oklahoma.*

18. See Swanton, *Source Material.*

19. J. Miller, "Changing Moons: A History of Caddo Religion," p. 243.

20. See J. D. Rogers, "The Caddos."

21. See Dee Ann Story, "Cultural History of the Native Americans"; Early, *Caddoan Saltmakers;* Frank F. Schambach, "Some New Interpretations of Spiroan Culture History"; R. H. Lafferty, "Prehistoric Exchange in the Lower Mississippi Valley"; Brown, *Spiro Ceremonial Center.*

22. Story, "Cultural History."

23. See Frank F. Schambach, "Mounds, Embankments, and Ceremonialism in the Trans-Mississippi South."

318 Notes to Pages 253–56

24. Don G. Wyckoff and Timothy G. Baugh, "Early Historic Hasinai Elites: A Model for the Material Culture of Governing Elites."

25. J. Peter Thurmond, *Archeology of the Cypress Creek Drainage Basin, Northeastern Texas and Northwestern Louisiana*; Timothy K. Perttula and B. Nelson,"Titus Phase Mortuary Practices in the Northeast Texas Pineywoods and Post Oak Savanna."

26. Lawrence A. Clayton, Vernon J. Knight, Jr., and Edward C. Moore, *The De Soto Chronicles: The Expedition of Hernando De Soto to North America in 1539–1543*; Charles Hudson, *Knights of Spain, Warriors of the Sun: Hernando de Soto and the South's Ancient Chiefdoms*.

27. Gentleman of Elvas, "True Relation of the Hardships Suffered by Governor Hernando De Soto & Certain Portuguese Gentlemen During the Discovery of the Province of Florida, Now Newly Set Forth by a Gentleman of Elvas," p. 145 (brackets added).

28. Cf. Ann F. Ramenofsky and Patricia Galloway, "Diseases and the Soto Entrada."

29. Thomas N. Campbell and Tommy Jo Campbell, *Indian Groups Associated with Spanish Missions of the San Antonio Missions National Historical Park*, pp. 53–54.

30. Timothy K. Perttula, "Caddoan Area Archaeology Since 1990."

31. Cf. Hiram F. Gregory, "Eighteenth-Century Caddoan Archaeology: A Study in Models and Interpretation."

32. George Sabo III, "Rituals of Encounter: Interpreting Native American Views of European Explorers," pp. 85–87; Sabo, "Encounters and Images"; George Sabo III, "The Structure of Caddo Leadership in the Colonial Era."

33. Hudson, *Knights of Spain*, p. 362; La Vere, *Caddo Chiefdoms*, p. 5; Sabo, "Rituals of Encounter," pp. 86–87.

34. For example, see P. Nick Kardulias, "Fur Production as a Specialized Activity in a World System: Indians in the North American Fur Trade."

35. Perttula, "French and Spanish," pp. 86–87.

36. See George Sabo III, "Reordering Their World: A Caddoan Ethnohistory," pp. 42–44.

37. Early, "With their friends," p. 4.

38. See Gregory, "Eighteenth-Century Caddoan," pp.15–16; Daniel A. Hickerson, "The Development and Decline of the Hasinai Confederacy"; Daniel A. Hickerson, "Historical Processes, Epidemic Disease, and the Formation of the Hasinai Confederacy"; Perttula, *The Caddo Nation*, pp. 179–182, 217–221.

39. John Canfield Ewers, "The Influence of Epidemics on the Indian Populations and Cultures of Texas"; Perttula, *The Caddo Nation*; Peter H. Wood, "The Changing Population of the Colonial South: An Overview by Race and Region, 1685–1790," pp. 82–84 and table 1.

40. See Perttula, *The Caddo Nation*, p. 87 and fig. 13.

41. E.g., Ewers, "Influence of Epidemics."

42. Cf. Swanton, *Source Material*.

43. Barbara Burnett, "Adaptive Efficiency of Arkansas Populations," p. 194.

44. E.g., J. W. Wood, George R. Milner, H. C. Harpending, and K. M. Weiss, "The Osteological Paradox: Problems of Inferring Prehistoric Health from Skeletal Samples"; Donald J. Ortner, "Skeletal Paleopathology: Probabilities, Possibilities, and Impossibilities."

45. See Burnett, "Adaptive Efficiency"; Early, *Caddoan Saltmakers*; M. L. Powell, "Foreword for Special Papers on Caddoan Bioarcheological Research."

46. Lisa Kealhofer and Brenda J. Baker, "Counterpoint to Collapse: Depopulation and Adaptation," pp. 210–211.

47. Burnett, "Adaptive Efficiency."

48. C. Lee, "Paleopathology of the Hatchel-Mitchell-Moores Sites, Bowie County, Texas"; Dorothy Thompson Lippert, "A Combination of Perspectives on Caddo Indian Health"; D. Wilson, "Dental Paleopathology in the Sanders (41LR2) and Mitchell (41BW4) Populations from the Red River Valley, Northeast Texas."

49. Powell, "Foreword," p. 136.
50. Powell, "Foreword," p. 137.
51. Thurmond, *Archeology*; Timothy K. Perttula, "Late Caddoan Societies in the Northeast Texas Pineywoods."
52. Nancy Adele Kenmotsu and Timothy K. Perttula, "Historical Processes and the Political Organization of the Hasinai Caddo Indians: A Reply"; Hudson, *Knights of Spain*, p. 372.
53. R. L. Brooks, "Warfare on the Southern Plains"; George R. Milner, "Warfare in Prehistoric and Early Historic Eastern North America."
54. David H. Dye, "Warfare in the Sixteenth-Century Southeast: The de Soto Expedition in the Interior"; Milner, "Warfare."
55. Hickerson, "Historical Processes."
56. Thomas N. Campbell, "Nabiri Indians"; Thomas N. Campbell, "Nondacau Indians."
57. Henri Joutel, *The La Salle Expedition to Texas: The Journal of Henri Joutel, 1684–1687*, pp. 302–303.
58. See Wallace Chafe, "Caddo Names in the de Soto Documents," p. 222.
59. From Pierre Margry, *Découvertes et Établissements des Français Dans l'Ouest et Dans le Sud de l'Amérique Septentrionale (1614–1754)*, Roll 3, p. 397.
60. William Joyce Griffith, *The Hasinai Indians of East Texas as seen by Europeans, 1687–1772*, p. 118.
61. Juan Bautista Chapa, *Texas & Northeastern Mexico, 1630–1690*, pp. 136, 161, 189; William C. Foster, *Spanish Expeditions into Texas, 1689–1768*, pp. 119, 305, fn. 20; Governor Salinas Varona, "The 1693 Expedition of Governor Salinas Varona to Sustain the Missionaries among the Tejas Indians"; Alston V. Thoms, *The Upper Keechi Creek Archaeological Project: Survey and Test Excavations at the Keechi Creek Wildlife Management Area, Leon County, Texas*, pp. 24, 26; Robert S. Weddle, "The Talon Interrogations: A Rare Perspective."
62. Griffith, *Hasinai Indians*, p. 145.
63. I.e., Ann F. Ramenofsky, "Evolutionary Theory and Native American Artifact Change in the Postcontact Period," pp. 139–141; Perttula, *The Caddo Nation*, pp. 202–207.
64. Smith, *Caddo Indians*, p. 13.
65. Cf. L. Johnson, Jr., "Notes on Mazanet's Stream Names, with Comments on their Linguistic and Ethnohistorical Value."
66. Perttula, "French and Spanish."
67. Margry, *Découvertes*, Roll 3, p. 397; see also Joutel, *The La Salle Expedition*, p. 185, fn 12.
68. Willard H. Rollings, *The Osage: An Ethnohistorical Study of Hegemony on the Prairie-Plains*.
69. Elizabeth Ann Harper John, *Storms Brewed in Other Men's Worlds: The Confrontation of Indians, Spanish, and French in the Southwest, 1540–1795*; José Maria Cortés y de Olarte, *Views from the Apache Frontier: Report on the Northern Provinces of New Spain by Jose Cortes, Lieutenant in the Royal Corps of Engineers, 1799*.
70. Gregory, "Eighteenth-Century Caddoan," p. 287.
71. Garrick Alan Bailey, *Changes in Osage Social Organization, 1673–1906*, p. 40.
72. Nancy Adele Kenmotsu, James E. Bruseth, and James E. Corbin, "Moscoso and the Route in Texas: A Reconstruction"; Frank F. Schambach, "The End of the Trail: The Route of Hernando de Soto's Army through Southwest Arkansas and East Texas"; Hudson, *Knights of Spain*, pp. 353–379 and map 8.
73. Dee Ann Story and Darrell G. Creel, "The Cultural Setting."
74. Hudson, *Knights of Spain*.
75. Margry, *Découvertes*, Roll 3, pp. 274–275.
76. See Hudson, *Knights of Spain*, map 8.

77. Cf. Jack Jackson, *Flags along the Coast: Charting the Gulf of Mexico, 1519–1759: A Reappraisal.*

78. See Henri Joutel, *The La Salle Expedition,* and Robert S. Weddle and Ann Linda Bell, "Voyage to the Mississippi through the Gulf of Mexico."

79. Margry, *Découvertes,* Roll 3, p. 397.

80. Swanton, *Source Material,* p. 50.

81. Perttula, *The Caddo Nation,* p. 182.

82. Carter, *Caddo Indians;* La Vere, *Caddo Chiefdoms;* Smith, *Caddo Indians.*

83. Hadley et al., *Presidio and Militia,* p. 323 (brackets added).

84. Chapa, *Texas,* p. 138.

85. Hadley et al., *Presidio and Militia,* p. 323.

86. Hudson, *Knights of Spain,* pp. 361, 375.

87. Kelley, *Two Caddoan Farmsteads,* fig. 15.

88. Chapa, *Texas,* p. 149; see also Elizabeth Cargill Erickson and James E. Corbin, *Archaeological Survey and Cultural Resource Assessment of Mission Tejas State Historical Park, Houston County, Texas.*

89. Perttula, "Caddoan Area," p. 310.

90. Perttula and Nelson, "Titus Phase."

91. Schambach, "Mounds, Embankments."

92. Schambach, "Mounds, Embankments," p. 41.

93. Schambach, "Mounds, Embankments," p. 41.

94. M. A. Hatcher, "The Expedition of Don Domingo Teran de los Rios into Texas."

95. Swanton, *Source Material,* plate 1.

96. Schambach, "Mounds, Embankments," p. 41.

97. Wilbur Sturtevant Nye, *Plains Indian Raiders: The Final Phases of Warfare from the Arkansas to the Red River, with Original Photographs by William S. Soule,* pp. 400–401.

98. Chapa, *Texas,* p. 138.

99. Schambach, "Archeology of the Great Bend Region," p. 7.

100. See Mildred M. Wedel, *La Harpe's 1719 Post on Red River and Nearby Caddo Settlements;* Darrell G. Creel, "Hatchel-Mitchell Site."

101. Creel, "Hatchel-Mitchell Site."

102. Creel, "Hatchel-Mitchell Site," p. 505.

103. Michael Claude Sierzchula, M. J. Guccione, R. H. Lafferty III, and M. T. Oates, *Archeological Investigations in the Great Bend Region, Miller County, Arkansas, Levee Items 2 and 3.*

104. See Clarence H. Webb, *The Belcher Mound, a Stratified Caddoan Site in Caddo Parish, Louisiana;* Michael P. Hoffman, "Changing Mortuary Patterns in the Little River Region, Arkansas"; Ann M. Early, *Standridge: Caddoan Settlement in a Mountain Environment.*

105. See Kelley, *Two Caddoan Farmsteads.*

106. Perttula and Nelson, "Titus Phase," p. 393.

107. Swanton, *Source Material,* p. 208.

108. Perttula and Nelson, "Titus Phase," table 25.

109. Perttula and Nelson, "Titus Phase," p. 396.

110. S. M. Derrick and D. Wilson, "Cranial Modeling as an Ethnic Marker among the Prehistoric Caddo," fig. 5.

111. See Perttula and Nelson, "Titus Phase," table 22.

112. E.g., Elise Worthington Clews Parsons, *Notes on the Caddo;* Swanton, *Source Material,* pp. 204–210.

113. Perttula and Nelson, "Titus Phase," p. 386 and table 24.

114. Perttula and Nelson, "Titus Phase."

115. Robert L. Turner, Jr., *Prehistoric Mortuary Remains at the Tuck Carpenter Site, Camp County, Texas,* p. 98 and table 17.

116. Perttula and Nelson, "Titus Phase," fig. 159.

117. Perttula, *The Caddo Nation*, pp. 172–177.

118. Perttula and Nelson, "Titus Phase," p. 393.

119. Perttula, "Two Worlds Meet."

120. Miller, "Changing Moons."

121. Carter, *Caddo Indians*; Smith, *Caddo Indians*; F. Todd Smith, *The Caddos, The Wichitas, and the United States, 1846–1901*.

122. Smith, *Caddo Indians*, p. 103.

Bibliography

ARCHIVES

Archives Hydrographiques. Transcription in Mississippi Department of Archives and History, Series 681, French Provincial Records, Transcripts of Letters and Documents, 1725–1740: 1732, Volume XXXV, "Traverse of the Pearl River."
Archivo General de Indias, Audiencia of Santo Domingo. Original papers in Seville, Spain. Microfilm copies of certain documents available at the P. K. Yonge Library of Florida History, Gainesville, Stetson Collection, or the John E. Worth Collection, Coosawattee Foundation, Calhoun, Georgia.
Archivo General de Indias, Audiencia of Mexico. Original papers in Seville, Spain. Microfilm copies of certain documents available at the P. K. Yonge Library of Florida History, Gainesville, or the John E. Worth Collection, Coosawattee Foundation, Calhoun, Georgia.
British Public Record Office. Colonial Office. Class Five Files. London, England. Microfilm transcript in the Library of Congress, Washington D.C.
British Public Records Office. Records Relating to South Carolina. London, England.
Charles City County, Virginia Records 1655–1665. Library of Virginia Archives, Richmond, Virginia.
Georgia State Department of Archives and History, Atlanta, Georgia.
Journal of the Commons House of Assembly, South Carolina, 1707–1721. Transcribed by Ruth and John Green. South Carolina Department of Archives and History, Columbia.
The Lyttleton Papers: The Papers of William Henry Lyttleton, Governor of South Carolina. Original Manuscripts and Letterbooks. William L. Clements Library, Ann Arbor, Michigan.
The Mary Ross Papers. Georgia State Department of Archives and History, Atlanta, Georgia.
Old Tappahannock County, Virginia Records. Essex County Courthouse, Tappahannock, Virginia.
Norfolk County Virginia Records, City of Chesapeake, Virginia.
Westmoreland County, Virginia Records.

PUBLISHED SOURCES

Ackerknecht, Erwin. *History and Geography of the Most Important Diseases.* New York: Hafner Publishing Co., 1965.
Adair, James. *Adair's History of the American Indians.* London, England, 1775. Reprint edited by Samuel Cole Williams. Johnson City, TN: The Watauga Press, 1930.
Adkins, Lesley, and Roy A. Adkins. *A Thesaurus of British Archaeology.* London, England: David and Charles, 1982.
Aldenderfer, Mark S., and Charles Stanish. "Domestic Architecture, Household Archaeology, and the Past in the South-Central Andes." In *Domestic Architecture, Ethnicity, and Complementarity in the South-Central Andes,* edited by Mark S. Aldenderfer, pp. 1–12. Iowa City: University of Iowa Press, 1993.
Alvord, Clarence W., and Lee Bidgood. *The First Explorations of the Trans-Allegheny Region by the Virginians, 1650–1674.* Cleveland, OH: Arthur H. Clark Co., 1912.
Anderson, David G. "Examining Prehistoric Settlement Distribution in Eastern North America." *Archaeology of Eastern North America* 19(1991):1–22.

————. *The Savannah River Chiefdoms: Political Change in the Late Prehistoric South-east*. Tuscaloosa: University of Alabama Press, 1994.

————. "Stability and Change in Chiefdom-Level Societies: An Examination of Missis-sippian Political Evolution on the South Atlantic Slope." In *Lamar Archaeology*, edited by Gary Shapiro. Tuscaloosa: University of Alabama Press, 1987.

Anderson, David G., David J. Hally, and James L. Rudolph. "The Mississippian Occupa-tion of the Savannah River Valley." *Southeastern Archaeology* 5(1986):32–51.

Anonymous. "Monongahela Village Site Donated." *The Archaeological Conservancy Newsletter* (spring 1994):1–4.

Anonymous. "Virginias Deploured Condition; Or an Impartiall Narrative of the Murders Comitted by the Indians There, and of the Sufferings of His Majesties Loyall Subjects under the Rebellious Outrages of Mr. Nathaniell Bacon, June to the Tenth Day of August Anno Domini 1676." *Collections of the Massachusetts Historical Society*, 4th series, 9(1871):162–176.

Anthony, David W. "Migration in Archeology: The Baby and the Bathwater." *American Anthropologist* 92(1990):895–914.

Anyon, Roger, T. J. Ferguson, Loretta Jackson, and Lillie Lane. "Native American Oral Traditions and Archaeology." *Society for American Archaeology Bulletin* 14, no. 2(1996):14–17.

Aquila, Richard. "Down the Warrior's Path: The Causes of the Southern Wars of the Iro-quois." *American Indian Quarterly* 4(1978):211–221.

————. *The Iroquois Restoration: Iroquois Diplomacy on the Colonial Frontier, 1701–1754*. 2d ed. Lincoln: University of Nebraska Press, 1977.

Archdale, John. "A New Description of that Fertile and Pleasant Province of South Caro-lina." In *Historical Collections of South Carolina*, 2 vols., edited by Bartholomew R. Carroll. New York, NY: Harper & Brothers, 1836.

Arnade, Charles W. *The Seige of St. Augustine in 1702*. Gainesville: University of Florida Press, 1959.

Atkin, Edmund. *The Appalachian Indian Frontier: The Edmund Atkin Report and Plan of 1755*, edited by Wilbur R. Jacobs. Lincoln: University of Nebraska Press, 1967.

Atkinson, James R. "Historic Chickasaw Cultural Material: A More Comprehensive Definition." *Mississippi Archaeology* 22, no. 2(1987):32–62.

————. "The De Soto Expedition through North Mississippi." *Mississippi Archaeology* 22, no. 1(1987):61–73.

Avery, G. "Eighteenth Century Spanish, French, and Caddoan Interactions as seen from Los Adaes." *Journal of Northeast Texas Archaeology* 7(1996):27–68.

Axtell, James. *The Indians' New South: Cultural Change in the Colonial Southeast*. Baton Rouge: Louisiana State University Press, 1997.

Baden, William W. *Tomotley: An Eighteenth Century Cherokee Village*. Report of Investi-gations 36, Department of Anthropology, University of Tennessee, Knoxville, 1983.

Bailey, Garrick Alan. *Changes in Osage Social Organization, 1673–1906*. Anthropological Papers No. 5, Department of Anthropology, University of Oregon, Eugene, 1973.

Baird, W. David. *The Quapaw Indians: A History of the Downstream People*. Norman: University of Oklahoma Press, 1980.

————. *The Quapaws*. Indians of North America. New York: Chelsea House Publishers, 1989.

Baker, C. Michael. "Archaeological Investigation of a Late Prehistoric Settlement in the Little Tennessee Drainage, Macon County, North Carolina." In *Collected Papers on the Archaeology of North Carolina*, edited by Joseph B. Mountjoy, pp. 29–55. North Caro-lina Archaeological Council Publications in Archaeology 19, Raleigh, 1982.

Baker, Stanley W. "Neale's Landing Site Ceramics: A Perspective on the Protohistoric Period from Blennerhasset Island." *West Virginia Archaeologist* 40(1988):40–53.

Bareis, Charles J., and James W. Porter, editors. *American Bottom Archaeology: A Sum-mary of the FAI-270 Project Contribution to the Culture History of the Mississippi River Valley*. Urbana: University of Illinois Press, 1984.

Barker, Eirlys Mair. "Much Blood and Treasure: South Carolina's Indian Traders, 1670–1755." Ph.D. dissertation, Department of History, College of William and Mary, 1993.

Bartram, William. *Travels of William Bartram*, edited by Mark Van Doren. New York, NY: Dover Publications, 1955.

———. *William Bartram on the Southeastern Indians*, edited by Gregory A. Waselkov and Kathryn E. Holland Braund. Lincoln: University of Nebraska Press, 1995.

Beck, Robin A., Jr. "From Joara to Chiaha: Spanish Exploration of the Appalachian Summit Area, 1540–1568." *Southeastern Archaeology* 16(1997):162–169.

Belmont, John S. "The Peabody Excavations, Coahoma County, Mississippi, 1901–1902." Senior honors thesis, Department of Anthropology, Harvard University, 1961.

Benenson, Abram S., editor. *The Control of Communicable Diseases in Man: An Official Report of the American Public Health Association*. Washington, DC: American Public Health Association, 1990.

Bense, Judith A. *Archaeology of the Southeastern United States: Paleoindian to World War I*. New York, NY: Academic Press, 1994.

Billings, Warren M., editor. *The Old Dominion in the Seventeenth Century*. Chapel Hill: University of North Carolina Press, 1975.

Binford, Lewis R. *An Archaeological Perspective*. New York, NY: Seminar Press, 1972.

———. *Cultural Diversity Among Aboriginal Cultures of Coastal Virginia and North Carolina*. New York, NY: Garland Publishing, Inc., 1991.

———. "In Pursuit of the Future." In *American Archaeology, Past and Future: A Celebration of the Society for American Archaeology, 1935–1985*, edited by David J. Meltzer, Don D. Fowler, and Jeremy A. Sabloff, pp. 459–479. Washington, DC: Smithsonian Institution Press, 1986.

Blakely, Robert L., and B. Detweiler Blakely. "The Impact of European Diseases in the Sixteenth Century Southeast: A Case Study." *Midcontinental Journal of Archaeology* 14(1989):62–89.

Blakeslee, Donald J. "The Origin and Spread of the Calumet Ceremony." *American Antiquity* 46(1981):759–768.

Bland, Edward. *The Discovery of New Brittaine*. London, England: Thomas Harper, 1651.

Bland, Edward, Abraham Wood, Sackford Brewster, and Elias Pennant. "The Discovery of New Brittaine, Began August 27, Anno Dom. 1650." In *Narratives of Early Carolina, 1650–1708*, edited by Alexander S. Salley, pp. 5–19. New York, NY: Charles Scribner's Sons, 1911.

Blanton, Wyndham B. *Medicine in Virginia in the Seventeenth Century*. New York, NY: Arno Press, 1972.

Blitz, John F. *Ancient Chiefdoms of the Tombigbee*. Tuscaloosa: University of Alabama Press, 1993.

———. *An Archaeological Study of the Mississippi Choctaw Indians*. Archaeological Report No. 16, Mississippi Department of Archives and History, Jackson, 1985.

———. "Choctaw Archaeology in Mississippi." *Journal of Alabama Archaeology* 41(1995):135–161.

———. "Mississippian Chiefdoms and the Fission-Fusion Process." *American Antiquity* 64(1999):577–592.

Bloch, Marc. *Feudal Society*, translated by L. A. Manyon. Chicago, IL: University of Chicago Press, 1964.

Bolton, Herbert Eugene, and Mary Ross. *The Debatable Land, A Sketch of the Anglo-Spanish Contest for the Georgia Country*. Berkeley: University of California Press, 1959.

Booker, Karen M., Charles M. Hudson, and Robert L. Rankin. "Place Name Identification and Multilingualism in the Sixteenth-Century Southeast." *Ethnohistory* 39(1992):399–451.

Boone, James L., and Eric Alden Smith. "Is It Evolution Yet? A Critique of Evolutionary Archaeology." *Current Anthropology* 39(1998):S141–S173.

Bowman, Greg, and Janel Curry-Roper. *The Houma People of Louisiana: A Story of Indian Survival.* Akron, PA: United Houma Nation and Mennonite Central Committee, 1982.

Bowne, Eric E. "The Rise and Fall of the Westo Indians: An Evaluation of the Documentary Evidence." *Early Georgia* 28(2000): 56–78.

Boyce, Douglas W. "Iroquois Tribes of the Virginia–North Carolina Coastal Plain." In *Handbook of North American Indians. Vol. 15, Northeast,* edited by Bruce G. Trigger, pp. 282–289. Washington, DC: Smithsonian Institution, 1978.

Boyd, Mark F. "Expedition of Marcos Delgado, 1686." *Florida Historical Quarterly* 16(1937):2–32.

———. "An Historical Sketch of the Prevalence of Malaria in North America." *American Journal of Tropical Medicine* 21(1941):223–244.

Bradley, James W., and S. Terry Childs. "Basque Earrings and Panther's Tails: The Form of Cross-Cultural Contact in 16th Century Iroquoia." In *Metals in Society: Theory Beyond Analysis,* edited by Robert M. Ehrenreich, pp. 7–17. MASCA Research Papers in Science and Archaeology, Vol. 8, Part 2, University Museum of Archaeology and Anthropology, University of Pennsylvania, Philadelphia, 1991.

Brain, Jeffrey P. "The Archaeological Phase: Ethnographic Fact or Fancy?" In *Archaeological Essays in Honor of Irving B. Rouse,* edited by Robert C. Dunnell and Edward S. Hall, Jr., pp. 307–314. The Hague: Mouton, 1978.

———. "Artifacts of the Adelantado." *The Conference on Historic Site Archaeology Papers* 8(1975):129–138.

———. "La Salle at the Natchez: An Archaeological and Historical Perspective." In *La Salle and His Legacy,* edited by Patricia Kay Galloway, pp. 49–59. Jackson: University Press of Mississippi, 1982.

———. "Late Prehistoric Settlement Patterning in the Yazoo Basin and Natchez Bluffs Regions of the Lower Mississippi Valley." In *Mississippian Settlement Patterns,* edited by Bruce D. Smith, pp. 331–368. New York, NY: Academic Press, 1978.

———. "The Natchez 'Paradox.'" *Ethnology* 10(1971): 215–222.

———. "A Note on the River of Anilco." *Mississippi Archaeology* 33, no. 2(1998):115–124.

———. *On the Tunica Trail.* Anthropological Study No. 1, Louisiana Archaeological Survey and Antiquities Commission, Department of Culture, Recreation, and Tourism, Baton Rouge, 1977.

———. *Tunica Archaeology.* Papers of the Peabody Museum of Anthropology and Ethnology, Vol. 78, Harvard University, Cambridge, MA, 1988.

———. *Tunica Treasure.* Papers of the Peabody Museum of Anthropology and Ethnology, Vol. 71, Harvard University, Cambridge, MA, 1979.

———. "Update of De Soto Studies Since the United States De Soto Expedition Commission Report." In *Final Report of the United States De Soto Expedition Commission,* by John R. Swanton, pp. xi–lxxii. 1939. Reprint, Washington, DC: Smithsonian Institution Press, 1985.

———. *Winterville: Late Prehistoric Culture Contact in the Lower Mississippi Valley.* Archaeological Report No. 23, Mississippi Department of Archives and History, Jackson, 1989.

Brain, Jeffrey P., Alan Toth, and Antonio Rodriguez-Buckingham. "Ethnohistoric Archaeology and the De Soto Entrada into the Lower Mississippi Valley." *Conference on Historic Site Archaeology Papers* 7(1974):232–289.

Braley, Chad. *Yuchi Town (1Ru63) Revisited: Analysis of the 1958–1962 Excavations.* Southeastern Archaeological Services, Inc., Athens, Georgia. Report submitted to Environmental Management Division, Directorate of Public Works, U. S. Army Infantry Center, Fort Benning, Georgia, 1988.

Brashler, Janet G., and Ronald W. Moxley. "Late Prehistoric Engraved Shell Gorgets of West Virginia." *West Virginia Archaeologist* 42(1990):1–10.

Braudel, Fernand. "History and the Social Sciences: The *Longue Dureé*." In *On History*, by Fernand Braudel, translated by Sarah Mathews, pp. 25–54. Chicago, IL: University of Chicago Press, 1980.

————. *The Mediterranean and the Mediterranean World in the Age of Philip II*. 2 vols. New York, NY: Harper, 1975.

Braun, E. Lucy. *Deciduous Forests of Eastern North America*. 1950. Reprint, New York, NY: Hafner Publishing Co., 1964.

Braund, Kathryn E. Holland. *Deerskins and Duffels: The Creek Indian Trade with Anglo-America, 1685–1815*. Lincoln: University of Nebraska Press, 1993.

Briceland, Alan. *Westward from Virginia: The Exploration of the Virginia-Carolina Frontier, 1650–1710*. Charlottesville: University Press of Virginia, 1987.

Brooks, R. L. "Warfare on the Southern Plains." In *Skeletal Biology in the Great Plains: Migration, Warfare, Health, and Subsistence*, edited by Douglas W. Owsley and Richard L. Jantz, pp. 317–323. Washington, DC: Smithsonian Institution Press, 1994.

Brown, Ian W. "An Archaeological Study of Culture Contact and Change in the Natchez Bluffs Region." In *La Salle and His Legacy: Frenchmen and Indians in the Lower Mississippi Valley*, edited by Patricia Galloway, pp. 176–193. Jackson: University Press of Mississippi, 1982.

————. "The Calumet Ceremony in the Southeast and its Archaeological Manifestations." *American Antiquity* 54(1989):311–331.

————. *Natchez Indian Archaeology: Culture Change and Stability in the Lower Mississippi Valley*. Archaeological Report No. 15, Mississippi Department of Archives and History, Jackson, 1985.

————. "Plaquemine Architectural Patterns in the Natchez Bluffs and Surrounding Regions of the Lower Mississippi Valley." *Midcontinental Journal of Archaeology* 10(1985):251–305.

Brown, James. "A Reconsideration of the Southern Cult." *Midcontinental Journal of Archaeology* 1(1976):115–135.

————. *The Spiro Ceremonial Center: The Archaeology of Arkansas Valley Caddoan Culture in Eastern Oklahoma*. 2 vols. Memoirs of the Museum of Anthropology No. 29, University of Michigan, Ann Arbor, 1996.

————. "On Style Divisions of the Southeastern Ceremonial Complex: A Revisionist Perspective." In *The Southeastern Ceremonial Complex: Artifacts and Analysis*, edited by Patricia Galloway, pp. 183–204. Lincoln: University of Nebraska Press, 1989.

————, editor. *The Zimmerman Site: A Report on Excavations at the Grand Village of Kaskaskia, La Salle County, Illinois*. Report of Investigations No. 9, Illinois State Museum, Springfield, 1961.

Brown, James A., and John Willis. "Re-Examination of Danner Pottery from the Starved Rock Area." Paper presented at the Annual Midwest Archaeological Conference, Beloit, Wisconsin, 1995.

Browne, William Hand, et al., editors. *The Archives of Maryland*. 72 vols. Baltimore: Maryland Historical Society, 1883–1972.

Bruseth, James E. "The Development of Caddoan Polities along the Middle Red River Valley of Eastern Texas and Oklahoma." In *The Native History of the Caddo: Their Place in Southeastern Archaeology and Ethnohistory*, edited by Timothy K. Perttula and James E. Bruseth, pp. 47–68. Studies in Archeology No. 30, Archeological Research Laboratory, University of Texas, Austin, 1998.

Bureau of Indian Affairs. *Proposed Finding: United Houma Nation, Inc.* United States Department of the Interior, Bureau of Indian Affairs, Branch of Acknowledgment and Research, December 13, 1994.

Burnett, Barbara. "Adaptive Efficiency of Arkansas Populations." In *Caddoan Saltmakers in the Ouachita Valley: The Hardman Site*, edited by Ann M. Early and Barbara Burnett, pp. 187–223. Research Series No. 43, Arkansas Archeological Survey, Fayetteville, 1993.

Byrd, William. *The Prose Works of William Byrd of Westover*, edited by Louis B. Wright. Cambridge, MA: The Belknap Press of Harvard University Press, 1966.

Cabeza de Vaca, Alvar Núñez. "La Relación dio Alvar Núñez Cabeza de Vaca." In *New American World: A Documentary History of North America*. 5 vols., edited by David B. Quinn. New York, NY: Arno Press, 1979.

Callender, Charles. *Social Organization of the Central Algonkian Indians*. Publications in Anthropology. Milwaukee, WI: Milwaukee Public Museum, 1962.

————. "Fox." In *Handbook of North American Indians. Vol. 15, Northeast*, edited by Bruce G. Trigger. Washington, DC: Smithsonian Institution, 1978.

————. "Shawnee." In *Handbook of North American Indians. Vol. 15, Northeast*, edited by Bruce G. Trigger. Washington, DC: Smithsonian Institution, 1978.

Campbell, Thomas N. "Nabiri Indians." In *The New Handbook of Texas*, vol. 4, edited by Ronnie C. Tyler, p. 922. Austin: The Texas State Historical Association, 1996.

————. "Nondacau Indians." In *The New Handbook of Texas*, vol. 4, edited by Ronnie C. Tyler, p. 1030. Austin: The Texas State Historical Association, 1996.

Campbell, Thomas N., and Tommy Jo Campbell. *Indian Groups Associated with Spanish Missions of the San Antonio Missions National Historical Park*. Special Report No. 16, Center for Archaeological Research, University of Texas at San Antonio, 1985.

Cappon, Lester J., editor. *Atlas of Early American History*. Princeton, NJ: Princeton University Press, 1976.

Cardoso, Fernando Henrique. "Dependency and Development in Latin America." *New Left Review*, 74(1972):100–104.

Cardross, Lord, and William Dunlop. "Cardross and William Dunlap to Peter Colleton, March 27, 1685." *Scottish Historical Review* 25(1928):100–104.

Carr, Christopher, editor. *For Concordance in Archaeological Analysis: Bridging Data Structure, Quantitative Technique, and Theory*. Kansas City, MO: Westport Press, 1985.

Carskadden, Jeff. "The Bosman Site, Muskingum County, Ohio." *Field Notes: The Newsletter of the West Virginia Archaeological Society* 34, no. 3(1992):3–4.

Carskadden, Jeff, Larry Edmister, and James Morton. "Scenes from the Bosman Site Excavation, Muskingum County, Ohio." *Ohio Archaeologist* 42(1992): 60–63.

Carskadden, Jeff, and James Morton. *Where the Frolics and War Dances Are Held: The Indian Wars and the Early European Exploration and Settlement of Muskingum County and the Central Muskingum Valley*. Baltimore, MD: Gateway Press, 1997.

————. "Fort Ancient in the Central Muskingam Valley of Eastern Ohio; A View from the Philo II Site." In *Cultures Before Contact: The Late Prehistory of Ohio and Surrounding Regions*, edited by Robert A. Genheimer, pp. 158–193. Columbus, OH: The Ohio Archaeological Council, 2000.

Carter, Cecile Elkins. *Caddo Indians: Where We Come From*. Norman: University of Oklahoma Press, 1995.

Chafe, Wallace. "Caddo Names in the de Soto Documents." In *The Expedition of Hernando de Soto West of the Mississippi, 1541–1543: Proceedings of the De Soto Symposia 1988 and 1990*, edited by Gloria A. Young and Michael P. Hoffman, pp. 222–226. Fayetteville: University of Arkansas Press, 1993.

Champagne, Duane. "Symbolic Structure and Political Change in Cherokee Society." *Journal of Cherokee Studies* 8(1983):87–96.

————. "Institutional and Cultural Order in Early Cherokee Society: A Sociological Interpretation." *Journal of Cherokee Studies* 15(1990):3–26.

————. *Social Order and Political Change: Constitutional Governments Among the Cherokee, the Chickasaw, the Choctaw, and the Creek*. Stanford, CA: Stanford University Press, 1992.

Chapa, Juan Bautista. *Texas & Northeastern Mexico, 1630–1690*, edited and with an introduction by William C. Foster. Austin: University of Texas Press, 1997.

Chapman, Jefferson. *Tellico Archaeology: Twelve Thousand Years of Native American His-*

tory. Report of Investigations No. 43, Department of Anthropology, University of Tennessee, Knoxville, 1985.

Chilcote, Ronald. *Theories of Development and Underdevelopment*. London, England: Westview Press, 1984.

Clancy, Phyllis. "The Carden's Bottom Puzzle Elucidated." Master's thesis, Department of Anthropology, University of Arkansas, Fayetteville, 1985.

Clark, Jerry E. *The Shawnee*. Lexington: University Press of Kentucky, 1977.

Clay, R. Berle. "The Mississippian Succession on the Lower Ohio." *Southeastern Archaeology* 16(1997):16–32.

Clayton, Lawrence A., Vernon J. Knight, Jr., and Edward C. Moore, editors. *The De Soto Chronicles: The Expedition of Hernando De Soto to North America in 1539–1543*. 2 vols. Tuscaloosa: University of Alabama Press, 1993.

Coe, Joffre Lanning. "Cherokee Archaeology." In *The Symposium on Cherokee and Iroquois Culture*, edited by William N. Fenton and John Gulick, pp. 151–160. Bureau of American Ethnology Bulletin 180, Smithsonian Institution, Washington, DC, 1961.

Colley, Linda. *Britons: Forging the Nation, 1707–1837*. London, England: Pimlico, 1992.

Collins, Susan M. *A Prehistoric Community at the Macon County Industrial Park Site*. North Carolina Archaeological Council Publications in Archaeology 2, Raleigh, 1977.

Connaway, John M., editor. *The Oliver Site in Northwest Mississippi*. Jackson: Mississippi Department of Archives and History, in press.

Cook, Noble David, and W. George Lovell, editors. *"Secret Judgements of God": Old World Diseases in Colonial Spanish America*. Norman: University of Oklahoma Press, 1991.

Corkran, David H. *The Creek Frontier, 1540–1783*. Norman: University of Oklahoma Press, 1967.

———. *The Cherokee Frontier, 1740–1762*. Norman: University of Oklahoma Press, 1962.

Cortés y de Olarte, José Maria. *Views from the Apache Frontier: Report on the Northern Provinces of New Spain by José Cortés, Lieutenant in the Royal Corps of Engineers, 1799*, edited by Elizabeth Ann Harper John, translated by J. Wheat. Norman: University of Oklahoma Press, 1989.

Cowan, C. Wesley. "The Dawn of History and the Demise of the Fort Ancient Cultures of the Central Ohio Valley." Paper presented at the annual meeting of the Society for American Archaeology, Pittsburgh, Pennsylvania, 1992.

Coxe, Daniel. "Coxe's Account of the Activities of the English in the Mississippi Valley in the Seventeenth Century." In *The First Explorations of the Trans-Allegheny Region by the Virginians, 1650–1674*, edited by Clarence Walworth Alvord and Lee Bidgood. Cleveland, OH: Arthur Clark, 1912.

Crane, Verner W. *The Southern Frontier, 1670–1732*. Raleigh, NC: Duke University Press, 1928, and Ann Arbor: University of Michigan Press, 1919, 1929. Reprint, New York, NY: W. W. Norton & Co., 1981.

Creel, Darrell G. "Hatchel-Mitchell Site." In *The New Handbook of Texas*, vol. 3, edited by Ronnie C. Tyler, pp. 504–505. Austin: Texas State Historical Association, 1996.

Cronon, William. *Changes in the Land: Indians, Colonists, and the Ecology of New England*. New York, NY: Hill and Wang, 1983.

Crosby, Alfred. *The Columbian Exchange: Biological and Cultural Consequences of 1492*. Westport, CT: Greenwood Press, 1972.

———. *Ecological Imperialism: The Biological Expansion of Europe, 900–1900*. New York, NY: Cambridge University Press, 1986.

———. "Virgin Soil Epidemics as a Factor in the Aboriginal Depopulation in America." *William and Mary Quarterly*, 3d ser., 33(1976):289–299.

Curren, Caleb. *The Protohistoric Period in Central Alabama*. Alabama-Tombigbee Regional Commission, 1984.

Daniels, John D. "The Indian Population of North America in 1492." *William and Mary Quarterly*, 3d ser., 49(1992):298–320.

Davis, Hester A., editor. *A State Plan for the Conservation of Archeological Resources in Arkansas*. Research Series No. 21, Arkansas Archeological Survey, Fayetteville, 1982.

Davis, Natalie Zeamon. *The Return of Martin Guerre*. Cambridge, MA: Harvard University Press, 1983.

Davis, R. P. Stephen, Jr., and H. Trawick Ward. "The Evolution of Siouan Communities in Piedmont North Carolina." *Southeastern Archaeology* 10, no. 1(1991):40–53.

———. "The Occaneechi and Their Role as Middlemen in the Seventeenth-Century Virginia–North Carolina Trade Network." In *Excavating Occaneechi Town: Archaeology of an Eighteenth-Century Indian Village in North Carolina*, edited by R. P. Stephen Davis, Jr., Patrick C. Livingood, H. Trawick Ward, and Vincas P. Steponaitis, pp. 244–249. CD-ROM. Chapel Hill: University of North Carolina Press, 1998.

Davis, R. P. Stephen, Jr., Patrick C. Livingood, H. Trawick Ward, and Vincas P. Steponaitis, editors. *Excavating Occaneechi Town: Archaeology of an Eighteenth-Century Indian Village in North Carolina*. CD-ROM. Chapel Hill: University of North Carolina Press, 1998.

DeMontigny. "Letter of Mr. DeMontigny, January 2, 1699." In *Early Voyages Up and Down the Mississippi*, edited by John Dawson Gilmary Schea. Originally published by J. Munsell, Albany, NY, 1861. Reprint, Albany, NY: J. McDonough, 1902.

DePratter, Chester. "The Chiefdom of Cofitachequi." In *The Forgotten Centuries: Indians and Europeans in the American South, 1521–1704*, edited by Charles Hudson and Carmen Chaves Tesser, pp. 197–226. Athens: University of Georgia Press, 1994.

———. "Cofitachequi: Ethnohistorical and Archaeological Evidence." In *Studies in South Carolina Archaeology: Essays in Honor of Robert L. Stephenson*, edited by Albert C. Goodyear III and Glen T. Hanson, pp. 133–156. Anthropological Studies 9, Occasional Papers of the South Carolina Institute of Archaeology and Anthropology, University of South Carolina, Columbia, 1989.

———. *Late Prehistoric and Early Historic Chiefdoms in the Southeastern United States*. New York, NY: Garland Publishing, 1991.

———. "The Role of Carolina in the Transformation of Native American Societies." Paper presented at the Porter L. Fortune, Jr., History Symposium entitled "Early Social History of the Southeastern Indians," University of Mississippi, Oxford, October 1998.

Derrick, S. M., and D. Wilson. "Cranial Modeling as an Ethnic Marker among the Prehistoric Caddo." *Bulletin of the Texas Archeological Society* 68(1997): 139–146.

DeVorsey, Louis, Jr. "The Impact of the La Salle Expedition of 1682 on European Cartography." In *La Salle and His Legacy: Frenchmen and Indians in the Lower Mississippi Valley*, edited by Patricia Kay Galloway, pp. 60–78. Jackson: University Press of Mississippi, 1982.

Diamond, Jared M. *Guns, Germs, and Steel: The Fates of Human Societies*. New York, NY: W. W. Norton & Co., 1999.

Dickens, Roy S., Jr. *Cherokee Prehistory: The Pisgah Phase in the Appalachian Summit*. Knoxville: University of Tennessee Press, 1976.

———. "An Evolutionary-Ecological Interpretation of Cherokee Cultural Development." In *The Conference on Cherokee Prehistory*, compiled by David G. Moore, pp. 81–94. Swannanoa, NC: Warren Wilson College, 1986.

———. "Mississippian Settlement Patterns in the Appalachian Summit Area: The Pisgah and Qualla Phases." In *Mississippian Settlement Patterns*, edited by Bruce D. Smith, pp. 115–139. New York, NY: Academic Press, 1978.

———. "The Origins and Development of Cherokee Culture." In *The Cherokee Indian Nation: A Troubled History*, edited by Duane H. King, pp. 3–32. Knoxville: University of Tennessee Press, 1979.

———. "The Route of Rutherford's Expedition Against the North Carolina Cherokees." *Southern Indian Studies* 19(1967):3–24.

Dickens, Roy, Trawick Ward, and R. P. Stephen Davis. *The Siouan Project: Seasons I and*

II. Monograph Series No. 1, Research Laboratories of Anthropology, University of North Carolina, Chapel Hill, 1987.

Dickinson, Samuel D. "Historic Tribes of the Ouachita Drainage System in Arkansas." *The Arkansas Archeologist* 21(1980):1–11.

———. "The River of Cayas: The Ouachita or the Arkansas River?" *Arkansas Archeological Society Field Notes* 209(1986):5–11.

Dimmick, Frederica R. "A Survey of Upper Creek Sites in Central Alabama." *Journal of Alabama Archaeology* 35, no. 2(1989):1–86.

Dobyns, Henry. *Their Number Become Thinned: Native American Population Dynamics in Eastern North America.* Knoxville: University of Tennessee Press, 1983.

Dos Santos, Theotonio. "The Structure of Dependence." *American Economic Review* 60, no. 2(1970):231–236.

Drechsel, Emanuel J. "Mobilian Jargon in the 'Prehistory' of Southeastern North America." In *Perspectives on the Southeast: Linguistics, Archaeology, Ethnohistory,* edited by Patricia Kwachka, pp. 25–43. Athens: University of Georgia Press, 1994.

Drooker, Penelope B. "Exotic Ceramics at Madisonville: Implications for Interaction." In *Taming the Taxonomy: Toward a New Understanding of Great Lakes Prehistory,* edited by Ron Williamson, pp. 171–181. Toronto: Ontario Archaeological Society 1999.

———. "External Relations: Exotic Materials and Artifacts at Madisonville." Paper presented at the annual meeting of the Society for American Archaeology, St. Louis, April 1993.

———. "Fort Ancient and the Southeast: Late Prehistoric and Protohistoric Interaction." Paper presented at the Southeastern Archaeological Conference, Lexington, Kentucky, 1994.

———. "Madisonville Metal and Glass Artifacts: Implications for Western Fort Ancient Chronology and Interaction Networks." *Midcontinental Journal of Archaeology* 21, no. 2(1996):1–46.

———. "Pots and Pipes as 'Smoking Guns'—Tracking the Early Historical Iroquois–Fort Ancient Relationship." Lecture presented at the annual meeting of the West Virginia Archeological Society, Charleston, West Virginia, 1999.

———. "The Shawnee Female Deity in Political Perspective." Manuscript in possession of author, Albany, NY, 1991.

———. *The View from Madisonville: Protohistoric Western Fort Ancient Interaction Patterns.* Memoirs of the Museum of Anthropology No. 31, University of Michigan, Ann Arbor, 1997.

———. *Zoom-in to Madisonville.* CD-ROM to accompany *The View from Madisonville: Protohistoric Western Fort Ancient Interaction Patterns.* Memoirs of the Museum of Anthropology No. 31, University of Michigan, Ann Arbor, 1998.

Drooker, Penelope B., and C. Wesley Cowan. "The Dawn of History and the Transformation of the Fort Ancient Cultures of the Central Ohio Valley." In *Societies in Eclipse,* edited by David S. Brose, Robert C. Mainfort, Jr., and C. Wesley Cowan. Washington, DC: Smithsonian Institution Press, 2001.

Dunaway, Wilma. "Incorporation as an Interactive Process: Cherokee Resistance to Expansion of the Capitalist World System." *Sociological Inquiry* 66, no. 4(1996):455–470.

Dye, David H. "Introduction." In *The Protohistoric Period in the Mid-South: 1500–1700,* edited by David H. Dye and Ronald C. Brister, pp. xi–xiv. Archaeological Report No. 18, Mississippi Department of Archives and History, Jackson, 1986.

———. "Reconstruction of the De Soto Expedition Route in Arkansas: The Mississippi Alluvial Plain." In *The Expedition of Hernando de Soto West of the Mississippi, 1541–1543,* edited by Gloria Young and Michael Hoffman, pp. 36–57. Fayetteville: University of Arkansas Press, 1993.

———. "Warfare in the Sixteenth-Century Southeast: The De Soto Expedition in the Interior." In *Columbian Consequences: Archaeological and Historical Perspectives on the Spanish Borderlands East*, 2 vols., edited by David Hurst Thomas, pp. 211–222. Washington, DC: Smithsonian Institution, 1990.

Dye, David H., and Ronald C. Brister, editors. *The Protohistoric Period in the Mid-South: 1500–1700.* Archaeological Report No. 18, Mississippi Department of Archives and History, Jackson, 1986.

Earle, Timothy K. "Comment on 'Is It Evolution Yet?' by James L. Boone and Eric Alden Smith." *Current Anthropology* 39, suppl.(1998):S158.

––––––. *How Chiefs Come to Power: The Political Economy in Prehistory.* Stanford, CA: Stanford University Press, 1997.

Early, Ann M. "Finding the Middle Passage: The Spanish Journey from the Swamplands to Caddo Country." In *The Expedition of Hernando de Soto West of the Mississippi, 1541–1543*, edited by Gloria A. Young and Michael P. Hoffman, pp. 68–77. University of Arkansas Press, Fayetteville, 1993.

––––––. *Standridge: Caddoan Settlement in a Mountain Environment.* Research Series No. 29, Arkansas Archeological Survey, Fayetteville, 1988.

––––––. " 'With Their Friends They Keep Unchangeable Peace': The Caddo of the Trans-Mississippi South." In *Indians of the Greater Southeast During the Historic Period*, edited by B. G. McEwan. Gainesville: University Press of Florida, 1998.

––––––, editor. *Caddoan Saltmakers in the Ouachita Valley: The Hardman Site.* Research Series No. 43, Arkansas Archeological Survey, Fayetteville, 1993.

Egloff, Brian J. "An Analysis of Ceramics from Historic Cherokee Towns." Master's thesis, Department of Anthropology, University of North Carolina, Chapel Hill, 1967.

Egloff, Keith T. "Methods and Problems of Mound Excavation in the South Appalachian Area." Master's thesis, Department of Anthropology, University of North Carolina, Chapel Hill, 1971.

Elias, Norbert. *The Civilizing Process*, translated by Edmund Jephcott. Oxford, England: B. Blackwell, 1982.

Ellis, Chris J., and Neal Ferris, editors. *The Archaeology of Southern Ontario to A.D. 1650.* London, Ontario: London Chapter, Ontario Archaeological Society, 1990.

Elvas, Gentleman of. "True Relation of the Hardships Suffered by Governor Hernando De Soto & Certain Portuguese Gentlemen During the Discovery of the Province of Florida, Now Newly Set Forth by a Gentleman of Elvas," edited and translated by J. A. Robertson. In *The De Soto Chronicles: The Expedition of Hernando de Soto to North America in 1539–1543*, vol. 1, edited by Lawrence A. Clayton, Vernon J. Knight, Jr., and Edward C. Moore, pp. 19–219. Tuscaloosa: University of Alabama Press, 1993.

Emberling, Geoffrey. "Ethnicity in Complex Societies." *Journal of Archaeological Research* 5(1995):295–344.

Erickson, Elizabeth Cargill, and James E. Corbin. *Archaeological Survey and Cultural Resource Assessment of Mission Tejas State Historical Park, Houston County, Texas.* Public Lands Division, Cultural Resource Program, Texas Parks and Wildlife Department, Austin, 1996.

Essenpreis, Patricia S. "Fort Ancient Settlement: Differential Response at a Mississippian–Late Woodland Interface." In *Mississippian Settlement Patterns*, edited by Bruce D. Smith, pp. 141–167. New York, NY: Academic Press, 1978.

Ethridge, Robbie, and Charles Hudson. "The Early Historic Transformation of the Southeastern Indians." In *Cultural Diversity in the U. S. South: Anthropological Contributions to a Region in Transition*, edited by Patricia Beaver and Carole Hill, pp. 34–50. Proceedings of the Southern Anthropological Society No. 31. Athens: University of Georgia Press, 1998.

Ewers, John Canfield. "The Influence of Epidemics on the Indian Populations and Cultures of Texas." *Plains Anthropologist* 18, no. 59(1973):104–115.

Fallam, Robert. "A Journal from Virginia Beyond the Appalachian Mountains, in Sept. 1671, Sent to the Royal Society by Mr. Clayton, and Read Aug. 1, 1688, before the Said Society." In *The First Explorations of the Trans-Allegheny Region by the Virginians,*

1650–1674, edited by Clarence W. Alvord and Lee Bidgood, pp. 183–205. Cleveland, OH: Arthur H. Clark Co., 1912.

Fenneman, Nevin. *Physiography of Eastern United States.* New York, NY: McGraw-Hill, 1938.

Ferguson, Leland G. "South Appalachian Mississippian." Ph.D. dissertation, Department of Anthropology, University of North Carolina, Chapel Hill, 1971.

Fisk, Harold N. *Geological Investigation of the Alluvial Valley of the Lower Mississippi River.* Mississippi River Commission Publications No. 52, Washington, DC, 1944.

Fitzgerald, William R., Laurier Turgeon, Ruth Holmes Whitehead, and James W. Bradley. "Late Sixteenth-Century Basque Banded Copper Kettles." *Historical Archaeology* 27(1993):44–57.

Fogelson, Raymond D. "Cherokee Notions of Power." In *The Anthropology of Power*, edited by Raymond D. Fogelson and Richard N. Adams, pp. 185–195. New York, NY: Academic Press, 1977.

Fontaine, John. *The Journal of John Fontaine, An Irish Huguenot Son in Spain and Virginia 1710–1719*, edited by Edward P. Alexander. Charlottesville: University Press of Virginia, 1972.

Ford, James A. *Menard Site: The Quapaw Village of Osotouy on the Arkansas River.* Anthropological Papers of the American Museum of Natural History No. 48, Part 2, American Museum of Natural History, New York, NY, 1961.

Fortescue, John William, Sir, editor. *Calendar of State Papers, Colonial Series: America and West Indies, 1574–1660*, vols. 11–16. London, England: Great Britain Public Record Office, 1860.

Foster, William C. *Spanish Expeditions into Texas, 1689–1768.* Austin: University of Texas Press, 1995.

Fox, Gregory L. "An Examination of Mississippian Period Phases in Southeastern Missouri." In *Changing Perspectives on the Archaeology of the Central Mississippi Valley*, edited by Michael J. O'Brien and Robert C. Dunnell, pp. 31–58. Tuscaloosa: University of Alabama Press, 1998.

Franklin, Wayne. *Discoverers, Explorers, Settlers: The Diligent Writers of Early America.* Chicago, IL: University of Chicago Press, 1979.

Fried, Morton H. *The Evolution of Political Society: An Essay on Political Anthropology.* New York, NY: Random House, 1967.

Friedman, Jonathan. "Tribes, States, and Transformations." In *Marxist Analyses and Social Anthropology*, edited by Maurice Bloch, pp. 161–202. New York, NY: John Wiley, 1975.

Fritz, Gayle J., and Tristram R. Kidder. "Recent Investigations into Prehistoric Agriculture in the Lower Mississippi Valley." *Southeastern Archaeology* 12(1993):1–14.

Galloway, Patricia K. *Choctaw Genesis: 1500–1700.* University of Nebraska Press, Lincoln, 1995.

———. "Confederacy as a Solution to Chiefdom Dissolution: Historical Evidence in the Choctaw Case." In *The Forgotten Centuries: Indians and Europeans in the American South, 1521–1704*, edited by Charles Hudson and Carmen Chaves Tesser, pp. 393–420. Athens: University of Georgia Press, 1994.

———. "*Conjoncture* and *Longue Durée*: History, Anthropology, and the Hernando de Soto Expedition." In *The Hernando de Soto Expedition: History, Historiography, and "Discovery" in the Southeast*, edited by Patricia K. Galloway, pp. 283–294. Lincoln: University of Nebraska Press, 1997.

———. "The Direct Historical Approach and Early Historical Documents: The Ethnohistorian's View." In *The Protohistoric Period in the Mid-South: 1500–1700*, edited by David H. Dye and Ronald C. Brister, pp. 14–23. Archaeological Report No. 18, Mississippi Department of Archives and History, Jackson, 1986.

———. "The Incestuous Soto Narratives." In *The Hernando de Soto Expedition: History, Historiography, and "Discovery" in the Southeast*, edited by Patricia K. Galloway, pp. 11–44. University of Nebraska Press, Lincoln, 1997.

―――. "Prehistoric Population of Mississippi: A First Approximation." *Mississippi Archaeology* 29, no. 2(1994):44–71.

Galloway, Patricia, Robert S. Weddle, and Mary Morkovsky. *La Salle, the Mississippi and the Gulf: Three Primary Documents*. College Station: Texas A&M University, 1987.

Galloway, William A. *Old Chillicothe: Shawnee and Pioneer History: Conflicts and Romances in the Northwest Territory*. Xenia, OH: The Buckeye Press, 1934.

Gatschet, Albert S. "Grammatic Sketch of the Catawba Language." *American Anthropologist* n.s. 2, no. 3(1900):527–549.

Gearing, Frederick O. "The Structural Poses of the Eighteenth-Century Cherokee Villages." *American Anthropologist* 60(1958):1148–1157.

―――. *Priests and Warriors: Social Structures for Cherokee Politics in the Eighteenth Century*. American Anthropological Association Memoirs 93, Washington, DC, 1962.

Gibson, Jon L. "Review of 'Archaeology and Ceramics at the Marksville Site,' by Alan Toth." *Louisiana Archaeology* 4(1979):127–137.

Ginzburg, Carlo. *The Cheese and the Worms: The Cosmos of a Sixteenth-Century Miller*, translated by John and Ann Tedeschi. Baltimore, MD: The Johns Hopkins University Press, 1980.

Girard, J. S. "Historic Caddoan Occupation in the Natchitoches Area: Recent Attempts to Locate Residential Sites." *Caddoan Archeology* 8, no. 3(1997): 19–31.

Giraud, Marcel. *Histoire de la Louisiane Française: L'époque de John Law*. Paris, France: Presses Universitaires de France, 1966.

―――. *A History of French Louisiana. Vol. 1, The Reign of Louis XIV, 1698–1715*, translated by Joseph Lambert. Baton Rouge: Louisiana State University Press, 1974.

Goddard, Ives. "Central Algonquian Languages." In *Handbook of North American Indians. Vol. 15, Northeast*, edited by Bruce G. Trigger. Washington, DC: Smithsonian Institution, 1978.

―――. "The Classification of the Native Languages of North America." In *Handbook of North American Indians. Vol. 17, Languages*, edited by Ives Goddard, pp. 290–323. Washington, DC: Smithsonian Institution Press, 1996.

―――. "Introduction." In *Handbook of North American Indians. Vol. 17, Languages*, edited by Ives Goddard, pp. 1–16. Washington, DC: Smithsonian Institution Press, 1996.

Goodwin, Gary C. *Cherokees in Transition: A Study of Changing Culture and Environment Prior to 1775*. Research Paper 181, Department of Geography, University of Chicago, Chicago, 1977.

Gravier, Father James. "Journal of . . . Gravier." In *Early Voyages Up and Down the Mississippi*, edited by John Dawson Gilmar Schea. Originally published by J. Munsell, Albany, NY, 1861. Reprint, Albany, NY: J. McDonough, 1902.

Graybill, Jeffrey R. "The Eastern Periphery of Fort Ancient (A.D. 1050–1650): A Diachronic Approach to Settlement Variability." Ph.D. dissertation, Department of Anthropology, University of Washington, Seattle, 1981.

―――. "Fort Ancient–East: Origins, Change, and External Correlations." Paper presented at the annual meeting of the Midwestern Archaeological Conference, Columbus, Ohio, 1986.

―――. "Fort Ancient–Madisonville Horizon: Protohistoric Archeology in the Middle Ohio Valley." Paper presented at the Third Annual Uplands Archaeology in the East Symposium, Harrisonburg, West Virginia, 1987.

Green, Thomas J., and Cheryl A. Munson. "Mississippian Settlement Patterns in Southwestern Indiana." In *Mississippian Settlement Patterns*, edited by Bruce D. Smith, pp. 293–330. New York, NY: Academic Press, 1978.

Green, William. "The Search for Altamaha: The Archaeology and Ethnohistory of an Early 18th-Century Yamasee Indian Town." Master's thesis, Department of Anthropology, University of South Carolina, Columbia, 1991.

Greenblatt, Stephen. *Marvelous Possessions: The Wonder of the New World*. Chicago, IL: University of Chicago Press, 1991.

Greene, Lance K. "The Archaeology and History of the Cherokee Out Towns." Master's thesis, Department of Anthropology, University of Tennessee, Knoxville, 1996.

Gregory, Hiram F. "Eighteenth-Century Caddoan Archæology: A Study in Models and Interpretation." Ph.D. dissertation, Department of Anthropology, Southern Methodist University, Dallas, 1973.

Griffin, James B. "Eastern North American Archaeology: A Summary." *Science* 156(1967):175–191.

———. *The Fort Ancient Aspect: Its Cultural and Chronological Position in Mississippi Valley Archaeology.* Anthropological Papers of the University of Michigan Museum of Anthropology No. 28. Ann Arbor: University of Michigan Press, 1943.

———. "Foreword." In *Mississippian Settlement Patterns,* edited by Bruce D. Smith, pp. xv–xxii. New York, NY: Academic Press, 1978.

Griffith, William Joyce. *The Hasinai Indians of East Texas as Seen by Europeans, 1687–1772.* Philological and Documentary Studies, vol. 2, no. 3. Middle American Research Institute, Tulane University, New Orleans, 1954.

Guthe, Alfred K. "The Eighteenth Century Overhill Cherokee." In *For the Director: Research Essays in Honor of James Griffin,* edited by Charles E. Cleland, pp. 112–129. Anthropological Papers of the University of Michigan Museum of Anthropology No. 61. Ann Arbor: University of Michigan Press, 1977.

Guthe, Alfred K., and E. Marian Bistline. *Excavations of Tomotley, 1973–74, and the Tukegee Area: Two Reports.* Report of Investigations No. 24, Department of Anthropology, University of Tennessee, Tennessee Valley Authority Publications in Anthropology, Knoxville, 1981.

Haas, Mary R. *Tunica Texts.* Berkeley: University of California Press, 1950.

Hadley, D., Thomas H. Naylor, and M. K. Schuetz-Miller, compilers and editors. *The Presidio and Militia on the Northern Frontier of New Spain: A Documentary History. Vol. 2, Part 2, The Central Corridor and the Texas Corridor, 1700–1765.* Tucson: University of Arizona Press, 1997.

Hale, Horatio. "The Tutelo Tribe and Language." *Proceedings of the American Philosophical Society* 21, no.114(1883):1–41.

Hall, Robert L. "The Evolution of the Calumet Pipe." In *Prairie Archaeology: Papers in Honor of David A. Baerris,* edited by Guy E. Gibbon. Minneapolis: University of Minnesota, 1983.

———. "Calumet Ceremonialism, Mourning Ritual, and Mechanisms of Inter-tribal Trade." In *Mirror and Metaphor: Material and Social Construction of Reality,* edited by D. W. Ingersoll, Jr., and G. Bronitsky. Lanham, MD: University Press of America, 1987.

Hally, David J. "The Cherokee Archaeology of Georgia." In *The Conference on Cherokee Prehistory,* compiled by David G. Moore, pp. 95–121. Swannanoa, NC: Warren Wilson College, 1986.

———. "The Chiefdom of Coosa." In *The Forgotten Centuries: Indians and Europeans in the American South, 1521–1704,* edited by Charles Hudson and Carmen Chaves Tesser, pp. 227–253. Athens: University of Georgia Press, 1994.

———. "The Identification of Vessel Function: A Case Study from Northwest Georgia." *American Antiquity* 51(1986):267–295.

———. "An Overview of Lamar Culture." In *Ocmulgee Archaeology, 1936–1986,* edited by David J. Hally, pp. 144–174. Athens: University of Georgia Press, 1994.

———. "Lamar Archaeology." In *Ocmulgee Archaeology, 1936–1986,* edited by David J. Hally, pp. 144–174. Athens: University of Georgia Press, 1994.

———. "The Plaquemine and Mississippian Occupations of the Upper Tensas Basin, Louisiana." Ph.D. dissertation, Department of Anthropology, Harvard University, Cambridge, MA 1972.

———. "The Settlement Pattern of Mississippian Chiefdoms in Northern Georgia." In *Settlement Pattern Studies in the Americas: Fifty Years Since Virú,* edited by Brian R.

Billman and Gary M. Feinman, pp. 96–115. Washington, DC: Smithsonian Institution Press, 1999.
———. "The Territorial Size of Mississippian Chiefdoms." In *Archaeology of Eastern North America: Papers in Honor of Stephen Williams*, edited by James A. Stoltman, pp. 143–168. Archaeological Report No. 25, Mississippi Department of Archives and History, Jackson, 1993.
Hally, David J., and Hypatia Kelly. "The Nature of Mississippian Towns in Northern Georgia: The King Site Example." In *Mississippian Towns and Sacred Spaces: Searching for an Architectural Grammar*, edited by R. Barry Lewis and Charles B. Stout, pp. 49–63. Tuscaloosa: University of Alabama Press, 1998.
Hally, David J., and James B. Langford. *Mississippi Period Archaeology of the Georgia Valley and Ridge Province*. Laboratory of Archaeology Report No. 25, Department of Anthropology, University of Georgia, Athens, 1988.
Hally, David J., and James L. Rudolph. *Mississippi Period Archaeology of the Georgia Piedmont*. Laboratory of Archaeology Report No. 24, Department of Anthropology, University of Georgia, Athens, 1986.
Hally, David J., Marvin T. Smith, and James B. Langford, Jr. "The Archaeological Reality of de Soto's Coosa." In *Columbian Consequences: Archaeological and Historical Perspectives on the Spanish Borderlands East*, 2 vols., edited by David Hurst Thomas, pp. 121–138. Washington, DC: Smithsonian Institution Press, 1990.
Hann, John. *Apalachee: The Land between the Rivers*. Gainesville: University Press of Florida, 1988.
———. *A History of the Timucua Indians and Missions*. Gainesville: University Press of Florida, 1996.
———. "Political Leadership among the Natives of Spanish Florida." *Florida Historical Quarterly* 71, no. 2(1992):188–208.
———. "St. Augustine's Fallout from the Yamasee War." *Florida Historical Quarterly* 68(1989):180–200.
———. "Visitations and Revolts in Florida, 1656–1695." *Florida Archaeology* 7(1993).
Hanna, Charles A. *The Wilderness Trail; or, the Ventures and Adventures of the Pennsylvania Traders on the Allegheny Path, With Some New Annals of the Old West, and the Records of Some Strong Men and Some Bad Ones*. New York, NY: G. P. Putnam's Sons, 1911.
Hanson, Lee H. *The Hardin Village Site*. Studies in Anthropology No. 4. Lexington: University of Kentucky Press, 1966.
———. *The Buffalo Site: A Late Seventeenth Century Indian Village Site (46PU31) in Putnam County, West Virginia*. Reports of Archaeological Investigations No. 5, West Virginia Geological and Economic Survey, Morgantown, 1975.
Harmon, Michael A. *Eighteenth Century Lower Cherokee Adaptation and Use of Material Cultures*. Volumes in Historical Archaeology 2, South Carolina Institute of Archaeology and Anthropology, Columbia, 1986.
Harrington, Mark R. "A Pot-Hunters' Paradise." *Indian Notes* 1, no. 2(1924): 84–90.
Harriot, Thomas. "A Briefe and True Report of the New Found Land of Virginia (1588)." In *New American World: A Documentary History of North America*, 5 vols., edited by David B. Quinn. New York, NY: Arno Press, 1979.
Harris, Marvin. *The Rise of Anthropological Theory: A History of Theories of Culture*. New York, NY: Thomas Y. Crowell, 1968.
———. *Cultural Materialism: The Struggle for a Science of Culture*. New York, NY: Random House, 1979.
Hatch, James W. "Lamar Period Upland Farmsteads of the Oconee River Valley, Georgia." In *Mississippian Communities and Households*, edited by J. Daniel Rogers and Bruce D. Smith, pp. 135–155. Tuscaloosa: University of Alabama Press, 1995.
Hatcher, M. A. "The Expedition of Don Domingo Teran de los Rios into Texas." *Preliminary Studies of the Texas Catholic Historical Society* 2(1932):3–62.

Hatley, M. Thomas. "Cherokee Women Farmers Hold Their Ground." In *Appalachian Frontiers: Settlement, Society, and Development in the Preindustrial Era*, edited by Robert D. Mitchell, pp. 37–51. Lexington: University Press of Kentucky, 1991.

———. *The Dividing Paths: Cherokees and South Carolinians through the Revolutionary Era*. New York, NY: Oxford University Press, 1995.

Helms, Mary. *Ancient Panama: Chiefs in Search of Power*. Austin: University of Texas Press, 1979.

Henderson, A. Gwynn, Cynthia E. Jobe, and Christopher A. Turnbow. *Indian Occupation and Use in Northern and Eastern Kentucky During the Contact Period (1540–1795): An Initial Investigation*. Manuscript on file, Kentucky Heritage Council, Frankfort, 1986.

Henderson, A. Gwynn, David Pollack, and Christopher A. Turnbow. "Chronology and Cultural Patterns." In *Fort Ancient Cultural Dynamics in the Middle Ohio Valley*, edited by A. Gwynn Henderson. Monographs in World Archaeology No. 8. Madison, WI: Prehistory Press, 1992.

Henige, David. "Millennarian Archaeology, Double Discourse, and the Unending Quest for de Soto." *Midcontinental Journal of Archaeology* 21(1996):191–215.

———. *Oral Historiography*. New York, NY: Longman, 1982.

———. "Primary Source by Primary Source? On the Role of Epidemics in New World Depopulation." *Ethnohistory* 33(1986):293–312.

———. " 'So Unbelievable It Has To Be True': Inca Garcilaso in Two Worlds." In *The Hernando de Soto Expedition: History, Historiography, and "Discovery" in the Southeast*, edited by Patricia K. Galloway, pp. 155–177. Lincoln: University of Nebraska Press, 1997.

Hening, William Walker, compiler. *The Statutes at Large, Being a Collection of all the Laws of Virginia from the First Session of the Legislature*. 13 vols. New York, NY: R. & W. & G. Bartow, 1809–1823.

Hickerson, Daniel A. "The Development and Decline of the Hasinai Confederacy." Ph.D. dissertation, Department of Anthropology, University of Georgia, Athens, 1996.

———. "Historical Processes, Epidemic Disease, and the Formation of the Hasinai Confederacy." *Ethnohistory* 44, no. 1(1997):31–52.

Hickerson, Harold. *The Southwestern Chippewa; an Ethnohistorical Study*. American Anthropological Association, Memoir 92. Menasha, WI: George Barton Co., Inc., 1962.

Higginbotham, Jay. *Old Mobile: Fort Louis de la Louisiane, 1702–1711*. Mobile, AL: Museum of the City of Mobile, 1977.

Hill, Sarah H. *Weaving New Worlds: Southeastern Cherokee Women and Their Basketry*. Chapel Hill: University of North Carolina Press, 1997.

Hilliard, Sam Bowers. *Atlas of Antebellum Southern Agriculture*. Baton Rouge: Louisiana State University Press, 1984.

Hinderaker, Eric. *Elusive Empires: Constructing Colonialism in the Ohio Valley, 1673–1800*. New York, NY: Cambridge University Press, 1997.

Hoffman, Darla S. "From the Southeast to Fort Ancient: A Survey of Shell Gorgets in West Virginia." Master's thesis, Department of Sociology, Marshall University, Huntington, West Virginia, 1998.

———. "From the Southeast to Fort Ancient: A Survey of Shell Gorgets in West Virginia." *West Virginia Archeologist* 49, nos. 1 and 2(1999):1–40.

Hoffman, Michael P. "Changing Mortuary Patterns in the Little River Region, Arkansas." In *Southeastern Natives and Their Pasts*, edited by Don G. Wyckoff and Jack L. Hofman, pp. 163–182. Studies in Oklahoma's Past No. 11, Oklahoma Archeological Survey, Norman, 1983.

———. "Ethnic Identities and Cultural Change in the Protohistoric Period of Eastern Arkansas." In *Perspectives on the Southeast: Linguistics, Archaeology, and Ethnohistory*, edited by Patricia B. Kwachka, pp. 61–70. Athens: University of Georgia Press, 1994.

———. "The Kinkead-Mainard Site, 3PU2: A Late Prehistoric Quapaw Phase Site near Little Rock, Arkansas." *The Arkansas Archeologist* 16,17,18(1977): 1–41.

———. "The Protohistoric Period in the Lower and Central Arkansas River Valley in Arkansas." In *The Protohistoric Period in the Mid-South: 1500–1700*, edited by David H. Dye and Ronald C. Brister, pp. 24–37. Archaeological Report No. 18, Mississippi Department of Archives and History, Jackson, 1986.

———. "Protohistoric Tunican Indians in Arkansas." *Arkansas Historical Quarterly* LI, no. 1(1992):30–53.

———. "Protohistoric Tunican Indians in Arkansas." In *Cultural Encounters in the Early South*, edited by Jeannie Whayne, pp. 61–75. Fayetteville: University of Arkansas Press, 1995.

———. "Quapaw Structures, 1673–1834, and Their Comparative Significance." In *Arkansas before the Americans*, edited by Hester A. Davis, pp. 55–68. Research Series, No. 40, Arkansas Archeological Survey, Fayetteville, 1991.

———. "The Terminal Mississippian Period in the Arkansas River Valley and Quapaw Ethnogenesis." In *Towns and Temples Along the Mississippi*, edited by David H. Dye and Cheryl Anne Cox, pp. 208–226. Tuscaloosa: University of Alabama Press, 1990.

Hollinger, R. Eric. "Residence Patterns and Oneota Cultural Dynamics." In *Oneota Archaeology: Past, Present and Future*, edited by William Green, pp. 141–174. Report of the Office of the State Archaeologist No. 20, University of Iowa, Iowa City, 1995.

Holmes, William F. S. "Hardin Village: A Northern Kentucky Late Fort Ancient Site's Mortuary Patterns and Social Organization." Master's thesis, Department of Anthropology, University of Kentucky, Lexington, 1994.

House, John H. "Continuing Field Studies at the Sarassa Lake Site."*Arkansas Archeological Society Field Notes* 251(1993):10–11.

———. "Flat-bottomed Shell-tempered Pottery in the Ozarks: A Preliminary Discussion." *The Arkansas Archeologist* 19(1978):44–49.

———. " 'The Most Historic Place in Arkansas': The 1997 Society-Survey Training Program at the Menard-Hodges Archeological Site, Arkansas County, Arkansas." *Arkansas Archeological Society Field Notes* 275, erroneously numbered "276"(1997):1, 3–5.

———. "Noble Lake: A Protohistoric Archeological Site on the Lower Arkansas River." *The Arkansas Archeologist* 36(1997):47–97.

———. "Time, People, and Material Culture at the Kuykendall Brake Site, Pulaski County, Arkansas." Paper presented at the annual meeting of the Southeastern Archaeological Conference, Baton Rouge, LA, 1997.

House, John H., and Henry S. McKelway. "Mississippian and Quapaw on the Lower Arkansas." In *A State Plan for the Conservation of Archeological Resources in Arkansas*, edited by Hester A. Davis, pp. SE41–SE47. Research Series No. 21, Arkansas Archeological Survey, Fayetteville, 1982.

House, John H., Mary Evelyn Starr, and Leslie C. Stewart-Abernathy. "Rediscovering Menard." *Mississippi Archaeology* 34, no. 2(1999):156–177.

Howard, A. Eric. *An Intrasite Spatial Analysis of Surface Collections at Chattooga: A Lower Cherokee Village*. Report submitted to the United States Forest Service, Francis Marion and Sumter National Forests, SC, 1997.

Hudson, Charles. *The Catawba Nation*. Athens: University of Georgia Press, 1970.

———. "De Soto in Arkansas: A Brief Synopsis." *Arkansas Archeological Society Field Notes* 205(1985):3–12.

———. "The Hernando de Soto Expedition, 1539–1543." In *Forgotten Centuries: Indians and Europeans in the American South, 1521–1704*, edited by Charles Hudson and Carmen Chaves Tesser, pp. 74–103. Athens: University of Georgia Press, 1994.

———. *The Juan Pardo Expeditions: Exploration of the Carolinas and Tennessee, 1566–1568*, translated by Paul Hoffman. Washington, DC: Smithsonian Institution Press, 1990.

———. *Knights of Spain, Warriors of the Sun: Hernando de Soto and the South's Ancient Chiefdoms*. Athens: University of Georgia Press, 1997.

————. "Reconstructing the de Soto Expedition Route West of the Mississippi River: Summary and Comments." In *The Expedition of Hernando de Soto West of the Mississippi, 1541–1543*, edited by Gloria A. Young and Michael P. Hoffman, pp. 143–154. Fayetteville: University of Arkansas Press, 1993.

————. *The Southeastern Indians.* Knoxville: University of Tennessee Press, 1976.

————. "An Unknown South: Spanish Explorers and Southeastern Chiefdoms." In *Visions and Revisions: Ethnohistoric Perspectives on Southeastern Cultures*, edited by George Sabo and William Schneider, pp. 6–24. Proceedings of the Southern Anthropological Society No. 20. Athens: University of Georgia Press, 1987.

Hudson, Charles M., Marvin T. Smith, and Chester B. DePratter. "The Hernando De Soto Expedition: From Apalachee to Chiaha." *Southeastern Archaeology* 3, no. 1(1984):65–77.

Hudson, Charles, Marvin Smith, D. Hally, R. Polhemus, and C. DePratter. "Coosa: A Chiefdom in the Sixteenth Century Southeastern United States." *American Antiquity* 50(1985):723–737.

Hudson, Charles, Marvin T. Smith, Chester B. DePratter, and Emilia Kelley. "The Tristán de Luna Expedition, 1559–1561." *Southeastern Archaeology* 8(1989):31–45.

Hudson, Charles, and Carmen Chaves Tesser, editors. *The Forgotten Centuries: Indians and Europeans in the American South, 1521–1704.* Athens: University of Georgia Press, 1994.

Hunt, George T. *Wars of the Iroquois.* Madison: University of Wisconsin Press, 1940.

Hunter, William A. "History of the Ohio Valley." In *Handbook of North American Indians. Vol. 15, Northeast*, edited by Bruce G. Trigger. Washington, DC: Smithsonian Institution, 1978.

Iberville, Pierre Le Moyne, Sieur d'. *Iberville's Gulf Journals*, edited and translated by Richebourg Gaillard McWilliams. Tuscaloosa: University of Alabama Press, 1981.

Insh, George Pratt. *Scottish Colonial Schemes, 1620–1686.* Glasgow, Scotland: Maclehouse, Jackson & Co., 1922.

Jackson, H. Edwin. *The Ables Creek Site: A Protohistoric Cemetery in Southeast Arkansas.* Research Series No. 42, Arkansas Archeological Survey, Fayetteville, 1992.

Jackson, Jack. *Flags along the Coast: Charting the Gulf of Mexico, 1519–1759: A Reappraisal.* Austin: The Book Club of Texas, 1995.

Jarcho, Saul. "Some Observations on Disease in Prehistoric North America." *Bulletin of the History of Medicine* 38(1964):1–19.

Jeane, David R. "Osotouy: The Quapaw Village Relocated Again?" Paper presented at the annual meeting of the Southeastern Archaeological Conference, Greenville, SC, 1998.

Jennings, Francis. *The Ambiguous Iroquois Empire: The Covenant Chain Confederation of Indian Tribes with English Colonies from Its Beginnings to the Lancaster Treaty of 1744.* New York, NY: W. W. Norton, 1984.

————. "Susquehannock." In *Handbook of North American Indians. Vol. 15, Northeast*, edited by Bruce G. Trigger, pp. 362–367. Washington, DC: Smithsonian Institution Press, 1978.

Jeter, Marvin D. "The Archeology of Southeast Arkansas: An Overview for the 1980s." In *Arkansas Archeology*, edited by Neal L. Trubowitz and Marvin D. Jeter, pp. 76–131. Research Series No. 15, Arkansas Archeological Survey, Fayetteville, 1982.

————. "Edward Palmer and Other Victorian Pioneers in Mid-South Archeology." In *The History of Archeology in the Mid-South* (working title), edited by Martha Ann Rolingson. Arkansas Archeological Survey Research Series, in progress.

————. "Ethnohistorical and Archeological Backgrounds." In *Goldsmith Oliver 2 (3Pu306): A Protohistoric Archaeological Site Near Little Rock, Arkansas*, 3 vols., edited by Marvin Jeter, Kathleen Cande, and John Mintz, pp. 32–96. Report submitted to the Federal Aviation Administration, SW Region by the Arkansas Archeological Survey, Fayetteville, 1990.

————. *The Goldsmith Oliver 2 Site (3PU306): Protohistoric Archeology, Ethnohistory, and Interactions in the Arkansas-Mississippi Valleys and Beyond.* Arkansas Archeological Survey Research Series, in progress.

———. "Oliver, as Seen from Goldsmith Oliver—and Beyond." In *The Oliver Site in Northwest Mississippi* (working title), edited by John M. Connaway. Archaeological Report, Mississippi Department of Archives and History, Jackson, in progress.

———. "Review of *Tunica Archaeology,* by Jeffrey P. Brain." *Southeastern Archaeology* 9(1990):147–149.

———. "Review of *French Colonial Archaeology,* edited by John A. Walthall, and *Calumet and Fleur-de-Lys,* edited by John A. Walthall and Thomas E. Emerson." *Arkansas Historical Quarterly* 52, no. 3(1993):354–357.

———. "Tunicans West of the Mississippi: A Summary of Early Historic and Archaeological Evidence." In *The Protohistoric Period in the Mid-South: 1500–1700,* edited by David H. Dye and Ronald C. Brister, pp. 38–63. Archaeological Report No. 18, Mississippi Department of Archives and History, Jackson, 1986.

———, editor. *Edward Palmer's Arkansas Mounds.* Fayetteville: University of Arkansas Press, 1990.

Jeter, Marvin D., Kathleen H. Cande, and John J. Mintz. *Goldsmith Oliver 2 (3PU306): A Protohistoric Archeological Site near Little Rock, Arkansas.* Report submitted to Federal Aviation Administration, Fort Worth, Texas, by Sponsored Research Program, Arkansas Archeological Survey, Fayetteville, 1990.

Jeter, Marvin D., and Ann M. Early. "Prehistory of the Saline River Drainage Basin, Central to Southeast Arkansas." In *Arkansas Archaeology: Essays in Honor of Dan and Phyllis Morse,* edited by Robert C. Mainfort, Jr., and Marvin D. Jeter, pp. 31–63. Fayetteville: University of Arkansas Press, 1999.

Jeter, Marvin D., David B. Kelley, and George P. Kelley. "The Kelley-Grimes Site: A Mississippi Period Burial Mound, Southeast Arkansas, Excavated in 1936." *The Arkansas Archeologist* 20(1979):1–51.

Jeter, Marvin D., Jerome C. Rose, G. Ishmael Williams, Jr., and Anna M. Harmon. *Archeology and Bioarcheology of the Lower Mississippi Valley and Trans-Mississippi South in Arkansas and Louisiana.* Research Series No. 37, Arkansas Archeological Survey, Fayetteville, 1989.

John, Elizabeth A. H. *Storms Brewed in Other Men's Worlds: The Confrontation of Indians, Spanish, and French in the Southwest, 1540–1795.* 1st ed., College Station: Texas A&M University Press, 1975; 2d ed., Norman: University of Oklahoma Press, 1975.

Johnson, Jay K. "From Chiefdom to Tribe in Northeast Mississippi: The Soto Expedition as a Window on a Culture in Transition." In *The Hernando de Soto Expedition: History, Historiography, and "Discovery" in the Southeast,* edited by Patricia Galloway, pp. 295–312. Lincoln: University of Nebraska Press, 1997.

———. "Stone Tools, Politics, and the Eighteenth Century Chickasaw in Northeast Mississippi." *American Antiquity* 62(1997):215–230.

Johnson, Jay K., and John T. Sparks. "Protohistoric Settlement Patterns in Northeastern Mississippi." In *The Protohistoric Period in the Mid-South: 1500–1700,* edited by David H. Dye and Ronald C. Brister, pp. 64–81. Archaeological Report No. 18, Mississippi Department of Archives and History, Jackson, 1986.

Johnson, L., Jr. "Notes on Mazanet's Stream Names, with Comments on their Linguistic and Ethnohistorical Value." In *A Texas Legacy: The Old San Antonio Road and the Caminos Reales. A Tricentennial History, 1691–1991,* edited by A. Joachim McGraw, John Wilburn Clark, and Elizabeth A. Robbins, pp. 121–128. Austin: Texas State Department of Highways and Public Transportation, Highway Design Division, 1991.

Johnson, William C. "The Protohistoric Monongahela and the Case for an Iroquois Connection." In *Societies in Eclipse,* edited by David Brose, Robert Mainfort, Jr., and C. Wesley Cowan. Washington, DC: Smithsonian Institution, 2001.

———. "The Protohistoric Monongahela and the Case for an Iroquois Connection." Paper presented at the Fifty-Seventh Annual Meeting of the Society for American Archaeology, Pittsburgh, Pennsylvania, 1992.

Jones, Sian. *The Archaeology of Ethnicity: Constructing Identities in the Past and Present.* London, England: Routledge, 1997.

Joutel, Henri. *The La Salle Expedition to Texas: The Journal of Henri Joutel, 1684–1687,* edited by William C. Foster. Austin: Texas State Historical Association, 1998.

Kardulias, P. Nick. "Fur Production as a Specialized Activity in a World System: Indians in the North American Fur Trade." *American Indian Culture and Research Journal* 14(1990):25–60.

Kealhofer, Lisa, and Brenda J. Baker. "Counterpoint to Collapse: Depopulation and Adaptation." In *Bioarchaeology of Native American Adaptation in the Spanish Borderlands,* edited by Brenda J. Baker and Lisa Kealhofer, pp. 209–222. Gainesville: University Press of Florida, 1996.

Keel, Bennie C. *Cherokee Archaeology: A Study of the Appalachian Summit.* Knoxville: University of Tennessee Press, 1976.

Kelley, David B., and Whitney J. Autin, editors. *Two Caddoan Farmsteads in the Red River Valley: The Archeology of the McLelland and Joe Clark Sites.* Research Series No. 51, Arkansas Archeological Survey, Fayetteville, 1997.

Kelton, Paul. "Not All Disappeared: Disease and Southeastern Indian Survival, 1500–1800." Ph.D. dissertation, Department of History, University of Oklahoma, Norman, 1998.

Kenmotsu, Nancy Adele, and Timothy K. Perttula. "Historical Processes and the Political Organization of the Hasinai Caddo Indians: A Reply." *Caddoan Archeology* 7, no. 2(1996):9–24.

Kenmotsu, Nancy Adele, James E. Bruseth, and James E. Corbin. "Moscoso and the Route in Texas: A Reconstruction." In *The Expedition of Hernando de Soto West of the Mississippi, 1541–1543: Proceedings of the De Soto Symposia 1988 and 1990,* edited by Gloria A. Young and Michael P. Hoffman, pp. 106–131. Fayetteville: University of Arkansas Press, 1993.

Kent, Barry C. *Susquehanna's Indians.* Anthropological Series No. 6. Harrisburg: Pennsylvania Historical and Museum Commission, 1984.

Kidder, Tristram R. "The Koroa Indians of the Lower Mississippi Valley." *Mississippi Archaeology* 23, no. 2(1988):1–42.

———. "Excavations at the Jordan Site (16MO1), Morehouse Parish, Louisiana." *Southeastern Archaeology* 11(1992):109–131.

———. "The Glendora Phase: Protohistoric–Early Historic Culture Dynamics on the Lower Ouachita River." In *Archaeology of Eastern North America: Papers in Honor of Stephen Williams,* edited by James B. Stoltman, pp. 231–260. Archaeological Report No. 25, Mississippi Department of Archives and History, Jackson, 1993.

King, Adam. "De Soto's Itaba and the Nature of Sixteenth Century Paramount Chiefdoms." *Southeastern Archaeology* 18(1999):110–123.

King, Duane, editor. *The Cherokee Indian Nation: A Troubled History.* Knoxville: University of Tennessee Press, 1979.

Knight, Vernon J. "The Formation of the Creeks." In *The Forgotten Centuries: Indians and Europeans in the American South, 1521–1704,* edited by Charles Hudson and Carmen Chaves Tesser, pp. 373–392. Athens: University of Georgia Press, 1994.

———. "Moundville as a Diagrammatic Ceremonial Center." In *Archaeology of the Moundville Chiefdom,* edited by Vernon J. Knight, Jr., and Vincas P. Steponaitis, pp. 44–62. Washington, DC: Smithsonian Institution Press, 1998.

———. "Social Organization and the Evolution of Hierarchy in Southeastern Chiefdoms." *Journal of Anthropological Research* 46(1990):1–23.

———. *Tukabatchee: Archaeological Investigations at an Historic Creek Town, Elmore County, Alabama, 1984.* Report of Investigations No. 45, Office of Archaeological Research, Alabama State Museum of Natural History, Tuscaloosa, 1985.

Knight, Vernon J., Jr., and Vincas P. Steponaitis, editors. *Archaeology of the Moundville Chiefdom.* Washington, DC: Smithsonian Institution Press, 1998.

Ladurie, Emmanuel Le Roy. *Montaillou: The Promised Land of Error*, abridged edition, translated by Barbara Bray. New York, NY: George Braziller, 1978.

Lafferty, R. H. "Prehistoric Exchange in the Lower Mississippi Valley." In *Prehistoric Exchange Systems in North America*, edited by Timothy G. Baugh and Jonathon E. Ericson, pp. 177–213. New York, NY: Plenum Press, 1994.

Lamarre, Lora A. "The Buffalo Site Ceramics: An Analysis of an Archaeological Assemblage from a Fort Ancient Village Site in West Virginia." Master's thesis, Department of Anthropology, University of Cincinnati, 1999.

Lankford, George E. *Native American Legends*. Little Rock: August House, 1987.

Larson, Lewis. "Settlement Distribution during the Mississippi Period." *Southeastern Archaeological Conference Bulletin* 13(1971):19–25.

La Salle, René-Robert Cavelier de. *Relation of the Discoveries and Voyages of Cavelier de La Salle from 1679 to 1681*, translated by Melville B. Anderson. Chicago, IL: The Caxton Club, 1901.

La Vere, David. *The Caddo Chiefdoms: Caddo Economics and Politics, 1700–1835*. Lincoln: University of Nebraska Press, 1998.

Lawson, John. *A New Voyage to Carolina*, edited by Hugh Talmage Lefler. Chapel Hill: University of North Carolina Press, 1967.

Lawson, Sarah, and W. John Faupel. *A Foothold in Florida: The Eye-Witness Account of Four Voyages made by the French to that Region*. Ease Grinstead, England: Antique Atlas Publications, 1992.

Lederer, John. *The Discoveries of John Lederer*, translated by William Talbot. London, England: Samuel Heyrick, 1672. Reprint edited by William P. Cumming. Charlottesville: University of Virginia Press, 1958.

Lee, C. "Paleopathology of the Hatchel-Mitchell-Moores Sites, Bowie County, Texas." *Bulletin of the Texas Archeological Society* 68(1997):161–177.

Lee, Dayna Bowker. "A Social History of Caddoan Peoples: Cultural Adaptation and Persistence in a Native American Community." Ph.D. dissertation, Department of Anthropology, University of Oklahoma, Norman, 1998.

Lee, E. Lawrence. *Indian Wars in North Carolina 1663–1763*. Raleigh, NC: The Carolina Charter Tercentenary Commission, 1963.

Levasseur, Charles. "A Voyage to the Mobile and Tomeh in 1700, with notes on the interior of Alabama." *Journal of Alabama Archaeology* 27(1981):32–56.

Lewis, Clifford M., and Albert J. Loomie. *The Spanish Jesuit Mission in Virginia, 1570–1572*. Chapel Hill: University of North Carolina Press, 1953.

Limerick, Patricia Nelson. "The Startling Ability of Culture to Bring Critical Inquiry to a Halt." *The Chronicle of Higher Education*, October 24(1997):A 76.

Lippert, Dorothy Thompson. "A Combination of Perspectives on Caddo Indian Health." Ph.D. dissertation, Department of Anthropology, University of Texas, Austin, 1997.

Little, Keith J., and Caleb Curren, "Conquest Archaeology of Alabama." In *Columbian Consequences: Archaeological and Historical Perspectives on the Spanish Borderlands East*, 2 vols., edited by David Hurst Thomas. Washington, DC: Smithsonian Institution Press, 1989.

Lolley, Terry L. "Ethnohistory and Archaeology: A Map Method for Locating Historic Upper Creek Indian Towns and Villages." *Journal of Alabama Archaeology* 42, no. 1(1996): i–93.

Luna, Tristán de. *The Luna Papers*, 2 vols., edited and translated by Herbert Priestly. Deland: Florida State Historical Society, 1928.

Lyman, R. Lee, and Michael J. O'Brien. "The Goals of Evolutionary Archaeology: History and Explanation." *Current Anthropology* 39(1998):615–652.

Lyon, Eugene. *The Enterprise of Florida*. Gainesville: University Press of Florida, 1976.

MacCord, Howard A., Sr. "Prehistoric Territoriality in Virginia." *Southern Indian Studies* 45(1996):57–77.

Mainfort, Robert C., Jr. "Late Period Phases in the Central Mississippi Valley: A Multivariate Approach." In *Arkansas Archaeology: Essays in Honor of Dan and Phyllis Morse*, edited by Robert C. Mainfort, Jr., and Marvin D. Jeter, pp. 143–167. Fayetteville: University of Arkansas Press, 1999.

Mallon, Florencia. *The Defense of Community in Peru's Central Highlands*. Princeton, NJ: Princeton University Press, 1983.

Manson, Joni L. "Trans-Mississippi Trade and Travel: The Buffalo Plains and Beyond." *Plains Anthropologist* 43, no. 166(1998):385–394.

Margry, Pierre. *Découvertes et Établissements des Français Dans l'Ouest et Dans le Sud de l'Amérique Septentrionale (1614–1754)*. 6 vols. Burton Historical Collections, Detroit Public Library, Detroit, Michigan.

Martin, Joel W. "Southeastern Indians and the English Trade in Skins and Slaves." In *The Forgotten Centuries: Indians and Europeans in the American South, 1521–1704*, edited by Charles Hudson and Carmen Chaves Tesser, pp. 304–324. Athens: University of Georgia Press, 1994.

Marx, Karl. "The Modern Theory of Colonization" (*Das Kapital*, vol.1, ch. 33). In *The Portable Karl Marx*, edited by Eugene Kamenka, pp. 493–504. New York, NY: Viking Press, 1983.

Mason, Carol I. "The Archaeology of Ocmulgee Old Fields, Macon, Georgia." Ph.D. dissertation, Department of Anthropology, University of Michigan, Ann Arbor, 1963.

———. "Eighteenth-Century Culture Change among the Lower Creeks." *The Florida Anthropologist* 16(1963):65–80.

Mathew, Thomas. "The Beginning, Progress and Conclusion of Bacon's Rebellion in Virginia in the Years 1675 & 1676." 1705. Reprinted in *Tracts and Other Papers*, vol. 1, edited by Peter Force. New York, NY: Peter Smith, 1947.

Mayr, Ernst. *The Growth of Biological Thought: Diversity, Evolution, and Inheritance*. Cambridge, MA: Belknap Press of Harvard University Press, 1982.

McConnell, Michael N. "Peoples 'In Between': The Iroquois and the Ohio Indians, 1720–1768." In *Beyond the Covenant Chain: The Iroquois and their Neighbors in Indian North America 1600–1800*, edited by Daniel K. Richter and James H. Merrell. Syracuse, NY: Syracuse University Press, 1987.

McCrady, Edward. *History of South Carolina*. New York, NY: MacMillan, 1897.

McDowell, William L., Jr., editor. *Journals of the Commissioners of the Indian Trade, September 20, 1710–August 29, 1718*. 1955. Reprint. Columbia: South Carolina Department of Archives and History, 1992.

McEwan, Bonnie G., editor. *The Spanish Missions of La Florida*. Gainesville: University Press of Florida, 1993.

McIlwaine, H. R., compiler. *Minutes of the Council and General Court of Virginia, 1622–1632, 1670–1676*. 2d ed., 1924. Reprint, Richmond: Virginia State Library, 1979.

McNeill, William. *Plagues and Peoples*. Garden City, NY: Doubleday, 1976.

McNutt, Charles H. "Review of *Changing Perspectives on the Archaeology of the Central Mississippi Valley*, edited by Michael J. O'Brien and Robert C. Dunnell." *Mississippi Archaeology* 34, no. 1(1999):77–102.

———, editor. *Prehistory of the Central Mississippi Valley*. Tuscaloosa: University of Alabama Press, 1996.

Merbs, Charles. "A New World of Infectious Diseases." In *Yearbook of Physical Anthropology*, vol. 35, pp. 3–42. New York, NY: Arno Press, 1992.

Merrell, James. *The Indians' New World: Catawbas and Their Neighbors from European Contact through the Era of Removal*. Chapel Hill: University of North Carolina Press, 1989.

———. "'Their Very Bones Shall Fight': The Catawba-Iroquois Wars." In *Beyond the Covenant Chain: The Iroquois and Their Neighbors in Indian North America 1600–1800*, edited by Daniel K. Richter and James H. Merrell. Syracuse, NY: Syracuse University Press, 1987.

Milanich, Jerald T. *Florida Indians and the Invasion from Europe*. Gainesville: University Press of Florida, 1995.

―――. *Laboring in the Fields of the Lord: Spanish Missions and Southeastern Indians.* Washington, DC: Smithsonian Institution Press, 1999.

Milanich, Jerald, and Charles Hudson. *Hernando de Soto and the Indians of Florida.* Gainesville: University Press of Florida, 1993.

Miller, J. "Changing Moons: A History of Caddo Religion." *Plains Anthropologist* 41, no. 157(1996):243–259.

Milner, George R. *The Cahokia Chiefdom: The Archaeology of a Mississippian Society.* Washington, DC: Smithsonian Institution Press, 1999.

―――. "Epidemic Disease in the Postcontact Southeast." *Mid-Continental Journal of Archaeology* 5(1980):39–56.

―――. "Warfare in Prehistoric and Early Historic Eastern North America." *Journal of Archaeological Research* 7, no. 2(1999):105–151.

Milner, George, David G. Anderson, and Marvin T. Smith. "The Distribution of Eastern Woodlands Peoples at the Prehistoric and Historic Interface." In *Societies in Eclipse,* edited by David Brose, Robert Mainfort, Jr., and C. Wesley Cowan. Washington, DC: Smithsonian Institution Press, 2001.

Mitchem, Jeffrey M. "Village Life at Parkin in the 1500s." Paper presented at the annual meeting of the Southeastern Archaeological Conference, Knoxville, TN, 1995.

―――. "Investigations of the Possible Remains of de Soto's Cross at Parkin." *The Arkansas Archeologist* 35(1996):87–95.

―――. "The 1996 Field Season at Parkin Archeological State Park." Paper presented at the annual meeting of the Southeastern Archaeological Conference, Birmingham, AL, 1996.

―――. "Results of 1998 Research at Parkin." *Arkansas Archeological Society Field Notes* 287(1999):10–11.

Mitchem, Jeffrey M., and Bonnie G. McEwan. "New Data on Early Bells from Florida." *Southeastern Archaeology* 7(1988):39–49.

Mithen, Steven. "Comment on 'Is It Evolution Yet?' by James L. Boone and Eric Alden Smith." *Current Anthropology* 39(1988):S163–S164.

Monahan, Elizabeth I., R. P. Stephen Davis, Jr., and H. Trawick Ward. "Piedmont Siouans and Mortuary Archaeology on the Eno River, North Carolina." In *Archaeological Studies of Gender in the Southeast,* edited by Jane M. Eastman and Christopher B. Rodning. Gainesville: University Press of Florida, in press.

Mooney, James. *The Siouan Tribes of the East.* Bureau of Ethnology Bulletin 22, Smithsonian Institution, Washington, DC, 1894.

Mooney, Timothy Paul. "Migration of the Chickasawhay into the Choctaw Homeland." *Mississippi Archaeology* 27(1992):28–39.

―――. "Choctaw Culture Compromise and Change Between the Eighteenth and Early Nineteenth Centuries: An Analysis of the Collections from Seven Sites from the Choctaw Homeland in East-Central Mississippi." *Journal of Alabama Archaeology* 41(1995):162–179.

―――. *Many Choctaw Standing: An Archaeological Study of Culture Change in the Early Historic Period.* Archaeological Report No. 27, Mississippi Department of Archives and History, Jackson, 1997.

Moore, Clarence B. "Certain Mounds of Arkansas and of Mississippi." 1908. Reprinted in *The Lower Mississippi Valley Expeditions of Clarence Bloomfield Moore,* edited by Dan F. Morse and Phyllis A. Morse. Tuscaloosa: University of Alabama Press, 1998.

―――. "Some Aboriginal Sites on the Mississippi River." *Journal of the Academy of Natural Science of Philadelphia* 14(1911):364–480.

Moore, David G. "Late Prehistoric and Early Historic Period Aboriginal Settlement in the Catawba Valley, North Carolina." Ph.D. dissertation, Department of Anthropology, University of North Carolina, Chapel Hill, 1999.

―――. "An Overview of Historic Aboriginal Public Architecture in Western North Carolina." Paper presented at the annual meeting of the Southeastern Archaeological Conference, Mobile, Alabama, 1990.

Moorehead, Warren K. *A Narrative of Explorations in New Mexico, Arizona, Indiana, etc.* Bulletin III, Department of Archaeology, Phillips Academy, Andover, MA, 1906.

Morgan, Catherine. "Ethnicity and Early Greek States: Historical and Material Perspectives." *Proceedings of the Cambridge Philological Society* 37(1991): 131–163.

Morgan, Edmund S. *American Slavery, American Freedom: The Ordeal of Colonial Virginia.* New York, NY: W. W. Smith, 1975.

Morse, Dan F. "The Nodena Phase." In *Towns and Temples Along the Mississippi*, edited by David H. Dye and Cheryl Anne Cox, pp. 69–97. Tuscaloosa: University of Alabama Press, 1990.

———. "On the Possible Origin of the Quapaws in Northeast Arkansas." In *Arkansas Before the Americans*, edited by Hester A. Davis, pp. 40–54. Research Series No. 40, Arkansas Archeological Survey, Fayetteville, 1991.

———. "The Seventeenth Century Michigamea Village Location in Arkansas." In *Calumet and Fleur-de-Lys: Archaeology of Indian and French Contact in the Midcontinent*, edited by John A. Walthall and Thomas E. Emerson, pp. 55–74. Washington DC: Smithsonian Institution Press, 1992.

———, editor. *Nodena: An Account of 90 years of Archeological Investigation in Southeast Mississippi County, Arkansas.* Research Series No. 30, Arkansas Archeological Survey, Fayetteville, 1989.

Morse, Dan F., and Phyllis A. Morse. *Archaeology of the Central Mississippi Valley.* New York, NY: Academic Press, 1983.

———. "Changes in Interpretation in the Archaeology of the Central Mississippi Valley since 1983." *North American Archaeologist* 17(1996):1–35.

———. "Northeast Arkansas." In *Prehistory of the Central Mississippi Valley*, edited by Charles H. McNutt, pp. 119–135. Tuscaloosa: University of Alabama Press, 1996.

———. "The Spanish Exploration of Arkansas." In *Columbian Consequences*, vol. 2, edited by David Hurst Thomas, pp. 197–210. Washington, DC: Smithsonian Institution Press, 1990.

———, editors. *The Lower Mississippi Valley Expeditions of Clarence Bloomfield Moore.* Tuscaloosa: University of Alabama Press, 1998.

Morse, Phyllis A. *Parkin: The 1978–1979 Archeological Investigation of a Cross County, Arkansas, Site.* Research Series No. 13, Arkansas Archeological Survey, Fayetteville, 1981.

Muller, Jon. *Mississippian Political Economy.* New York, NY: Plenum Press, 1997.

Munson, Cheryl Ann, Marjorie M. Jones, Jocelyn C. Turner, and Besse LaBudde. *Archaeology at the Hovey Lake Village Site.* Evansville: Historic Southern Indiana USI Foundation, University of Southern Indiana, 1998.

Nairne, Thomas. *Nairne's Muskogean Journals: Journal of Expedition to the Mississippi River, 1708*, edited by Alexander Moore. Jackson: University Press of Mississippi, 1988.

Nance, C. Roger. "Artifact Attribute Covariation as the Product of Inter-level Site Mixing." *Midcontinental Journal of Archaeology* 2(1976):229–235.

Naroll, Raoul. "The Causes of the Fourth Iroquois War." *Ethnohistory* 16(1969):51–81.

Needham, James, and Gabriel Arthur. "The Travels of James Needham and Gabriel Arthur Through Virginia, North Carolina, and Beyond, 1673–1674," edited by R. P. Stephen Davis, Jr. *Southern Indian Studies* 39(1990):31–55.

Neill, Edward D. *Virginia Carolorum: The Colony Under the Rule of Charles the First and Second*, A.D. *1625–*A.D. *1685: Based Upon Manuscripts and Documents of the Period.* Albany, NY: John Munsell's Sons, 1866.

Neitzel, Robert S. *Archaeology of the Fatherland Site: The Grand Village of the Natchez.* Anthropological Papers of the American Museum of Natural History, vol. 51, part 1, American Museum of Natural History, New York, NY, 1965. Reprint, Archaeological Report No. 28, Mississippi Department of Archives and History, Jackson, 1997.

———. *The Grand Village of the Natchez Indians Revisited: Excavations at the Fatherland Site, Adams County, Mississippi, 1972.* Archaeological Report No. 12, Mississippi Department of Archives and History, Jackson, 1983.

Nugent, Nell Marion, compiler. *Cavaliers and Pioneers: Abstracts of Virginia Land Patents and Grants, 1623–1800*, vol. 1. Richmond, VA: Dietz Press, 1934.

————. *Cavaliers and Pioneers: Abstracts of Virginia Land Patents and Grants, 1623–1800*, vol. 2. Richmond: Virginia State Library, 1977.

Nye, Wilbur Sturtevant. *Plains Indian Raiders: The Final Phases of Warfare from the Arkansas to the Red River, with Original Photographs by William S. Soule*. Norman: University of Oklahoma Press, Norman, 1968.

Oatis, Steven James. "A Colonial Complex: South Carolina's Changing Frontiers in the Era of the Yamasee War, 1680–1730." Ph.D. dissertation, Department of History, Emory University, Atlanta, 1999.

O'Brien, Michael J., and Robert C. Dunnell, editors. *Changing Perspectives on the Archaeology of the Central Mississippi Valley*. Tuscaloosa: University of Alabama Press, 1998.

O'Brien, Michael J., and W. Raymond Wood. *The Prehistory of Missouri*. Columbia: University of Missouri Press, 1998.

Olafson, Sigfus. "Gabriel Arthur and the Fort Ancient People." *The West Virginia Archeologist* 12(1960):32–42.

Ortner, Donald J. "Skeletal Paleopathology: Probabilities, Possibilities, and Impossibilities." In *Disease and Demography in the Americas*, edited by John W. Verano and Douglas H. Ubelaker, pp. 5–13. Washington, DC: Smithsonian Institution Press, 1992.

O'Shea, John M., and John Ludwickson. *Archaeology and Ethnohistory of the Omaha Indians: The Big Village Site*. Lincoln: University of Nebraska Press, 1992.

Oviedo, Gonzalo Fernández de. "*Historia General y Natural de las Indias*." In *New American World: A Documentary History of North America*, vol. 4, edited by David B. Quinn, pp. 325–330. New York, NY: Arno Press, 1979.

Parsons, Elise Worthington Clews. *Notes on the Caddo*. Memoirs of the American Anthropological Association No. 57. Menasha, WI: The American Anthropological Association, 1941.

Peabody, Charles. *Exploration of Mounds, Coahoma County, Mississippi*. Papers of the Peabody Museum of Anthropology and Ethnology, vol. 3, no. 2, Harvard University, Cambridge, MA, 1904.

Peckham, Howard. *The Colonial Wars, 1689–1762*. Chicago, IL: University of Chicago Press, 1964.

Peebles, Christopher. "Paradise Lost, Strayed and Stolen: Prehistoric Social Devolution in the Southeast." In *The Burden of Being Civilized: An Anthropological Perspective on the Discontents of Civilization*, edited by Miles Richardson and Malcolm C. Webb, pp. 24–40. Athens: University of Georgia Press, 1986.

————. "The Rise and Fall of Moundville in Western Alabama: The Moundville and Summerville Phases, AD 1000 to 1600." *Mississippi Archaeology*, 22 (1987):1–31.

Pendergast, James. *The Massawomeck: Raiders and Traders into the Chesapeake Bay in the Seventeenth Century*. Transactions of the American Philosophical Society No. 81. Philadelphia, PA: American Philosophical Society, 1991.

Pendergast, James F., William Engelbrecht, Martha Sempowski, William Johnson, and James Herbstritt. "Discussion of Archaeological Evidence of the Massawomek." Symposium presented at the Conference on Iroquois Research, Rensselaer, NY, 1991.

Pénicaut, André. *Fleur de Lys and Calumet: Being the Pénicaut Narrative of French Adventure in Louisiana*, edited and translated by Richebourg Gaillard McWilliams. Baton Rouge: Louisiana State University, 1953.

Percy, George. "Observations Gathered out of a Discourse of the Plantation of the Southern Colonie in Virginia by the English 1606." In *The Jamestown Voyages Under the First Charter*, edited by Philip L. Barbour, series 2, vol. 136, pp. 129–146. London, England: The Hakluyt Society, 1969.

Perdue, Theda. *Cherokee Women: Gender and Culture Change, 1700–1835*. Lincoln: University of Nebraska Press, 1998.

Peregrine, Peter N. *Mississippian Evolution: A World-System Perspective*. Monographs in World Archaeology No. 9. Madison, WI: Prehistory Press, 1992.

Perrot, Nicolas. *The Indian Tribes of the Upper Mississippi Valley and Region of the Great Lakes, as Described by Nicolas Perrot, French Commandant in the Northwest; Bacqueville de la Potherie, French Royal Commissioner to Canada; Morrell Marston, American Army Officer; and Thomas Forsyth, United States Agent at Fort Armstrong,* 2 vols., edited by Emma H. Blair. Cleveland, OH: Arthur H. Clark, 1911–1912.

Persico, V. Richard, Jr. "Early Nineteenth-Century Cherokee Political Organization." In *The Cherokee Indian Nation: A Troubled History*, edited by Duane H. King, pp. 92–109. Knoxville: University of Tennessee Press, 1979.

Perttula, Timothy K. *"The Caddo Nation": Archaeological and Ethnohistoric Perspectives.* Austin: University of Texas Press, 1992, 1997.

———. "Caddoan Area Archaeology Since 1990." *Journal of Archaeological Research* 4, no. 4(1996):295–348.

———. "French and Spanish Colonial Trade Policies and the Fur Trade among the Caddoan Indians of the Trans-Mississippi South." In *The Fur Trade Revisited: Selected Papers of the Sixth North American Fur Trade Conference, Mackinac Island, Michigan, 1991*, edited by Jennifer S. H. Brown, W. J. Eccles, and Donald P. Heldman, pp. 71–91. East Lansing: Michigan State University Press, 1994.

———. "Late Caddoan Societies in the Northeast Texas Pineywoods." In *The Native History of the Caddo: Their Place in Southeastern Archaeology and Ethnohistory*, edited by Timothy K. Perttula and James E. Bruseth, pp. 69–90. Studies in Archaeology 30, Texas Archeological Research Laboratory, University of Texas, Austin, 1998.

———, compiler. *Caddo Archeological and Historical Workshop Sourcebook for the Caddo Tribe of Oklahoma.* Binger, OK: Caddo Tribe of Oklahoma, 1995.

———, moderator. "Two Worlds Meet: The Caddoan People and Missions." *Journal of Northeast Texas Archaeology* 7(1996):69–91.

Perttula, Timothy K., and B. Nelson. "Titus Phase Mortuary Practices in the Northeast Texas Pineywoods and Post Oak Savanna." In *Analysis of the Titus Phase Mortuary Assemblage at the Mockingbird or "Kahbakayammaahin" Site (41TT550)*, edited by Timothy K. Perttula, M. Tate, H. Neff, J. W. Cogswell, M. D. Glasscock, E. Skokan, S. Mulholland, R. Rogers, and B. Nelson, pp. 328–401. Document No. 970849, Espey, Huston & Associates, Inc., Austin, TX, 1998.

Phillips, Philip. *Archaeological Survey in the Lower Yazoo Basin, Mississippi, 1949–1955.* Papers of the Peabody Museum of Anthropology and Ethnology, vol. 60, Harvard University, Cambridge, MA, 1970.

Phillips, Philip, James A. Ford, and James B. Griffin. *Archaeological Survey in the Lower Mississippi Alluvial Valley, 1940–1947.* Papers of the Peabody Museum of Anthropology and Ethnology, vol. 25, Harvard University, Cambridge, MA, 1951.

Pillsbury, Richard. "The Europeanization of the Cherokee Settlement Landscape Prior to Removal: A Georgia Case Study." In *Historical Archaeology of the Eastern United States*, edited by Robert W. Neuman, pp. 59–69. Baton Rouge: Louisiana State University, 1983.

Polhemus, Richard R. "Dallas Phase Architecture and Sociopolitical Structure." In *Lamar Archaeology: Mississippian Chiefdoms of the Deep South*, edited by Mark Williams and Gary Shapiro, pp. 125–138. Tuscaloosa: University of Alabama Press, 1990.

———, editor. *The Toqua Site: A Late Mississippian Dallas Phase Town.* Report of Investigations 41, Department of Anthropology, University of Tennessee, Knoxville, 1987.

Pollack, David. "Intraregional and Intersocietal Relationships of the Late Mississippian Caborn-Welborn Phase of the Lower Ohio River Valley." Ph.D. dissertation, University of Kentucky, Lexington, 1998.

Pollack, David, and A. Gwynn Henderson. "A Mid-Eighteenth Century Historic Indian Occupation in Greenup County, Kentucky." In *Late Prehistoric Research in Kentucky*, edited by David Pollack, Charles D. Hockensmith, and Thomas N. Sanders. Frankfort: Kentucky Heritage Council, 1984.

Pollack, David, and Cheryl Ann Munson. "Caborn-Welborn Ceramics: Inter-Site Comparisons and Extra-Regional Interaction." Paper presented at the annual meeting of the Southeastern Archaeological Conference, Lexington, Kentucky, 1994, and the Kentucky Heritage Council Archaeology Conference, 1995.

————. "The Angel to Caborn-Welborn Transition: Late Mississippian Developments in Southwestern Indiana, Northwestern Kentucky, and Southwestern Illinois." Paper presented at the 43rd Midwestern Archaeological Conference, Muncie, Indiana, 1998.

Pollack, David, Cheryl Ann Munson, and A. Gwynn Henderson. *Slack Farm and the Caborn-Welborn People.* Education Series No. 1, Kentucky Archaeological Survey, Lexington, 1996.

Pollack, David, Mary Lucas Powell, and Audrey Adkins. " Preliminary Study of Mortuary Patterns at the Larkin Site, Bourbon County, Kentucky." In *Current Archaeological Research in Kentucky,* vol 1., edited by David Pollack. Frankfort: Kentucky Heritage Council, 1987.

Powell, M. L. "Foreword for Special Papers on Caddoan Bioarchaeological Research." *Bulletin of the Texas Archeological Society* 68(1997):135–138.

Pratz, Antoine Simon Le Page du. *Histoire de la Louisiane.* 3 vols. Paris, France: De Bure, 1758.

Price, James, and Cynthia Price. "Protohistoric/Early Historic Manifestations in Southeastern Missouri." In *Towns and Temples Along the Mississippi,* edited by David Dye and Cheryl Cox, pp. 59–69. Tuscaloosa: University of Alabama Press, 1990.

Purrington, Burton L. "Ancient Mountaineers: An Overview of the Prehistoric Archaeology of North Carolina's Western Mountain Region." In *The Prehistory of North Carolina: An Archaeological Symposium,* edited by Mark A. Mathis and Jeffrey J. Crow, pp. 83–180. Raleigh: North Carolina Division of Archives and History, 1983.

Quinn, David Beers, editor. *The Roanoke Voyages, 1584–1590,* series 2, vol. 104. London, England: The Hakluyt Society, 1955.

Ramenofsky, Ann F. "Evolutionary Theory and Native American Artifact Change in the Postcontact Period." In *Evolutionary Archaeology: Methodological Issues,* edited by Patricia A. Teltser, pp. 129–147. Tucson: University of Arizona Press, 1995.

————. *Vectors of Death: The Archaeology of European Contact.* Albuquerque: University of New Mexico Press, 1987.

Ramenofsky, Ann F., and Patricia Galloway. "Disease and the Soto Entrada." In *The Hernando de Soto Expedition: History, Historiography, and "Discovery" in the Southeast,* edited by Patricia Galloway, pp. 259–279. Lincoln: University of Nebraska Press, 1997.

Ramenofsky, Ann F., and Anastasia Steffen. *Unit Issues in Archaeology: Measuring Time, Space, and Material.* Salt Lake City: University of Utah Press, 1998.

Randolph, J. Ralph. *British Travelers Among the Southern Indians, 1660–1763.* Norman: University of Oklahoma Press, 1973.

Rankin, Robert L. "Language Affiliations of Some de Soto Place Names in Arkansas." In *The Expedition of Hernando de Soto West of the Mississippi, 1541–1543,* edited by Gloria A. Young and Michael P. Hoffman, pp. 210–221. Fayetteville: University of Arkansas Press, 1993.

————. "Oneota and Historical Linguistics." Paper presented at the Annual Oneota Conference, Iowa City, IA, 1997.

————. "Quapaw: Genetic and Areal Affiliations." In *In Honor of Mary Haas,* edited by W. Shipley, pp. 629–650. New York, NY: Mouton de Gruyter, 1988.

Reff, Daniel. *Disease, Depopulation, and Culture Change in Northwestern New Spain, 1518–1764.* Salt Lake City: University of Utah Press, 1991.

Reid, John Philip. *A Better Kind of Hatchet: Law, Trade and Diplomacy in the Cherokee Nation during the Early Years of European Contact.* University Park: Pennsylvania State University, 1976.

Richter, Daniel K. *The Ordeal of the Longhouse: The Peoples of the Iroquois League in the Era of European Colonization.* Chapel Hill: University of North Carolina Press, 1997.

————. "War and Culture: The Iroquois Experience." *William and Mary Quarterly* 40(1983):528–559.

Richter, Daniel K., and James H. Merrell, editors. *Beyond the Covenant Chain: The Iroquois and Their Neighbors in Indian North America 1600–1800.* Syracuse, NY: Syracuse University Press, 1987.

Riggs, Brett H. "Interhousehold Variability Among Early Nineteenth Century Cherokee Artifact Assemblages." In *Households and Communities*, edited by Scott MacEachern, David J. W. Archer, and Richard D. Garvin, pp. 328–338. Archaeological Association of the University of Calgary 21, Calgary, Alberta, Canada, 1989.

Riggs, Brett H., M. Scott Shumate, and Patti Evans-Shumate. *Archaeological Data Recovery at Site 31Jk291, Jackson County, North Carolina.* Report submitted to the North Carolina Division of Archives and History, Asheville, 1997.

————. *Archaeological Site Survey and Testing at Site 31Jk291, Jackson County, North Carolina.* Report submitted to the North Carolina Division of Archives and History, Asheville, 1996.

Riggs, Brett H., M. Scott Shumate, Patti Evans-Shumate, and Brad Bowden. *An Archaeological Survey of the Ferguson Farm, Swain County, North Carolina.* Report submitted to the Eastern Band of the Cherokee Indians, Cherokee, NC, 1998.

Rights, Douglas L. *The American Indian in North Carolina.* Winston-Salem, NC: John F. Blair, 1957.

Robertson, Thomas B. "An Indian King's Will." *Virginia Magazine of History and Biography* 36(1928):193.

Rodning, Christopher B. "Archaeological Perspectives on Gender and Women in Traditional Cherokee Society." *Journal of Cherokee Studies* 20(1999):3–27.

Rogers, J. D. "Markers of Social Integration: The Development of Centralized Authority in the Spiro Region." In *Political Structure and Change in the Prehistoric Southeastern United States*, edited by John F. Scarry, pp. 53–68. Gainesville: University Press of Florida, 1996.

————. "The Caddos." In *Handbook of North American Indians. Vol. Southeast*, in preparation. Washington, DC: Smithsonian Institution Press, n.d.

Roland, Dunbar, and A. G. Saunders, editors. *Mississippi Provincial Archives. French Dominion, Vol. 1, 1729–1740.* Jackson: Mississippi Department of Archives and History, 1927.

————. *Mississippi Provincial Archives. French Dominion, Vol. 3, 1704–1743.* Jackson: Mississippi Department of Archives and History, 1932.

Rolingson, Martha Ann. "Archeology along Bayou Bartholomew, Southeast Arkansas." *The Arkansas Archeologist* 32(1993):1–138.

————, editor. *History of Archeology in the Mid-South* (working title). Volume in preparation for publication in the Arkansas Archeological Survey Research Series, in progress.

Rollings, Willard H. *The Osage: An Ethnohistorical Study of Hegemony on the Prairie-Plains.* Columbia: University of Missouri Press, 1992.

————. "Living in a Graveyard: Native Americans in Colonial Arkansas." In *Cultural Encounters in the Early South: Indians and Europeans in Arkansas*, compiled by Jeannie M. Whayne, pp. 38–60. Fayetteville: University of Arkansas Press, 1995.

Rountree, Helen C. *Pocahontas's People: The Powhatan Indians of Virginia Through Four Centuries.* Norman: University of Oklahoma Press, 1990.

————. *The Powhatan Indians of Virginia: Their Traditional Culture.* Norman: University of Oklahoma Press, 1989.

————. "The Powhatans and Other Woodland Indians as Travelers." In *Powhatan Foreign Relations, 1500–1722*, edited by Helen C. Rountree, pp. 20–52. Charlottesville: University Press of Virginia, 1993.

————. "Trouble Coming Southward: Emanations Through and From Virginia, 1607–1675." Paper presented at the Porter L. Fortune, Jr., History Symposium entitled

"Early Social History of the Southeastern Indians," University of Mississippi, Oxford, 1997.

Rountree, Helen C., and E. Randolph Turner III. "The Evolution of the Powhatan Paramount Chiefdom in Virginia." In *Chiefdoms and Chieftaincy: An Integration of Archaeological, Ethnohistorical, and Ethnographic Approaches*, edited by Elsa M. Redmond, pp. 265–296. Gainesville: University Press of Florida, 1999.

———. "On the Fringe of the Southeast: The Powhatan Paramount Chiefdom in Virginia." In *The Forgotten Centuries: Europeans and Indians in the American South, 1513–1704*, edited by Charles Hudson and Carmen Chaves Tesser, pp. 355–72. Athens: University of Georgia Press, 1994.

Russ, Kurt C., and Jefferson Chapman. *Archaeological Investigations at the Eighteenth Century Overhill Cherokee Town of Mialoquo*. Report of Investigations No. 37, Department of Anthropology, University of Tennessee, Knoxville, 1983.

Rutman, Darret B., and Anita H. Rutman. "Of Agues and Fevers: Malaria in the Early Chesapeake." *William and Mary Quarterly*, 3d Ser., 33(1976):32–60.

Sabo, George III. "Encounters and Images: European Contact and Caddo Indians." *Historical Reflections/Réflexions Historiques* 21, no. 2(1995):217–242.

———. *Paths of our Children: Historic Indians of Arkansas*. Popular Series No. 3, Arkansas Archeological Survey, Fayetteville, 1992.

———. "Reordering Their World: A Caddoan Ethnohistory." In *Visions and Revisions: Ethnohistoric Perspectives on Southern Cultures*, edited by George Sabo III and William M. Schneider, pp. 25–47. Athens: University of Georgia Press, 1987.

———. "Rituals of Encounter: Interpreting Native American Views of European Explorers." In *Cultural Encounters in the Early South: Indians and Europeans in Arkansas*, compiled by Jeannie M. Whayne, pp. 76–87. Fayetteville: University of Arkansas Press, 1995.

Sabo, George III, Ann M. Early, Jerome C. Rose, et al. *Human Adaptation in the Ozark-Ouachita Mountains*. Report submitted to the U. S. Army Corps of Engineers, Southwestern Division, by Arkansas Archeological Survey, Fayetteville, 1988.

———. "The Structure of Caddo Leadership in the Colonial Era." In *The Native History of the Caddo: Their Place in Southeastern Archeology and Ethnohistory*, edited by Timothy K. Perttula and James E. Bruseth, pp. 159–174. Studies in Archeology 30, Texas Archeological Research Laboratory, University of Texas, Austin, 1998.

Sabo, George III, Randall L. Guendling, W. Fredrick Limp, et al. *Archeological Investigations at 3MR80—Area D in the Rush Development Area, Buffalo National River, Arkansas*. Southwest Cultural Resources Center Professional Papers No. 38, U. S. Department of the Interior, National Park Service, 1990.

Sainsbury, William Noel, editor. *Calendar of State Papers, Colonial Series: America and West Indies, 1574–1660*, vols. 1–10. London, England: Great Britain Public Record Office, 1860.

Saint Cosme, J. F. Buisson. "Letter to Bishop of Quebec, 1699." In *Early Voyages Up and Down the Mississippi*, edited by John Dawson Gilmar Schea. Originally published by J. Munsell, Albany, NY, 1861. Reprint, Albany, NY: J. McDonough, 1902.

Salley, Alexander S., editor. *Commissions and Instructions from the Lords Proprietors of Carolina to Public Officials of South Carolina, 1685–1715*. Columbia: South Carolina Department of History and Archives, 1916.

———, editor. *Journal of the Commons House of Assembly of South Carolina, 1697*. Columbia: South Carolina Department of History and Archives, 1907.

Sattler, Richard A. "Women's Status Among the Muskogee and Cherokee." In *Women and Power in Native North America*, edited by Laura F. Klein and Lillian A. Ackerman, pp. 214–229. Norman: University of Oklahoma Press, 1995.

Saucier, Roger T. *Quaternary Geology of the Lower Mississippi Valley*. Research Series No. 6, Arkansas Archeological Survey, Fayetteville, 1974.

———. *Geomorphology and Geologic History of the Lower Mississippi Valley*. U. S. Army Corps of Engineers, Waterways Experiment Station, Vicksburg, Mississippi, 1994.

Sauer, Carl. *Sixteenth Century North America: The Land and People as Seen by the Europeans.* Berkeley: University of California Press, 1971.

Saunders, William Laurence, editor. *The Colonial Records of North Carolina.* Vol. 1, *1662–1712.* Raleigh, NC: P. M. Hale, State Printer, 1886–1890.

Sauvole, de la Villantray De. *The Journal of Sauvole [1699–1701],* edited by Prieur Jay Higginbotham. Mobile, AL: Colonial Books, 1969.

Scarry, John F. "How Great Were the Southeastern Polities?" In *Great Towns and Regional Polities in the Prehistoric American Southwest and Southeast,* edited by Jill E. Neitzel, pp. 59–74. Albuquerque: University of New Mexico Press, 1999.

———. "The Late Prehistoric Southeast." In *The Forgotten Centuries: Indians and Europeans in the American South, 1521–1704,* edited by Charles Hudson and Carmen Chaves Tesser, pp. 17–35. Athens: University of Georgia Press, 1994.

———. "Looking for and at Mississippian Political Change." In *Political Structure and Change in the Prehistoric Southeastern United States,* edited by John F. Scarry, pp. 3–11. Gainesville: University Press of Florida, 1996.

———. "The Nature of Mississippian Societies." In *Political Structure and Change in the Prehistoric Southeastern United States,* edited by John F. Scarry, pp. 12–24. Gainesville: University Press of Florida, 1996.

Schaffer, Gary D. "An Examination of the Bead Hill Site in the Wyoming Valley." *Pennsylvania Archaeologist* 68, no. 2(1998):18–41.

Schambach, Frank F. "The Archeology of the Great Bend Region in Arkansas." In *Contributions to the Archeology of the Great Bend Region,* edited by Frank F. Schambach and Frank Rackerby, pp. 1–11. Research Series No. 22, Arkansas Archeological Survey, Fayetteville, 1983.

———. "A Description and Analysis of the Ceramics." In *The Shallow Lake Site (3UN9/52) and Its Place in Regional Prehistory,* edited by Martha A. Rolingson and Frank F. Schambach, pp. 101–176. Research Series No. 12, Arkansas Archeological Survey, Fayetteville, 1981.

———. "The End of the Trail: The Route of Hernando de Soto's Army through Southwest Arkansas and East Texas." *The Arkansas Archeologist* 27/28(1989): 9–33.

———. "Mounds, Embankments, and Ceremonialism in the Trans-Mississippi South." In *Mounds, Embankments, and Ceremonialism in the Midsouth,* edited by Robert C. Mainfort and Richard Walling, pp. 36–43. Research Series No. 46, Arkansas Archeological Survey, Fayetteville, 1996.

———. *Pre-Caddoan Cultures in the Trans-Mississippi South: A Beginning Sequence.* Research Series No. 53, Arkansas Archeological Survey, Fayetteville, 1998.

———. "A Probable Spiroan Entrepôt in the Red River Valley in Northeast Texas." *Caddoan Archaeology Newsletter* 6, no. 1(1995):10–25.

———. "Some New Interpretations of Spiroan Culture History." In *Archaeology of Eastern North America: Papers in Honor of Stephen Williams,* edited by James B. Stoltman, pp. 187–230. Archaeological Report No. 25, Mississippi Department of Archives and History, Jackson, 1993.

———. "Spiro and the Tunica: A New Interpretation of the Role of the Tunica in the Culture History of the Southeast and the Southern Plains, A.D. 11–1750." In *Arkansas Archeology: Essays in Honor of Dan and Phyllis Morse,* edited by Robert C. Mainfort, Jr., and Marvin D. Jeter, pp. 169–224. Fayetteville: University of Arkansas Press, 1999.

Schambach, Frank F., and John E. Miller. "A Description and Analysis of the Ceramics." In *Cedar Grove: An Interdisciplinary Investigation of a Late Caddo Farmstead in the Red River Valley,* edited by Neal L. Trubowitz. Research Series No. 23, Arkansas Archeological Survey, Fayetteville, 1984.

Schambach, Frank F., and David B. Waddell. "The Pottery from the Bangs Slough Site." In *Coles Creek and Mississippi Period Foragers in the Felsenthal Region of the Lower Mississippi Valley,* edited by Frank F. Schambach, pp. 19–62. Research Series No. 39, Arkansas Archeological Survey, Fayetteville, 1990.

Schroedl, Gerald F. "Louis-Phillipe's Journal and Archaeological Investigations at the Overhill Town of Toqua." *Journal of Cherokee Studies* 3(1978):206–220.

———. "Mississippian Towns in the Eastern Tennessee Valley." In *Mississippian Towns and Sacred Spaces*, edited by R. Barry Lewis and Charles B. Stout, pp. 64–92. Tuscaloosa: University of Alabama Press, 1998.

———. "Overhill Cherokee Household and Village Patterns in the Eighteenth Century." In *Households and Communities*, edited by Scott MacEachern, David J. W. Archer, and Richard D. Garvin, pp. 350–360. Archaeological Association of the University of Calgary 21, Calgary, Alberta, Canada, 1989.

———. *A Summary of Archaeological Activities Conducted at the Chattooga Site, Oconee County, South Carolina*. Report submitted to the United States Forest Service, Francis Marion and Sumter National Forests, SC, 1994.

———. "Toward an Explanation of Cherokee Origins in East Tennessee." In *The Conference on Cherokee Prehistory*, compiled by David G. Moore, pp. 122–138. Swannanoa, NC: Warren Wilson College, 1986.

———, editor. *Overhill Cherokee Archaeology at Chota-Tanasee*. Report of Investigations No. 38, Department of Anthropology, University of Tennessee, Knoxville, 1986.

Schroedl, Gerald F., and Brett H. Riggs. "Cherokee Lower Town Archaeology at the Chattooga Site." Paper presented at the annual meeting of the Southeastern Archaeological Conference, Tampa, Florida, 1989.

———. "Investigations of Cherokee Village Patterning and Public Architecture at the Chattooga Site." Paper presented at the annual meeting of the Southeastern Archaeological Conference, Mobile, Alabama, 1990.

Sempowski, Martha L. "Early Historic Exchange Between the Seneca and the Susquehannock." In *Proceedings of the 1992 People to People Conference*, edited by Charles F. Hayes III, Connie C. Bodner, and Lorraine P. Saunders, pp. 51–64. Research Records No. 23, Rochester Museum and Science Center Rochester, New York, NY, 1994.

Service, Elman R. *Primitive Social Organization: An Evolutionary Perspective*, 2d ed. New York, NY: Random House, 1971.

Setzler, Frank M., and Jesse D. Jennings. *Peachtree Mound and Village Site, Cherokee County, North Carolina*. Bureau of American Ethnology Bulletin 131, Smithsonian Institution, Washington, DC, 1941.

Sheldon, Craig T., and Ned J. Jenkins. "Protohistoric Development in Central Alabama." In *The Protohistoric Period in the Mid-South: 1500–1700*, edited by David H. Dye and Ronald C. Brister, pp. 95–102. Archaeological Report No. 18, Mississippi Department of Archives and History, Jackson, 1986.

Shennan, Stephen J. "Archaeological Approaches to Cultural Identity." In *Archaeological Approaches to Cultural Identity*, edited by Stephen J. Shennan, pp. 1–32. London: Routledge, 1994.

Shumate, M. Scott, and Larry R. Kimball. *Archaeological Data Recovery at 31Sw273 on the Davis Cemetery Tract, Nantahala National Forest, Swain County, North Carolina*. Report submitted to National Forests in North Carolina, Asheville, 1997.

Shurkin, Joel N. *The Invisible Fire: The Story of Mankind's Victory over the Ancient Scourge of Smallpox*. New York, NY: Putnam, 1979.

Sierzchula, Michael Claude, M. J. Guccione, R. H. Lafferty III, and M. T. Oates. *Archeological Investigations in the Great Bend Region, Miller County, Arkansas, Levee Items 2 and 3*. Report No. 94–5, Mid-Continental Research Associates, Inc., Lowell, AR, 1995.

Simmons, Marc. *The Last Conquistador: Juan de Oñate and the Settling of the Far Southwest*. Norman: University of Oklahoma Press, 1991.

Simpkins, Daniel L. *Aboriginal Intersite Settlement System Change in the Northeastern North Carolina Piedmont During the Contact Period*. Ph.D. dissertation, Department of Anthropology, University of North Carolina, Chapel Hill, 1992.

Smith, Alan G. R. *The Emergence of a Nation State: The Commonwealth of England, 1529–1660*. Foundations of Modern Britain Series. London, England: Longman Press, 1984.

Smith, Betty A. "Distribution of Eighteenth-Century Cherokee Settlements." In *The Cherokee Indian Nation: A Troubled History*, edited by Duane H. King, pp. 46–60. Knoxville: University of Tennessee Press, 1979.

Smith, F. Todd. *The Caddo Indians: Tribes at the Convergence of Empires, 1542–1854*. College Station: Texas A&M University Press, 1995.

———. *The Caddos, The Wichitas, and the United States, 1846–1901*. College Station: Texas A&M University Press, 1996.

Smith, John. "The Generall Historie of Virginia, New England, and the Summer Isles, 1624." In *The Complete Works of Captain John Smith (1580–1631)*, vol. 2, edited by Philip L. Barbour, pp. 25–488. Chapel Hill: University of North Carolina Press, 1986.

———. "A Map of Virginia." In *The Complete Works of Captain John Smith (1580–1631)*, vol. 1, edited by Philip L. Barbour, pp. 119–190. Chapel Hill: University of North Carolina Press, 1986.

———. *Travels and Works of Captain John Smith*, 2 vols., edited by Edward Arber and A. G. Bradley. Edinburgh, England: John Grant, 1910.

———. "A True Relation." In *The Complete Works of Captain John Smith (1580–1631)*, vol. 1, edited by Philip L. Barbour, pp. 3–118. Chapel Hill: University of North Carolina Press, 1986.

Smith, Kevin E. "The Middle Cumberland Region: Mississippian Archaeology in North Central Tennessee." Ph.D. dissertation, Department of Anthropology, University of Tennessee, Knoxville, 1992.

Smith, Marvin T. "Aboriginal Depopulation in the Postcontact Southeast." In *The Forgotten Centuries: Indians and Europeans in the American South, 1521–1704*, edited by Charles Hudson and Carmen Chaves Tesser, pp. 257–275. Athens: University of Georgia Press, 1994.

———. "Aboriginal Population Movements in the Early Historic Period Interior Southeast." In *Powhatan's Mantle: Indians in the Colonial Southeast*, edited by Peter H. Wood, Gregory A. Waselkov, and M. Thomas Hatley, pp. 20–34. Lincoln: University of Nebraska Press, 1989.

———. "Aboriginal Population Movements in the Postcontact Southeast." Paper presented at the Porter L. Fortune, Jr., History Symposium entitled "Early Social History of the Southeastern Indians, 1526–1715," University of Mississippi, Oxford, Mississippi, 1998.

———. *Archaeology of Aboriginal Culture Change in the Interior Southeast: Depopulation During the Early Historic Period*. Gainesville: University Press of Florida, 1987.

———. *Coosa: The Rise and Fall of a Southeastern Mississippian Chiefdom*. Gainesville: University Press of Florida, in preparation.

———. "Glass Beads from the Goldsmith Oliver 2 Site." In *Goldsmith Oliver 2 (3PU306): A Protohistoric Archeological Site near Little Rock, Arkansas*, edited by Marvin D. Jeter, Kathleen H. Cande, and John J. Mintz, pp. 217–223. Report submitted to Federal Aviation Administration, Fort Worth, Texas, by Sponsored Research Program, Arkansas Archeological Survey, Fayetteville, 1990.

———. *Historic Period Indian Archaeology of Northern Georgia*. Laboratory of Archaeology Report No. 30, Department of Anthropology, University of Georgia, Athens, 1992.

———. "In the Wake of De Soto: Alabama's Seventeenth-Century Indians on the Coosa River." Report submitted to the Alabama De Soto Commission, Tuscaloosa, 1989.

Smith, Marvin T., and Julie B. Smith. "Engraved Shell Masks in North America." *Southeastern Archaeology* 8(1989):9–18.

Smith, Marvin T., and Mark Williams. "Mississippian Mound Refuse Disposal Patterns and Implications for Archaeological Research." *Southeastern Archaeology* 13(1994):27–35.

Snapp, J. Russel. *John Stuart and the Struggle for Empire on the Southern Frontier*. Baton Rouge: Louisiana State University Press, 1996.

Snow, Dean, and Kim M. Lanphear. "European Contact and Indian Depopulation in the Northeast: The Timing of the First Epidemics." *Ethnohistory* 35(1988):15–33.

Snow, Dean R., and William A. Starna. "Sixteenth-Century Depopulation: A View from the Mohawk Valley." *American Anthropologist* 91(1989):142–149.

Sonderegger, Richard. "The Southern Frontier to the End of King George's War." Ph.D. dissertation, Department of History, University of Michigan, Ann Arbor, 1964.

South Carolina Historical Society. *Collections of the South Carolina Historical Society*, vol. 5. Richmond, VA: William Ellis Jones, 1897.

Spaulding, Albert C. "Review of 'Method and Theory in American Archaeology' by Philip Phillips and Gordon R. Willey." *American Antiquity* 23(1957): 85–87.

Speck, Frank G. "Siouan Tribes of the Carolinas." *American Anthropologist* 37, no. 2(1935):201–225.

Spelman, Henry. "Relation of Virginea." In *The Travels and Works of Captain John Smith*, edited by Edward Arber and A. G. Bradley, pp. ci–cxiv. New York, NY: Burt Franklin, 1910.

Springer, James W., and Stanley R. Witkowski. "Siouan Historical Linguistics and Oneota Archaeology." In *Oneota Studies*, edited by Guy E. Gibbon, pp. 69–117. Publications in Anthropology No. 1, Department of Anthropology, University of Minnesota, Minneapolis, 1982.

Stanish, Charles. "Household Archaeology: Testing Models of Zonal Complementarity in the South Central Andes." *American Anthropologist* 91(1989): 7–24.

Stewart-Abernathy, Leslie C. "The Carden Bottom Project, Yell County, Arkansas: From Dalton to Trade Beads, So Far." *Arkansas Archeological Society Field Notes* 261(1994):3–7.

Story, Dee Ann. "Cultural History of the Native Americans." In *The Archeology and Bioarcheology of the Gulf Coastal Plain*, 2 vols., edited by Dee Ann Story, J. A. Guy, B. A. Burnett, M. D. Freeman, J. C. Rose, D. G. Steele, B. W. Olive, and K. J. Reinhard, pp. 163–366. Research Series No. 38, Arkansas Archeological Survey, Fayetteville 1990.

―――, editor. *The Deshazo Site, Nacogdoches County, Texas. Vol. 1, The Site, Its Setting, Investigation, Cultural Features, Artifacts of Non-Native Manufacture, and Subsistence Remains*. Texas Antiquities Permit Series No. 7, Texas Antiquities Committee, Austin, 1982.

―――, editor. *The Deshazo Site, Nacogdoches County, Texas. Vol. 2, Artifacts of Native Manufacture*. Studies in Archeology 21, Texas Archeological Research Laboratory, University of Texas, Austin, 1995.

Story, Dee Ann, and Darrell G. Creel. "The Cultural Setting." In *The Deshazo Site, Nacogdoches County, Texas. Vol. 1, The Site, Its Setting, Investigation, Cultural Features, Artifacts of Non-Native Manufacture, and Subsistence Remains*, edited by Dee Ann Story, pp. 20–34. Texas Antiquities Permit Series No. 7, Texas Antiquities Committee, Austin, 1982.

Strachey, William. *The Historie of Travell into Virginia Britania*, series 2, vol. 103, edited by Louis B. Wright and Virginia Freund. London, England: The Hakluyt Society, 1953.

Sullivan, Lynne P. "Household, Community, and Society: An Analysis of Mouse Creek Settlements." In *Households and Communities*, edited by Scott MacEachern, David J.W. Archer, and Richard D. Garvin, pp. 317–327. Archaeological Association of the University of Calgary 21, Calgary, Alberta, Canada, 1989.

―――. "Mississippian Community and Household Organization in Eastern Tennessee." In *Mississippian Communities and Households*, edited by J. Daniel Rogers and Bruce D. Smith, pp. 99–123. Tuscaloosa: University of Alabama Press, 1995.

Sutton, Richard E. "New Approaches for Identifying Prehistoric Iroquoian Migrations." In *Origins of the People of the Longhouse*, edited by Andre Bekerman and Gary Warrick. Proceedings of the 21st Annual Symposium of the Ontario Archaeological Society. North York, Ontario: Ontario Archaeological Society Inc., 1995.

Swanton, John R. "Early History of the Eastern Siouan Tribes." In *Essays in Anthropology in Honor of Alfred Louis Kroeber*, edited by Robert H. Lowie, pp. 371–381. Berkeley: University of California Press, 1936.

————. *Final Report of the United States De Soto Expedition Commission*. 1939. Reprint, House Document 71, 76th Congress, 1st Session. Washington, DC: Smithsonian Institution Press, 1985.

————. *The Indians of the Southeastern United States*. Bureau of American Ethnology Bulletin No. 137, Smithsonian Institution, Washington, DC, 1946.

————. *Indian Tribes of the Lower Mississippi Valley and Adjacent Coast of the Gulf of Mexico*. Bureau of American Ethnology Bulletin 43, Smithsonian Institution, Washington, DC, 1911.

————. "The Relation of the Southeast to General Culture Problems of American Pre-history." Paper presented at the Conference on Southern Pre-history, Birmingham, Alabama, December 18–20, 1932, pp. 60–74. Limited–distribution transcript issued by the National Research Council, Washington, DC, 1932. Reprinted in 1976 by the Southeastern Archaeological Conference.

————. "The Social Significance of the Creek Confederacy." In *Proceedings of the 19th International Congress of Americanists*, pp. 327–324. Washington, DC: Government Printing Office, 1915. Reprinted in *Ethnology of the Southeastern Indians: A Source Book*, edited by Charles M. Hudson. New York, NY: Garland Publishing, Inc., 1985.

————. *Source Material on the History and Ethnology of the Caddo Indians*. Bureau of American Ethnology Bulletin 132, Smithsonian Institution, Washington, DC, 1942.

Tanner, Helen Hornbeck. "The Land and Water Communication Systems of the Southeastern Indians." In *Powhatan's Mantle: Indians in the Colonial Southeast*, edited by Peter Wood, Gregory Waselkov, and Thomas Hatley, pp. 6–20. Lincoln: University of Nebraska Press, 1989.

Temple, Wayne C. *Indian Villages of the Illinois Country*. 2d ed. Scientific Papers, vol. 2, pt. 2, Illinois State Museum, Springfield, 1966.

Thaumer de la Source. "Letter of Mr. Thaumer de la Source, 1699." In *Early Voyages Up and Down the Mississippi*, edited by John Dawson Gilmar Schea. Originally published by J. Munsell, Albany, NY, 1861. Reprint, Albany, NY: J. McDonough, 1902.

Thomas, Cyrus. "Burial Mounds of the Northern Sections of the United States." Fifth Annual Report of the Bureau of Ethnology, pp. 3–119. Smithsonian Institution, Washington, DC, 1887.

————. "The Story of a Mound: Or, the Shawnees in Pre-Columbian Times." *American Anthropologist* 4(1891):109–159, 237–273.

Thomas, Daniel H. *Fort Toulouse: The French Outpost at the Alabamas on the Coosa*. Tuscaloosa: University of Alabama Press, 1989.

Thomas, David Hurst, editor. *Columbian Consequences: Archaeological and Historical Perspectives on the Spanish Borderlands East*. 2 vols. Washington, DC: Smithsonian Institution Press, 1990.

Thoms, Alston V., editor. *The Upper Keechi Creek Archaeological Project: Survey and Test Excavations at the Keechi Creek Wildlife Management Area, Leon County, Texas*. Technical Report No. 3, Center for Environmental Archaeology, Texas A&M University, College Station, 1997.

Thornton, Russell. *American Indian Holocaust and Survival*. Norman: University of Oklahoma Press, 1987.

————. *The Cherokees: A Population History*. Lincoln: University of Nebraska Press, 1987.

Thornton, Russell, Tim Miller, and Jonathan Warren. "American Indian Population Recovery following Smallpox Epidemics." *American Anthropologist* 93(1991):28–45.

Thurman, Melburn D. "Conversations with Lewis R. Binford on Historical Archaeology." *Historical Archaeology* 32, no. 2(1998):28–55.

Thurmond, J. Peter. *Archeology of the Cypress Creek Drainage Basin, Northeastern Texas and Northwestern Louisiana*. Studies in Archeology No. 5, Texas Archeological Research Laboratory, University of Texas, Austin, 1990.

Thwaites, Reuben G., editor. *The Jesuit Relations and Allied Documents; Travel and*

Explorations of the Jesuit Missionaries in New France, 1610–1791. 73 vols. Cleveland, OH: Burrows Brothers, 1896–1901.

Tonti, Henri de. *Relation of Henri de Tonti Concerning the Exploration of La Salle from 1678 to 1683*, translated by Melville B. Anderson. Chicago, IL: The Caxton Club, 1898.

———. "Tonty's Account of the Route from the Illinois, by the River Mississippi to the Gulf of Mexico." In *Historical Collections of Louisiana*, 5 vols., edited by B. F. French. New York, NY: Wiley and Putnam, 1846.

Trigger, Bruce G. "Early Iroquoian Contacts with Europeans." In *Handbook of North American Indians. Vol. 15, Northeast*, edited by Bruce G. Trigger. Washington, DC: Smithsonian Institution, 1978.

———. "The Mohawk-Mahican War (1624–1628): The Establishment of a Pattern." *Canadian Historical Review* 52(1971):276–286.

———. *Natives and Newcomers: Canada's "Heroic Age" Reconsidered*. Kingston, Ontario: McGill–Queen's University Press, 1986.

———, editor. *Handbook of North American Indians. Vol. 15, Northeast*. Washington, DC: Smithsonian Institution, 1978.

Trigger, Bruce G., and William R. Swagerty. "Entertaining Strangers: North America in the Sixteenth Century." In *The Cambridge History of the Native Peoples of the Americas. Vol. I, North America, Part 1*, edited by Bruce G. Trigger and Wilcomb E. Washburn, pp. 325–398. New York, NY: Cambridge University Press, 1996.

Trowbridge, C. C. *Shawnese Traditions: C. C. Trowbridge's Account*, edited by W. Vernon Kinietz and Erminie Wheeler Voegelin. Occasional Contributions from the Museum of Anthropology of the University of Michigan No. 9. Ann Arbor: University of Michigan Press, 1939.

Turner, Robert L., Jr. *Prehistoric Mortuary Remains at the Tuck Carpenter Site, Camp County, Texas*. Studies in Archeology 10, Texas Archeological Research Laboratory, University of Texas, Austin, 1992.

Urban, Greg. "The Social Organization of the Southeast." In *North American Indian Anthropology: Essays on Society and Culture*, edited by Raymond J. DeMallie and Alfonso Ortiz, pp. 172–193. Norman: University of Oklahoma Press, 1994.

Usner, Daniel H., Jr. *Indians, Settlers, and Slaves in a Frontier Exchange Economy: The Lower Mississippi Valley Before 1782*. Chapel Hill: University of North Carolina Press, 1992.

Vansina, Jan. *Oral Tradition as History*. Madison: University of Wisconsin Press, 1985.

Varona, Governor Salinas. "The 1693 Expedition of Governor Salinas Varona to Sustain the Missionaries among the Tejas Indians," edited by William C. Foster and Jack Jackson, translated by N. F. Brierley. *Southwestern Historical Quarterly* 97, no. 2(1993):264–311.

Vehik, Susan C. "Wichita Culture History." *Plains Anthropologist* 37, no. 141(1992):311–332.

———. "Dhegiha Origins and Plains Archaeology." *Plains Anthropologist* 38, no.146(1993):231–252.

Vietzen, Raymond C. *The Riker Site*. Sugar Creek Valley Chapter of the Archaeological Society of Ohio, 1974.

Wallace, Anthony F. C. "Origins of Iroquois Neutrality: The Grand Settlement of 1701." *Pennsylvania History* 24(1957):223–235.

Wallerstein, Immanuel. *The Modern World-System: Capitalist Agriculture and the Origins of the European World Economy in the 16th Century*. New York, NY: Academic Press, 1974.

Walthall, John A. "Aboriginal Pottery and the Eighteenth-Century Illini." In *Calumet and Fleur-de-Lys: Archaeology of Indian and French Contact in the Midcontinent*, edited by John A. Walthall and Thomas E. Emerson, pp. 155–174. Washington DC: Smithsonian Institution Press, 1992.

Ward, H. Trawick. "Social Implications of Storage and Disposal Patterns." In *Structure* and Process in Southeastern Archaeology, edited by Roy S. Dickens, Jr., and H. Trawick Ward, pp. 82–101. Tuscaloosa: University of Alabama Press, 1985.

Ward, Trawick, and R. P. Stephen Davis, Jr. "The Impact of Old World Diseases on the Native Inhabitants of the North Carolina Piedmont." Archaeology of Eastern North America 19(1991):171–181.

———. Indian Communities on the North Carolina Piedmont A.D. 1000–1700. Monograph No. 2, Research Laboratories of Anthropology, University of North Carolina, Chapel Hill, 1993.

———. Time Before History: The Archaeology of North Carolina. Chapel Hill: University of North Carolina Press, 1999.

Waselkov, Gregory. "Changing Strategies of Indian Field Location in the Early Historic Southeast." In People, Plants, and Landscapes: Studies in Paleoethnobotany, edited by Kristen J. Gremillion, pp. 179–194. Tuscaloosa: University of Alabama Press, 1997.

———. "The Eighteenth-Century Anglo-Indian Trade in Southeastern North America." In New Faces of the Fur Trade: Selected Papers of the Seventh North American Fur Trade Conference, Halifax, Nova Scotia, 1995, edited by Jo-Anne Fiske, Susan Sleeper-Smith, and William Wicken. East Lansing: Michigan State University Press, 1998.

———. "Historic Creek Indian Responses to European Trade and the Rise of Political Factions." In Ethnohistory and Archaeology: Approaches to Postcontact Change in the Americas, edited by J. Daniel Rogers and Samuel M. Wilson, pp. 123–131. New York, NY: Plenum Press, 1993.

———. "The Macon Trading House and Early European-Indian Contact in the Colonial Southeast." In Ocmulgee Archaeology, 1936–1986, edited by David J. Hally, pp. 190–196. Athens: University of Georgia Press, 1994.

———. "Seventeenth-Century Trade in the Colonial Southeast." Southeastern Archaeology 8(1989):117–133.

Waselkov, Gregory A., and John W. Cottier. "European Perceptions of Eastern Muskogean Ethnicity." Proceedings of the French Colonial Historical Society 10(1985):23–45.

Webb, Clarence H. The Belcher Mound, a Stratified Caddoan Site in Caddo Parish, Louisiana. Memoirs No. 16, Society for American Archaeology, Salt Lake City, 1959.

Weddle, Robert. Spanish Sea: The Gulf of Mexico in North American Discovery, 1500–1685. College Station: Texas A&M University Press, 1985.

———. "The Talon Interrogations: A Rare Perspective." In La Salle, the Mississippi, and the Gulf: Three Primary Documents, edited by Robert S. Weddle, pp. 209–224. College Station: Texas A&M University Press, 1987.

Weddle, Robert S., annotator, and Ann Linda Bell, translator. "Voyage to the Mississippi through the Gulf of Mexico." In La Salle, the Mississippi, and the Gulf: Three Primary Documents, edited by Robert S. Weddle, pp. 225–258. College Station: Texas A&M University Press, 1987.

Wedel, Mildred M. "The Indian They Called Turco." 1982. Reprint, in The Wichita Indians 1541–1750: Ethnohistorical Essays, edited by Mildred M. Wedel, pp. 38–52. Lincoln, NE: J & L Reprint Company, 1988.

———. La Harpe's 1719 Post on Red River and Nearby Caddo Settlements. Bulletin 30, Texas Memorial Museum, University of Texas, Austin, 1978.

———. "Oneota Sites on the Upper Iowa River." Missouri Archaeologist 21 (1959):1–180.

Wedel, Waldo R. An Introduction to Kansas Archeology. Bureau of American Ethnology Bulletin 174, Smithsonian Institution, Washington DC, 1959.

———. "The Ioway, Oto, and Omaha Indians in 1700." Journal of the Iowa Archeological Society (1981):1–13.

———. "Peering at the Ioway Indians Through the Mist of Time: 1650–circa 1700." Journal of the Iowa Archaeological Society (1986):1–74.

Weinstein, Richard A., et al. Cultural Resources Survey of the Upper Steele Bayou Basin, West-Central Mississippi. Report submitted to Vicksburg District, U. S. Army Corps of Engineers, by Coastal Environments, Inc., Baton Rouge, LA, 1979.

358 Bibliography

Weinstein, Richard A., and Thurston H. G. Hahn III. *Cultural Resources Survey of the Lake Beulah Landside Berm, Item L-583, Bolivar County, Mississippi*. Report submitted to Vicksburg District, U. S. Army Corps of Engineers, by Coastal Environments, Inc., Baton Rouge, LA, 1992.

Weisman, Brent R. *Excavations on the Franciscan Frontier: Archaeology at the Fig Springs Mission*. Gainesville: University Press of Florida, 1992.

Wesson, Cameron B. "Chiefly Power and Food Storage in Southeastern North America." *World Archaeology* 31(1999):145–164.

Wetmore, Ruth Y. "The Green Corn Ceremony of the Eastern Cherokees." *Journal of Cherokee Studies* 8(1983):46–56.

White, Richard. *The Middle Ground: Indians, Empires, and Republics in the Great Lakes Region, 1650–1815*. New York, NY: Cambridge University Press, 1991.

———. *The Roots of Dependency: Subsistence, Environment, and Social Change among the Choctaws, Pawnees, and Navajos*. Lincoln: University of Nebraska Press, 1983.

Whitman, Janice K. "An Analysis of the Ceramics from the Riker site, Tuscarawas County, Ohio." Master's thesis, Department of Anthropology, Kent State University, 1975.

Widmer, Randolph J. "Structure of Southeastern Chiefdoms." In *Forgotten Centuries: Indians and Europeans in the American South, 1521–1704*, edited by Charles Hudson and Carmen Chaves Tesser, pp. 125–155. Athens: University of Georgia Press, 1994.

Willey, Gordon R., and Philip Phillips. *Method and Theory in American Archaeology*. Chicago, IL: University of Chicago Press, 1958.

Williams, Mark. "Growth and Decline of the Oconee Province." In *Forgotten Centuries: Indians and Europeans in the American South, 1521–1704*, edited by Charles Hudson and Carmen Chaves Tesser, pp. 179–196. Athens: University of Georgia Press, 1994.

Williams, Stephen, and Jeffrey P. Brain. *Excavations at the Lake George Site, Yazoo County, Mississippi, 1958–1960*. Papers of the Peabody Museum of Anthropology and Ethnology, vol. 74, Harvard University, Cambridge, MA, 1983.

Wilms, Douglas C. "Cherokee Land Use in Georgia Before Removal." In *Cherokee Removal, Before and After*, edited by William L. Anderson, pp. 1–28. Athens: University of Georgia Press, 1991.

———. "Cherokee Settlement Patterns in Nineteenth-Century Georgia." *Southeastern Geographer* 14(1974):46–53.

Wilson, D. "Dental Paleopathology in the Sanders (41LR2) and Mitchell (41BW4) Populations from the Red River Valley, Northeast Texas." *Bulletin of the Texas Archeological Society* 68(1997):147–159.

Wilson, Edward O. *Consilience: The Unity of Knowledge*. New York, NY: Knopf, 1998.

Wilson, Jack H., Jr. *A Study of Late Prehistoric, Protohistoric, and Historic Indians of the Carolina and Virginia Piedmont: Structure, Process, and Ecology*. Ph.D. dissertation, Department of Anthropology, University of North Carolina, Chapel Hill, 1983.

Witthoft, John, and William A. Hunter. "The Seventeenth-Century Origins of the Shawnee." *Ethnohistory* 2(1955):42–57.

Wood, Abraham. "Letter to John Richards, August 23, 1674." In *The First Explorations of the Trans-Allegheny Region by the Virginians, 1650–1674*, edited by Clarence W. Alvord and Lee Bidgood, pp. 210–26. Cleveland, OH: Arthur H. Clark Co., 1912.

Wood, J. W., George R. Milner, H. C. Harpending, and K. M. Weiss. "The Osteological Paradox: Problems of Inferring Prehistoric Health from Skeletal Samples." *Current Anthropology* 33, no. 4(1992):343–370.

Wood, Peter H. *Black Majority: Negroes in Colonial South Carolina from 1670 through the Stono Rebellion*. New York, NY: W. W. Norton, 1974.

———. "The Changing Population of the Colonial South: An Overview by Race and Region, 1685–1790." In *Powhatan's Mantle: Indians in the Colonial Southeast*, edited by Peter H. Wood, Thomas Hatley, and Gregory Waselkov, pp. 35–103. Lincoln: University of Nebraska Press, 1989.

———. "The Impact of Smallpox on the Native Population of the 18th-Century South." *New York State Journal of Medicine* 87(1987):30–36.

Woodall, J. Ned. *The Donnaha Site: 1973, 1975 Excavations.* North Carolina Archaeological Council Publication 22, Raleigh, 1984.

Worth, John E. "The Ethnohistorical Context of Bioarchaeology in Spanish Florida." In *Bioarchaeology in Northern Frontier New Spain: The Case of La Florida,* edited by Clark Spencer Larsen. Gainesville: University Press of Florida, in press.

———. "Late Spanish Military Expeditions in the Interior Southeast, 1597–1628." In *The Forgotten Centuries: Indians and Europeans in the American South, 1521–1704,* edited by Charles Hudson and Carmen Chaves Tesser, pp. 104–122. Athens: University of Georgia Press, 1994.

———. "The Lower Creeks: Origins and Early History." In *Indians of the Greater Southeast During the Historic Period,* edited by Bonnie McEwan. Gainesville: University Press of Florida, 2000.

———. "Recollections of the Juan Pardo Expeditions: The Domingo de León Account." Draft manuscript in possession of the author.

———. *The Struggle for the Georgia Coast: An Eighteenth-Century Spanish Retrospective on Guale and Mocama.* Athens: University of Georgia Press, 1995.

———. *The Timucuan Chiefdoms of Spanish Florida.* 2 vols. Gainesville: University Press of Florida, 1998.

———. "Yamassee Origins and the Development of the Carolina-Florida Frontier." Paper presented at the annual conference of the Omohundro Institute of Early American History and Culture, Austin, Texas, June 12, 1999.

Wren, Christopher. "Description of Indian Graves on Bead Hill, Plymouth, Pennsylvania." *Proceedings and Collections of the Wyoming Historical and Geological Society* 12(1912):199–204.

Wright, J. Leitch. *Anglo-Spanish Rivalry in North America.* Athens: University of Georgia Press, 1971.

———. *Creeks and Seminoles: The Destruction and Regeneration of the Muscogulge People.* Lincoln: University of Nebraska Press, 1986.

———. *The Only Land They Knew.* New York, NY: The Free Press, 1981.

Wright, Ronald. "On the Rampage in Florida: Hernando de Soto's Cruel Life and Death." *Times Literary Supplement,* August 1, 1997.

Wyckoff, Don G., and Timothy G. Baugh. "Early Historic Hasinai Elites: A Model for the Material Culture of Governing Elites." *Midcontinental Journal of Archaeology* 5(1980):225–288.

Wynn, Jack T. *The Mississippi Period Archaeology of the Georgia Blue Ridge.* Laboratory of Archaeology Report No. 27, Department of Anthropology, University of Georgia, Athens, 1990.

Young, Gloria A., and Michael P. Hoffman, editors. *The Expedition of Hernando de Soto West of the Mississippi, 1541–1543.* Fayetteville: University of Arkansas Press, 1993.

Zinsser, Hans. *Rats, Lice, and History.* Boston, MA: Little, Brown, and Company, 1935.

Contributors

R. P. STEPHEN DAVIS, JR., is research archaeologist and associate director at the Research Laboratories of Archaeology, University of North Carolina at Chapel Hill. He received his doctorate in anthropology from the University of Tennessee in 1986. He has spent the past two decades investigating the late prehistory of central North Carolina and the impact of Europeans on native peoples in the region during the seventeenth and early eighteenth centuries.

PENELOPE B. DROOKER is curator of anthropology at the New York State Museum, Albany, New York. She is the author of several works on the Indians of the Ohio Valley, including *The View from Madisonville: Protohistoric Western Fort Ancient Interaction Patterns*.

ROBBIE ETHRIDGE is McMullan Assistant Professor of Southern Studies and assistant professor of anthropology at the University of Mississippi in Oxford. She received her doctorate in anthropology from the University of Georgia in 1996, and she is the author of several works on the social history of the Southeastern Indians, including her dissertation entitled "Creek Country: The Creek Indians and Their World, 1796–1816." She is the recipient of the 1999 Anderson Award for innovative research.

PATRICIA GALLOWAY is assistant professor at the Graduate School of Library and Information Science at the University of Texas at Austin. She received her doctorate in comparative literature from the University of North Carolina at Chapel Hill in 1973 and is currently a doctoral candidate in anthropology there, as well. She is the author of *Choctaw Genesis, 1500–1700* and the editor of *The Hernando de Soto Expedition: History, Historiography, and "Discovery" in the Southeast*.

STEVEN C. HAHN is assistant professor of history at St. Olaf College in Minnesota. He received his doctorate in history from Emory University in 2000. He is the author of several works on the history of the Southeastern Indians, including his dissertation, "The Invention of the Creek Nation: A Political History of the Creek Indians in the South's Imperial Period, 1540–1763."

CHARLES HUDSON is Emeritus Franklin Professor of Anthropology and History at the University of Georgia. He is the author of *The Southeastern Indians; Knights of Spain, Warriors of the Sun: Hernando de Soto and the South's Ancient Chiefdoms;* and other works.

MARVIN D. JETER is the UAM Station Archeologist for the Arkansas Archeological Survey, based in Monticello. He has also worked in his home state of Alabama, plus Tennessee, Louisiana, and Arizona, mainly but not exclusively on late prehistoric to early historic-contact sites.

PAUL KELTON is assistant professor of history at the University of Kansas. He received his doctorate in history from the University of Oklahoma in 1998. He is the author of several works on the history of the Southeastern Indians, including his dissertation entitled, "Not All Disappeared: Disease and Southeastern Indian Survival, 1500–1800."

TIMOTHY K. PERTTULA is a principal in Archeological & Environmental Consultants, a private cultural resources management firm (Austin and Pittsburg, Texas). He received

361

his doctorate in archaeology from the University of Washington in 1989, and he specializes in Caddoan archaeology and ethnohistory.

CHRISTOPHER B. RODNING is a doctoral candidate in anthropology at the University of North Carolina at Chapel Hill. His dissertation is an archaeological study of architecture and social history at the Coweeta Creek site in southwestern North Carolina.

HELEN C. ROUNTREE is Emeritus Professor of Anthropology at Old Dominion University. She is the author of many works on the Indians of Virginia, including *The Powhatan Indians of Virginia: Their Traditional Culture* and *Pocahontas's People: The Powhatan Indians of Virginia through Four Centuries;* she is the editor of *Powhatan Foreign Relations, 1500–1722,* and co-author (with Thomas Davidson) of *Eastern Shore Indians of Virginia and Maryland,* and co-author (with E. Randolph Turner III) of the forthcoming book (May 2002), *Before and After Jamestown: The Virginia Algonquian Indians Over the Last Millennium.* She is active in contemporary Virginia Indian affairs as well, and she is an honorary member of the Nansemond Indian Tribe and the Upper Mattaponi Tribe.

MARVIN T. SMITH is professor of anthropology at Valdosta State University. He received his doctorate in anthropology from the University of Florida in 1984. He is the author of *Archaeology of Aboriginal Culture Change in the Interior Southeast: Depopulation during the Early Historic Period* and *Coosa: The Rise and Fall of a Southeastern Mississippian Chiefdom.* He is the recipient of the C. B. Moore Award for Excellence in Southeastern Archaeology.

JOHN E. WORTH is coordinator at the Florida Museum of Natural History's Randell Research Center near Fort Myers. He has conducted research for many years on the social history of the Indians of the Southeast, and especially those of Spanish Florida. He is the author of *The Struggle for the Georgia Coast: An Eighteenth-Century Spanish Retrospective on Guale and Mocama* and *The Timucuan Chiefdoms of Spanish Florida.*

Index

Abihka, 41, 60, 83, 102. *See also* Creeks
Alabama River archaeological tradition, 10, 16
Alabamas, 102, 245; language of, 159. *See also* Creeks
Algonkian. *See* Algonquian
Algonquian, 66–67, 116, 123, 124–27, 136, 216, 311 n 268
Apache, xxxvi, 257, 260
Apalachees, xxxvi, 7, 8, 27, 41, 56, 88, 90, 92, 95, 100, 242; language of, 159. *See also* Spanish Missions
Apalachicola, 40, 41, 60, 83, 89, 90; European interest in, 90–94. *See also* Creeks
Appalachia physiographic province. *See* Southern Appalachia
Appamattucks, 70, 75, 76
Arthur, Gabriel, xxix, 123, 141, 149, 154
Atlantic seaboard, European colonization of, 46, 65–78

Bacon's Rebellion, 33, 142, 150, 151
Balero. *See* Tickhonabe
Bartram, William, 42
Bayagoulas, 28, 34. *See also* Gulf Coast; Mississippi River Valley, Lower
Berkeley, William, xxxii
Biloxi Indians, 34. *See also* Gulf Coast; Mississippi River Valley, Lower
Bison, xxxv, 117, 131–32, 192, 203, 258–60
Bland, Edward, 139, 148
Brave Dog, 79–81, 102–03, 106, 107, 113
British. *See* English
Buffalo. *See* Bison

Caborn-Welborn archaeological tradition, 118, 119, 120, 215, 310 n 248, 312 n 274; sites of, 120
Caddos, xiv, xxxv–xxxvi, 191, 203–09, 249–69; chiefdoms, 262–68; disease among, 253–54, 255–57; formation of, 255–65, 267–68; and French, 249, 255, 257–62, 268–69; Hasinai Caddo, xxxvi, 249, 252, 255, 257, 259, 261, 262, 268–69; Kadohadacho Caddo, xxxvi, 252, 255, 260, 261, 262, 263, 265, 268–69; kinship, 252, 268; language of,

xiv, xxxv, 257; mortuary practices of, 265–68; Natchitoches Caddo, 252, 268; population movements among, 255–57, 260–65; in the protohistoric period, 251–55, 260–61; and Spanish, 192–93, 199, 204, 249, 254, 255, 257, 259, 263, 268–69; and trade, 254–55, 257–65, 268–69; and war, 257–60. *See also* Trans-Mississippi South
Carden Bottoms archaeological tradition, 181, 197–98
Carolina, colony of: as commercial colony, 83–84; and Creeks, 79–114, 144; disease in, 33–34; and Indian slave trade, 79–114; in Queen Anne's War, 96–114; and Shawnees, 126, 130–33; and traders, xxix, 31–37; and Westos, 85–99. *See also* English
Catawbas, xxxiii, xxxix, 7, 12, 117, 135, 136, 137, 139, 140, 142, 144, 154; formation of, 138, 143, 145; language, xxxiii, 136–37, 156, 157
Charles Town, xxxiii, 88, 91, 94, 101, 126, 130, 131, 135, 144. *See also* English; Carolina, colony of
Charleston. *See* Charles Town
Chehaws, 99. *See also* Creeks
Cheraw War, 143, 145, 153–54. *See also* Southern Indian Wars
Cherokees, xi, xx, xxiii, xxxiv, xxxvi, xxxix; clans, 158, 159, 172; Coweeta Creek town, 165, 167–71; and Creeks, 103, 155, 170; disease among, 35–36, 280 n 74; and English, 142, 144, 157, 170; formation of, 155–75; households, 158, 172–73; Iroquois, 157, 171; Mississippian chiefdoms, 161–66, 170–75; and Natchez, 8, 9, 19; political organization, 157–60, 171–75; populations, movement of, 159–60, 170–71; territory of, xxxiv–xxxv; and Tomahittans, 140; towns of, xxxiv–xxxv, 155, 158–62, 164, 165, 167–69; trade, 171–75. *See also* Southern Appalachia; North Carolina Piedmont
Chesapeakes, 66, 68
Chicasa, 237. *See also* Chickasaws
Chickasaws, xxxiii, xxxv, xxxvi, xxxix, 4, 6,

31, 32, 88, 89, 191, 205, 206, 225, 229, 241–47, 260, 314 n 13, 315 n 31, 315 n 32, 316 n 44; disease among, 35; and Natchez, 8, 9, 19; population movements of, 17; in protohistoric period, 232–34, 237, 240–41
Chiouanons. See Shawnees
Chiscas, 52, 93, 281–82 n 27. See also Trade, Indian slave
Choctaws, xi, xx, xxv, xxxvi, xxxix, 12, 16, 117, 191, 205, 225, 229, 241–47, 315 n 31, 316 n 44; and Creeks, 99; disease among, 35–36; formation of, 16, 159; in protohistoric period, 232–34, 240–41. See also Mississippi River Valley, Lower
Chowanoes, 70
Coalescent societies, xxvii; Caddos, 255–65; Catawbas, 138, 143, 145; Cherokees, 155–75; Choctaws, 16, 159; Coosa-Abihka, 15; Creeks, 40–41, 159; formation of, xxvii, xxxvi, 4–5, 159; Natchez, 18–19; in North Carolina Piedmont, 138–54; and population loss, 51–52
Cofitachequi, xv, xxxiii, 28, 60, 86; disease in, 137–38, 278 n 36
Congarees, 33
Cooper, Anthony Ashley. See Earl of Shaftsbury
Coosa, xiv, xxiii, 14–16, 19, 30, 51. See also Mississippian chiefdoms
Cowetas, 41, 79, 80, 88, 90, 91, 94, 95, 105. See also Creeks
Creek Confederacy. See Creeks
Creeks, xi, xx, xxxvi, xxxix, 4, 5, 8, 19, 27, 31, 32, 42, 45, 83, 159, 242, 315 n 32; and Abihkas, 41, 60, 83, 102; and Alabamas, 102, 245; and Carolina colony, 79–114, 144; and Chehaws, 99; and Cherokees, 103, 155, 170; and Choctaws, 99; and Cowetas, 41, 79, 80, 88, 90, 91, 94, 95, 105; and Cussitas, 86–87, 88, 89, 90, 91, 99; disease among, 35; formation of, 40–41, 159; and French, 102, 103, 106; and Indian slave trade, 99, 108; and Natchez, 8, 9, 19; and Oakfuskees, 104; Ocmulgee, 95; policy of neutrality, 105; political organization of, 41; population movements of, 95–98; population of, 44; Shawnees, 125, 127, 130–31; and Spanish, 79–114; and Talisi, 101, 109; and Tallapoosas, 41, 60, 83, 98, 101, 102, 110; and Tiguales, 101; and trade, 79–114; Tuckabatche, xxx, 101, 125, 127, 130–31; wars of, 96–114, 145

Cromwell, Oliver, 83, 84
Culture, concept of, xii, xv, 179–80
Cussitas, 86–87, 88, 89, 90, 91, 99. See also Creeks

Dan River archaeological tradition, 136, 138, 140
De Soto. See Soto, Hernando de
Delawares, 115, 127, 132
Delgado, Marcos, 5, 7, 19
Dhegihan Siouan language. See Siouan, Dhegiha Siouan
Diseases, Old World, 24, 25, 36; and buffer zones, 27–28; among the Caddos, xxxv, 253–54, 255–57; among the Cherokees, xxxiv, 35–36, 280 n 74; among the Chickasaws, 35–36; among the Choctaws, 35–36; in Cofitachequi, 137, 278 n 36; among the Creeks, 35; and decline of Mississippian chiefdoms, xxii–xxiv, xxxvi, 17, 25–26, 28–29, 48–50; and the English, 22, 30–37; evidence for, 29–31, 228; malaria, 29; in Mississippi River Valley, 31–32, 183–84, 187–88, 202–03, 205, 233, 237; and population loss, 22, 28–29, 36–37, 46–53, 138, 144, 151–53, 239, 240, 275 n 4, 282 n 28; and population movements, 4, 7, 19, 116, 131; and Spanish expeditions, xxii–xxv, 25–26, 276 n 14; in Spanish Florida, 22, 275 n 3; and trade, 21, 26–28, 31–37; transmission of, 276 n 12; in trans-Mississippi South, 253–54, 255–57; typhoid fever, 24, 36; virgin soil epidemics, 21, 23, 25, 30, 274 n 2; whooping cough, 275 n 8; yellow fever, 23, 275–76 n 9. See also Smallpox
DNA analysis, 195–96, 307 n 136
Doegs, 72, 74, 284 n 30
Dutch traders, xxv–xxxi, 131. See also Trade, European

Earl of Shaftsbury, 86
English: colonial strategies of, xxxi, xxxviii; 44–45, 79–114; and disease, 22, 30–37; expeditions of, 65, 72–78, 139–43; in Gulf coast, 96; in Mississippi River Valley, 32, 96, 241–47; in North Carolina Piedmont, 139–54; and plantation system, xxxi–xxxii, 69, 144; and trade, 27–28, 44–64, 69–78, 79–114, 139–54. See also Carolina, colony of; Charles Town; Jamestown; Trade, European; Trade, Indian slave; Virginia, colony of

Osage, 194, 260, 312 n 274; and Quapaws, 216–19, 311 n 261
Ospogue, Francisco, 39
Oumas, 28

Parkin archaeological tradition, 199–200
Patawomecks, 74
Percival, Andrew, 86
Petuns, 116, 290 n 11
Piedmont. *See* North Carolina Piedmont
Piscataways, 72, 74
Pisgah archaeological tradition, 163–66
Plantation system. *See* English: and plantation system
Plaquemine archaeological tradition, 16, 18, 184–88, 194, 210, 211, 231, 233, 237
Pocoughtraonacks. *See* Massawomecks
Population loss. *See* Diseases, Old World: and population loss
Population movements, 3, 51, 117, 165, 174; in Atlantic seaboard, 72–78; and Cherokees, 159–60, 170–71; and Chickasaws, 17; and Creeks, 95–98; and disease, 4, 7, 19, 116, 131; and the environment, 5, 16, 17; factors of, 3–9, 115–18, 128–33, 143–45; maps of, 9–19, 145–54; in Mississippi River Valley, 187–88, 240; in North Carolina Piedmont, 135–43; in Ohio River Valley, 115–18, 122–23, 128–33; Opechancanough, 70, 71; and Portobaccos, 74; Powhatan paramount chiefdom, xxxiii, 65, 66, 69–72, 136, 139; and Shawnees, 126–28, 132–33; and Siouan, 199; in Southern Appalachia, 4, 7, 18, 19, 159–60; and Spanish missions, 5, 7; and trade, 5, 8–9, 16–17, 131–33; in trans-Mississippi South, 256–57. *See also* North Carolina Piedmont; Virginia

Qualla archaeological tradition, 161–65, 166
Quapaws, xxx, xxxi, xxxv, 6, 32, 35, 178, 183, 188–91, 196–221, 244, 310 n 237, 311 n 252, 311 n 261, 312 n 274, 312 n 275, 313 n 2; language of, 194–96; and Menard archaeological tradition, 181, 189, 197, 200, 213–19, 312 n 275; oral traditions of, 216; origins of, 181, 209, 213–19; and Osage, 216–19, 311 n 261; Quapaw archaeological tradition, 188–89, 197–201, 213–19
Queen Anne's War (War of Spanish Succession), 96–114, 245

Richahecrians, 75, 283 n 46. *See also* Westos
Roanoke, 65, 69

St. Augustine. *See* Spanish Florida
Saponi, 135, 136, 138, 140, 142–44, 147, 150–53. *See also* Siouan
Sara, 138, 141–43, 149, 150. *See also* Siouan
Savannahs. *See* Shawnees
Seminoles, xxxix, 7
Senecas, 72, 115, 123, 124, 127, 143–44, 149, 217. *See also* Iroquois, League of
Sewees, 33
Shawnees, xxix, xxxi, 4, 6, 12, 17, 115–33, 216, 217, 311 n 268; archaeology of, 124–28; and Carolina colony, 126, 130–33; and Creeks, 25, 127, 130–31; divisions of, 124, 126; and French, 127, 130; historical documentation of, 124–30; and Indian slave trade, 131; Lower Shawneetown, 125; population movements of, 126–28, 132–33; and Spanish, 124
Siouan, xxxi, xxxiii, 7, 66, 74, 77, 132; Dhegiha Siouan speakers, 194–97, 200, 215–19; divisions of, 136–38; eastern Siouan, 135–36, 147–54; historical documentation of, 138–43; in Mississippi River Valley, 194–96, 209, 215–19, 234, 315 n 31; Omaha-Ponca, 195, 217; Osage-Kansa, 195, 217; population movements of, 199; Saponi, 136, 138; Sara, 138; territory of, 136
Slave trade, Indian. *See* Trade, Indian slave
Smallpox, xxiii, 21–37; and Creeks, 35; and Cherokees, 35–36, 280 n 74; and Chickasaws, 35; and Choctaws, 35–36; epidemiology of, 23–25; Great Southeastern Small Pox Epidemic, 21–37; in Gulf Coast, 34; in Mississippi River Valley, 34–35; in North Carolina Piedmont, 138; in South Carolina, 33–34; in Virginia, 32. *See also* Diseases, Old World
Smith, John, 65
Soto, Hernando de, xii, xxx, xxxiv, 9, 14–16, 17, 28, 46, 139, 146, 160, 177–221, 228, 235–40, 247, 253, 260–65, 268, 278 n 36; 279 n 41. *See also* Spanish, expeditions of
South Carolina. *See* Carolina, colony of

South, the: antiquity of, xxxvii–xxxix;
foodways of, xxxvii
Southern Appalachia: Indians of, 155–75;
and Mississippian chiefdoms, 161–64,
170–75; population movements in,
159–60, 165, 170–71. *See also*
Cherokees; North Carolina Piedmont
Southern Indian Wars, 144–45, 154. *See
also* Cheraw War; Tuscarora War;
Yamassee War
Spanish, expeditions of, xxii, 3, 46, 139,
146, 160, 177–221, 235–39, 240, 254,
255, 257, 259, 263, 268–69, 276–77 n 17;
and disease, xxii–xxv, 25–26, 29, 276 n
14. *See also* Soto, Hernando de
Spanish Florida: and Creeks, 79–114; and
disease, 22, 275 n 3; economics of,
54–56; and Indian labor, 55–56; as
military outpost, 54; missions in, 47; and
Mississippian chiefdoms, 53–59; in
Queen Anne's War, 96–114; St.
Augustine, 12, 54, 56, 86, 87, 88, 90, 92,
102, 126, 193; and Shawnees, 124; and
trade, 27, 79–114. *See also* Spanish
missions
Spanish missions, xxiv–xxv; as a colonial
strategy, 44, 52–59; destruction of, 43,
79; in Guale, 39; and Indian slave trade,
43–44, 88, 95–99; and Mississippian
chiefdoms, 39–64; population
movements in, 5, 7; population of, 44; in
trans-Mississippi South, xxxv–xxxvi, 249,
254, 255, 257, 259, 263, 268–69
Spiro archaeological tradition, 181, 203,
205; trade relations of, 203
Summerville archaeological tradition, 16
Susquehannocks, 6, 66, 72, 74, 117,
121–28, 130, 131, 142, 149, 150

Taensa, 190, 194, 210, 211, 309 n 213
Talisi. *See* Tallassees
Tallapoosas, 41, 60, 83, 98, 101, 102, 110.
See also Creeks
Tallassees, 101, 109. *See also* Creeks
Texas. *See* Trans-Mississippi South
Tickhonabe, 109–14
Tiguale, 101
Timucuan, 7, 12, 41, 45, 52, 56, 58, 88, 92.
See also Spanish Florida; Spanish
Missions
Tomahittans, 123, 140
Tomichichi, 40
Tonicas. *See* Tunican

Trade, aboriginal, 65, 66, 117, 233–34,
252–53
Trade, European: archaeological evidence
of, 9, 16, 18; and Cherokees, 171–75; as
a colonial strategy, 44–45, 79–114; and
disease, 21, 26–28, 31–37; and Dutch,
xxv–xxxi, 131; and English, 27, 44–64,
69–78, 79–114, 139–54; and French,
xxv–xxxi; and Indian consumers, 63–64,
95–114; and Indian debt, 98–114; and
Iroquois, xxv–xxxi, 122, 131; and
Mississippian chiefdoms, 44–45; and
native political economy, 53, 60–64,
97–114; in North Carolina Piedmont,
139–44, 149–54; in northeast, xxv–xxvi;
in Ohio River Valley, 121; and
population movements, 5, 8–9, 16–17,
131–33; in Spanish Florida, 27, 79–114.
See also Trade, Indian slave
Trade goods, 92–94, 104–14; guns, 104,
108, 258; list of, 110–12
Trade, Indian slave, 8, 19, 31–37, 77, 99;
and Chiscas, 52, 93, 281–82 n 27; and
Creeks, 99, 108; in North Carolina
Piedmont, 138; and Shawnees, 131; and
social transformation, 52, 60–64; of
Spanish missions, 43–44, 88, 95–99; in
Virginia, 77; and Westos, xxvii, xxxi,
xxxiii, 4, 6, 7, 10, 17, 27, 60, 83, 85, 87,
89, 90, 130, 214–15, 217
Traders, European, 91–94, 100, 101–02
Trading Path, 142–43, 144, 148, 149, 151,
152
Trans-Mississippi South: disease in,
253–54, 255–57; French in, xxxv–xxxvi,
249, 255, 257, 261–65, 268–69; Indians
of, 249–69; and Mississippian
chiefdoms, 251–69; Spanish in, 249, 254,
255, 257, 259, 263, 268–69. *See also*
Caddos
Tuckabatchee, xxx, 101, 125, 127, 130–31.
See also Creeks
Tugalo archaeological tradition, 161–65
Tula, 192–93, 199, 202, 204, 209
Tunican, xxxi, 12, 17, 18, 35, 183, 189–90,
195–99, 206, 201–21, 229, 231, 234,
312 n 275, 314 n 12, 316 n 44;
archaeology of, 181; disease among,
202–03; during historic period, 225,
240–41, 244, 246, 247; oral traditions of,
207; population movements of, 18;
Tuscaroras, xxxiii, 8, 12, 27, 65, 66, 70,
71, 135, 136, 139, 144–45, 148. *See also*
North Carolina Piedmont

Printed in the United States
128161LV00003B/6/P

9 781604 731842

Made in the USA
Lexington, KY
11 May 2010